Holt Online Learning

go.hrw.com

All the help you need, any time you need it.

Log on to **www.go.hrw.com** to access Holt's online resources.

Interactive Online Edition
- Complete Student Edition with Audio
- **Interactive Tutorials**
- Additional practice with feedback

Extra Practice
- Homework Help Online
- Intervention and enrichment exercises
- State test practice

Online Tools
- Graphing calculator
- Algebra tiles
- Multilingual glossary

HOLT

Pre-Algebra

Jennie M. Bennett

David J. Chard

Audrey Jackson

Janet K. Scheer

Bert K. Waits

HOLT, RINEHART AND WINSTON

A Harcourt Education Company

Orlando • Austin • New York • San Diego • London

Pre-Algebra Contents in Brief

Student Handbook

Printed in the United States of America

Cover Photo: Reflections in Cloud Gate, Millenium Park, Chicago, Illinois, USA © Gail Mooney/Masterfile

ISBN 978-0-03-093468-1
ISBN 0-03-093468-0

2 3 4 5 048 09 08 07

AUTHORS

Jennie M. Bennett, Ph.D. is a mathematics teacher at Hartman Middle School in Houston, Texas. Jennie is past president of the Benjamin Banneker Association, the Second Vice-President of NCSM, and a former board member of NCTM.

Janet K. Scheer, Ph.D., Executive Director of Create A VisionTM, is a motivational speaker and provides customized K-12 math staff development. She has taught internationally and domestically at all grade levels.

David J. Chard, Ph.D., is an Associate Dean of Curriculum and Academic Programs at the University of Oregon. He is the President of the Division for Research at the Council for Exceptional Children, is a member of the International Academy for Research on Learning Disabilities, and is the Principal Investigator on two major research projects for the U.S. Department of Education.

Bert K. Waits, Ph.D., is a Professor Emeritus of Mathematics at The Ohio State University and co-founder of T3 (Teachers Teaching with Technology), a national professional development program.

Audrey L. Jackson is on the Board of Directors for NCTM. She is the Program Coordinator for Leadership Development with the St. Louis, public schools and is a former school administrator for the Parkway School District.

Contributing Authors

Linda Antinone
Fort Worth, TX

Ms. Antinone teaches mathematics at R. L. Paschal High School in Fort Worth, Texas. She has received the Presidential Award for Excellence in Teaching Mathematics and the National Radio Shack Teacher award. She has coauthored several books for Texas Instruments on the use of technology in mathematics.

Carmen Whitman
Pflugerville, TX

Ms. Whitman travels nationally helping districts improve mathematics education. She has been a program coordinator on the mathematics team at the Charles A. Dana Center, and has served as a secondary math specialist for the Austin Independent School District.

Reviewers

Marilyn Adams
Mathematics Department Chair
Eanes ISD
Austin, TX

Thomas J. Altonjy
Assistant Principal
Robert R. Lazar Middle School
Montville, NY

Jane Bash, M.A.
Math Education
Eisenhower Middle School
San Antonio, TX

Charlie Bialowas
District Math Coordinator
Anaheim Union High School District
Anaheim, CA

Lynn Bodet
Math Teacher
Eisenhower Middle School
San Antonio, TX

Chandra Budd
Mathematics Teacher
Amarillo ISD
Amarillo, TX

Terry Bustillos
Mathematics Teacher
El Paso ISD
El Paso, TX

Louis D'Angelo, Jr.
Math Teacher
Archmere Academy
Claymont, DE

Troy Deckebach
Math Teacher
Tredyffrin-Easttown Middle School
Berwyn, PA

Linda Foster
Mathematics Department Chair
Abilene ISD
Abilene, TX

Mary Gorman
Math Teacher
Sarasota, FL

Brian Griffith
Supervisor of Mathematics, K-12
Mechanicsburg Area School District
Mechanicsburg, PA

Ruth Harbin-Miles
District Math Coordinator
Instructional Resource Center
Olathe, KS

Jo Ann Hawkins
Mathematics Department Chair
Lake Travis ISD
Austin, TX

Kim Hayden
Math Teacher
Milford Jr. High School
Milford, OH

Susan Howe
Math Teacher
Lime Kiln Middle School
Fulton, MD

Emily Hyatt
Mathematics Teacher, retired
Klein ISD
Klein, TX

Paul Jenniges
Austin, TX

Ronald J. Labrocca
District Mathematics Coordinator
Manhasset Public Schools
Plainview, NY

Victor R. Lopez
Math Teacher
Washington School
Union City, NJ

George Maguschak
Math Teacher/Building Chairperson
Wilkes-Barre Area
Wilkes-Barre, PA

Dianne McIntire
Math Teacher
Garfield School
Kearny, NJ

Kenneth McIntire
Math Teacher
Lincoln School
Kearny, NJ

Francisco Pacheco
Math Teacher
IS 125
Bronx, NY

Vivian Perry
Edwards, IL

Vicki Perryman Petty
Math Teacher
Central Middle School
Murfreesbro, TN

Teresa Roy
Mathematics Curriculum Specialist
Round Rock, ISD
Round Rock, TX

Jennifer Sawyer
Math Teacher
Shawboro, NC

Russell Sayler
Math Teacher
Longfellow Middle School
Wauwatosa, WI

Raymond Scacalossi
Math Chairperson
Hauppauge Schools
Hauppauge, NY

Richard Seavey
Math Teacher, retired
Metcalf Jr. High
Eagan, MN

Sherry Shaffer
Math Teacher
Honeoye Central School
Honeoye Falls, NY

Diane Shaver
Mathematics Department Chair
Round Rock ISD
Round Rock, TX

Gail M. Sigmund
Math Teacher
Charles A. Mooney Preparatory School
Cleveland, OH

Jonathan Simmons
Math Teacher
Manor Middle School
Killeen, TX

Jeffrey L. Slagel
Math Department Chair
South Eastern Middle School
Fawn Grove, PA

Karen Smith, Ph.D.
Math Teacher
East Middle School
Braintree, MA

Melba Smithwick
Mathematics Department Chair
Corpus Christi ISD
Corpus Christi, TX

Bonnie Thompson
Math Teacher
Tower Heights Middle School
Dayton, OH

Mary Thoreen
Mathematics Subject Area Leader
Wilson Middle School
Tampa, FL

Paul Turney
Math Teacher
Ladue School District
St. Louis, MO

Lori Van Houton
Mathematics Teacher
Abilene ISD
Abilene, TX

Pam Walker
Curriculum Teacher Specialist
Nacogdoches ISD
Nacogdoches, TX

Preparing for Standardized Tests

Holt Mathematics Pre–Algebra provides many opportunities for you to prepare for standardized tests.

Test Prep Exercises

Use the Test Prep Exercises for daily practice of standardized test questions.

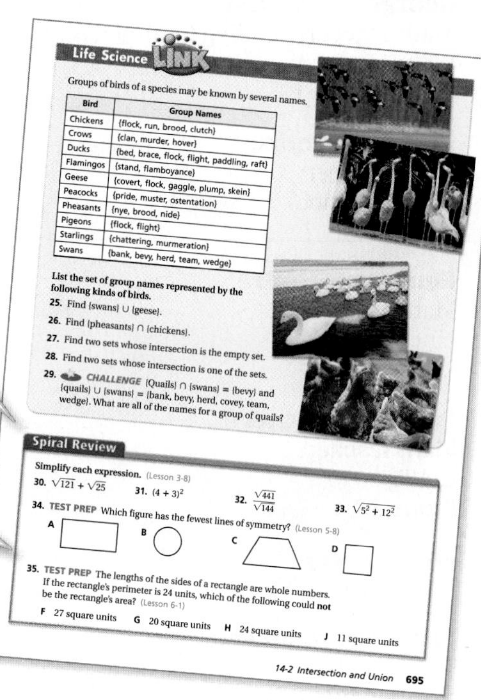

Life Science LINK

Groups of birds of a species may be known by several names.

Bird	Group Names
Chickens	{flock, run, brood, clutch}
Crows	{clan, murder, hover}
Ducks	{bed, brace, flock, flight, paddling, raft}
Flamingos	{stand, flamboyance}
Geese	{covert, flock, gaggle, plump, skein}
Peacocks	{pride, muster, ostentation}
Pheasants	{nye, brood, nide}
Pigeons	{flock, flight}
Starlings	{chattering, murmeration}
Swans	{bank, bevy, herd, team, wedge}

List the set of group names represented by the following kinds of birds.

25. Find {swans} ∪ {geese}.
26. Find {pheasants} ∩ {chickens}.
27. Find two sets whose intersection is the empty set.
28. Find two sets whose intersection is one of the sets.
29. CHALLENGE {Quails} ∩ {swans} = {bevy} and {quails} ∪ {swans} = {bank, bevy, herd, covey, team, wedge}. What are all of the names for a group of quails?

Spiral Review

Simplify each expression. (Lesson 3-8)

30. $\sqrt{121} + \sqrt{25}$ 31. $(4 + 3)^2$ 32. $\frac{\sqrt{441}}{\sqrt{144}}$ 33. $\sqrt{5^2 + 12^2}$

34. TEST PREP Which figure has the fewest lines of symmetry? (Lesson 5-8)

A B C D

35. TEST PREP The lengths of the sides of a rectangle are whole numbers. If the rectangle's perimeter is 24 units, which of the following could **not** be the rectangle's area? (Lesson 6-1)

F 27 square units G 20 square units H 24 square units J 11 square units

14-2 Intersection and Union 695

Spiral Review—Helps you practice previously covered material.

Multiple Choice—Provides cumulative practice in a format common to most standardized tests.

Performance Assessment

Use the Performance Assessment to become familiar with and practice short and extended problem solving exercises.

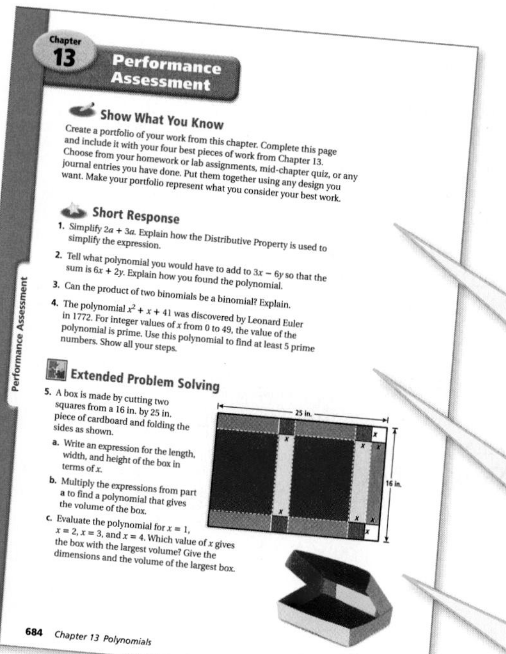

Chapter 13 Performance Assessment

Show What You Know

Create a portfolio of your work from this chapter. Complete this page and include it with your four best pieces of work from Chapter 13. Choose from your homework or lab assignments, mid-chapter quiz, or any journal entries you have done. Put them together using any design you want. Make your portfolio represent what you consider your best work.

Short Response

1. Simplify $2a + 3a$. Explain how the Distributive Property is used to simplify the expression.
2. Tell what polynomial you would have to add to $3x - 6y$ so that the sum is $6x + 2y$. Explain how you found the polynomial.
3. Can the product of two binomials be a binomial? Explain.
4. The polynomial $x^2 + x + 41$ was discovered by Leonhard Euler in 1772. For integer values of x from 0 to 49, the value of the polynomial is prime. Use this polynomial to find at least 5 prime numbers. Show all your steps.

Extended Problem Solving

5. A box is made by cutting two squares from a 16 in. by 25 in. piece of cardboard and folding the sides as shown.
   a. Write an expression for the length, width, and height of the box in terms of x.
   b. Multiply the expressions from part a to find a polynomial that gives the volume of the box.
   c. Evaluate the polynomial for $x = 1$, $x = 2$, $x = 3$, and $x = 4$. Which value of x gives the box with the largest volume? Give the dimensions and the volume of the largest box.

Performance Assessment

684 Chapter 13 Polynomials

Show What You Know explains how to create a portfolio that represents your best work.

Short Response takes basic skill problems to a new level by asking you to show and explain your work.

Extended Problem Solving guides you through the problem solving process using key exercise questions.

Standardized Test Prep

Use the Standardized Test Prep to apply test-taking strategies.

The Hot Tip provides test-taking tips to help you succeed on your tests.

This page includes practice with multiple choice and short response test items.

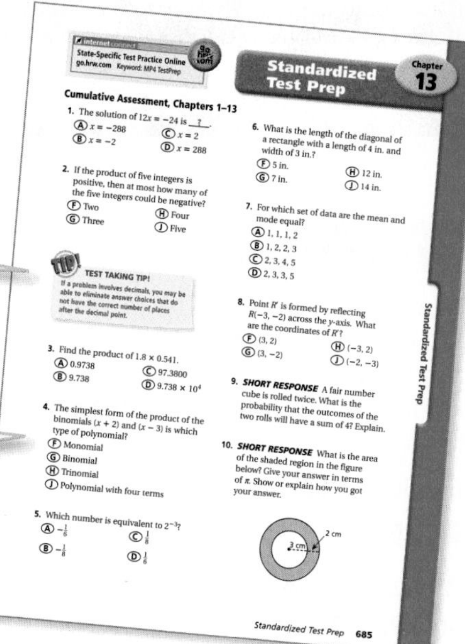

internet connect
State-Specific Test Practice Online
go.hrw.com Keyword: MP4 TestPrep

Standardized Test Prep — Chapter 13

Cumulative Assessment, Chapters 1–13

1. The solution of $12x = -24$ is __?__.
   - Ⓐ $x = -288$
   - Ⓑ $x = -2$
   - Ⓒ $x = 2$
   - Ⓓ $x = 288$
2. If the product of five integers is positive, then at most how many of the five integers could be negative?
   - Ⓕ Two
   - Ⓖ Three
   - Ⓗ Four
   - Ⓙ Five

TEST TAKING TIP! If a problem involves decimals, you may be able to eliminate answer choices that do not have the correct number of places after the decimal point.

3. Find the product of 1.8×0.541.
   - Ⓐ 0.9738
   - Ⓑ 9.738
   - Ⓒ 97.3800
   - Ⓓ 9.738×10^4
4. The simplest form of the product of the binomials $(x + 2)$ and $(x - 3)$ is which type of polynomial?
   - Ⓕ Monomial
   - Ⓖ Binomial
   - Ⓗ Trinomial
   - Ⓙ Polynomial with four terms
5. Which number is equivalent to 2^{-3}?
   - Ⓐ $-\frac{1}{6}$
   - Ⓑ $-\frac{1}{8}$
   - Ⓒ $\frac{1}{8}$
   - Ⓓ $\frac{1}{6}$
6. What is the length of the diagonal of a rectangle with a length of 4 in. and width of 3 in.?
   - Ⓕ 5 in.
   - Ⓖ 7 in.
   - Ⓗ 12 in.
   - Ⓙ 14 in.
7. For which set of data are the mean and mode equal?
   - Ⓐ 1, 1, 1, 2
   - Ⓑ 1, 2, 2, 3
   - Ⓒ 2, 3, 4, 5
   - Ⓓ 2, 3, 3, 5
8. Point R' is formed by reflecting $R(-3, -2)$ across the y-axis. What are the coordinates of R'?
   - Ⓕ (3, 2)
   - Ⓖ (3, −2)
   - Ⓗ (−3, 2)
   - Ⓙ (−2, −3)
9. ***SHORT RESPONSE*** A fair number cube is rolled twice. What is the probability that the outcomes of the two rolls will have a sum of 4? Explain.
10. ***SHORT RESPONSE*** What is the area of the shaded region in the figure below? Give your answer in terms of π. Show or explain how you got your answer.

Standardized Test Prep

Standardized Test Prep 685

Countdown to Testing — WEEK 9

DAY 1
George gets paid an hourly rate to deliver pizza, in addition to a small nightly amount for using his own car. Which of the following shows how much George makes for 1 hour, 2 hours, 3 hours, and 4 hours of work?
- Ⓐ \$3.00, \$6.00, \$12.00, \$24.00
- Ⓑ \$10.50, \$16.00, \$21.50, \$27.00
- Ⓒ \$2.00, \$4.00, \$6.00, \$8.00
- Ⓓ \$5.50, \$11.00, \$16.50, \$22.00

DAY 2
Maria wants to enlarge a photo. If the photo is 5 inches by 7 inches and Maria wants to enlarge it 2.75 times, what is the best estimate of the size of the enlarged photo?
- Ⓕ 10 inches by 14 inches
- Ⓖ 12 inches by 14 inches
- Ⓗ 15 inches by 21 inches
- Ⓙ 16 inches by 22 inches

DAY 3
Identify which sequence does not have a proportional relationship?
- Ⓐ 10, 30, 90, 270, …
- Ⓑ 0.6, 0.12, 0.24, 0.48, …
- Ⓒ $\frac{1}{2}, \frac{4}{8}, \frac{16}{32}, \frac{64}{128}, \ldots$
- Ⓓ \$2.50, \$3.00, \$3.50, \$4.00, …

DAY 4
Steve's wood-burning stove can heat his house 6°F an hour. He first lights the stove at 6:00 AM when it is 52°F. How many hours will it take for the temperature to reach 82°F?

Hour	0	1	2	3	4
Temperature (°F)	52	58	64		

- Ⓕ 3
- Ⓖ 4
- Ⓗ 5
- Ⓙ 6

DAY 5
If the pattern continues, how many white tiles will there be in the next set of tiles?
- Ⓐ 3
- Ⓑ 6

C12 Countdown to Testing

Countdown to Testing

Use the Countdown to Testing to practice for your state test every day.

There are 24 pages of practice for your state test. Each page is designed to be used in a week so that all practice will be completed before your state test is given.

Each week's page has five practice test items, one for each day of the week.

Test-Taking Tips

- ☑ Get plenty of sleep the night before the test. A rested mind thinks more clearly and you won't feel like falling asleep while taking the test.
- ☑ Draw a figure when one is not provided with the problem. If a figure is given, write any details from the problem on the figure.
- ☑ Read each problem carefully. As you finish each problem, read it again to make sure your answer is reasonable.
- ☑ Review the formula sheet that will be supplied with the test. Make sure you know when to use each formula.
- ☑ First answer problems that you know how to solve. If you do not know how to solve a problem, skip it and come back to it when you have finished the others.
- ☑ Use other test-taking strategies that can be found throughout this book, such as working backward and eliminating answer choices.

Countdown to Testing

Week 1

Day 1

Six friends went to the movies. Admission cost $7.50. Two of them bought a bag of popcorn for $3.50. Which expression can be used to find the total amount they spent?

Ⓐ 6(7.50 + 3.50)

Ⓑ 6(7.50) + 2(3.50)

Ⓒ 6 · (7.50 + 3.50)

Ⓓ 6(7.50) + 2 + (3.50)

Day 2

How many feet of wood molding would Jeremy need to trim all the walls of his bedroom?

16 ft Bedroom

20 ft

Ⓕ 4 feet

Ⓖ 32 feet

Ⓗ 72 feet

Ⓙ 320 feet

Day 3

In which month were the savings greatest?

Ⓐ June

Ⓑ July

Ⓒ August

Ⓓ September

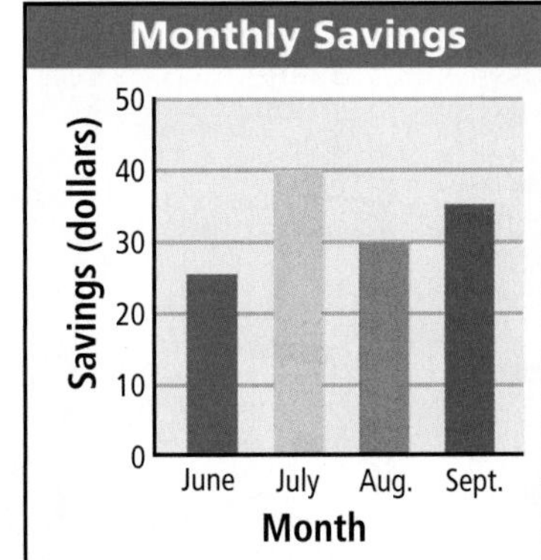

Day 4

Ravi is studying fruit flies. What is the length of the smallest fly?

2.605 mm

2.456 mm

2.508 mm

2.6 mm

Ⓕ 2.605 mm

Ⓖ 2.501 mm

Ⓗ 2.6 mm

Ⓙ 2.456 mm

Day 5

The science club is raising money for a trip. It needs to raise $240.50 so that the entire club can go. So far it has raised $169.75. How much more money does it need to raise?

Ⓐ $70.50

Ⓑ $70.75

Ⓒ $70.85

Ⓓ $71.75

Countdown to Testing

WEEK 2

DAY 1

Craig has 0.38 milliliters of a solution to pour into four equal parts. He determines that each part will contain 0.095 milliliters of the solution. Which of the following shows that Craig's solution is reasonable?

Ⓐ $4 \cdot 0.01 = 0.04$

Ⓑ $0.4 \cdot 4 = 1.6$

Ⓒ $0.1 \cdot 4 = 0.4$

Ⓓ $0.4 \cdot 0.01 = 0.004$

DAY 2

Missy's car can travel 30 miles per gallon. If Missy fills up her tank with 16 gallons of gas, which equation can be used to show how many gallons of gas are left in Missy's tank after she travels 90 miles?

Ⓕ $16(90 \div 30)$

Ⓖ $16 - \frac{90}{30}$

Ⓗ $30 + 30 + 30 - 16$

Ⓙ $90 \cdot 16 - 30$

DAY 3

What information does the circle graph not tell you about Chris?

Ⓐ Chris spends more time at soccer practice than at the library.

Ⓑ Chris spends the most amount of time doing his chores.

Ⓒ Chris spends less time at guitar practice than at soccer practice.

Ⓓ Chris spends more time doing chores than at the library.

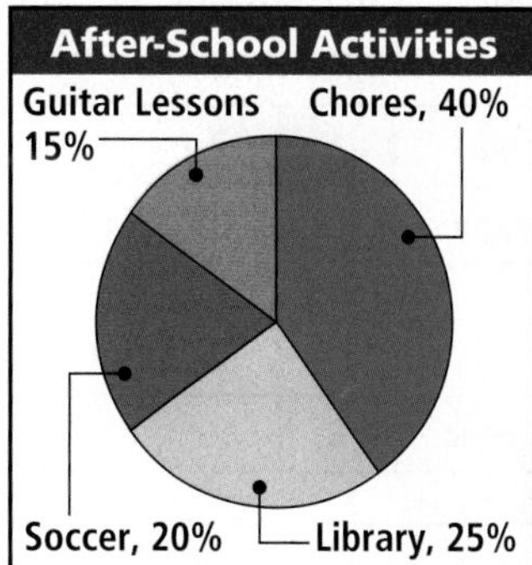

DAY 4

Ivy's Fresh Eggs transports its eggs in crates. How many crates will 8 trucks carry?

Trucks	2	3	4	5
Crates	80	120	160	200

Ⓕ 220

Ⓖ 280

Ⓗ 320

Ⓙ 360

DAY 5

When Kit woke up, it was –15°C outside. By that afternoon, the temperature had risen 20 degrees. What was the afternoon temperature?

Ⓐ –5°C

Ⓑ 5°C

Ⓒ 20°C

Ⓓ 35°C

Countdown to Testing

WEEK 3

DAY 1

Annie makes gift baskets of mini muffins. If Annie needs 20 baskets with 25 muffins in each basket, which equation shows how many dozens of muffins she must make?

Ⓐ 12(20) – 25

Ⓑ 25(20) + 12

Ⓒ 20(25) ÷ 12

Ⓓ 12(25 + 20)

DAY 2

Beth saved $2,200. A laptop costs $2199.99, extra memory is $149.50, and an extra battery is $59.95. Beth also has a coupon for $300 off one purchase at the store. Which of the following shows that Beth has saved enough for all of these items?

Ⓕ 2200 – 300 + 150 – 60 = 1,890

Ⓖ 2200 – 150 – 60 – 300 = 1,690

Ⓗ 2200 + 150 + 60 = 2,410

Ⓙ 2200 + 150 + 60 – 300 = 2,110

DAY 3

At a restaurant, a rectangular table can seat 1 person on each end and 2 on each side. When 2 tables are pushed together end to end, 10 people can sit. Which table shows the number of people who can sit at 4 tables pushed together?

Ⓐ

Tables	1	2	3	4
People	6	10	14	18

Ⓑ

Tables	1	2	3	4
People	6	10	18	24

Tables	1	2	3	4
People	6	10	12	16

Tables	1	2	3	4
People	6	10	24	48

DAY 4

Rita is playing a board game. If she had 13 points before landing on the shown spot, how many points does she have now?

Ⓕ –33

Ⓖ –7

Ⓗ 7

Ⓙ 33

DAY 5

Jorge recorded the following information while studying the effects of sunlight on plant growth. Which plant grew the most?

Plant	1	2	3	4
Change in Height (in.)	$\frac{1}{2}$	$-\frac{3}{8}$	$-\frac{1}{4}$	$\frac{7}{16}$

Ⓐ 1

Ⓑ 2

Ⓒ 3

Ⓓ 4

Countdown to Testing WEEK 4

DAY 1

Juan deposits $200 at his bank. The first quarter, Juan withdraws $150. He deposits another $100 in each of the next two quarters. How much money does Juan have now?

Ⓐ $50

Ⓑ $250

Ⓒ $350

Ⓓ $450

DAY 2

Sandra uses 3.6 meters of ribbon to weave a small rug and 4.2 meters to weave a large rug. Which expression can be used to find the total length of ribbon used for 12 small rugs and 18 large rugs?

Ⓕ 12(3.6) + 18(4.2)

Ⓖ 18(3.6) + 12(4.2)

Ⓗ 12 + 18(3.6 · 4.2)

Ⓙ 12 + 18 + 3.6 + 4.2

DAY 3

To do his homework, Ethan estimates that he will need about 185 minutes, or 4 hours. What mistake did Ethan make?

Ⓐ He rounded 185 minutes to 200.

Ⓑ He multiplied 4 by 60.

Ⓒ He underestimated the time needed.

Ⓓ He divided 185 by 60 incorrectly.

DAY 4

Andre recorded the high temperature for each day this week. What was the temperature on the warmest day?

Day	M	T	W	Th	F
(°C)	5	−15	−10	−10	−20

Ⓕ −20 Ⓗ −10

Ⓖ −15 Ⓙ 5

DAY 5

At the factory, boxes of paper clips are packed into shipping cases. How many boxes come in 5 cases?

Cases	2	3	4	5
Boxes	192	288	384	?

Ⓐ 384 Ⓒ 500

Ⓑ 480 Ⓓ 672

Countdown to Testing

WEEK 5

DAY 1

Ari had 15.3 centimeters of metal pipe. He needed to make 3 equal-size pieces for a project. Should he add, subtract, multiply, or divide to find the length of each piece?

Ⓐ Add 15.3 and 3

Ⓑ Subtract 3 from 15.3

Ⓒ Multiply 15.3 by 3

Ⓓ Divide 15.3 by 3

DAY 2

Sue needed $3\frac{2}{7}$ yards of fringe to trim each drape. If she had 8 drapes to trim, how much fringe did she need?

Ⓕ $4\frac{6}{7}$ yards

Ⓖ $11\frac{2}{7}$ yards

Ⓗ $24\frac{3}{7}$ yards

Ⓙ $26\frac{2}{7}$ yards

DAY 3

Cara used the following table to predict the number of sit-ups she would do on Sunday. She predicted 40. Is her prediction reasonable?

Day	M	T	W	Th	F	S	Su
Number of Sit-ups	2	3	5	8	12		

Ⓐ Yes, it is about right.

Ⓑ No, it is too low.

Ⓒ No, it is too high.

Ⓓ No, there is no pattern in the table.

DAY 4

The table shows how much different numbers of tickets to a hockey game cost. How many dollars would 10 tickets cost?

Tickets	2	3	5	8
Cost ($)	4.80	7.20	12.00	19.20

Ⓕ $21.60

Ⓖ $24.00

Ⓗ $29.20

Ⓙ $32.00

DAY 5

Which is the greatest number in the list?

3.3, $3\frac{1}{4}$, 3.1, 3.13, 3.11, 3.31

Ⓐ 3.13

Ⓑ $3\frac{1}{4}$

Ⓒ 3.3

Ⓓ 3.31

Countdown to Testing

WEEK 6

DAY 1

Which point is located at (2, –3)?

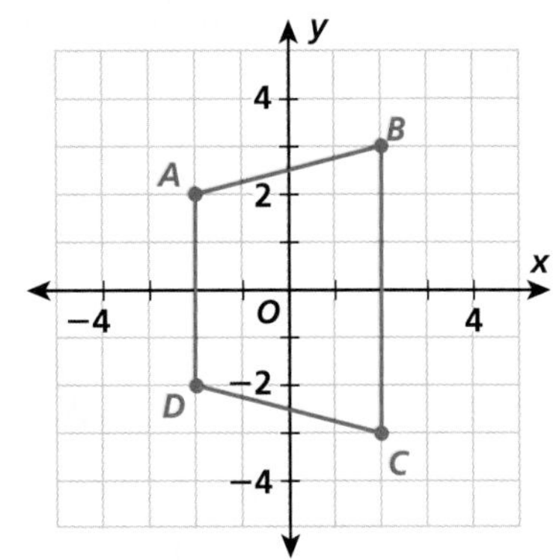

Ⓐ *A*
Ⓑ *B*
Ⓒ *C*
Ⓓ *D*

DAY 2

What are the coordinates of *F*?

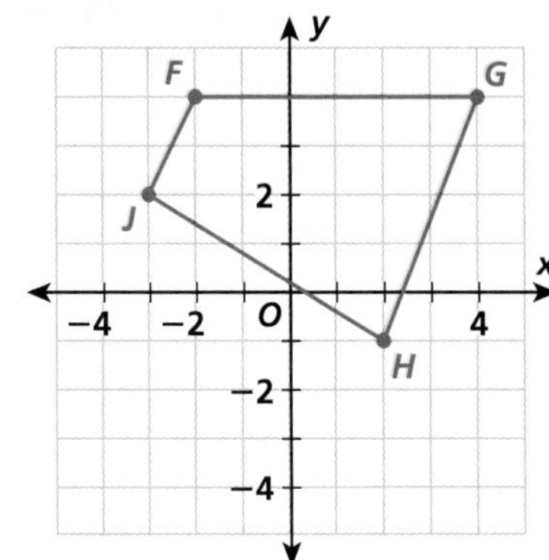

Ⓕ (–3, 2)
Ⓖ (–2, 4)
Ⓗ (4, 4)
Ⓙ (2, –1)

DAY 3

Carla is making a table based on the information in the graph. Complete the table for Monday.

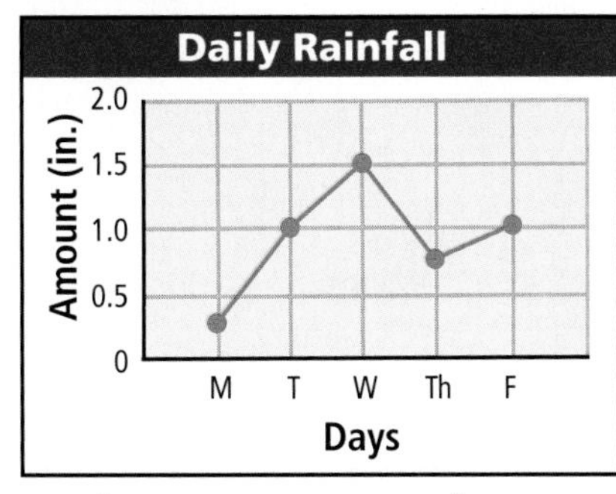

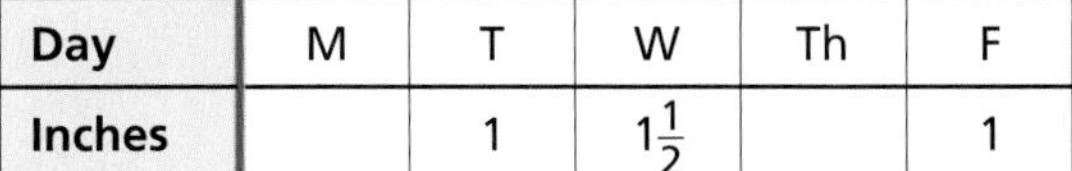

Day	M	T	W	Th	F
Inches		1	$1\frac{1}{2}$		1

Ⓐ $\frac{1}{4}$
Ⓑ $\frac{1}{2}$
Ⓒ $\frac{3}{4}$
Ⓓ 1

DAY 4

Blake works in a cheese store. The table shows how many cheese tidbits he has made at the end of each hour. If he continues at the same pace, how many tidbits will Blake have made in 6 hours?

Hours	2	3	4	5	6
Cheese Tidbits	234	351	468		

Ⓕ 585
Ⓖ 702
Ⓗ 819
Ⓙ 1404

DAY 5

Six samples of water (A, B, C, D, E, F) were collected from the lake.

A = 591.25 mL, B = 591.85 mL,
C = 591.5 mL, D = 591.75 mL,
E = 591.8 mL

If sample F measured between the greatest and least amounts, which of the following could be the amount of sample F?

Ⓐ 591.15 mL
Ⓑ 591.2 mL
Ⓒ 591.45 mL
Ⓓ 591.90 mL

Countdown to Testing — WEEK 7

DAY 1

Chandra gets paid 1.5 times her hourly wage of $12.50 per hour when she works overtime. This month she worked 20 hours of overtime.

Which of the following expressions shows how much extra money Chandra will earn this month?

Ⓐ $1.5(12.50) + 20$

Ⓑ $12.50 \div 1.5 \cdot 20$

Ⓒ $1.5(12.50) \cdot 20$

Ⓓ $20 \div 12.50 \cdot 1.5$

DAY 2

Which of the following describes the distance of the E ring from the surface of Saturn?

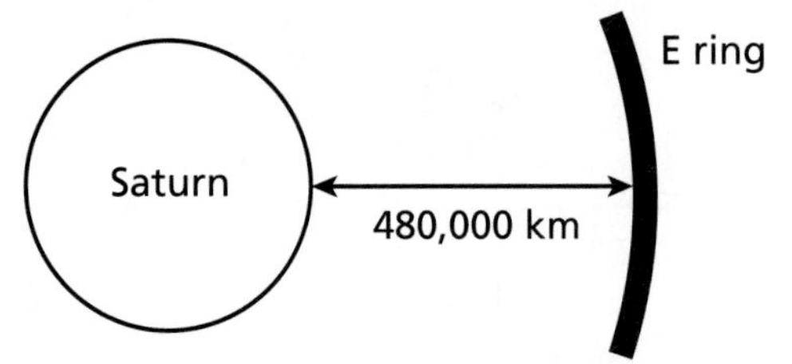

Ⓕ $4.8 \cdot 10^5$

Ⓖ $4.8 \cdot 10^6$

Ⓗ $0.48 \cdot 10^4$

Ⓙ $48 \cdot 10^5$

DAY 3

Which expression describes the following sequence?

10, 17, 31, 59, ...

Ⓐ $x + 7$

Ⓑ $2x - 3$

Ⓒ $2(x - 2)$

Ⓓ $3x - 13$

DAY 4

How many dots could be in the next figure in this sequence?

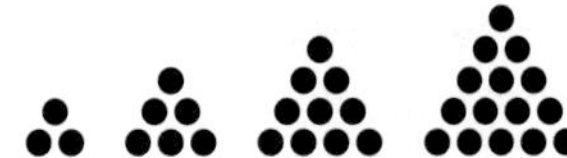

Ⓕ 20

Ⓖ 21

Ⓗ 22

Ⓙ 23

DAY 5

Every 2 hours, a hive of honeybees can produce 150 grams of honey. How many grams of honey does the hive produce in 5 hours?

Ⓐ 300

Ⓑ 375

Ⓒ 450

Ⓓ 750

Countdown to Testing

WEEK 8

DAY 1

Ronnie ties his dog to an 8-foot length of rope attached to a pole. What is the distance around the circle the dog can run? Use 3.14 for π.

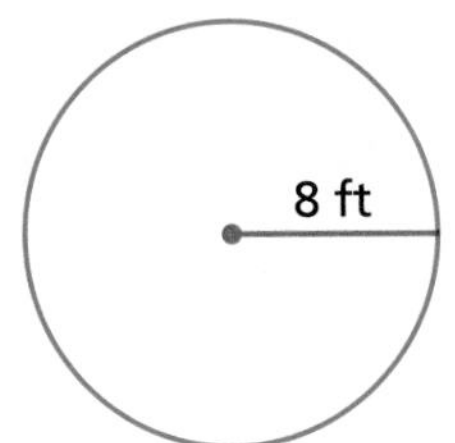

Ⓐ 25.12 feet
Ⓑ 50.24 feet
Ⓒ 100.48 feet
Ⓓ 200.96 feet

DAY 2

Shawn uses a ramp to get in and out of his house. What is the height of the ramp? Round your answer to the nearest tenth.

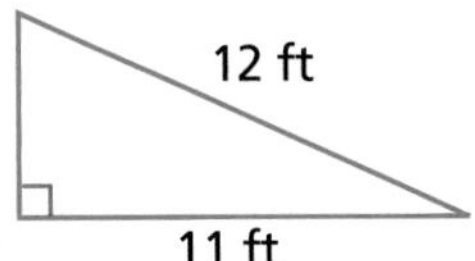

Ⓕ 1.09 feet
Ⓖ 2.5 feet
Ⓗ 3.6 feet
Ⓙ 4.8 feet

DAY 3

Carla receives a special offer from an online bookseller. For every \$50 she spends, she'll receive \$5 off her purchases. Carla spends \$142.50 and estimates she'll pay about \$133. Which of the following shows that Carla's estimate is reasonable?

Ⓐ 142.50 – 50 = 92.50
Ⓑ 142.50 + 50 – 50 = 197.50
Ⓒ 142.50 – 2(5) = 132.50
Ⓓ 142.50 – 3(5) = 127.50

DAY 4

Jerry is building two triangular tables from a piece of rectangular wood. If the wood measures 24 inches by 36 inches, how many inches will the third side of each table be? Round to the nearest tenth.

Ⓕ 24.7 inches
Ⓖ 36.3 inches
Ⓗ 43.3 inches
Ⓙ 60 inches

DAY 5

Carolyn is building a triangular headboard for her bed. What is its height? Round your answer to the nearest tenth.

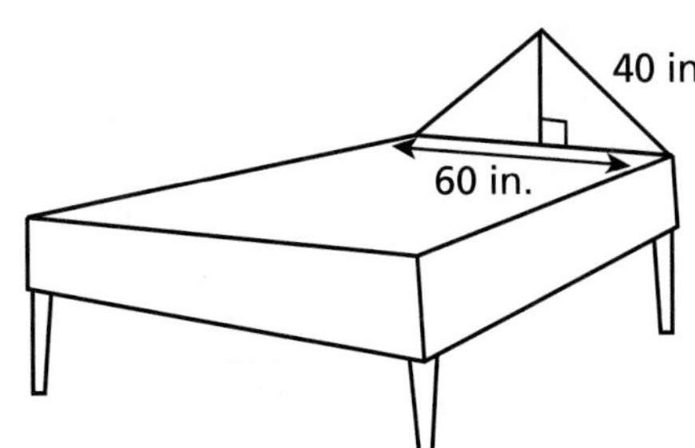

Ⓐ 8.3 inches
Ⓑ 10 inches
Ⓒ 26.5 inches
Ⓓ 100 inches

Countdown to Testing

WEEK 9

DAY 1

George gets paid an hourly rate to deliver pizza, in addition to a small nightly amount for using his own car. Which of the following shows how much George makes for 1 hour, 2 hours, 3 hours, and 4 hours of work?

Ⓐ $3.00, $6.00, $12.00, $24.00

Ⓑ $10.50, $16.00, $21.50, $27.00

Ⓒ $2.00, $4.00, $6.00, $8.00

Ⓓ $5.50, $11.00, $16.50, $22.00

DAY 2

Maria wants to enlarge a photo. If the photo is 5 inches by 7 inches and Maria wants to enlarge it 2.75 times, what is the best estimate of the size of the enlarged photo?

Ⓕ 10 inches by 14 inches

Ⓖ 12 inches by 14 inches

Ⓗ 15 inches by 21 inches

Ⓙ 16 inches by 22 inches

DAY 3

Identify which sequence does not have a proportional relationship?

Ⓐ 10, 30, 90, 270, ...

Ⓑ 0.6, 0.12, 0.24, 0.48, ...

Ⓒ $\frac{1}{2}, \frac{4}{8}, \frac{16}{32}, \frac{64}{128}, \ldots$

Ⓓ $2.50, $3.00, $3.50, $4.00, ...

DAY 4

Steve's wood-burning stove can heat his house 6°F an hour. He first lights the stove at 6:00 AM when it is 52°F. How many hours will it take for the temperature to reach 82°F?

Hour	0	1	2	3	4
Temperature (°F)	52	58	64		

Ⓕ 3

Ⓖ 4

Ⓗ 5

Ⓙ 6

DAY 5

If the pattern continues, how many white tiles will there be in the next set of tiles?

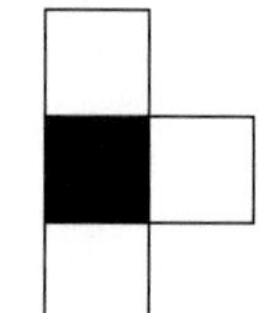

Ⓐ 3

Ⓑ 6

Ⓒ 10

Ⓓ 12

Countdown to Testing

WEEK 10

DAY 1

The table shows the typing rates of four applicants for a job. Based on typing rates, which applicant is the best choice to hire?

Applicant	Words	Minute
Ann	112	6
Theo	206	8
June	195	7
Andy	120	5

Ⓐ June
Ⓑ Ann
Ⓒ Andy
Ⓓ Theo

DAY 2

If figure *ABCD* is dilated by a scale factor of 3, which ordered pair describes the new location of *C*?

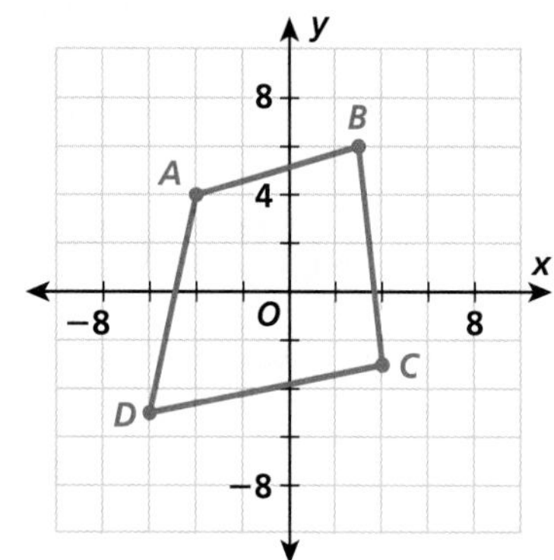

Ⓕ (−12, 9)
Ⓖ (9, 18)
Ⓗ (4, −3)
Ⓙ (12, −9)

DAY 3

Dylan is making a circular garden. Its diameter is 3.2 ft. What is its circumference? Use 3.14 for π. Round to the nearest tenth.

Ⓐ 6.4 ft
Ⓑ 10 ft
Ⓒ 20.1 ft
Ⓓ 32.2 ft

DAY 4

A chandelier uses three different sizes of bulbs. Each bulb is twice as large as the previous one. What is the diameter of the largest bulb?

C = 6.28 in.

Ⓕ 2 inches
Ⓖ 3.14 inches
Ⓗ 8 inches
Ⓙ 12.56 inches

DAY 5

Mr. Bryce bought a hybrid car that can travel 240 miles on 8 gallons of gas. How far can Mr. Bryce travel on 10 gallons of gas?

Ⓐ 280 miles
Ⓑ 300 miles
Ⓒ 480 miles
Ⓓ 2400 miles

DAY 1

Simon is shopping for a new mountain bike. He finds one that costs $179.95, but he has a coupon. By which number should Simon multiply the price of the bike to calculate how much money he'll save?

Metro Bikes	10% OFF The purchase of any bike offer good until 9/1

Ⓐ 0.01
Ⓑ 0.1
Ⓒ 1.0
Ⓓ 10.0

DAY 2

Christina wants to paint a circle with a radius of 4 feet on her bedroom wall. If 1 can of paint covers 26 square feet, how many cans of paint will Christina need to buy?

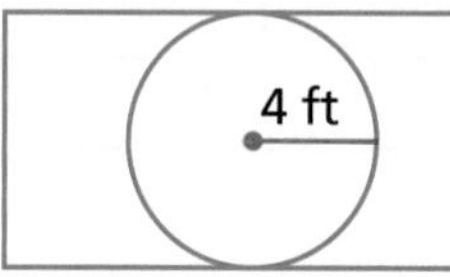

Ⓕ 1
Ⓖ 2
Ⓗ 3
Ⓙ 4

DAY 3

Jake is a reporter for a local newspaper. He has rewritten 68% of an interview that lasted 87 minutes. Which is the best estimate of the number of minutes Jake has transcribed?

Ⓐ 18 minutes
Ⓑ 48 minutes
Ⓒ 54 minutes
Ⓓ 63 minutes

DAY 4

Four people are playing a trivia game. Their scores are shown in the table. Which player has the lowest score?

Player	1	2	3	4
Score	−30	10	−25	50

Ⓕ 1
Ⓖ 2
Ⓗ 3
Ⓙ 4

DAY 5

For every 3 scarves that Kendall knits, Rhonda can knit 4 hats. When Kendall has knit 15 scarves, how many hats will Rhonda have knit?

Kendall	3	6	9	12
Rhonda	4	8		

Ⓐ 20
Ⓑ 24
Ⓒ 30
Ⓓ 60

Countdown to Testing

WEEK 12

DAY 1

A manufacturer of doll clothes produces more white dresses than blue dresses by a factor of 3.5. Given *b*, the number of blue dresses produced, which equation shows *w*, the number of white dresses produced?

Ⓐ $w = b \div 3.5$

Ⓑ $w = \frac{3.5}{b}$

Ⓒ $w = 3.5b$

Ⓓ $w = 3.5 + b$

DAY 2

At dinner, Mr. and Mrs. Brandt decide to leave a 20% tip for their server. Which is the best estimate of their tip if their meals total $63.20?

Ⓕ $1.20

Ⓖ $12.00

Ⓗ $14.00

Ⓙ $120.00

DAY 3

Tom is working with his lab group on a chemistry project. Each group member recorded the weight of a sample after a chemical reaction. Which number, rounded to the nearest hundredth, should be used for the weight of solution B?

Solution	A	B	C	D
Weight (g)	42.28	$47\frac{12}{17}$	50.16	44.09

Ⓐ 47.17 grams

Ⓑ 47.7 grams

Ⓒ 47.71 grams

Ⓓ 48.42 grams

DAY 4

Ronald followed this recipe for fruit punch. How many cups did he make? Write your answer in simpest terms.

Fantastic Fruit Punch

$1\frac{3}{4}$ cups orange juice

$\frac{2}{3}$ cup cranberry juice

$1\frac{1}{3}$ cups white grape juice

$\frac{1}{4}$ cup lime juice

Combine ingredients. Chill until ready to serve.

Ⓕ 3 cups

Ⓖ $3\frac{1}{2}$ cups

Ⓗ 4 cups

Ⓙ $4\frac{2}{3}$ cups

DAY 5

Mark is researching the effects of diet on mice. The table below shows the percent change in weight of each mouse studied. If the mice weighed the same at the start of the experiment, which mouse lost the most weight?

Mouse	% Change in Weight
1	−9.2
2	3.25
3	−9.05
4	−9.095

Ⓐ 1

Ⓑ 2

Ⓒ 3

Ⓓ 4

Countdown to Testing WEEK 13

DAY 1

Which of the following correctly shows the length of the Earth's equator?

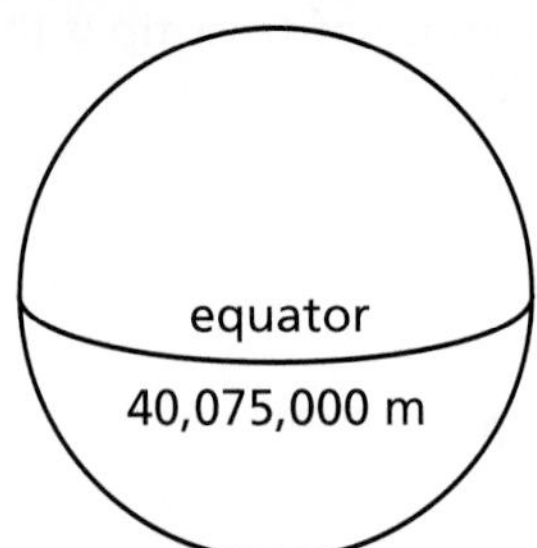

Ⓐ 0.40075×10^7 meters

Ⓑ 4.0075×10^7 meters

Ⓒ 40.075×10^7 meters

Ⓓ $4{,}007.5 \times 10^7$ meters

DAY 2

Figure *ABCD* is dilated by a scale factor of $\frac{3}{2}$. What are the coordinates of *C* after the dilation?

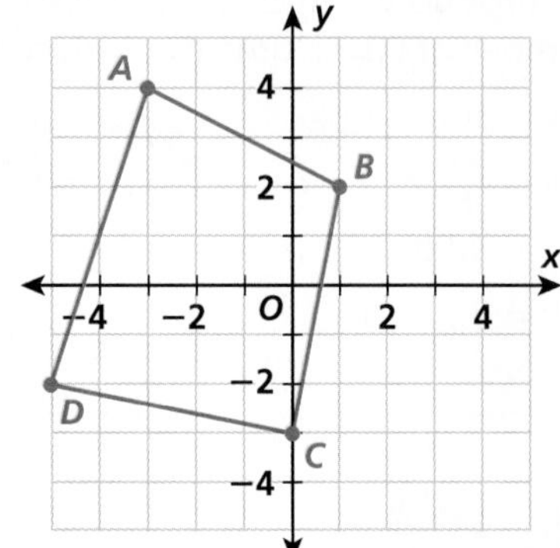

Ⓕ (2, –4)

Ⓖ $(0, -4\frac{1}{2})$

Ⓗ $(0, -1\frac{1}{2})$

Ⓙ (0, –2)

DAY 3

The Gordon family is driving to the Grand Canyon from Lubbock, Texas. If they drive an average of 55 miles per hour for *h* hours, which equation shows *d*, the distance they traveled?

Ⓐ $d = 55h$

Ⓑ $d = 55 \div h$

Ⓒ $d = \frac{h}{55}$

Ⓓ $d = 55 + h$

DAY 4

This rectangle is enlarged by a scale factor of 3. What is the new length in centimeters?

Ⓕ 9 centimeters

Ⓖ 10 centimeters

Ⓗ 20 centimeters

Ⓙ 21 centimeters

DAY 5

If these two figures are similar, what is the missing length of figure B?

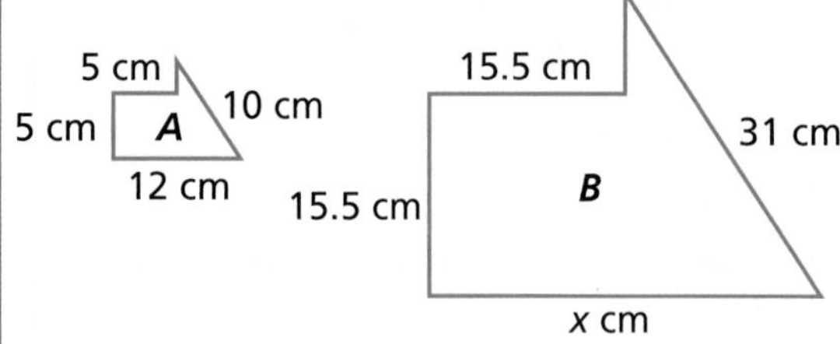

Ⓐ 3.1 centimeters

Ⓑ 22.5 centimeters

Ⓒ 25.2 centimeters

Ⓓ 37.2 centimeters

Countdown to Testing

WEEK 14

DAY 1

Television screen size is measured on the diagonal. What is the height of this screen? Round your answer to the nearest tenth.

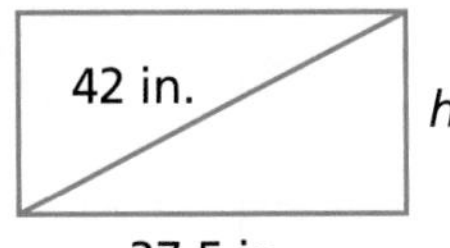

Ⓐ 4.5 inches
Ⓑ 9.0 inches
Ⓒ 18.9 inches
Ⓓ 20.3 inches

DAY 2

Which point is at $(-5, -\frac{1}{2})$?

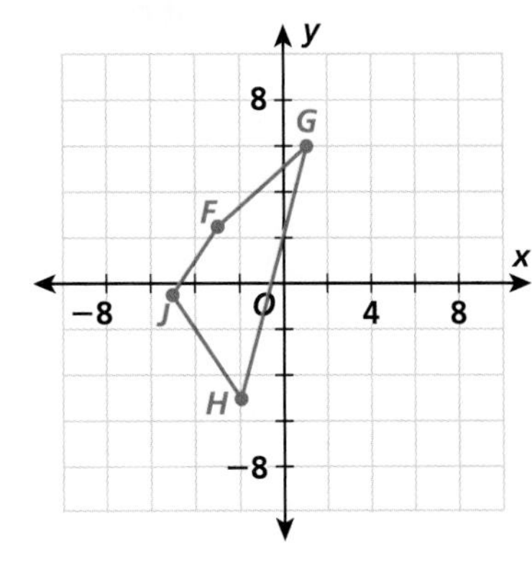

Ⓕ *F*
Ⓖ *G*
Ⓗ *H*
Ⓙ *J*

DAY 3

Martin can repair 7 watches in 1 hour when he begins work in the morning. The next hour, Martin repairs one less watch. If this pattern continues, which of the following shows how many watches Martin repairs in the third, fourth, fifth, and sixth hours?

Ⓐ 5, 4, 3, 2
Ⓑ 6, 4, 2, 1
Ⓒ 14, 21, 28, 35
Ⓓ 8, 9, 10, 11

DAY 4

If these two figures are similar, what is the missing measure in figure B?

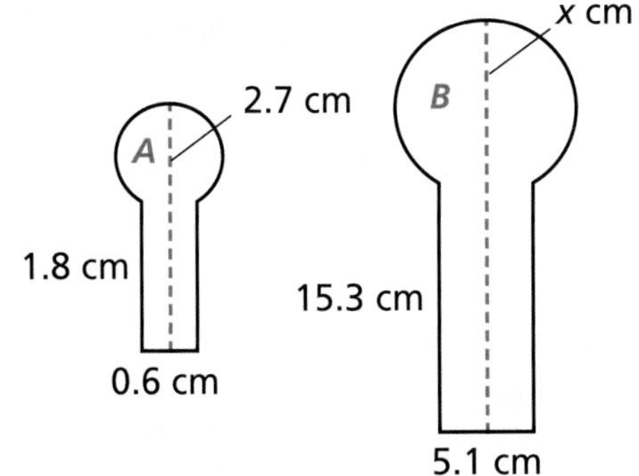

Ⓕ 18 centimeters
Ⓖ 20.4 centimeters
Ⓗ 22.95 centimeters
Ⓙ 30.6 centimeters

DAY 5

Gina is drawing a scale model of a park. If the scale factor is 1 inch = 4 feet, what is the perimeter of the actual park?

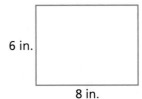

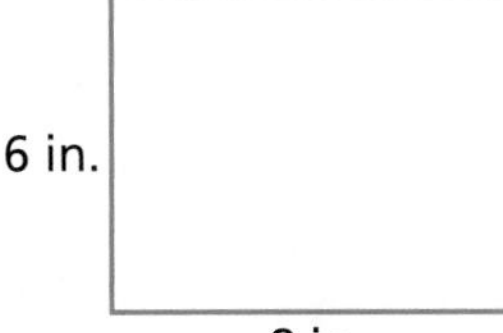

Ⓐ 28 feet
Ⓑ 56 feet
Ⓒ 112 feet
Ⓓ 768 feet

Countdown to Testing

WEEK 15

DAY 1

If figure *LMNO* is reflected across the *x*-axis, which point(s) will **not** change locations?

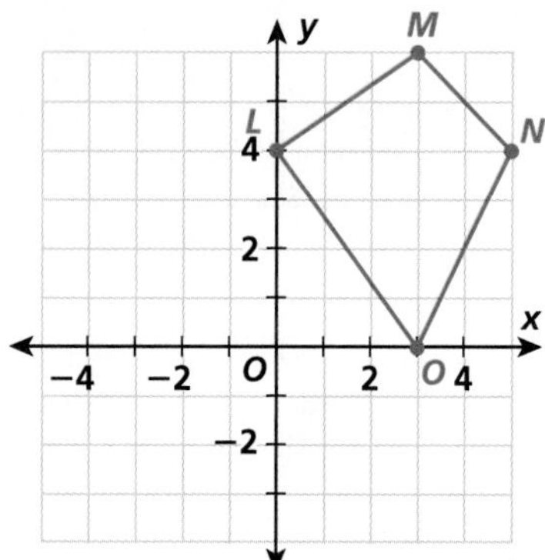

Ⓐ *L* and *O*

Ⓑ *L*

Ⓒ *O*

Ⓓ *L* and *N*

DAY 2

If figure *PQRS* is dilated by a scale factor of $\frac{1}{2}$, which point will be located at $\left(2, -1\frac{1}{2}\right)$?

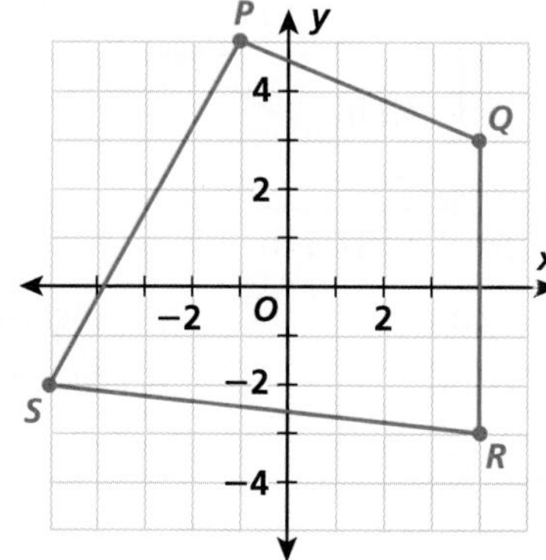

Ⓕ *P*

Ⓖ *Q*

Ⓗ *R*

Ⓙ *S*

DAY 3

The number 48 is 6% of which number?

Ⓐ 28.8

Ⓑ 80

Ⓒ 288

Ⓓ 800

DAY 4

Which figure does **not** form a tessellation?

Figure 1

Figure 2

Figure 3

Figure 4

Ⓕ Figure 1

Ⓖ Figure 2

Ⓗ Figure 3

Ⓙ Figure 4

DAY 5

What is the side length of this square? Round your answer to the nearest tenth.

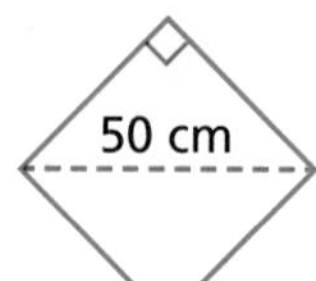

Ⓐ 5.0 centimeters

Ⓑ 11.2 centimeters

Ⓒ 25.0 centimeters

Ⓓ 35.4 centimeters

Countdown to Testing

WEEK 16

DAY 1

A computer's hard drive spins at 5400 revolutions per minute. If the hard drive has been running for *m* minutes, which expression shows *r*, the number of revolutions?

(A) $r = m \div 5400$

(B) $r = 5400 \cdot m$

(C) $r = 5400 + m$

(D) $r = \frac{5400}{m}$

DAY 2

Which expression describes this sequence?

…, 23, 25, 27, 29, …

(F) $3x - 3$

(G) $3 + 2x$

(H) $2x - 2$

(J) $x^2 + 1$

DAY 3

Figures A and B are similar. If the area of Figure A is 218.75 square centimeters, which expression could you use to determine the area of Figure B?

Figure A

17.5 cm | 218.75 cm^2

Figure B

? | 3.5 cm

(A) $17.5 \div 3.5$

(B) $218.75 \div 25$

(C) $5 \cdot 218.75$

(D) $3.5 \cdot 17.5$

DAY 4

Katie wants to frame this stained-glass window with wood. What length of wood does she need to buy? Round your answer to the nearest tenth.

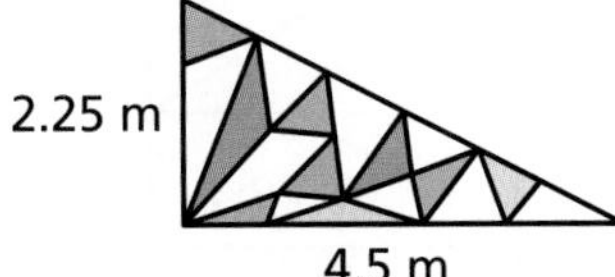

(F) 5 meters

(G) 6.8 meters

(H) 11.8 meters

(J) 13.5 meters

DAY 5

What is the length of side *c*?

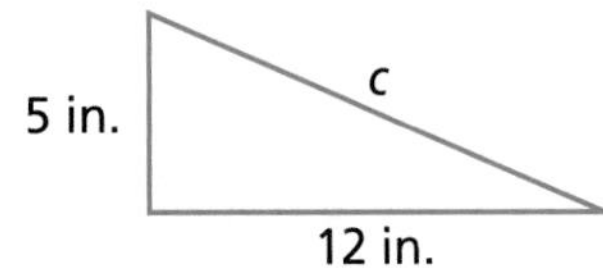

(A) 12 inches

(B) 13 inches

(C) 25 inches

(D) 169 inches

Countdown to Testing

WEEK 17

DAY 1

The Great Pyramid in Giza, Egypt, is a rectangular pyramid. Which formula could you use to determine the volume of the pyramid?

Ⓐ $V = \frac{1}{2}Bh$

Ⓑ $V = \frac{1}{3}Bh$

Ⓒ $V = Bh$

Ⓓ $V = \frac{4}{3}\pi r^3$

DAY 2

For which of the following shapes could you **not** use the formula $V = Bh$ to find the volume?

Ⓕ hexagonal prism

Ⓖ cylinder

Ⓗ rectangular prism

Ⓙ triangular pyramid

DAY 3

Nick buys a new fish tank for his living room. Which is the best estimate of the volume of water Nick needs to fill the tank?

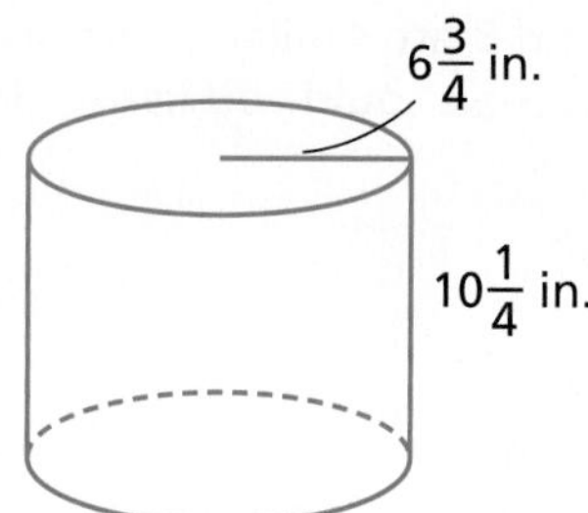

Ⓐ 70 cubic inches

Ⓑ 147 cubic inches

Ⓒ 1080 cubic inches

Ⓓ 1470 cubic inches

DAY 4

If $\triangle ACE$ is similar to $\triangle BCD$, what is the length of AC?

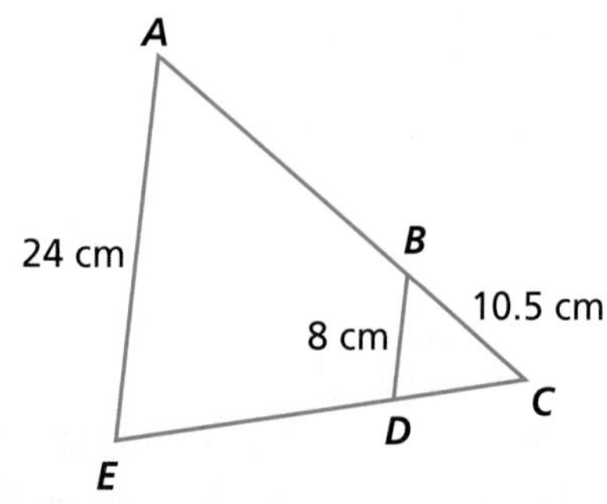

Ⓕ 5.5 centimeters

Ⓖ 13.5 centimeters

Ⓗ 21.5 centimeters

Ⓙ 31.5 centimeters

DAY 5

Candace is building a bookcase with shelves that are right triangles. What is the measure across the front of the bookcase? Round your answer to the nearest whole unit.

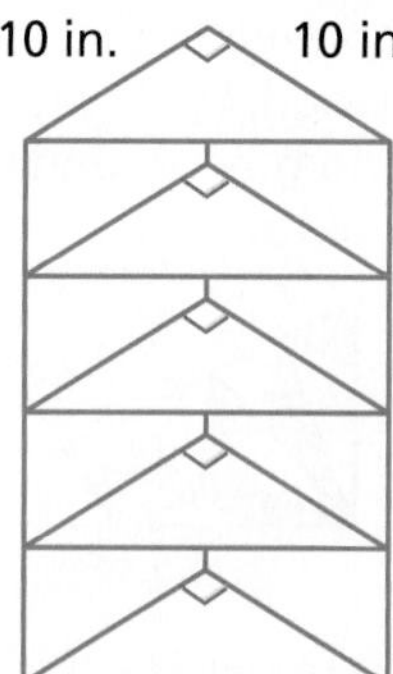

Ⓐ 4 inches

Ⓑ 14 inches

Ⓒ 50 inches

Ⓓ 72 inches

Countdown to Testing

WEEK 18

DAY 1

What is the surface area of this square pyramid?

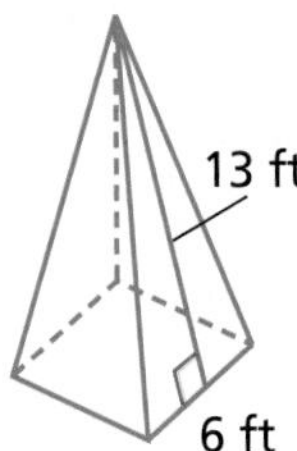

Ⓐ 75 square feet

Ⓑ 156 square feet

Ⓒ 192 square feet

Ⓓ 348 square feet

DAY 2

Sherman wants to paint the lateral surface area of the base for a sculpture he made. Which is the best estimate of the area Sherman wants to paint?

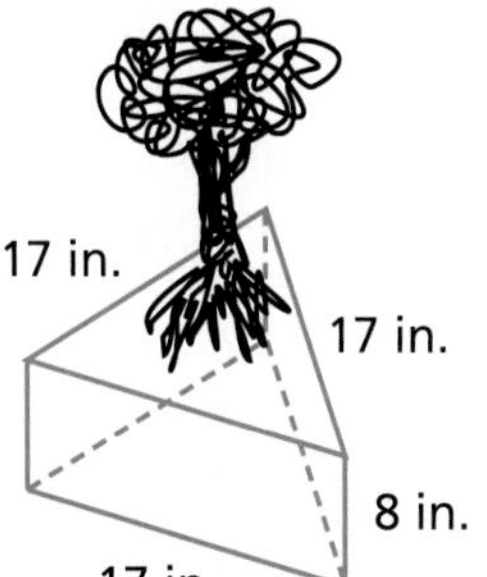

Ⓕ 51 square inches

Ⓖ 136 square inches

Ⓗ 408 square inches

Ⓙ 533 square inches

DAY 3

At a garage sale, Curtis buys a planter for his backyard. With base area *B* and height *h*, which formula should Curtis use to find the volume of soil he will need to fill the planter?

Ⓐ $V = Bh$

Ⓑ $V = \frac{1}{2}Bh$

Ⓒ $V = \frac{4}{3}\pi r^3$

Ⓓ $V = \frac{1}{3}Bh$

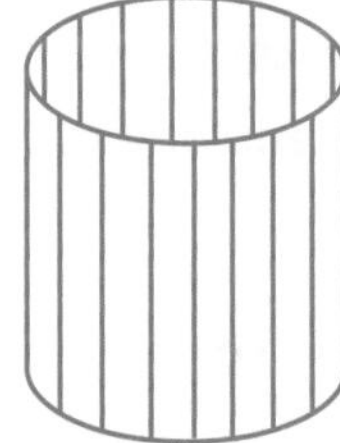

DAY 4

Nina is designing a pattern that is made up of equilateral triangles. If all the triangles are similar, what is the combined area of three shaded triangles?

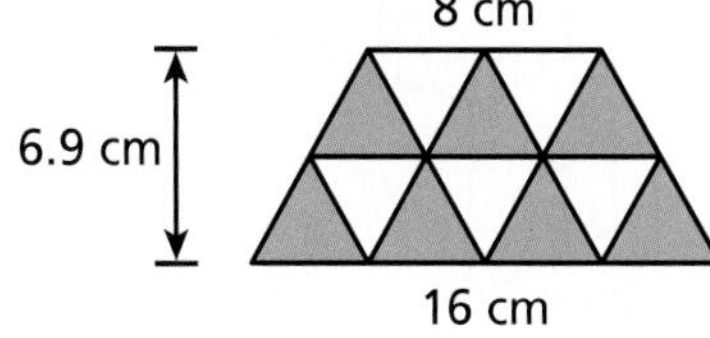

Ⓕ 6.9 square centimeters

Ⓖ 20.7 square centimeters

Ⓗ 27.6 square centimeters

Ⓙ 82.8 square centimeters

DAY 5

What percent of the larger rectangle's area is the smaller rectangle's area?

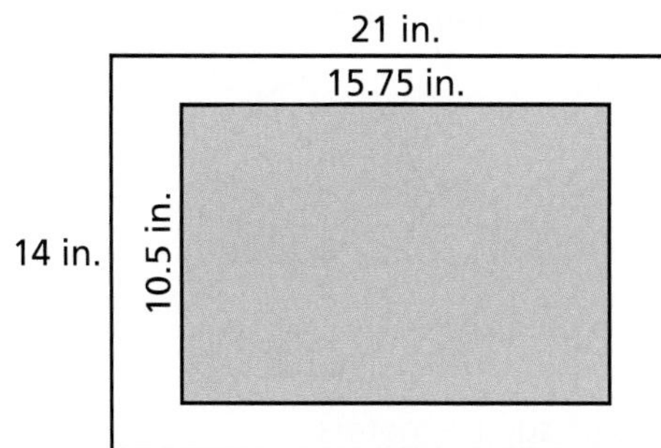

Ⓐ 0.75%

Ⓑ 5.25%

Ⓒ 56.25%

Ⓓ 103%

Countdown to Testing

WEEK 19

DAY 1

Which formula would you use to find the volume of this globe?

Ⓐ $V = \frac{4}{3}\pi r^3$

Ⓑ $V = Bh$

Ⓒ $V = \frac{1}{3}Bh$

Ⓓ $V = \frac{1}{2}Bh$

DAY 2

What is the best estimate of the lateral surface area of this vase if the radius is 6 inches and the slant height is 13 inches?

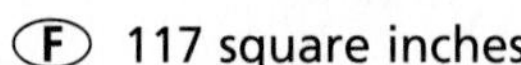

Ⓕ 117 square inches

Ⓖ 234 square inches

Ⓗ 468 square inches

Ⓙ 1404 square inches

DAY 3

Mia made this net of a triangular prism. What is the surface area of the prism?

Ⓐ 615 square centimeters

Ⓑ 840 square centimeters

Ⓒ 877.5 square centimeters

Ⓓ 915 square centimeters

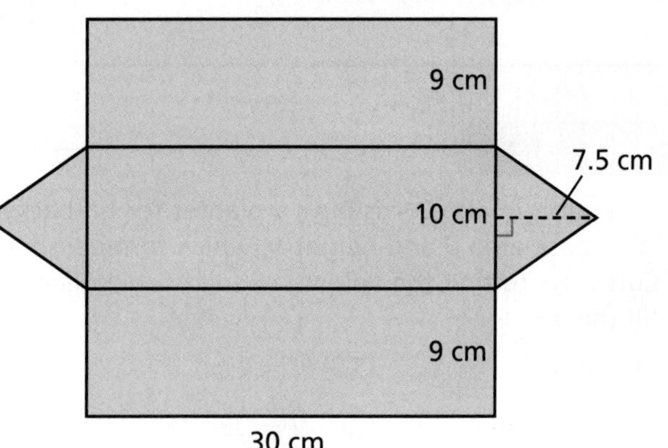

DAY 4

Paola drew a circle with four congruent circles inside it. If the area of the large circle is 167.2 square meters, what is the area of one small circle?

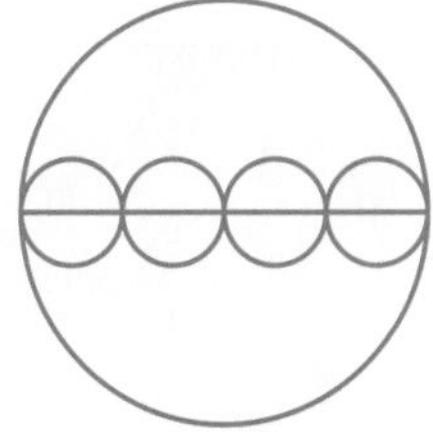

Ⓕ 5.65 square meters

Ⓖ 10.45 square meters

Ⓗ 18.54 square meters

Ⓙ 41.83 square meters

DAY 5

The roof of the greenhouse, which forms half a cylinder, is covered in glass. What is the surface area of the glass roof?

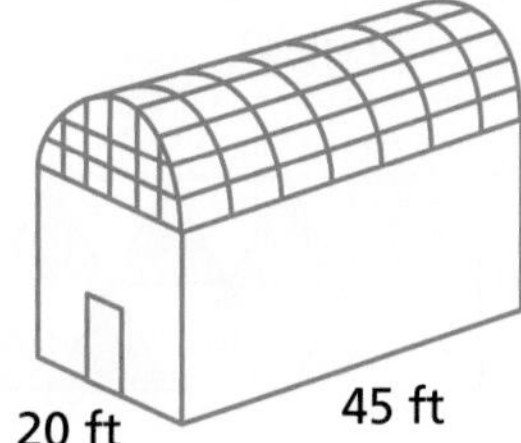

Ⓐ 1,727 square feet

Ⓑ 2,041 square feet

Ⓒ 3,140 square feet

Ⓓ 3,454 square feet

Countdown to Testing

WEEK 20

DAY 1

What is the best measure of the central tendency of these test scores?

92, 85, 89, 93, 74, 94

Ⓐ mean
Ⓑ median
Ⓒ mode
Ⓓ range

DAY 2

What is the lateral surface area of this pentagonal prism? Every side on the base has the same measurement.

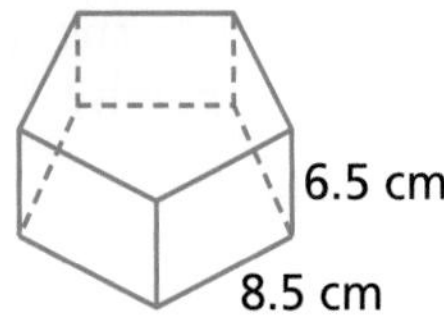

Ⓕ 120 square centimeters
Ⓖ 211.25 square centimeters
Ⓗ 212.5 square centimeters
Ⓙ 276.25 square centimeters

DAY 3

Philip created this table for the data in the graph. What mistake did he make?

Plant	A	B	C	D
Height (in.)	$1\frac{1}{2}$	3	1	$2\frac{1}{4}$

Ⓐ He confused the data for plants A and C.
Ⓑ He misread the data for plant C.
Ⓒ He rounded the data to the nearest $\frac{1}{4}$ inch.
Ⓓ He misread the data for plant D.

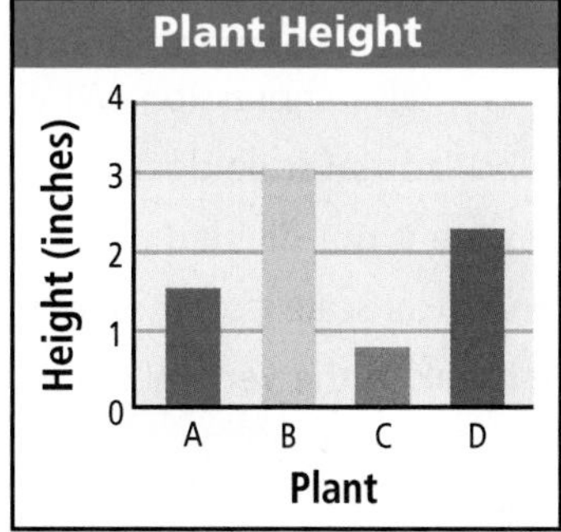

DAY 4

In this figure, each rectangle has $\frac{1}{4}$ less area than the rectangle directly enclosing it. What is the area of the smallest rectangle in this figure?

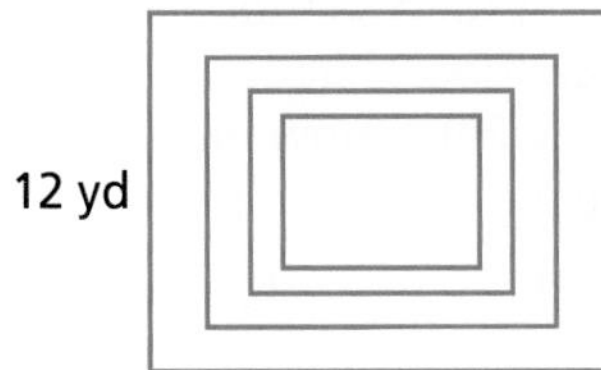

Ⓕ 81 square yards
Ⓖ 108 square yards
Ⓗ 144 square yards
Ⓙ 192 square yards

DAY 5

What is the possible next term in this pattern?

1, 8, 64, 512, ▢

Ⓐ 576
Ⓑ 582
Ⓒ 2,048
Ⓓ 4,096

Countdown to Testing

WEEK 21

DAY 1

Liu is researching the speeds of some of the fastest animals on Earth. Which of the following is the most appropriate method for her to display the data she finds on animals and their top speeds?

Ⓐ stem-and-leaf plot

Ⓑ scatter plot

Ⓒ line graph

Ⓓ bar graph

DAY 2

Bruno surveys his classmates about their favorite pet. What is the best measure of central tendency of this data?

Ⓕ mode

Ⓖ range

Ⓗ mean

Ⓙ median

DAY 3

This graph shows a company's monthly profits, but it gives a false impression. Why?

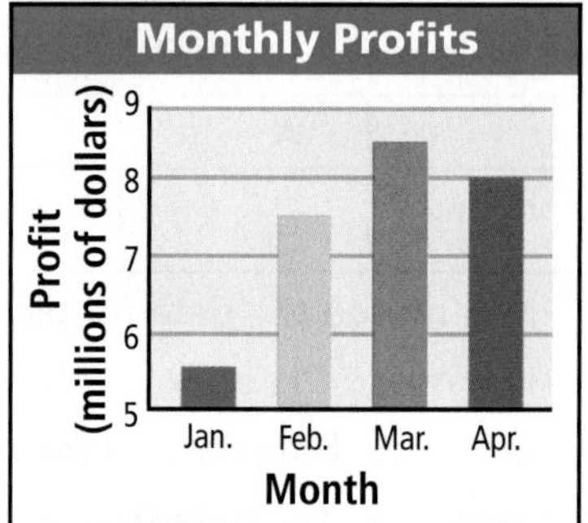

Ⓐ The horizontal scale does not start with 0.

Ⓑ The scale is not divided into equal increments.

Ⓒ The vertical scale does not start at 0.

Ⓓ The break in the vertical scale exaggerates the data.

DAY 4

Keenan creates a sequence using blocks. The pattern of the sequence is shown in the table. How many blocks will he use for the fourteenth figure in the sequence?

Figure	1	2	3	4
Blocks	1	3	6	9

Ⓕ 36

Ⓖ 39

Ⓗ 42

Ⓙ 45

DAY 5

Jimmy buys 44 feet of wood to build a square frame for a sandbox. He decides to make the sandbox smaller and reduces its perimeter by 20%. How much wood will be left over?

Ⓐ 8.8 feet

Ⓑ 17.6 feet

Ⓒ 26.4 feet

Ⓓ 35.2 feet

Countdown to Testing — WEEK 22

DAY 1

Which conclusion can you draw about worker productivity based on the scatter plot?

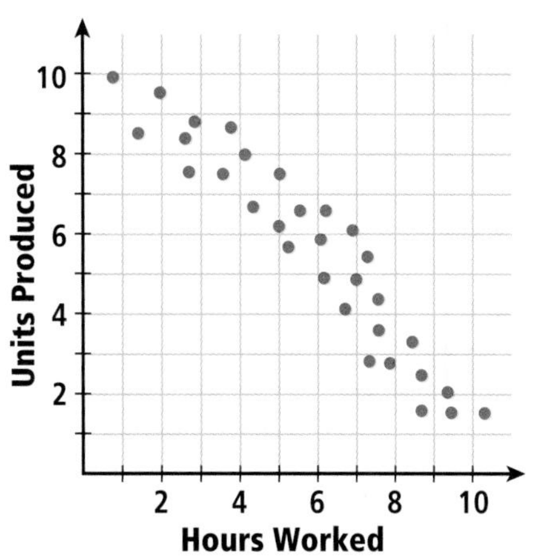

Ⓐ Productivity increases during the work day.

Ⓑ There is no trend for productivity in the scatter plot.

Ⓒ As the work day progresses, productivity declines.

Ⓓ Productivity remains constant during the work day.

DAY 2

Why is this bar graph misleading?

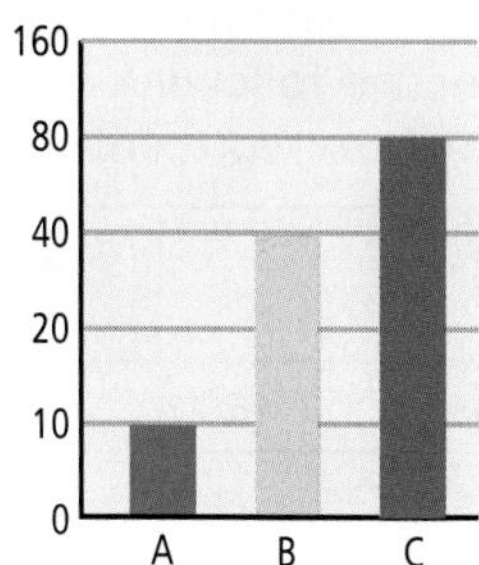

Ⓕ The scale is not divided into equal intervals, so the differences among the data seems less than they really are.

Ⓖ The horizontal scale does not start at 0, which skews the data.

Ⓗ The scale is not divided into equal intervals, so the differences among the data seems greater than they really are.

Ⓙ The bar graph is not misleading.

DAY 3

Kyle is studying the speed of cars as they drive by his house. Which of the following is the most appropriate way for Kyle to display his data?

Ⓐ circle graph　　Ⓒ stem-and-leaf plot

Ⓑ bar graph　　Ⓓ line graph

DAY 4

Ben is building a wall. What length of wood does Ben need to buy to create two cross beams for the frame? Round your answer to the nearest tenth.

Ⓕ 4.3 meters

Ⓖ 5.8 meters

Ⓗ 8.5 meters

Ⓙ 11.6 meters

2.1 m

3.7 m

DAY 5

If this pattern continues, how many circles will be in the eighth group in this sequence?

○ , ○△ , ○△□ ,

○△□○ , ○△□○△ , ...

Ⓐ 2　　Ⓒ 4

Ⓑ 3　　Ⓓ 5

Countdown to Testing WEEK 23

DAY 1

The frequency table shows the number of days of rain in each month for one year. Which of the following is the most appropriate way to represent this data?

Days of Rain	0–2	3–5	6–8	9–11
Frequency	4	6	2	0

Ⓐ histogram
Ⓑ bar graph
Ⓒ circle graph
Ⓓ line plot

DAY 2

Which conclusion can you draw based on the data in this scatter plot?

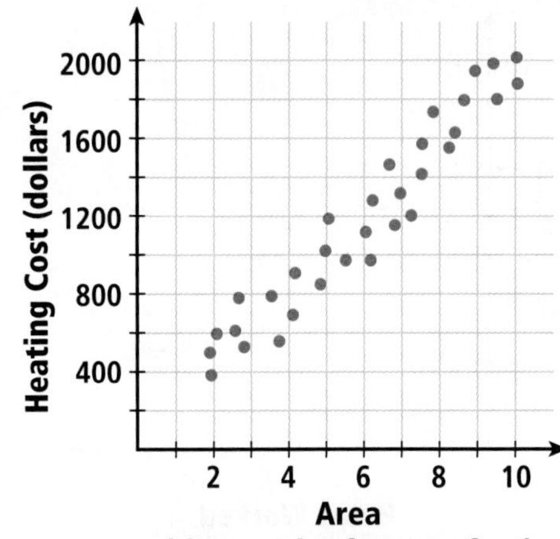

Ⓕ The smaller the area, the more expensive the heating costs.
Ⓖ Heating costs remain constant.
Ⓗ The scatter plot does not show a trend.
Ⓙ The larger the area, the greater the heating costs.

DAY 3

Tamara records the high temperature for each day this month. Which would be the most appropriate way for Tamara to display the data if she wants to see the change in temperature over time?

Ⓐ circle graph
Ⓑ line plot
Ⓒ line graph
Ⓓ scatter plot

DAY 4

If the two rectangles are similar, what is the length of the smaller rectangle?

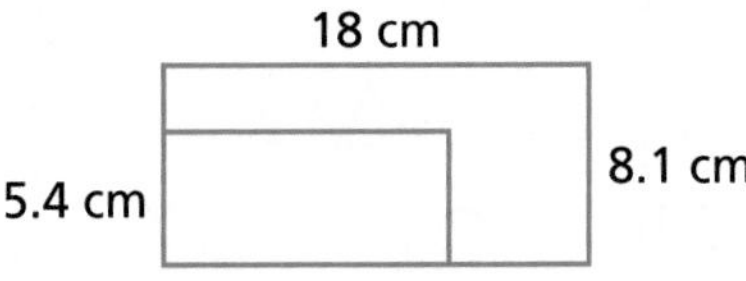

Ⓕ 6.7 centimeters
Ⓖ 12 centimeters
Ⓗ 14.1 centimeters
Ⓙ 15 centimeters

DAY 5

If the side of this triangle is increased by a factor of 1.3, what is the perimeter of the new triangle?

Ⓐ 7.3 meters
Ⓑ 7.8 meters
Ⓒ 21.9 meters
Ⓓ 23.4 meters

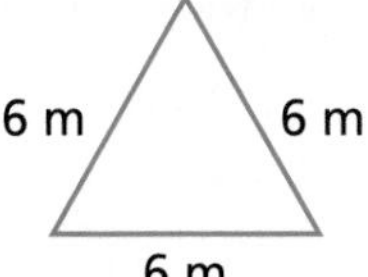

Countdown to Testing

WEEK 24

DAY 1

What kind of correlation would you expect to find in a scatter plot comparing people's ages and favorite colors?

Ⓐ negative

Ⓑ no correlation

Ⓒ positive

Ⓓ There is not enough information to answer the question.

DAY 2

Megan recorded the weight of each tomato in her garden this week. Which is the best measure of the central tendency for this data set?

220 grams, 225 grams,
213 grams, 140 grams,
210 grams, 209 grams

Ⓕ mean

Ⓖ range

Ⓗ mode

Ⓙ median

DAY 3

This graph shows a local politician's approval ratings for the last four months. What effect does the unequal scale interval have on the visual impression of the data?

Ⓐ It makes the drop in his approval ratings look more dramatic.

Ⓑ It makes the drop in his approval ratings look less dramatic.

Ⓒ It makes the politician appear less popular than he is.

Ⓓ It does not have any effect.

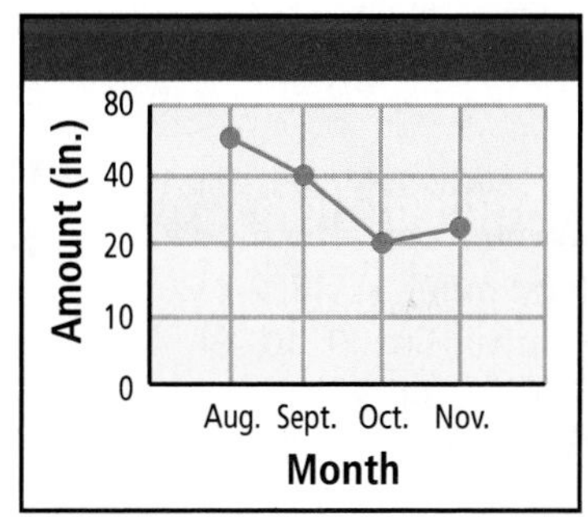

DAY 4

Mrs. Weyland is making 7 cups of juice for her children's friends. If she wants to serve each guest $\frac{3}{4}$ cup of juice, how many children will the juice serve?

Ⓕ 8

Ⓖ 9

Ⓗ 10

Ⓙ 11

DAY 5

Which number is missing from this sequence?

254, ▒, 22.86, 6.858, …

Ⓐ 76.2

Ⓑ 99.06

Ⓒ 115.57

Ⓓ 138.43

Algebra Toolbox

Interdisciplinary LINKS

Life Science 7, 37
Earth Science 47
Physical Science 5, 41
Entertainment 7, 12, 17
Sports 12, 27, 31
Social Studies 16, 17, 22
Money 20
Business 27, 31, 37
Retail 35
History 37
Music 41

Student Help

Remember 4, 18, 24, 29
Helpful Hint 9, 10, 14, 23, 28, 34, 35, 38
Test Taking Tip 57

internet connect go.hrw.com

Homework Help Online

6, 11, 16, 21, 26, 36, 40, 45

KEYWORD: MP4 HWHelp

Algebra *Indicates algebra included in lesson development*

Integers and Exponents

Assessment

Interdisciplinary LINKS

Student Help

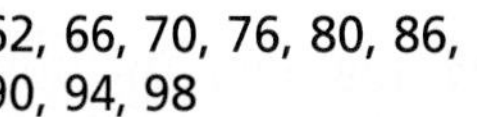

Homework Help Online

KEYWORD: MP4 HWHelp

Rational and Real Numbers

Assessment

Interdisciplinary LINKS

Student Help

internet connect go.hrw.com

Homework Help Online

KEYWORD: MP4 HWHelp

Algebra *Indicates algebra included in lesson development*

Collecting, Displaying, and Analyzing Data

Assessment

Interdisciplinary LINKS

Student Help

Homework Help Online

KEYWORD: MP4 HWHelp

Plane Geometry

Assessment

Interdisciplinary LINKS

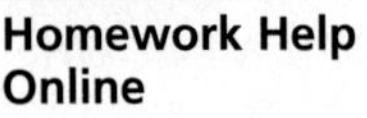

Student Help

internet connect

Homework Help Online

KEYWORD: MP4 HWHelp

Algebra *Indicates algebra included in lesson development*

Perimeter, Area, and Volume

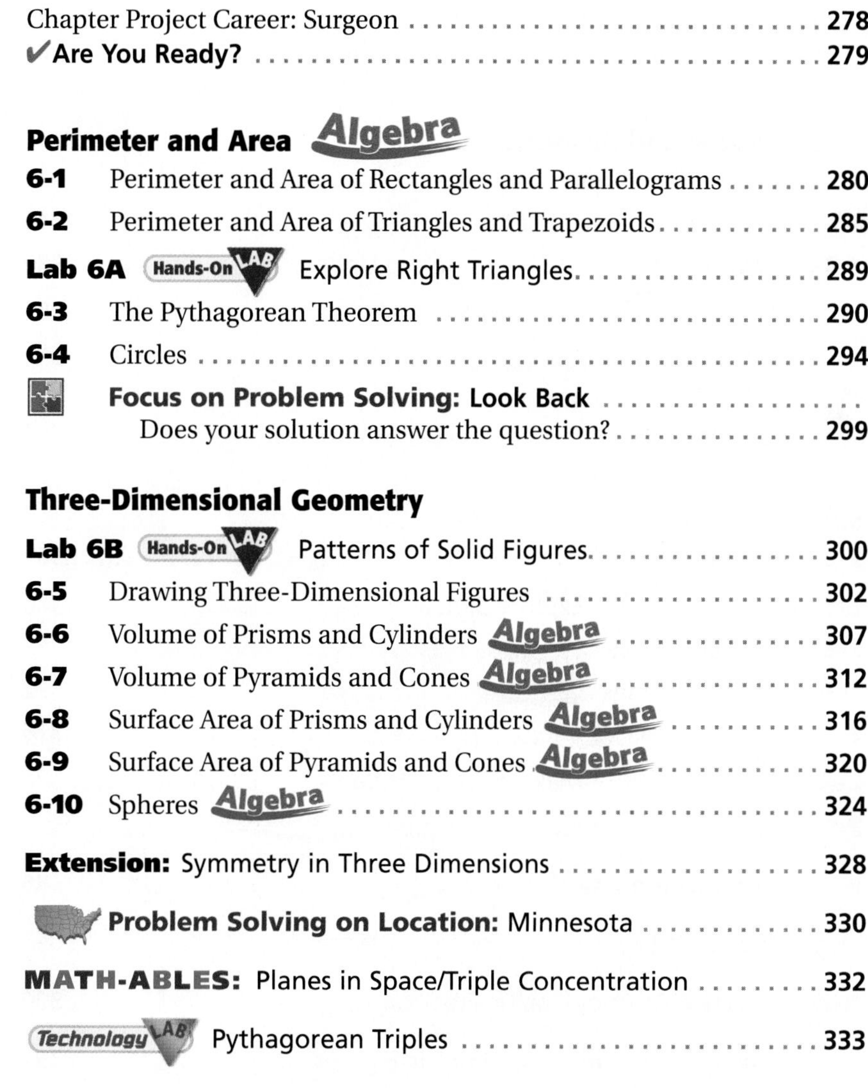

Assessment

State Test Preparation Online .... KEYWORD: MP4 TestPrep

Interdisciplinary LINKS

Student Help

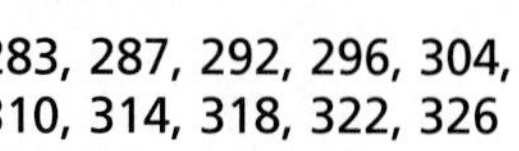

Homework Help Online

283, 287, 292, 296, 304, 310, 314, 318, 322, 326

KEYWORD: MP4 HWHelp

Ratios and Similarity

Assessment

State Test Preparation Online .... KEYWORD: MP4 TestPrep

Interdisciplinary LINKS

Student Help

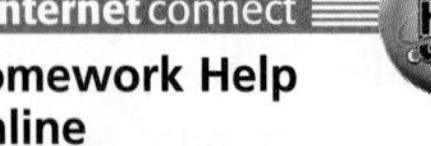

Homework Help Online

344, 348, 353, 358, 364, 370, 374, 378, 384

KEYWORD: MP4 HWHelp

Algebra *Indicates algebra included in lesson development*

Percents

Interdisciplinary LINKS

Student Help

Homework Help Online

402, 407, 412, 418

KEYWORD: MP4 HWHelp

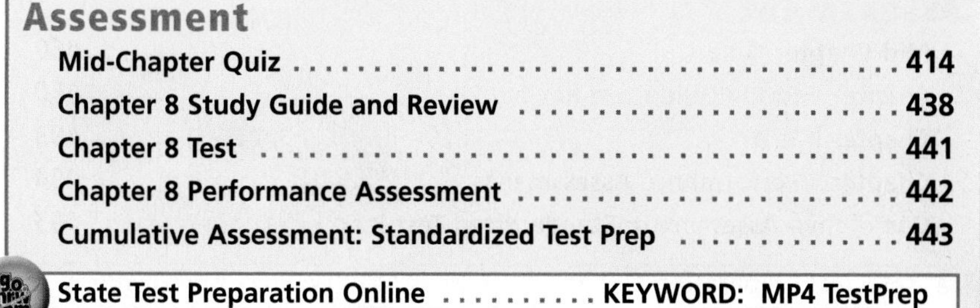

Assessment

State Test Preparation Online .... **KEYWORD: MP4 TestPrep**

Probability

Interdisciplinary LINKS

Student Help

internet connect go.hrw.com
Homework Help Online
449, 453, 458, 465, 469, 474, 480, 484
KEYWORD: MP4 HWHelp

Assessment

Algebra *Indicates algebra included in lesson development*

More Equations and Inequalities

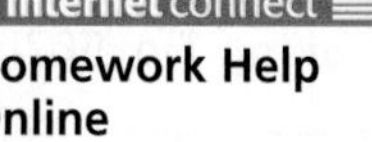

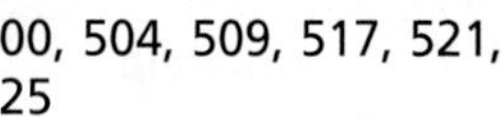

Graphing Lines

Assessment

Interdisciplinary LINKS

Student Help

internet connect go.hrw.com

Homework Help Online

543, 548, 553, 558, 565, 570, 574

KEYWORD: MP4 HWHelp

Algebra *Indicates algebra included in lesson development*

Sequences and Functions

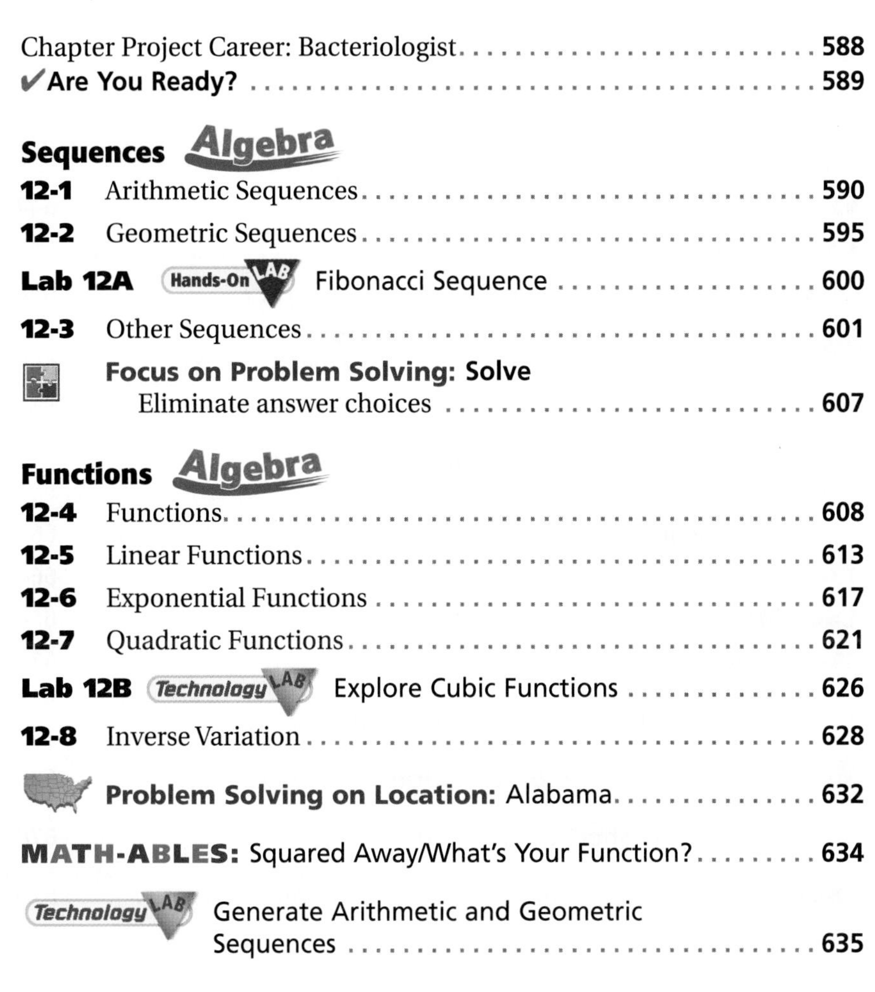

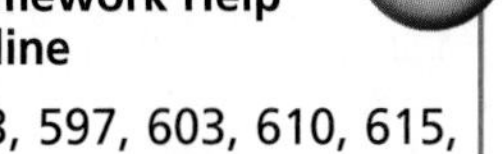

internet connect

Homework Help Online

593, 597, 603, 610, 615, 619, 624, 630

KEYWORD: MP4 HWHelp

Polynomials

Assessment

Student Help

internet connect

Homework Help Online

646, 652, 658, 662, 666, 672

Keyword: MP4 HWHelp

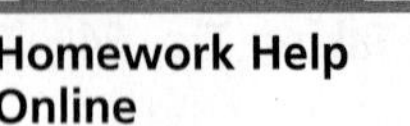

Indicates algebra included in lesson development

Set Theory and Discrete Math

Student Handbook

Using Your Book for Success

This book has many features designed to help you learn and study math. Becoming familiar with these features will prepare you for greater success on your exams.

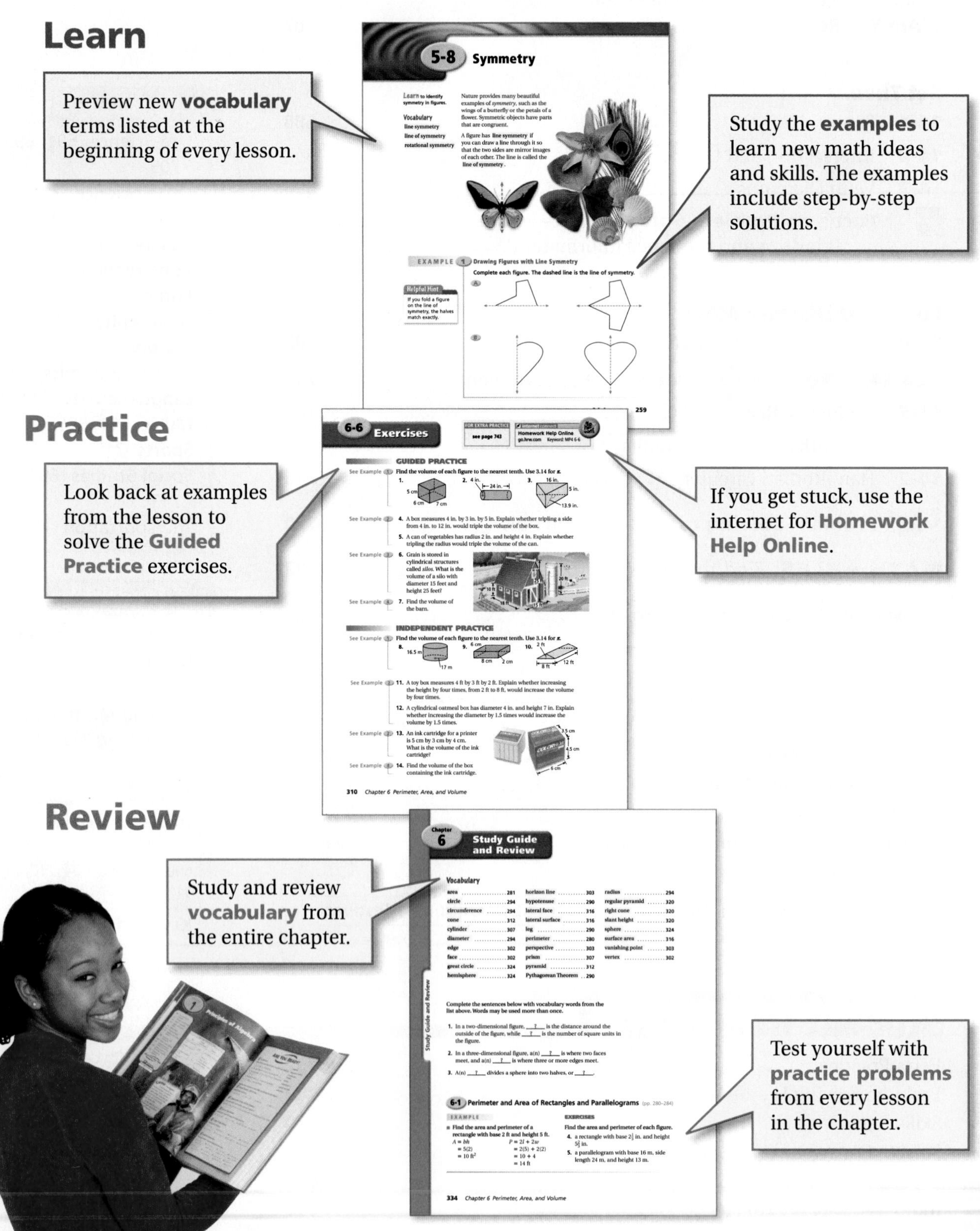

Learn
Preview new vocabulary terms listed at the beginning of every lesson.
5-8 Symmetry
Study the examples to learn new math ideas and skills. The examples include step-by-step solutions.
Practice
6-6 Exercises
Look back at examples from the lesson to solve the Guided Practice exercises.
If you get stuck, use the internet for Homework Help Online.
Review
Chapter 6 Study Guide and Review
Study and review vocabulary from the entire chapter.
Test yourself with practice problems from every lesson in the chapter.

Focus on Problem Solving

The Problem Solving Plan

In order to be a good problem solver, you need to use a good problem-solving plan. The plan used in this book is detailed below. If you have another plan that you like to use, you can use it as well.

UNDERSTAND the Problem

■ **What are you asked to find?**	Restate the question in your own words.
■ **What information is given?**	Identify the important facts in the problem.
■ **What information do you need?**	Determine which facts are needed to answer the question.
■ **Is all the information given?**	Determine whether all the facts are given.
■ **Is there any information given**	Determine which facts, if any, are that you will not use? unnecessary to solve the problem.

Make a PLAN

■ **Have you ever solved a similar problem?**	Think about other problems like this that you successfully solved.
■ **What strategy or strategies can you use?**	Determine a strategy that you can use and how you will use it.

SOLVE

■ **Follow your plan.**	Show the steps in your solution. Write your answer as a complete sentence.

LOOK BACK

■ **Have you answered the question?**	Be sure that you answered the question that is being asked.
■ **Is your answer reasonable?**	Your answer should make sense in the context of the problem.
■ **Is there another strategy you could use?**	Solving the problem using another strategy is a good way to check your work.
■ **Did you learn anything that could help you solve similar problems in the future?**	Try to remember the problems you have solved and the strategies you used to solve them.

Chapter 1

Algebra Toolbox

TABLE OF CONTENTS

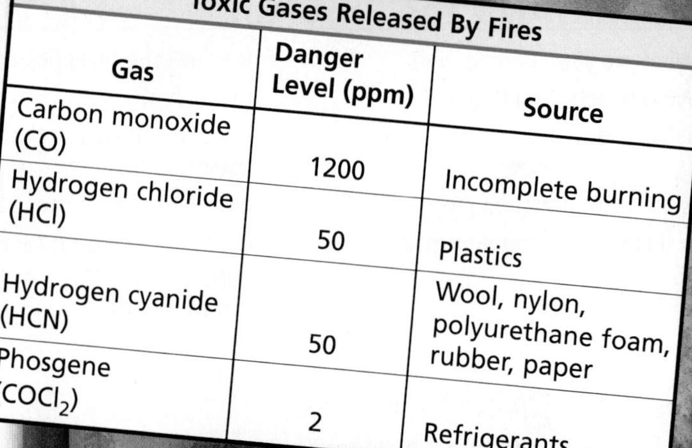

Toxic Gases Released By Fires

Gas	Danger Level (ppm)	Source
Carbon monoxide (CO)	1200	Incomplete burning
Hydrogen chloride (HCl)	50	Plastics
Hydrogen cyanide (HCN)	50	Wool, nylon, polyurethane foam, rubber, paper
Phosgene ($COCl_2$)	2	Refrigerants

Career *Firefighter*

A firefighter approaching a fire should be aware of ventilation, space, what is burning, and what could be ignited. Oxygen, fuel, heat, and chemical reactions are at the core of a fire, but the amounts and materials differ.

The table above lists some of the toxic gases that firefighters frequently encounter.

internet connect go.hrw.com

Chapter Opener Online
go.hrw.com
KEYWORD: MP4 Ch1

ARE YOU READY?

Choose the best term from the list to complete each sentence.

1. ___?___ is the ___?___ of addition.
2. The expressions 3 · 4 and 4 · 3 are equal by the ___?___.
3. The expressions 1 + (2 + 3) and (1 + 2) + 3 are equal by the ___?___.
4. Multiplication and ___?___ are opposite operations.
5. ___?___ and ___?___ are commutative.

addition
Associative Property
Commutative Property
division
opposite operation
multiplication
subtraction

Complete these exercises to review skills you will need for this chapter.

✔ Whole Number Operations

Simplify each expression.

6. 8 + 116 + 43 **7.** 2431 − 187 **8.** 204 · 38 **9.** 6447 ÷ 21

✔ Compare and Order Whole Numbers

Order each sequence of numbers from least to greatest.

10. 1050; 11,500; 105; 150 **11.** 503; 53; 5300; 5030 **12.** 44,400; 40,040; 40,400; 44,040

✔ Inverse Operations

Rewrite each expression using the inverse operation.

13. 72 + 18 = 90 **14.** 12 · 9 = 108 **15.** 100 − 34 = 66 **16.** 56 ÷ 8 = 7

✔ Order of Operations

Simplify each expression.

17. 2 + 3 · 4 **18.** 50 − 2 · 5 **19.** 6 · 3 · 3 − 3 **20.** (5 + 2)(5 − 2)

21. 5 − 6 ÷ 2 **22.** 16 ÷ 4 + 2 · 3 **23.** (8 − 3)(8 + 3) **24.** 12 ÷ 3 ÷ 2 + 5

✔ Evaluate Expressions

Determine whether the given expressions are equal.

25. (4 · 7) · 2 and 4 · (7 · 2) **26.** (2 · 4) ÷ 2 and 2 · (4 ÷ 2) **27.** 2 · (3 − 3) · 2 and (2 · 3) − 3 **28.** 5 · (50 − 44) and 5 · 50 − 44

29. 9 − (4 · 2) and (9 − 4) · 2 **30.** 2 · 3 + 2 · 4 and 2 · (3 + 4) **31.** (16 ÷ 4) + 4 and 16 ÷ (4 + 4) **32.** 5 + (2 · 3) and (5 + 2) · 3

1-1 Variables and Expressions

Learn to evaluate algebraic expressions.

Vocabulary

variable

coefficient

algebraic expression

constant

evaluate

substitute

The nautilus is a sea creature whose shell has a series of chambers. Every lunar month (about 30 days), the nautilus creates and moves into a new chamber of the shell.

Let n be the number of chambers in the shell. You can approximate the age, in days, of the nautilus using the following expression:

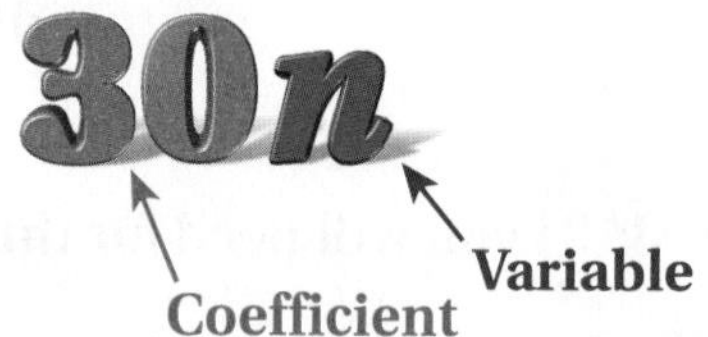

Coefficient

Variable

This nautilus shell has about 34 chambers. Using this information, you can determine its approximate age.

A **variable** is a letter that represents a value that can change or vary. The **coefficient** is the number multiplied by the variable. An **algebraic expression** has one or more variables.

In the algebraic expression $x + 6$, 6 is a **constant** because it does not change. To **evaluate** an algebraic expression, **substitute** a given number for the variable, and find the value of the resulting numerical expression.

EXAMPLE 1 Evaluating Algebraic Expressions with One Variable

Evaluate each expression for the given value of the variable.

A $x + 6$ for $x = 13$

$13 + 6$ *Substitute 13 for x.*

19 *Add.*

B $2a + 3$ for $a = 4$

$2(4) + 3$ *Substitute 4 for a.*

$8 + 3$ *Multiply.*

11 *Add.*

C $3(5 + n) - 1$ for $n = 0, 1, 2$

n	Substitute	Parentheses	Multiply	Subtract
0	$3(5 + 0) - 1$	$3(5) - 1$	$15 - 1$	**14**
1	$3(5 + 1) - 1$	$3(6) - 1$	$18 - 1$	**17**
2	$3(5 + 2) - 1$	$3(7) - 1$	$21 - 1$	**20**

Remember!

Order of Operations

PEMDAS:

1. Parentheses
2. Exponents
3. Multiply and Divide from left to right.
4. Add and Subtract from left to right.

EXAMPLE 2 Evaluating Algebraic Expressions with Two Variables

Evaluate each expression for the given values of the variables.

A $2x + 3y$ for $x = 15$ and $y = 12$

$2(15) + 3(12)$	*Substitute 15 for x and 12 for y.*
$30 + 36$	*Multiply.*
66	*Add.*

B $1.5p - 2q$ for $p = 18$ and $q = 7.5$

$1.5(18) - 2(7.5)$	*Substitute 18 for p and 7.5 for q.*
$27 - 15$	*Multiply.*
12	*Subtract.*

EXAMPLE 3 *Physical Science Application*

If *c* is a temperature in degrees Celsius, then 1.8*c* + 32 can be used to find the temperature in degrees Fahrenheit. Convert each temperature from degrees Celsius to degrees Fahrenheit.

A freezing point of water: 0°C

$1.8c + 32$

$1.8(0) + 32$	*Substitute 0 for c.*
$0 + 32$	*Multiply.*
32	*Add.*

0°C = 32°F

Water freezes at 32°F.

B world's highest recorded temperature (El Azizia, Libya): 58°C

$1.8c + 32$

$1.8(58) + 32$	*Substitute 58 for c.*
$104.4 + 32$	*Multiply.*
136.4	*Add.*

58°C = 136.4°F

The highest recorded temperature in the world is 136.4°F.

Think and Discuss

1. **Give an example** of an expression that is algebraic and of an expression that is not algebraic.
2. **Tell** the steps for evaluating an algebraic expression for a given value.
3. **Explain** why you cannot find a numerical value for the expression $4x - 5y$ for $x = 3$.

1-1 Exercises

FOR EXTRA PRACTICE

see page 732

internet connect

Homework Help Online

go.hrw.com Keyword: MP4 1-1

GUIDED PRACTICE

See Example 1 Evaluate each expression for the given value of the variable.

1. $x + 5$ for $x = 12$ **2.** $3a + 5$ for $a = 6$ **3.** $2(4 + n) - 5$ for $n = 0$

See Example 2 Evaluate each expression for the given values of the variables.

4. $3x + 2y$ for $x = 8$ and $y = 10$ **5.** $1.2p - 2q$ for $p = 3.5$ and $q = 1.2$

See Example 3 You can make cornstarch slime by mixing $\frac{1}{2}$ as many tablespoons of water as cornstarch. How many tablespoons of water do you need for each number of tablespoons of cornstarch?

6. 10 tbsp **7.** 16 tbsp **8.** 23 tbsp **9.** 34 tbsp

INDEPENDENT PRACTICE

See Example 1 Evaluate each expression for the given value of the variable.

10. $x + 7$ for $x = 23$ **11.** $5t + 3$ for $t = 6$ **12.** $6(2 + k) - 5$ for $k = 0$

See Example 2 Evaluate each expression for the given values of the variables.

13. $5x + 4y$ for $x = 7$ and $y = 8$ **14.** $4m - 2n$ for $m = 25$ and $n = 2.5$

See Example 3 If q is the number of quarts, then $\frac{1}{4}q$ can be used to find the number of gallons. Find the number of gallons for each of the following.

15. 16 quarts **16.** 24 quarts **17.** 8 quarts **18.** 32 quarts

PRACTICE AND PROBLEM SOLVING

Evaluate each expression for the given value of the variable.

19. $12d$ for $d = 0$ **20.** $x + 3.2$ for $x = 5$ **21.** $30 - n$ for $n = 8$

22. $5t + 5$ for $t = 1$ **23.** $2a - 5$ for $a = 7$ **24.** $3 + 5b$ for $b = 1.2$

25. $12 - 2m$ for $m = 3$ **26.** $3g + 8$ for $g = 14$ **27.** $x + 7.5$ for $x = 2.5$

28. $15 - 5y$ for $y = 3$ **29.** $4y + 2$ for $y = 3.5$ **30.** $2(z + 8)$ for $z = 5$

Evaluate each expression for $t = 0, x = 1.5, y = 6$, and $z = 23$.

31. $y + 5$ **32.** $2y + 7$ **33.** $z - 2x$ **34.** $3z - 3y$

35. $2z - 2y$ **36.** xy **37.** $2.6y - 2x$ **38.** $1.2z - y$

39. $4(y - x)$ **40.** $3(4 + y)$ **41.** $4(2 + z) + 5$ **42.** $2(y - 6) + 3$

43. $3(6 + t) - 1$ **44.** $y(4 + t) - 5$ **45.** $x + y + z$ **46.** $10x + z - y$

47. $3y + 4(x + t)$ **48.** $3(z - 2t) + 1$ **49.** $7tyz$ **50.** $z - 2xy$

51. ***LIFE SCIENCE*** Measuring your heart rate is one way to check the intensity of exercise. Studies show that a person's maximum heart rate depends on his or her age. The expression $220 - a$ approximates a person's maximum heart rate in beats per minute, where a is the person's age. Find your maximum heart rate.

52. ***LIFE SCIENCE*** In the Karvonen Formula, a person's resting heart rate r, age a, and desired intensity I are used to find the number of beats per minute the person's heart rate should be during training.

$$\text{training heart rate (THR)} = I(220 - a - r) + r$$

What is the THR of a person who is 45 years old, and who has a resting heart rate of 85 and a desired intensity of 0.5?

53. ***ENTERTAINMENT*** There are 24 frames, or still shots, in one second of movie footage.

a. Write an expression to determine the number of frames in a movie.

b. Using the running time of *E.T. the Extra-Terrestrial,* determine how many frames are in the movie.

E.T. the Extra-Terrestrial (1982) has a running time of 115 minutes, or 6900 seconds.

54. ***CHOOSE A STRATEGY*** A baseball league has 192 players and 12 teams, with an equal number of players on each team. If the number of teams were reduced by four but the total number of players remained the same, there would be ________ players per team.

A four more B eight fewer C four fewer D eight more

55. ***WRITE ABOUT IT*** A student says that for any value of x the expression $5x + 1$ will always give the same result as $1 + 5x$. Is the student correct? Explain.

56. ***CHALLENGE*** Can the expressions $2x$ and $x + 2$ ever have the same value? If so, what must the value of x be?

Spiral Review

Identify the odd number(s) in each list of numbers. (Previous course)

57. 15, 18, 22, 34, 21, 62, 71, 100

58. 101, 114, 122, 411, 117, 121

59. 4, 6, 8, 16, 18, 20, 49, 81, 32

60. 9, 15, 31, 47, 65, 93, 1, 3, 43

61. **TEST PREP** Which is **not** a multiple of 21? (Previous course)

A 21 **C** 7
B 42 **D** 105

62. **TEST PREP** Which is a factor of 12? (Previous course)

F 4 **H** 8
G 24 **J** 36

1-2 Write Algebraic Expressions

Problem Solving Skill

Learn to write algebraic expressions.

Each 30-second block of commercial time during Super Bowl XXXV cost an average of $2.2 million.

This information can be used to write an algebraic expression to determine how much a given number of 30-second blocks would have cost.

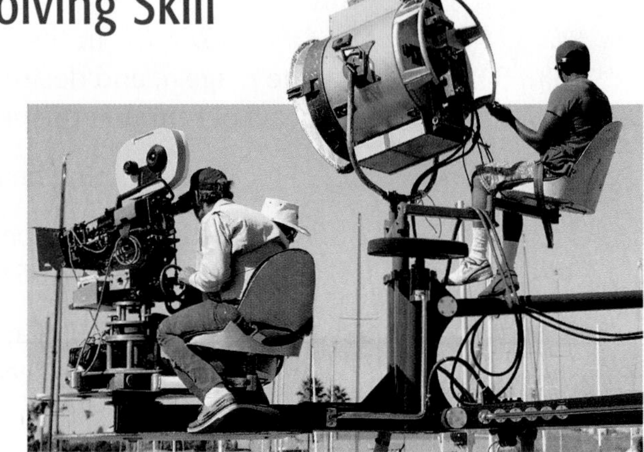

Eighty-three commercials aired during the 2002 Super Bowl.

	Word Phrases	Expression
+	• a number plus 5 • add 5 to a number • sum of a number and 5 • 5 more than a number • a number increased by 5	$n + 5$
−	• a number minus 11 • subtract 11 from a number • difference of a number and 11 • 11 less than a number • a number decreased by 11	$x - 11$
×	• 3 times a number • 3 multiplied by a number • product of 3 and a number	$3m$
÷	• a number divided by 7 • 7 divided into a number • quotient of a number and 7	$\frac{a}{7}$ or $a \div 7$

EXAMPLE 1 Translating Word Phrases into Math Expressions

Write an algebraic expression for each word phrase.

A **a number n decreased by 11**

n decreased by 11

n − 11

$n - 11$

Write an algebraic expression for each word phrase.

B **the quotient of 3 and a number h**

	quotient of	3 and h
3	$\div$	h

$\frac{3}{h}$

Helpful Hint

In Example 1C parentheses are not needed because multiplication is performed first by the order of operations.

C **1 more than the product of 12 and p**

1	more than	the	product of	12 and p
1	$+$	(12	$\cdot$	p)

$1 + 12p$

D **3 times the sum of q and 1**

3	times	the	sum of	q and 1
3	$\cdot$	(q	$+$	1)

$3(q + 1)$

To solve a word problem, you must first interpret the action you need to perform and then choose the correct operation for that action. When a word problem involves groups of equal size, use multiplication or division. Otherwise, use addition or subtraction. The table gives more information to help you decide which operation to use to solve a word problem.

Action	Operation	Possible Question Clues
Combine	Add	How many altogether?
Combine equal groups	Multiply	How many altogether?
Separate	Subtract	How many more? How many less?
Separate into equal groups	Divide	How many equal groups?

EXAMPLE 2 Interpreting Which Operation to Use in Word Problems

A **Monica got a 200-minute calling card and called her brother at college. After talking with him for t minutes, she had t less than 200 minutes remaining on her card. Write an expression to determine the number of minutes remaining on the calling card.**

$200 - t$ *Separate t minutes from the original 200.*

B **If Monica talked with her brother for 55 minutes, how many minutes does she have left on her calling card?**

$200 - 55 = 145$ *Evaluate the expression for $t = 55$.*

There are 145 minutes remaining on her calling card.

EXAMPLE 3 Writing and Evaluating Expressions in Word Problems

Write an algebraic expression to evaluate each word problem.

A **Rob and his friends buy a set of baseball season tickets. The 81 tickets are to be divided equally among *p* people. If he divides them among 9 people, how many tickets does each person get?**

$81 \div p$ — *Separate the tickets into p equal groups.*

$81 \div 9 = 9$ — *Evaluate for p = 9.*

Each person gets 9 tickets.

B **A company airs its 30-second commercial *n* times during Super Bowl XXXV at a cost of \$2.2 million each time. What will the cost be if the commercial is aired 2, 3, 4, and 5 times?**

$2.2 million · *n* — *Combine n equal amounts of \$2.2 million.*

$2.2n$ — *In millions of dollars*

n	2.2*n*	Cost
2	2.2(2)	\$4.4 million
3	2.2(3)	\$6.6 million
4	2.2(4)	\$8.8 million
5	2.2(5)	\$11 million

Evaluate for n = 2, 3, 4, and 5.

Helpful Hint

Some word problems give more numbers than are necessary to find the answer. In Example 3B, 30 seconds describes the length of a commercial, and the number is not needed to solve the problem.

C **Before Benny took his road trip, his car odometer read 14,917 miles. After the trip, his odometer read *m* miles more than 14,917. If he traveled 633 miles on the trip, what did the odometer read after his trip?**

$14{,}917 + m$ — *Combine 14,917 miles and m miles.*

$14{,}917 + 633 = 15{,}550$ — *Evaluate for m = 633.*

The odometer read 15,550 miles after the trip.

Think and Discuss

1. Give two words or phrases that can be used to express each operation: addition, subtraction, multiplication, and division.

2. Express $5 + 7n$ in words in at least two different ways.

1-2 Exercises

FOR EXTRA PRACTICE

see page 732

internet connect

Homework Help Online
go.hrw.com Keyword: MP4 1-2

GUIDED PRACTICE

See Example  **Write an algebraic expression for each word phrase.**

1. the quotient of 6 and a number t

2. a number y decreased by 25

3. 7 times the sum of m and 6

4. the sum of 7 times m and 6

See Example 

5. a. Carl walked n miles for charity at a rate of \$8 per mile. Write an expression to find out how much money Carl raised.

b. How much money would Carl have raised if he had walked 23 miles?

See Example 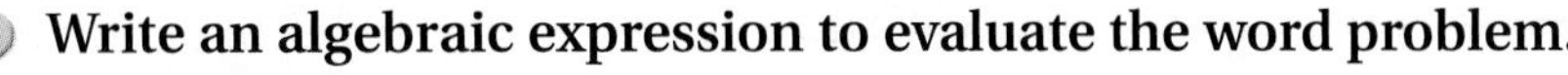 **Write an algebraic expression to evaluate the word problem.**

6. Cheryl and her friends buy a pizza for \$15.00 plus a delivery charge of d dollars. If the delivery charge is \$2.50, what is the total cost?

INDEPENDENT PRACTICE

See Example  **Write an algebraic expression for each word phrase.**

7. a number k increased by 34

8. the quotient of 12 and a number h

9. 5 plus the product of 5 and z

10. 6 times the difference of x and 4

See Example 

11. a. Mr. Gimble's class is going to a play. The 42 students will be seated equally among p rows. Write an expression to determine how many people will be seated in each row.

b. If there are 6 rows, how many students will be in each row?

See Example  **Write an algebraic expression and evaluate each word problem.**

12. Julie bought a card good for 35 visits to a health club and began a workout routine. After y visits, she had y fewer than 35 visits remaining on her card. After 18 visits, how many visits did she have left?

13. Myron bought n dozen eggs for \$1.75 per dozen. If he bought 8 dozen eggs, how much did they cost?

PRACTICE AND PROBLEM SOLVING

Write an algebraic expression for each word phrase.

14. 7 more than a number y

15. 6 times the sum of 4 and y

16. 11 less than a number t

17. half the sum of m and 5

18. 9 more than the product of 6 and a number y

19. 6 less than the product of 13 and a number y

20. 2 less than a number m divided by 8

21. twice the quotient of a number m and 35

Translate each algebraic expression into words.

22. $4b - 3$ **23.** $t + 12$ **24.** $3(m + 4)$

25. ***ENTERTAINMENT*** Ron bought two comic books on sale. Each comic book was discounted \$1 off the regular price r. Write an expression to find what Ron paid before taxes. If each comic book was regularly \$2.50, what was the total cost before taxes?

26. ***SPORTS*** In basketball, players score 2 points for each field goal, 3 points for each three-point shot, and 1 point for each free throw made. Write an expression for the total score for a team that makes g field goals, t three-point shots, and f free throws. Find the total score for a team that scores 23 field goals, 6 three-pointers, and 11 free throws.

27. At age 2, a cat or dog is considered 24 "human" years old. Each year after age 2 is equivalent to 4 "human" years. Fill in the expression [24 + ▇ $(a - 2)$] so that it represents the age of a cat or dog in human years. Copy the chart and use your expression to complete it.

Age	24 + ▇ $(a - 2)$	Age (human years)
2		
3		
4		
5		
6		

DO NOT WRITE IN BOOK

28. ***WHAT'S THE ERROR?*** A student says $3(n - 5)$ is equal to $3n - 5$. What's the error?

29. ***WRITE ABOUT IT*** Paul used addition to solve a word problem about the weekly cost of commuting by toll road for \$1.50 each day. Fran solved the same problem by multiplying. They both had the correct answer. How is this possible?

30. ***CHALLENGE*** Write an expression for the sum of 1 and twice a number n. If you let n be any odd number, will the result always be an odd number?

Spiral Review

Find each sum, difference, product, or quotient. (Previous course)

31. $200 + 2$ **32.** $200 \div 2$ **33.** $200 \cdot 2$ **34.** $200 - 2$

35. $200 + 0.2$ **36.** $200 \div 0.2$ **37.** $200 \cdot 0.2$ **38.** $200 - 0.2$

39. **TEST PREP** Which is **not** a factor of 24? (Previous course)

A 24 **C** 48

B 8 **D** 12

40. **TEST PREP** Which is a multiple of 15? (Previous course)

F 1 **H** 3

G 5 **J** 15

1-3 Solving Equations by Adding or Subtracting

Learn to solve equations using addition and subtraction.

Vocabulary

equation

solve

solution

inverse operation

isolate the variable

Addition Property of Equality

Subtraction Property of Equality

Mexico City is built on top of a large underground water source. Over the 100 years between 1900 and 2000, as the water was drained, the city sank as much as 30 feet in some areas.

In 1910, the Monumento a la Independencia was built at ground level. It now requires 23 steps to reach the base because the ground around the monument has sunk.

If you know the altitude of Mexico City in 2000 was 7350 feet above sea level, you can use an *equation* to estimate the altitude in 1900.

An **equation** uses an equal sign to show that two expressions are equal. All of these are equations.

$3 + 8 = 11$ $\quad r + 6 = 14$ $\quad 24 = x - 7$ $\quad 9n = 27$ $\quad \frac{100}{2} = 50$

To **solve** an equation that contains a variable, find the value of the variable that makes the equation true. This value of the variable is called the **solution** of the equation.

EXAMPLE 1 Determining Whether a Number Is a Solution of an Equation

Determine which value of x is a solution of the equation.

$x - 4 = 16$; $x = 12, 20,$ or 21

Substitute each value for x in the equation.

$x - 4 = 16$

$12 - 4 \stackrel{?}{=} 16$ *Substitute 12 for x.*

$8 \stackrel{?}{=} 16$ ✗

So 12 is not a solution.

$x - 4 = 16$

$20 - 4 \stackrel{?}{=} 16$ *Substitute 20 for x.*

$16 \stackrel{?}{=} 16$ ✓

So 20 is a solution.

$x - 4 = 16$

$21 - 4 \stackrel{?}{=} 16$ *Substitute 21 for x.*

$17 \stackrel{?}{=} 16$ ✗

So 21 is not a solution.

Helpful Hint

The phrase "subtraction 'undoes' addition" can be understood with this example:
If you start with 3 and add 4, you can get back to 3 by subtracting 4.

$$\begin{array}{r} 3+4 \\ \underline{-\ 4} \\ 3 \end{array}$$

Addition and subtraction are **inverse operations**, which means they "undo" each other. To solve an equation, use inverse operations to **isolate the variable**. In other words, get the variable alone on one side of the equal sign.

To solve a subtraction equation, like $y - 15 = 7$, you would use the **Addition Property of Equality**.

ADDITION PROPERTY OF EQUALITY		
Words	**Numbers**	**Algebra**
You can add the same number to both sides of an equation, and the statement will still be true.	$\begin{array}{rr} 2+3= & 5 \\ \underline{+\ 4} & \underline{+\ 4} \\ 2+7= & 9 \end{array}$	$x = y$ $x + z = y + z$

There is a similar property for solving addition equations, like $x + 9 = 11$. It is called the **Subtraction Property of Equality**.

SUBTRACTION PROPERTY OF EQUALITY		
Words	**Numbers**	**Algebra**
You can subtract the same number from both sides of an equation, and the statement will still be true.	$\begin{array}{rr} 4+7= & 11 \\ \underline{-\ 3} & \underline{-\ 3} \\ 4+4= & 8 \end{array}$	$x = y$ $x - z = y - z$

EXAMPLE  2 Solving Equations Using Addition and Subtraction Properties

Solve.

A $3 + t = 11$

$$\begin{array}{rr} 3+t= & 11 \\ \underline{-3\qquad} & \underline{-3} \\ 0+t= & 8 \\ t= & 8 \end{array}$$

Subtract 3 from both sides.

Identity Property of Zero: 0 + t = t

Check

$3 + t = 11$

$3 + 8 \stackrel{?}{=} 11$ *Substitute 8 for t.*

$11 \stackrel{?}{=} 11$ ✔

Solve.

B $m - 7 = 11$

$$\begin{array}{rcll} m - 7 &=& 11 & \\ \underline{+7} && \underline{+7} & \textit{Add 7 to both sides.} \\ m + 0 &=& 18 & \\ m &=& 18 & \end{array}$$

C $15 = w + 14$

$$\begin{array}{rcll} 15 &=& w + 14 & \\ 15 - 14 &=& w + 14 - 14 & \textit{Subtract 14 from both sides.} \\ 1 &=& w + 0 & \\ 1 &=& w & \\ w &=& 1 & \textit{Definition of Equality} \end{array}$$

EXAMPLE 3 *Geography Applications*

A **The altitude of Mexico City in 2000 was about 7350 ft above sea level. What was the approximate altitude of Mexico City in 1900 if it sank 30 ft during the 100-year period?**

beginning altitude	−	altitude sank	=	altitude in 2000
Solve: x	−	30	=	7350

$$\begin{array}{rcll} x - 30 &=& 7350 & \\ \underline{+30} && \underline{+30} & \textit{Add 30 to both sides.} \\ x + 0 &=& 7380 & \\ x &=& 7380 & \end{array}$$

In 1900, Mexico City was at an altitude of 7380 ft.

B **From 1954 to 1999, shifting plates increased the height of Mount Everest from 29,028 ft to 29,035 ft. By how many feet did Mount Everest's altitude increase during the 45-year period?**

Solve: 29,028 ft + h = 29,035 ft

$$\begin{array}{rcll} 29{,}028 + h &=& 29{,}035 & \\ \underline{-29{,}028} && \underline{-29{,}028} & \textit{Subtract 29,028 from both sides.} \\ 0 + h &=& 7 & \\ h &=& 7 & \end{array}$$

Mount Everest's altitude increased 7 ft between 1954 and 1999.

Geography LINK

Mexico City, above, sank 19 inches in one year while Venice, Italy, possibly the most famous sinking city, has sunk only 9 inches in the last century.

Web Extra!
KEYWORD: MP4 Sinking

Think and Discuss

1. **Explain** whether you would use addition or subtraction to solve $x - 9 = 25$.

2. **Explain** what it means to isolate the variable.

1-3 Exercises

FOR EXTRA PRACTICE

see page 732

internet connect

Homework Help Online
go.hrw.com Keyword: MP4 1-3

GUIDED PRACTICE

See Example 1 **Determine which value of x is a solution of each equation.**

1. $x + 9 = 14$; $x = 2, 5,$ or 23
2. $x - 7 = 14$; $x = 2, 7,$ or 21

See Example 2 **Solve.**

3. $m - 9 = 23$
4. $8 + t = 13$
5. $13 = w - 4$

See Example 3

6. At what altitude did a climbing team start if it descended 3600 feet to a camp at an altitude of 12,035 feet?

INDEPENDENT PRACTICE

See Example 1 **Determine which value of x is a solution of each equation.**

7. $x - 14 = 8$; $x = 6, 22,$ or 32
8. $x + 7 = 35$; $x = 5, 28,$ or 42

See Example 2 **Solve.**

9. $9 = w + 8$
10. $m - 11 = 33$
11. $4 + t = 16$

See Example 3

12. If a team camps at an altitude of 18,450 feet, how far must it ascend to reach the summit of Mount Everest at an altitude of 29,035 feet?

PRACTICE AND PROBLEM SOLVING

Determine which value of the variable is a solution of the equation.

13. $d + 4 = 24$; $d = 6, 20,$ or 28
14. $m - 2 = 13$; $m = 11, 15,$ or 16
15. $y - 7 = 23$; $y = 30, 26,$ or 16
16. $k + 3 = 4$; $k = 1, 7,$ or 17
17. $12 + n = 19$; $n = 7, 26,$ or 31
18. $z - 15 = 15$; $z = 0, 15,$ or 30
19. $x + 48 = 48$; $x = 0, 48,$ or 96
20. $p - 2.5 = 6$; $p = 3.1, 3.5,$ or 8.5

Solve the equation and check the solution.

21. $7 + t = 12$
22. $h - 21 = 52$
23. $15 = m - 9$
24. $m - 5 = 10$
25. $h + 8 = 11$
26. $6 + t = 14$
27. $1785 = t - 836$
28. $m + 35 = 172$
29. $x - 29 = 81$
30. $p + 8 = 23$
31. $n - 14 = 31$
32. $20 = 8 + w$
33. $0.8 + t = 1.3$
34. $5.7 = c - 2.8$
35. $9.87 = w + 7.97$

36. ***SOCIAL STUDIES*** In 1990, the population of Cheyenne, Wyoming, was 73,142. By 2000, the population had increased to 81,607. Write and solve an equation to find n, the increase in Cheyenne's population from 1990 to 2000.

37. ***SOCIAL STUDIES*** In 1804, explorers Lewis and Clark began their journey to the Pacific Ocean at the mouth of the Missouri River. Use the map to determine the following distances.

a. from Blackbird Hill, Nebraska, to Great Falls, Montana

b. from the meeting point, or confluence, of the Missouri and Yellowstone Rivers to Great Falls, Montana

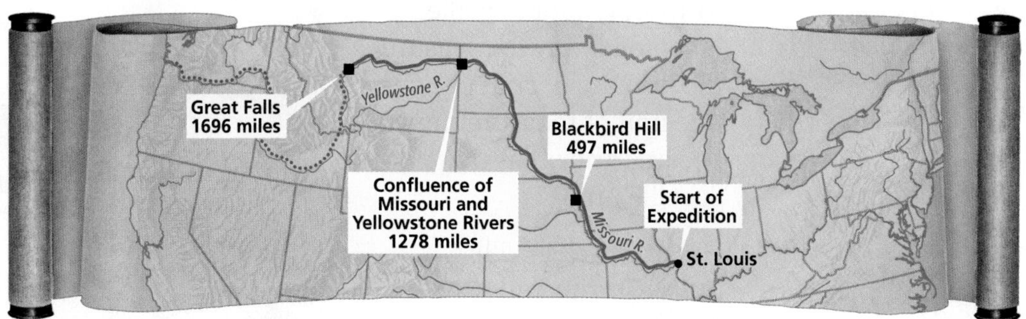

38. ***SOCIAL STUDIES*** The United States flag had 15 stars in 1795. How many stars have been added since then to make our present-day flag with 50 stars? Write and solve an equation to find s, the number of stars that have been added to the United States flag since 1795.

39. ***ENTERTAINMENT*** Use the bar graph about movie admission costs to write and solve an equation for each of the following.

a. Find c, the increase in cost of a movie ticket from 1940 to 1990.

b. The cost c of a movie ticket in 1950 was \$3.82 less than in 1995. Find the cost of a movie ticket in 1995.

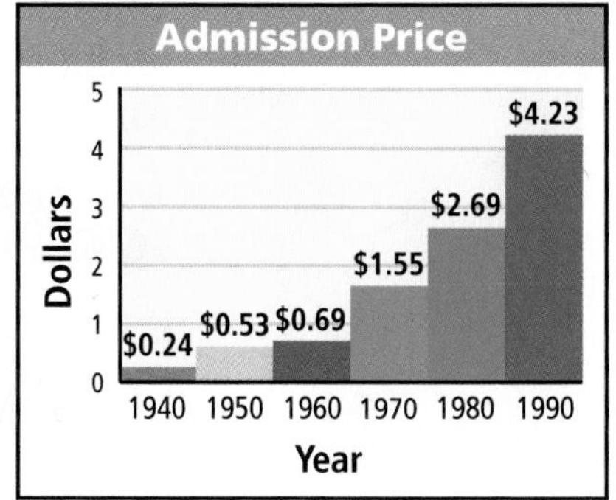

40. ***WRITE A PROBLEM*** Write a subtraction problem using the graph about admission costs. Explain your solution.

41. ***WRITE ABOUT IT*** Write a set of rules to use when solving addition and subtraction equations.

42. ***CHALLENGE*** Explain how you could solve for h in the equation $14 - h = 8$ using algebra. Then find the value of h.

Spiral Review

Evaluate each expression for the given value of the variable. (Lesson 1-1)

43. $x + 9$ for $x = 13$ **44.** $x - 8$ for $x = 18$ **45.** $14 + x$ for $x = 12$

46. **TEST PREP** Which is "3 times the difference of y and 4"? (Lesson 1-2)

A $3 \cdot y - 4$ **B** $3 \cdot (y + 4)$ **C** $3 \cdot (y - 4)$ **D** $3 - (y - 4)$

1-4 Solving Equations by Multiplying or Dividing

Learn to solve equations using multiplication and division.

Vocabulary

Division Property of Equality

Multiplication Property of Equality

In 1912, Wilbur Scoville invented a way to measure the hotness of chili peppers. The unit of measurement became known as the Scoville unit.

You can use Scoville units to write and solve multiplication equations for substituting one kind of pepper for another in a recipe.

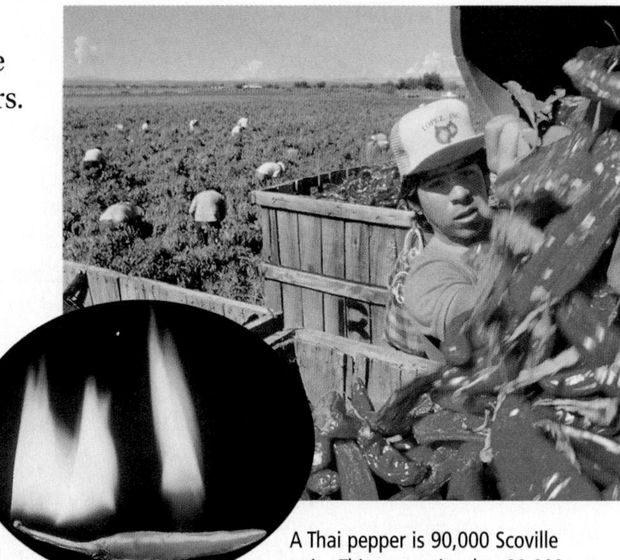

A Thai pepper is 90,000 Scoville units. This means it takes 90,000 cups of sugar water to neutralize the hotness of one cup of Thai peppers.

You can solve a multiplication equation using the **Division Property of Equality**.

DIVISION PROPERTY OF EQUALITY

Words	Numbers	Algebra
You can divide both sides of an equation by the same nonzero number, and the statement will still be true.	$4 \cdot 3 = 12$ $\frac{4 \cdot 3}{2} = \frac{12}{2}$ $\frac{12}{2} = 6$	$x = y$ $\frac{x}{z} = \frac{y}{z}$

EXAMPLE 1 Solving Equations Using Division

Solve $7x = 35$.

$7x = 35$

$\frac{7x}{7} = \frac{35}{7}$ *Divide both sides by 7.*

$1x = 5$ *$1 \cdot x = x$*

$x = 5$

Check

$7x = 35$

$7(5) \stackrel{?}{=} 35$ *Substitute 5 for x.*

$35 \stackrel{?}{=} 35$ ✔

Remember!

Multiplication and division are inverse operations.

$\frac{8 \cdot 3}{3} = 8$

You can solve division equations using the **Multiplication Property of Equality**.

MULTIPLICATION PROPERTY OF EQUALITY		
Words	**Numbers**	**Algebra**
You can multiply both sides of an equation by the same number, and the statement will still be true.	$2 \cdot 3 = 6$ $4 \cdot 2 \cdot 3 = 4 \cdot 6$ $8 \cdot 3 = 24$	$x = y$ $zx = zy$

EXAMPLE 2 **Solving Equations Using Multiplication**

Solve $\frac{h}{3} = 6$.

$\frac{h}{3} = 6$

$3 \cdot \frac{h}{3} = 3 \cdot 6$ *Multiply both sides by 3.*

$h = 18$

EXAMPLE 3 ***Food Application***

A recipe calls for 1 tabasco pepper, but Jennifer wants to use jalapeño peppers. How many jalapeño peppers should she substitute in the dish to equal the Scoville units of 1 tabasco pepper?

Scoville Units of Selected Peppers	
Pepper	**Scoville Units**
Ancho (Poblano)	1,500
Bell	100
Cayenne	30,000
Habanero	360,000
Jalapeño	5,000
Serrano	10,000
Tabasco	30,000
Thai	90,000

Scoville units of 1 jalapeño	$\cdot$	number of jalapeños	=	Scoville units of 1 tabasco
5000	$\cdot$	n	=	30,000

$5{,}000n = 30{,}000$ *Write the equation.*

$\frac{5{,}000n}{5{,}000} = \frac{30{,}000}{5{,}000}$ *Divide both sides by 5000.*

$n = 6$

Six jalapeños are about as hot as one tabasco pepper. Jennifer should substitute 6 jalapeños for the tabasco pepper in her recipe.

EXAMPLE 4 *Money Application*

Helene's band needs money to go to a national competition. So far, band members have raised \$560, which is only one-third of what they need. What is the total amount needed?

fraction of total amount raised so far	•	total amount needed	=	amount raised so far
$\frac{1}{3}$	•	x	=	\$560

$\frac{1}{3}x = 560$ *Write the equation.*

$3 \cdot \frac{1}{3}x = 3 \cdot 560$ *Multiply both sides by 3.*

$x = 1680$

The band needs to raise a total of \$1680.

Sometimes it is necessary to solve equations by using two inverse operations. For instance, the equation $6x - 2 = 10$ has multiplication and subtraction.

Variable term

Multiplication → $6x - 2 = 10$

Subtraction

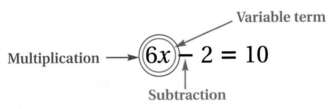

To solve this equation, add to isolate the term with the variable in it. Then divide to solve.

EXAMPLE 5 Solving a Simple Two-Step Equation

Solve $2x + 1 = 7$.

Step 1:

$$\begin{aligned} 2x + 1 &= 7 \\ -1 &= -1 \\ \hline 2x &= 6 \end{aligned}$$

Subtract 1 from both sides to isolate the term with x in it.

Step 2:

$$\frac{2x}{2} = \frac{6}{2}$$

Divide both sides by 2.

$$x = 3$$

Think and Discuss

1. **Explain** what property you would use to solve $\frac{k}{2.5} = 6$.
2. **Give** the equation you would solve to figure out how many ancho peppers are as hot as one cayenne pepper.

1-4 Exercises

FOR EXTRA PRACTICE

see page 732

internet connect

Homework Help Online
go.hrw.com Keyword: MP4 1-4

GUIDED PRACTICE

See Example 1 **Solve.**

1. $4x = 28$ **2.** $7t = 49$ **3.** $3y = 42$ **4.** $2w = 26$

See Example 2

5. $\frac{l}{15} = 4$ **6.** $\frac{k}{8} = 9$ **7.** $\frac{h}{19} = 3$ **8.** $\frac{m}{6} = 1$

See Example 3

9. One serving of milk contains 8 grams of protein, and one serving of steak contains 32 grams of protein. Write and solve an equation to find the number of servings of milk n needed to get the same amount of protein as there is in one serving of steak.

See Example 4

10. Gary needs to buy a suit to go to a formal dance. Using a coupon, he can save \$60, which is only one-fourth of the cost of the suit. Write and solve an equation to determine the cost c of the suit.

See Example 5 **Solve.**

11. $3x + 2 = 23$ **12.** $\frac{k}{5} - 1 = 7$ **13.** $3y - 8 = 1$ **14.** $\frac{m}{6} + 4 = 10$

INDEPENDENT PRACTICE

See Example 1 **Solve.**

15. $3d = 57$ **16.** $7x = 105$ **17.** $4g = 40$ **18.** $16y = 112$

See Example 2

19. $\frac{n}{9} = 63$ **20.** $\frac{h}{27} = 2$ **21.** $\frac{a}{6} = 102$ **22.** $\frac{j}{8} = 12$

See Example 3

23. An orange contains about 80 milligrams of vitamin C, which is 10 times as much as an apple contains. Write and solve an equation to find n, the number of milligrams of vitamin C in an apple.

See Example 4

24. Fred gathered 150 eggs on his family's farm today. This is one-third the number he usually gathers. Write and solve an equation to determine the number n that he usually gathers.

See Example 5 **Solve.**

25. $6x - 5 = 7$ **26.** $\frac{n}{3} - 4 = 1$ **27.** $2y + 5 = 9$ **28.** $\frac{h}{7} + 2 = 2$

PRACTICE AND PROBLEM SOLVING

Solve.

29. $2x = 14$ **30.** $4y = 80$ **31.** $6y = 12$ **32.** $9m = 9$

33. $\frac{k}{8} = 7$ **34.** $\frac{1}{5}x = 121$ **35.** $\frac{b}{6} = 12$ **36.** $\frac{n}{15} = 1$

37. $3x = 51$ **38.** $15g = 75$ **39.** $16y + 18 = 66$ **40.** $3z - 14 = 58$

41. $\frac{b}{4} = 12$ **42.** $\frac{m}{24} = 24$ **43.** $\frac{n}{5} - 3 = 4$ **44.** $\frac{a}{2} + 8 = 14$

Social Studies LINK

In 1956, during President Eisenhower's term, construction began on the United States interstate highway system. The original plan was for 42,000 miles of highways to be completed within 16 years. It actually took 37 years to complete. The last part, Interstate 105 in Los Angeles, was completed in 1993.

45. Write and solve an equation to show how many miles m needed to be completed per year for 42,000 miles of highways to be built in 16 years.

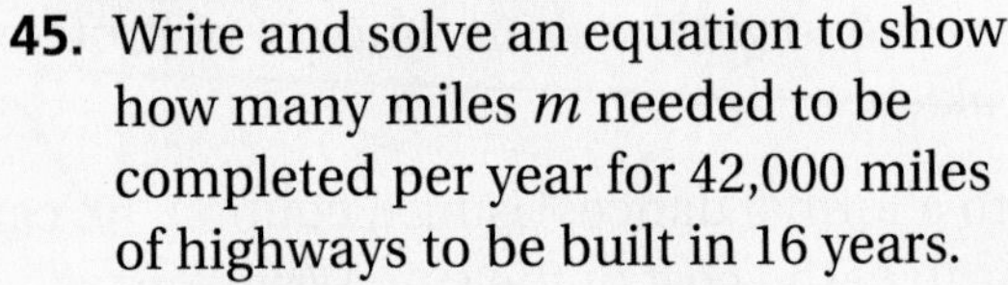

46. Interstate 35 runs north and south from Laredo, Texas, to Duluth, Minnesota, covering 1568 miles. There are 505 miles of I-35 in Texas and 262 miles in Minnesota. Write and solve an equation to find m, the number of miles of I-35 that are not in either state.

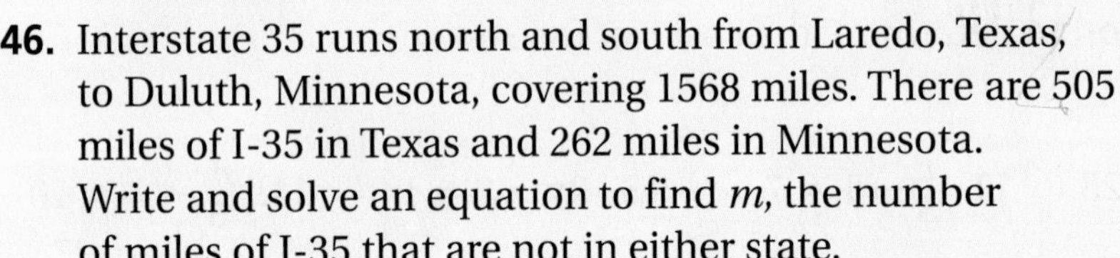

47. A portion of I-476 in Pennsylvania, known as the Blue Route, is about 22 miles long. The length of the Blue Route is about one-sixth the total length of I-476. Write and solve an equation to calculate the length of I-476 in miles m.

48. ***CHALLENGE*** Interstate 80 extends from California to New Jersey. At right are the number of miles of Interstate 80 in each state the highway passes through.

a. __?__ has 134 more miles than __?__.

b. __?__ has 174 fewer miles than __?__.

Number of I-80 Miles

State	Miles
California	195 mi
Nevada	410 mi
Utah	197 mi
Wyoming	401 mi
Nebraska	455 mi
Iowa	301 mi
Illinois	163 mi
Indiana	167 mi
Ohio	236 mi
Pennsylvania	314 mi
New Jersey	68 mi

Spiral Review

Solve. (Lesson 1-3)

49. $3 + x = 11$

50. $y - 6 = 8$

51. $13 = w + 11$

52. $5.6 = b - 4$

53. TEST PREP Which is the prime factorization of 72? (Previous Course)

A $3 \cdot 3 \cdot 2 \cdot 2 \cdot 2$

B $3^3 \cdot 2^2$

C $3 \cdot 2 \cdot 2 \cdot 6$

D $3^2 \cdot 4 \cdot 2$

54. TEST PREP What is the value of the expression $3x + 4$ for $x = 2$? (Lesson 1-1)

F 4

G 6

H 9

J 10

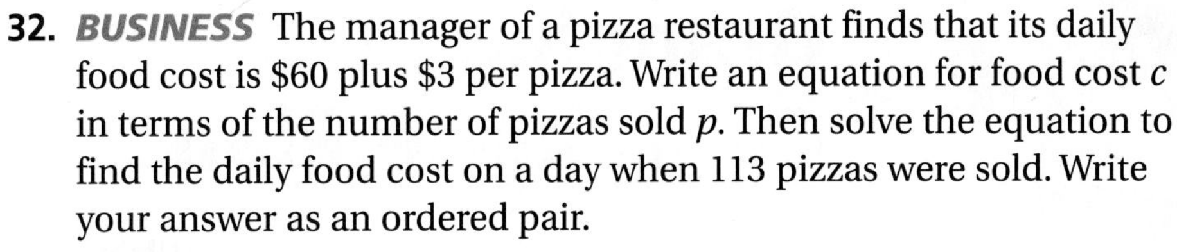

32. ***BUSINESS*** The manager of a pizza restaurant finds that its daily food cost is \$60 plus \$3 per pizza. Write an equation for food cost c in terms of the number of pizzas sold p. Then solve the equation to find the daily food cost on a day when 113 pizzas were sold. Write your answer as an ordered pair.

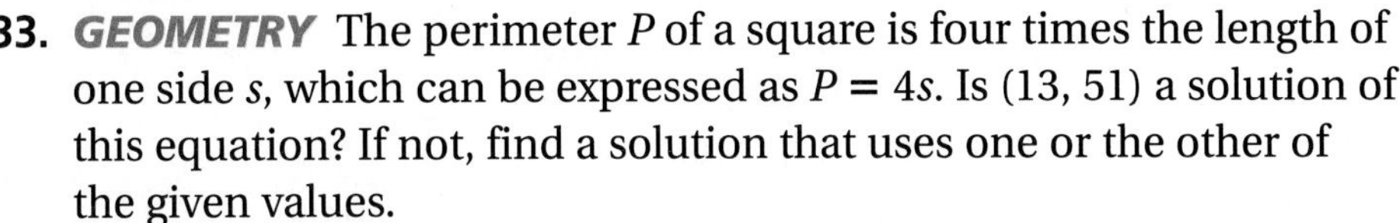

33. ***GEOMETRY*** The perimeter P of a square is four times the length of one side s, which can be expressed as $P = 4s$. Is (13, 51) a solution of this equation? If not, find a solution that uses one or the other of the given values.

History LINK

In 1513, Ponce de León went in search of the legendary Fountain of Youth, which people believed would give them eternal youth. While searching, he discovered Florida, which he named Pascua de Florida.

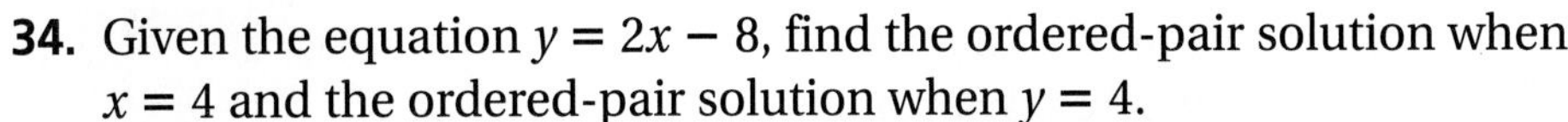

34. Given the equation $y = 2x - 8$, find the ordered-pair solution when $x = 4$ and the ordered-pair solution when $y = 4$.

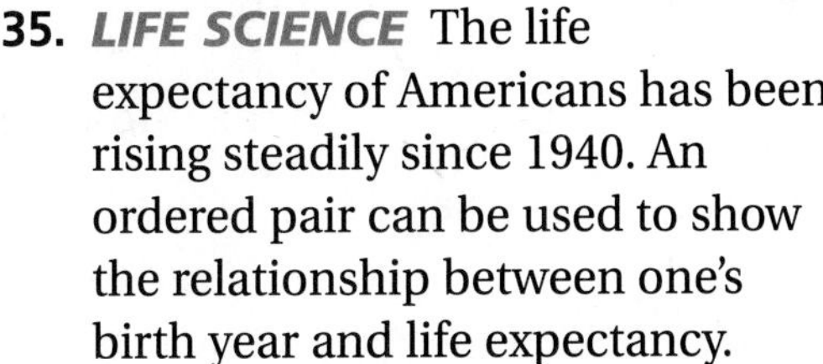

35. ***LIFE SCIENCE*** The life expectancy of Americans has been rising steadily since 1940. An ordered pair can be used to show the relationship between one's birth year and life expectancy.

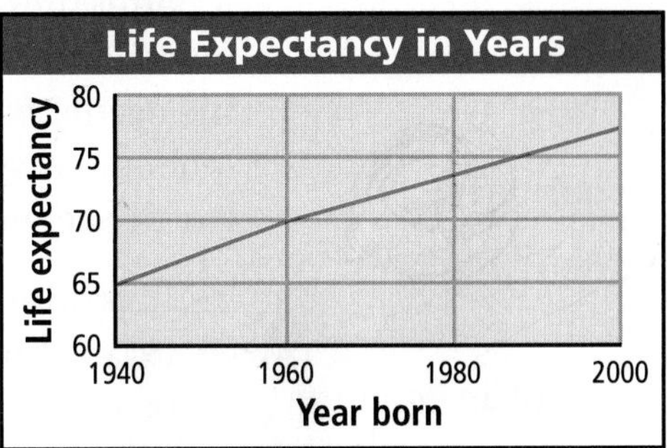

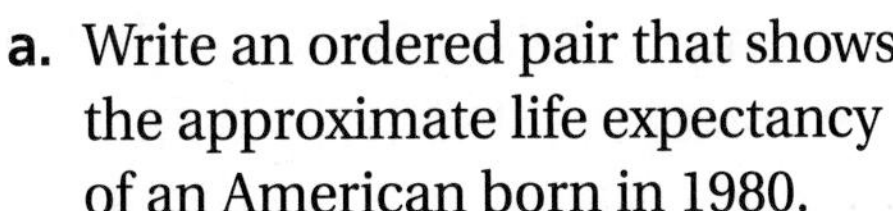

a. Write an ordered pair that shows the approximate life expectancy of an American born in 1980.

b. The data on the chart can be approximated by the equation $L = 0.2n - 323$, where L is the life expectancy and n is the year of birth. Use the equation to find an ordered pair that shows the approximate life expectancy for an American born in 2020.

36. ***WHAT'S THE ERROR?*** A table of solutions shows that (4, 10) is a solution to the equation $y = \frac{x}{2} - 1$. What's the error?

37. ***WRITE ABOUT IT*** Write an equation that has (3, 5) as a solution. Explain how you found the equation.

38. ***CHALLENGE*** In football, a touchdown is worth 6 points and a field goal is worth 3 points. If x equals the number of touchdowns scored, and y equals the number of field goals scored, find the possible solutions of the equation $54 = 6x + 3y$.

Spiral Review

Evaluate each expression for the given value of the variable. (Lesson 1-1)

39. $x - 4$ for $x = 11$ **40.** $2x + 3$ for $x = 9$ **41.** $3x - 2$ for $x = 2$

42. $4(x + 1)$ for $x = 8$ **43.** $3(x - 1)$ for $x = 5$ **44.** $2(x + 4)$ for $x = 3$

45. TEST PREP Determine which value of x is the solution of $x + 3 = 14$. (Lesson 1-3)

A 9 **C** 17
B 11 **D** 21

46. TEST PREP Determine which value of x is the solution of $x - 4 = 3$. (Lesson 1-3)

F 1 **H** −1
G 12 **J** 7

1-8 Graphing on a Coordinate Plane

Learn to graph points and lines on the coordinate plane.

Vocabulary

- coordinate plane
- *x*-axis
- *y*-axis
- *x*-coordinate
- *y*-coordinate
- origin
- graph of an equation

Kim left a message for José that read, "Meet me on Second Street."

But José did not know where on Second Street. A better message would have been "Meet me at the corner of East Jefferson Avenue and North Second Street."

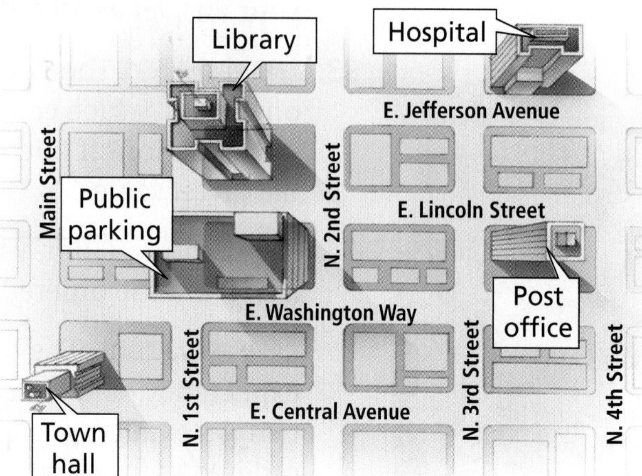

The **coordinate plane** is like a map formed by two number lines, the **x-axis** and the **y-axis**, that intersect at right angles. Ordered pairs are the locations, or points, on the map. The **x-coordinate** and **y-coordinate** of an ordered pair tell the direction and number of units to move.

x-coordinate *move right or left*  *y*-coordinate *move up or down*

Helpful Hint

The sign of a number indicates which direction to move.
Positive: up or right
Negative: down or left

To plot an ordered pair, begin at the **origin**, the point (0, 0), which is the intersection of the *x*-axis and the *y*-axis. The first coordinate tells how many units to move left or right; the second coordinate tells how many units to move up or down.

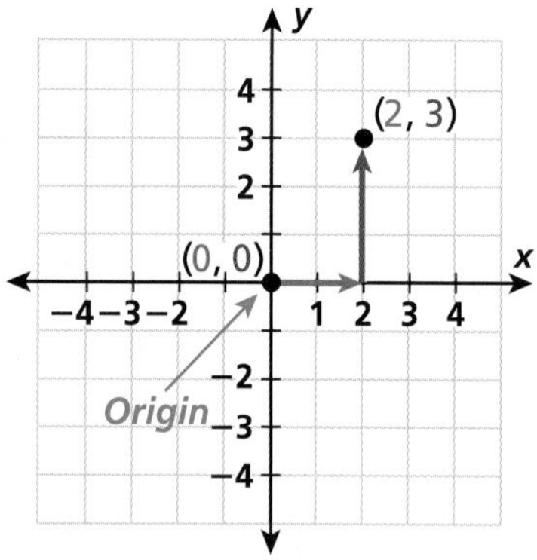

move right 2 units **(2, 3)** *move up 3 units*

EXAMPLE 1 Finding the Coordinates of Points on a Plane

Give the coordinates of each point.

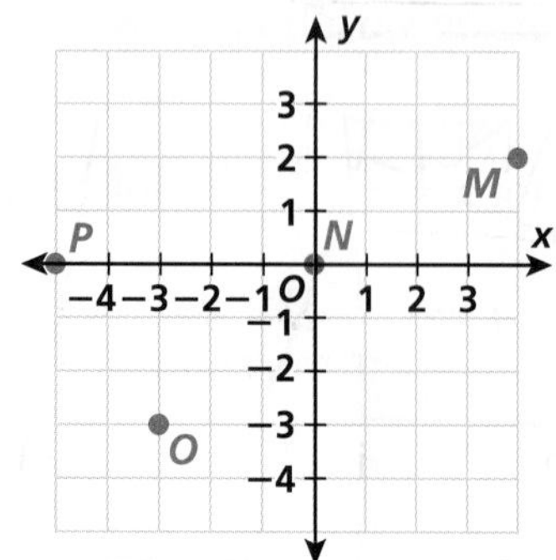

Point *M* is (4, 2).
4 units right, 2 units up

Point *N* is (0, 0).
0 units right, 0 units up

Point *O* is (−3, −3).
3 units left, 3 units down

Point *P* is (−5, 0).
5 units left, 0 units up

internet connect

State-Specific Test Practice Online
go.hrw.com Keyword: MP4 TestPrep

Standardized Test Prep

Chapter 1

Cumulative Assessment, Chapter 1

1. Which algebraic equation represents the word sentence "15 less than the number of computers c is 32"?

   (A) $\frac{c}{15} = 32$ (C) $15 - c = 32$
   (B) $15c = 32$ (D) $c - 15 = 32$

2. Which inequality is represented by this graph?

   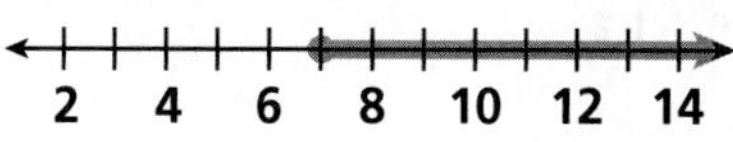

   (F) $x < 7$ (H) $7 < x$
   (G) $x \leq 7$ (J) $7 \leq x$

3. Bill is 3 years older than his cat. The sum of their ages is 25. If c represents the cat's age, which equation could be used to find c?

   (A) $c + 25 = c + 3$ (C) $c + 3c = 25$
   (B) $c + 25 = 3c$ (D) $c + (c + 3) = 25$

4. The solution of $k + 3(k - 2) = 34$ is

   (F) $k = 10$ (H) $k = 8$
   (G) $k = 9$ (J) $k = 7$

5. Jamal brings \$20 to a pizza restaurant where a plain slice costs \$2.25, including tax. Which inequality can he use to find the number of plain slices he can buy?

   (A) $2.25 + s \leq 20$ (C) $2.25s \leq 20$
   (B) $2.25 + s \geq 20$ (D) $2.25s \geq 20$

6. When twice a number is decreased by 4, the result is 236. What is the number?

   (F) 29.5 (H) 116
   (G) 59 (J) 120

7. A number n is increased by 5 and the result is multiplied by 5. This result is decreased by 5. What is the final result?

   (A) $5n$ (C) $5n + 10$
   (B) $5n + 5$ (D) $5n + 20$

8. Which has the greatest value?

   (F) $(2 + 3)(2 + 3)$ (H) $(2 \cdot 3)(2 \cdot 3)$
   (G) $2 + 3 \cdot 3$ (J) $2 \cdot 2 + 3 \cdot 3$

TEST TAKING TIP!

To convert from a larger unit of measure to a smaller unit, multiply by the conversion factor. To convert from a smaller unit of measure to a larger unit, divide by the conversion factor.

9. ***SHORT RESPONSE*** Jo has 197 fund-raising posters. She decides to use four 5-inch strips of tape to hang each poster. Each roll of tape is 250 feet long. Estimate the number of whole rolls Jo will need to hang all of the posters. Explain in words how you determined your estimate. (*Hint:* 12 in. = 1 ft)

10. ***SHORT RESPONSE*** Mrs. Morton recorded the lengths of the telephone calls she made this week.

Length of call (min)	2	5	7	12	15
Number of calls	7	x	2	2	3

The number of calls shorter than 6 minutes is equal to the number of calls longer than 6 minutes. Write an equation that could be used to determine the number of 5-minute calls Mrs. Morton made. Solve your equation.

Standardized Test Prep

Chapter

2

Integers and Exponents

TABLE OF CONTENTS

Atomic Particle	Independent Life Span (s)
Electron	Indefinite
Proton	Indefinite
Neutron	920
Muon	2.2×10^{-6}

Career *Nuclear Physicist*

The atom was defined by the ancient Greeks as the smallest particle of matter. We now know that atoms are made up of many smaller particles.

Nuclear physicists study these particles using large machines—such as linear accelerators, synchrotrons, and cyclotrons—that can smash atoms to uncover their component parts.

Nuclear physicists use mathematics along with the data they discover to create models of the atom and the structure of matter.

ARE YOU READY?

Choose the best term from the list to complete each sentence.

expression
inequality
order of operations
variable
equation

1. According to the __?__, you must multiply or divide before you add or subtract when simplifying a numerical __?__.
2. An algebraic expression is a mathematical sentence that has at least one __?__.
3. In a(n) __?__, an equal sign is used to show that two quantites are the same.
4. You use a(n) __?__ to show that one quantity is greater than another quantity.

Complete these exercises to review skills you will need for this chapter.

✔ Order of Operations

Simplify by using the order of operations.

5. $(12) + 4(2)$ **6.** $12 + 8 \div 4$ **7.** $15(14 - 4)$

8. $(23 - 5) - 36 \div 2$ **9.** $12 \div 2 + 10 \div 5$ **10.** $40 \div 2 \cdot 4$

✔ Equations

Solve.

11. $x + 9 = 21$ **12.** $3z = 42$ **13.** $\frac{w}{4} = 16$

14. $24 + t = 24$ **15.** $p - 7 = 23$ **16.** $12m = 0$

✔ Match a Number Line to an Inequality

Write an inequality that describes the set of points shown on each number line.

17. −6 −4 −2 0 2 4 6

18. 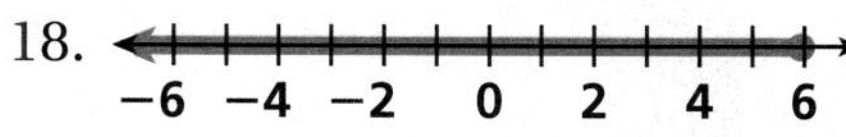

19. −4 −2 0 2 4 6 8

20. −4 −2 0 2 4 6 8

✔ Multiply and Divide by Powers of Ten

Multiply or divide.

21. $358(10)$ **22.** $358(1000)$ **23.** $358(100,000)$

24. $\frac{358}{10}$ **25.** $\frac{358}{1000}$ **26.** $\frac{358}{100,000}$

2-1 Adding Integers

Learn to add integers.

Vocabulary
integer
opposite
absolute value

Katrina keeps a health journal. She knows that when she eats she adds calories and when she exercises she subtracts calories. So she uses *integers* to find her daily total.

Integers are the set of whole numbers, including 0, and their **opposites**. The sum of two opposite integers is zero.

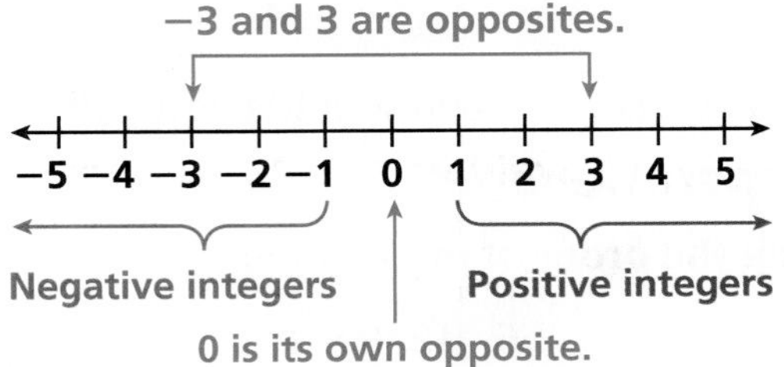

EXAMPLE 1 Using a Number Line to Add Integers

Helpful Hint

To add a **positive** number, move to the **right**. To add a **negative** number, move to the **left**.

Use a number line to find the sum.

$4 + (-6)$

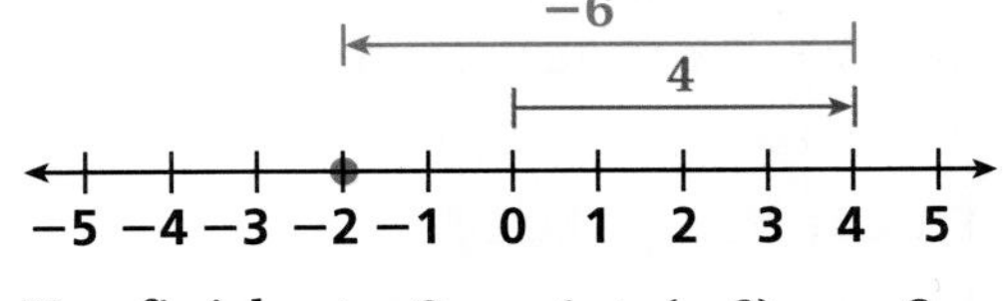

Move right 4 units. From 4, move left 6 units.

You finish at -2, so $4 + (-6) = -2$.

Another way to add integers is to use absolute value. The **absolute value** of a number is its distance from 0. The absolute value of -4, written as $|-4|$, is 4; and the absolute value of 5 is 5.

ADDING INTEGERS	
If the signs are the same. . .	**If the signs are different. . .**
find the sum of the absolute values. Use the same sign as the integers.	find the difference of the absolute values. Use the sign of the integer with the larger absolute value.

EXAMPLE 2 Using Absolute Value to Add Integers

Add.

A $-3 + (-5)$

$-3 + (-5)$	*Think: Find the sum of 3 and 5.*
-8	*Same sign; use the sign of the integers.*

B $4 + (-7)$

$4 + (-7)$	*Think: Find the difference of 7 and 4.*
-3	*7 > 4; use the sign of 7.*

C $-3 + 6$

$-3 + 6$	*Think: Find the difference of 6 and 3.*
3	*6 > 3; use the sign of 6.*

EXAMPLE 3 Evaluating Expressions with Integers

Evaluate $b + 12$ for $b = -5$.

$b + 12$	
$(-5) + 12$	*Replace b with −5.*
	Think: Find the difference of 12 and 5.
$-5 + 12 = 7$	*12 > 5; use the sign of 12.*

EXAMPLE 4 *Health Application*

Katrina wants to check her calorie count after breakfast and exercise. Use information from the journal entry to find her total.

$145 + 62 + 111 + (-110) + (-40)$	*Use a positive sign for calories and a negative sign for calories burned.*
$(145 + 62 + 111) + (-110 + -40)$	*Group integers with same signs.*
$318 + (-150)$	*Add integers within each group.*
168	*318 > 150; use the sign of 318.*

Katrina's calorie count after breakfast and exercise is 168 calories.

Think and Discuss

1. Compare the sums $10 + (-22)$ and $-10 + 22$.

2. Explain whether an absolute value is ever negative.

2-1 Exercises

FOR EXTRA PRACTICE
see page 734

internet connect
Homework Help Online
go.hrw.com Keyword: MP4 2-1

GUIDED PRACTICE

See Example 1 **Use a number line to find each sum.**

1. $3 + 2$ **2.** $6 + (-4)$ **3.** $-6 + 10$ **4.** $-4 + (-2)$

See Example 2 **Add.**

5. $-11 + 3$ **6.** $8 + (-2)$ **7.** $-12 + 15$ **8.** $-7 + (-9)$

See Example 3 **Evaluate each expression for the given value of the variable.**

9. $t + 16$ for $t = -5$ **10.** $m + 8$ for $m = -4$ **11.** $p + (-4)$ for $p = -4$

See Example 4 **12.** Ron is balancing his checkbook. Use the information at right to find the difference in his checking account. Note that checks represent account withdrawals.

Checks	Deposits
$128	$500
$46	$175
$204	

INDEPENDENT PRACTICE

See Example 1 **Use a number line to find each sum.**

13. $5 + (-7)$ **14.** $-5 + 5$ **15.** $5 + (-8)$ **16.** $-4 + 7$

See Example 2 **Add.**

17. $9 + 12$ **18.** $-7 + (-8)$ **19.** $-9 + (-9)$ **20.** $16 + (-4)$

See Example 3 **Evaluate each expression for the given value of the variable.**

21. $q + 10$ for $q = 12$ **22.** $x + 16$ for $x = -6$ **23.** $z + (-7)$ for $z = 16$

See Example 4 **24.** A hospital clerk is checking her records. Use the information at right to find the net change in the number of patients for the week.

	Admissions	Discharges
Monday	14	8
Tuesday	25	4
Wednesday	13	11
Thursday	17	0
Friday	9	5

PRACTICE AND PROBLEM SOLVING

Write an addition equation for each number line diagram.

25.

−8 −6 −4 −2 0 2 4

26.

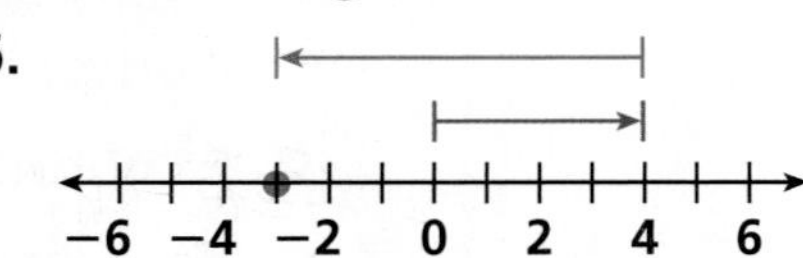

Use a number line to find each sum.

27. $-8 + (-5)$ **28.** $16 + (-22)$ **29.** $-36 + 18$

30. $55 + 27$ **31.** $57 + (-59)$ **32.** $-14 + 85$

33. $52 + (-9)$ **34.** $-26 + (-26)$ **35.** $-41 + 41$

36. $-7 + 9 + (-8)$ **37.** $-11 + (-6) + (-2)$ **38.** $32 + (-4) + (-15)$

Evaluate each expression for the given value of the variable.

39. $c + 16$ for $c = -8$ **40.** $k + (-12)$ for $k = 4$

41. $b + (-3)$ for $b = -17$ **42.** $15 + r$ for $r = -18$

43. $-9 + w$ for $w = -6$ **44.** $1 + n + (-7)$ for $n = 6$

45. Evaluate $2 + x + y$ for $x = 7$ and $y = -4$.

Economics LINK

The number one port for foreign trade by water in the United States is the Port of Houston. In 2000, the port recorded 6801 vessel calls totaling over 175 million tons of cargo.

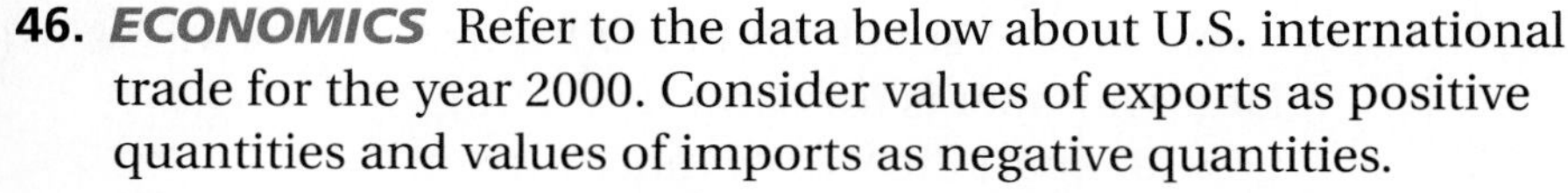

46. ***ECONOMICS*** Refer to the data below about U.S. international trade for the year 2000. Consider values of exports as positive quantities and values of imports as negative quantities.

	Exports	Imports
Goods	$772,210,000,000	$1,224,417,000,000
Services	$293,492,000,000	$217,024,000,000

Source: 2000 U.S. Census

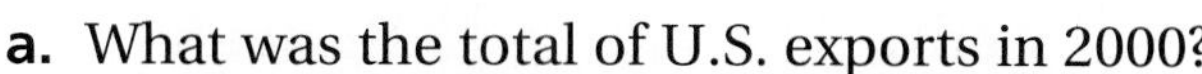

a. What was the total of U.S. exports in 2000?

b. What was the total of U.S. imports in 2000?

c. The sum of exports and imports is called the *balance of trade.* Write an addition equation to show the 2000 U.S. balance of trade.

47. ***WHAT'S THE ERROR?*** A student evaluating $-3 + f$ for $f = -4$ gave an answer of 1. What could be wrong?

48. ***WRITE ABOUT IT*** Explain the different ways it is possible to add two integers and get a negative answer.

49. ***CHALLENGE*** What is the sum of $1 + (-1) + 1 + (-1) + \ldots$ when there are 12 terms? 17 terms? 20 terms? 23 terms? Explain any patterns that you find.

Spiral Review

Solve. (Lessons 1-3 and 1-4)

50. $p - 8 = 12$ **51.** $f + 9 = 15$ **52.** $\frac{m}{4} = 16$ **53.** $7q = 42$

54. **TEST PREP** Which number below is **not** a solution of $n - 7 < 1$? (Lesson 1-5)

A 2 **B** 4 **C** 6 **D** 8

2-2 Subtracting Integers

Learn to subtract integers.

Some roller coasters have maximum drops that are greater than their heights.

Riders enter underground tunnels at speeds of up to 85 miles per hour. The underground depths of the rides can be represented by negative integers.

Subtracting a smaller number from a larger number is the same as finding how far apart the two numbers are on a number line. Subtracting an integer is the same as adding its opposite.

SUBTRACTING INTEGERS

Words	Numbers	Algebra
Change the subtraction sign to an addition sign and change the sign of the second number.	$2 - 3 = 2 + (-3)$ $4 - (-5) = 4 + 5$	$a - b = a + (-b)$ $a - (-b) = a + b$

EXAMPLE 1 Subtracting Integers

Subtract.

A $-5 - 5$

$-5 - 5 = -5 + (-5)$ *Add the opposite of 5.*

$= -10$ *Same sign; use the sign of the integers.*

B $2 - (-4)$

$2 - (-4) = 2 + 4$ *Add the opposite of −4.*

$= 6$ *Same signs; use the sign of the integers.*

C $-11 - (-8)$

$-11 - (-8) = -11 + 8$ *Add the opposite of −8.*

$= -3$ *11 > 8; use the sign of 11.*

EXAMPLE 2 Evaluating Expressions with Integers

Evaluate each expression for the given value of the variable.

A $4 - t$ **for** $t = -3$**.**

$4 - t$	
$4 - (-3)$	*Substitute −3 for t.*
$= 4 + 3$	*Add the opposite of −3.*
$= 7$	*Same sign; use the sign of the integers.*

B $-5 - s$ **for** $s = -7$**.**

$-5 - s$	
$-5 - (-7)$	*Substitute −7 for s.*
$= -5 + 7$	*Add the opposite of −7.*
$= 2$	*7 > 5; use the sign of 7.*

C $-1 - x$ **for** $x = 8$**.**

$-1 - x$	
$-1 - 8$	*Substitute 8 for x.*
$= -1 + (-8)$	*Add the opposite of 8.*
$= -9$	*Same sign; use the sign of the integers.*

EXAMPLE 3 *Architecture Application*

The roller coaster Desperado has a maximum height of 209 ft and maximum drop of 225 ft. How far underground does the roller coaster go?

$209 - 225$	*Subtract the drop from the height.*
$209 + (-225)$	*Add the opposite of 225.*
$= -16$	*225 > 209; use the sign of 225.*

Desperado goes 16 ft underground.

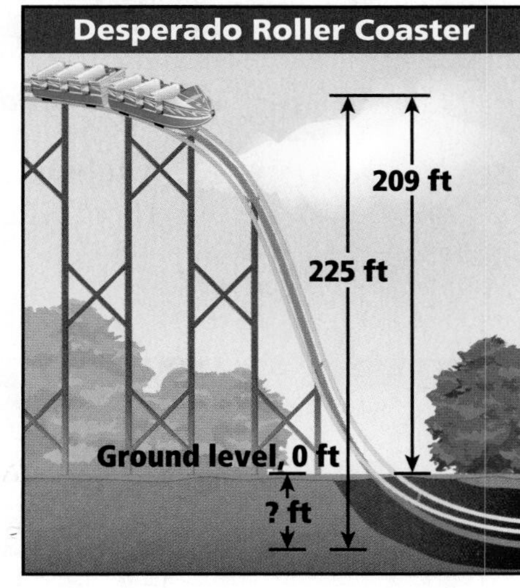

Think and Discuss

1. Explain why $10 - (-10)$ does not equal $-10 - 10$.

2. Describe the answer that you get when you subtract a larger number from a smaller number.

2-2 Exercises

FOR EXTRA PRACTICE
see page 734

internet connect
Homework Help Online
go.hrw.com Keyword: MP4 2-2

GUIDED PRACTICE

See Example 1

Subtract.

1. $-7 - 8$
2. $-7 - (-4)$
3. $9 - (-5)$
4. $-10 - (-3)$

See Example 2

Evaluate each expression for the given value of the variable.

5. $7 - h$ for $h = -6$
6. $-8 - m$ for $m = -2$
7. $-3 - k$ for $k = 12$

See Example 3

8. The temperature rose from -4°F to 45°F in Spearfish, South Dakota, on January 22, 1943, in only 2 minutes! By how many degrees did the temperature change? *Source: The Weather Book,* Random House, Inc.

INDEPENDENT PRACTICE

See Example 1

Subtract.

9. $-2 - 9$
10. $12 - (-7)$
11. $11 - (-6)$
12. $-9 - (-3)$
13. $-8 - (-11)$
14. $-14 - 8$
15. $-5 - (-9)$
16. $30 - (-12)$

See Example 2

Evaluate each expression for the given value of the variable.

17. $12 - b$ for $b = -4$
18. $-9 - q$ for $q = -12$
19. $-7 - f$ for $f = 10$
20. $7 - d$ for $d = 16$
21. $-7 - w$ for $w = 7$
22. $-3 - p$ for $p = -3$

See Example 3

23. A submarine cruising at 25 m below sea level, or -25 m, descends 15 m. What is its new depth?

PRACTICE AND PROBLEM SOLVING

Write a subtraction equation for each number line diagram.

24.

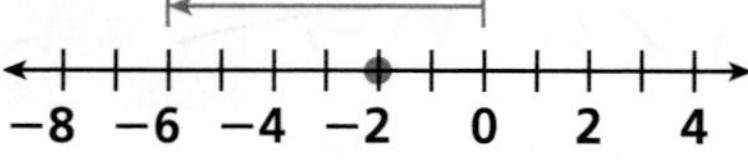

25.

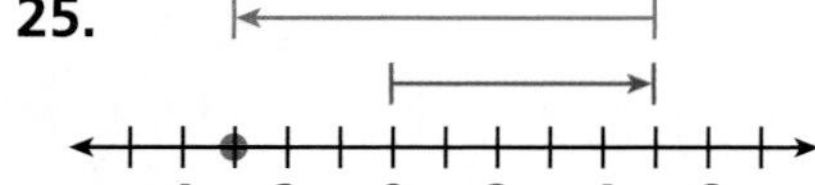

Perform the given operations.

26. $-7 - (-10)$
27. $24 - (-27)$
28. $-31 - 11$
29. $-31 - 31$
30. $-12 - 9 + (-4)$
31. $-13 - (-5) + (-8)$

Evaluate each expression for the given value of the variable.

32. $x - 15$ for $x = -3$
33. $6 - t$ for $t = -7$
34. $-14 - y$ for $y = 9$
35. $s - (-21)$ for $s = -19$
36. $1 - r - (-2)$ for $r = 5$
37. $-3 - w + 3$ for $w = 42$

Social Studies LINK

go.hrw.com
Web Extra!
KEYWORD: MP4 Egypt

Use the timeline to answer the questions. Use negative numbers for years B.C. Assume that there was a year 0 (there wasn't) and that there have been no major changes to the calendar (there have been).

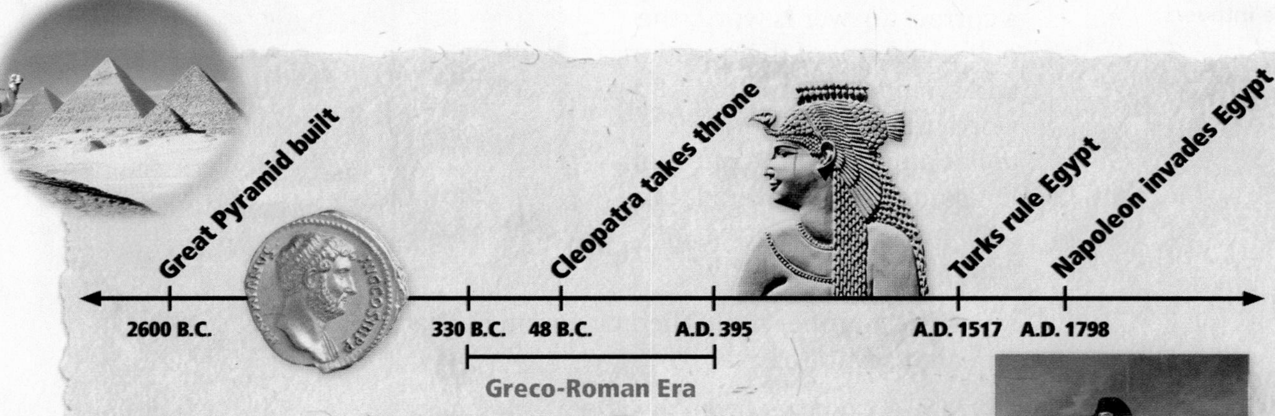

38. How long was the Greco-Roman era, when Greece and Rome ruled Egypt?

39. Which was a longer period of time: from the Great Pyramid to Cleopatra, or from Cleopatra to the present? By how many years?

40. Queen Neferteri ruled Egypt about 2900 years before the Turks ruled. In what year did she rule?

41. There are 1846 years between which two events on this timeline?

42. ***WRITE ABOUT IT*** What is it about years B.C. that makes negative numbers a good choice for representing them?

43. ***CHALLENGE*** How would your calculations differ if you took into account the fact that there was no year 0?

Spiral Review

Combine like terms. (Lesson 1-6)

44. $9m + 8 - 4m + 7 - 5m$ **45.** $6t + 3k - 15$ **46.** $5a + 3 - b + 1$

47. **TEST PREP** Which of the following is **not** a solution of $y = 5x + 1$? (Lesson 1-7)

A (0, 1) **B** (1, 6) **C** (21, 4) **D** (22, 111)

48. **TEST PREP** Which of the following is the value of $-7 + 3h$ when $h = 5$? (Lesson 2-1)

F -8 **G** -22 **H** 8 **J** 22

2-3 Multiplying and Dividing Integers

Learn to multiply and divide integers.

On *Jeopardy! Teen Tournament,* a correct answer is worth the dollar amount of the question, and an incorrect answer is worth the opposite of the dollar amount of the question. If a contestant answered three $200 questions incorrectly, what would the score be?

A positive number multiplied by an integer can be written as repeated addition.

$3(-200) = -200 + (-200) + (-200) = -600$

From what you know about adding integers, you can see that a positive integer times a negative integer is negative.

You know that multiplying two positive integers together gives you a positive answer. Look for a pattern in the integer multiplication at right to understand the rules for multiplying two negative integers.

$3(-200) = -600$
+ 200
$2(-200) = -400$
+ 200
$1(-200) = -200$
+ 200
$0(-200) = 0$
$-1(-200) = 200$
$-2(-200) = 400$
$-3(-200) = 600$

The product of two negative integers is a positive integer.

MULTIPLYING AND DIVIDING TWO INTEGERS

If the signs are the same, the sign of the answer is **positive.**

If the signs are different, the sign of the answer is **negative.**

EXAMPLE  1 Multiplying and Dividing Integers

Multiply or divide.

A $6(-7)$ — *Signs are different.*

-42 — *Answer is* ***negative.***

B $\frac{-45}{9}$ — *Signs are different.*

-5 — *Answer is* ***negative.***

C $-12(-4)$ — *Signs are the same.*

48 — *Answer is* ***positive.***

D $\frac{18}{-6}$ — *Signs are different.*

-3 — *Answer is* ***negative.***

EXAMPLE 2 Using the Order of Operations with Integers

Simplify.

A $-2(3 - 9)$

$-2(3 - 9)$ *Subtract inside the parentheses.*

$= -2(-6)$ *Think: The signs are the same.*

$= \mathbf{12}$ *The answer is positive.*

Remember!

Order of Operations
1. Parentheses
2. Exponents
3. Multiply and divide from left to right.
4. Add and subtract from left to right.

B $4(-7 - 2)$

$4(-7 - 2)$ *Subtract inside the parentheses.*

$= 4(-9)$ *Think: The signs are different.*

$= \mathbf{-36}$ *The answer is negative.*

C $-3(16 - 8)$

$-3(16 - 8)$ *Subtract inside the parentheses.*

$= -3(8)$ *Think: The signs are different.*

$= \mathbf{-24}$ *The answer is negative.*

The order of operations can be used to find ordered pair solutions of integer equations. Substitute an integer value for one variable to find the value of the other variable in each ordered pair.

EXAMPLE 3 Plotting Integer Solutions of Equations

Complete a table of solutions for $y = -2x - 1$ for $x = -2$, -1, 0, 1, and 2. Plot the points on a coordinate plane.

x	$-2x - 1$	y	(x, y)
−2	−2(−2) − 1	3	(−2, 3)
−1	−2(−1) − 1	1	(−1, 1)
0	−2(0) − 1	−1	(0, −1)
1	−2(1) − 1	−3	(1, −3)
2	−2(2) − 1	−5	(2, −5)

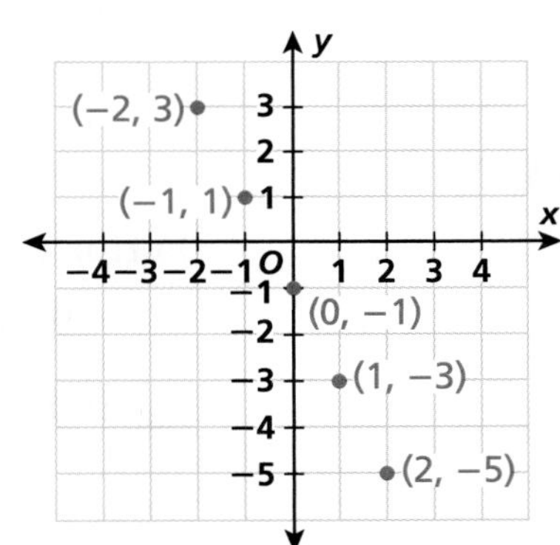

Think and Discuss

1. List all possible multiplication and division statements for the integers with absolute values of 5, 6, and 30. For example, $5 \cdot 6 = 30$.

2. Compare the sign of the product of two negative integers with the sign of the sum of two negative integers.

2-3 Exercises

FOR EXTRA PRACTICE

see page 734

internet connect

Homework Help Online

go.hrw.com Keyword: MP4 2-3

GUIDED PRACTICE

See Example 1 **Multiply or divide.**

1. $9(-3)$
2. $\frac{-56}{7}$
3. $-6(-5)$
4. $\frac{32}{-8}$

See Example 2 **Simplify.**

5. $-7(5 - 12)$
6. $7(-3 - 8)$
7. $-6(-5 + 9)$
8. $12(-8 + 2)$

See Example 3 **Complete a table of solutions for each equation for $x = -2, -1, 0, 1,$ and 2. Plot the points on a coordinate plane.**

9. $y = 3x + 1$
10. $y = -3x - 1$
11. $y = 2x + 2$

INDEPENDENT PRACTICE

See Example 1 **Multiply or divide.**

12. $-4(-9)$
13. $\frac{77}{-7}$
14. $12(-7)$
15. $\frac{-42}{6}$

See Example 2 **Simplify.**

16. $10(7 - 15)$
17. $-13(-2 - 8)$
18. $15(9 - 12)$
19. $10 + 4(5 - 8)$

See Example 3 **Complete a table of solutions for each equation for $x = -2, -1, 0, 1,$ and 2. Plot the points on a coordinate plane.**

20. $y = -2x$
21. $y = -2x + 1$
22. $y = -x - 3$

PRACTICE AND PROBLEM SOLVING

Perform the given operations.

23. $-9(5)$
24. $\frac{-121}{11}$
25. $-6(-6)$
26. $\frac{100}{-25}$
27. $3(-4)(-2)$
28. $\frac{-96}{-12}$
29. $12(3)(-2)$
30. $\frac{-15(3)}{-5}$
31. $-10(-1)(-8)$
32. $\frac{3(-8)}{2}$
33. $-9(2 - 9)$
34. $\frac{-12(-6)}{-2}$

Evaluate the expressions for the given value of the variable.

35. $-3t - 4$ for $t = 5$
36. $-x + 2$ for $x = -9$
37. $-7(s + 8)$ for $s = -10$
38. $\frac{-r}{7}$ for $r = 49$
39. $\frac{-27}{t}$ for $t = -9$
40. $\frac{y - 10}{-3}$ for $y = 37$

Complete a table of solutions for each equation for $x = -2, -1, 0, 1,$ and 2. Plot the points on a coordinate plane.

41. $y = 2x + 4$
42. $y = 5 - 4x$
43. $y = 1 + 3x$

Anoplogaster cornuta, often called a fangtooth or ogrefish, is a predatory fish that reaches a maximum length of 15 cm. It can be found in tropical and temperate waters at −16,000 ft.

44. ***EARTH SCIENCE*** The ocean floor is extremely uneven. It includes underwater mountains, ridges, and extremely deep areas called *trenches.* To the nearest foot, find the average depth of the trenches shown.

Depths of Ocean Trenches

(Sea level) 0
Depth (ft)
−20,000
−25,000
−30,000
−35,000
−40,000
Bonin −32,788
Kuril −31,988
Mariana −35,840
Yap −27,976

45. ***BUSINESS*** A leak in a commercial water tank changes the amount of water in the tank each day by −6 gallons. When the total change is −192 gallons, the pump will stop working. How many days will it take from the time the tank is full until the pump fails?

46. ***EARTH SCIENCE*** Ocean tides are the result of the gravitational force between the sun, the moon and the earth. When ocean tides occur, the earth also moves. This is called an earth tide. The formula for the height of an earth tide is $y = \frac{x}{3}$, where x is the height of the ocean tide. Fill in the table and plot the points on a coordinate plane.

Ocean Tide (x)	$\frac{x}{3}$	Earth Tide (y)
High: 12		
Low: −9		
High: 6		
Low: −12		

47. ***CHOOSE A STRATEGY*** P is the set of positive factors of 20, and Q is the set of negative factors of 12. If x is a member of set P and y is a member of set Q, what is the greatest possible value of $x \cdot y$?

A 220 **B** 212 **C** 210 **D** −1

48. ***WRITE ABOUT IT*** If you know that the product of two integers is negative, what can you say about the two integers? Give examples.

49. ***CHALLENGE*** Complete a table of solutions of $x + y = 10$ for $x = -2, -1, 0, 1$, and 2. Plot the points on a coordinate plane.

Spiral Review

Solve. (Lessons 1-3 and 1-4)

50. $z - 13 = 5$ **51.** $8 + w = 19$ **52.** $\frac{x}{5} = 25$ **53.** $3h = 0$

54. TEST PREP Which ordered pair is a solution of $2y - 3x = 8$? (Lesson 1-7)

A (6, 13) **B** (19, 4) **C** (10, 4) **D** (4, 0)

55. TEST PREP Which of the following is equivalent to $|7 - (-3)|$? (Lesson 2-2)

F $|7| - |-3|$ **G** $|7| + |-3|$ **H** −10 **K** 4

Model Solving Equations

Use with Lesson 2-4

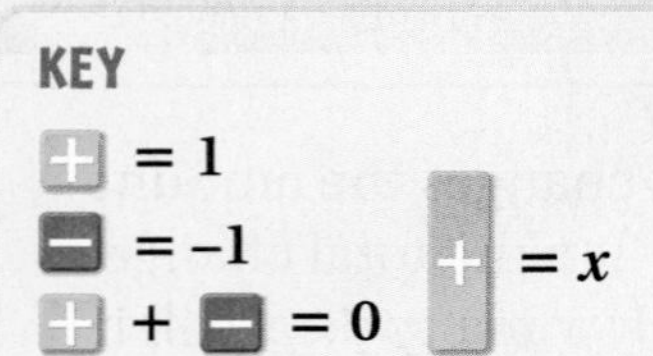

REMEMBER
It will not change the value of an expression if you add or remove zero.

You can use algebra tiles to help you solve equations.

Activity

To solve the equation $x + 3 = 5$, you need to get x alone on one side of the equal sign. You can add or remove tiles as long as you add the same amount or remove the same amount on both sides.

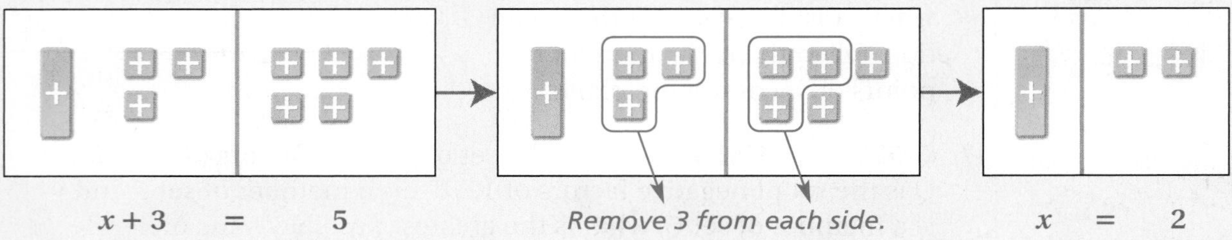

1 Use algebra tiles to model and solve each equation.

a. $x + 1 = 2$ **b.** $x + 2 = 7$ **c.** $x + (-6) = -9$ **d.** $x + 4 = 4$

The equation $x + 4 = 2$ is more difficult to solve because there are not enough yellow tiles on the right side. You can use the fact that $1 + (-1) = 0$ to help you solve the equation.

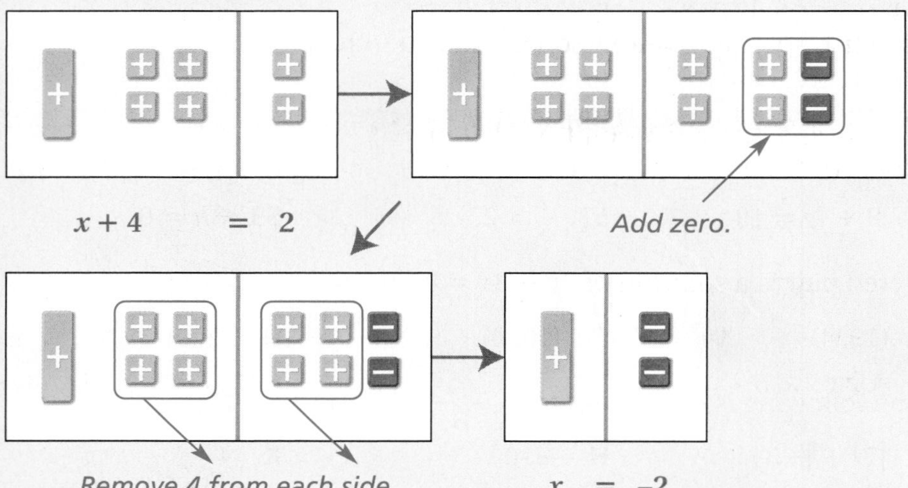

2 Use algebra tiles to model and solve each equation.

a. $x + 3 = 7$ **b.** $x + 9 = 2$ **c.** $x + (-3) = -1$ **d.** $x + (-11) = -4$

Modeling $x - 4 = 2$ is similar to modeling $x + 4 = 2$. Remember that you can add zero to an equation and the equation's value does not change.

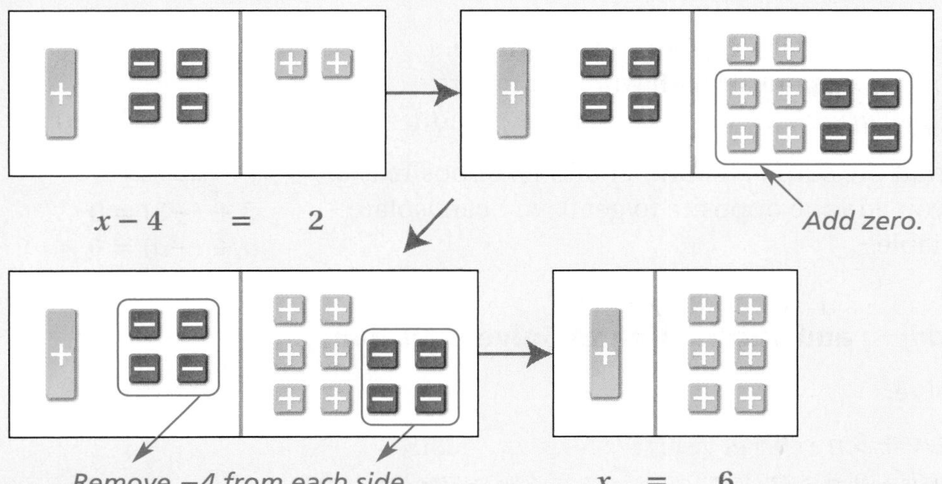

Remove −4 from each side. $x = 6$

3 Use algebra tiles to model and solve each equation.

a. $x - 1 = 2$ **b.** $x - 2 = 5$ **c.** $x - 4 = -3$ **d.** $x - 7 = 4$

Think and Discuss

1. When you add zero to an equation, how do you know the numbers of yellow square tiles and red square tiles that you need to represent the addition?
2. When you remove tiles, what operation are you representing? When you add tiles, what operation are you representing?
3. How can you use the original model to check your solution?
4. Give an example of an equation with a negative solution that would require your adding 2 red square tiles and 2 yellow square tiles to model and solve it.
5. Give an example of an equation with a positive solution that would require your adding 2 red square tiles and 2 yellow square tiles to model and solve it.

Try This

Use algebra tiles to model and solve each equation.

1. $x - 7 = 10$ **2.** $x + 5 = -8$ **3.** $x + 3 = 4$ **4.** $x + 2 = -1$

5. $x + (-4) = 8$ **6.** $x - 6 = 2$ **7.** $x + (-1) = -9$ **8.** $x - 7 = -6$

2-4 Solving Equations Containing Integers

Learn to solve equations with integers.

When you are solving equations with integers, your goal is the same as with whole numbers: *isolate the variable* on one side of the equation.

Recall that the sum of a number and its opposite is 0. When you add the opposite to get 0, you can isolate the variable.

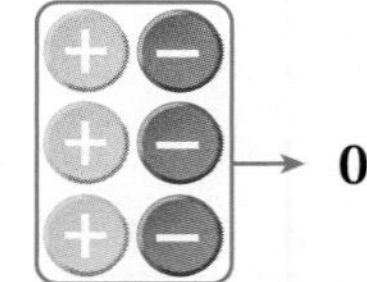

$3 + (-3) = 0$
$a + (-a) = 0$

EXAMPLE 1 Adding and Subtracting to Solve Equations

Solve.

A $y + 8 = 6$

$y + 8 = 6$ — *Add −8 to each side.*

$\underline{\quad -8 \quad -8}$

$y = -2$

B $-5 + t = -25$

$-5 + t = -25$

$-5 + t + 5 = -25 + 5$ — *Add 5 to each side.*

$t + (-5) + 5 = -20$ — *Commutative Property*

$t = -20$ — $t + \underbrace{(-5) + 5}_{0} = -20$

C $x = -7 + 13$

$x = -7 + 13$ — *The variable is already isolated.*

$x = 6$ — *Add integers.*

EXAMPLE 2 Multiplying and Dividing to Solve Equations

Solve.

A $\frac{k}{-7} = -1$

$\frac{k}{-7} = -1$

$-7 \cdot \frac{k}{-7} = -7 \cdot (-1)$ — *Multiply both sides by −7.*

$k = 7$

B $-51 = 17b$

$\frac{-51}{17} = \frac{17b}{17}$ — *Divide both sides by 17.*

$-3 = b$

EXAMPLE 3 PROBLEM SOLVING APPLICATION

PROBLEM SOLVING

Net force is the sum of all forces acting on an object. Expressed in newtons (N), it tells you in which direction and how quickly the object will move. If two dogs are playing tug-of-war, and the dog on the right pulls with a force of 12 N, what force is the dog on the left exerting on the rope if the net force is 2 N?

> **Helpful Hint**
>
> Force is measured in newtons (N). The number of newtons tells the size of the force and the sign tells its direction. Positive is to the right, and negative is to the left.

1 Understand the Problem

The **answer** is the force that the left dog exerts on the rope.

List the **important information:**

- The dog on the right pulls with a force of 12 N.
- The net force is 2 N.

Show the **relationship** of the information:

net force	=	left dog's force	+	right dog's force

2 Make a Plan

Write an equation and solve it. Let f represent the left dog's force on the rope, and use the equation model.

$$2 = f + 12$$

3 Solve

$$\begin{aligned} 2 &= f + 12 \\ \underline{-12} \quad & \quad \underline{\quad -12} \\ -10 &= f \end{aligned}$$

Subtract 12 from both sides.

The left dog is exerting a force of –10 newtons on the rope.

4 Look Back

The left dog exerts force to the left, so the force is negative. Its absolute value is smaller than the force the right dog exerts. This makes sense, since the net force is positive; thus the rope is moving to the right.

Think and Discuss

1. **Explain** what the result would be in the tug-of-war match in Example 3 if another dog pulled on the tail of the dog on the left with a force of -7 N.
2. **Describe** the steps to solve $y - 5 = 16$.

2-4 Exercises

FOR EXTRA PRACTICE
see page 734

internet connect
Homework Help Online
go.hrw.com Keyword: MP4 2-4

GUIDED PRACTICE

Solve.

See Example 1
1. $y - 8 = -2$ **2.** $d = 5 - (-7)$ **3.** $3 + x = -8$ **4.** $b + 4 = -3$

See Example 2
5. $\frac{t}{4} = -4$ **6.** $8g = -32$ **7.** $\frac{a}{-6} = -2$ **8.** $-65 = 13f$

See Example 3

9. Mercury's surface temperature has a range of 600°C. This range is the broadest of any planet in the solar system. If the lowest temperature on Mercury's surface is −173°C, write and solve an equation to find the highest temperature.

INDEPENDENT PRACTICE

See Example 1

Solve.

10. $-8 + b = 4$ **11.** $a - 17 = -4$ **12.** $f = -9 + 16$ **13.** $4 + b = 1$

14. $t - 9 = -22$ **15.** $y + 6 = -31$ **16.** $7 + x = -8$ **17.** $h + 3 = -28$

See Example 2
18. $-42 = 6a$ **19.** $\frac{n}{-3} = 13$ **20.** $34 = -2m$ **21.** $\frac{c}{-7} = -12$

22. $-51 = 3f$ **23.** $\frac{a}{-5} = -9$ **24.** $-63 = 7g$ **25.** $\frac{r}{4} = -16$

See Example 3
26. Kayleigh bought stock for \$15 a share. The next day the value of her stock went up \$5. At the end of the third day, her stock was worth \$17 a share. What change in value occurred on the third day?

PRACTICE AND PROBLEM SOLVING

Solve.

27. $s + 3 = -8$ **28.** $-12 = 4b$ **29.** $6x = 24$ **30.** $t - 14 = 15$

31. $\frac{m}{3} = -9$ **32.** $p = -18 + 7$ **33.** $z - 12 = 4$ **34.** $\frac{n}{-6} = 13$

35. $16 = -4h$ **36.** $-13 + p = 8$ **37.** $-15 = \frac{y}{7}$ **38.** $4 + z = -13$

39. $\frac{x}{-3} = -8$ **40.** $g - 7 = -31$ **41.** $9p = -54$ **42.** $-8 + f = 8$

43. While scuba diving Tom descended at a rate of −4 m per minute.

a. Write an expression to find Tom's depth after t minutes.

b. What would Tom's depth be after 17 minutes?

c. If Tom has −24 m left to get to the ocean floor, how long will it take him to travel the remaining distance at the same rate?

44. ***PHYSICAL SCIENCE*** An ion is a charged particle. Each proton in an ion has a +1 charge and each electron has a −1 charge. The ion charge is the electron charge plus the proton charge. Write and solve an equation to find the electron charge for each ion.

Hydrogen sulfate ion (HSO_4^-)

Name of Ion	Proton Charge	Electron Charge	Ion Charge
Aluminum ion (Al^{3+})	+13	■	+3
Hydroxide ion (OH^-)	+9	■	−1
Oxide ion (O^{2-})	+8	■	−2
Sodium ion (Na^+)	+11	■	+1

45. ***WHAT'S THE ERROR?*** A fan used the graph at right to find the net yardage gained during a series of plays by adding the number of yards gained during each play: $1 + 2 + 8 + 3 + 0 + 8 = 22$. What is wrong with this calculation?

46. ***WRITE ABOUT IT*** Explain what a gain of negative yardage means in a football game.

47. ***CHALLENGE*** During a series of plays in the fourth quarter of Superbowl XXXV, the Ravens gained x yards on one play and $-2x$ yards on the next play for a net gain of −3 yards. How many yards were gained during the first play?

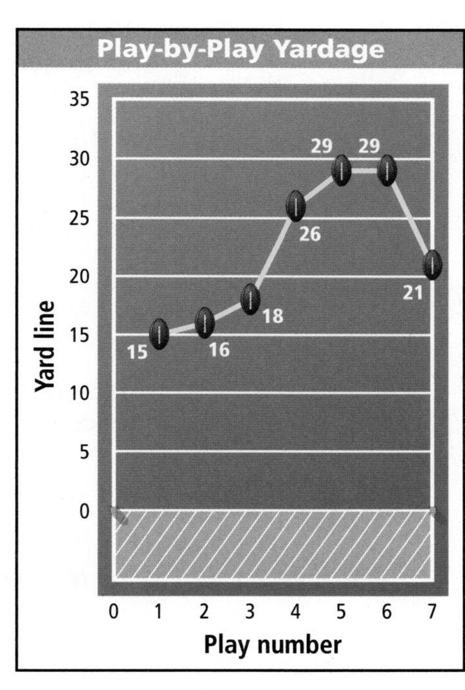

Spiral Review

Solve by combining like terms. (Lesson 1-6)

48. $17x - 16x = 14 + 27$　　**49.** $12w + w = 29 - 3$　　**50.** $5k - (2 + 1)k = 13 - 7$

51. **TEST PREP** Which of the following is the value of $7x + 9$ when $x = 2$? (Lesson 1-1)

A 2　　**B** 16　　**C** 23　　**D** 81

52. **TEST PREP** Which value of y is a solution of $y - 3 = 15$? (Lesson 1-3)

F $y = 18$　　**G** $y = 12$　　**H** $y = 5$　　**J** $y = 45$

2-5 Solving Inequalities Containing Integers

Learn to solve inequalities with integers.

When you pour salt on ice, the ice begins to melt. If enough salt is added, the resulting saltwater will have a freezing point of −21°C, which is much less than water's freezing point of 0°C.

Adding rock salt to the ice lowers the freezing point and helps to freeze the ice cream mixture.

At its freezing point, a substance begins to freeze. To stay frozen, the substance must maintain a temperature that is less than or equal to its freezing point.

If you add salt to ice that is at a temperature of −4°C, what must the temperature change be to keep the ice from melting?

This problem can be expressed as the following inequality:

$$-4 + t \leq -21$$

When you add 4 to both sides and solve, you find that if $t \leq -17$, the ice will remain frozen.

EXAMPLE 1 Adding and Subtracting to Solve Inequalities

Remember!

The graph of an inequality shows all of the numbers that satisfy the inequality. When graphing inequalities on a number line, use solid circles (●) for ≥ and ≤ and open circles (○) for > and <.

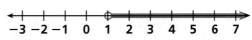

Solve and graph.

A $w + 3 \leq -1$

$w + 3 \leq -1$

$\underline{-3 \quad -3}$ *Subtract 3 from both sides.*

$w \leq -4$

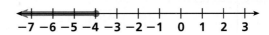

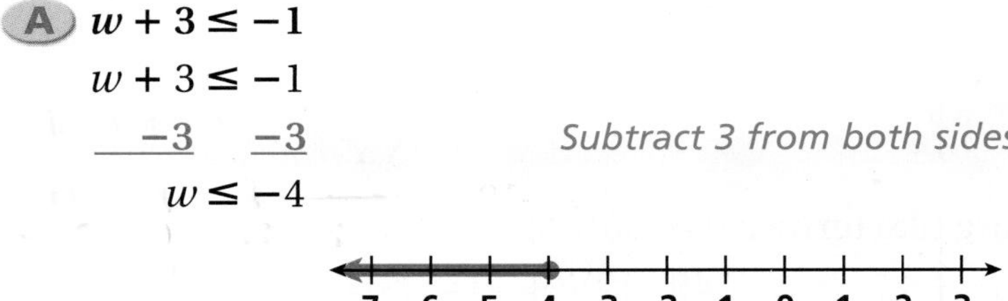

B $n - 6 > -5$

$n - 6 > -5$

$n - 6 + 6 > -5 + 6$ *Add 6 to both sides.*

$n > 1$

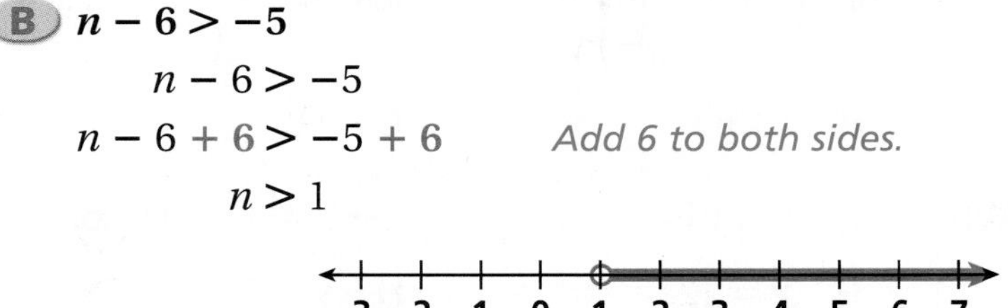

Sometimes you must multiply or divide to isolate the variable. Multiplying or dividing both sides of an inequality by a negative number gives a surprising result.

$5 > -1$	*5 is greater than −1.*
$-1 \cdot 5 \ \square\ -1 \cdot (-1)$	*Multiply both sides by −1.*
$-5 \ \square\ 1$	*> or < ?*

You know −5 is less than 1, so you should use <.

$$-5 < 1$$

$-5 < 1$

−7 −6 −5 −4 −3 −2 −1 0 1 2 3 4 5 6 7

$5 > -1$

MULTIPLYING INEQUALITIES BY NEGATIVE INTEGERS

Words	Original Inequality	Multiply/Divide	Result
Multiplying or dividing by a negative number reverses the inequality symbol.	$3 > 1$	Multiply by −2	$-6 < -2$
	$-4 \leq 12$	Divide by −4	$1 \geq -3$

EXAMPLE 2 Multiplying and Dividing to Solve Inequalities

Solve and graph.

A $-2d > 12$

$\frac{-2d}{-2} < \frac{12}{-2}$ *Divide each side by (−2); > changes to <.*

$d < -6$

−10 −9 −8 −7 −6 −5 −4 −3 −2 −1 0

B $\frac{-y}{2} \leq 5$

$-2 \cdot \frac{-y}{2} \geq -2 \cdot 5$ *Multiply each side by −2; ≤ changes to ≥.*

$y \geq -10$

−12 −11 −10 −9 −8 −7 −6

Helpful Hint

The direction of the inequality changes **only** if the number you are using to multiply or divide by is negative.

Think and Discuss

1. **Explain** how multiplying a number by −1 changes the number's location with respect to 0.
2. **Tell** when to reverse the direction of the inequality symbol when you are solving an inequality.

2-5 Exercises

FOR EXTRA PRACTICE

see page 734

internet connect

Homework Help Online
go.hrw.com Keyword: MP4 2-5

GUIDED PRACTICE

See Example 1 **Solve and graph.**

1. $x + 2 \geq -3$
2. $y + 2 < 4$
3. $b + 6 \leq -1$
4. $h - 2 < -1$
5. $f - 3 > 1$
6. $k - 2 \leq 3$

See Example 2

7. $-11x > 33$
8. $2y < -4$
9. $-4w \geq -12$
10. $\frac{x}{-3} \leq 1$
11. $\frac{z}{4} > -2$
12. $\frac{n}{-2} \geq -3$

INDEPENDENT PRACTICE

See Example 1 **Solve and graph.**

13. $k + 4 > 1$
14. $z - 5 \leq 4$
15. $x - 2 < -3$
16. $b + 1 \leq -3$
17. $r + 2 \geq 4$
18. $p - 3 > 3$
19. $n - 3 > 2$
20. $g + 1 \leq 5$
21. $x + 2 \geq -2$

See Example 2

22. $-7h < 49$
23. $3x > -15$
24. $3p \leq 15$
25. $-8x < 16$
26. $-5y \leq -25$
27. $\frac{k}{2} \geq 5$
28. $\frac{b}{-4} > -2$
29. $\frac{a}{3} \leq -4$
30. $\frac{z}{-2} \geq 4$

PRACTICE AND PROBLEM SOLVING

Solve and graph.

31. $r + 1 \leq 0$
32. $\frac{x}{-1} > 3$
33. $-2t = -4$
34. $s - 4 \geq -1$
35. $-4b < 0$
36. $\frac{a}{-2} \geq -2$
37. $\frac{f}{3} = -6$
38. $5 + h \geq 1$
39. $c - 3 \leq -1$
40. $y + 5 < 1$
41. $\frac{n}{-2} > 3$
42. $k - 3 \geq -3$
43. $g - 5 = 3$
44. $3 + f > -1$
45. $3p = -27$

46. The freezing point of helium is −272°C. The original temperature of a sample of helium is 3°C.
    a. How much must the temperature change to ensure that helium freezes?
    b. Assume the temperature changed at a steady rate for 25 minutes. Using your answer from part **a** for how much the temperature must change to freeze the helium, write and solve an inequality to determine how much the temperature must change each minute.

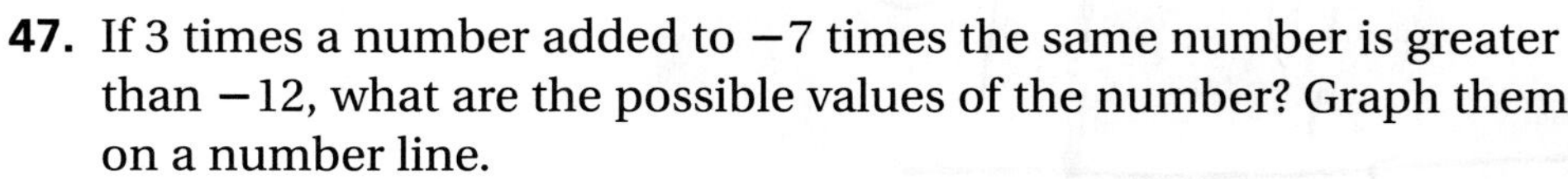

47. If 3 times a number added to -7 times the same number is greater than -12, what are the possible values of the number? Graph them on a number line.

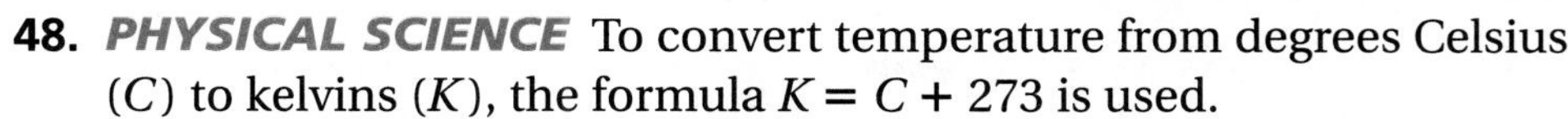

48. ***PHYSICAL SCIENCE*** To convert temperature from degrees Celsius (C) to kelvins (K), the formula $K = C + 273$ is used.

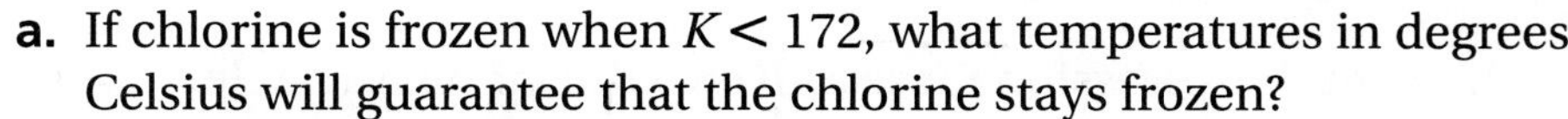

a. If chlorine is frozen when $K < 172$, what temperatures in degrees Celsius will guarantee that the chlorine stays frozen?

b. If nitrogen is frozen when $C < -210$, what temperatures in kelvins will guarantee that the nitrogen stays frozen?

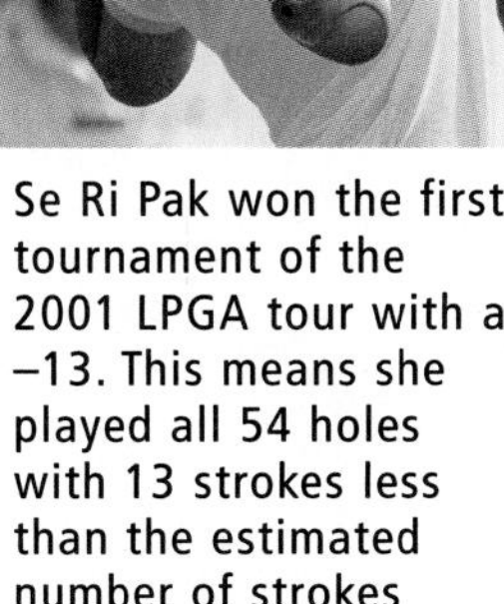

Se Ri Pak won the first tournament of the 2001 LPGA tour with a -13. This means she played all 54 holes with 13 strokes less than the estimated number of strokes needed, which is called *par.*

go.hrw.com
Web Extra!
KEYWORD: MP4 LPGA

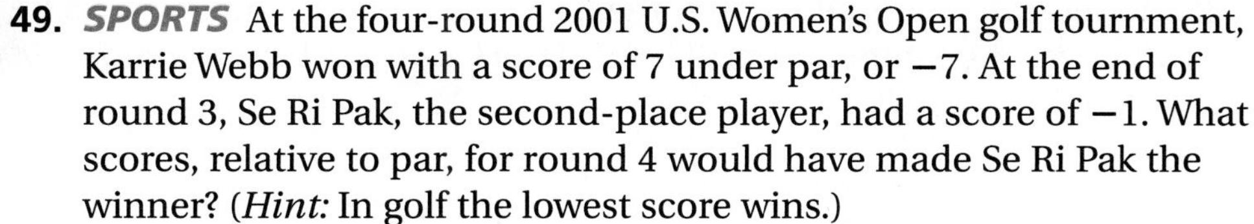

49. ***SPORTS*** At the four-round 2001 U.S. Women's Open golf tournment, Karrie Webb won with a score of 7 under par, or -7. At the end of round 3, Se Ri Pak, the second-place player, had a score of -1. What scores, relative to par, for round 4 would have made Se Ri Pak the winner? (*Hint:* In golf the lowest score wins.)

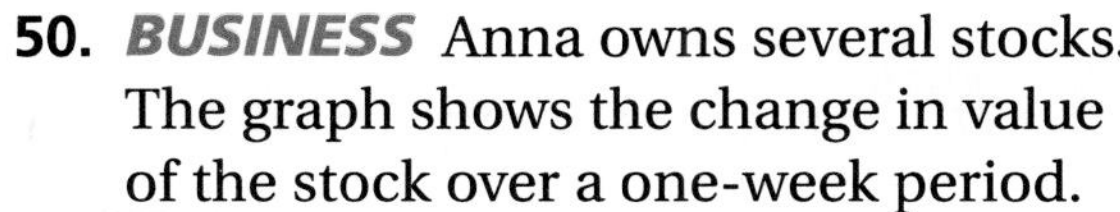

50. ***BUSINESS*** Anna owns several stocks. The graph shows the change in value of the stock over a one-week period.

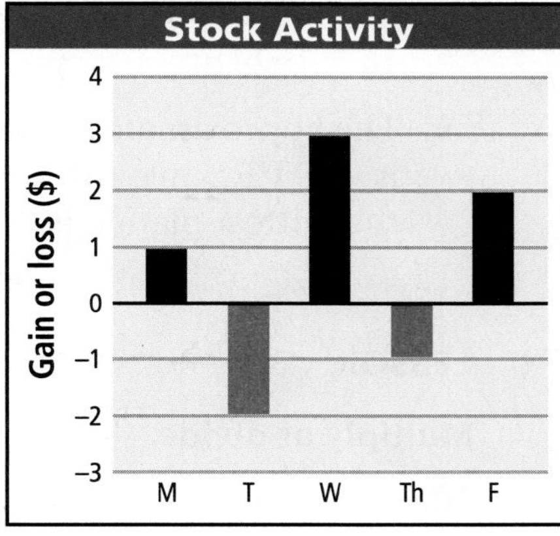

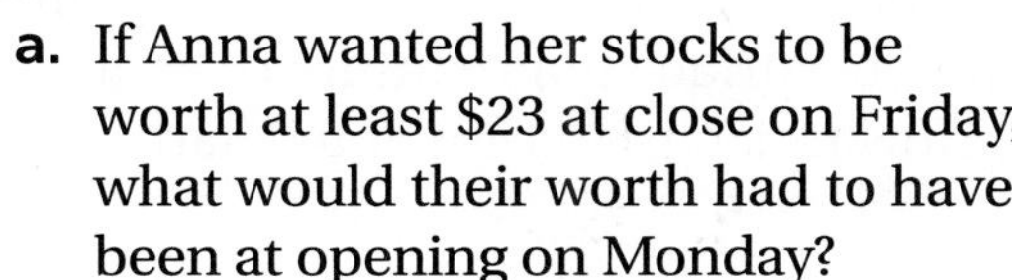

a. If Anna wanted her stocks to be worth at least \$23 at close on Friday, what would their worth had to have been at opening on Monday?

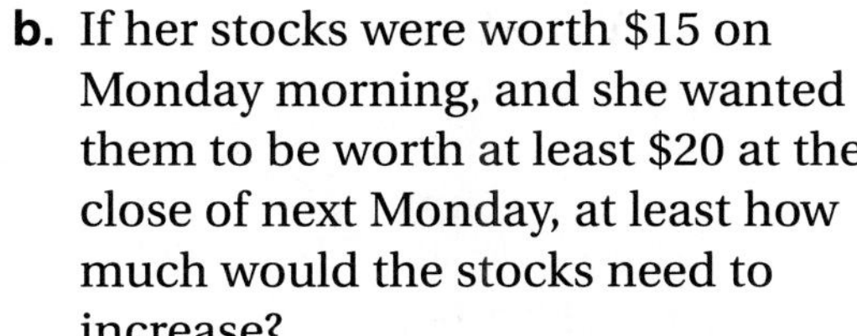

b. If her stocks were worth \$15 on Monday morning, and she wanted them to be worth at least \$20 at the close of next Monday, at least how much would the stocks need to increase?

51. ***WHAT'S THE ERROR?*** $-3n > 15; \frac{-3n}{-3} > \frac{15}{-3}; n > -5$. Why is this incorrect?

52. ***WRITE ABOUT IT*** Given $4x \leq -16$, explain whether the direction of the inequality symbol changes when you solve the inequality.

53. ***CHALLENGE*** Solve $4 - x < 6$.

Spiral Review

Add or subtract. (Lessons 2-1 and 2-2)

54. $-7 + 3$ **55.** $5 - (-4)$ **56.** $-3 + (-6)$ **57.** $-513 - (-259)$

58. $-37 - (-42) + 3$ **59.** $71 + (-83) - 4$ **60.** $-354 - 266 + 100$ **61.** $24 + (-31) - (-10)$

62. **TEST PREP** Solve $\frac{x}{7} = 5$. (Lesson 1-4)

A $x = 12$ **C** $x = 2$

B $x = 0.71$ **D** $x = 35$

63. **TEST PREP** Evaluate the expression $12 - y$ for the value $y = -8$. (Lesson 2-2)

F -4 **H** 20

G 4 **J** -20

Chapter 2

Mid-Chapter Quiz

LESSON 2-1 (pp. 60–63)

Evaluate each expression for the given value of the variable.

1. $p + 12$ for $p = -5$
2. $w + (-9)$ for $w = -4$
3. $t + (-14)$ for $t = 8$
4. In a 12-hour time period in Granville, North Dakota, on Feb. 21, 1918, the temperature increased 83°F. If the beginning temperature was −33°F, what was the temperature 12 hours later? *(Source: Time Almanac 2000)*

LESSON 2-2 (pp. 64–67)

Subtract.

5. $12 - (-8)$
6. $-9 - (-3)$
7. $-5 - (-16)$
8. $-20 - 7$
9. The approximate surface temperature of Pluto, the coldest planet, is −391°F, while the approximate surface temperature of Venus, the hottest planet, is 864°F. How much hotter is Venus than Pluto?

LESSON 2-3 (pp. 68–71)

Multiply or divide.

10. $(-8)(-6)$
11. $\frac{-21}{3}$
12. $\frac{39}{-3}$
13. $(-4)(-7)(-3)$
14. In a *magic square,* all sums—horizontal, vertical, and diagonal—are the same.

    Start with magic square A and create magic square B by dividing each entry of A by 2. What is the magic sum of B?

8	−6	4
−2	2	6
0	10	−4

Magic square A

LESSON 2-4 (pp. 74–77)

Solve.

15. $t - 12 = -4$
16. $\frac{x}{-2} = -16$
17. $7x = -91$
18. $10 + y = 24$
19. After balancing her checkbook Barbara had exactly $0. Her bank said her balance was −$18. She realized she had not been recording her daily $2 debit charge for cups of coffee. For how many days had she forgotten to record her coffee purchases?

LESSON 2-5 (pp. 78–81)

Solve and graph.

20. $m + 1 \geq -2$
21. $t - 5 < -3$
22. $\frac{r}{-2} \geq 4$
23. $-3k \leq 15$

Focus on Problem Solving

Look Back

• **Is your answer reasonable?**

After you solve a word problem, ask yourself if your answer makes sense. You can round the numbers in the problem and estimate to find a reasonable answer. It may also help to write your answer in sentence form.

Read the problems below and tell which answer is most reasonable.

1. Tonia makes $1836 per month. Her total expenses are $1005 per month. How much money does she have left each month?
   A. about −$800 per month
   B. about $1000 per month
   C. about $800 per month
   D. about −$1000 per month

2. The Qin Dynasty in China began about 2170 years before the People's Republic of China was formed in 1949. When did the Qin Dynasty begin?
   A. before 200 B.C.
   B. between 200 B.C. and A.D. 200
   C. between A.D. 200 and A.D. 1949
   D. after A.D 1949

3. On Mercury, the coldest temperature is about 600°C below the hottest temperature of 430°C. What is the coldest temperature on the planet?
   A. about 1030°C
   B. about −1030°C
   C. about −170°C
   D. about 170°C

4. Julie is balancing her checkbook. Her beginning balance is $325.46, her deposits add up to $285.38, and her withdrawals add up to $683.27. What is her ending balance?
   A. about −$70
   B. about −$600
   C. about $700
   D. about $1300

2-6 Exponents

Learn to evaluate expressions with exponents.

Vocabulary

power

exponential form

exponent

base

Fold a piece of $8\frac{1}{2}$-by-11-inch paper in half. If you fold it in half again, the paper is 4 sheets thick. After the third fold in half, the paper is 8 sheets thick. How many sheets thick is the paper after 7 folds?

With each fold the number of sheets doubles.

$2 \cdot 2 \cdot 2 \cdot 2 \cdot 2 \cdot 2 \cdot 2 = 128$ sheets thick after 7 folds.

This multiplication problem can also be written in *exponential form.*

$2 \cdot 2 \cdot 2 \cdot 2 \cdot 2 \cdot 2 \cdot 2 = 2^7$

The number 2 is a factor 7 times.

The term 2^7 is called a **power**. If a number is in **exponential form**, the **exponent** represents how many times the **base** is to be used as a factor.

EXAMPLE 1 Writing Exponents

Write in exponential form.

A $3 \cdot 3 \cdot 3 \cdot 3 \cdot 3 \cdot 3$

$3 \cdot 3 \cdot 3 \cdot 3 \cdot 3 \cdot 3 = 3^6$ *Identify how many times 3 is a factor.*

Reading Math

Read 3^6 as "3 to the 6th power."

B $(-2) \cdot (-2) \cdot (-2) \cdot (-2)$

$(-2) \cdot (-2) \cdot (-2) \cdot (-2) = (-2)^4$ *Identify how many times −2 is a factor.*

C $n \cdot n \cdot n \cdot n \cdot n$

$n \cdot n \cdot n \cdot n \cdot n = n^5$ *Identify how many times n is a factor.*

D 12

$12 = 12^1$ *12 is used as a factor 1 time, so $12 = 12^1$.*

EXAMPLE 2 Evaluating Powers

Helpful Hint

Always use parentheses to raise a negative number to a power.

$(-8)^2 = (-8) \cdot (-8)$
$= 64$

$-8^2 = -(8 \cdot 8)$
$= -64$

Evaluate.

A 2^6

$2^6 = 2 \cdot 2 \cdot 2 \cdot 2 \cdot 2 \cdot 2$ *Find the product of six 2's.*

$= 64$

B $(-8)^2$

$(-8)^2 = (-8) \cdot (-8)$ *Find the product of two −8's.*

$= 64$

Evaluate.

C $(-5)^3$

$(-5)^3 = (-5) \cdot (-5) \cdot (-5)$ — *Find the product of three −5's.*

$= -125$

EXAMPLE 3 Simplifying Expressions Containing Powers

Simplify $50 - 2(3 \cdot 2^3)$.

$50 - 2(3 \cdot 2^3)$

$= 50 - 2(3 \cdot 8)$ — *Evaluate the exponent.*

$= 50 - 2(24)$ — *Multiply inside the parentheses.*

$= 50 - 48$ — *Multiply from left to right.*

$= 2$ — *Subtract from left to right.*

EXAMPLE 4 *Geometry Application*

The number of diagonals of an *n*-sided figure is $\frac{1}{2}(n^2 - 3n)$. Use the formula to find the number of diagonals for a 5-sided figure.

$\frac{1}{2}(n^2 - 3n)$

$\frac{1}{2}(5^2 - 3 \cdot 5)$ — *Substitute the number of sides for n.*

$\frac{1}{2}(25 - 3 \cdot 5)$ — *Evaluate the exponent.*

$\frac{1}{2}(25 - 15)$ — *Multiply inside the parentheses.*

$\frac{1}{2}(10)$ — *Subtract inside the parentheses.*

5 diagonals — *Multiply.*

Verify your answer by sketching the diagonals.

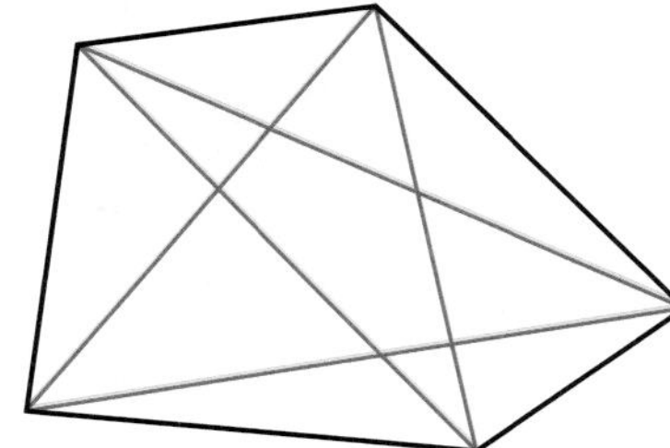

Think and Discuss

1. **Describe** a rule for finding the sign of a negative number raised to a whole number power.
2. **Compare** $3 \cdot 2$, 3^2, and 2^3.
3. **Show** that $(4 - 11)^2$ is not equal to $4^2 - 11^2$.

2-6 Exercises

FOR EXTRA PRACTICE

see page 735

internet connect
Homework Help Online
go.hrw.com Keyword: MP4 2-6

GUIDED PRACTICE

See Example 1 **Write in exponential form.**

1. 14 **2.** $15 \cdot 15$ **3.** $b \cdot b \cdot b \cdot b$ **4.** $(-1) \cdot (-1) \cdot (-1)$

See Example 2 **Evaluate.**

5. 3^4 **6.** $(-5)^2$ **7.** $(-3)^5$ **8.** 7^4

See Example 3 **Simplify.**

9. $(3 - 6^2)$ **10.** $42 + (3 \cdot 4^2)$ **11.** $(8 - 5^3)$ **12.** $61 - (4 \cdot 3^3)$

See Example 4 **13.** The sum of the first n positive integers is $\frac{1}{2}(n^2 + n)$. Check the formula for the first four positive integers. Then use the formula to find the sum of the first 12 positive integers.

INDEPENDENT PRACTICE

See Example 1 **Write in exponential form.**

14. $6 \cdot 6 \cdot 6 \cdot 6 \cdot 6 \cdot 6 \cdot 6$ **15.** $(-7) \cdot (-7) \cdot (-7)$

16. -6 **17.** $c \cdot c \cdot c \cdot c \cdot c$

See Example 2 **Evaluate.**

18. 6^6 **19.** $(-4)^4$ **20.** 8^4 **21.** $(-2)^9$

See Example 3 **Simplify.**

22. $(1 - 7^2)$ **23.** $27 + (2 \cdot 5^2)$

24. $(8 - 10^3)$ **25.** $45 - (5 \cdot 3^4)$

See Example 4 **26.** A circle can be divided by n lines into a maximum of $\frac{1}{2}(n^2 + n) + 1$ regions. Use the formula to find the maximum number of regions for 7 lines.

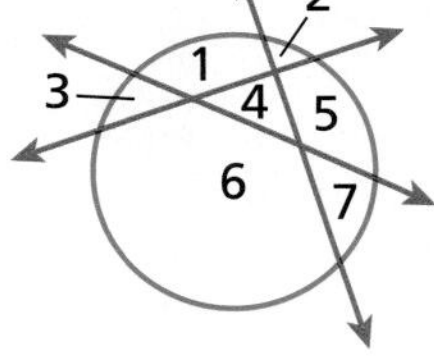

3 lines → 7 regions

PRACTICE AND PROBLEM SOLVING

Write in exponential form.

27. $(-2) \cdot (-2) \cdot (-2)$ **28.** $h \cdot h \cdot h \cdot h$

29. $4 \cdot 4 \cdot 4 \cdot 4$ **30.** $(5)(5)(5)(5)(5)$

Evaluate.

31. 7^3 **32.** 8^2 **33.** $(-12)^3$ **34.** $(-6)^5$

35. $(-3)^6$ **36.** $(-9)^3$ **37.** 4^1 **38.** 2^9

Simplify.

39. $(9 - 5^3)$ 40. $(18 - 7^3)$ 41. $42 + (8 - 6^3)$ 42. $16 + (2 + 8^3)$

43. $32 - (4 \cdot 3^2)$ 44. $(5 + 5^5)$ 45. $(5 - 6^1)$ 46. $86 - [6 - (-2)^5]$

Evaluate each expression for the given value of the variable.

47. a^3 for $a = 6$ 48. x^7 for $x = -1$ 49. $n^4 + 1$ for $n = 4$ 50. $1 - y^5$ for $y = 2$

Life Science LINK

Most bacteria reproduce by a type of simple cell division known as binary fission. Each species reproduces best at a specific temperature and moisture level.

51. ***LIFE SCIENCE*** Bacteria can divide every 20 minutes, so one bacterium can multiply to 2 in 20 minutes, 4 in 40 minutes, 8 in 1 hour, and so on. How many bacteria will there be in 6 hours? Write your answer using exponents, and then evaluate.

52. Make a table with the column headings n, n^2, and $2n$. Complete the table for $n = -5, -4, -3, -2, -1, 0, 1, 2, 3, 4,$ and 5.

53. For any whole number n, $5^n - 1$ is divisible by 4. Verify this for $n = 3$ and $n = 5$.

54. The chart shows Han's genealogy. Each generation consists of twice as many people as the generation after it.

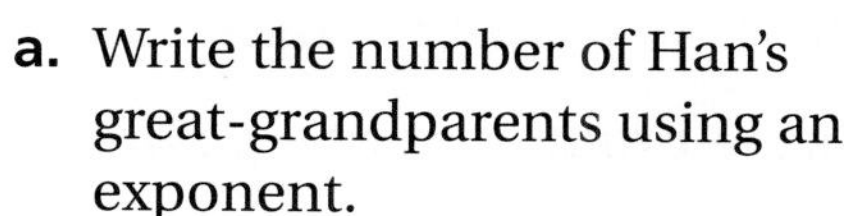

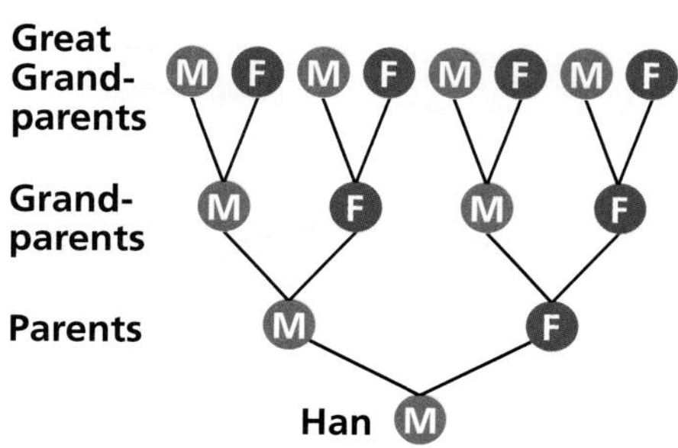

a. Write the number of Han's great-grandparents using an exponent.

b. How many ancestors were in the fifth generation back from Han?

55. ***CHOOSE A STRATEGY*** Place the numbers 1, 2, 3, 4, and 5 in the boxes to make a true statement: $\square \cdot \square^3 = \square^2 - \square^{\square}$

56. ***WRITE ABOUT IT*** Compare 10^3 and 3^{10}. For any two numbers, which usually gives the greater number, using the larger number as the base or as the exponent? Give at least one exception.

57. ***CHALLENGE*** Write $(3^2)^3$ using a single exponent.

Spiral Review

Multiply or divide. (Lesson 2-3)

58. $7(-8)$ 59. $\frac{-63}{-7}$ 60. $\frac{38}{-19}$ 61. $-8(-13)$ 62. $-6(15)$

63. **TEST PREP** Which represents the phrase *the difference of a number and 32*? (Lesson 1-2)

A $n + 32$ C $n - 32$

B $n \times 32$ D $32 \div n$

64. **TEST PREP** Which of the values -2, -1, and 0 are solutions of $x - 2 > -3$? (Lesson 2-5)

F -1 and 0 H -2 and -1

G only 0 J $-2, -1,$ and 0

2-7 Properties of Exponents

Learn to apply the properties of exponents and to evaluate the zero exponent.

The factors of a power, such as 7^4, can be grouped in different ways. Notice the relationship of the exponents in each product.

$$7 \cdot 7 \cdot 7 \cdot 7 = 7^4$$
$$(7 \cdot 7 \cdot 7) \cdot 7 = 7^3 \cdot 7^1 = 7^4$$
$$(7 \cdot 7) \cdot (7 \cdot 7) = 7^2 \cdot 7^2 = 7^4$$

MULTIPLYING POWERS WITH THE SAME BASE

Words	Numbers	Algebra
To multiply powers with the same base, keep the base and add the exponents.	$3^5 \cdot 3^8 = 3^{5+8} = 3^{13}$	$b^m \cdot b^n = b^{m+n}$

EXAMPLE 1 Multiplying Powers with the Same Base

Multiply. Write the product as one power.

A $3^5 \cdot 3^2$

$3^5 \cdot 3^2$

3^{5+2} *Add exponents.*

3^7

B $a^{10} \cdot a^{10}$

$a^{10} \cdot a^{10}$

a^{10+10} *Add exponents.*

a^{20}

C $16 \cdot 16^7$

$16 \cdot 16^7$

$16^1 \cdot 16^7$ *Think: $16 = 16^1$*

16^{1+7} *Add exponents.*

16^8

D $6^4 \cdot 4^4$

$6^4 \cdot 4^4$ *Cannot combine; the bases are not the same.*

Notice what occurs when you divide powers with the same base.

$$\frac{5^5}{5^3} = \frac{5 \cdot 5 \cdot 5 \cdot 5 \cdot 5}{5 \cdot 5 \cdot 5} = \frac{\cancel{5} \cdot \cancel{5} \cdot \cancel{5} \cdot 5 \cdot 5}{\cancel{5} \cdot \cancel{5} \cdot \cancel{5}} = 5 \cdot 5 = 5^2$$

DIVIDING POWERS WITH THE SAME BASE

Words	Numbers	Algebra
To divide powers with the same base, keep the base and subtract the exponents.	$\frac{6^9}{6^4} = 6^{9-4} = 6^5$	$\frac{b^m}{b^n} = b^{m-n}$

EXAMPLE 2 Dividing Powers with the Same Base

Divide. Write the quotient as one power.

A $\frac{100^9}{100^3}$

$\frac{100^9}{100^3}$

100^{9-3} *Subtract exponents.*

100^6

B $\frac{x^8}{y^5}$

$\frac{x^8}{y^5}$ *Cannot combine; the bases are not the same.*

Helpful Hint

0^0 does not exist because 0^0 represents a quotient of the form

$$\frac{0^n}{0^n}.$$

But the denominator of this quotient is 0, which is impossible, since you cannot divide by 0.

When the numerator and denominator of a fraction have the same base and exponent, subtracting the exponents results in a 0 exponent.

$$1 = \frac{4^2}{4^2} = 4^{2-2} = 4^0 = 1$$

This result can be confirmed by writing out the factors.

$$\frac{4^2}{4^2} = \frac{(4 \cdot 4)}{(4 \cdot 4)} = \frac{(\cancel{4} \cdot \cancel{4})}{(\cancel{4} \cdot \cancel{4})} = \frac{1}{1} = 1$$

THE ZERO POWER

Words	Numbers	Algebra
The zero power of any number except 0 equals 1.	$100^0 = 1$ $(-7)^0 = 1$	$a^0 = 1$, if $a \neq 0$

EXAMPLE 3 *Physical Science Application*

There are about 10^{25} molecules in a cubic meter of air at sea level, but only 10^{23} molecules at a high altitude (33 km). How many times more molecules are there at sea level than at 33 km?

You want to find the number that you must multiply by 10^{23} to get 10^{25}. Set up and solve an equation. Use x as your variable.

$(10^{23})x = 10^{25}$ *"10^{23} times some number x equals 10^{25}."*

$\frac{(10^{23})x}{10^{23}} = \frac{10^{25}}{10^{23}}$ *Divide both sides by 10^{23}.*

$x = 10^{25-23}$ *Subtract the exponents.*

$x = 10^2$

There are 10^2 times more molecules per cubic meter of air at sea level than at 33 km.

Think and Discuss

1. **Explain** why the exponents cannot be added in the product $14^3 \cdot 18^3$.
2. **List** two ways to express 4^5 as a product of powers.

2-7 Exercises

FOR EXTRA PRACTICE
see page 735

internet connect
Homework Help Online
go.hrw.com Keyword: MP4 2-7

GUIDED PRACTICE

See Example 1 **Multiply. Write the product as one power.**

1. $3^4 \cdot 3^7$ **2.** $12^3 \cdot 12^2$ **3.** $m \cdot m^5$ **4.** $14^5 \cdot 8^5$

See Example 2 **Divide. Write the quotient as one power.**

5. $\frac{8^7}{8^5}$ **6.** $\frac{a^9}{a^1}$ **7.** $\frac{12^5}{12^5}$ **8.** $\frac{7^{18}}{7^6}$

See Example 3 **9.** A scientist estimates that a sweet corn plant produces 10^8 grains of pollen. If there are 10^{10} grains of pollen, how many plants are there?

INDEPENDENT PRACTICE

See Example 1 **Multiply. Write the product as one power.**

10. $10^{10} \cdot 10^7$ **11.** $2^3 \cdot 2^3$ **12.** $r^5 \cdot r^4$ **13.** $16 \cdot 16^3$

See Example 2 **Divide. Write the quotient as one power.**

14. $\frac{7^{12}}{7^8}$ **15.** $\frac{m^{10}}{d^3}$ **16.** $\frac{t^8}{t^5}$ **17.** $\frac{10^8}{10^8}$

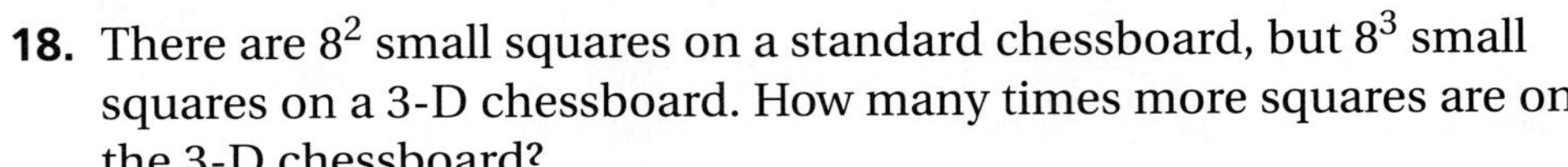

See Example 3 **18.** There are 8^2 small squares on a standard chessboard, but 8^3 small squares on a 3-D chessboard. How many times more squares are on the 3-D chessboard?

PRACTICE AND PROBLEM SOLVING

Multiply or divide. Write the product or quotient as one power.

19. $\frac{6^8}{6^5}$ **20.** $7^9 \cdot 7^1$ **21.** $\frac{a^3}{a^2}$ **22.** $\frac{10^{18}}{10^9}$

23. $x^3 \cdot x^7$ **24.** $a^7 \cdot b^8$ **25.** $6^4 \cdot 6^2$ **26.** $4 \cdot 4^2$

27. $\frac{12^5}{6^3}$ **28.** $\frac{11^7}{11^6}$ **29.** $\frac{y^9}{y^9}$ **30.** $\frac{2^9}{2^3}$

31. $x^5 \cdot x^3$ **32.** $c^9 \cdot d^3$ **33.** $4^4 \cdot 4^2$ **34.** $9^2 \cdot 9^2$

35. $10^5 \cdot 10^9$ **36.** $\frac{k^6}{p^2}$ **37.** $n^8 \cdot n^8$ **38.** $\frac{9^{11}}{9^6}$

39. $4^9 \div 4^5$ **40.** $2^{12} \div 2^6$ **41.** $6^2 \cdot 6^3 \cdot 6^4$ **42.** $5^3 \cdot 5^6 \cdot 5^0$

43. There are 26^3 ways to make a 3-letter "word" (from *aaa* to *zzz*) and 26^5 ways to make a 5-letter word. How many times more ways are there to make a 5-letter word than a 3-letter word?

44. ***ASTRONOMY*** The mass of the known universe is about 10^{23} solar masses, which is 10^{50} metric tons. How many metric tons is one solar mass?

45. ***BUSINESS*** Using the manufacturing terms below, tell how many dozen are in a great gross. How many gross are in a great gross?

1 dozen	$= 12^1$ items
1 gross	$= 12^2$ items
1 great gross	$= 12^3$ items

46. A googol is the number 1 followed by 100 zeros.

 a. What is a googol written as a power?

 b. What is a googol times a googol written as a power?

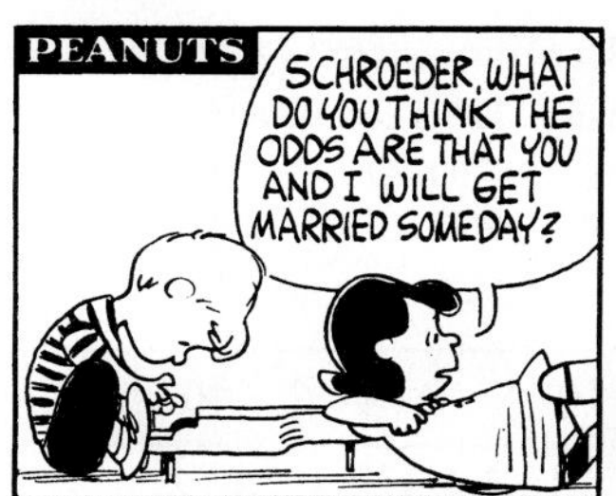

47. ***ASTRONOMY*** The distance from Earth to the moon is about 22^4 miles. The distance from Earth to Neptune is about 22^7 miles. How many one-way trips from Earth to the moon are about equal to one trip from Earth to Neptune?

48. ***WHAT'S THE ERROR?*** A student said that $\frac{4^7}{8^7}$ is the same as $\frac{1}{2}$. What mistake has the student made?

49. ***WRITE ABOUT IT*** Why do you add exponents when multiplying powers with the same base?

50. ***CHALLENGE*** A number to the 10th power divided by the same number to the 7th power equals 125. What is the number?

Spiral Review

Evaluate each expression for $m = -3$. (Lesson 2-1)

51. $m + 6$ 52. $m + -5$ 53. $-9 + m$ 54. $m + 3$

Subtract. (Lesson 2-2)

55. $-8 - 8$ 56. $-3 - (-7)$ 57. $-10 - 2$ 58. $11 - (-9)$

59. **TEST PREP** Which is **not** a solution to $-3x > 15$? (Lesson 2-5)

 A -20 **B** -100 **C** -6 **D** -5

 2-8 Look for a Pattern in Integer Exponents

Problem Solving Skill

Learn to evaluate expressions with negative exponents.

The nanoguitar is the smallest guitar in the world. It is no larger than a single cell, at about 10^{-5} meters long. Can you imagine 10^{-5} meters?

Look for a pattern in the table to extend what you know about exponents to include negative exponents. Start with what you know about positive and zero exponents.

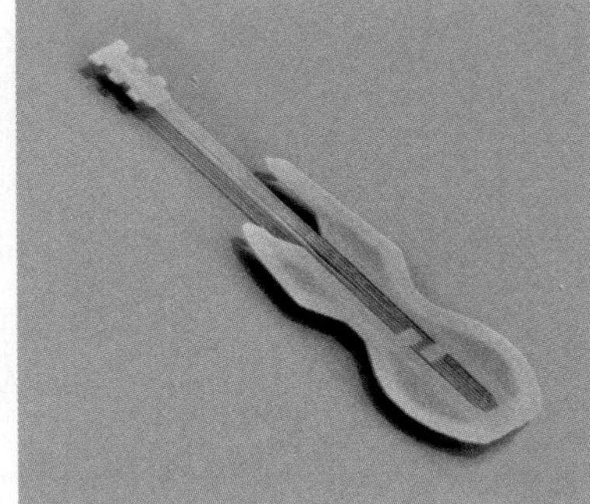

The nanoguitar is carved from crystalline silicon. It has 6 strings that are each about 100 atoms wide.

10^2	10^1	10^0	10^{-1}	10^{-2}
$10 \cdot 10$	10	1	$\frac{1}{10}$	$\frac{1}{10 \cdot 10}$
100	10	1	$\frac{1}{10} = 0.1$	$\frac{1}{100} = 0.01$

$\div 10$ $\div 10$ $\div 10$ $\div 10$

EXAMPLE 1 Using a Pattern to Evaluate Negative Exponents

Evaluate the powers of 10.

A 10^{-3}

$$10^{-3} = \frac{1}{10 \cdot 10 \cdot 10}$$ *Extend the pattern from the table.*

$$10^{-3} = \frac{1}{1000} = 0.001$$

B 10^{-4}

$$10^{-4} = \frac{1}{10 \cdot 10 \cdot 10 \cdot 10}$$ *Extend the pattern from Example 1A.*

$$10^{-4} = \frac{1}{10{,}000} = 0.0001$$

C 10^{-5}

$$10^{-5} = \frac{1}{10 \cdot 10 \cdot 10 \cdot 10 \cdot 10}$$ *Extend the pattern from Example 1B.*

$$10^{-5} = \frac{1}{100{,}000} = 0.00001$$

So how long is 10^{-5} meters?

$10^{-5}\text{ m} = \frac{1}{100{,}000}\text{ m} \longrightarrow$ "one hundred-thousandth of a meter"

NEGATIVE EXPONENTS		
Words	**Numbers**	**Algebra**
A power with a negative exponent equals 1 divided by that power with its opposite exponent.	$5^{-3} = \frac{1}{5^3} = \frac{1}{125}$	$b^{-n} = \frac{1}{b^n}$

EXAMPLE 2 Evaluating Negative Exponents

Remember!

The reciprocal of a number is 1 divided by that number.

Evaluate $(-2)^{-3}$.

$(-2)^{-3}$

$\frac{1}{(-2)^3}$ *Write the reciprocal; change the sign of the exponent.*

$\frac{1}{(-2)(-2)(-2)}$

$-\frac{1}{8}$

EXAMPLE 3 Evaluating Products and Quotients of Negative Exponents

Evaluate.

A $10^3 \cdot 10^{-3}$

$10^3 \cdot 10^{-3}$

$10^{3 + (-3)}$ *Bases are the same, so add the exponents.*

$10^0 = 1$ ***Check*** $10^3 \cdot 10^{-3} = 10^3 \cdot \frac{1}{10^3} = \frac{10^3}{10^3} = \frac{\cancel{10} \cdot \cancel{10} \cdot \cancel{10}}{\cancel{10} \cdot \cancel{10} \cdot \cancel{10}} = 1$

B $\frac{2^4}{2^7}$

$\frac{2^4}{2^7}$

2^{4-7} *Bases are the same, so subtract the exponents.*

2^{-3}

$\frac{1}{2^3}$ *Write the reciprocal; change the sign of the exponent.*

$\frac{1}{8}$ ***Check*** $\frac{2^4}{2^7} = \frac{\cancel{2} \cdot \cancel{2} \cdot \cancel{2} \cdot \cancel{2}}{\cancel{2} \cdot \cancel{2} \cdot \cancel{2} \cdot \cancel{2} \cdot 2 \cdot 2 \cdot 2} = \frac{1}{8}$

Think and Discuss

1. **Express** $\frac{1}{2}$ using an exponent.
2. **Tell** whether the statement is true or false: If a power has a negative exponent, then the power is negative. Justify your answer.
3. **Tell** whether an integer raised to a negative exponent can ever be greater than 1.

2-8 Exercises

FOR EXTRA PRACTICE
see page 735

internet connect
Homework Help Online
go.hrw.com Keyword: MP4 2-8

GUIDED PRACTICE

See Example 1 Evaluate the powers of 10.

1. 10^{-7} **2.** 10^{-3} **3.** 10^{-6} **4.** 10^{-1}

See Example 2 Evaluate.

5. $(-2)^{-4}$ **6.** $(-3)^{-2}$ **7.** 2^{-3} **8.** $(-2)^{-5}$

See Example 3 **9.** $10^7 \cdot 10^{-4}$ **10.** $3^5 \cdot 3^{-7}$ **11.** $\frac{6^8}{6^5}$ **12.** $\frac{3^6}{3^9}$

INDEPENDENT PRACTICE

See Example 1 Evaluate the powers of 10.

13. 10^{-2} **14.** 10^{-9} **15.** 10^{-5} **16.** 10^{-11}

See Example 2 Evaluate.

17. $(-4)^{-3}$ **18.** 3^{-2} **19.** $(-10)^{-4}$ **20.** $(-2)^{-1}$

See Example 3 **21.** $10^5 \cdot 10^{-1}$ **22.** $\frac{2^3}{2^5}$ **23.** $\frac{5^2}{5^2}$ **24.** $\frac{3^7}{3^2}$

25. $\frac{2^1}{2^4}$ **26.** $4^2 \cdot 4^{-3}$ **27.** $10^3 \cdot 10^{-6}$ **28.** $6^4 \cdot 6^{-2}$

PRACTICE AND PROBLEM SOLVING

Evaluate.

29. 2^7 **30.** $\frac{5^7}{5^5}$ **31.** $\frac{m^9}{m^2}$

32. $x^{-5} \cdot x^7$ **33.** $\frac{(-3)^2}{(-3)^4}$ **34.** $8^4 \cdot 8^{-4}$

35. $4^9 \cdot 4^{-4}$ **36.** $\frac{7^2}{8^6}$ **37.** $2^{-2} \cdot 2^{-2} \cdot 2^3$

38. $\frac{(7-3)^3}{(5-1)^6}$ **39.** $(5-3)^{-7} \cdot (7-5)^5$ **40.** $\frac{(4-11)^5}{(1-8)^2}$

41. $(2 \cdot 6)^{-5} \cdot (4 \cdot 3)^3$ **42.** $\frac{(3+2)^4}{5(7-2)^3}$ **43.** $(2+2)^{-5} \cdot (1+3)^6$

44. ***COMPUTER SCIENCE*** Computer files are measured in bytes. One byte contains approximately 1 character of text.

	Byte	Kilobyte (KB)	Megabyte (MB)	Gigabyte (GB)
Value (bytes)	$2^0 = 1$	2^{10}	2^{20}	2^{30}

a. If a hard drive on a computer holds 2^{35} bytes of data, how many gigabytes does the hard drive hold?

b. A Zip® disk holds about 2^8 MB of data. How many bytes is that?

Ship crews in the Great Lakes refer to the *J. W. Westcott II* mail deliveries as "mail by the pail."

J. W. Westcott Company

Since 1895 the J. W. Westcott Company has been making mid-river mail deliveries by tugboat to the riverboats and lake boats of the Great Lakes area. The company runs the only floating post office in the world, and the Westcott Boat Station is the only boat station in the United States with its own postal code. The mail boat makes approximately 30 trips per day, 275 days per season. In 1968 the mail boat delivered nearly a million pieces of mail. Now it delivers closer to 400,000 pieces.

1. The *J. W. Westcott II* has a 220-horsepower diesel engine. One horsepower is the power needed to raise 550 pounds through a height of 1 foot in 1 second. So 1 horsepower (hp) is equal to 550 foot pounds force per second (550 ft lb f/s). How many ft lb f/s does the engine of the *J. W. Westcott II* have? What is this number estimated to the nearest power of ten?

2. Suppose the J. W. Westcott Company delivered an average of 750,000 pieces of mail per year over all the years it has been in operation. Approximately how many pieces of mail would have been delivered by the 100th anniversary in 1995? Write your answer in scientific notation.

3. The J. W. Westcott Company provides mail service 24 hours a day from April through December. That is 275 days.

   a. Find the number of hours the mail boat offers service. Write your answer in scientific notation.

   b. Write and solve an equation to find the number of eight-hour shifts from April through December.

4. The mail boat delivers to freighters that weigh more than 250 tons. One ton is 2000 pounds. How many pounds do these freighters weigh? Write your answer in scientific notation.

MATH-ABLES

Magic Squares

A *magic square* is a square with numbers arranged so that the sums of the numbers in each row, column, and diagonal are the same.

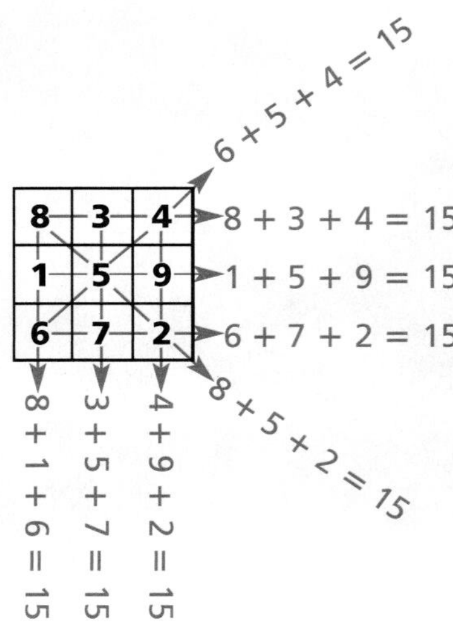

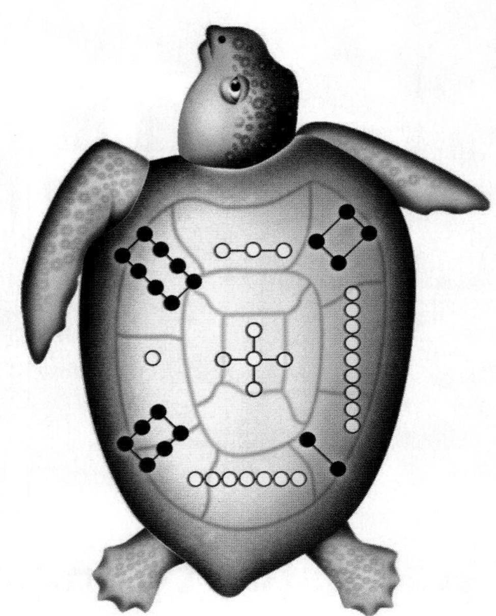

According to an ancient Chinese legend, a tortoise from the Lo river had the pattern of this magic square on its shell.

1. Complete each magic square below.

6		4
1	3	
	7	

	−6	−1
−4		0
−3	2	

−7		6	−4
4	−2		1
	2	3	−3
5	−5	−6	

2. Use the numbers −4, −3, −2, −1, 0, 1, 2, 3, and 4 to make a magic square with row, column, and diagonal sums of 0.

Equation Bingo

Each bingo card has numbers on it. The caller has a collection of equations. The caller reads an equation, and then the players solve the equation for the variable. If players have the solution on their cards, they place a chip on it. The winner is the first player with a row of chips either down, across, or diagonally.

internet connect

For a complete set of rules and cards, visit ***go.hrw.com***
KEYWORD: MP4 Game2

Evaluate Expressions

Use with Lesson 2-8

internet connect
Lab Resources Online
go.hrw.com
KEYWORD: MP4 TechLab2

A graphing calculator can be used to evaluate expressions that have negative exponents.

Activity

1 Use the STO▶ button to evaluate x^{-3} for $x = 2$. View the answer as a decimal and as a fraction.

2 STO▶ X,T,θ,n ENTER   X,T,θ,n ^ (−) 3 ENTER   MATH ENTER ENTER

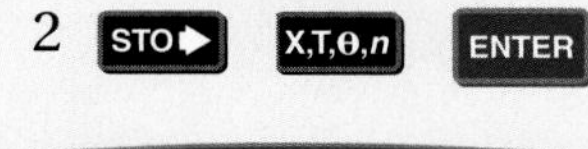

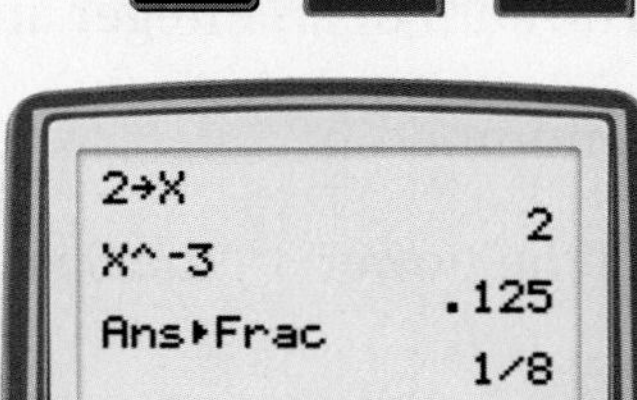

Notice that $2^{-3} = 0.125$, which is equivalent to $\frac{1}{2^3}$, or $\frac{1}{8}$.

2 Use the **TABLE** feature to evaluate 2^{-x} for several x-values. Match the settings shown.

Y= 2 ^ (−) X,T,θ,n ENTER   2nd TBLSET WINDOW   2nd TABLE GRAPH

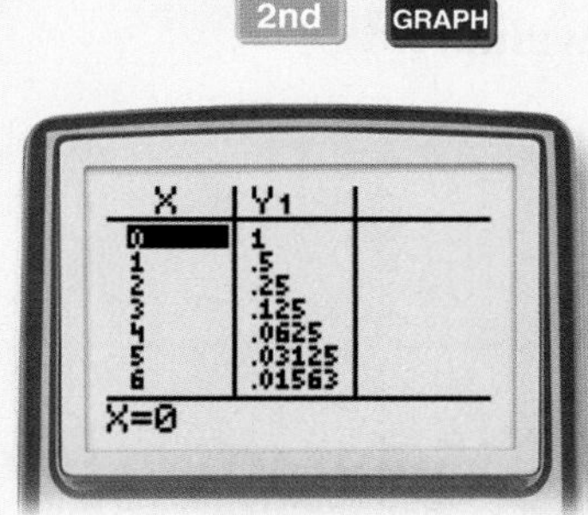

The **Y1** list shows the value of 2^{-x} for several x-values.

Think and Discuss

1. When you evaluated 2^{-3} in Activity 1, the result was not a negative number. Is this surprising? Why or why not?

Try This

Evaluate each expression for the given x-value(s). Give your answers as fractions and as decimals rounded to the nearest hundredth.

1. 4^{-x}; $x = 2$

2. 3^{-x}; $x = 1, 2$

3. x^{-2}; $x = 1, 2, 5$

Chapter 2

Study Guide and Review

Vocabulary

absolute value 60	exponential form 84	power 84
base 84	integer 60	scientific notation 96
exponent 84	opposite 60	

Complete the sentences below with vocabulary words from the list above. Words may be used more than once.

1. The sum of an integer and its ___?___ is 0.
2. A number in ___?___ is a number from 1 to 10 times a(n) ___?___ of 10.
3. In the power 3^5, the 5 is the ___?___ and the 3 is the ___?___ .

2-1 Adding Integers (pp. 60–63)

EXAMPLE

■ **Add.**

$-8 + 2$ — *Find the difference of 8 and 2.*
-6 — *8 > 2; use the sign of the 8.*

■ **Evaluate.**

$-4 + a$ for $a = -7$
$-4 + (-7)$ — *Substitute.*
-11 — *Same sign*

EXERCISES

Add.

4. $-6 + 4$
5. $-3 + (-9)$
6. $4 + (-7)$
7. $4 + (-3)$
8. $-11 + (-5) + (-8)$

Evaluate.

9. $k + 11$ for $k = -3$
10. $-6 + m$ for $m = -2$

2-2 Subtracting Integers (pp. 64–67)

EXAMPLE

■ **Subtract.**

$-3 - (-5)$
$-3 + 5$ — *Add the opposite of −5.*
2 — *5 > 3; use the sign of the 5.*

■ **Evaluate.**

$-9 - d$ for $d = 2$
$-9 - 2$ — *Substitute.*
$-9 + (-2)$ — *Add the opposite of 2.*
-11 — *Same sign*

EXERCISES

Subtract.

11. $-7 - 9$
12. $8 - (-9)$
13. $-2 - (-5)$
14. $13 - (-2)$
15. $-5 - 17$
16. $16 - 20$

Evaluate.

17. $9 - h$ for $h = -7$
18. $12 - z$ for $z = 17$

2-3 Multiplying and Dividing Integers (pp. 68–71)

EXAMPLE

Multiply or divide.

- $4(-9)$ *The signs are **different**.*
  -36 *The answer is **negative**.*
- $\frac{-33}{-11}$ *The signs are the **same**.*
  3 *The answer is **positive**.*

EXERCISES

Multiply or divide.

19. $7(-5)$ **20.** $\frac{72}{-4}$ **21.** $-4(-13)$

22. $\frac{-100}{-4}$ **23.** $8(-3)(-5)$ **24.** $\frac{10(-5)}{-25}$

2-4 Solving Equations with Integers (pp. 74–77)

EXAMPLE

Solve.

- $$\begin{aligned} x - 9 &= -12 \\ +9 &= +9 \\ x &= -3 \end{aligned}$$
- $$\begin{aligned} y + 4 &= -11 \\ -4 &= -4 \\ y &= -15 \end{aligned}$$
- $$\begin{aligned} 4m &= 20 \\ \frac{4m}{4} &= \frac{20}{4} \\ m &= 5 \end{aligned}$$
- $$\begin{aligned} \frac{t}{-2} &= 10 \\ (-2) \cdot \frac{t}{-2} &= (-2) \cdot 10 \\ t &= -20 \end{aligned}$$

EXERCISES

Solve.

25. $p - 8 = 1$ **26.** $t + 4 = 7$

27. $6 + k = 9$ **28.** $-7g = 42$

29. $\frac{w}{-4} = 20$ **30.** $10 = \frac{b}{-2}$

31. $8 = -2a$ **32.** $-13 = \frac{h}{7}$

33. $-15 + s = 23$

2-5 Solving Inequalities with Integers (pp. 78–81)

EXAMPLE

Solve and graph.

- $$\begin{aligned} x + 5 &\le -1 \\ -5 &\quad -5 \\ x &\le -6 \end{aligned}$$

−10 −8 −6 −4 −2

- $$\begin{aligned} -3q &> 21 \\ \frac{-3q}{-3} &> \frac{21}{-3} \\ q &< -7 \end{aligned}$$

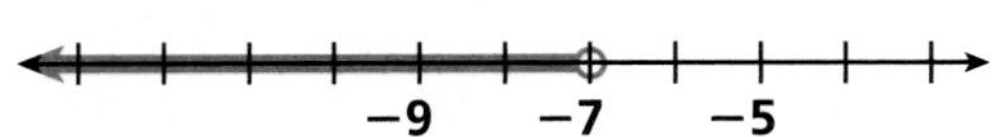

EXERCISES

Solve and graph.

34. $b + 3 < 1$ **35.** $r - 2 > 4$

36. $2m \ge 6$ **37.** $4p < -8$

38. $-2z > 10$ **39.** $-3q \le -9$

40. $\frac{m}{2} \ge 2$ **41.** $\frac{x}{-3} < 1$

42. $\frac{y}{-1} > -4$ **43.** $4 + x > 1$

44. $-3b \ge 0$ **45.** $-2 + y < 4$

2-6 Exponents (pp. 84–87)

EXAMPLE

- Write in exponential form.

  $4 \cdot 4 \cdot 4$

  4^3

- Evaluate the power.

  $(-2)^3$

  $(-2) \cdot (-2) \cdot (-2)$

  -8

EXERCISES

Write in exponential form.

46. $7 \cdot 7 \cdot 7$ **47.** $(-3) \cdot (-3)$

48. $k \cdot k \cdot k \cdot k$

Evaluate each power.

49. 5^4 **50.** $(-2)^5$ **51.** $(-1)^9$

2-7 Properties of Exponents (pp. 88–91)

EXAMPLE

Write the product or quotient as one power.

- $2^5 \cdot 2^3$

  2^{5+3}

  2^8

- $\frac{10^9}{10^2}$

  10^{9-2}

  10^7

EXERCISES

Write the product or quotient as one power.

52. $4^2 \cdot 4^5$ **53.** $9^2 \cdot 9^4$ **54.** $p \cdot p^3$

55. $\frac{8^5}{8^2}$ **56.** $\frac{9^3}{9}$ **57.** $\frac{m^7}{m^2}$

58. $5^0 \cdot 5^3$ **59.** $y^6 \div y$ **60.** $k^4 \div k^4$

2-8 Looking for a Pattern in Integer Exponents (pp. 92–95)

EXAMPLE

Evaluate.

- $(-3)^{-2}$

  $\frac{1}{(-3)^2}$

  $\frac{1}{9}$

- $\frac{2^5}{2^5}$

  2^{5-5}

  2^0

  1

EXERCISES

Evaluate.

61. 5^{-3} **62.** $(-4)^{-3}$

63. 11^{-1} **64.** $\frac{7^4}{7^4}$

65. $\frac{5^7}{5^7}$ **66.** $\frac{x^3}{x^3}$

67. $(9-7)^{-3}$ **68.** $(6-9)^{-3}$

2-9 Scientific Notation (pp. 96–99)

EXAMPLE

Write in standard notation.

- 3.58×10^4

  $3.58 \times 10{,}000$

  $35{,}800$

- 3.58×10^{-4}

  $3.58 \times \frac{1}{10{,}000}$

  $3.58 \div 10{,}000$

  0.000358

Write in scientific notation.

- $0.000007 = 7 \times 10^{-6}$
- $62{,}500 = 6.25 \times 10^4$

EXERCISES

Write in standard notation.

69. 1.62×10^3 **70.** 1.62×10^{-3}

71. 9.1×10^5 **72.** 9.1×10^{-5}

Write in scientific notation.

73. 0.000000008 **74.** 73,000,000

75. 0.0000096 **76.** 56,400,000,000

Chapter Test

Perform the given operations.

1. $-9 + (-12)$
2. $11 - 17$
3. $6(-22)$
4. $(-20) \div (-4)$
5. $42 - (-5)$
6. $-18 \div 3$
7. $-9 - (-13)$
8. $12 - (-6) + (-5)$
9. $-2(-21 - 17)$
10. $(-15 + 3) \div (-4)$
11. $(54 \div 6) - (-1)$
12. $-(16 + 4) -20$
13. The temperature on a winter day increased 37°F. If the beginning temperature was −9°F, what was the temperature after the increase?

Evaluate each expression for the given value of the variable.

14. $16 - p$ for $p = -12$
15. $t - 7$ for $t = -14$
16. $13 - x + (-2)$ for $x = 4$
17. $-8y + 27$ for $y = -9$

Solve.

18. $y + 19 = 9$
19. $4z = -32$
20. $52 = p - 3$
21. $\frac{w}{3} = 9$
22. $t + 1 < 7$
23. $z - 4 \geq 7$
24. $\frac{m}{-2} \leq 6$
25. $-3q > 15$

Graph each inequality.

26. $x > -4$
27. $n \leq 3$

Evaluate each power.

28. 4^3
29. $(-5)^4$
30. $(-3)^5$

Multiply or divide. Write the product or quotient as one power.

31. $7^4 \cdot 7^5$
32. $\frac{12^5}{12^2}$
33. $x \cdot x^3$

Evaluate.

34. $(12 - 3)^2$
35. $40 + 5^3$
36. $\frac{3^4}{3^7}$
37. $10^4 \cdot 10^{-4}$

Write each number in standard notation.

38. 3×10^6
39. 3.1×10^{-6}
40. 4.52×10^5

Write each number in scientific notation.

41. 3000
42. 42,000,000
43. 0.00000092
44. A sack of cocoa beans weighs about 132 lb. How much would one thousand sacks of cocoa beans weigh? Write the answer in scientific notation.

Chapter 2

Performance Assessment

Show What You Know

Create a portfolio of your work from this chapter. Complete this page and include it with your four best pieces of work from Chapter 2. Choose from your homework or lab assignments, mid-chapter quiz, or any journal entries you have done. Put them together using any design you want. Make your portfolio represent what you consider your best work.

Short Response

1. a. Complete the following rules for operations involving odd and even numbers:

even + even = __?__ odd + odd = __?__ odd + even = __?__
even · even = __?__ odd · odd = __?__ even · odd = __?__

b. Compare the rules from part **a** with the rules for finding the sign when multiplying two integers.

2. Write the subtraction equation $4 - 6 = -2$ as an addition equation. Draw a number-line diagram to illustrate the addition equation.

3. Consider the statement "Half of a number is less than or equal to -2." Write an inequality for this word sentence and solve it. Show your work.

Extended Problem Solving

4. The formula for converting degrees Celsius (°C) to degrees Fahrenheit (°F) is $F = \frac{9}{5}C + 32$. A way to estimate the temperature in degrees Fahrenheit is to double the temperature in degrees Celsius and add 30.

a. Write the way of estimating as a formula.

b. Compare the results for the exact formula and the estimate formula for −10°C, 0°C, 30°C, and 100°C.

c. For which of the values was the estimate closest to the exact answer? Find a temperature in degrees Celsius for which the estimate and the exact answer are the same. Show your work.

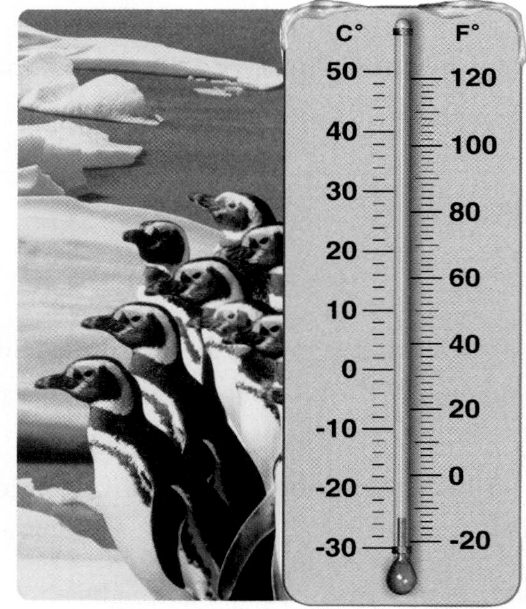

Performance Assessment

internet connect
State-Specific Test Practice Online
go.hrw.com Keyword: MP4 TestPrep

Standardized Test Prep

Chapter 2

Cumulative Assessment, Chapters 1–2

1. If $(n + 3)(9 - 5) = 16$, then what does n equal?

   (A) 1 (C) 4
   (B) 7 (D) 9

2. If $x = -\frac{1}{4}$, which is least?

   (F) $1 - x$ (H) x
   (G) $x - 1$ (J) $1 \div x$

TEST TAKING TIP!

Make comparisons: Express quantities in a common number base.

3. Which ratio compares the value of a hundred \$1000 bills with the value of a thousand \$100 bills?

   (A) 1 to 10 (C) 5 to 1
   (B) 1 to 1 (D) 10 to 1

4. Which is $3 \times 3 \times 3 \times 3 \times 11 \times 11 \times 11$ expressed in exponential form?

   (F) $4^3 \times 3^{11}$ (H) 33^7
   (G) $3^4 \times 11^3$ (J) 33^3

5. Which number is equivalent to 2^{-5}?

   (A) $\frac{1}{10}$ (C) $-\frac{1}{10}$
   (B) $\frac{1}{32}$ (D) $-\frac{1}{32}$

6. Which is 8.1×10^{-5}?

   (F) 8,100,000 (H) 0.000081
   (G) 810,000 (J) 0.0000081

7. Which power is equivalent to $5^{12} \div 5^4$?

   (A) 1^3 (C) 5^3
   (B) 1^8 (D) 5^8

8. The bar graph shows the average daily temperatures in Sturges, Michigan, for five months. Between which two months did the average temperature change by the greatest amount?

   (F) January and February
   (G) February and March
   (H) March and April
   (J) April and May

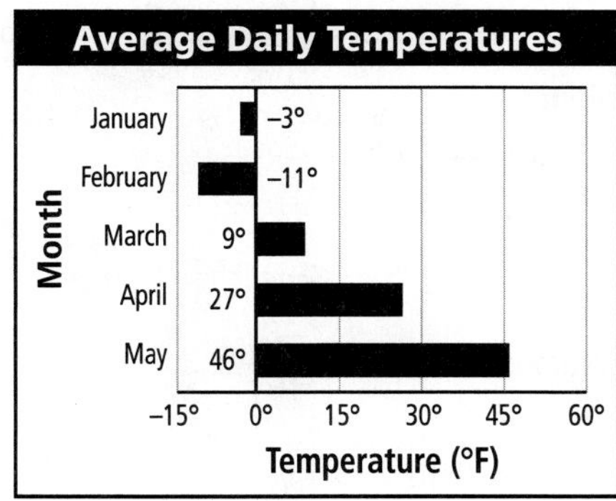

9. ***SHORT RESPONSE*** Linda takes her grandson Colin to the ice cream parlor every Wednesday and spends \$6.50. During a 30-day month that began on a Monday, how much money did Linda spend at the ice cream parlor? Explain how you found your answer.

10. ***SHORT RESPONSE*** An elevator begins 7 floors above ground level and descends to a floor that is 2 floors below ground level. Each floor is 12 feet high. Draw a diagram to determine the number of feet the elevator traveled.

Chapter

3

Rational and Real Numbers

TABLE OF CONTENTS

internet connect

Chapter Opener Online
go.hrw.com
KEYWORD: MP4 Ch3

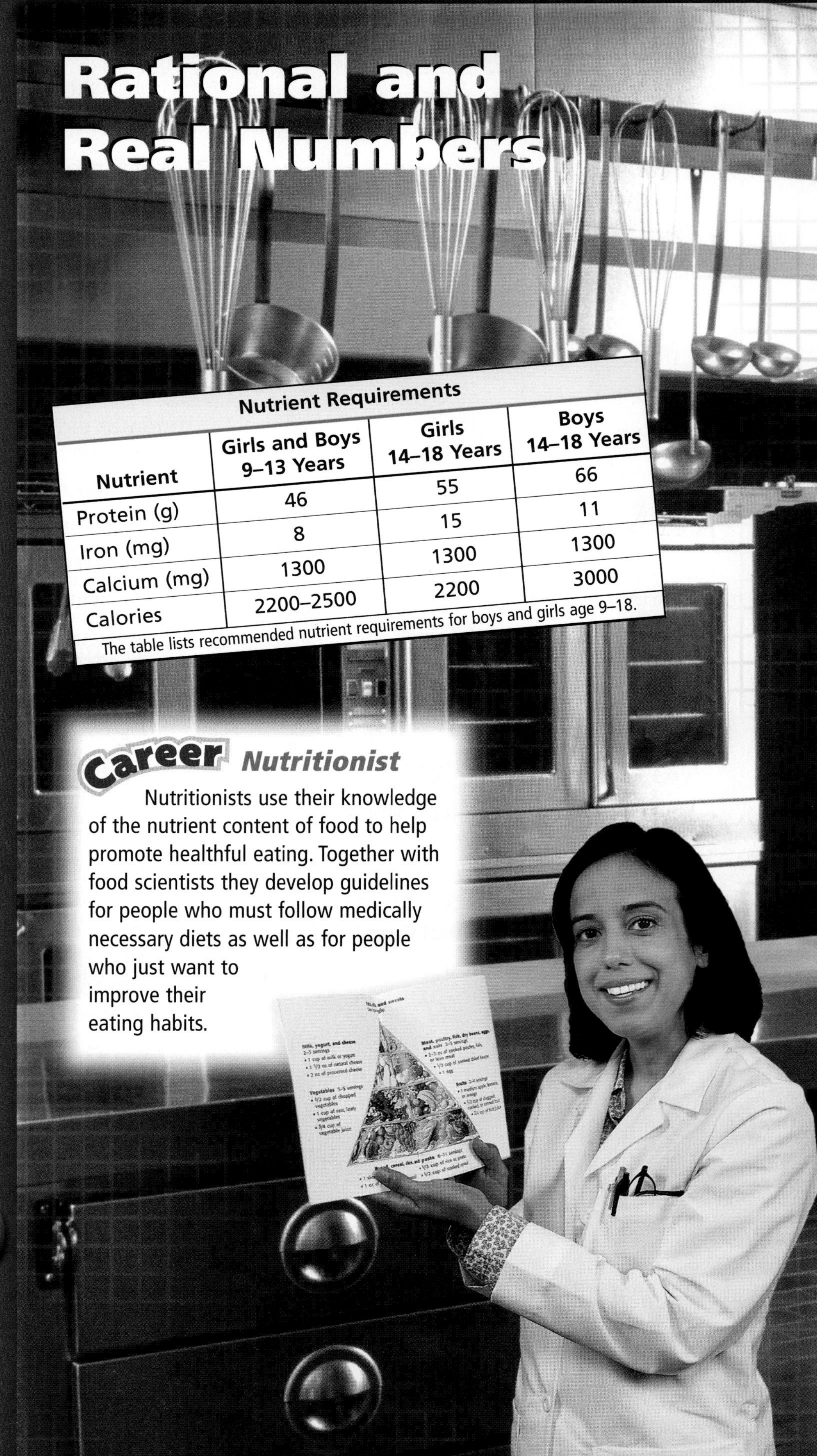

Nutrient Requirements

Nutrient	Girls and Boys 9–13 Years	Girls 14–18 Years	Boys 14–18 Years
Protein (g)	46	55	66
Iron (mg)	8	15	11
Calcium (mg)	1300	1300	1300
Calories	2200–2500	2200	3000

The table lists recommended nutrient requirements for boys and girls age 9–18.

Career ***Nutritionist***

Nutritionists use their knowledge of the nutrient content of food to help promote healthful eating. Together with food scientists they develop guidelines for people who must follow medically necessary diets as well as for people who just want to improve their eating habits.

3-1 Exercises

FOR EXTRA PRACTICE

see page 736

internet connect
Homework Help Online
go.hrw.com Keyword: MP4 3-1

GUIDED PRACTICE

See Example 1 **Simplify.**

1. $\frac{12}{15}$ **2.** $\frac{6}{10}$ **3.** $-\frac{16}{24}$ **4.** $\frac{11}{27}$

5. $\frac{57}{69}$ **6.** $-\frac{20}{24}$ **7.** $-\frac{7}{27}$ **8.** $\frac{49}{112}$

See Example 2 **Write each decimal as a fraction in simplest form.**

9. 0.75 **10.** 1.125 **11.** 0.431 **12.** 0.8

13. −2.2 **14.** 0.625 **15.** 3.21 **16.** −0.3878

See Example 3 **Write each fraction as a decimal.**

17. $\frac{7}{8}$ **18.** $\frac{3}{5}$ **19.** $\frac{5}{12}$ **20.** $\frac{3}{4}$

21. $\frac{16}{4}$ **22.** $\frac{1}{8}$ **23.** $\frac{12}{5}$ **24.** $\frac{9}{4}$

INDEPENDENT PRACTICE

See Example 1 **Simplify.**

25. $\frac{21}{28}$ **26.** $\frac{25}{60}$ **27.** $-\frac{17}{34}$ **28.** $-\frac{18}{21}$

29. $\frac{13}{17}$ **30.** $\frac{22}{35}$ **31.** $\frac{64}{76}$ **32.** $-\frac{78}{126}$

See Example 2 **Write each decimal as a fraction in simplest form.**

33. 0.4 **34.** 3.5 **35.** 0.71 **36.** –0.183

37. 1.377 **38.** 1.450 **39.** −1.4 **40.** −2.9

See Example 3 **Write each fraction as a decimal.**

41. $\frac{3}{8}$ **42.** $\frac{11}{12}$ **43.** $\frac{7}{5}$ **44.** $\frac{9}{20}$

45. $\frac{34}{50}$ **46.** $\frac{23}{5}$ **47.** $\frac{29}{25}$ **48.** $\frac{7}{3}$

PRACTICE AND PROBLEM SOLVING

49. Make up a fraction that cannot be simplified that has 36 as its denominator.

50. Make up a fraction that cannot be simplified that has 27 as its denominator.

51. a. Simplify each fraction below.

$\frac{9}{12}$	$\frac{5}{30}$	$\frac{15}{27}$	$\frac{68}{80}$
$\frac{39}{96}$	$\frac{22}{50}$	$\frac{57}{72}$	$\frac{32}{60}$

b. Write the denominator of each simplified fraction as the product of prime factors.

c. Write each simplified fraction as a decimal. Label each as a terminating or repeating decimal.

52. The ruler is marked at every $\frac{1}{16}$ in. Do the labeled measurements convert to terminating or repeating decimals?

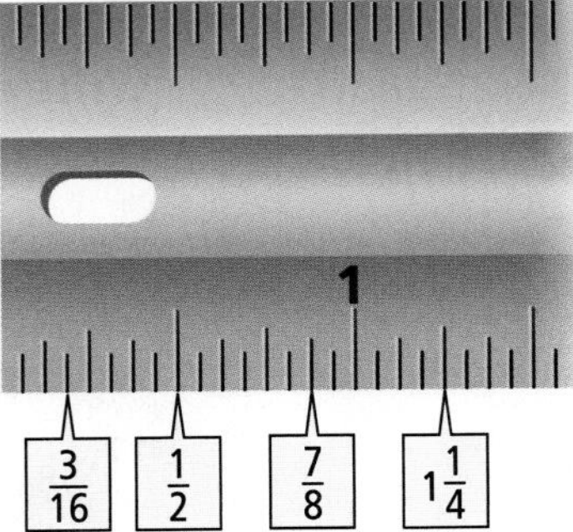

53. Remember that the greatest common factor, GCF, is the largest common factor of two or more given numbers. Find and remove the GCF of 48 and 76 from the fraction $\frac{48}{76}$. Can the resulting fraction be further simplified? Explain.

54. Prices on one stock market are shown using decimal equivalents for fractions or mixed numbers. Write the stock price 13.625 as a mixed number.

55. ***WHAT'S THE ERROR?*** A student simplified a fraction in this manner: $\frac{-12}{-18} = -\frac{2}{3}$. What error did the student make?

56. ***WRITE ABOUT IT*** Using your answers to Exercise 51, examine the prime factors in the denominators of the simplified fractions that are equivalent to terminating decimals. Then examine the prime factors in the denominators of the simplified fractions that are equivalent to repeating decimals. What pattern do you see?

57. ***CHALLENGE*** A student simplified a fraction to $-\frac{3}{7}$ by removing the common factors, which were 3 and 7. What was the original fraction?

Spiral Review

Evaluate each expression for the given values of the variable. (Lesson 1-1)

58. $3x + 5$ for $x = 2$ and $x = 3$

59. $4(x + 1)$ for $x = 6$ and $x = 11$

60. $2x - 4$ for $x = 5$ and $x = 7$

61. $7(3x + 2)$ for $x = 1$ and $x = 0$

62. TEST PREP Solve the inequality $7 > \frac{x}{3}$. (Lesson 1-5)

A $21 < x$ **B** $x < 21$ **C** $2.333 > x$ **D** $\frac{7}{3} > x$

63. TEST PREP Solve the inequality $8x \leq 24$. (Lesson 1-5)

F $x \leq 32$ **G** $x < 3$ **H** $x \leq 3$ **J** $x \leq 16$

3-3 Multiplying Rational Numbers

Learn to multiply fractions, mixed numbers and decimals.

Kendall invited 36 people to a party. She needs to triple the recipe for a dip, or multiply the amount of each ingredient by 3. Remember that multiplication by a whole number can be written as repeated addition.

Favorite Vegetable Dip
1 c sour cream
1/2 c mayonnaise
1 envelope dry Italian dressing mix
1/2 tsp thyme
1/4 tsp curry powder
Mix and chill 24 hours. Serves 12.

Repeated addition	Multiplication
$\frac{1}{4} + \frac{1}{4} + \frac{1}{4} = \frac{3}{4}$	$3\left(\frac{1}{4}\right) = \frac{3 \cdot 1}{4} = \frac{3}{4}$

Notice that multiplying a fraction by a whole number is the same as multiplying the whole number by just the numerator of the fraction and keeping the same denominator.

RULES FOR MULTIPLYING TWO RATIONAL NUMBERS

If the signs of the factors are the same, the product is positive.

$(+) \cdot (+) = (+)$ **or** $(-) \cdot (-) = (+)$

If the signs of the factors are different, the product is negative.

$(+) \cdot (-) = (-) \cdot (+) = (-)$

EXAMPLE 1 Multiplying a Fraction and an Integer

Helpful Hint

To write $\frac{12}{5}$ as a mixed number, divide:

$\frac{12}{5} = 2 \text{ R}2$

$= 2\frac{2}{5}$

Multiply. Write each answer in simplest form.

A $6\left(\frac{2}{3}\right)$

$6\left(\frac{2}{3}\right)$

$= \frac{6 \cdot 2}{3}$

$= \frac{12}{3}$

$= 4$

B $-4\left(2\frac{3}{5}\right)$

$-4\left(2\frac{3}{5}\right)$

$= -4\left(\frac{13}{5}\right)$ *$2\frac{3}{5} = \frac{2(5) + 3}{5} = \frac{13}{5}$*

$= -\frac{52}{5}$ *Multiply.*

$= -10\frac{2}{5}$ *Simplify.*

A model of $\frac{3}{5} \cdot \frac{2}{3}$ is shown. Notice that to multiply fractions, you multiply the numerators and multiply the denominators.

If you place the first rectangle on top of the second, the number of green squares represents the numerator, and the number of total squares represents the denominator.

$$\frac{3}{5} \cdot \frac{2}{3} = \frac{6}{15}$$

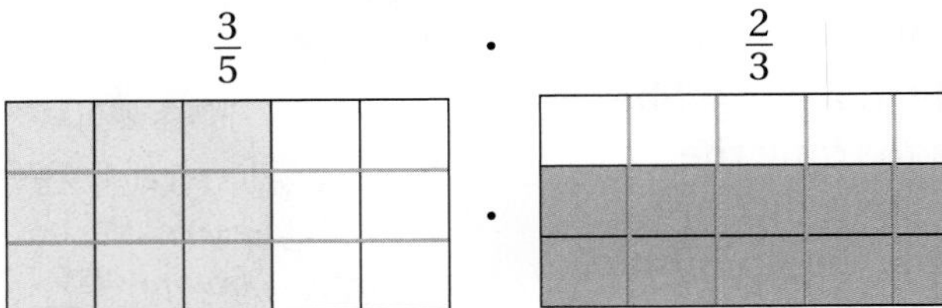

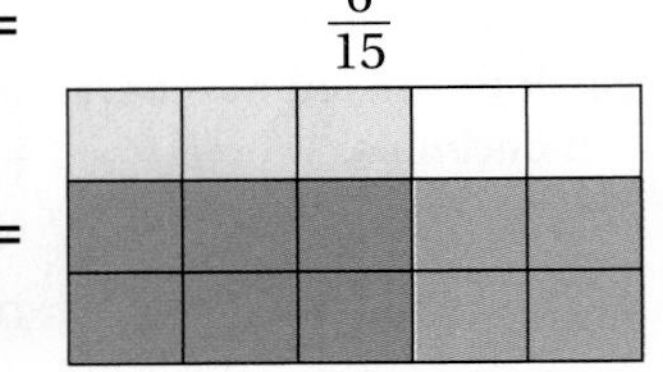

To simplify the product, rearrange the six green squares into the first two columns. You can see that this is $\frac{2}{5}$.

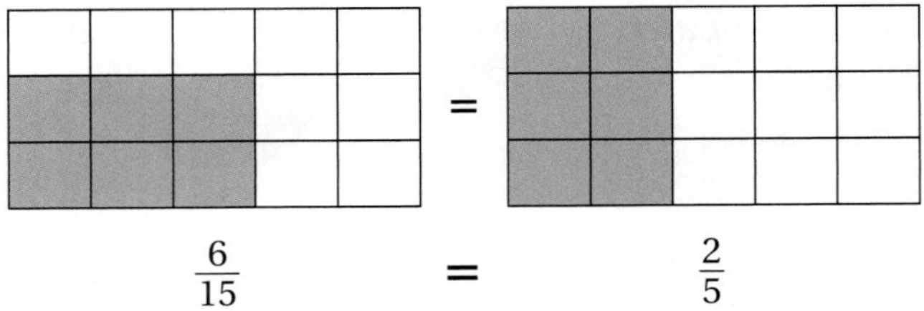

$$\frac{6}{15} = \frac{2}{5}$$

EXAMPLE 2 **Multiplying Fractions**

Multiply. Write each answer in simplest form.

A $-\frac{1}{2}\left(-\frac{3}{5}\right)$

$$-\frac{1}{2}\left(-\frac{3}{5}\right) = \frac{-1}{2}\left(\frac{-3}{5}\right)$$

$$= \frac{(-1)(-3)}{2(5)}$$ *Multiply numerators. Multiply denominators.*

$$= \frac{3}{10}$$ *Simplest form*

B $\frac{5}{12}\left(-\frac{12}{5}\right)$

$$\frac{5}{12}\left(-\frac{12}{5}\right) = \frac{5}{12}\left(\frac{-12}{5}\right)$$

$$= \frac{{}^{1}\cancel{5}(\cancel{-12})^{-1}}{{}_{1}\cancel{12}(\cancel{5})_{1}}$$ *Look for common factors: 12, 5.*

$$= \frac{-1}{1} = -1$$ *Simplest form*

C $6\frac{2}{3}\left(\frac{7}{20}\right)$

$$6\frac{2}{3}\left(\frac{7}{20}\right) = \frac{20}{3}\left(\frac{7}{20}\right)$$ *Write as an improper fraction.*

$$= \frac{{}^{1}\cancel{20}(7)}{3(\cancel{20})_{1}}$$ *Look for common factors: 20.*

$$= \frac{7}{3}, \text{ or } 2\frac{1}{3}$$ *7 ÷ 3 = 2 R1*

Helpful Hint

A fraction is in lowest terms, or simplest form, when the numerator and denominator have no common factors.

EXAMPLE 3 Multiplying Decimals

Multiply.

A $-2.5(-8)$

$-2.5 \cdot (-8) = 20.0$ *Product is positive with 1 decimal place.*

You can drop the zero after the decimal point.

$= 20$

B $-0.07(4.6)$

$-0.07 \cdot 4.6 = -0.322$ *Product is negative with 3 decimal places.*

EXAMPLE 4 Evaluating Expressions with Rational Numbers

Evaluate $-5\frac{1}{2}t$ for each value of t.

A $t = -\frac{2}{3}$

$-5\frac{1}{2}t$

$= -5\frac{1}{2}\left(-\frac{2}{3}\right)$ *Substitute $-\frac{2}{3}$ for t.*

$= -\frac{11}{2}\left(-\frac{2}{3}\right)$ *Write as an improper fraction.*

$= \frac{11 \cdot \cancel{2}^{1}}{{}_{1}\cancel{2} \cdot 3}$ *The product of 2 negative numbers is positive.*

$= \frac{11}{3}$, or $3\frac{2}{3}$ *$11 \div 3 = 3$ R2*

B $t = 8$

$-5\frac{1}{2}t$

$= -\frac{11}{2}(8)$ *Substitute 8 for t.*

$= -\frac{88}{2}$

$= -44$

Think and Discuss

1. **Name** the number of decimal places in the product of 5.625 and 2.75.
2. **Explain** why products of fractions are like products of integers.
3. **Give an example** of two fractions whose product is an integer due to common factors.

3-3 Exercises

FOR EXTRA PRACTICE
see page 736

internet connect
Homework Help Online
go.hrw.com Keyword: MP4 3-3

GUIDED PRACTICE

See Example 1

Multiply. Write each answer in simplest form.

1. $4\left(\frac{1}{3}\right)$ **2.** $-6\left(2\frac{2}{5}\right)$ **3.** $3\left(\frac{5}{8}\right)$ **4.** $-2\left(1\frac{9}{10}\right)$

5. $7\left(\frac{4}{9}\right)$ **6.** $-5\left(1\frac{8}{11}\right)$ **7.** $9\left(\frac{3}{4}\right)$ **8.** $3\left(2\frac{1}{8}\right)$

See Example 2

Multiply. Write each answer in simplest form.

9. $-\frac{1}{3}\left(-\frac{4}{7}\right)$ **10.** $\frac{3}{8}\left(-\frac{7}{10}\right)$ **11.** $6\frac{2}{5}\left(\frac{5}{9}\right)$ **12.** $-\frac{2}{3}\left(-\frac{3}{8}\right)$

13. $\frac{5}{13}\left(-\frac{5}{6}\right)$ **14.** $4\frac{7}{8}\left(\frac{5}{12}\right)$ **15.** $-\frac{7}{8}\left(-\frac{2}{3}\right)$ **16.** $\frac{5}{12}\left(-\frac{11}{16}\right)$

See Example 3

Multiply.

17. $-3.1(-4)$ **18.** $0.04(3.6)$ **19.** $-7.3(-5)$ **20.** $-0.15(2.8)$

21. $-5.9(-7)$ **22.** $0.5(7.3)$ **23.** $-4.7(-3)$ **24.** $-0.08(5.2)$

See Example 4

Evaluate $3\frac{2}{7}x$ for each value of x.

25. $x = 4$ **26.** $x = 1\frac{3}{4}$ **27.** $x = -2$ **28.** $x = -\frac{3}{7}$

29. $x = 7$ **30.** $x = 2\frac{1}{3}$ **31.** $x = -3$ **32.** $x = -\frac{3}{10}$

INDEPENDENT PRACTICE

See Example 1

Multiply. Write each answer in simplest form.

33. $3\left(\frac{1}{5}\right)$ **34.** $-4\left(1\frac{5}{8}\right)$ **35.** $2\left(\frac{9}{16}\right)$ **36.** $-5\left(1\frac{3}{4}\right)$

37. $9\left(\frac{14}{15}\right)$ **38.** $-2\left(4\frac{7}{8}\right)$ **39.** $6\left(\frac{2}{3}\right)$ **40.** $-7\left(3\frac{1}{5}\right)$

See Example 2

Multiply. Write each answer in simplest form.

41. $-\frac{2}{3}\left(-\frac{5}{6}\right)$ **42.** $\frac{2}{5}\left(-\frac{9}{10}\right)$ **43.** $2\frac{5}{7}\left(\frac{2}{9}\right)$ **44.** $-\frac{1}{2}\left(-\frac{11}{12}\right)$

45. $\frac{4}{5}\left(-\frac{3}{8}\right)$ **46.** $5\frac{1}{3}\left(\frac{13}{16}\right)$ **47.** $-\frac{3}{4}\left(-\frac{1}{8}\right)$ **48.** $\frac{7}{8}\left(\frac{3}{5}\right)$

See Example 3

Multiply.

49. $-2.9(-3)$ **50.** $-0.02(5.9)$ **51.** $-6.2(-7)$ **52.** $-0.25(3.5)$

53. $-4.8(-7)$ **54.** $-0.07(4.8)$ **55.** $-3.6(-8)$ **56.** $-0.04(9.2)$

See Example 4

Evaluate $2\frac{3}{4}x$ for each value of x.

57. $x = 6$ **58.** $x = 2\frac{1}{3}$ **59.** $x = -4$ **60.** $x = -\frac{3}{8}$

61. $x = 3$ **62.** $x = 4\frac{7}{8}$ **63.** $x = -7$ **64.** $x = -\frac{7}{9}$

PRACTICE AND PROBLEM SOLVING

Career LINK

Becoming a veterinarian requires at least two years at an undergraduate college and four years at a veterinary college. There are fewer than 30 veterinary colleges in the United States.

65. ***HEALTH*** As a rule of thumb, people should drink $\frac{1}{2}$ ounce of water for each pound of body weight per day. How much water should a 145-pound person drink per day?

66. People who are physically active should increase the daily amount of water they drink to $\frac{2}{3}$ ounce per pound of body weight. How much water should a 245-pound football player drink per day?

67. ***ANIMALS*** The label on a bottle of pet vitamins lists dosage guidelines. What dosage would you give to each of these animals?
    - **a.** a 50 lb adult dog
    - **b.** a 12 lb cat
    - **c.** a 40 lb pregnant dog

Do-Good Pet Vitamins

- **Adult dogs:** $\frac{1}{2}$ tsp per 20 lb body weight
- **Puppies, pregnant dogs, or nursing dogs:** $\frac{1}{2}$ tsp per 10 lb body weight
- **Cats:** $\frac{1}{4}$ tsp per 2 lb body weight

68. ***CONSUMER ECONOMICS*** At a clothing store, the ticketed price of a sweater is $\frac{1}{2}$ the original price. You have a discount coupon for $\frac{1}{2}$ off the ticketed price. What fraction of the original price is the additional discount?

69. ***WHAT'S THE ERROR?*** A student multiplied two mixed numbers in the following fashion: $3\frac{3}{8} \cdot 4\frac{1}{3} = 12\frac{1}{8}$. What's the error?

70. ***WRITE ABOUT IT*** In the pattern $\frac{1}{3} + \frac{1}{4} + \frac{1}{5} + \ldots$, which fraction makes the sum greater than 1? Explain.

71. ***CHALLENGE*** On January 20, 2001, George W. Bush was inaugurated as the forty-third president of the United States. Of the 42 presidents before him, $\frac{1}{3}$ had served as vice-president. Of those previous vice-presidents, $\frac{3}{7}$ served as president for more than four years. What fraction of the first 42 presidents were former vice-presidents who also served more than four years as president?

Spiral Review

Solve. (Lesson 1-3)

72. $7 + x = 13$ **73.** $x - 5 = 7$ **74.** $x + 8 = 19$

75. $12 + x = 46$ **76.** $x - 27 = 54$ **77.** $x + 31 = 75$

78. TEST PREP Solve the inequality $-3a \geq 24$. (Lesson 2-5)

A $a \geq -8$ **B** $a > 8$ **C** $a < 8$ **D** $a \leq -8$

79. TEST PREP Solve the inequality $\frac{a}{2} < -22$. (Lesson 2-5)

F $a < -44$ **G** $a > -44$ **H** $a > -11$ **J** $a < 11$

3-4 Dividing Rational Numbers

Learn to divide fractions and decimals.

Vocabulary

reciprocal

A number and its **reciprocal** have a product of 1. To find the reciprocal of a fraction, exchange the numerator and the denominator. Remember that an integer can be written as a fraction with a denominator of 1.

Number	Reciprocal	Product
$\frac{3}{4}$	$\frac{4}{3}$	$\frac{3}{4}\left(\frac{4}{3}\right) = 1$
$-\frac{5}{12}$	$-\frac{12}{5}$	$-\frac{5}{12}\left(-\frac{12}{5}\right) = 1$
6	$\frac{1}{6}$	$6\left(\frac{1}{6}\right) = 1$

Multiplication and division are inverse operations. They undo each other.

$$\frac{1}{3}\left(\frac{2}{5}\right) = \frac{2}{15} \longrightarrow \frac{2}{15} \div \frac{2}{5} = \frac{1}{3}$$

Notice that multiplying by the reciprocal gives the same result as dividing.

$$\left(\frac{2}{15}\right)\left(\frac{5}{2}\right) = \frac{2 \cdot 5}{15 \cdot 2} = \frac{1}{3}$$

DIVIDING RATIONAL NUMBERS IN FRACTION FORM

Words	Numbers	Algebra
To divide by a fraction, multiply by the reciprocal.	$\frac{1}{5} \div \frac{2}{3} = \frac{1}{5} \cdot \frac{3}{2} = \frac{3}{10}$	$\frac{a}{b} \div \frac{c}{d} = \frac{a}{b} \cdot \frac{d}{c} = \frac{ad}{bc}$

EXAMPLE 1 Dividing Fractions

Divide. Write each answer in simplest form.

A $\frac{7}{12} \div \frac{2}{3}$

$\frac{7}{12} \div \frac{2}{3} = \frac{7}{12} \cdot \frac{3}{2}$ *Multiply by the reciprocal.*

$= \frac{7 \cdot \cancel{3}^{1}}{{}_{4}\cancel{12} \cdot 2}$ *Reduce common factors.*

$= \frac{7}{8}$ *Simplest form*

Divide. Write each answer in simplest form.

B $3\frac{1}{4} \div 4$

$3\frac{1}{4} \div 4 = \frac{13}{4} \div \frac{4}{1}$ *Write as improper fractions.*

$= \frac{13}{4}\left(\frac{1}{4}\right)$ *Multiply by the reciprocal.*

$= \frac{13 \cdot 1}{4 \cdot 4}$ *No common factors.*

$= \frac{13}{16}$ *Simplest form*

When dividing a decimal by a decimal, multiply both numbers by a power of 10 so you can divide by a whole number. To decide which power of 10 to multiply by, look at the denominator. The number of decimal places is the number of zeros to write after the 1.

$$\frac{1.32}{0.4} = \frac{1.32}{0.4}\left(\frac{10}{10}\right) = \frac{13.2}{4}$$

1 decimal place *1 zero*

EXAMPLE 2 Dividing Decimals

Divide.

2.92 ÷ 0.4

$2.92 \div 0.4 = \frac{2.92}{0.4}\left(\frac{10}{10}\right) = \frac{29.2}{4}$

$= 7.3$ *Divide.*

EXAMPLE 3 Evaluating Expressions with Fractions and Decimals

Evaluate each expression for the given value of the variable.

A $\frac{7.2}{n}$ **for** $n = 0.24$

$\frac{7.2}{0.24} = \frac{7.2}{0.24}\left(\frac{100}{100}\right)$ *0.24 has 2 decimal places, so use* $\frac{100}{100}$.

$= \frac{720}{24}$ *Divide.*

$= 30$

When $n = 0.24$, $\frac{7.2}{n} = 30$.

B $m \div \frac{3}{8}$ **for** $m = 7\frac{1}{2}$

$7\frac{1}{2} \div \frac{3}{8} = \frac{15}{2} \cdot \frac{8}{3}$

$= \frac{\cancel{15}^{5} \cdot \cancel{8}^{4}}{{}_{1}\cancel{2} \cdot \cancel{3}_{1}} = \frac{20}{1} = 20$

When $m = 7\frac{1}{2}$, $m \div \frac{3}{8} = 20$.

EXAMPLE 4 PROBLEM SOLVING

You pour $\frac{2}{3}$ cup of a sports drink into a glass. The serving size is 6 ounces, or $\frac{3}{4}$ cup. How many servings will you consume? How many calories will you consume?

Nutrition Facts
Serving size 6 fl oz (240 mL)
Servings per container: 2
Amount per serving
Calories 50
% daily value
Total fat 0 g 0%
Sodium 110 mg 5%
Potassium 30 mg 1%
Total carbohydrates 0 g 5%
Sugar 14 g 5%
Protein 0 g 0%

1 Understand the Problem

The number of calories you consume is the number of calories in the fraction of a serving.

List the **important information:**

- The amount you plan to drink is $\frac{2}{3}$ cup.
- The amount of a full serving is $\frac{3}{4}$ cup.
- The number of calories in one serving is 50.

2 Make a Plan

Set up an equation to find the number of servings you will drink.

amount you drink ÷ serving size = number of servings

Using the number of servings, you can find the calories consumed.

number of servings · calories per serving = total calories

3 Solve

Let n = number of servings. Let c = total calories.

Servings:

$$\frac{2}{3} \div \frac{3}{4} = n$$
$$\frac{2}{3} \cdot \frac{4}{3} = n$$
$$\frac{8}{9} = n$$

Calories:

$$\frac{8}{9} \cdot 50 = c$$
$$\frac{8 \cdot 50}{9} = c$$
$$\frac{400}{9} = c \approx 44.4$$

You will drink $\frac{8}{9}$ of a serving, which is about 44.4 calories.

4 Look Back

You did not pour a full serving, so $\frac{8}{9}$ is a reasonable answer. It is less than 1, and 44.4 calories is less than the calories in a full serving, 50.

Think and Discuss

1. **Tell** what happens when you divide a fraction by itself. Show that you are correct using multiplication by the reciprocal.
2. **Model** the product of $\frac{2}{3}$ and $\frac{1}{4}$.

EXAMPLE 2 Changing from Base 10 to Base 8

Helpful Hint

There is at least one multiple of 8^2 in 185, but no multiples of $8^3, 8^4, 8^5, \ldots$, since these are all greater than 185.

Change 185_{decimal} to base 8.

185 is between $8^2 = 64$ and $8^3 = 512$.

Do repeated divisions, by 8^2, 8^1, and finally 8^0.

$185 \div 8^2 = 2$ remainder 57
$57 \div 8^1 = 7$ remainder 1
$1 \div 8^0 = 1$ remainder 0

$185_{\text{decimal}} = 271_{\text{octal}}$

Check

$2 \times 8^2 + 7 \times 8^1 + 1 \times 8^0 = 185$

EXTENSION Exercises

Change each number in base 8 to base 10.

1. 63_{octal}
2. 357_{octal}
3. 1042_{octal}

Change each number in base 10 to base 8.

4. 74_{decimal}
5. 229_{decimal}
6. 3339_{decimal}

Base 2, or the **binary** system, is the number system used by computers. The binary system works in the same way as base 10 and base 8, except the place values are powers of 2 and the only digits are 0 and 1.

Change each number in base 2 to base 10.

7. 11_{binary}
8. 1010_{binary}
9. 111010_{binary}

Change each number in base 10 to base 2.

10. 13_{decimal}
11. 222_{decimal}
12. 1024_{decimal}

The binary system can be used in a code to represent symbols such as letters, numbers, and punctuation. There are four possible two-digit codes.

Possible Two-Digit Codes
00, 01, 10, 11

13. **a.** Write the possible binary three-digit codes.
    b. Write the possible binary four-digit codes.

14. ***WHAT'S THE ERROR?*** The binary number 1010110_{binary} is supposed to equal 78_{decimal}. Correct the mistake in the binary number.

15. ***CHALLENGE*** What would be the digits for base 5? for base n?

Problem Solving on Location

NEW YORK

Adirondack Park

Adirondack Park covers one-fifth of the state of New York, making the park larger than Connecticut, Delaware, Hawaii, New Jersey, or Rhode Island. The park can be broken up into six regions plus the Northville–Lake Placid trail. There are 589 trails, totaling over 2000 miles in length. The 135-mile Northville–Lake Placid trail is the longest.

Adirondack Park	
Region	**Trails**
High Peaks	139
Northern	84
Central	74
West-central	129
Eastern	100
Southern	62
Total	588

For 1–3, use the table. Simplify your answers.

1. a. Express the number of trails in the northern region as a fraction of the total number of trails in the table.

b. Express the number of trails in the central region as a fraction of the total number of trails in the table.

c. What fraction of the trails in the table do the High Peaks region and the central region combined make up?

2. The High Peaks region combined with which other region contain $\frac{67}{147}$ of the trails?

3. The northern region has $\frac{21}{25}$ as many trails as which region?

4. Bradley walked one trail each day on a three-day trip to Adirondack Park. On the first day, he walked the Black Mountain trail, which is 8.5 miles. On the second day, he walked the Dead Creek Flow trail, which is a round-trip distance of 12.2 miles. And on the third day, he walked the Mount Marcy–Elk Lake trail. If his three-day total mileage was 31.15 miles, how long is the Mount Marcy–Elk Lake trail?

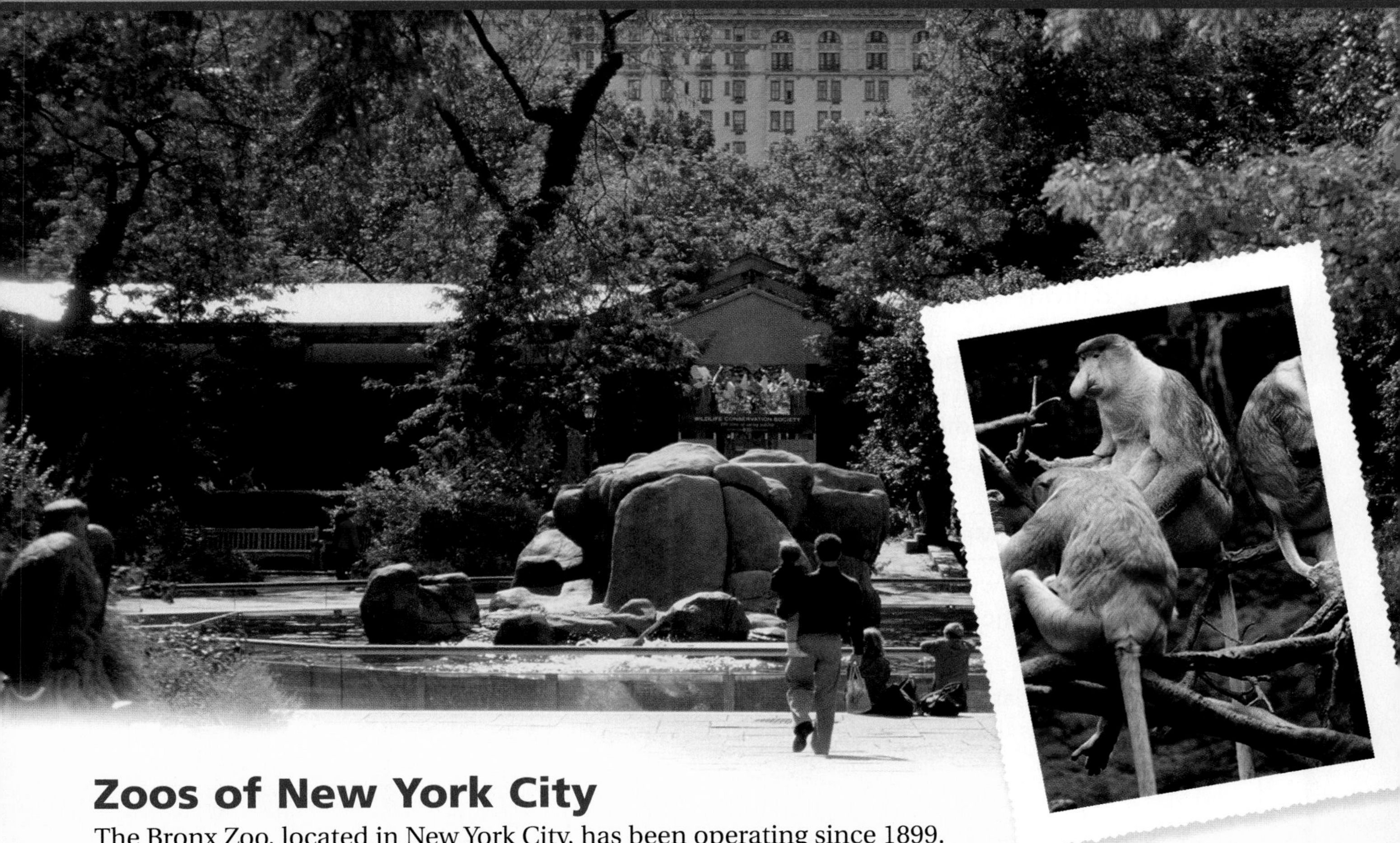

Zoos of New York City

The Bronx Zoo, located in New York City, has been operating since 1899. It opened with 22 exhibits and 843 animals. Currently, workers at the Bronx Zoo system care for more than 15,000 animals at five facilities in New York City, including Central Park Zoo in Manhattan.

Unusual species at the Bronx Zoo include snow leopards, lowland gorillas, Mauritius pink pigeons, and Chinese alligators.

The Congo Gorilla Forest is the zoo's 6.5 acre African rain forest habitat. It features 400 animals and 55 species. The exhibit's 23 lowland gorillas make up one of the largest breeding groups in the United States.

1. What fraction of the species in the African rain-forest habitat are lowland gorillas?
2. What fraction of the animals in the African rain-forest habitat are lowland gorillas?
3. If the 6.5-acre African rain-forest habitat were divided equally, about what fraction of an acre would each of the 400 animals have?
4. Central Park Zoo has 1400 animals and 130 species. The Queens Zoo has 400 animals and 70 species. Which represents a larger fraction, a comparison of the species at the Queens Zoo with those at Central Park Zoo, or a comparison of the number of animals at each zoo?

MATH-ABLES

Egyptian Fractions

If you were to divide 9 loaves of bread among 10 people, you would give each person $\frac{9}{10}$ of a loaf. The answer was different on the ancient Egyptian Ahmes papyrus, because ancient Egyptians used only *unit fractions,* which have a numerator of 1. All other fractions were written as sums of different unit fractions. So $\frac{5}{6}$ could be written as $\frac{1}{2} + \frac{1}{3}$, but not as $\frac{1}{6} + \frac{1}{6} + \frac{1}{6} + \frac{1}{6} + \frac{1}{6}$.

Method	Example
Suppose you want to write a fraction as a sum of different unit fractions.	$\frac{9}{10}$
Step 1. Choose the largest fraction of the form $\frac{1}{n}$ that is less than the fraction you want.	0, $\frac{1}{5}$ $\frac{1}{4}$ $\frac{1}{3}$, $\frac{1}{2}$, $\frac{9}{10}$, $\frac{1}{1}$
Step 2. Subtract $\frac{1}{n}$ from the fraction you want.	$\frac{9}{10} - \frac{1}{2} = \frac{2}{5}$ remaining
Step 3. Repeat steps 1 and 2 using the difference of the fractions until the result is a unit fraction.	0, $\frac{1}{5}$ $\frac{1}{4}$ $\frac{1}{3}$ $\frac{2}{5}$ $\frac{1}{2}$, $\frac{1}{1}$ $\frac{2}{5} - \frac{1}{3} = \frac{1}{15}$ remaining
Step 4. Write the fraction you want as the sum of the unit fractions.	$\frac{9}{10} = \frac{1}{2} + \frac{1}{3} + \frac{1}{15}$

Write each fraction as a sum of different unit fractions.

1. $\frac{3}{4}$ **2.** $\frac{5}{8}$ **3.** $\frac{11}{12}$ **4.** $\frac{3}{7}$ **5.** $\frac{7}{5}$

Egg Fractions

This game is played with an empty egg carton. Each compartment represents a fraction with a denominator of 12. The goal is to place tokens in compartments with a given sum.

internet connect

Go to ***go.hrw.com*** for a complete set of rules and instructions.
KEYWORD: MP4 Game3

Add and Subtract Fractions

Use with Lesson 3-5

You can add and subtract fractions using your graphing calculator. To display decimals as fractions, use the MATH key.

Activity

1 Use a graphing calculator to add $\frac{7}{12} + \frac{3}{8}$. Write the sum as a fraction.

Type 7 ÷ 12 and press ENTER.

You can see that the decimal equivalent is a repeating decimal, $0.58\overline{3}$.

Type + 3 ÷ 8 ENTER. The decimal form of the sum is displayed.

Press MATH ENTER ENTER.

The fraction form of the sum, $\frac{23}{24}$, is displayed as 23/24.

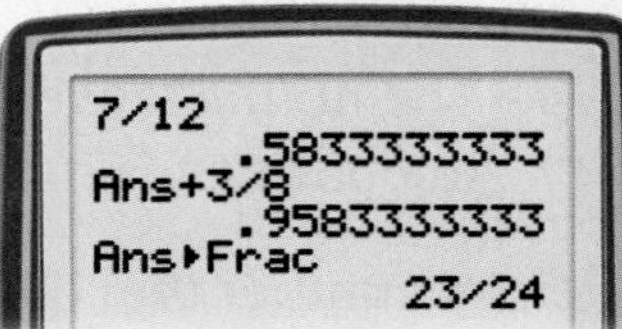

2 Use a graphing calculator to subtract $\frac{3}{5} - \frac{2}{3}$. Write the difference as a fraction.

Type 3 ÷ 5 − 2 ÷ 3 MATH ENTER ENTER.

The answer is $-\frac{1}{15}$.

Think and Discuss

1. Why is the difference in **2** negative?
2. Type 0.33333… (pressing 3 at least twelve times). Press MATH ENTER ENTER to write $0.\overline{3}$ as a fraction. Now do the same for $0.\overline{9}$. What happens to $0.\overline{9}$? How does the fraction for $0.\overline{3}$ help to explain this result?

Try This

Use a calculator to add or subtract. Write each result as a fraction.

1. $\frac{1}{2} + \frac{2}{5}$ **2.** $\frac{7}{8} - \frac{2}{3}$ **3.** $\frac{7}{17} + \frac{1}{10}$ **4.** $\frac{1}{3} - \frac{5}{7}$

5. $\frac{5}{32} + \frac{2}{11}$ **6.** $\frac{33}{101} - \frac{3}{7}$ **7.** $\frac{4}{15} + \frac{7}{16}$ **8.** $\frac{1}{35} - \frac{1}{37}$

Chapter 3

Study Guide and Review

Vocabulary

Complete the sentences below with vocabulary words from the list above. Words may be used more than once.

1. Any number that can be written as a fraction $\frac{n}{d}$ (where n and d are integers and $d \neq 0$) is called a __?__.
2. The set of __?__ is made up of the set of rational numbers and the set of __?__.
3. Integers that have no common factors other than 1 are __?__.
4. The nonnegative square root of a number is called the __?__ of the number.
5. A number that has rational numbers as its square roots is a __?__.

3-1 Rational Numbers (pp. 112–116)

EXAMPLE

- **Write the decimal as a fraction.**

$0.8 = \frac{8}{10}$ *8 is in the tenths place.*

$= \frac{8 \div 2}{10 \div 2}$ *Divide numerator and denominator by 2.*

$= \frac{4}{5}$

EXERCISES

Write each decimal as a fraction.

6. 0.6
7. 0.25
8. 0.525

Simplify.

9. $\frac{14}{21}$
10. $\frac{22}{33}$
11. $\frac{75}{100}$

3-2 Adding and Subtracting Rational Numbers (pp. 117–120)

EXAMPLE

- **Add or subtract.**

$\frac{3}{7} + \frac{4}{7} = \frac{3+4}{7} = \frac{7}{7} = 1$

$\frac{8}{11} - \left(\frac{-2}{11}\right) = \frac{8-(-2)}{11} = \frac{8+2}{11} = \frac{10}{11}$

EXERCISES

Add or subtract.

12. $\frac{-8}{13} + \frac{2}{13}$
13. $\frac{3}{5} - \left(\frac{-4}{5}\right)$
14. $\frac{-2}{9} + \frac{7}{9}$
15. $\frac{-5}{12} - \left(\frac{-7}{12}\right)$

3-3 Multiplying Rational Numbers (pp. 121–125)

EXAMPLE

- **Multiply. Write the answer in simplest form.**

$5\left(3\frac{1}{4}\right) = \left(\frac{5}{1}\right)\left(\frac{3(4)+1}{4}\right)$

$= \left(\frac{5}{1}\right)\left(\frac{13}{4}\right)$ *Write as improper fractions.*

$= \frac{65}{4}$ *Multiply.*

$= 16\frac{1}{4}$ *Write in simplest form.*

EXERCISES

Multiply. Write each answer in simplest form.

16. $3\left(-\frac{2}{5}\right)$

17. $2\left(3\frac{4}{5}\right)$

18. $\frac{-2}{3}\left(\frac{-4}{5}\right)$

19. $\frac{8}{11}\left(\frac{-22}{4}\right)$

20. $5\frac{1}{4}\left(\frac{3}{7}\right)$

21. $2\frac{1}{2}\left(1\frac{3}{10}\right)$

3-4 Dividing Rational Numbers (pp. 126–130)

EXAMPLE

- **Divide. Write the answer in simplest form.**

$\frac{7}{8} \div \frac{3}{4} = \frac{7}{8} \cdot \frac{4}{3}$ *Multiply by the reciprocal.*

$= \frac{7 \cdot 4}{8 \cdot 3}$ *Write as one fraction.*

$\frac{7 \cdot \cancel{4}^{1}}{{}_{2}\cancel{8} \cdot 3} = \frac{7 \cdot 1}{2 \cdot 3}$ *Divide by common factor, 4.*

$\frac{7}{6} = 1\frac{1}{6}$

EXERCISES

Divide. Write each answer in simplest form.

22. $\frac{3}{4} \div \frac{1}{8}$

23. $\frac{3}{10} \div \frac{4}{5}$

24. $\frac{2}{3} \div 3$

25. $4 \div \frac{-1}{4}$

26. $3\frac{3}{4} \div 3$

27. $1\frac{1}{3} \div \frac{2}{3}$

3-5 Adding and Subtracting with Unlike Denominators (pp. 131–134)

EXAMPLE

- **Add.**

$\frac{3}{4} + \frac{2}{5}$ *Multiply denominators, 4 • 5 = 20.*

$\frac{3 \cdot 5}{4 \cdot 5} = \frac{15}{20}$ $\frac{2 \cdot 4}{5 \cdot 4} = \frac{8}{20}$ *Rename fractions with the LCD 20.*

$\frac{15}{20} + \frac{8}{20} = \frac{15 + 8}{20} = \frac{23}{20} = 1\frac{3}{20}$ *Add and simplify.*

EXERCISES

Add or subtract.

28. $\frac{5}{6} + \frac{1}{3}$

29. $\frac{5}{6} - \frac{5}{9}$

30. $3\frac{1}{2} + 7\frac{4}{5}$

31. $7\frac{1}{10} - 2\frac{3}{4}$

3-6 Solving Equations with Rational Numbers (pp. 136–139)

EXAMPLE

- **Solve.**

$x - 13.7 = -22$

$\underline{+13.7} = \underline{+13.7}$ *Add 13.7 to each side.*

$x = -8.3$

EXERCISES

Solve.

32. $y + 7.8 = -14$

33. $2.9z = -52.2$

34. $w + \frac{3}{4} = \frac{1}{8}$

35. $\frac{3}{8}p = \frac{3}{4}$

3-7 Solving Inequalities with Rational Numbers (pp. 140–143)

EXAMPLE

- **Solve.**

$-3x > \frac{6}{7}$

$-\frac{1}{3}(-3x) > -\frac{1}{3}\left(\frac{6}{7}\right)$ *Multiply each side by $-\frac{1}{3}$.*

$x < -\frac{2}{7}$ *Change > to <, since you multiplied by a negative.*

EXERCISES

Solve.

36. $4m > -\frac{1}{3}$

37. $-2.7t \leq 32.4$

38. $7\frac{1}{2} - y \geq 10\frac{3}{4}$

39. $x + \frac{4}{5} > \frac{3}{10}$

3-8 Squares and Square Roots (pp. 146–149)

EXAMPLE

- **Find the two square roots of 400.**

$20 \cdot 20 = 400$

$(-20) \cdot (-20) = 400$

The square roots are 20 and −20.

EXERCISES

Find the two square roots of each number.

40. 16 **41.** 900 **42.** 676

Evaluate each expression.

43. $\sqrt{4 + 21}$ **44.** $\frac{\sqrt{100}}{20}$ **45.** $\sqrt{3^4}$

3-9 Finding Square Roots (pp. 150–153)

EXAMPLE

- **Find the side length of a square with area 359 ft^2 to one decimal place. Then find the distance around the square.**

$18^2 = 324$, $19^2 = 361$

Side = $\sqrt{359} \approx 18.9$

Distance around $\approx 4(18.9) \approx 75.6$ feet

EXERCISES

Find the distance around each square with the area given. Answer to the nearest tenth.

46. Area of square *ABCD* is 500 in^2.

47. Area of square *MNOP* is 1750 cm^2.

3-10 The Real Numbers (pp. 156–159)

EXAMPLE

- **State if the number is rational, irrational, or not a real number.**

$-\sqrt{2}$ real, irrational *The decimal equivalent does not repeat or end.*

$\sqrt{-4}$ not real *Square roots of negative numbers are not real.*

EXERCISES

State if the number is rational, irrational, or not a real number.

48. $\sqrt{81}$ **49.** $\sqrt{122}$ **50.** $\sqrt{-16}$

51. $-\sqrt{5}$ **52.** $\frac{0}{-4}$ **53.** $\frac{7}{0}$

Chapter 3

Chapter Test

Simplify.

1. $\frac{36}{72}$ **2.** $\frac{21}{35}$ **3.** $\frac{16}{88}$ **4.** $\frac{18}{25}$

Write each decimal as a fraction in simplest form.

5. 0.225 **6.** 0.04 **7.** 0.101 **8.** 0.875

Write each fraction as a decimal.

9. $\frac{7}{8}$ **10.** $\frac{13}{25}$ **11.** $\frac{5}{12}$ **12.** $\frac{4}{33}$

Add or subtract. Write each answer in simplest form.

13. $\frac{-3}{11} - \left(\frac{-4}{11}\right)$ **14.** $7\frac{1}{4} - 2\frac{3}{4}$ **15.** $\frac{5}{6} + \frac{7}{18}$

16. $\frac{5}{6} - \frac{8}{9}$ **17.** $4\frac{1}{2} + 5\frac{7}{8}$ **18.** $8\frac{1}{5} - 1\frac{2}{3}$

Multiply or divide. Write each answer in simplest form.

19. $9\left(\frac{-2}{27}\right)$ **20.** $\frac{7}{8} \div \frac{5}{24}$ **21.** $\frac{2}{3}\left(\frac{-9}{20}\right)$

22. $3\frac{3}{7}\left(1\frac{5}{16}\right)$ **23.** $34 \div 3\frac{2}{5}$ **24.** $-4\frac{2}{3} \div 1\frac{1}{6}$

Solve.

25. $x - \frac{1}{4} = -\frac{3}{8}$ **26.** $-3.14y = 53.38$

27. $-2k < \frac{1}{4}$ **28.** $h - 3.24 \leq -1.1$

Find the two square roots of each number.

29. 196 **30.** 1 **31.** 0.25 **32.** 6.25

Each square root is between two integers. Name the integers.

33. $\sqrt{230}$ **34.** $\sqrt{125}$ **35.** $\sqrt{89}$ **36.** $-\sqrt{60}$

State whether the number is rational, irrational, or not real.

37. $-\sqrt{121}$ **38.** $-1.\overline{7}$ **39.** $\sqrt{-9}$

Solve.

40. Michelle wants to put a fence along one side of her square-shaped vegetable garden. The area of the garden is 1250 ft^2. How much fencing should she buy, to the nearest foot?

Chapter 3

Performance Assessment

Show What You Know

Create a portfolio of your work from this chapter. Complete this page and include it with your four best pieces of work from Chapter 3. Choose from your homework or lab assignments, mid-chapter quiz, or any journal entries you have done. Put them together using any design you want. Make your portfolio represent what you consider your best work.

Short Response

1. A square chessboard is made up of 64 squares. If you placed a knight in each of the squares around the edge of the board, how many knight pieces would you need? Show or explain how you determined your answer.

2. In a mechanical drawing, a hidden line is usually represented by dashes $\frac{1}{8}$ in. long with $\frac{1}{32}$ in. spaces between them. How long is a line represented by 26 dashes? Show or explain how you determined your answer.

3. Write the multiplication equation $\frac{3}{4} \cdot \frac{5}{7} = \frac{15}{28}$ as a division equation. Use your result to explain why dividing by a fraction is the same as multiplying by the fraction's reciprocal.

Extended Problem Solving

4. Use a diagram to model multiplication of fractions.
   a. Draw a diagram to model the fraction $\frac{5}{6}$.
   b. Shade $\frac{2}{5}$ of the part of your diagram that represents $\frac{5}{6}$. What product does this shaded area represent?
   c. Use your diagram to write the product in simplest form.

internet connect
State-Specific Test Practice Online
go.hrw.com Keyword: MP4 TestPrep

Standardized Test Prep

Chapter 3

Cumulative Assessment, Chapters 1–3

1. Which ordered pair lies on the negative portion of the y-axis?

Ⓐ $(-4, -4)$ Ⓒ $(4, -4)$
Ⓑ $(0, -4)$ Ⓓ $(-4, 0)$

2. The sum of two numbers that differ by 1 is x. In terms of x, what is the value of the greater of the two numbers?

Ⓕ $\frac{x-1}{2}$ Ⓗ $\frac{x+1}{2}$
Ⓖ $\frac{x}{2}$ Ⓙ $\frac{x}{2} + 1$

3. If the sum of the consecutive integers from -22 through x is 72, what is the value of x?

Ⓐ 23 Ⓒ 50
Ⓑ 25 Ⓓ 75

4. If $xy + y = x + 2z$, what is the value of y when $x = 2$ and $z = 3$?

Ⓕ $\sqrt{8}$ Ⓗ $\sqrt[3]{8}$
Ⓖ $\frac{8}{3}$ Ⓙ 24

5. A local library association has posted the results of community contributions to the building fund.

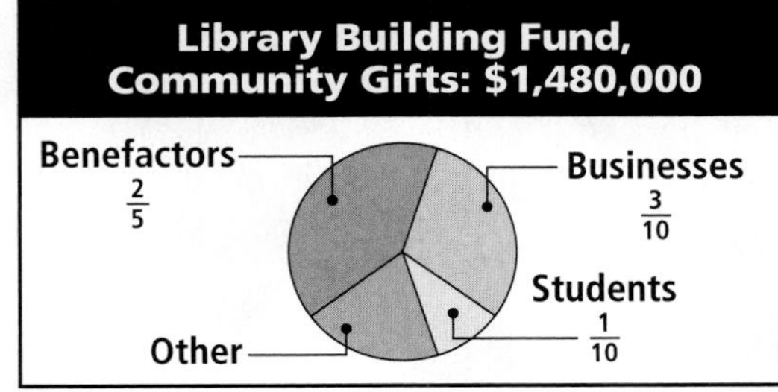

How much money does "Other" represent?

Ⓐ $148,000 Ⓒ $444,000
Ⓑ $296,000 Ⓓ $592,000

6. Which number is equivalent to 3^{-3}?

Ⓕ $\frac{1}{9}$ Ⓗ $-\frac{1}{9}$
Ⓖ $\frac{1}{27}$ Ⓙ $-\frac{1}{27}$

7. What is the value of $10 - 2 \cdot 3^2$?

Ⓐ -26 Ⓒ 72
Ⓑ -8 Ⓓ 576

TEST TAKING TIP!

Making comparisons: When assigning test values, try different kinds of numbers, such as negatives and fractions.

8. If x is any real number, then which statement **must** be true?

Ⓕ $x^2 > x$
Ⓖ $x^3 > x$
Ⓗ $x^3 > x^2$
Ⓙ No relationship can be determined.

9. ***SHORT RESPONSE*** The total weight of Sam and his son Dan is 250 pounds. Sam's weight is 10 pounds more than 3 times Dan's weight. Write an equation that could be used to determine Dan's weight. Solve your equation.

10. ***SHORT RESPONSE*** There was $1000 in the bank teller's drawer when the bank opened. After the first customer's withdrawal, the drawer still had greater than $900 in it, and it had an equal number of $1, $5, $10, $20, $50, and $100 bills in it. How much money did the first customer withdraw? Show or explain how you found your answer.

Standardized Test Prep

Chapter 4

Collecting, Displaying, and Analyzing Data

TABLE OF CONTENTS

internet connect

Chapter Opener Online
go.hrw.com
KEYWORD: MP4 CH4

Errors in Samples

Company Type	Sample Size	Errors
Software	25	2
Stoneworks	100	7
Tools	50	4
Pizza	75	3

Career *Quality Assurance Specialist*

How do manufacturers know that their products are well made? It is the job of the quality assurance specialist. QA specialists design tests and procedures that allow the companies to determine how good their products are. Because checking every product or procedure may not be possible, QA specialists use sampling to predict the margin of error.

Indiana Caves

Indiana has 2640 known caves in 31 counties. There are a total of 2872 known entrances, and 257 of the caves are over 1000 ft long. The Indiana Cave Survey database has maps of 1736 of the known caves.

For 1–4, use the table.

1. Organize the cave data into a frequency table showing the number of caves in each county. Use an interval of 50.
2. Make a histogram using the frequency table from problem **1**.
3. Tell which interval in problem **2** represents the largest number of counties and which interval represents the least number of counties.
4. Examine the data and determine the mode.
   a. In which interval on your histogram does the mode fall?
   b. Is it the interval with the highest frequency? Explain why or why not.

Indiana Caves by County

County Name	Number of Caves	County Name	Number of Caves
Bartholomew	10	Martin	85
Brown	1	Monroe	251
Clark	53	Morgan	12
Clay	1	Orange	240
Crawford	202	Owen	78
Decatur	15	Parke	2
Deleware	2	Perry	9
Dubois	11	Putman	13
Floyd	5	Ripley	20
Fountain	2	Scott	1
Greene	54	Shelby	5
Harrison	600	Tippecanoe	4
Jackson	4	Vanderburgh	4
Jefferson	156	Wabash	4
Jennings	197	Washington	155
Lawrence	444	**TOTAL**	**2640**

MATH-ABLES

Distribution of Primes

Remember that a prime number is only divisible by 1 and itself. There are infinitely many prime numbers, but there is no algebraic formula to find them. The largest known prime number, discovered on November 14, 2001, is $2^{13,466,917} - 1$. In standard form, this number would have 4,053,946 digits.

Sieve of Eratosthenes

One way to find prime numbers is called the sieve of Eratosthenes. Use a list of whole numbers in order. Cross off 1. The next number, 2, is prime. Circle it, and then cross off all multiples of 2, because they are not prime. Circle the next number on the list, and cross off all of its multiples. Repeat this step until all of the numbers are circled or crossed off. The circled numbers will all be primes.

~~1~~	(2)	3	~~4~~	5	~~6~~	7	~~8~~	9	~~10~~
11	~~12~~	13	~~14~~	15	~~16~~	17	~~18~~	19	~~20~~
21	~~22~~	23	~~24~~	25	~~26~~	27	~~28~~	29	~~30~~
31	~~32~~	33	~~34~~	35	~~36~~	37	~~38~~	39	~~40~~
41	~~42~~	43	~~44~~	45	~~46~~	47	~~48~~	49	~~50~~

1. Use the sieve of Eratosthenes to find all prime numbers less than 50.

2. Create a scatter plot of the first 15 prime numbers. Use the prime numbers as the x-coordinates and their positions in the sequence as the y-coordinates; 2 is the 1st prime, 3 is the 2nd prime, and so on.

Prime Number	2	3	5	7	■	■	■	■	■	■	■	■	■	■	■
Position in Sequence	1	2	3	4	5	6	7	8	9	10	11	12	13	14	15

3. Estimate the line of best fit and use it to guess the number of primes under 100. Use the sieve of Eratosthenes to check your guess.

Math in the Middle

This game can be played by two or more players. On your turn, roll 5 number cubes. The number of spaces you move is your choice of the mean, rounded to the nearest whole number; the median; or the mode, if it exists. The winner is the first player to land on the *Finish* square by exact count.

internet connect go.hrw.com

Go to ***go.hrw.com*** for a complete set of rules and the game board.
KEYWORD: MP4 Game4

Mean, Median, and Mode

The National Collegiate Athletic Association (NCAA) tournaments determine the champions of women's and men's college basketball. The victory margins for the championship games from 1995 through 2001 are shown below.

Margin of Victory, NCAA Championship Games							
Year	1995	1996	1997	1998	1999	2000	2001
Men's Game (points)	11	9	5	9	3	13	10
Women's Game (points)	6	18	9	18	17	19	2

Activity

1 Use a spreadsheet to find the mean, median, and mode of the men's championship-game victory margins from the table. Fill in rows 1 and 2 with the data and labels shown in the spreadsheet below.

The **AVERAGE, MEDIAN,** and **MODE** functions find the mean, median, and mode of the data in a given range of spreadsheet cells.

- Enter **=AVERAGE(B2:H2)** into cell H3 to find the mean of the data in cells B2 through H2.
- Enter **=MEDIAN(B2:H2)** into cell H4 to find the median of the data.
- Enter **=MODE(B2:H2)** into cell H5 to find the mode of the data.

	A	B	C	D	E	F	G	H
1	Year	1995	1996	1997	1998	1999	2000	2001
2	Margin (points)	11	9	5	9	3	13	10
3							Mean	8.571429
4							Median	9
5							Mode	9

Think and Discuss

1. If an eighth game with a victory margin of 30 points were added, what would happen to these three calculated values?

Try This

1. Use a spreadsheet to find the mean, median, and mode for the women's championship games (shown in the table above).

Chapter 4

Study Guide and Review

Vocabulary

Complete the sentences below with vocabulary words from the list above. Words may be used more than once.

1. The __?__ of a data set is the middle value, while the __?__ is the value that occurs most often.
2. __?__ describes how spread out a data set is. One measure of __?__ is the __?__.
3. The __?__ is the line that comes closest to all the points on a(n) __?__. __?__ describes the type of relationship between two data sets.

4-1 Samples and Surveys (pp. 174–177)

EXAMPLE

■ **Identify the population and sample. Give a reason why the sample could be biased.**

In a community of 1250 people, a pollster asks 250 people living near a railroad track if they want the tracks moved.

Population	Sample	Possible bias
1250 people who live in a community	250 residents living near tracks	People living near tracks are annoyed by the noise and want tracks moved.

EXERCISES

Identify the population and sample. Give a reason why the sample could be biased.

4. Of the 125 people in line for a *Star Wars* movie, 25 are asked to name their favorite type of movie.
5. Fifty parents of children attending Park Middle School are asked if the community should build a new Little League field.
6. This week, a U.S. senator asked 75 of the constituents who visited her office if she should run for reelection.

4-2 Organizing Data (pp. 179–183)

EXAMPLE

■ **Make a back-to-back stem-and-leaf plot.**

American League East
Final Standings 2000

Team	Wins	Losses
New York	87	74
Boston	85	77
Toronto	83	79
Baltimore	74	88
Tampa Bay	69	92

Wins		Losses
9	6	
4	7	4 7 9
7 5 3	8	8
	9	2

Key:
|9| 2 means 92
9 |6| means 69

EXERCISES

Make a back-to-back stem-and-leaf plot.

7.

President	Inaugural Age	Age at Death
George Washington	57	67
Thomas Jefferson	57	83
Abraham Lincoln	52	56
Franklin D. Roosevelt	51	63
John F. Kennedy	43	46

4-3 Central Tendency (pp. 184–187)

EXAMPLE

■ **Find the mean, median, and mode.**

30, 41, 46, 39, 46

mean: $\frac{30 + 41 + 46 + 39 + 46}{5} = \frac{202}{5} = 40.4$

median: 30 39 (41) 46 46

mode: 46

EXERCISES

Find the mean, median, and mode.

8. 450, 500, 500, 570, 650, 700, 1950

9. 8, 8, 8.5, 10, 10, 9, 9, 11.5

10. 2, 6, 6, 10, 2, 6, 6, 10

11. 1.1, 3.1, 3.1, 3.1, 7.1, 1.1, 3.1, 3.1

4-4 Variability (pp. 188–192)

EXAMPLE

■ **Find the range and quartiles.**

7, 10, 14, 16, 17, 17, 18, 20, 20

range = 20 − 7 = 13 *largest − smallest*

lower half *upper half*

(7 (10 14) 16) (17) (17 (18 20) 20)

1st quartile *3rd quartile*

$\frac{10 + 14}{2} = 12$ $\frac{18 + 20}{2} = 19$

EXERCISES

Find the range and quartiles.

12. 80, 80, 80, 82, 85, 87, 87, 90, 90, 90

13. 67, 68, 68, 80, 92, 99, 80, 99, 99, 99

Study Guide and Review

4-5 Displaying Data (pp. 196–199)

EXAMPLE

■ **Make a histogram of the data set.**

Heights of 20 people, in inches:

72, 64, 56, 60, 66, 72, 48, 66, 58, 60, 60, 50, 68, 72, 68, 62, 72, 58, 60, 68

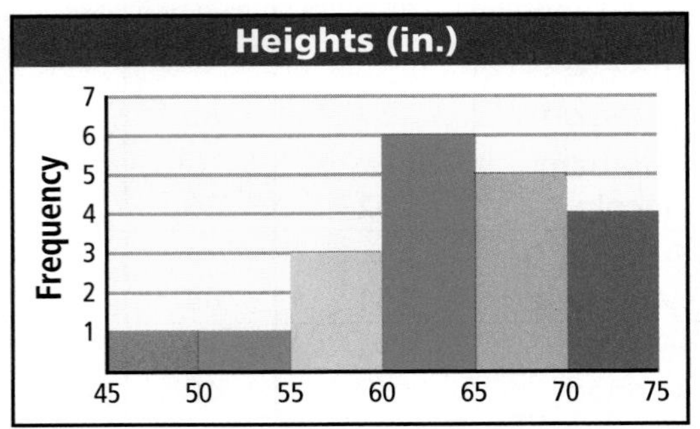

EXERCISES

Make a histogram of each data set.

14.

Test Scores	Frequency
91–100	6
81–90	8
71–80	11
61–70	4
51–60	0
41–50	3

15. TV viewing (hr/week): 19, 17, 11, 17, 3, 12, 27, 12, 20, 17, 25, 18, 23, 15, 16, 25, 23, 1, 14, 23, 17, 13, 19, 10, 21

4-6 Misleading Graphs and Statistics (pp. 200–203)

EXAMPLE

■ **Explain why the graph is misleading.**

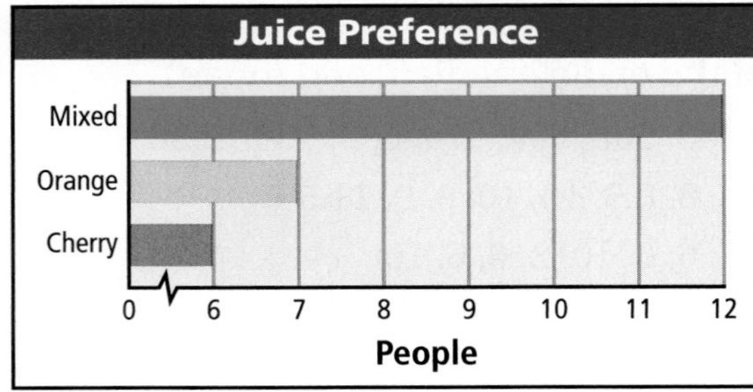

The bar for mixed juice is 7 times longer than the bar for cherry juice, but it is only preferred by 2 times as many people.

EXERCISES

Explain why the graph is misleading.

16.

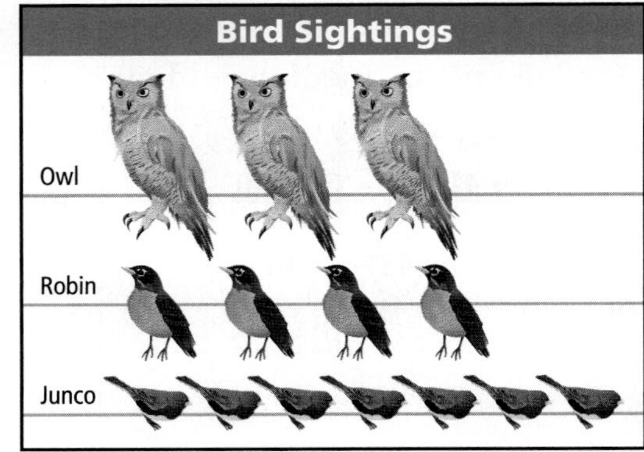

Each bird = 100 sightings

4-7 Scatter Plots (pp. 204–207)

EXAMPLE

■ **Does the data set have a positive, a negative, or no correlation? Explain.**

The age of a battery in a flashlight and the intensity of the flashlight beam.

Negative: The older the battery is, the less intense the flashlight beam will be.

EXERCISES

Do the data sets have a positive, a negative, or no correlation? Explain.

17. The price of an item and the dollar amount paid in sales tax.

18. Your height and the last digit of your phone number.

Chapter Test

Identify the sampling method used.

1. Twenty U.S. cities are randomly chosen and 100 people are randomly chosen from each city.

Use the data: **59, 21, 32, 33, 40, 51, 23, 23, 28, 26, 35, 49, 48, 41, 37, 39, 44, 54, 53, 29, 28, 29, 57, 58, 46**

2. Find the mean.
3. Find the median.
4. Find the mode.
5. Make a stem-and-leaf plot.
6. Find the range.
7. Find the first quartile.
8. Find the third quartile.
9. Make a box-and-whisker plot.

Use the data: **7, 7, 7, 7, 8, 8, 8, 5, 5, 8, 6, 6, 7, 7, 8, 8, 8, 5, 7, 5, 6, 7, 7, 6, 6, 6, 7, 7, 7, 7, 8**

10. Make a frequency table.
11. Make a bar graph.

Use the data: **155, 162, 168, 147, 152, 153, 178, 151, 180, 158, 163, 177, 171, 168, 183, 154, 180, 158, 157, 160, 171, 164, 171**

12. Make a frequency table.
13. Make a histogram.

Use the data in the table.

14. Make a line graph.
15. Use the line graph to estimate the population of Africa in the year 1800.
16. Use the line graph to estimate the population of Africa in the year 1900.

Year	Population of Africa
1650	100,000,000
1750	95,000,000
1850	95,000,000
1950	229,000,000
2000	805,000,000

17. **Give a reason why the statistic could be misleading.**

    A sign reads "Work at home—earn up to $1000 per week!"

Use the data in the table.

18. Make a scatter plot.
19. Draw the line of best fit.
20. Do the data sets have a positive, a negative, or no correlation? Explain.

Animal	Gestation Period (d)	Average Life (yr)
Baboon	187	20
Chipmunk	31	6
Elephant	645	40
Fox	52	7
Horse	330	20
Lion	100	15
Mouse	19	3

Chapter 4

Performance Assessment

Show What You Know

Create a portfolio of your work from this chapter. Complete this page and include it with your four best pieces of work from Chapter 4. Choose from your homework or lab assignments, mid-chapter quiz, or any journal entries you have done. Put them together using any design you want. Make your portfolio represent what you consider your best work.

Short Response

1. Determine the mean, median, and mode for the data set 2, 1, 8, 3, 500, 3, 1. Show your work.

2. Write a numeric expression that could be used to find the mean of the data in the frequency table. What is the mean of the data?

Number	1	2	3	4	5
Frequency	4	7	1	6	2

3. Name two ordered pairs (x, y) that satisfy these conditions: The mean of 0, x, and y is twice the median; $0 < x < y$; and $y = nx$ (y is a multiple of x). What is the value of n? Show your work or explain in words how you determined your answer.

Extended Problem Solving

4. Twenty students in a gym class kept a record of their jogging. The results are shown in the scatter plot.

   a. Describe the correlation of the data in the scatter plot.

   b. Find the average speeds of joggers who run 1, 2, 3, 4, 5, and 6 miles.

   c. Explain the relationship between your answer from part **a** and your answers from part **b**.

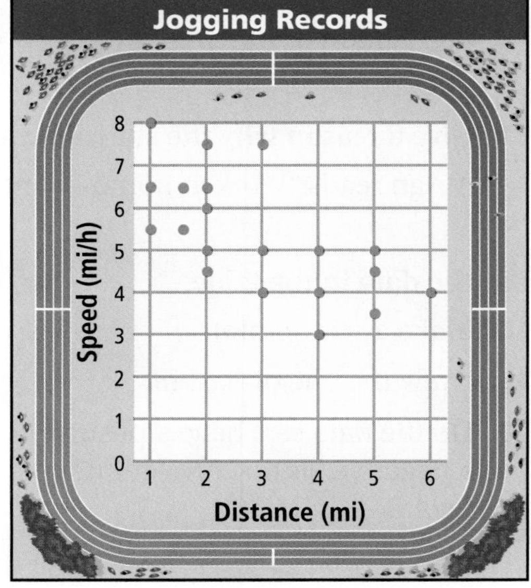

Performance Assessment

internet connect

State-Specific Test Practice Online
go.hrw.com Keyword: MP4 TestPrep

Standardized Test Prep

Chapter 4

Cumulative Assessment, Chapters 1–4

1. Dana bought 9 comic books for a total of \$30.50. Which equation is equivalent to the equation $9c = 30.5$?

   Ⓐ $c = 30.5 - 9$ Ⓒ $c = 9 - 30.5$

   Ⓑ $c = \frac{30.5}{9}$ Ⓓ $c = \frac{9}{30.5}$

2. On the number line, what number is the coordinate of point R?

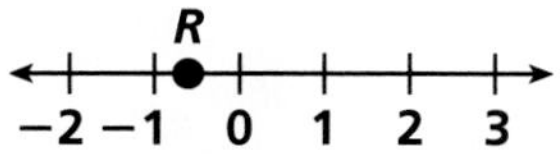

   [Number line from −2 to 3 with point R between −1 and 0]

   Ⓕ $-1\frac{3}{4}$ Ⓗ $-\frac{3}{4}$

   Ⓖ $-1\frac{1}{4}$ Ⓙ $-\frac{1}{4}$

3. If the product of five integers is negative, then, at most, how many of the five integers could be negative?

   Ⓐ five Ⓒ three

   Ⓑ four Ⓓ two

4. Which is equivalent to $3^8 \cdot 3^4$?

   Ⓕ 9^{32} Ⓗ 3^{32}

   Ⓖ 9^{12} Ⓙ 3^{12}

5. What is the value of $32 - 2 \cdot 4^2$?

   Ⓐ 14,400 Ⓒ 0

   Ⓑ 480 Ⓓ −32

TEST TAKING TIP!

To calculate the median, the data must be in order.

6. For which set of data are the mean, median, and mode all the same?

   Ⓕ 3, 1, 3, 3, 5 Ⓗ 2, 1, 1, 1, 5

   Ⓖ 1, 1, 2, 5, 6 Ⓙ 10, 1, 3, 5, 1

7. Which is true for the data 6, 6, 6.5, 8, 8.5?

   Ⓐ median < mode

   Ⓑ median = mean

   Ⓒ median < mean

   Ⓓ median = mode

8. The stem-and-leaf plot shows test scores for a teacher's first and second periods. What can you conclude?

1st period		2nd period
7	6	5 8
6 4 2	7	5 6 9
9 8 6 4 2 0	8	1 3 5 7 7 8 8
9 7 7 2 1	9	0 6 7 8 9

Key: |9|0 means 90
7|6| means 67

   Ⓕ More first period students scored in the 90's.

   Ⓖ Fewer first period students scored 80 or below.

   Ⓗ More second period students scored in the 70's.

   Ⓙ More second period students scored in the 80's.

9. ***SHORT RESPONSE*** Julie wants to make homemade bows for her presents. She buys $\frac{1}{2}$ yard of red ribbon and $\frac{3}{4}$ yard of green. If each bow takes $\frac{1}{8}$ yard to make, how many total bows can she create? Justify your answer.

10. ***SHORT RESPONSE*** Max scored 75, 73, 71, 70, and 71 on his last 5 tests. Max wants to bring up his test average to a 75. What would Max need to make on his next test to bring his average up to a 75? Show your work.

Chapter

5

Plane Geometry

TABLE OF CONTENTS

Chapter Opener Online
go.hrw.com
KEYWORD: MP4 CH5

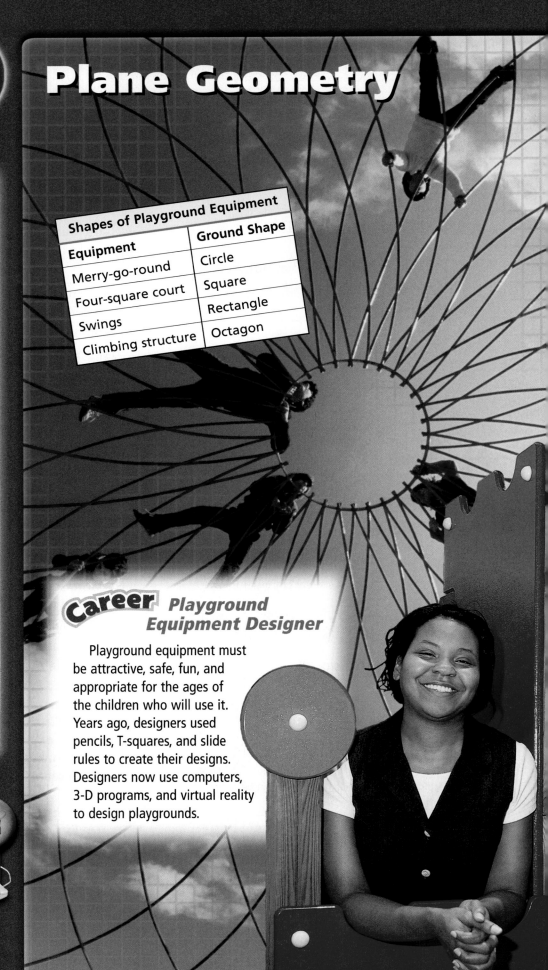

Shapes of Playground Equipment

Equipment	Ground Shape
Merry-go-round	Circle
Four-square court	Square
Swings	Rectangle
Climbing structure	Octagon

Career *Playground Equipment Designer*

Playground equipment must be attractive, safe, fun, and appropriate for the ages of the children who will use it. Years ago, designers used pencils, T-squares, and slide rules to create their designs. Designers now use computers, 3-D programs, and virtual reality to design playgrounds.

ARE YOU READY?

Choose the best term from the list to complete each sentence.

1. In the __?__ (4, −3), 4 is the __?__, and −3 is the __?__.
2. The __?__ divide the __?__ into four sections.
3. The point (0, 0) is called the __?__.
4. The point (0, −3) lies on the __?__, while the point (−2, 0) lies on the __?__.

coordinate axes
coordinate plane
origin
ordered pair
***x*-axis**
***y*-axis**
***x*-coordinate**
***y*-coordinate**

Complete these exercises to review skills you will need for this chapter.

✔ Ordered Pairs

Write the coordinates of the indicated points.

5. point *A*
6. point *B*
7. point *C*
8. point *D*
9. point *E*
10. point *F*
11. point *G*
12. point *H*

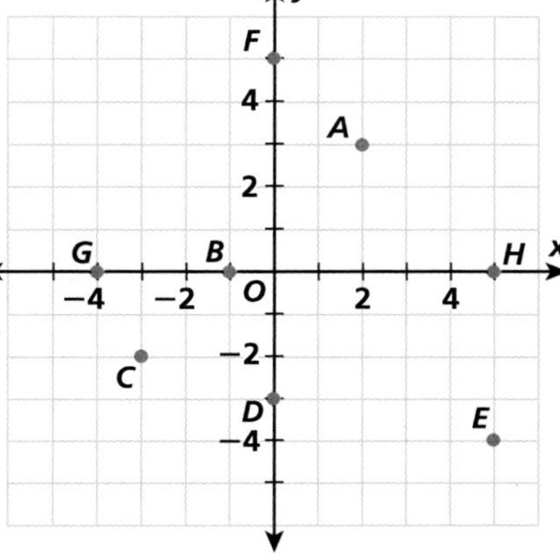

✔ Combine Like Terms

Simplify each expression by combining the like terms.

13. $5m + 7 - 2m - 1$
14. $2x - 4 - 6x + 1$
15. $6w + z - 5w - z$
16. $3r + 11s$
17. $12h - 9 + 2 - 3h$
18. $4y + 1 - 2y - x$

✔ Equations

Solve each equation.

19. $2p = 18$
20. $7 + h = 21$
21. $\frac{x}{3} = 9$
22. $y - 6 = 16$
23. $4d + 1 = 13$
24. $-2q - 3 = 3$
25. $4(z - 1) = 16$
26. $x + 3 + 4x = 23$

Determine whether the given values are solutions of the given equations.

27. $\frac{2}{3}x + 1 = 7$ $\quad x = 9$
28. $2x - 4 = 6$ $\quad x = -1$
29. $8 - 2x = -4$ $\quad x = 5$
30. $\frac{1}{2}x + 5 = -2$ $\quad x = -14$

5-1 Points, Lines, Planes, and Angles

Learn to classify and name figures.

Vocabulary

point, line, plane, segment, ray, angle, right angle, acute angle, obtuse angle, complementary angles, supplementary angles, congruent, vertical angles

Points, lines, and planes are the building blocks of geometry. Segments, rays, and angles are defined in terms of these basic figures.

A **point** names a location.	• A	point A
A **line** is perfectly straight and extends forever in both directions.	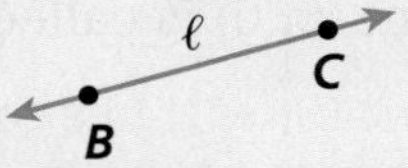 line through B and C, labeled ℓ	line ℓ, or $\overleftrightarrow{BC}$
A **plane** is a perfectly flat surface that extends forever in all directions.	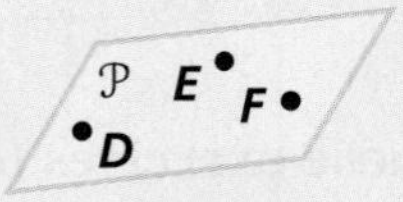 plane $\mathcal{P}$ with points D, E, F	plane $\mathcal{P}$, or plane DEF
A **segment**, or line segment, is the part of a line between two points.	segment from G to H	$\overline{GH}$
A **ray** is part of a line that starts at one point and extends forever in one direction.	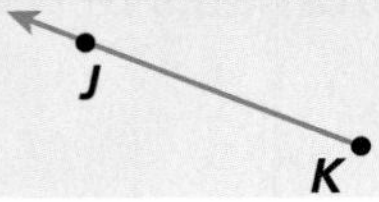 ray from K through J	$\overrightarrow{KJ}$

$\overleftrightarrow{BC}$ is read "line BC." $\overline{GH}$ is read "segment GH." $\overrightarrow{KJ}$ is read "ray KJ." To name a ray, always write the endpoint first.

EXAMPLE 1 Naming Points, Lines, Planes, Segments, and Rays

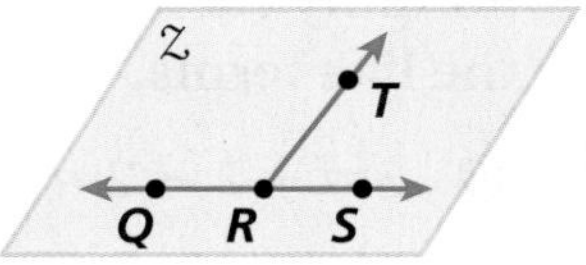

A Name four points in the figure.

point Q, point R, point S, point T

B Name a line in the figure.

$\overleftrightarrow{QS}$ or $\overleftrightarrow{QR}$ or $\overleftrightarrow{RS}$

Any 2 points on the line can be used.

C Name a plane in the figure.

plane $\mathcal{Z}$ or plane QRT *Any 3 points in the plane that form a triangle can be used.*

D Name four segments in the figure.

$\overline{QR}$, $\overline{RS}$, $\overline{RT}$, $\overline{QS}$

E Name five rays in the figure.

$\overrightarrow{RQ}$ $\overrightarrow{RS}$, $\overrightarrow{RT}$, $\overrightarrow{SQ}$, $\overrightarrow{QS}$

An **angle** ($\angle$) is formed by two rays with a common endpoint called the *vertex* (plural, *vertices*). Angles can be measured in degrees. One degree, or 1°, is $\frac{1}{360}$ of a circle. m$\angle$1 means the measure of $\angle$1. The angle can be named $\angle XYZ$, $\angle ZYX$, $\angle 1$, or $\angle Y$. The vertex must be the middle letter.

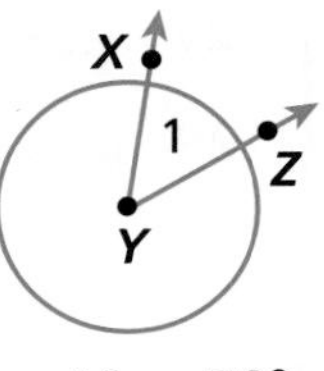

m$\angle 1 = 50°$

The measures of angles that fit together to form a straight line, such as ∠*FKG*, ∠*GKH*, and ∠*HKJ*, add to 180°.

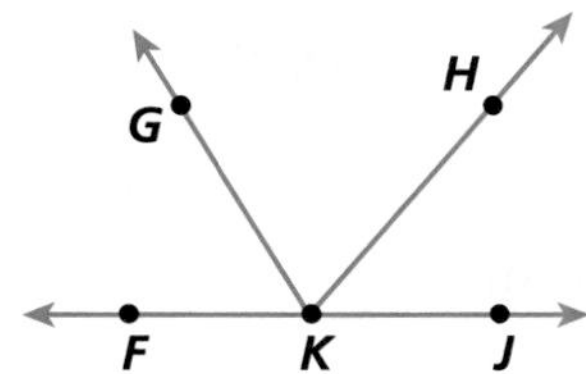

The measures of angles that fit together to form a complete circle, such as ∠*MRN*, ∠*NRP*, ∠*PRQ*, and ∠*QRM*, add to 360°.

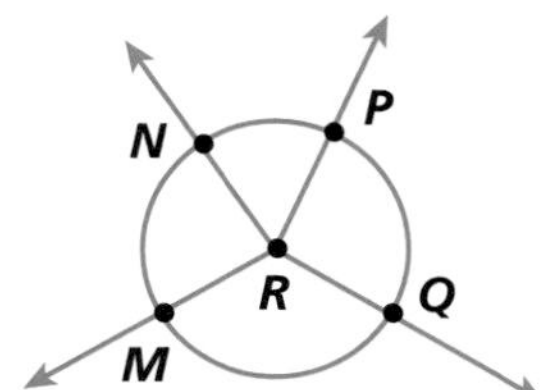

A **right angle** measures 90°. An **acute angle** measures less than 90°. An **obtuse angle** measures greater than 90° and less than 180°. **Complementary angles** have measures that add to 90°. **Supplementary angles** have measures that add to 180°.

EXAMPLE 2 Classifying Angles

Reading Math

A right angle can be labeled with a small box at the vertex.

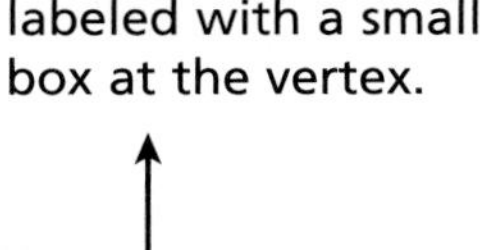

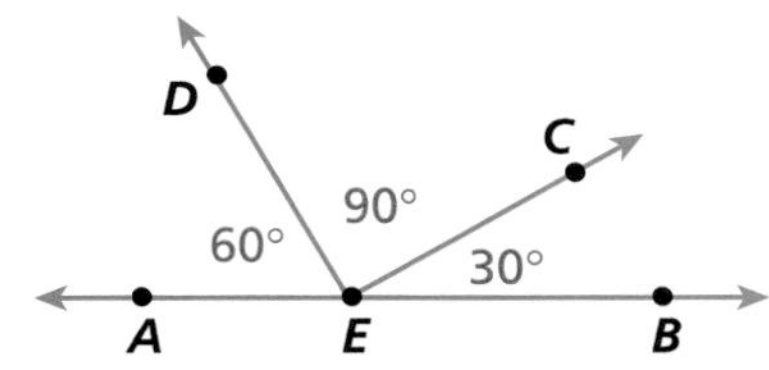

A **Name a right angle in the figure.**

∠*DEC*

B **Name two acute angles in the figure.**

∠*AED*, ∠*CEB*

C **Name two obtuse angles in the figure.**

∠*AEC*, ∠*DEB*

D **Name a pair of complementary angles in the figure.**

∠*AED*, ∠*CEB* $m\angle AED + m\angle CEB = 60° + 30° = 90°$

E **Name two pairs of supplementary angles in the figure.**

∠*AED*, ∠*DEB* $m\angle AED + m\angle DEB = 60° + 120° = 180°$

∠*AEC*, ∠*CEB* $m\angle AEC + m\angle CEB = 150° + 30° = 180°$

Congruent figures have the same size and shape.

- Segments that have the same length are congruent.
- Angles that have the same measure are congruent.
- The symbol for congruence is ≅, which is read "is congruent to."

Intersecting lines form two pairs of **vertical angles**. Vertical angles are always congruent, as shown in the next example.

EXAMPLE 3 Finding the Measures of Vertical Angles

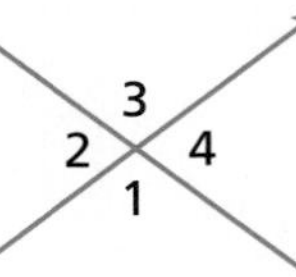

In the figure, $\angle 1$ and $\angle 3$ are vertical angles, and $\angle 2$ and $\angle 4$ are vertical angles.

A **If m$\angle 2 = 75°$, find m$\angle 4$.**

The measures of $\angle 2$ and $\angle 3$ add to 180° because they are supplementary, so m$\angle 3 = 180° - 75° = 105°$.

The measures of $\angle 3$ and $\angle 4$ add to 180° because they are supplementary, so m$\angle 4 = 180° - 105° = 75°$.

B **If m$\angle 3 = x°$, find m$\angle 1$.**

m$\angle 4 = 180° - x°$

m$\angle 1 = 180° - (180° - x°)$

$= 180° - 180° + x°$ *Distributive Property*

$= x°$ *m$\angle 1$ = m$\angle 3$*

Think and Discuss

1. Tell which statements are correct if $\angle X$ and $\angle Y$ are congruent.

a. $\angle X = \angle Y$ **b.** m$\angle X$ = m$\angle Y$ **c.** $\angle X \cong \angle Y$ **d.** m$\angle X \cong$ m$\angle Y$

2. Explain why vertical angles must always be congruent.

5-1 Exercises

FOR EXTRA PRACTICE
see page 740

internet connect
Homework Help Online
go.hrw.com Keyword: MP4 5-1

GUIDED PRACTICE

See Example 1

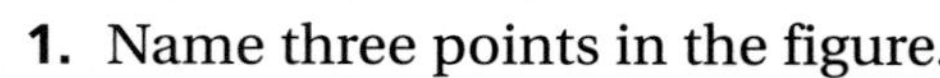

1. Name three points in the figure.
2. Name a line in the figure.
3. Name a plane in the figure.
4. Name three segments in the figure.
5. Name three rays in the figure.

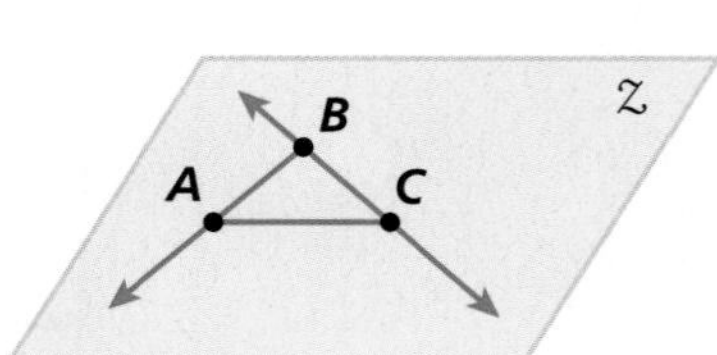

See Example 2

6. Name a right angle in the figure.
7. Name two acute angles in the figure.
8. Name an obtuse angle in the figure.
9. Name a pair of complementary angles in the figure.
10. Name two pairs of supplementary angles in the figure.

L
M
40°
90°
50°
H
J
K

See Example 3

In the figure, ∠1 and ∠3 are vertical angles, and ∠2 and ∠4 are vertical angles.

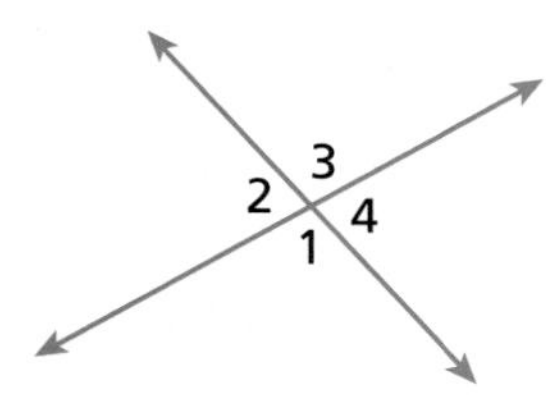

11. If m∠3 = 115°, find m∠1.

12. If m∠2 = a°, find m∠4.

INDEPENDENT PRACTICE

See Example 1

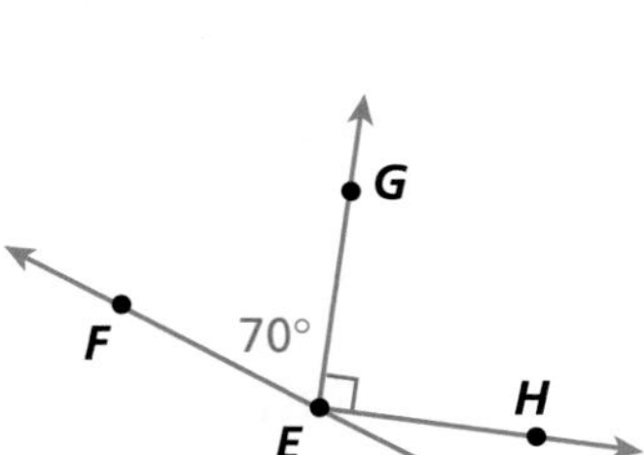

13. Name four points in the figure.

14. Name two lines in the figure.

15. Name a plane in the figure.

16. Name three segments in the figure.

17. Name five rays in the figure.

See Example 2

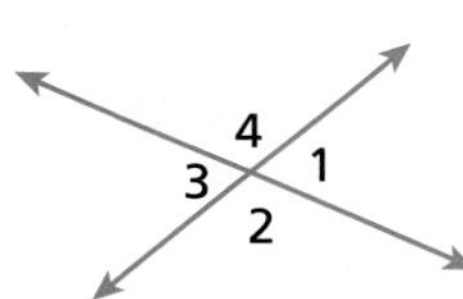

18. Name a right angle in the figure.

19. Name two acute angles in the figure.

20. Name two obtuse angles in the figure.

21. Name a pair of complementary angles in the figure.

22. Name two pairs of supplementary angles in the figure.

See Example 3

In the figure, ∠1 and ∠3 are vertical angles, and ∠2 and ∠4 are vertical angles.

23. If m∠2 = 117°, find m∠4.

24. If m∠1 = n°, find m∠3.

PRACTICE AND PROBLEM SOLVING

Use the figure for Exercises 25–34. Write *true* or *false*. If a statement is false, rewrite it so it is true.

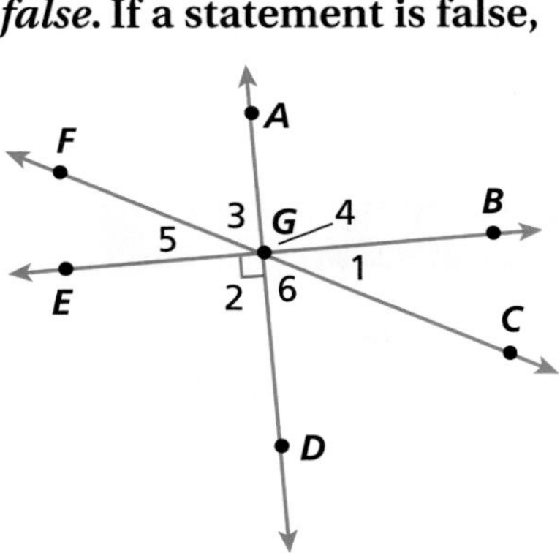

25. $\overleftrightarrow{AE}$ is a line in the figure.

26. Rays $\overrightarrow{GB}$ and $\overrightarrow{GE}$ make up line $\overleftrightarrow{EB}$.

27. ∠EGD is an obtuse angle.

28. ∠4 and ∠2 are supplementary.

29. ∠3 and ∠5 are supplementary.

30. ∠6 and ∠5 are complementary.

31. If m∠1 = 30°, then m∠6 = 45°.

32. If m∠FGD = 130°, then m∠DGC = 130°.

33. If m∠3 = x°, then m∠FGE = 180° − x°.

34. m∠1 + m∠3 + m∠5 + m∠6 = 180°.

Physical Science LINK

The archerfish can spit a stream of water up to 3 meters in the air to knock its prey into the water. This job is made more difficult by *refraction,* the bending of light waves as they pass from one substance to another. When you look at an object through water, the light between you and the object is refracted. Refraction makes the object appear to be in a different location. Despite refraction, the archerfish still catches its prey.

35. Suppose that the measure of the angle between the bug's actual location and the bug's apparent location is 35°.

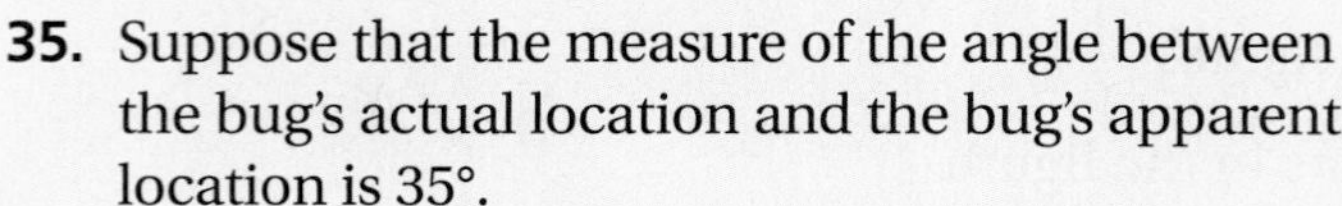

a. Refer to the diagram. Along the fish's line of vision, what is the measure of the angle between the fish and the bug's apparent location?

b. What is the relationship of the angles in the diagram?

36. In the photograph, the underwater part of the net appears to be 40° to the right of where it actually is. What is the measure of the angle formed by the image of the underwater part of the net and the part of the net above the water?

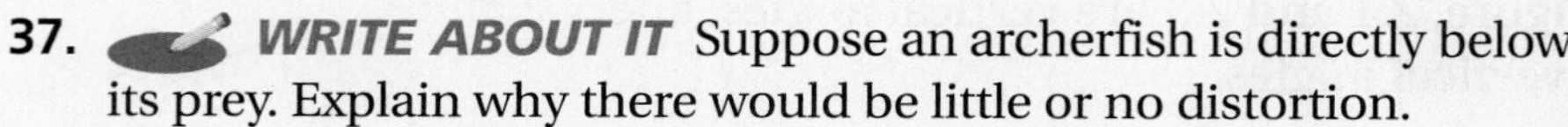

37. ***WRITE ABOUT IT*** Suppose an archerfish is directly below its prey. Explain why there would be little or no distortion.

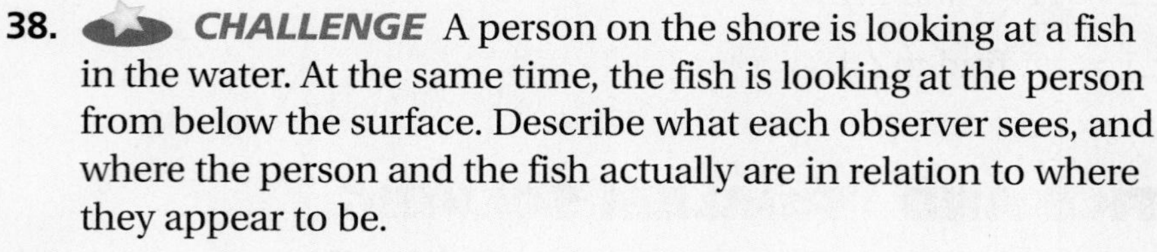

38. ***CHALLENGE*** A person on the shore is looking at a fish in the water. At the same time, the fish is looking at the person from below the surface. Describe what each observer sees, and where the person and the fish actually are in relation to where they appear to be.

Spiral Review

Find the mean, median, and mode of each data set. Round to the nearest tenth. (Lesson 4-3)

39. 16, 16, 14, 13, 20, 29, 14, 13, 16

40. 2.1, 2.3, 3.2, 2.2, 1.9, 2.3, 2.2

Find the range and the first and third quartiles of each data set. (Lesson 4-4)

41. 32, 26, 24, 14, 20, 32, 16, 25, 26

42. 221, 223, 352, 202, 139, 243, 232

43. **TEST PREP** Which fraction is greater than $\frac{1}{4}$? (Previous course)

A $\frac{12}{49}$ **B** $\frac{6}{23}$ **C** $\frac{15}{68}$ **D** $\frac{17}{99}$

Basic Constructions

Use with Lesson 5-1

internet connect
Lab Resources Online
go.hrw.com
KEYWORD: MP4 Lab5A

When you *bisect* a figure, you divide it into two congruent parts.

Activity

1 Follow the steps below to bisect a segment.

a. Draw $\overline{JK}$ on your paper. Place your compass point on J and draw an arc. Without changing your compass opening, place your compass point on K and draw an arc.

b. Connect the intersections of the arcs with a line. Measure $\overline{JM}$ and $\overline{KM}$. What do you notice?

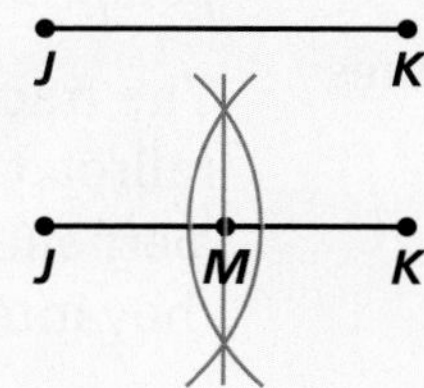

2 Follow the steps below to bisect an angle.

a. Draw acute $\angle H$ on your paper.

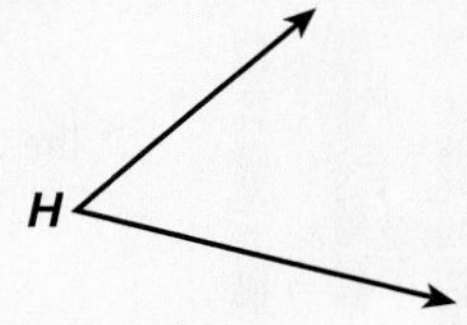

b. Place your compass point on H and draw an arc through both sides of the angle.

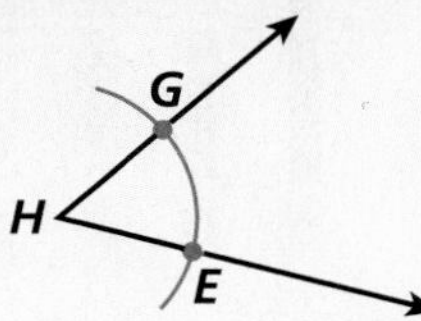

c. Without changing your compass opening, draw intersecting arcs from G and E. Label the intersection D.

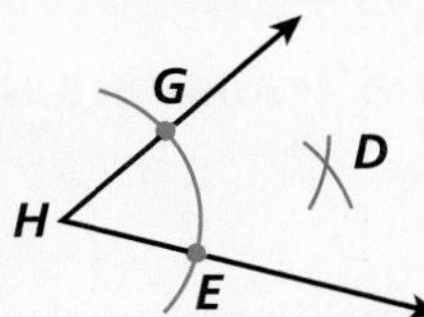

d. Draw $\overrightarrow{HD}$. Use a protractor to measure $\angle GHD$ and $\angle DHE$. What do you notice?

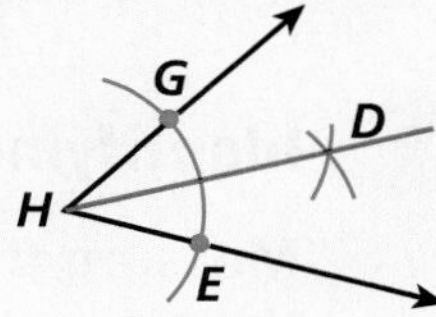

Think and Discuss

1. Explain how to use a compass and a straightedge to divide a segment into four congruent segments. Prove that the segments are congruent.

Try This

Draw each figure, and then use a compass and a straightedge to bisect it. Verify by measuring.

1. a 2-inch segment
2. a 1-inch segment
3. a 4-inch segment
4. a 64° angle
5. a 90° angle
6. a 120° angle

5-2 Parallel and Perpendicular Lines

Learn to identify parallel and perpendicular lines and the angles formed by a transversal.

Vocabulary

parallel lines

perpendicular lines

transversal

Parallel lines are two lines in a plane that never meet, like a set of perfectly straight, infinite train tracks. The tracks in the picture appear to meet at the horizon because of *perspective.*

The tracks and the railroad ties are like **perpendicular lines** ; that is, they intersect at 90° angles.

A **transversal** is a line that intersects any two or more other lines. Transversals to parallel lines have interesting properties.

EXAMPLE 1 Identifying Congruent Angles Formed by a Transversal

Remember!

Use a protractor to measure angles. You cannot tell if angles are congruent by measuring because measurement is not exact. See page 772.

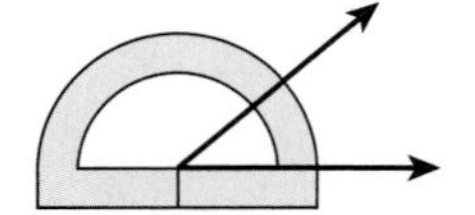

Measure the angles formed by the transversal and the parallel lines. Which angles seem to be congruent?

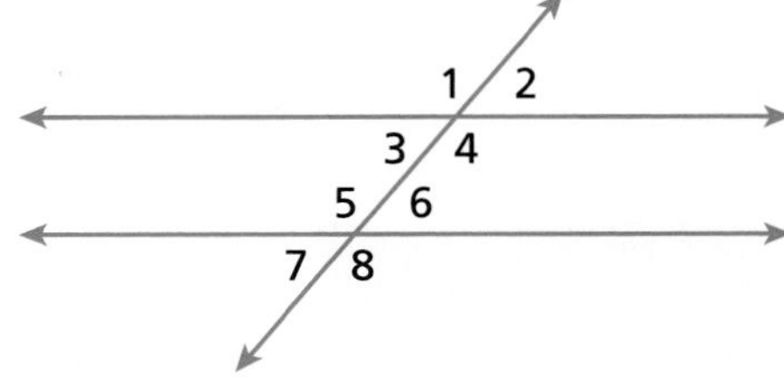

$\angle 1$, $\angle 4$, $\angle 5$, and $\angle 8$ all measure 130°.
$\angle 2$, $\angle 3$, $\angle 6$, and $\angle 7$ all measure 50°.

Angles marked in blue appear congruent to each other, and angles marked in red appear congruent to each other.

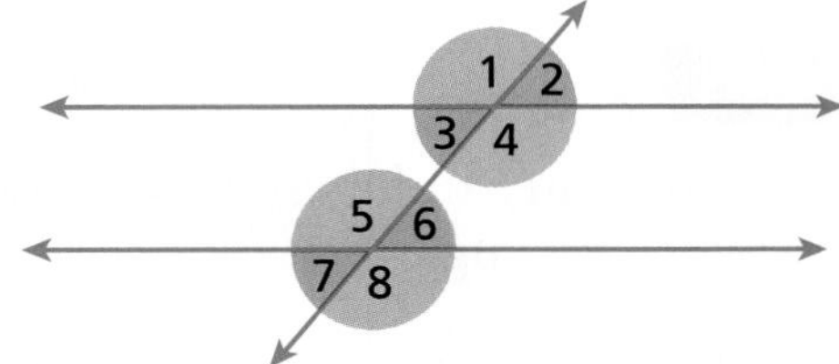

$\angle 1 \cong \angle 4 \cong \angle 5 \cong \angle 8$

$\angle 2 \cong \angle 3 \cong \angle 6 \cong \angle 7$

PROPERTIES OF TRANSVERSALS TO PARALLEL LINES

If two parallel lines are intersected by a transversal,

- the acute angles that are formed are all congruent,
- the obtuse angles are all congruent,
- and any acute angle is supplementary to any obtuse angle.

If the transversal is perpendicular to the parallel lines, all of the angles formed are congruent 90° angles.

Writing Math

The symbol for parallel is ||. The symbol for perpendicular is ⊥.

EXAMPLE 2 Finding Angle Measures of Parallel Lines Cut by Transversals

In the figure, line *r* || line *s*. Find the measure of each angle.

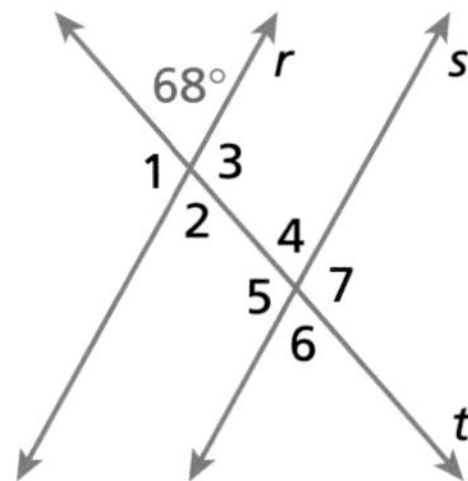

A $\angle 4$

$m\angle 4 = 68°$ *All acute angles in the figure are congruent.*

B $\angle 3$

$$\begin{aligned} m\angle 3 + 68° &= 180° \\ -68° &\quad -68° \\ m\angle 3 &= 112° \end{aligned}$$

∠3 is supplementary to the 68° angle.

C $\angle 7$

$m\angle 7 = 112°$ *All obtuse angles in the figure are congruent.*

If two lines are intersected by a transversal and any of the angle pairs shown below are congruent, then the lines are parallel. This fact is used in the construction of parallel lines.

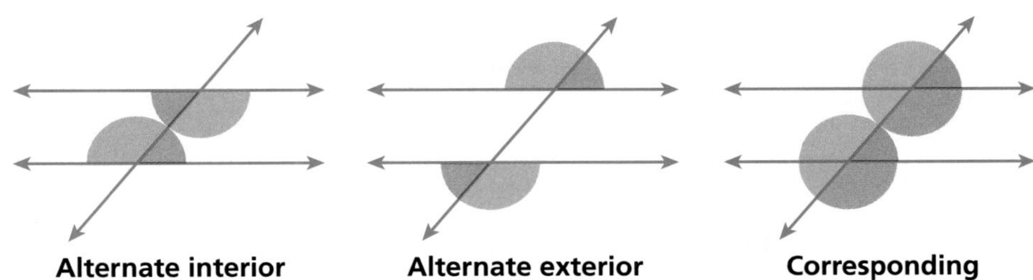

Think and Discuss

1. **Tell** how many different angles would be formed by a transversal intersecting three parallel lines. How many different angle measures would there be?
2. **Explain** how a transversal could intersect two other lines so that all of the acute angles formed are *not* congruent.

5-2 Exercises

FOR EXTRA PRACTICE
see page 740

GUIDED PRACTICE

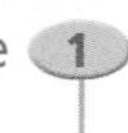

See Example 1

1. Measure the angles formed by the transversal and the parallel lines. Which angles seem to be congruent?

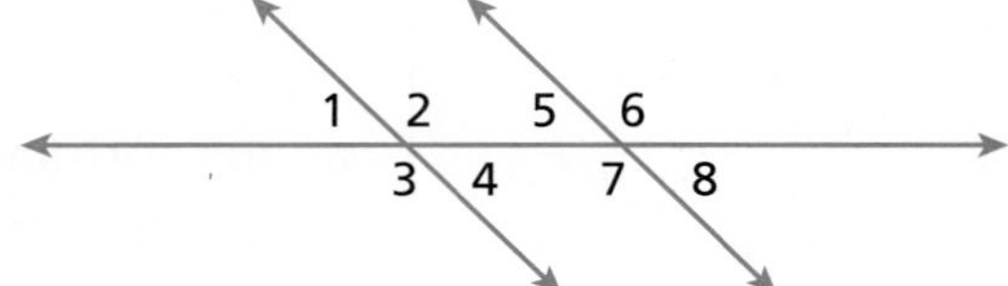

See Example 2

In the figure, line *m* || line *n*. Find the measure of each angle.

2. ∠1
3. ∠4
4. ∠6
5. ∠7

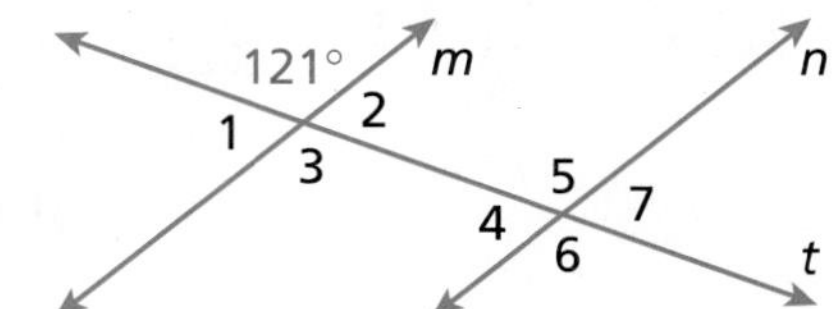

INDEPENDENT PRACTICE

See Example 1

6. Measure the angles formed by the transversal and the parallel lines. Which angles seem to be congruent?

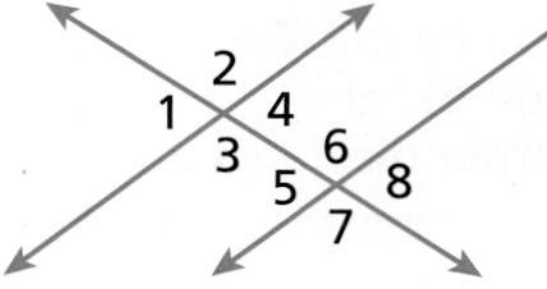

See Example 2

In the figure, line *p* || line *q*. Find the measure of each angle.

7. ∠1
8. ∠4
9. ∠6
10. ∠7

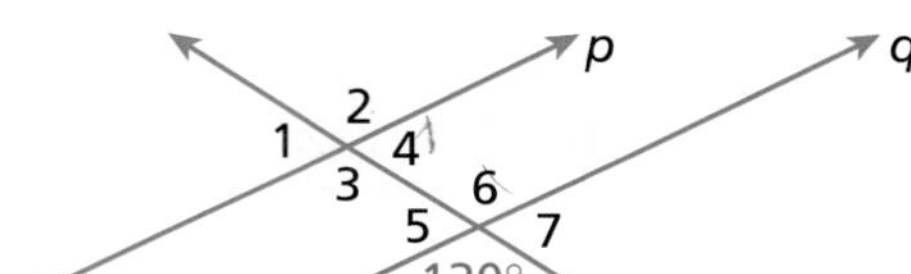

PRACTICE AND PROBLEM SOLVING

In the figure, line *t* || line *s*.

11. Name all angles congruent to ∠1.
12. Name all angles congruent to ∠2.
13. Name three pairs of supplementary angles.
14. Which line is the transversal?
15. If m∠4 is 129°, what is m∠2?
16. If m∠7 is 52°, what is m∠3?
17. If m∠5 is 90°, what is m∠2?

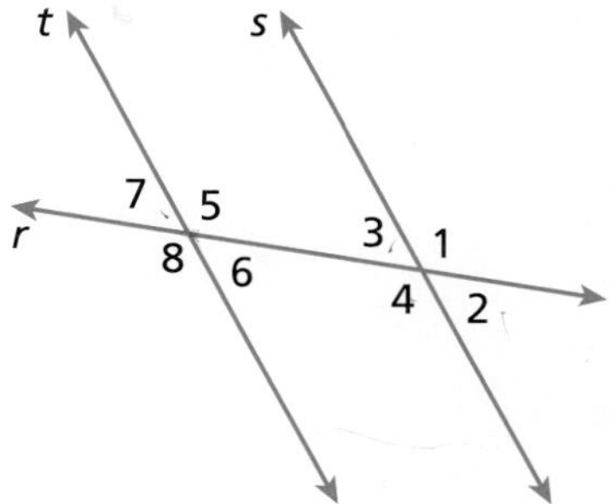

Draw a diagram to illustrate each of the following.

18. line *p* || line *q* || line *r* and line *s* transversal to lines *p*, *q*, and *r*
19. line *m* || line *n* and transversal *h* with congruent angles ∠1 and ∠3
20. line *h* || line *j* and transversal *k* with eight congruent angles

This hat from the 1937 British Industries Fair is equipped with a pair of parallel mirrors to enable the wearer to see above crowds.

21. ***PHYSICAL SCIENCE*** A periscope contains two parallel mirrors that face each other. With a periscope, a person in a submerged submarine can see above the surface of the water.

 a. Name the transversal in the diagram.

 b. If $m\angle 1 = 45°$, find $m\angle 2$, $m\angle 3$, and $m\angle 4$.

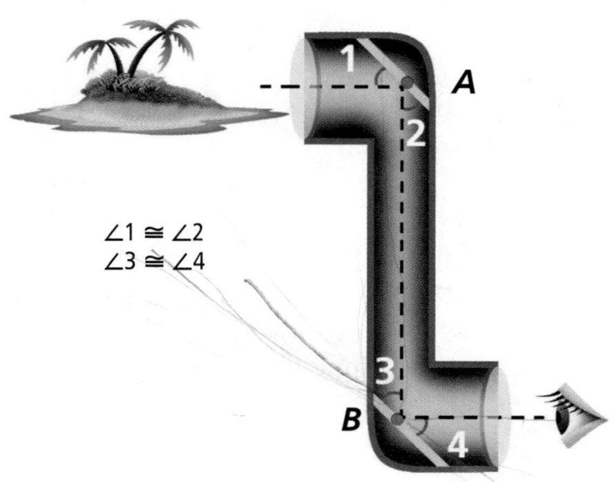

22. ***ART*** The corners of a picture frame are formed by two pieces of wood cut at 45° angles, as shown. Explain how a carpenter could use the guideline on the boards to be sure that both boards are cut at a 45° angle.

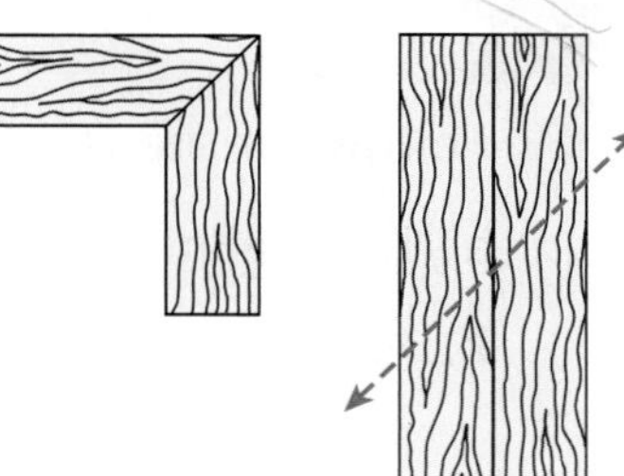

23. ***WHAT'S THE ERROR?*** Line a is parallel to line b. Line c is perpendicular to line b. Line c forms a 60° angle with line a. Why is this figure impossible to draw?

24. ***WRITE ABOUT IT*** Choose an example of abstract art or architecture with parallel lines. Explain how parallel lines, transversals, or perpendicular lines are used in the composition.

25. ***CHALLENGE*** In the figure, $\angle 1$, $\angle 4$, $\angle 6$, and $\angle 7$ are all congruent, and $\angle 2$, $\angle 3$, $\angle 5$, and $\angle 8$ are all congruent. Does this mean that line $s \parallel$ line t? Explain.

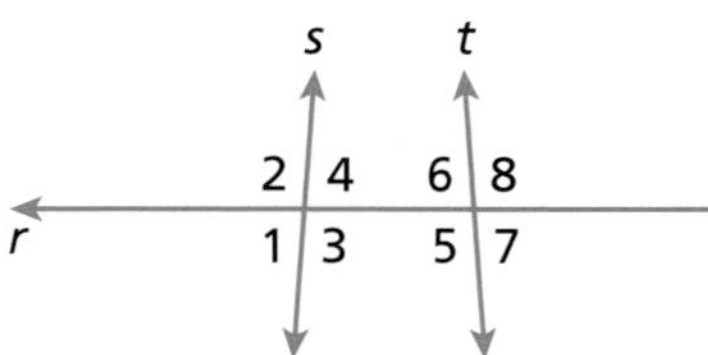

Spiral Review

Evaluate. (Lesson 2-8)

26. $\frac{3^9}{3^2}$ **27.** 2^5 **28.** $\frac{w^5}{w^1}$ **29.** $\frac{10^2}{10^{10}}$

30. 8^3 **31.** $2^3 \cdot 2^4$ **32.** $\frac{4^7}{4^5}$ **33.** $m^5 \cdot m^8$

Identify the population and sample. Give a reason why the sample could be biased. (Lesson 4-1)

34. In December, a store owner asks shoppers whether they are buying items for themselves or as gifts.

35. A market researcher pays a group of shoppers at a mall to fill out a questionnaire about products they are shown.

36. **TEST PREP** If $x + 5 = 16$, then $x - 7 =$ ▇ . (Lesson 1-3)

A 9 **B** 2 **C** 11 **D** 4

Advanced Constructions

Use with Lesson 5-2

internet connect
Lab Resources Online
go.hrw.com
KEYWORD: MP4 Lab5B

Copying an angle is an important step in the construction of parallel lines.

Activity

1 Follow the steps below to copy an angle.

a. Draw acute $\angle ABC$ on your paper. Draw $\overrightarrow{DE}$.

b. With your compass point on B, draw an arc through $\angle ABC$. With the same compass opening, place your compass point on D and draw an arc through $\overrightarrow{DE}$.

c. Adjust your compass to the width of the arc intersecting $\angle ABC$. Place your compass point on F and draw an arc that intersects the arc through $\overrightarrow{DE}$ at G. Draw $\overrightarrow{DG}$. Use your protractor to measure $\angle ABC$ and $\angle GDF$.

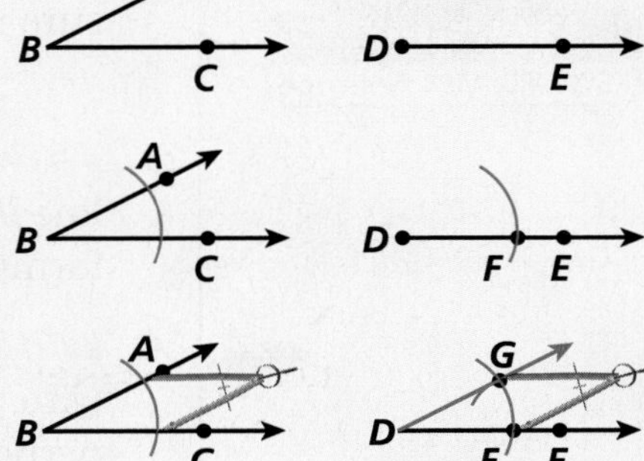

2 Follow the steps below to construct parallel lines.

1. Draw $\overleftrightarrow{QR}$ on your paper. Draw point S above or below $\overleftrightarrow{QR}$. Draw a line through point S that intersects $\overleftrightarrow{QR}$. Label the intersection T.

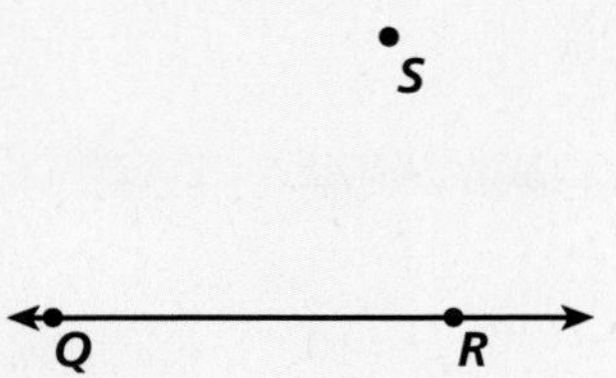

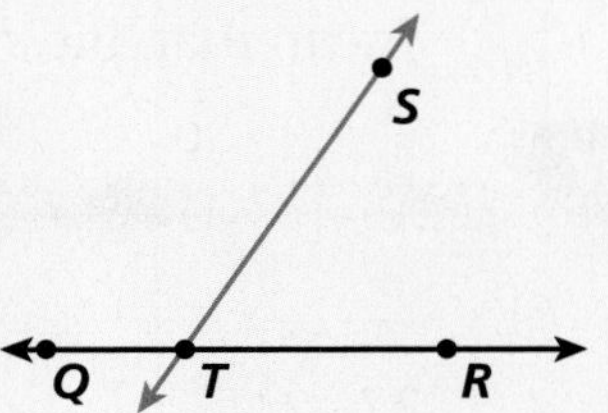

2. Make a copy of $\angle STR$ with its vertex at S using the method described in the first Activity. How do you know the lines are parallel?

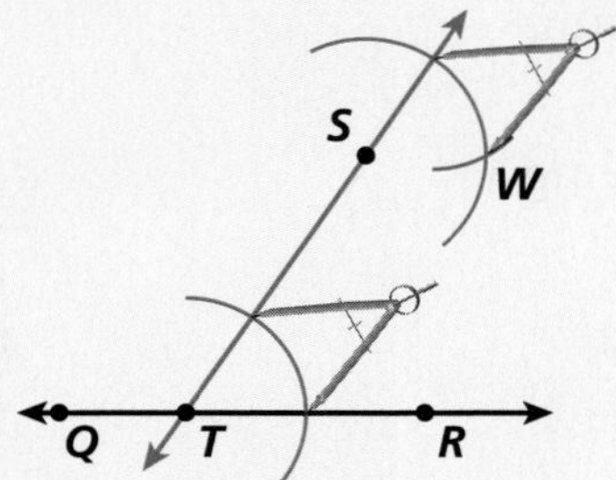

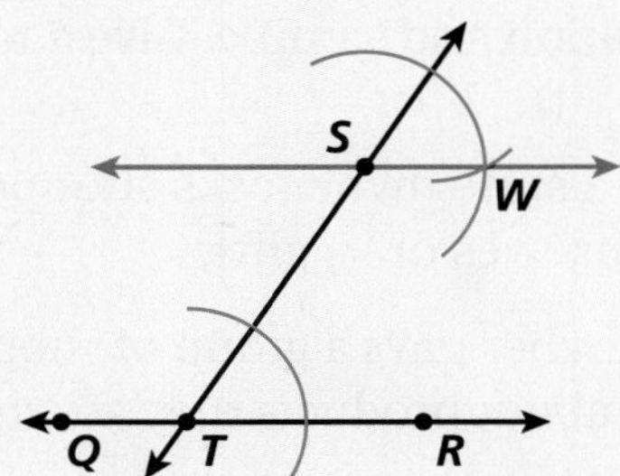

3 **Follow the steps below to construct perpendicular lines.**

a. Draw $\overleftrightarrow{MN}$ on your paper. Draw point P above or below $\overleftrightarrow{MN}$.

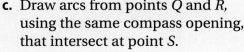

b. With your compass point at P, draw an arc intersecting $\overleftrightarrow{MN}$ at points Q and R.

c. Draw arcs from points Q and R, using the same compass opening, that intersect at point S.

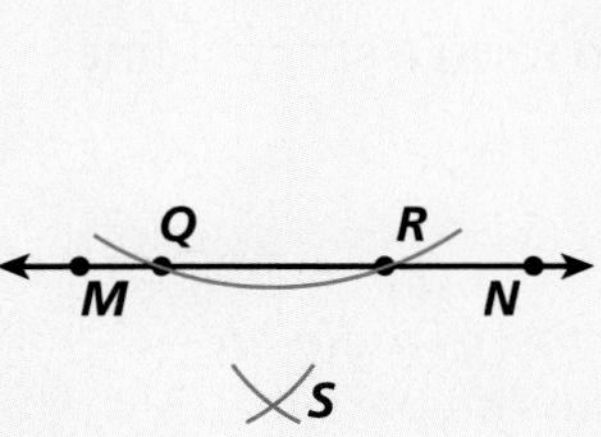

d. Draw $\overleftrightarrow{PS}$. What do you think is true about $\overleftrightarrow{MN}$ and $\overleftrightarrow{PS}$? Use a protractor to check your guess.

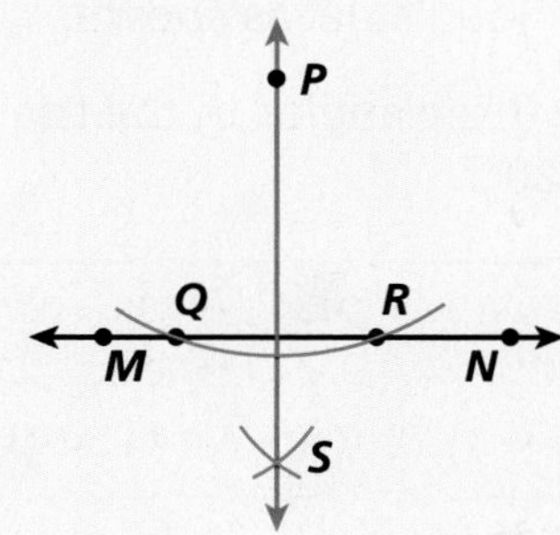

Think and Discuss

1. How many lines can be drawn that are perpendicular to a given line? Explain your answer.
2. Name three ways that you can determine if two lines are parallel.

Try This

Use a compass and a straightedge to construct each figure.

1. an angle congruent to $\angle LMN$

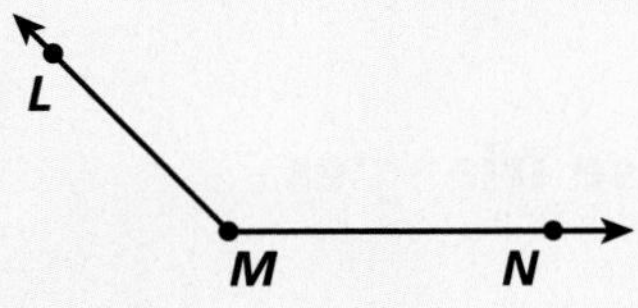

2. a line parallel to $\overleftrightarrow{ST}$

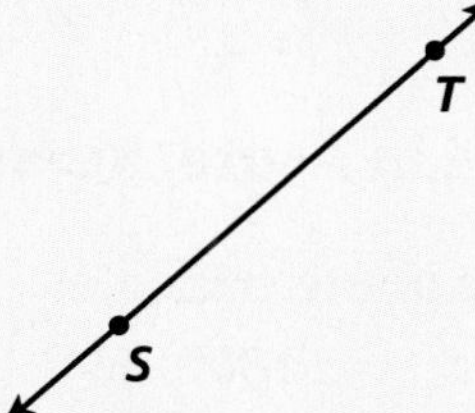
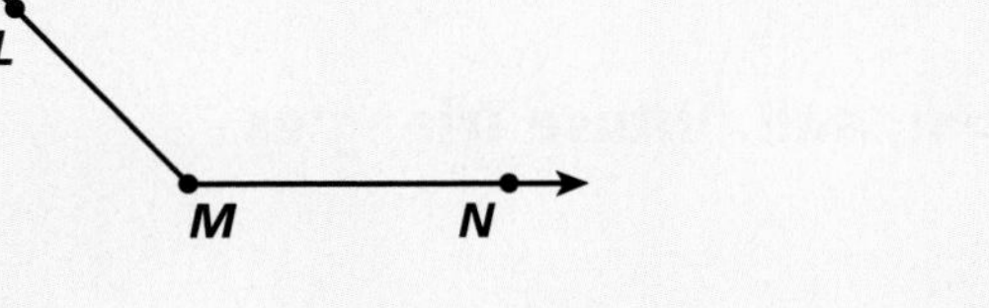

3. a line perpendicular to $\overleftrightarrow{GH}$

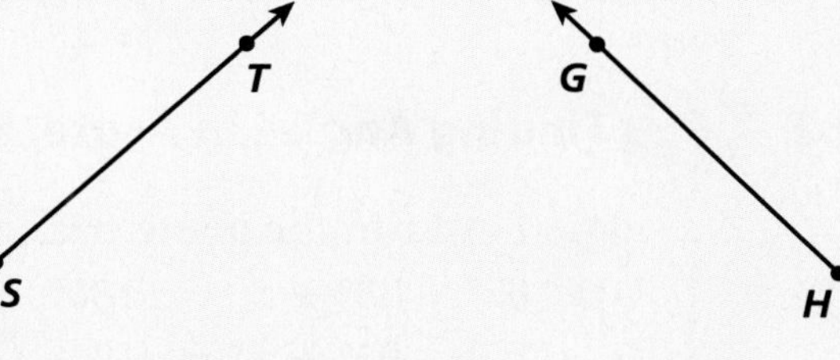

4. an angle congruent to $\angle DEF$

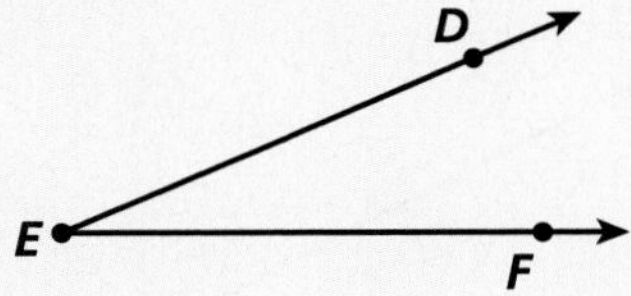

5. a line parallel to $\overleftrightarrow{AB}$

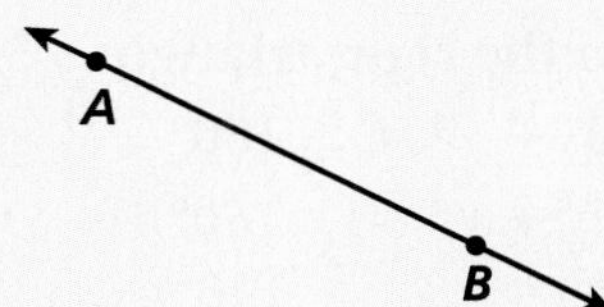

6. a line perpendicular to $\overleftrightarrow{CD}$

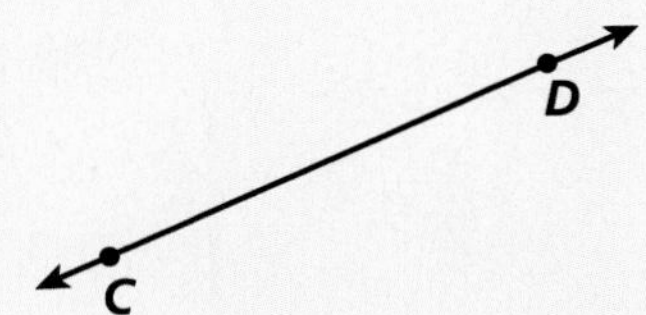

5-3 Triangles

Learn to find unknown angles in triangles.

Vocabulary

Triangle Sum Theorem

acute triangle

right triangle

obtuse triangle

equilateral triangle

isosceles triangle

scalene triangle

If you tear off two corners of a triangle and place them next to the third corner, the three angles seem to form a straight line.

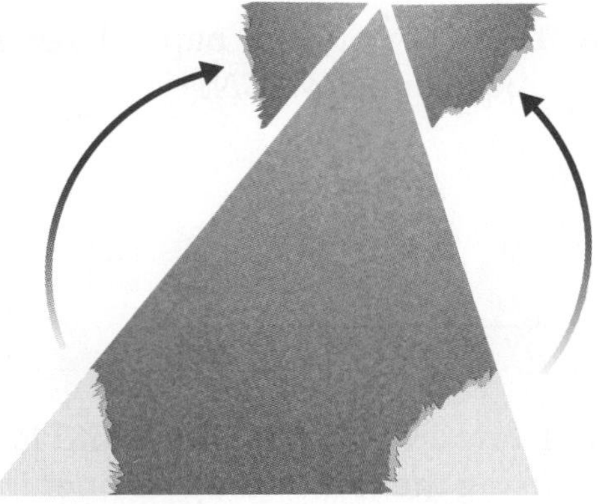

This torn triangle demonstrates an important geometry theorem called the Triangle Sum Theorem.

Draw a triangle and extend one side. Then draw a line parallel to the extended side, as shown.

The three angles in the triangle can be arranged to form a straight line, or 180°.

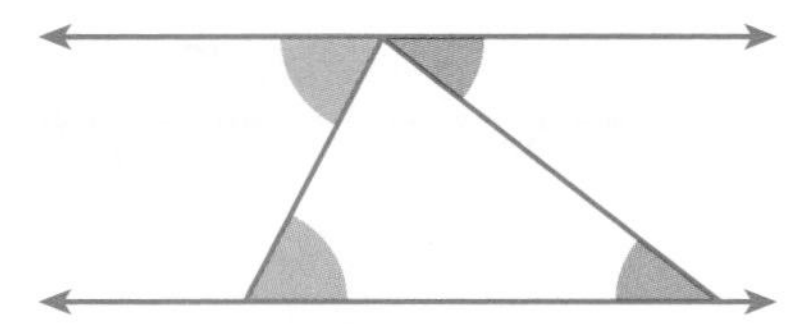

The sides of the triangle are transversals to the parallel lines.

TRIANGLE SUM THEOREM

Words	Numbers	Algebra
The angle measures of a triangle in a plane add to 180°.	43°, 58°, 79° $43° + 58° + 79° = 180°$	$r°$, $s°$, $t°$ $r° + s° + t° = 180°$

An **acute triangle** has 3 acute angles. A **right triangle** has 1 right angle. An **obtuse triangle** has 1 obtuse angle.

EXAMPLE 1 Finding Angles in Acute, Right, and Obtuse Triangles

A **Find x in the acute triangle.**

$$62° + 33° + x° = 180°$$
$$95° + x° = 180°$$
$$-95° \quad\quad -95°$$
$$x° = 85°$$

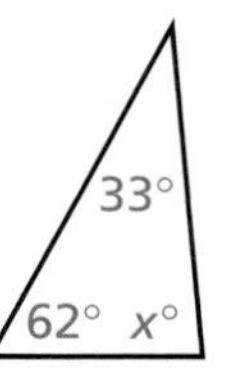

B **Find y in the right triangle.**

$$28° + 90° + y° = 180°$$
$$118° + y° = 180°$$
$$-118° \quad\quad -118°$$
$$y° = 62°$$

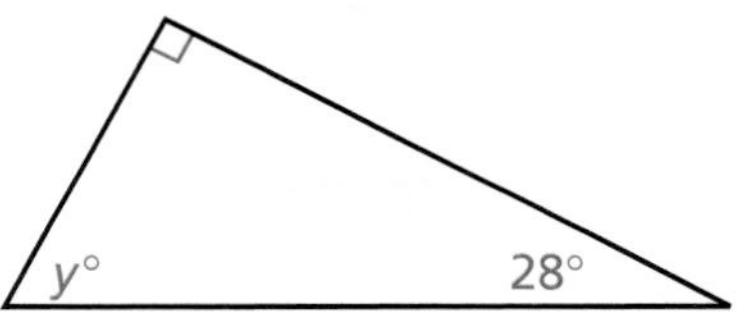

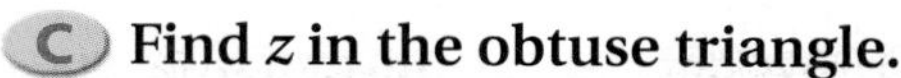

C **Find z in the obtuse triangle.**

$$14° + 51° + z° = 180°$$
$$65° + z° = 180°$$
$$\underline{-65°} \qquad \underline{-65°}$$
$$z° = 115°$$

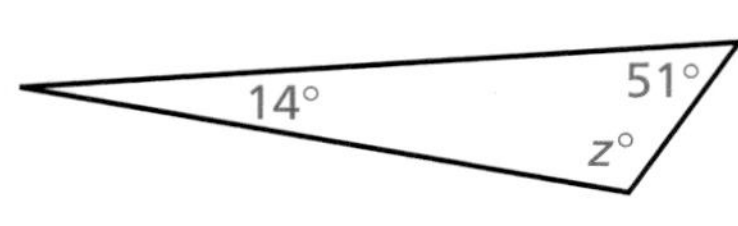

An **equilateral triangle** has 3 congruent sides and 3 congruent angles. An **isosceles triangle** has at least 2 congruent sides and 2 congruent angles. A **scalene triangle** has no congruent sides and no congruent angles.

EXAMPLE 2 Finding Angles in Equilateral, Isosceles, and Scalene Triangles

A **Find the angle measures in the equilateral triangle.**

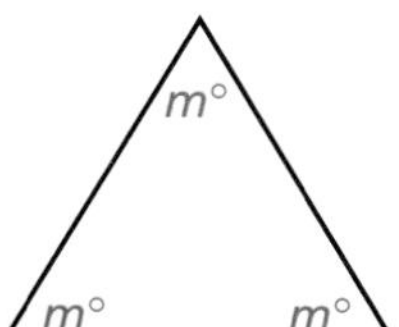

$3m° = 180°$ *Triangle Sum Theorem*

$$\frac{3m°}{3} = \frac{180°}{3}$$

$$m° = 60°$$

All three angles measure 60°.

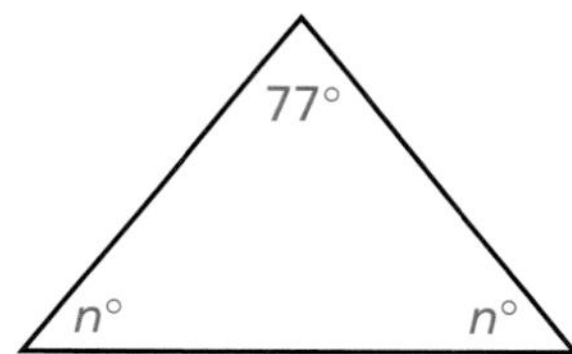

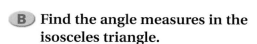

B **Find the angle measures in the isosceles triangle.**

$77° + n° + n° = 180°$ *Triangle Sum Theorem*

$77° + 2n° = 180°$ *Combine like terms.*

$\underline{-77°} \qquad \underline{-77°}$ *Subtract 77° from both sides.*

$2n° = 103°$

$\frac{2n°}{2} = \frac{103°}{2}$ *Divide both sides by 2.*

$n° = 51.5°$

The angles labeled $n°$ measure 51.5°.

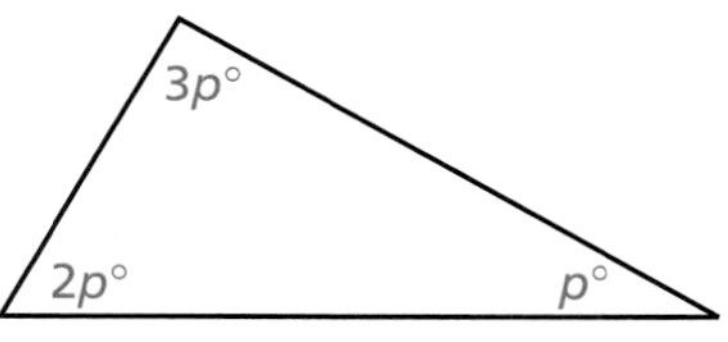

C **Find the angle measures in the scalene triangle.**

$p° + 2p° + 3p° = 180°$ *Triangle Sum Theorem*

$\frac{6p°}{6} = \frac{180°}{6}$ *Combine like terms.*

$p° = 30°$

The angle labeled $p°$ measures 30°, the angle labeled $2p°$ measures $2(30°) = 60°$, and the angle labeled $3p°$ measures $3(30°) = 90°$.

EXAMPLE 3 Finding Angles in a Triangle That Meets Given Conditions

The second angle in a triangle is twice as large as the first. The third angle is half as large as the second. Find the angle measures and draw a possible picture.

Let $x°$ = first angle measure. Then $2x°$ = second angle measure, and $\frac{1}{2}(2x)° = x°$ = third angle measure.

$x° + 2x° + x° = 180°$ *Triangle Sum Theorem*

$\frac{4x°}{4} = \frac{180°}{4}$ *Combine like terms.*

$x° = 45°$ *Divide both sides by 4.*

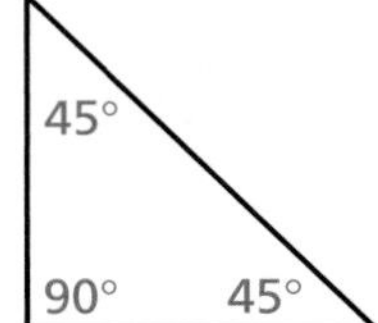

Two angles measure 45° and one angle measures 90°. The triangle has two congruent angles. The triangle is an isosceles right triangle.

Think and Discuss

1. Can a right triangle be equilateral? isosceles? scalene? Explain.

2. Can an isosceles triangle be acute? obtuse? Explain.

3. Can a triangle have 2 right angles? 2 obtuse angles? Explain.

5-3 Exercises

FOR EXTRA PRACTICE
see page 740

internet connect
Homework Help Online
go.hrw.com Keyword: MP4 5-3

GUIDED PRACTICE

See Example 1

1. Find q in the acute triangle.
2. Find r in the right triangle.
3. Find s in the obtuse triangle.

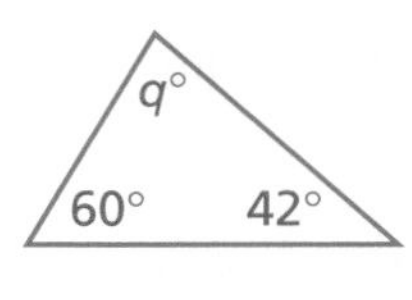

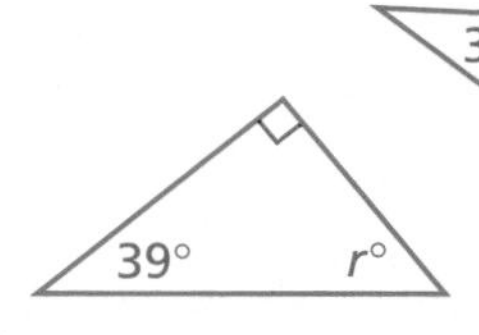

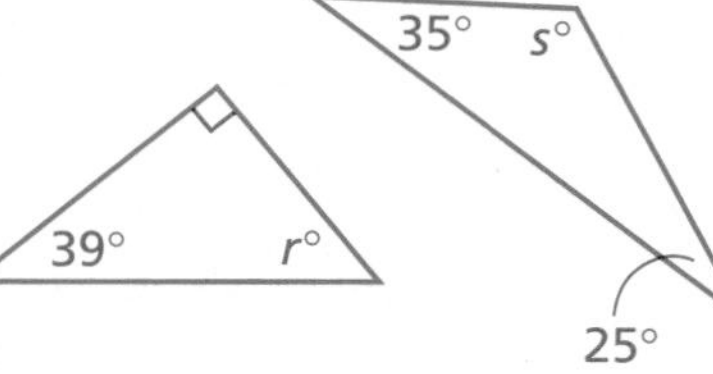

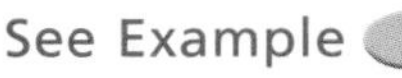

See Example 2

4. Find the angle measures in the equilateral triangle.
5. Find the angle measures in the isosceles triangle.
6. Find the angle measures in the scalene triangle.

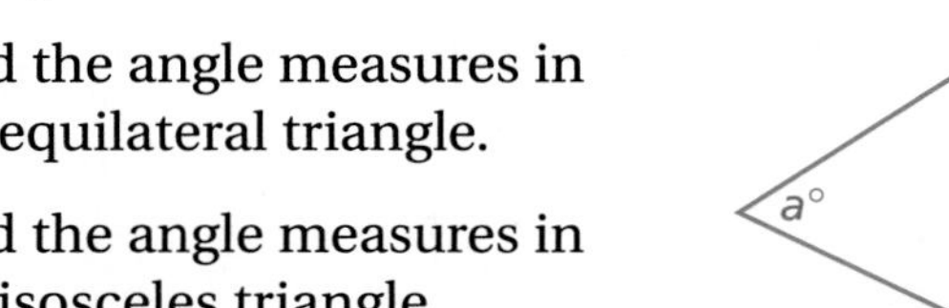

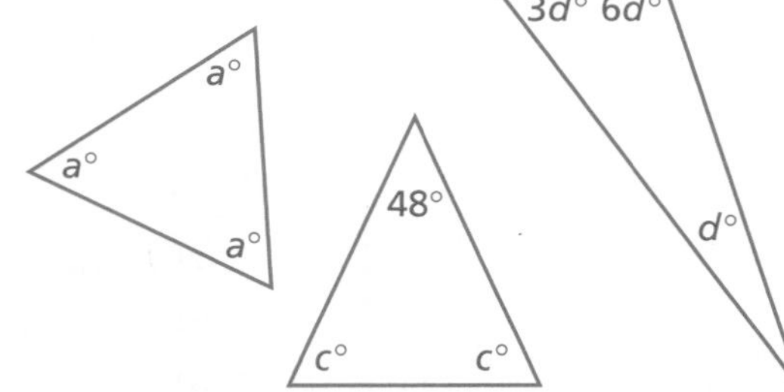

The sum of the angle measures of a polygon is given. Name the polygon.

25. 720° **26.** 360° **27.** 1980°

Graph the given vertices on a coordinate plane. Connect the points to draw a polygon and classify it by the number of its sides.

28. $A(1, 4), B(2, 3), C(4, 3), D(5, 4), E(4, 5), F(2, 5)$

29. $A(-2, 1), B(-2, -1), C(1, -2), D(3, 0), E(1, 2)$

30. $A(3, 3), B(5, 2), C(5, 1), D(3, -1), E(-2, -1), F(-3, 1), G(-3, 2), H(2, 3)$

Earth Science LINK

The master jeweler of Great Britain's crown jewels has thousands of diamonds in his care, including the world's two largest cut diamonds. The Imperial State Crown contains over 3000 precious stones, including 2800 diamonds.

Sketch a quadrilateral to fit each description. If no quadrilateral can be drawn, write *not possible.*

31. a parallelogram that is not a rectangle

32. a square that is not a rhombus

33. a quadrilateral that is not a trapezoid or a parallelogram

34. a rectangle that is not a square

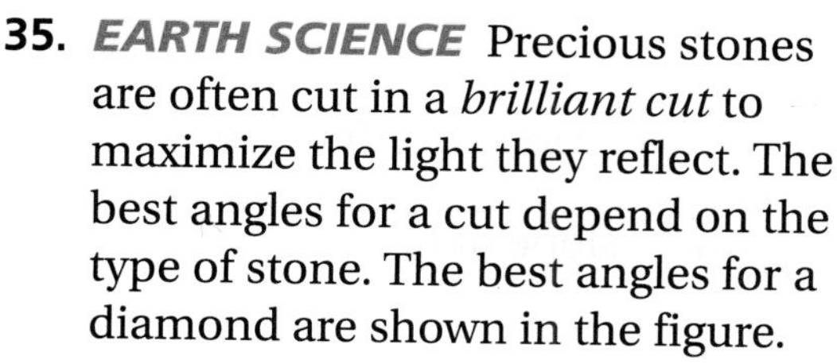

35. ***EARTH SCIENCE*** Precious stones are often cut in a *brilliant cut* to maximize the light they reflect. The best angles for a cut depend on the type of stone. The best angles for a diamond are shown in the figure.

a. Use the fact that the pavilion main angle is 41° to find x.

b. Use the fact that the crown angle is 35° to find y.

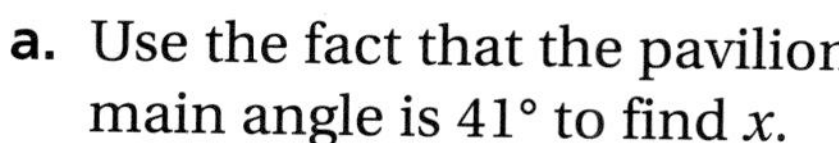

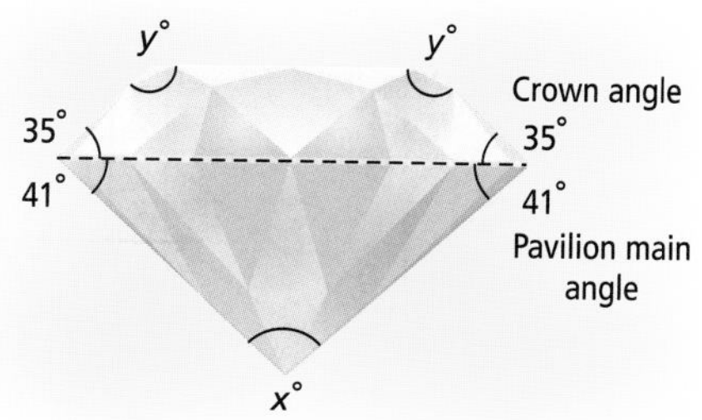

36. ***WHAT'S THE ERROR?*** A student said that all squares are rectangles, but not all squares are rhombuses. What was the error?

37. ***WRITE ABOUT IT*** Why is it possible to find the sum of the angle measures of an n-gon using the formula $(180n - 360)°$?

38. ***CHALLENGE*** Use properties of parallel lines to explain which angles in a parallelogram must be congruent.

Spiral Review

Write each number in scientific notation. (Lesson 2-9)

39. 0.00000064 **40.** 7,390,000,000 **41.** −0.0000016 **42.** −4,100,000

43. TEST PREP If the measure of one acute angle of a right triangle is 32°, then the measure of the other acute angle is ▇. (Lesson 5-3)

A 32° **B** 148° **C** 58° **D** 48°

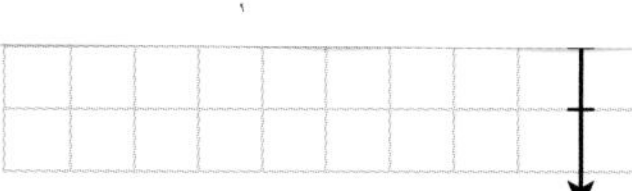

$\overleftrightarrow{JK} \parallel \overleftrightarrow{ML}$ and $\overleftrightarrow{MJ} \parallel \overleftrightarrow{LK}$
$\overleftrightarrow{JK} \perp \overleftrightarrow{LK}, \overleftrightarrow{JK} \perp \overleftrightarrow{MJ}$,
$\overleftrightarrow{ML} \perp \overleftrightarrow{LK}$ and $\overleftrightarrow{ML} \perp \overleftrightarrow{MJ}$
parallelogram, rectangle, square, rhombus

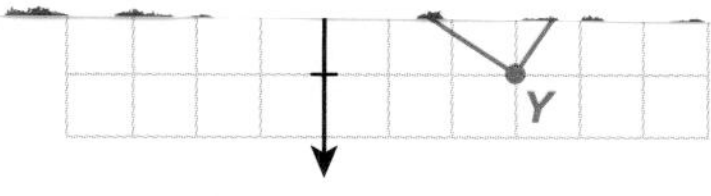

$\overleftrightarrow{WX} \parallel \overleftrightarrow{ZY}$ and $\overleftrightarrow{ZW} \parallel \overleftrightarrow{YX}$
$\overleftrightarrow{ZW} \perp \overleftrightarrow{WX}, \overleftrightarrow{ZW} \perp \overleftrightarrow{ZY}$,
$\overleftrightarrow{YX} \perp \overleftrightarrow{WX}$ and $\overleftrightarrow{YX} \perp \overleftrightarrow{ZY}$
parallelogram, rectangle

5-5 Coordinate Geometry

Learn to identify polygons in the coordinate plane.

In computer graphics, a coordinate system is used to create images, from simple geometric figures to realistic figures used in movies.

Graph the quadrilaterals with the given vertices. Give all of the names that apply to each quadrilateral.

C $E(-1, 6)$, $F(5, 6)$, $G(3, 4)$, $H(-3, 4)$

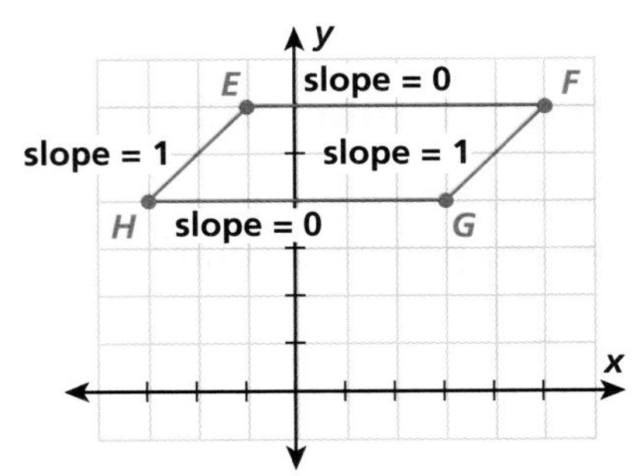

$\overleftrightarrow{EF} \parallel \overleftrightarrow{HG}$ and $\overleftrightarrow{HE} \parallel \overleftrightarrow{GF}$

parallelogram

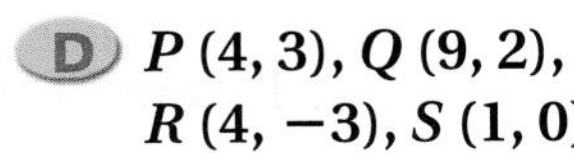

D $P(4, 3)$, $Q(9, 2)$, $R(4, -3)$, $S(1, 0)$

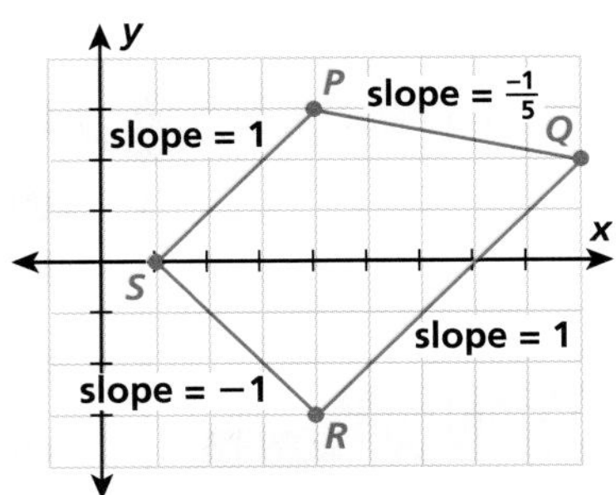

$\overleftrightarrow{SP} \parallel \overleftrightarrow{RQ}$

trapezoid

Think and Discuss

1. Explain why the slope of a horizontal line is 0.

2. Explain why the slope of a vertical line is undefined.

5-5 Exercises

FOR EXTRA PRACTICE
see page 740

GUIDED PRACTICE

See Example 1 **Determine if the slope of each line is positive, negative, 0, or undefined. Then find the slope of each line.**

1. $\overleftrightarrow{AD}$
2. $\overleftrightarrow{BE}$
3. $\overleftrightarrow{MN}$
4. $\overleftrightarrow{EF}$

See Example 2

5. Which lines are parallel?
6. Which lines are perpendicular?

See Example 3 **Graph the quadrilaterals with the given vertices. Give all of the names that apply to each quadrilateral.**

7. $D(-3, -2)$, $E(-3, 3)$, $F(2, 3)$, $G(2, -2)$
8. $R(3, -2)$, $S(3, 1)$, $T(-3, 5)$, $V(-3, -2)$

INDEPENDENT PRACTICE

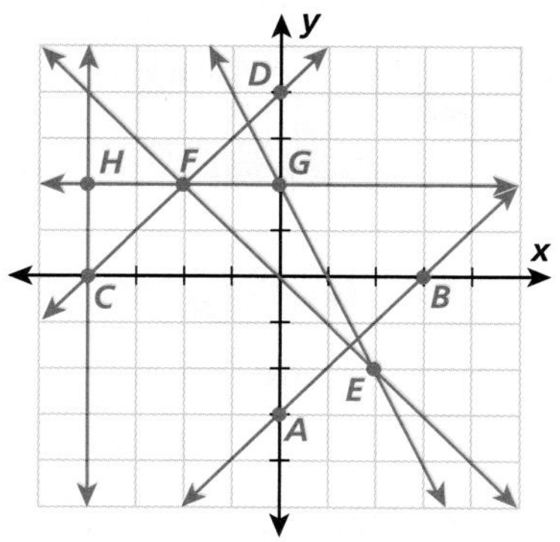

See Example 1

Determine if the slope of each line is positive, negative, 0, or undefined. Then find the slope of each line.

9. $\overleftrightarrow{AB}$ **10.** $\overleftrightarrow{EG}$

11. $\overleftrightarrow{HG}$ **12.** $\overleftrightarrow{CH}$

See Example 2

13. Which lines are parallel?

14. Which lines are perpendicular?

See Example 3

Graph the quadrilaterals with the given vertices. Give all of the names that apply to each quadrilateral.

15. $D(-3, 5)$, $E(3, 5)$, $F(3, -1)$, $G(-3, -1)$

16. $W(-2, 1)$, $X(-2, -2)$, $Y(4, 1)$, $Z(0, 2)$

PRACTICE AND PROBLEM SOLVING

Draw the line through the given points and find its slope.

17. $A(2, 1)$, $B(4, 7)$

18. $C(-2, 0)$, $D(-2, -5)$

19. $G(5, -4)$, $H(-2, -4)$

20. $E(-3, 1)$, $F(4, -2)$

21. On a coordinate grid draw a line s with slope 0 and a line t with slope 1. Then draw three lines through the intersection of lines s and t that have slopes between 0 and 1.

22. On a coordinate grid draw a line m with slope 0 and a line n with slope -1. Then draw three lines through the intersection of lines m and n that have slopes between 0 and -1.

23. ***WHAT'S THE ERROR?*** Points $P(3, 7)$, $Q(5, 2)$, $R(3, -3)$, and $S(1, 2)$ are vertices of a square. What is the error?

24. ***WRITE ABOUT IT*** Explain how using different points on a line to find the slope affects the answer.

25. ***CHALLENGE*** Use a square in a coordinate plane to explain why a line with slope 1 makes a 45° angle with the x-axis.

Spiral Review

The measures of two angles of a triangle are given. Find the measure of the third angle. (Lesson 5-3)

26. 45°, 45° **27.** 30°, 60° **28.** 21°, 82° **29.** 105°, 42°

30. **TEST PREP** Evaluate $[(4 \cdot 5) - 5] \div 2$. (Previous course)

A 2 **B** 5 **C** 7.5 **D** 0

Chapter 5

Mid-Chapter Quiz

LESSON 5-1 (pp. 222–226)

Refer to the figure.

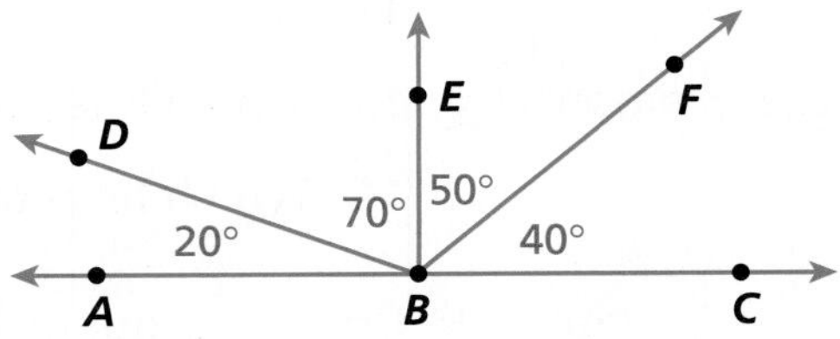

1. Name two pairs of complementary angles.
2. Name three pairs of supplementary angles.
3. Name two right angles.

LESSON 5-2 (pp. 228–231)

In the figure, line $m \parallel$ line n. Find the measure of each angle.

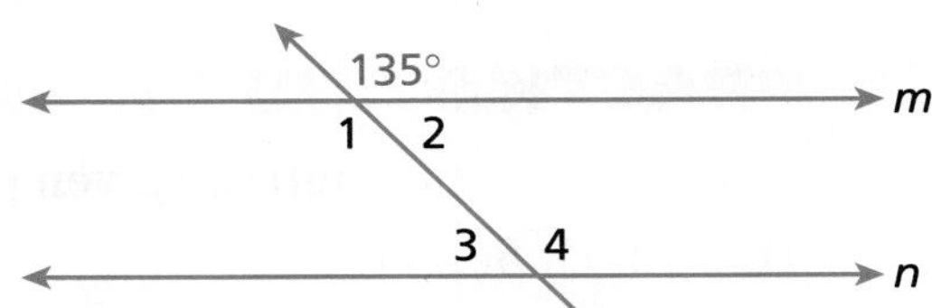

4. $\angle 1$
5. $\angle 2$
6. $\angle 3$
7. $\angle 4$

LESSON 5-3 (pp. 234–238)

Find x in each triangle.

8. 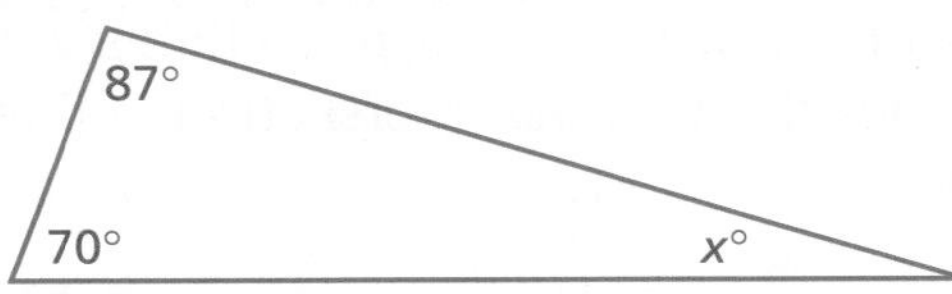

9. 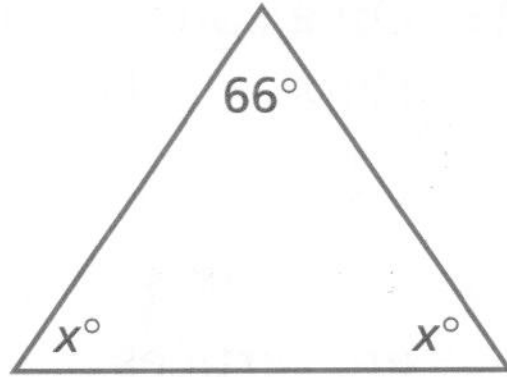

LESSON 5-4 (pp. 239–243)

Give all of the names that apply to each figure.

10. 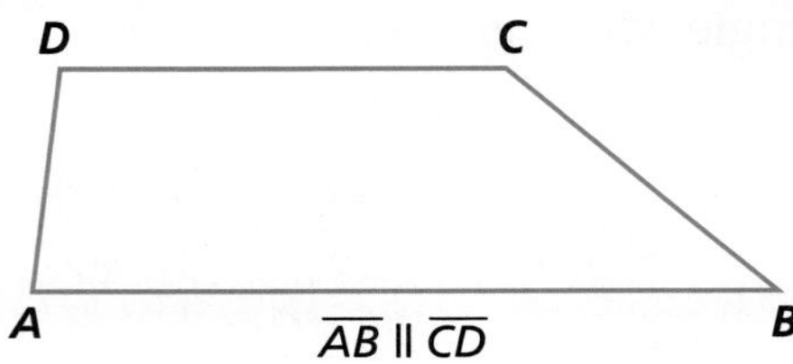

11. 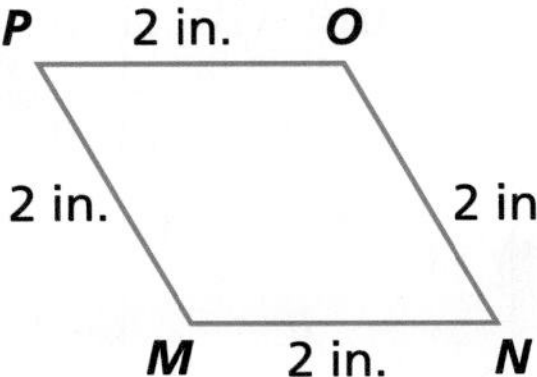

LESSON 5-5 (pp. 244–247)

Graph the quadrilaterals with the given vertices. Give all of the names that apply to each quadrilateral.

12. $A(-2, 1), B(3, 2), C(2, 0), D(-3, -1)$
13. $P(-4, 5), Q(3, 5), R(3, -2), S(-4, -2)$
14. $J(0, 2), K(4, 4), L(2, 1), M(0, 0)$
15. $U(4, 2), V(-2, 4), W(-3, 1), X(3, -1)$

internet connect
State-Specific Test Practice Online
go.hrw.com Keyword: MP4 TestPrep

Standardized Test Prep

Chapter 5

Cumulative Assessment, Chapters 1–5

1. Which of the following is $3.1415 \cdot 10^3$ written in standard notation?

(A) 31,415,000 (C) 3141.5
(B) 31,415 (D) 314.5

2. Which number is equivalent to 5^{-2}?

(F) $\frac{1}{10}$ (H) $\frac{1}{-10}$
(G) $\frac{1}{25}$ (J) $\frac{1}{-25}$

3. The cost of 3 sweatshirts is d dollars. At this rate, what is the cost in dollars of 30 sweatshirts?

(A) $30d$ (C) $10d$
(B) $\frac{10d}{3}$ (D) $\frac{30}{d}$

TEST TAKING TIP!

When a letter is used more than once in a statement, it always has the same value.

4. If $a \cdot k = a$ for all values of a, what is the value of k?

(F) $-a$ (H) 0
(G) -1 (J) 1

5. If $m^x \cdot m^7 = m^{28}$ and $\frac{m^y}{m^5} = m^3$ for all values of m, what is the value of $x + y$?

(A) 19 (C) 12
(B) 29 (D) 31

6. Laura wants to tile her kitchen floor. Which of the following shapes would **not** cover her floor with a tessellation?

(F) [square] (H) [parallelogram]
(G) [octagon] (J) [chevron]

7. The solution of $9x = -72$ is __?__.

(A) $x = 8$ (C) $x = -648$
(B) $x = 648$ (D) $x = -8$

8. In the histogram below, which interval contains the median score?

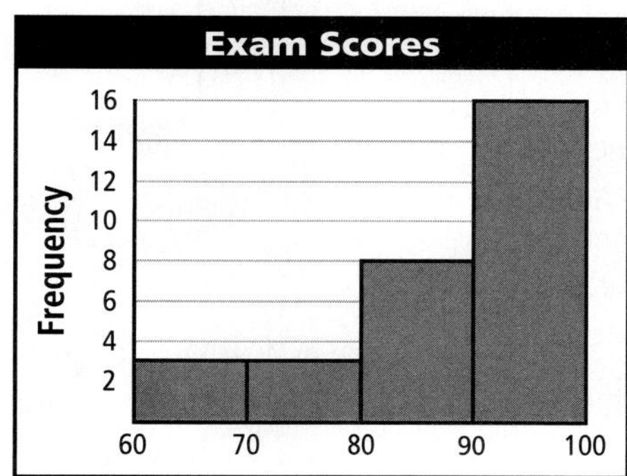

(F) 60–69 (H) 80–89
(G) 70–79 (J) 90–99

9. ***SHORT RESPONSE*** Triangle ABC, with vertices $A(2, 3)$, $B(4, -5)$, $C(6, 8)$, is reflected across the x-axis to triangle $A'B'C'$. On a coordinate grid, draw and label triangle ABC and triangle $A'B'C'$. Give the new coordinates for triangle $A'B'C'$.

10. ***SHORT RESPONSE*** Stephen bought 3 fish for his pond at a total cost of d dollars. At this rate what is the cost in dollars if he purchased 12 more fish? Show your work.

Standardized Test Prep

Chapter 6

Perimeter, Area, and Volume

TABLE OF CONTENTS

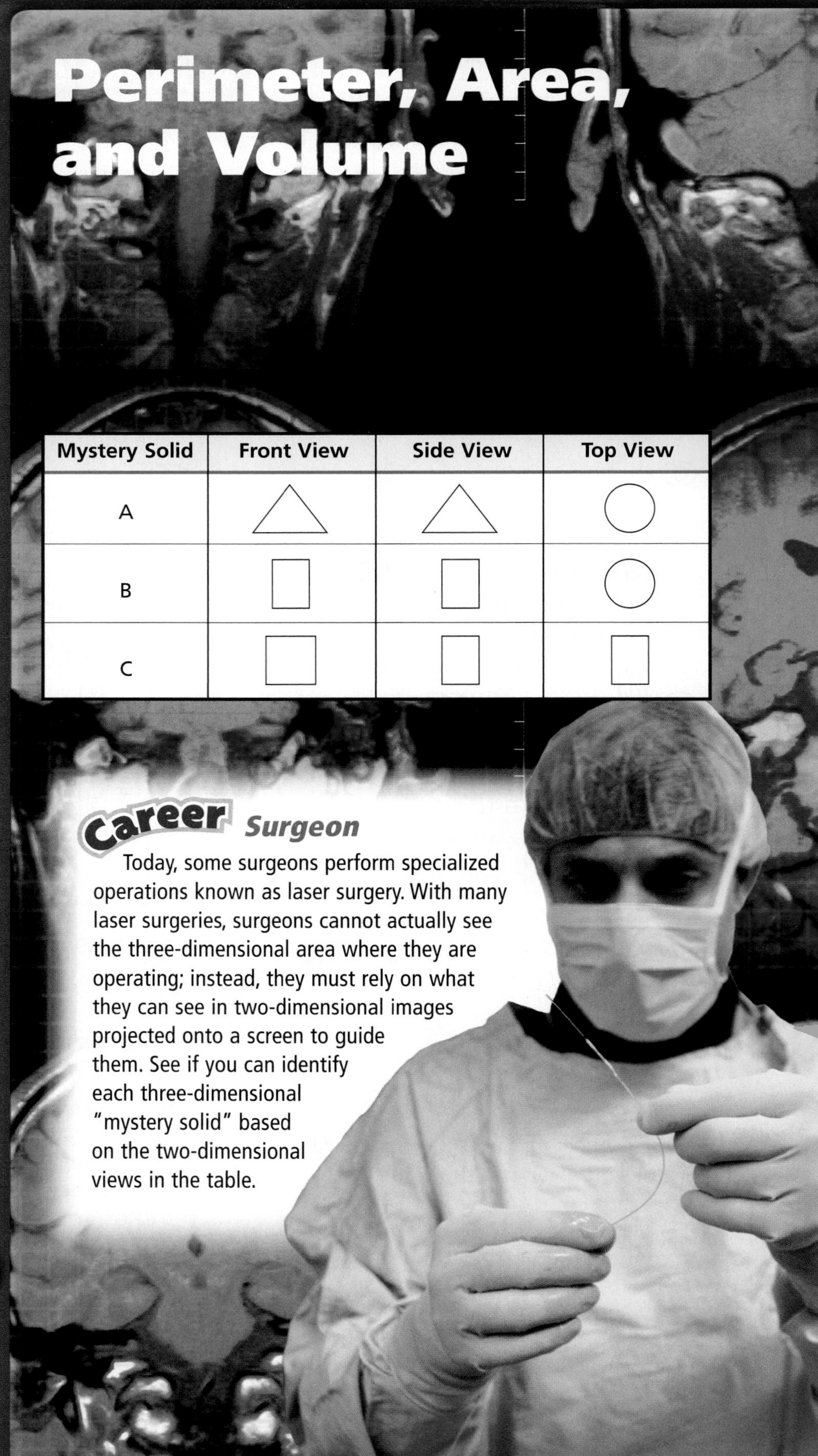

Mystery Solid	Front View	Side View	Top View
A	triangle	triangle	circle
B	rectangle	rectangle	circle
C	square	rectangle	rectangle

Career *Surgeon*

Today, some surgeons perform specialized operations known as laser surgery. With many laser surgeries, surgeons cannot actually see the three-dimensional area where they are operating; instead, they must rely on what they can see in two-dimensional images projected onto a screen to guide them. See if you can identify each three-dimensional "mystery solid" based on the two-dimensional views in the table.

internet connect

Chapter Opener Online
go.hrw.com
KEYWORD: MP4 Ch6

ARE YOU READY?

Choose the best term from the list to complete each sentence.

1. A(n) __?__ is a number that represents a part of a whole.
2. A(n) __?__ is another way of writing a fraction.
3. To multiply 7 by the fraction $\frac{2}{3}$, multiply 7 by the __?__ of the fraction and then divide the result by the __?__ of the fraction.
4. To round 7.836 to the nearest tenth, look at the digit in the __?__ place.

decimal
denominator
fraction
numerator
tenths
hundredths

Complete these exercises to review skills you will need for this chapter.

✔ Square and Cube Numbers

Evaluate.

5. 16^2 **6.** 9^3 **7.** $(4.1)^2$ **8.** $(0.5)^3$

9. $\left(\frac{1}{4}\right)^2$ **10.** $\left(\frac{2}{5}\right)^2$ **11.** $\left(\frac{1}{2}\right)^3$ **12.** $\left(\frac{2}{3}\right)^3$

✔ Multiply with Fractions

Multiply.

13. $\frac{1}{2}(8)(10)$ **14.** $\frac{1}{2}(3)(5)$ **15.** $\frac{1}{3}(9)(12)$ **16.** $\frac{1}{3}(4)(11)$

17. $\frac{1}{2}(8^2)16$ **18.** $\frac{1}{2}(5^2)24$ **19.** $\frac{1}{2}(6)(3 + 9)$ **20.** $\frac{1}{2}(5)(7 + 4)$

✔ Multiply with Decimals

Multiply. Write each answer to the nearest tenth.

21. $2(3.14)(12)$ **22.** $3.14(5^2)$ **23.** $3.14(4^2)(7)$ **24.** $3.14(2.3)^2(5)$

✔ Multiply with Fractions and Decimals

Multiply. Write each answer to the nearest tenth.

25. $\frac{1}{3}(3.14)(5^2)(7)$ **26.** $\frac{1}{3}\left(3.14\right)(5^3)$

27. $\frac{1}{3}(3.14)(3.2)^2(2)$ **28.** $\frac{4}{3}(3.14)(2.7)^3$

29. $\frac{1}{5}\left(\frac{22}{7}\right)(4^2)(5)$ **30.** $\frac{4}{11}\left(\frac{22}{7}\right)(3.2^3)$

31. $\frac{1}{2}\left(\frac{22}{7}\right)(1.7)^2(4)$ **32.** $\frac{7}{11}\left(\frac{22}{7}\right)(9.5)^3$

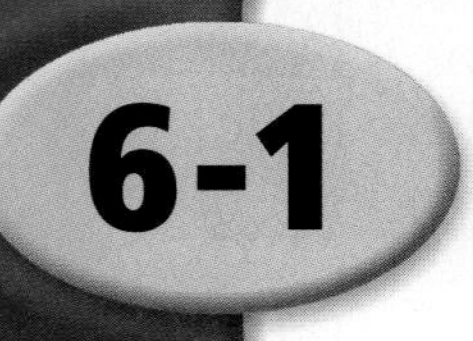

6-1 Perimeter & Area of Rectangles & Parallelograms

Learn to find the perimeter and area of rectangles and parallelograms.

Vocabulary

perimeter

area

In inlaid woodworking, artists use geometry to create a variety of beautiful patterns. One design can have thousands of pieces made from many different kinds of wood. In a design made entirely of parallelograms, the total area of the design is the sum of the areas of the parallelograms in the design.

Any side of a rectangle or parallelogram can be chosen as the base. The height is measured along a line perpendicular to the base.

Rectangle

Parallelogram

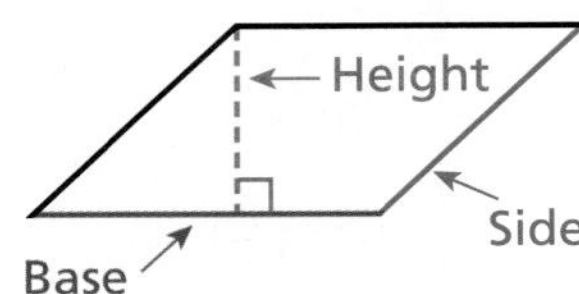

Perimeter is the distance around the outside of a figure. To find the perimeter of a figure, add the lengths of all its sides.

EXAMPLE 1 **Finding the Perimeter of Rectangles and Parallelograms**

Find the perimeter of each figure.

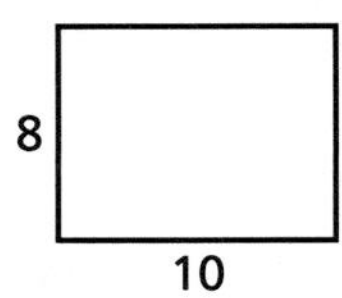

$P = 10 + 10 + 8 + 8$ *Add all side lengths.*

$= 36$ units

or $P = 2b + 2h$ *Perimeter of rectangle*

$= 2(10) + 2(8)$ *Substitute 10 for b and 8 for h.*

$= 20 + 16 = 36$ units

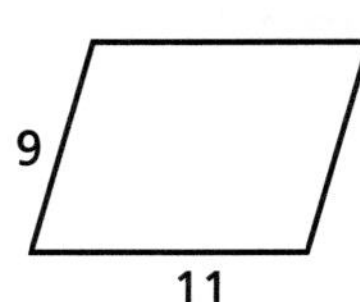

$P = 9 + 9 + 11 + 11$ *Add all side lengths.*

$= 40$ units

Helpful Hint

The formula for the perimeter of a rectangle can be written as $P = 2b + 2h$, where b is the length of the base and h is the height.

Area is the number of square units in a figure. A parallelogram can be cut and the cut piece shifted to form a rectangle with the same base length and height as the original parallelogram. So a parallelogram has the same area as a rectangle with the same base length and height.

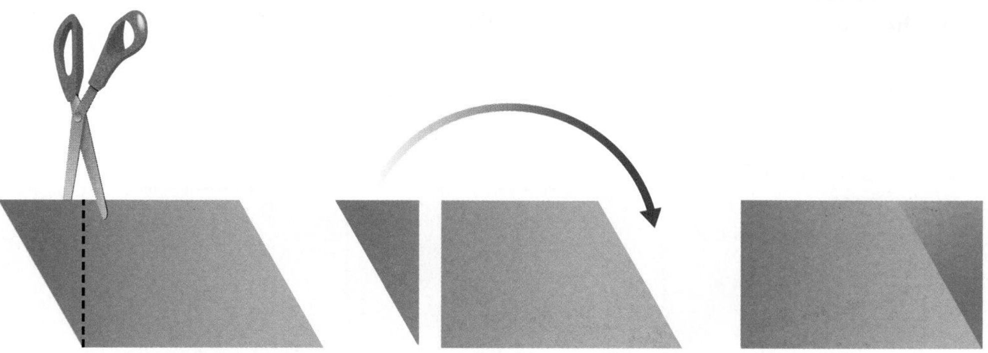

AREA OF RECTANGLES AND PARALLELOGRAMS

Words	Numbers		Formula
The area A of a rectangle or parallelogram is the base length b times the height h.	5, 3; $5 \cdot 3 = 15$ units^2 **Rectangle**	5, 3; $5 \cdot 3 = 15$ units^2 **Parallelogram**	$A = bh$

EXAMPLE 2 Using a Graph to Find Area

Graph each figure with the given vertices. Then find the area of each figure.

A $(-2, -1), (2, -1), (2, 2), (-2, 2)$

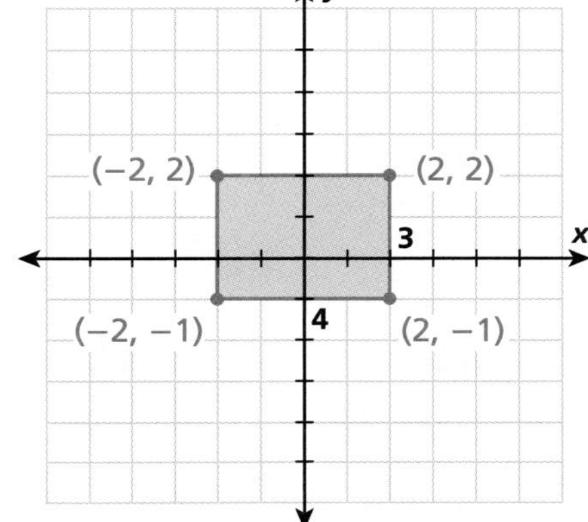

$A = bh$ *Area of rectangle*

$= 4 \cdot 3$ *Substitute 4 for b and 3 for h.*

$= 12$ units^2

Graph each figure with the given vertices. Then find the area of the figure.

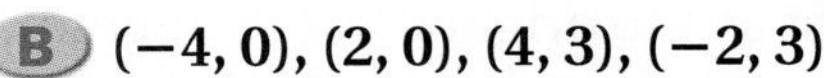

B $(-4, 0), (2, 0), (4, 3), (-2, 3)$

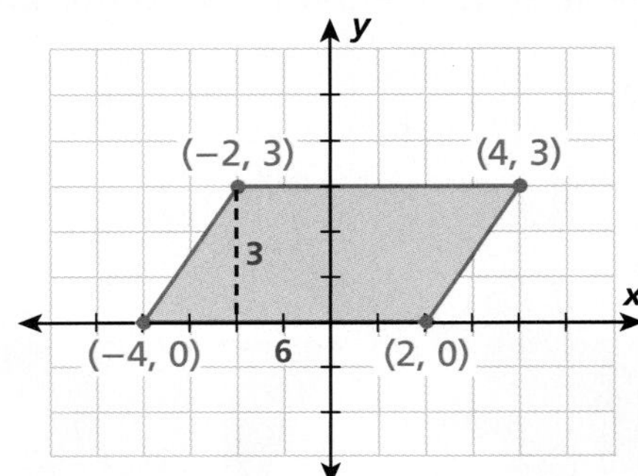

Helpful Hint

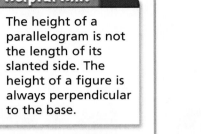

The height of a parallelogram is not the length of its slanted side. The height of a figure is always perpendicular to the base.

$A = bh$ — *Area of parallelogram*

$= 6 \cdot 3$ — *Substitute 6 for b and 3 for h.*

$= 18 \text{ units}^2$

EXAMPLE 3 Finding Area and Perimeter of a Composite Figure

Find the perimeter and area of the figure.

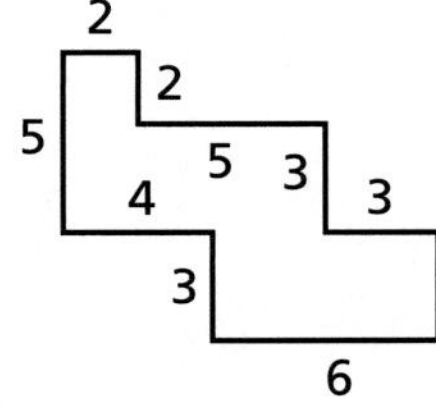

The length of the side that is not labeled is the same as the length of the opposite side, 3 units.

$P = 5 + 2 + 2 + 5 + 3 + 3 + 3 + 6 + 3 + 4$

$= 36 \text{ units}$

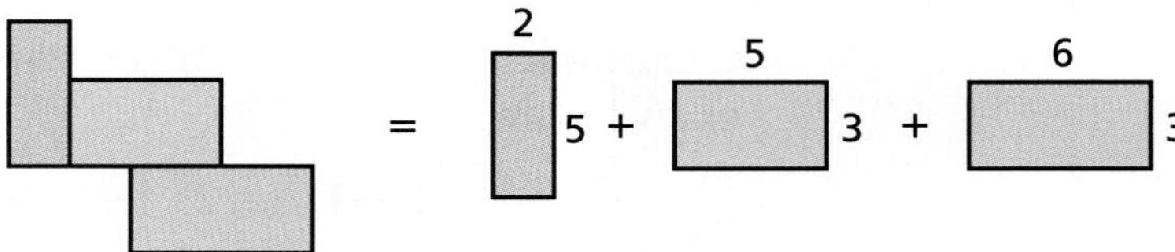

$A = 5 \cdot 2 + 5 \cdot 3 + 6 \cdot 3$ — *Add the areas together.*

$= 10 + 15 + 18$

$= 43 \text{ units}^2$

Think and Discuss

1. **Compare** the area of a rectangle with base b and height h with the area of a rectangle with base $2b$ and height $2h$.
2. **Express** the formulas for the area and perimeter of a square using s for the length of a side.

6-1 Exercises

FOR EXTRA PRACTICE
see page 742

internet connect
Homework Help Online
go.hrw.com Keyword: MP4 6-1

GUIDED PRACTICE

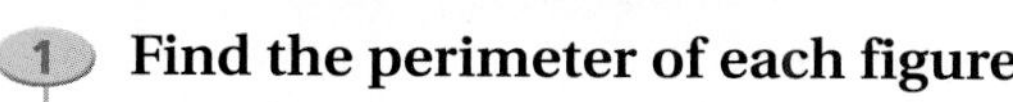

See Example 1 **Find the perimeter of each figure.**

1.

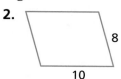

2.

8
10

3.

3.2x
6.5x

See Example 2 **Graph each figure with the given vertices. Then find the area of each figure.**

4. (−3, 2), (0, 2), (3, −3), (0, −3)

5. (−4, 0), (−4, 4), (3, 4), (3, 0)

6. (−4, 1), (4, 1), (3, −3), (−5, −3)

7. (−2, 3), (0, 3), (0, −4), (−2, −4)

See Example 3 **8.** Find the perimeter and area of the figure.

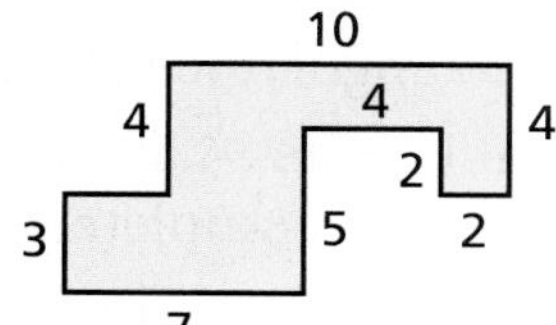

INDEPENDENT PRACTICE

See Example 1 **Find the perimeter of each figure.**

9.

10.

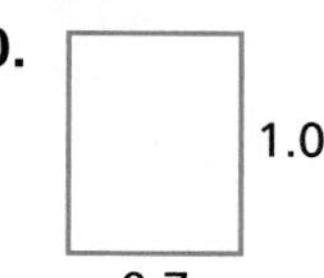

11.

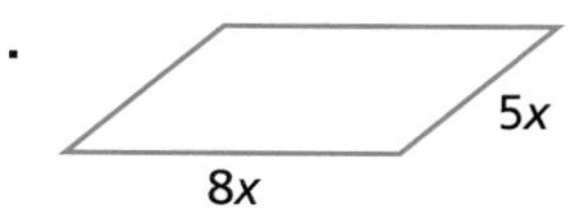

See Example 2 **Graph each figure with the given vertices. Then find the area of each figure.**

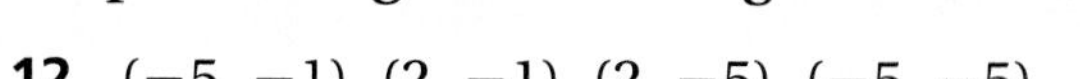

12. (−5, −1), (2, −1), (2, −5), (−5, −5)

13. (0, 3), (6, 3), (3, −1), (−3, −1)

14. (3, 5), (5, 3), (−3, 3), (−5, 5)

15. (2, 5), (5, 5), (5, −1), (2, −1)

See Example 3 **16.** Find the perimeter and area of the figure.

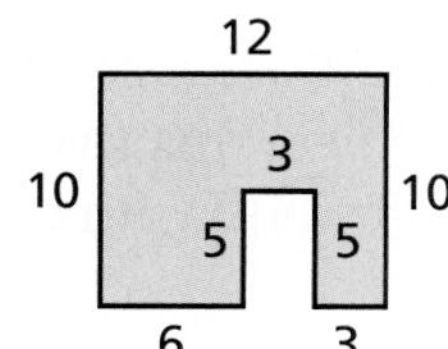

PRACTICE AND PROBLEM SOLVING

Find the perimeter of each figure.

17.

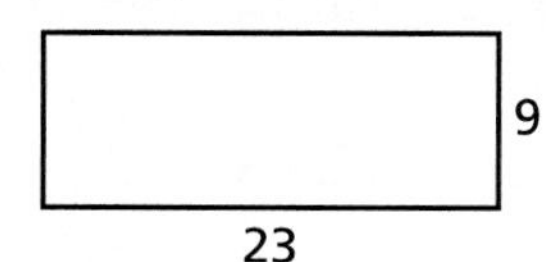

18.

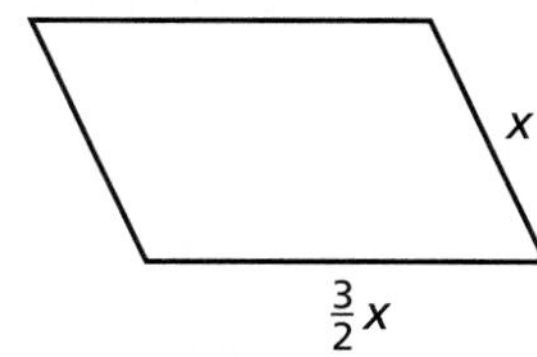

Find the perimeter and area of each figure.

19.

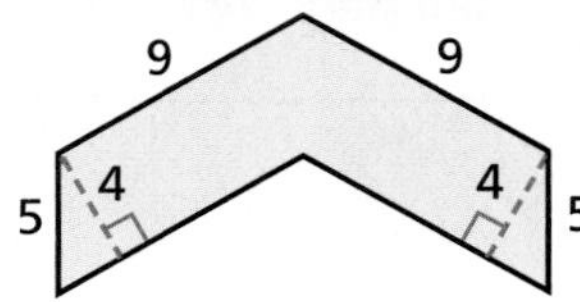

20.

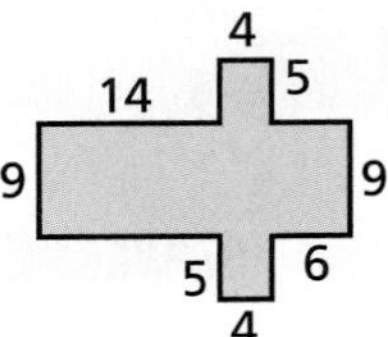

21. Find the perimeter and area of the figure with vertices $A(-8, 5)$, $B(-4, 5)$, $C(-4, 2)$, $D(3, 2)$, $E(3, -2)$, $F(6, -2)$, $G(6, -4)$, $H(-8, -4)$.

22. If the area of a parallelogram is 52.7 cm^2 and the height is 6.2 cm, what is the length of the base?

23. Find the height of a rectangle with perimeter 114 in. and base length 24 in. What is the area?

24. Find the height of a rectangle with area 143 cm^2 and base length 11 cm. What is the perimeter?

25. A rectangular ice-skating rink measures 50 ft by 75 ft.

a. If it costs $4.50 per foot to build a railing, how much would it cost to completely enclose the rink with a railing?

b. If the skating rink allows one person for every 10 ft^2 of ice, how many people are allowed in the rink at one time?

26. ***SOCIAL STUDIES*** The state of Tennessee is shaped approximately like a parallelogram. Estimate the area of the state.

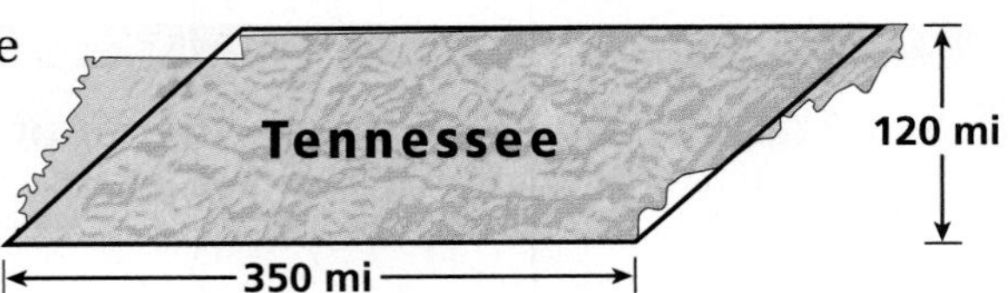

27. ***WHAT'S THE QUESTION?*** A rectangle has base 4 mm and height 3.7 mm. If the answer is 14.8 mm^2, what is the question?

28. ***WRITE ABOUT IT*** A rectangle and an identical rectangle with a smaller rectangle cut from the bottom and placed on top are shown. Do the two figures have the same area? Do they have the same perimeter? Explain.

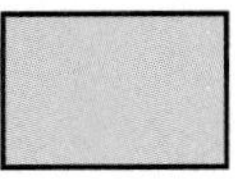

29. ***CHALLENGE*** A ruler is 12 in. long by 1 in. wide. How many rulers this size can be cut from a 72 in^2 rectangular piece of wood with base length 15 in.?

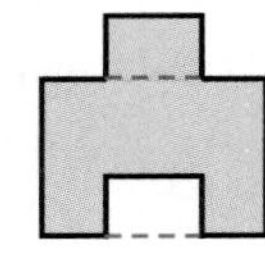

Spiral Review

Solve and graph. (Lesson 2-5)

30. $\frac{2}{3}n \leq 4$ **31.** $y + 4 < 2$ **32.** $-4x \geq 16$ **33.** $w - 5 > -2$

34. **TEST PREP** Estimate $\sqrt{46}$ to two decimal places. (Lesson 3-9)

A 7.12 **B** 6.78 **C** 6.05 **D** 5.98

6-2 Perimeter and Area of Triangles and Trapezoids

Learn to find the area of triangles and trapezoids.

The figures show a *fractal* called the Koch snowflake. It is constructed by first drawing an equilateral triangle. Then triangles with sides one-third the length of the original sides are added to the middle of each side. The second step is then repeated over and over again.

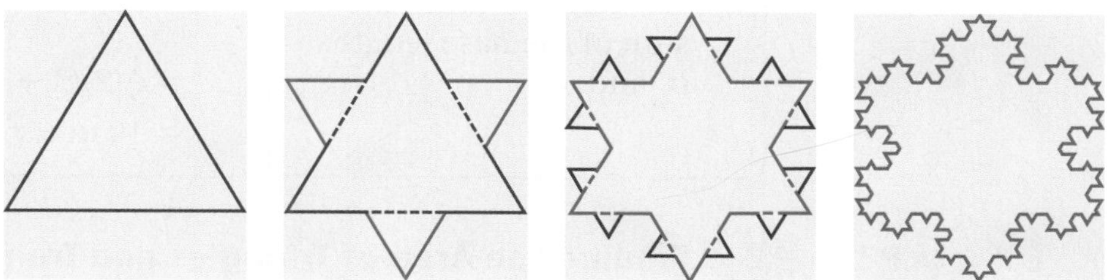

The area and perimeter of each figure is larger than that of the one before it. However, the area of any figure is never greater than the area of the shaded box, while the perimeters increase without bound. To find the area and perimeter of each figure, you must be able to find the area of a triangle.

EXAMPLE 1 Finding the Perimeter of Triangles and Trapezoids

Find the perimeter of each figure.

A

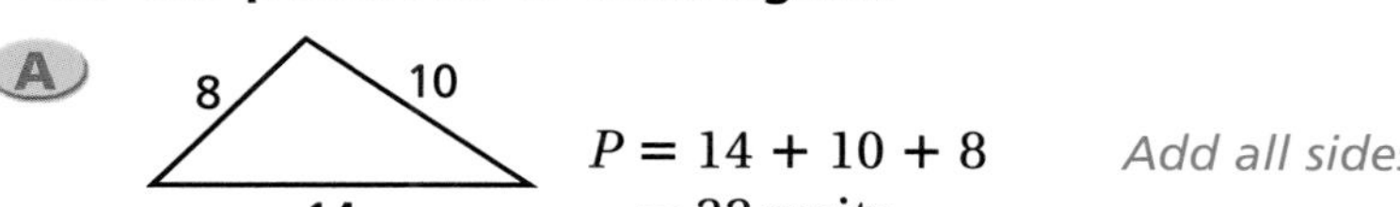

$P = 14 + 10 + 8$ *Add all sides.*
$= 32$ units

B

7
4
2
11

$P = 7 + 11 + 2 + 4$ *Add all sides.*
$= 24$ units

A triangle or a trapezoid can be thought of as half of a parallelogram.

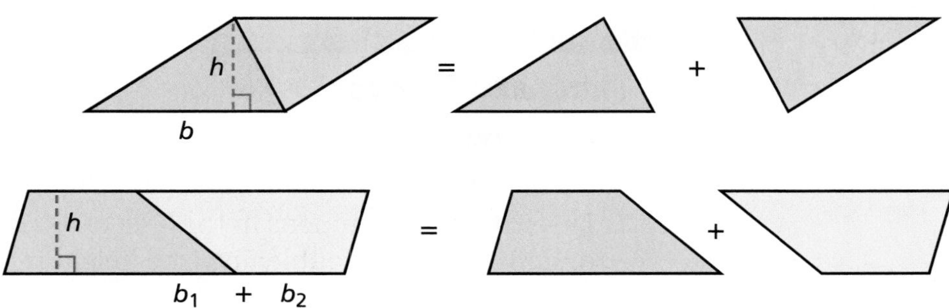

AREA OF TRIANGLES AND TRAPEZOIDS

Words	Numbers	Formula
Triangle: The area A of a triangle is one-half of the base length b times the height h.	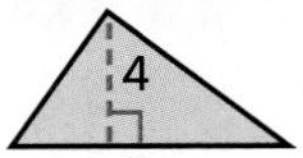 $A = \frac{1}{2}(8)(4)$ $= 16 \text{ units}^2$	$A = \frac{1}{2}bh$
Trapezoid: The area of a trapezoid is one-half the height h times the sum of the base lengths b_1 and b_2.	 $A = \frac{1}{2}(2)(3 + 7)$ $= 10 \text{ units}^2$	$A = \frac{1}{2}h(b_1 + b_2)$

Reading Math

In the term b_1, the number 1 is called a *subscript*.
It is read as "*b* one" or "*b* sub-one."

EXAMPLE 2 **Finding the Area of Triangles and Trapezoids**

Graph and find the area of each figure with the given vertices.

A $(-1, 1), (3, 1), (1, 5)$

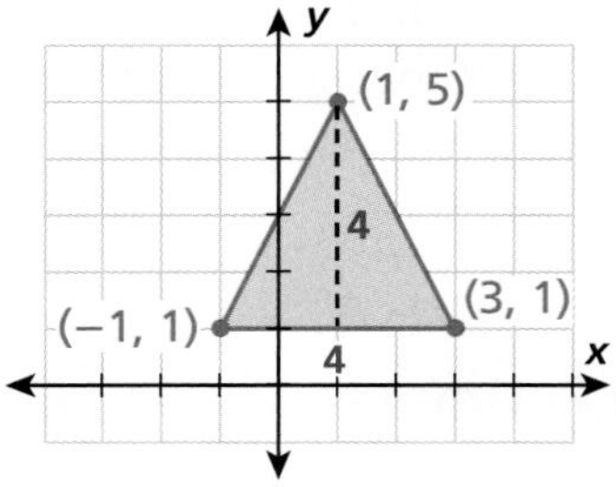

$A = \frac{1}{2}bh$ *Area of a triangle*

$= \frac{1}{2} \cdot 4 \cdot 4$ *Substitute for b and h.*

$= 8 \text{ units}^2$

B $(-3, -2), (-3, 1), (0, 1), (2, -2)$

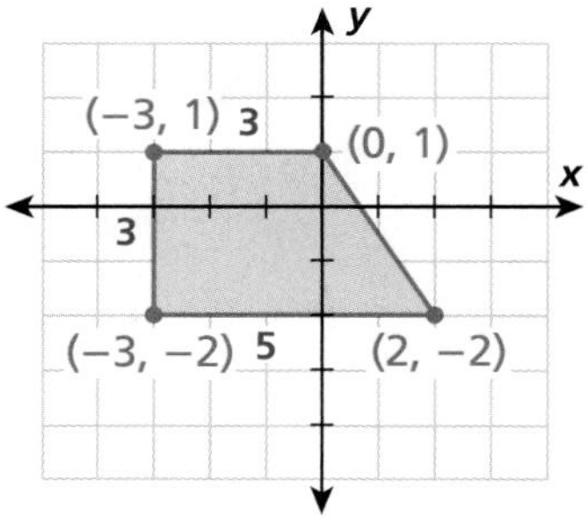

$A = \frac{1}{2}h(b_1 + b_2)$ *Area of a trapezoid*

$= \frac{1}{2} \cdot 3(3 + 5)$ *Substitute for h, b_1, and b_2.*

$= 12 \text{ units}^2$

Think and Discuss

1. **Describe** what happens to the area of a triangle when the base is doubled and the height remains the same.
2. **Describe** what happens to the area of a trapezoid when the length of both bases are doubled but the height remains the same.

6-2 Exercises

FOR EXTRA PRACTICE
see page 742

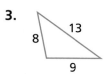

internet connect
Homework Help Online
go.hrw.com Keyword: MP4 6-2

GUIDED PRACTICE

See Example 1

Find the perimeter of each figure.

1. 4, 5, 7, 6

2. $3\frac{3}{4}$, $3\frac{1}{2}$, 4

3. 8, 13, 9

4. 9, 7.7, 6.3, 11.5

5. 27, 19, 17, 21

6. x, $2x - 3$, $x + 4$

See Example 2

Graph and find the area of each figure with the given vertices.

7. (−2, 3), (2, −3), (−3, −3)

8. (5, 2), (2, −2), (−3, −2), (−4, 2)

9. (4, 2), (5, −6), (2, −6)

10. (0, −1), (−7, −1), (−5, 4), (−2, 4)

INDEPENDENT PRACTICE

See Example 1

Find the perimeter of each figure.

11.

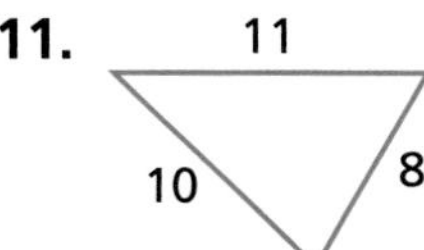

12.

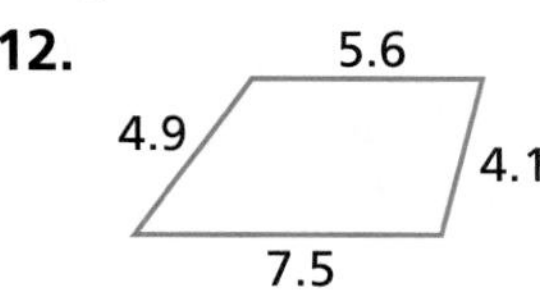

13.

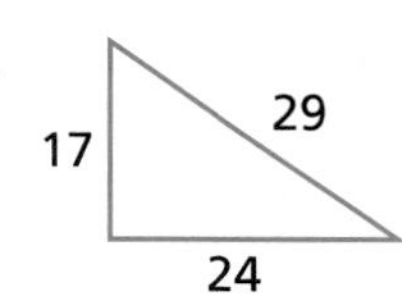

14. 4, $5\frac{1}{3}$, $2\frac{3}{4}$, $3\frac{1}{3}$

15.

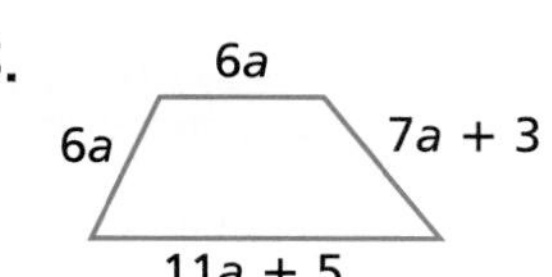

16.

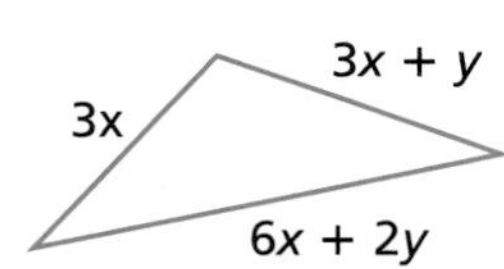

See Example 2

Graph and find the area of each figure with the given vertices.

17. (1, 5), (1, 1), (−3, 1), (−5, 5)

18. (−5, 2), (1, −3), (−3, −3)

19. (2, −3), (−1, −6), (−6, −3)

20. (1, 4), (4, −5), (−5, −5), (−3, 4)

PRACTICE AND PROBLEM SOLVING

Find the area of each figure with the given dimensions.

21. triangle: $b = 9$, $h = 11$

22. trapezoid: $b_1 = 6$, $b_2 = 10$, $h = 5$

23. triangle: $b = 7x$, $h = 6$

24. trapezoid: $b_1 = 4.5$, $b_2 = 8$, $h = 6.7$

25. The perimeter of a triangle is 37.4 ft. Two of its sides measure 16.4 ft and 11.9 ft, respectively. What is the length of its third side?

26. The area of a triangle is 63 mm^2. If its height is 14 mm, what is the length of its base?

Physical Science LINK

To fly, a plane must overcome gravity and achieve *lift*, the force that allows a flying object to have upward motion. The shape and size of a plane's wings affect the amount of lift that is created. The wings of high-speed airplanes are thin and usually angled back to give the plane more lift.

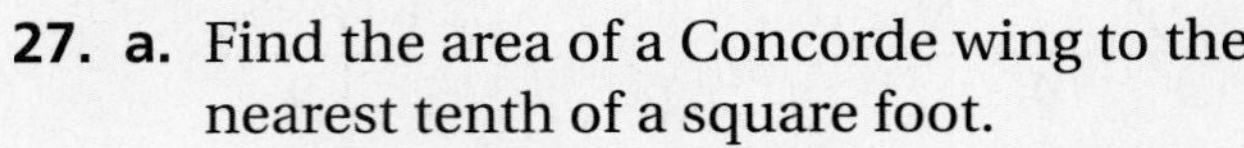

27. **a.** Find the area of a Concorde wing to the nearest tenth of a square foot.

b. Find the total perimeter of the two wings of a Concorde to the nearest tenth of a foot.

28. What is the area of a Boeing 747 wing to the nearest tenth of a square foot?

29. What is the perimeter of an F-18 wing to the nearest tenth of a foot?

30. What is the total area of the two wings of an F-18?

31. Find the area and perimeter of the wing of a space shuttle rounded to the nearest tenth.

32. ***CHALLENGE*** The wing of the Wright brothers' plane is about half the length of a Boeing 747 wing. Compare the area of the Wright brothers' wing with the area of a Boeing 747 wing. Is the area of the Wright brothers' wing half the area of the 747 wing? Explain.

go.hrw.com
Web Extra!
KEYWORD: MP4 Lift

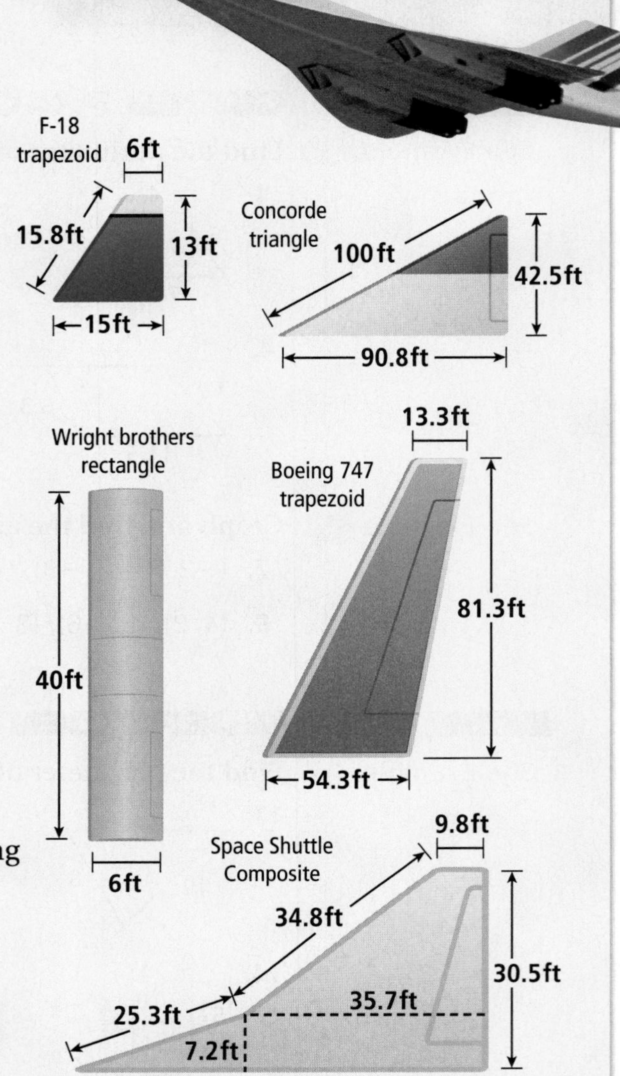

Spiral Review

Write each fraction as a decimal. (Lesson 3-1)

33. $\frac{3}{4}$ **34.** $\frac{1}{8}$ **35.** $\frac{10}{4}$ **36.** $\frac{9}{15}$

Do the data sets have a positive, a negative, or no correlation? (Lesson 4-7)

37. the number of shoes purchased and the amount of money left over

38. the length of a sub sandwich and the price of the sandwich

39. **TEST PREP** What name best describes a quadrilateral with vertices at (2, 4), (4, 1), (−3, 1), and (−5, 4)? (Lesson 5-5)

A Trapezoid **B** Parallelogram **C** Rhombus **D** Rectangle

Explore Right Triangles

Use with Lesson 6-3

WHAT YOU NEED
- scissors
- paper

REMEMBER
Right triangles have 1 right angle and 2 acute angles.

internet connect
Lab Resources Online
go.hrw.com
KEYWORD: MP4 Lab6A

Activity

1 The Pythagorean Theorem states that if a and b are the lengths of the legs of a right triangle, then c is the length of the hypotenuse, where $a^2 + b^2 = c^2$. Prove the Pythagorean Theorem using the following steps.

a. Draw two squares side by side. Label one with side a and one with side b.

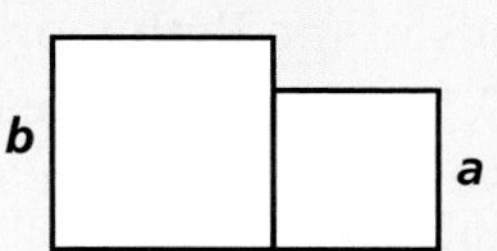

Notice that the area of this composite figure is $a^2 + b^2$.

b. Draw hypotenuses of length c, so that we have right triangles with sides a, b, and c.

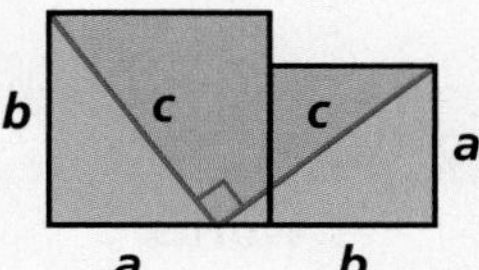

c. Cut out the triangles and the remaining piece.

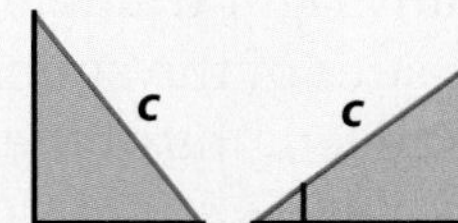

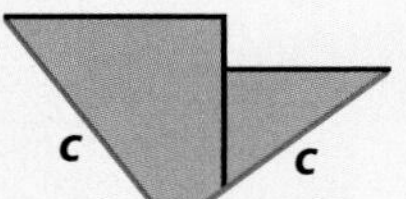

d. Fit the pieces together to make a square with sides c and area c^2. You have shown that the area $a^2 + b^2$ can be cut up and rearranged to form the area c^2, so $a^2 + b^2 = c^2$.

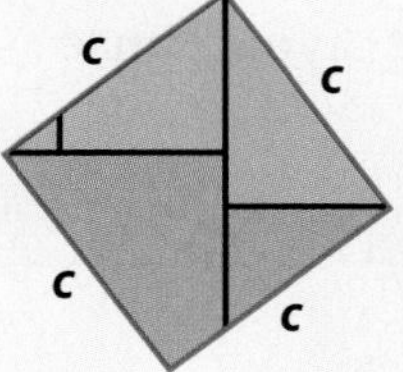

Think and Discuss

1. Does the Pythagorean Theorem work for triangles that are not right triangles?

Try This

1. If you know that the lengths of two legs of a right triangle are 9 and 12, can you find the length of the hypotenuse? Show your work.
2. Take a piece of paper and fold the right corner down so that the top edge of the paper matches the side edge. Crease the paper. Without measuring, find the diagonal's length.

6-3 The Pythagorean Theorem

Learn to use the Pythagorean Theorem and its converse to solve problems.

Vocabulary

Pythagorean Theorem

leg

hypotenuse

Pythagoras was born on the Aegean island of Samos sometime between 580 B.C. and 569 B.C. He is best known for the *Pythagorean Theorem,* which relates the side lengths of a right triangle.

A Babylonian tablet known as Plimpton 322 provides evidence that the relationship between the side lengths of right triangles was known as early as 1900 B.C. Many people, including U.S. president James Garfield, have written proofs of the Pythagorean Theorem. In 1940, E. S. Loomis presented 370 proofs of the theorem in *The Pythagorean Proposition.*

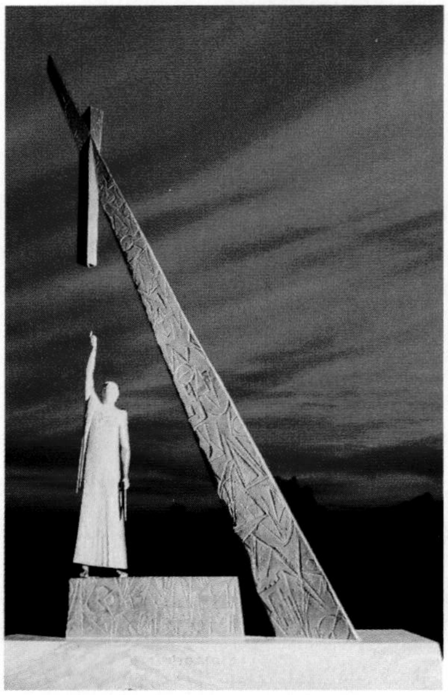

This statue of Pythagoras is located in the Pythagorion Harbor on the island of Samos.

THE PYTHAGOREAN THEOREM

Words	Numbers	Algebra
In any right triangle, the sum of the squares of the lengths of the two **legs** is equal to the square of the length of the **hypotenuse**.	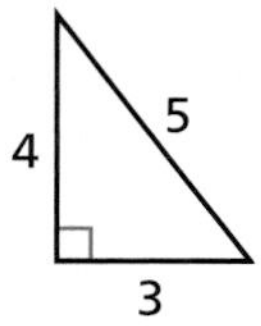 $3^2 + 4^2 = 5^2$ $9 + 16 = 25$	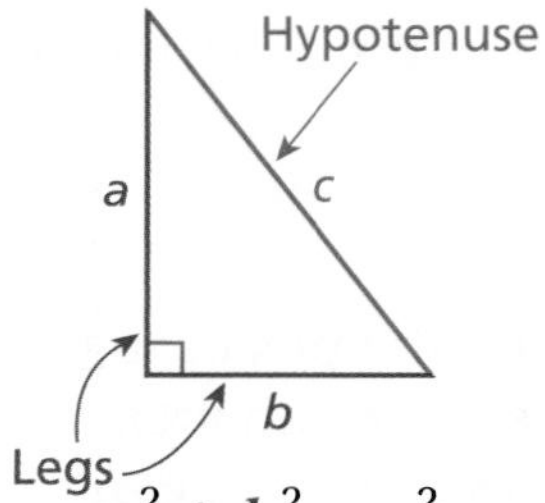 $a^2 + b^2 = c^2$

EXAMPLE 1 Finding the Length of a Hypotenuse

Helpful Hint

The triangle in the figure is an isosceles right triangle. It is also called a 45°-45°-90° triangle.

Find the length of the hypotenuse.

A

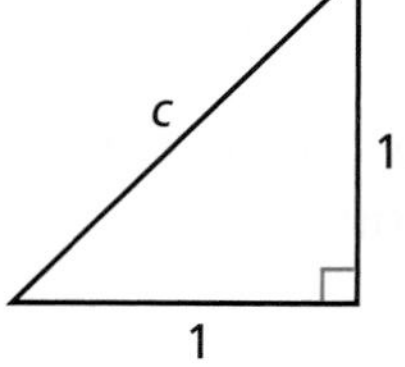

$a^2 + b^2 = c^2$	*Pythagorean Theorem*
$1^2 + 1^2 = c^2$	*Substitute for a and b.*
$1 + 1 = c^2$	*Simplify powers.*
$2 = c^2$	
$\sqrt{2} = c$	*Solve for c; $c = \sqrt{c^2}$.*
$1.41 \approx c$	

Find the length of the hypotenuse.

B **triangle with coordinates (6, 1), (0, 9), and (0, 1)**

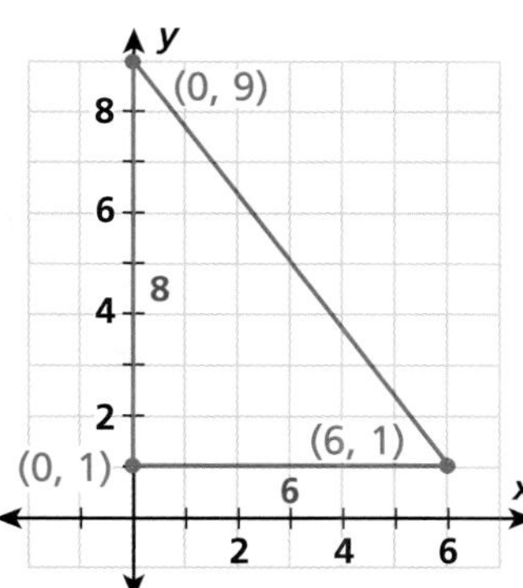

The points form a right triangle with $a = 8$ and $b = 6$.

$$a^2 + b^2 = c^2 \quad \textit{Pythagorean Theorem}$$
$$8^2 + 6^2 = c^2 \quad \textit{Substitute for a and b.}$$
$$64 + 36 = c^2 \quad \textit{Simplify powers.}$$
$$100 = c^2$$
$$10 = c \quad \sqrt{100} = 10$$

EXAMPLE 2 Finding the Length of a Leg in a Right Triangle

Solve for the unknown side in the right triangle.

$$a^2 + b^2 = c^2$$
$$5^2 + b^2 = 13^2$$
$$25 + b^2 = 169$$
$$\underline{-25 \qquad\quad -25}$$
$$b^2 = 144$$
$$b = 12 \quad \sqrt{144} = 12$$

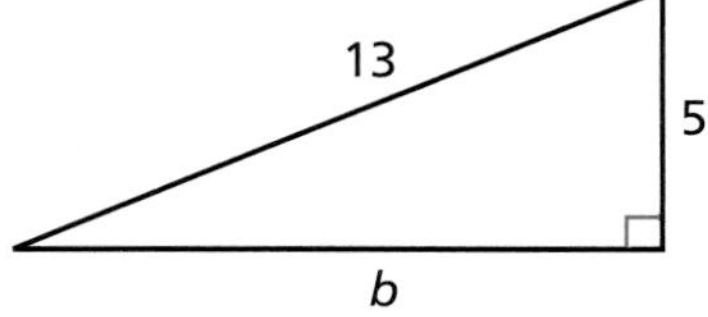

EXAMPLE 3 Using the Pythagorean Theorem to Find Area

Use the Pythagorean Theorem to find the height of the triangle. Then use the height to find the area of the triangle.

$$a^2 + b^2 = c^2$$
$$a^2 + 1^2 = 2^2 \quad \textit{Substitute 1 for b and 2 for c.}$$
$$a^2 + 1 = 4$$
$$a^2 = 3$$
$$a = \sqrt{3} \text{ units} \approx 1.73 \text{ units} \quad \textit{Find the square root of both sides.}$$

$$A = \frac{1}{2}bh = \frac{1}{2}(2)(\sqrt{3}) = \sqrt{3} \text{ units}^2 \approx 1.73 \text{ units}^2$$

Think and Discuss

1. Tell how to use the Pythagorean Theorem to find the height of any isosceles triangle when the side lengths are given.

2. Explain if 2, 3, and 4 cm could be side lengths of a right triangle.

6-3 Exercises

FOR EXTRA PRACTICE
see page 742

internet connect
Homework Help Online
go.hrw.com Keyword: MP4 6-3

GUIDED PRACTICE

See Example 1

Find the length of the hypotenuse in each triangle to the nearest tenth.

1. 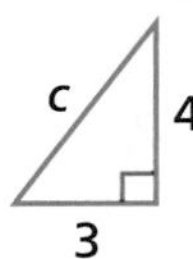

2. 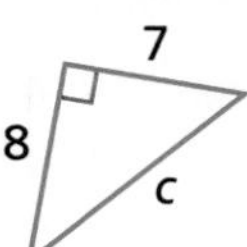

3. triangle with coordinates $(-5, 0)$, $(-5, 6)$, and $(0, 6)$

See Example 2

Solve for the unknown side in each right triangle to the nearest tenth.

4. 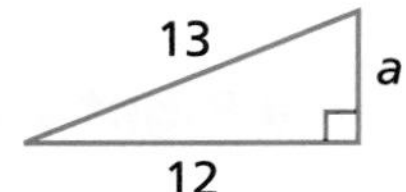

5. 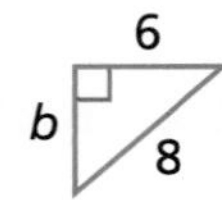

6. 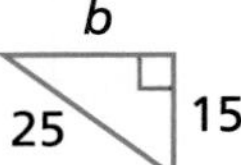

See Example 3 

7. Use the Pythagorean Theorem to find the height of the triangle. Then use the height to find the area of the triangle.

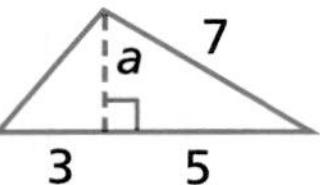

INDEPENDENT PRACTICE

See Example 1

Find the length of the hypotenuse in each triangle to the nearest tenth.

8. 

9. 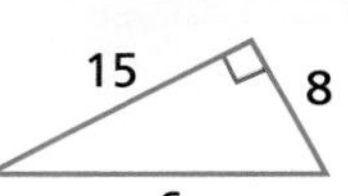

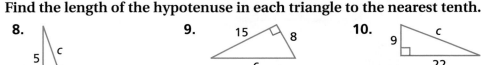

10. 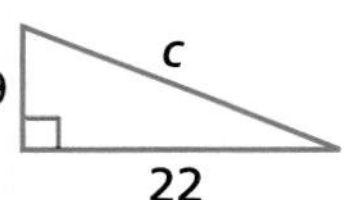

11. triangle with coordinates $(-4, 2)$, $(4, -2)$, and $(-4, -2)$

See Example 2 

Solve for the unknown side in each right triangle to the nearest tenth.

12. 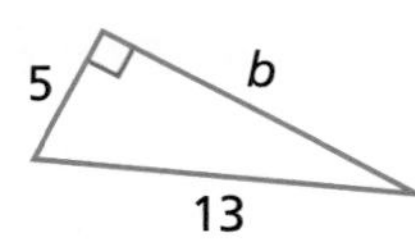

13. 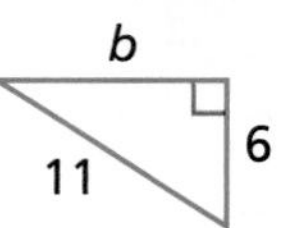

14. 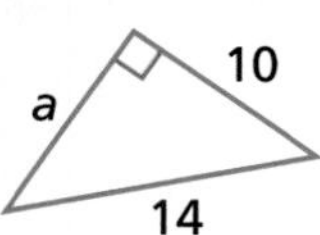

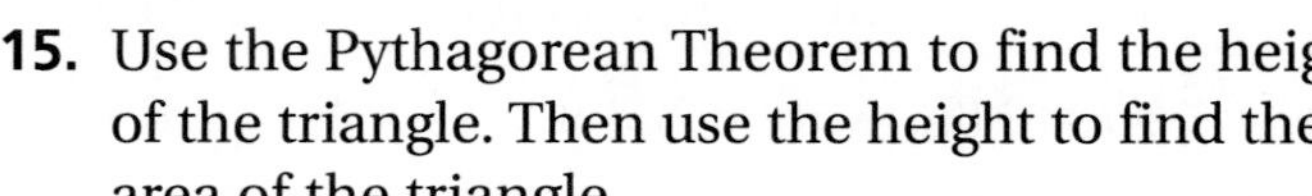
See Example 3

15. Use the Pythagorean Theorem to find the height of the triangle. Then use the height to find the area of the triangle.

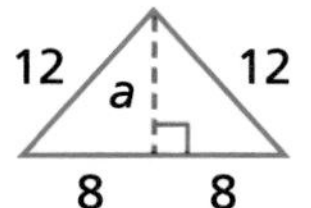

PRACTICE AND PROBLEM SOLVING

Find the missing length for each right triangle.

16. $a = 3, b = 6, c = $ ▭
17. $a = $ ▭, $b = 24, c = 25$
18. $a = 30, b = 72, c = $ ▭
19. $a = 20, b = $ ▭, $c = 46$
20. $a = $ ▭, $b = 53, c = 70$
21. $a = 65, b = $ ▭, $c = 97$

The *converse* of the Pythagorean Theorem states that any three positive numbers that make the equation $a^2 + b^2 = c^2$ true are the side lengths of a right triangle. If the side lengths are all whole numbers, they are called *Pythagorean triples.* Determine whether each set is a Pythagorean triple.

22. 2, 6, 8 **23.** 3, 4, 5 **24.** 8, 15, 17 **25.** 12, 16, 20

26. 10, 24, 26 **27.** 9, 13, 16 **28.** 11, 17, 23 **29.** 24, 32, 40

30. Use the Pythagorean Theorem to find the height of the figure. Then find the area, to the nearest whole number.

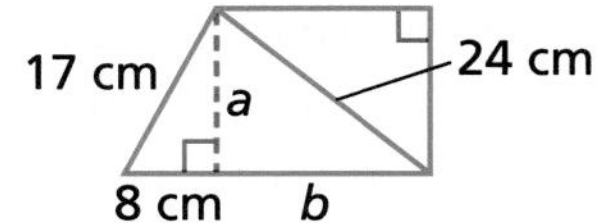

31. How far is the sailboat from the lighthouse, to the nearest kilometer?

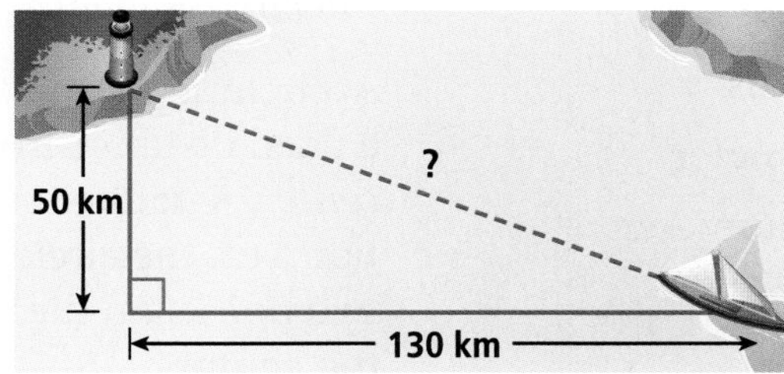

32. ***CONSTRUCTION*** A construction company is pouring a concrete foundation. The measures of two sides that meet in a corner are 33 ft and 56 ft. For the corner to be square (a right angle), what would the length of the diagonal have to be? (*Hint:* Draw a diagram.)

33. ***SOCIAL STUDIES*** The state of Colorado is shaped approximately like a rectangle. To the nearest mile, what is the distance between opposite corners of the state?

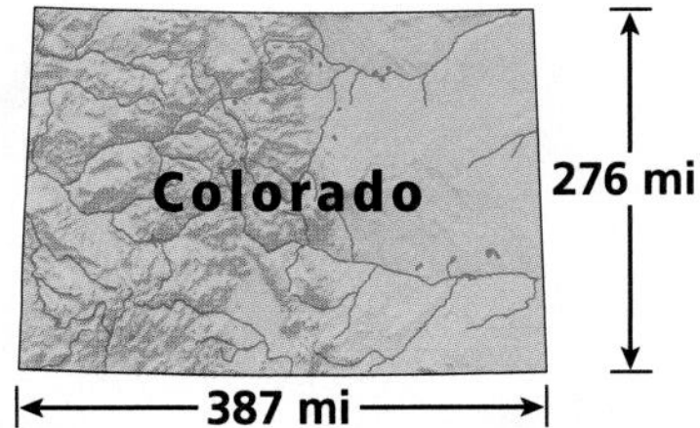

34. ***WRITE A PROBLEM*** Use a street map to write and solve a problem that requires the use of the Pythagorean Theorem.

35. ***WRITE ABOUT IT*** Explain how to use the converse of the Pythagorean Theorem to show that a triangle is a right triangle. (See Exercises 22–29.)

36. ***CHALLENGE*** A right triangle has legs of length $6x$ m and $8x$ m and hypotenuse of length 90 m. Find the lengths of the legs of the triangle.

Spiral Review

Solve. (Lesson 2-4)

37. $x + 13 = 22$ **38.** $b + 5 = -2$ **39.** $2y + 9 = 19$ **40.** $4a + 2 = -18$

41. **TEST PREP** Which real number lies between $3\frac{1}{5}$ and $3\frac{4}{7}$? (Lesson 3-10)

A 3.216 **B** 3.59 **C** 3.701 **D** 3.9

6-4 Circles

Learn to find the area and circumference of circles.

Vocabulary
circle
radius
diameter
circumference

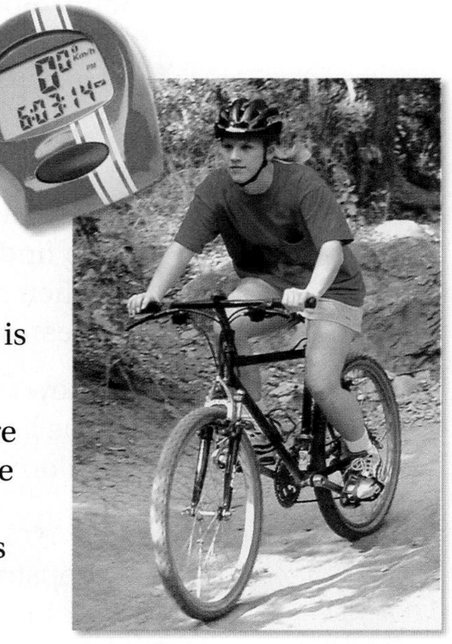

A bicycle odometer uses a magnet attached to a wheel and a sensor attached to the bicycle frame. Each time the magnet passes the sensor, the odometer registers the distance traveled. This distance is the *circumference* of the wheel.

A **circle** is the set of points in a plane that are a fixed distance from a given point, called the *center*. A **radius** connects the center to any point on the circle, and a **diameter** connects two points on the circle and passes through the center.

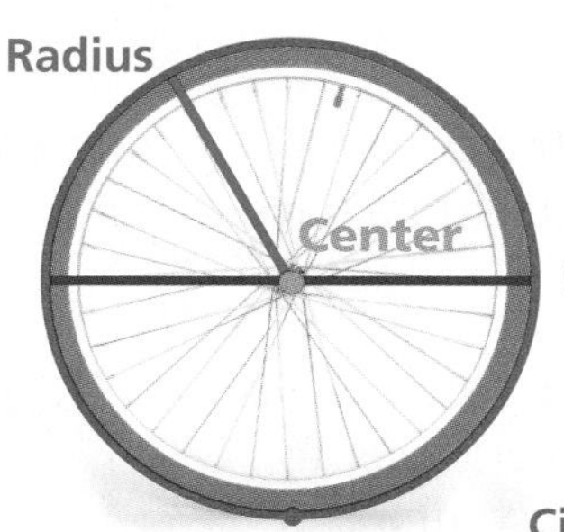

The diameter d is twice the radius r.

The **circumference** of a circle is the distance around the circle.

Remember!

Pi (π) is an irrational number that is often approximated by the rational numbers 3.14 and $\frac{22}{7}$.

CIRCUMFERENCE OF A CIRCLE		
Words	**Numbers**	**Formula**
The circumference C of a circle is π times the diameter d, or 2π times the radius r.	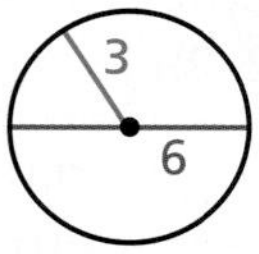 (circle: 3, 6) $C = \pi(6)$ $= 2\pi(3)$ ≈ 18.8 units	$C = \pi d$ or $C = 2\pi r$

EXAMPLE 1 **Finding the Circumference of a Circle**

Find the circumference of each circle, both in terms of π and to the nearest tenth. Use 3.14 for π.

A circle with radius 5 cm

$C = 2\pi r$

$= 2\pi(5)$

$= 10\pi \text{ cm} \approx 31.4 \text{ cm}$

B circle with diameter 1.5 in.

$C = \pi d$

$= \pi(1.5)$

$= 1.5\pi \text{ in.} \approx 4.7 \text{ in.}$

AREA OF A CIRCLE		
Words	**Numbers**	**Formula**
The area A of a circle is π times the square of the radius r.	$A = \pi(3^2)$ $= 9\pi$ ≈ 28.3 units^2	$A = \pi r^2$

EXAMPLE 2 Finding the Area of a Circle

Find the area of each circle, both in terms of π and to the nearest tenth. Use 3.14 for π.

A **circle with radius 5 cm**

$A = \pi r^2 = \pi(5^2)$

$= 25\pi \text{ cm}^2 \approx 78.5 \text{ cm}^2$

B **circle with diameter 1.5 in.**

$A = \pi r^2 = \pi(0.75^2)$ *$\frac{d}{2} = 0.75$*

$= 0.5625\pi \text{ in}^2 \approx 1.8 \text{ in}^2$

EXAMPLE 3 Finding Area and Circumference on a Coordinate Plane

Graph the circle with center (−1, 1) that passes through (−1, 3). Find the area and circumference, both in terms of π and to the nearest tenth. Use 3.14 for π.

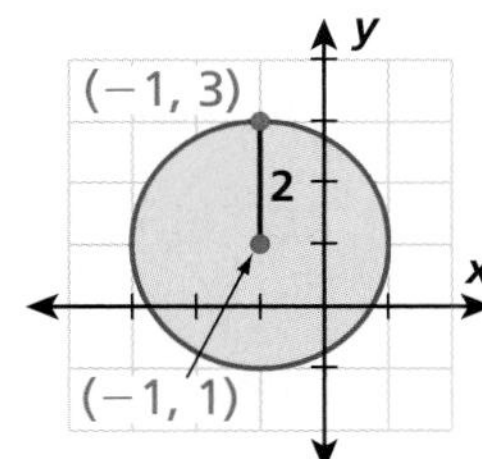

$A = \pi r^2$
$= \pi(2^2)$
$= 4\pi$ units^2
≈ 12.6 units^2

$C = \pi d$
$= \pi(4)$
$= 4\pi$ units
≈ 12.6 units

EXAMPLE 4 *Transportation Application*

A bicycle odometer recorded 147 revolutions of a wheel with diameter $\frac{4}{3}$ ft. How far did the bicycle travel? Use $\frac{22}{7}$ for π.

$C = \pi d = \pi\left(\frac{4}{3}\right) \approx \frac{22}{7}\left(\frac{4}{3}\right) = \frac{88}{21}$ *Find the circumference.*

The distance traveled is the circumference of the wheel times the number of revolutions, or about $\frac{88}{21} \cdot 147 = 616$ ft.

Think and Discuss

1. **Compare** the circumference of a circle with diameter x to the circumference of a circle with diameter $2x$.
2. **Give** the formula for area of a circle in terms of the diameter d.

6-4 Exercises

FOR EXTRA PRACTICE

see page 742

GUIDED PRACTICE

See Example 1

Find the circumference of each circle, both in terms of π and to the nearest tenth. Use 3.14 for π.

1. circle with diameter 8 cm
2. circle with radius 3.2 in.

See Example 2

Find the area of each circle, both in terms of π and to the nearest tenth. Use 3.14 for π.

3. circle with radius 1.5 ft
4. circle with diameter 15 cm

See Example 3

5. Graph a circle with center (3, −1) that passes through (0, −1). Find the area and circumference, both in terms of π and to the nearest tenth. Use 3.14 for π.

See Example 4

6. Estimate the diameter of a wheel that makes 9 revolutions and travels 50 feet. Use $\frac{22}{7}$ for π.

INDEPENDENT PRACTICE

See Example 1

Find the circumference of each circle, both in terms of π and to the nearest tenth. Use 3.14 for π.

7. circle with radius 7 in.
8. circle with diameter 11.5 m
9. circle with radius 20.2 cm
10. circle with diameter 2 ft

See Example 2

Find the area of each circle, both in terms of π and to the nearest tenth. Use 3.14 for π.

11. circle with diameter 24 cm
12. circle with radius 1.4 yd
13. circle with radius 18 in.
14. circle with diameter 17 ft

See Example 3

15. Graph a circle with center (−4, 2) that passes through (−4, −4). Find the area and circumference, both in terms of π and to the nearest tenth. Use 3.14 for π.

See Example 4

16. If the diameter of a wheel is 2 ft, about how many revolutions does the wheel make for every mile driven? Use $\frac{22}{7}$ for π. (*Hint:* 1 mi = 5280 ft.)

PRACTICE AND PROBLEM SOLVING

Find the circumference and area of each circle to the nearest tenth. Use 3.14 for π.

17.
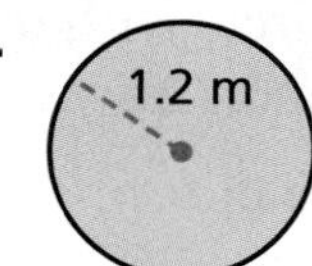

18.
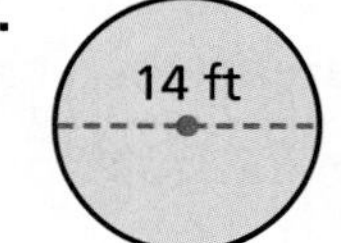

19.
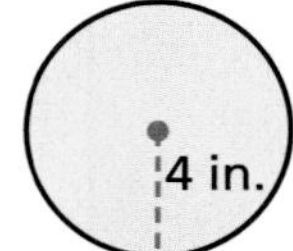

INDEPENDENT PRACTICE

See Example 1

4. Use isometric dot paper to sketch a rectangular box with a base 4 units long by 3 units wide and a height of 1 unit.

See Example 2

5. Sketch a one-point perspective drawing of a rectangular box.

See Example 3

6. Sketch a two-point perspective drawing of a triangular box.

PRACTICE AND PROBLEM SOLVING

Name all of the faces in each figure.

7. 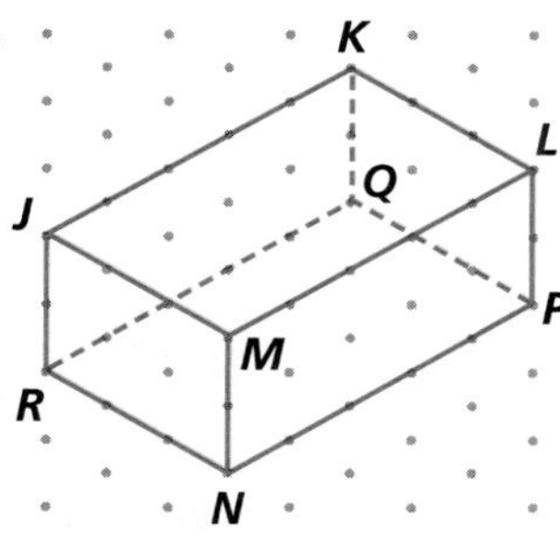

8. 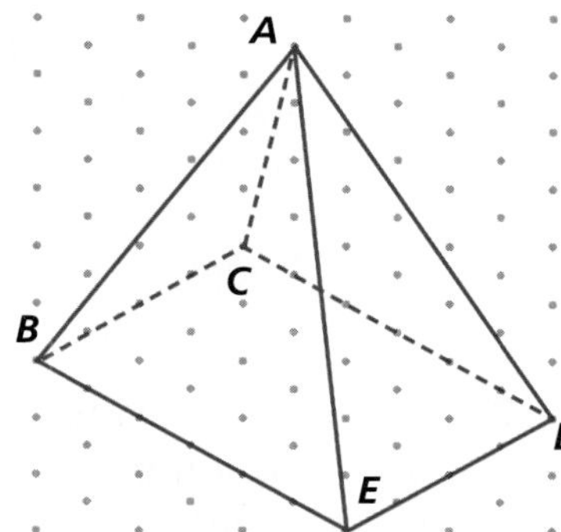

9. 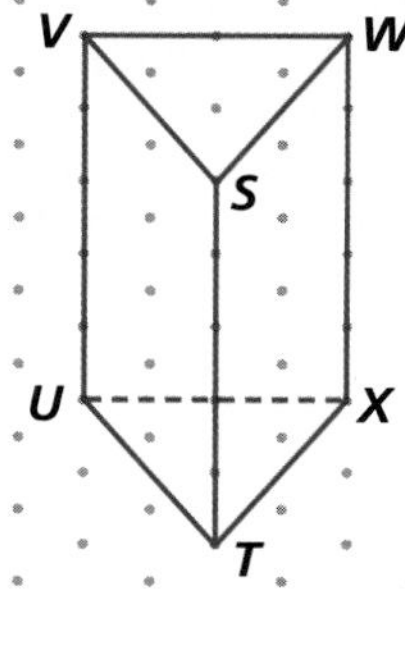

Use isometric dot paper to sketch each figure.

10. a cube 3 units on each side
11. a triangular box 5 units high
12. a rectangular box 7 units high, with base 5 units by 2 units
13. a box with parallel faces that are 3 units by 2 units and 4 units by 4 units
14. a box with parallel faces that are 2 units by 2 units and 5 units by 3 units

Use the one-point perspective drawing for Exercises 15–19.

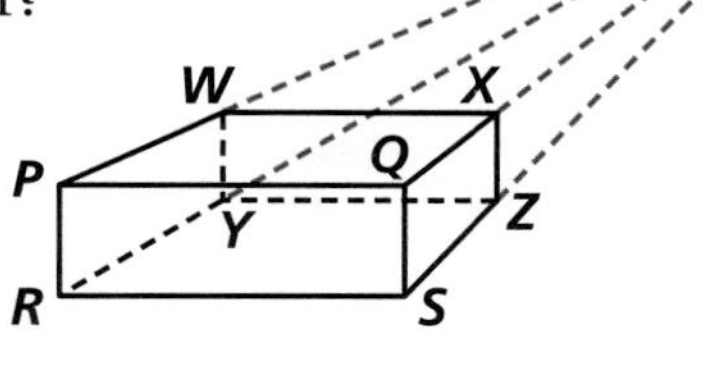

15. Name the vanishing point.
16. Which segments are parallel to each other?
17. Which face is the front face?
18. Which face is the back face?
19. Which segments are hidden edges of the figure?

Use the two-point perspective drawing for Exercises 20–24.

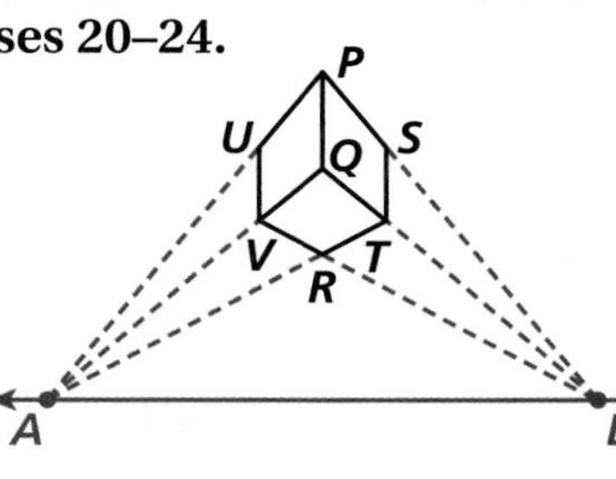

20. Name the vanishing points.
21. Which segments are parallel to each other?
22. Name the horizon line.
23. Which edge is nearest to the viewer?
24. Which segments are not edges of the figure?

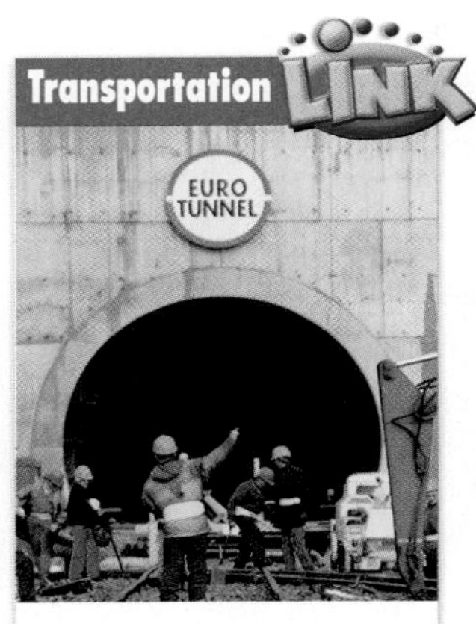

The Chunnel was built from both ends at the same time. Specially designed tunneling machines completed an average of 125 m per week.

25. ***TRANSPORTATION*** Engineers long dreamed of linking England with the European mainland. In 1994, the dream became a reality with the opening of the Channel Tunnel, or Chunnel, which links Britain and France. The drawing shows the train *Eurostar* in the Chunnel. Is this an example of one-point or two-point perspective?

26. ***TECHNOLOGY*** Architects often use CADD (Computer Aided Design/Drafting) programs to create 3-D images of their ideas. Is the image an example of one-point or two-point perspective?

27. Copy the drawing below, and add another building like the one shown, with its lower front edge at $\overline{AB}$.

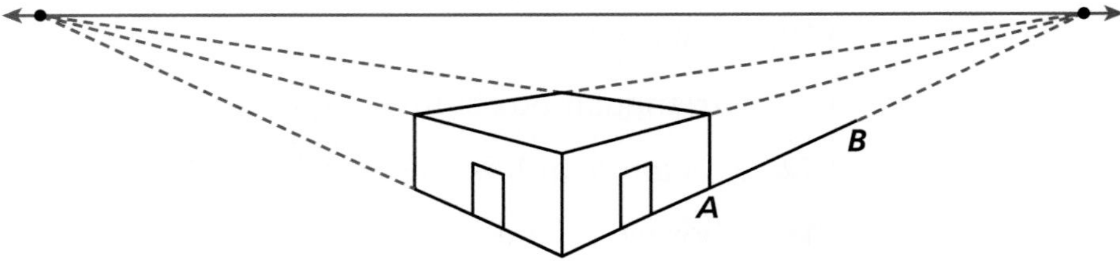

28. ***WHAT'S THE ERROR?*** A student sketched a 3-unit cube on dot paper. The student said that four faces and eight edges were visible in the sketch. What was the student's error?

29. ***WRITE ABOUT IT*** Describe the differences between a dot-paper drawing of a cube and a perspective drawing of a cube.

30. ***CHALLENGE*** Use one-point perspective to create a block-letter sign of your name.

Spiral Review

Write each number in standard notation. (Lesson 2-9)

31. 2.75×10^3 **32.** -4.2×10^2 **33.** 6.3×10^{-7} **34.** -1.9×10^{-4}

35. **TEST PREP** Which type of triangle can be constructed with a 50° angle between two 8-inch sides? (Lesson 5-3)

A Equilateral **B** Isosceles **C** Scalene **D** Obtuse

6-6 Volume of Prisms and Cylinders

Learn to find the volume of prisms and cylinders.

Vocabulary
prism
cylinder

Kansai International Airport, in Japan, is built on the world's largest man-made island. To find the amount of rock, gravel, and concrete needed to build the island, you need to know how to find the volume of a *rectangular prism.*

A **prism** is a three-dimensional figure named for the shape of its bases. The two bases are congruent polygons. All of the other faces are parallelograms. A **cylinder** has two circular bases.

Remember!

If all six faces of a rectangular prism are squares, it is a cube.

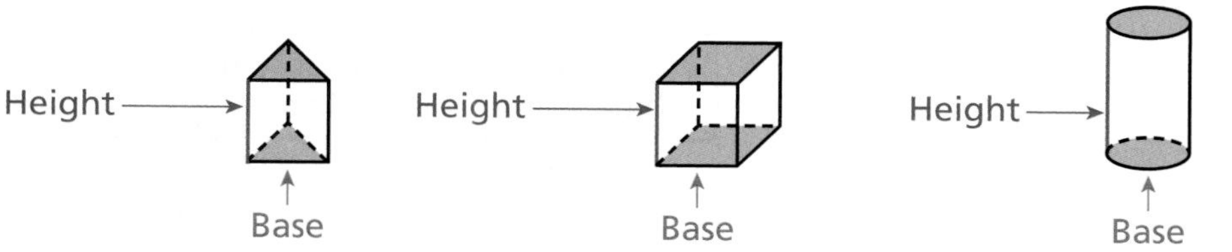

VOLUME OF PRISMS AND CYLINDERS

Words	Numbers	Formula
Prism: The volume V of a prism is the area of the base B times the height h.	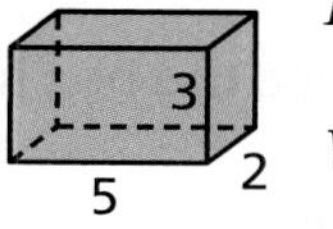 $B = 2(5) = 10$ units^2; $V = (10)(3) = 30$ units^3	$V = Bh$
Cylinder: The volume of a cylinder is the area of the base B times the height h.	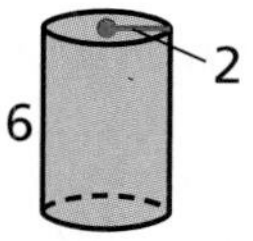 $B = \pi(2^2) = 4\pi$ units^2; $V = (4\pi)(6) = 24\pi \approx 75.4$ units^3	$V = Bh = (\pi r^2)h$

EXAMPLE 1 Finding the Volume of Prisms and Cylinders

Helpful Hint

Area is measured in *square units.* Volume is measured in *cubic units.*

Find the volume of each figure to the nearest tenth.

A **A rectangular prism with base 1 m by 3 m and height 6 m.**

$B = 1 \cdot 3 = 3\text{ m}^2$ *Area of base*

$V = Bh$ *Volume of prism*

$= 3 \cdot 6 = 18\text{ m}^3$

Find the volume of each figure to the nearest tenth.

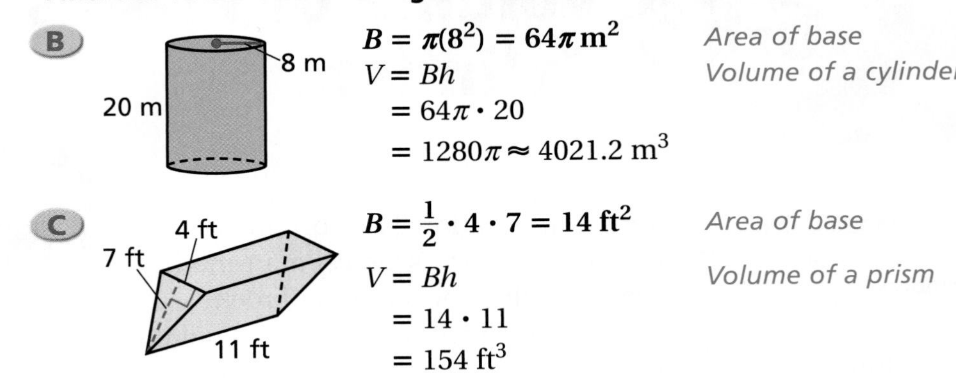

B $B = \pi(8^2) = 64\pi \text{ m}^2$ *Area of base*

$V = Bh$ *Volume of a cylinder*

$= 64\pi \cdot 20$

$= 1280\pi \approx 4021.2 \text{ m}^3$

C $B = \frac{1}{2} \cdot 4 \cdot 7 = 14 \text{ ft}^2$ *Area of base*

$V = Bh$ *Volume of a prism*

$= 14 \cdot 11$

$= 154 \text{ ft}^3$

The volume of a rectangular prism can be written as $V = \ell wh$, where ℓ is the length, w is the width, and h is the height.

EXAMPLE 2 Exploring the Effects of Changing Dimensions

A **A juice box measures 3 in. by 2 in. by 4 in. Explain whether doubling the length, width, or height of the box would double the amount of juice the box holds.**

Original Dimensions	Double the Length	Double the Width	Double the Height
$V = \ell wh$ $= 3 \cdot 2 \cdot 4$ $= 24 \text{ in}^3$	$V = (2\ell)wh$ $= 6 \cdot 2 \cdot 4$ $= 48 \text{ in}^3$	$V = \ell(2w)h$ $= 3 \cdot 4 \cdot 4$ $= 48 \text{ in}^3$	$V = \ell w(2h)$ $= 3 \cdot 2 \cdot 8$ $= 48 \text{ in}^3$

The original box has a volume of 24 in^3. You could double the volume to 48 in^3 by doubling any one of the dimensions. So doubling the length, width, or height would double the amount of juice the box holds.

B **A juice can has a radius of 1.5 in. and a height of 5 in. Explain whether doubling the height of the can would have the same effect on the volume as doubling the radius.**

Original Dimensions	Double the Radius	Double the Height
$V = \pi r^2 h$ $= 1.5^2\pi \cdot 5$ $= 11.25\pi \text{ in}^3$	$V = \pi(2r)^2 h$ $= 3^2\pi \cdot 5$ $= 45\pi \text{ in}^3$	$V = \pi r^2(2h)$ $= 1.5^2\pi \cdot (2 \cdot 5)$ $= 22.5\pi \text{ in}^3$

By doubling the height, you would double the volume. By doubling the radius, you would increase the volume to four times the original.

EXAMPLE 3 Construction Application

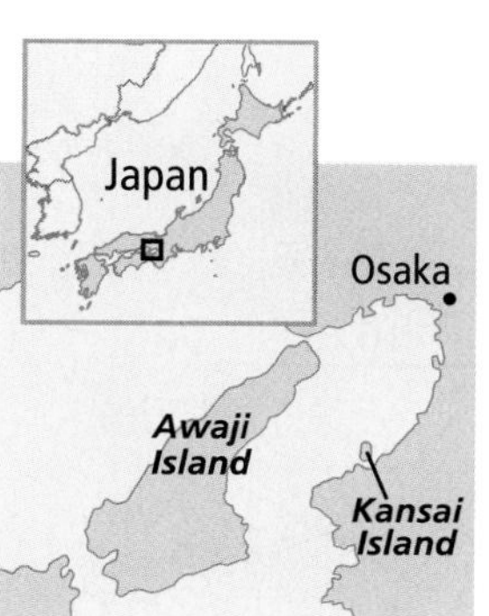

Kansai International Airport is on a man-made island that is a rectangular prism measuring 60 ft deep, 4000 ft wide, and 2.5 miles long. What is the volume of rock, gravel, and concrete that was needed to build the island?

length = 2.5 mi = 2.5(5280) ft
= 13,200 ft — *1 mi = 5280 ft*

width = 4000 ft

height = 60 ft

$V = 13{,}200 \cdot 4000 \cdot 60 \text{ ft}^3$ — *V = lwh*

$= 3{,}168{,}000{,}000 \text{ ft}^3$

The volume of rock, gravel, and concrete needed was 3,168,000,000 ft^3, which is equivalent to nearly 24 billion gallons of water.

To find the volume of a composite three-dimensional figure, find the volume of each part and add the volumes together.

EXAMPLE  4 Finding the Volume of Composite Figures

Find the volume of the milk carton.

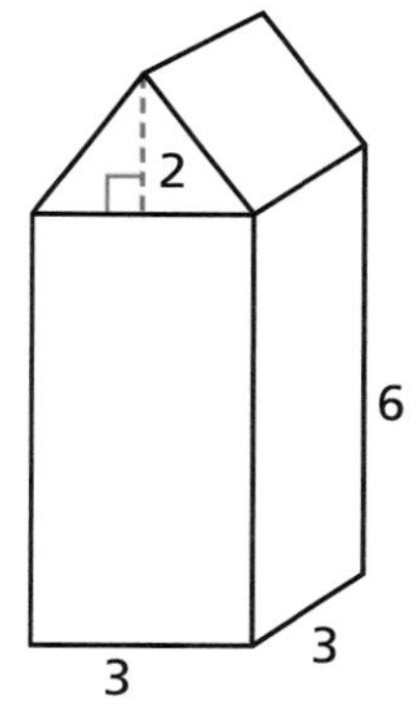

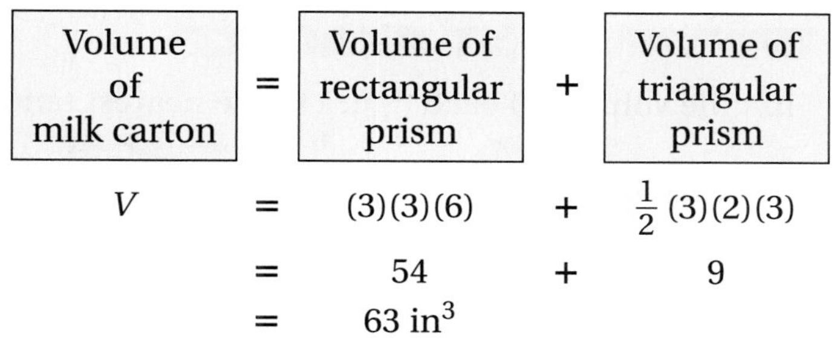

Volume of milk carton	=	Volume of rectangular prism	+	Volume of triangular prism
V	=	$(3)(3)(6)$	+	$\frac{1}{2}(3)(2)(3)$
	=	54	+	9
	=	63 in^3		

The volume is 63 in^3, or about 0.27 gallons.

Think and Discuss

1. **Give an example** that shows that two rectangular prisms can have different heights but the same volume.
2. **Apply** your results from Example 2 to make a conclusion about changing dimensions in a triangular prism.
3. **Describe** what happens to the volume of a cylinder when the diameter of the base is tripled.

6-6 Exercises

FOR EXTRA PRACTICE

see page 743

internet connect

Homework Help Online
go.hrw.com Keyword: MP4 6-6

GUIDED PRACTICE

See Example 1

Find the volume of each figure to the nearest tenth. Use 3.14 for π.

1. 5 cm, 6 cm, 7 cm

2. 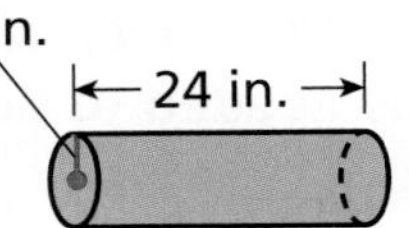

3. 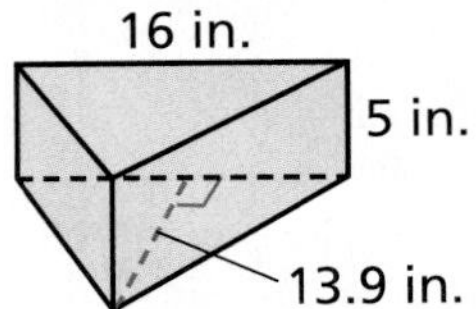

See Example 

4. A box measures 4 in. by 3 in. by 5 in. Explain whether tripling a side from 4 in. to 12 in. would triple the volume of the box.

5. A can of vegetables has radius 2 in. and height 4 in. Explain whether tripling the radius would triple the volume of the can.

See Example 

6. Grain is stored in cylindrical structures called *silos*. What is the volume of a silo with diameter 15 feet and height 25 feet?

See Example 4

7. Find the volume of the barn.

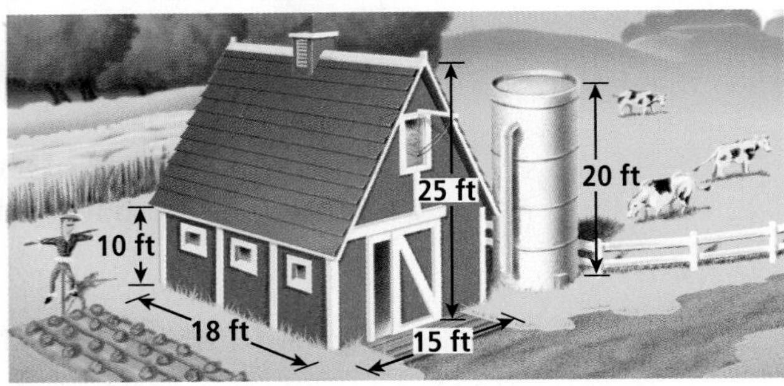

INDEPENDENT PRACTICE

See Example 

Find the volume of each figure to the nearest tenth. Use 3.14 for π.

8. 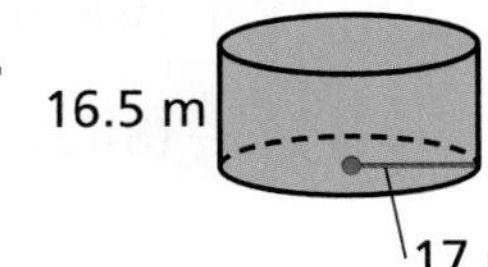

9. 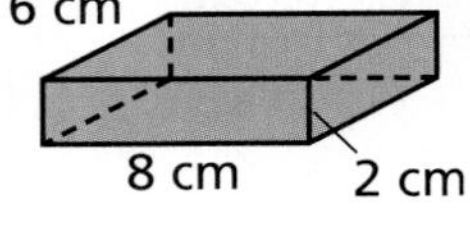

10. 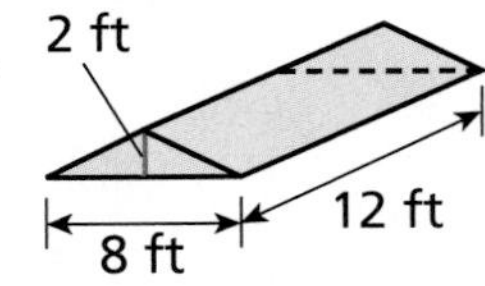

See Example 

11. A toy box measures 4 ft by 3 ft by 2 ft. Explain whether increasing the height by four times, from 2 ft to 8 ft, would increase the volume by four times.

12. A cylindrical oatmeal box has diameter 4 in. and height 7 in. Explain whether increasing the diameter by 1.5 times would increase the volume by 1.5 times.

See Example 

13. An ink cartridge for a printer is 5 cm by 3 cm by 4 cm. What is the volume of the ink cartridge?

See Example 

14. Find the volume of the box containing the ink cartridge.

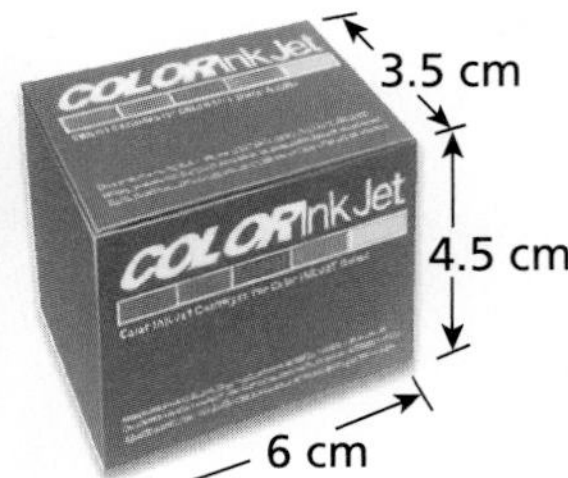

PRACTICE AND PROBLEM SOLVING

Through the 52 large windows of the Giant Ocean Tank, visitors can see 3000 corals and sponges as well as large sharks, sea turtles, barracudas, moray eels, and hundreds of tropical fishes.

15. ***LIFE SCIENCE*** The cylindrical Giant Ocean Tank at the New England Aquarium in Boston has a volume of 200,000 gallons.
    a. One gallon of water equals 231 cubic inches. How many cubic inches of water are in the Giant Ocean Tank?
    b. Use your answer from part **a** as the volume. The tank is 24 ft deep. Find the radius in feet of the Giant Ocean Tank.

16. ***ENTERTAINMENT*** An outdoor theater group sets up a portable stage. The stage comes in sections that are 48 in. by 96 in. by 36 in.
    a. What are the dimensions in feet of one stage section?
    b. What is the volume in cubic feet of one section?
    c. If the stage has a total volume of 864 ft^3, how many sections make up the stage?

17. ***SOCIAL STUDIES*** The tablet held by the Statue of Liberty is approximately a rectangular prism with volume 1,107,096 in^3. Estimate the thickness of the tablet.

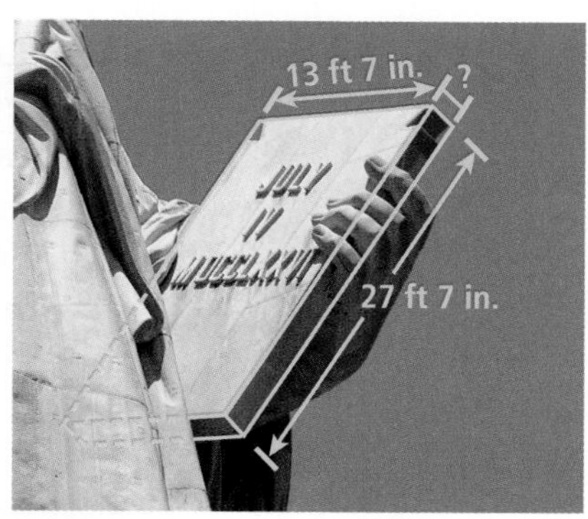

18. ***LIFE SCIENCE*** Air has about 4000 bacteria per cubic meter. There are about 120,000 bacteria in a room that is 3 m long by 4 m wide. What is the height of the room?

19. ***WHAT'S THE ERROR?*** A student read this statement in a book: "The volume of a triangular prism with height 10 cm and base area 25 cm is 250 cm^3." Correct the error in the statement.

20. ***WRITE ABOUT IT*** Explain why one cubic foot equals 1728 cubic inches.

21. ***CHALLENGE*** A 6 cm section of plastic water pipe has inner diameter 12 cm and outer diameter 15 cm. Find the volume of the plastic pipe, not the hollow interior, to the nearest tenth.

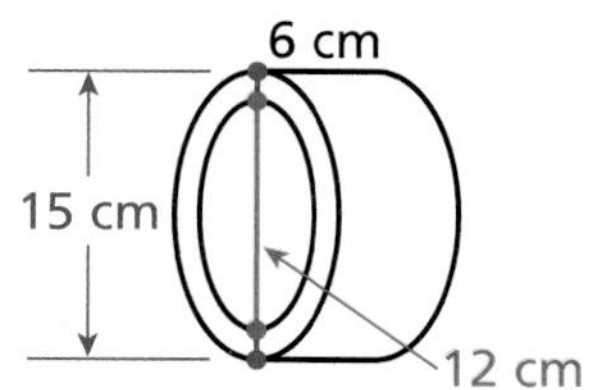

Spiral Review

Find the mean, median, and mode of each data set to the nearest tenth. (Lesson 4-3)

22. 3, 5, 5, 6, 9, 3, 5, 2, 5 **23.** 17, 15, 14, 16, 18, 13 **24.** 100, 75, 48, 75, 48, 63, 45

25. TEST PREP Find the sum of the angle measures of an octagon. (Lesson 5-4)

A 8° **B** 135° **C** 1080° **D** 1440°

6-7 Volume of Pyramids and Cones

Learn to find the volume of pyramids and cones.

Vocabulary
pyramid
cone

The Great Pyramid of Giza was built using about 2.5 million blocks of stone, each weighing at least two tons. It is believed that 20,000 to 30,000 workers took about 20 years to complete the pyramid.

The Great Pyramid's height is equivalent to that of a forty-story skyscraper. The pyramid covers an area of thirteen acres.

A **pyramid** is named for the shape of its base. The base is a polygon, and all of the other faces are triangles. A **cone** has a circular base. The height of a pyramid or cone is measured from the highest point to the base along a perpendicular line.

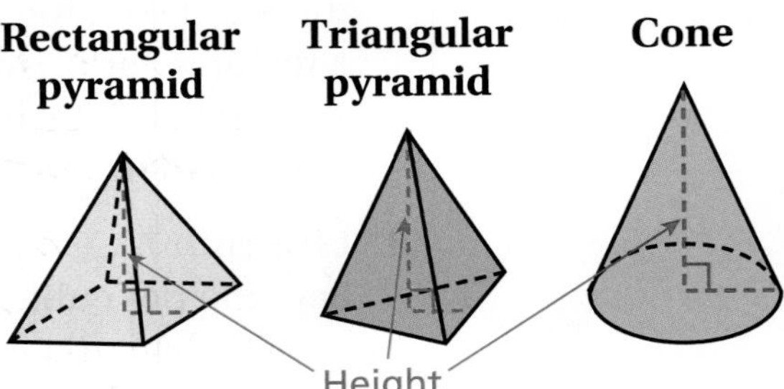

VOLUME OF PYRAMIDS AND CONES

Words	Numbers	Formula
Pyramid: The volume V of a pyramid is one-third of the area of the base B times the height h.	4, 3, 3 $B = 3(3)$ $= 9 \text{ units}^2$ $V = \frac{1}{3}(9)(4)$ $= 12 \text{ units}^3$	$V = \frac{1}{3}Bh$
Cone: The volume of a cone is one-third of the area of the circular base B times the height h.	3, 2 $B = \pi(2^2)$ $= 4\pi \text{ units}^2$ $V = \frac{1}{3}(4\pi)(3)$ $= 4\pi$ $\approx 12.6 \text{ units}^3$	$V = \frac{1}{3}Bh$ or $V = \frac{1}{3}\pi r^2 h$

EXAMPLE 1 Finding the Volume of Pyramids and Cones

Find the volume of each figure.

A

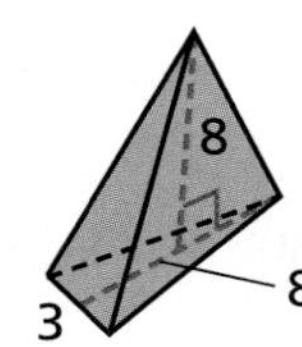

$B = \frac{1}{2}(3 \cdot 8) = 12 \text{ units}^2$

$V = \frac{1}{3} \cdot 12 \cdot 8$ $\quad V = \frac{1}{3}Bh$

$V = 32 \text{ units}^3$

Great Lakes Aquarium

The Great Lakes Aquarium in Duluth, Minnesota, is the only all-freshwater aquarium in the United States. It is located on the shore of Lake Superior and contains 170,000 gallons of water.

1. The aquarium has a glass water wall with etched panels. The water wall is 5 panels across and 7 panels tall.
   a. Find the number of panels that make up the water wall.
   b. If each panel is 10 feet across and 4 feet high, what is the area of one panel? What is the total area of the water wall?

2. You can compare Lake Superior to 40 different lakes, icecaps, and rivers at the 5 ft diameter globe and computer station. Find the surface area and volume of the aquarium's globe.

3. The St. Louis River tank is a trapezoidal prism. The height of the trapezoidal base is 24 ft, and the two bases are 3 ft and 7 ft. If the height of the tank is 3 ft 6 in., what is the volume of the tank?

The 85,000-gallon Isle Royale exhibit is made up of three back-to-back tanks. Each tank is a prism with a different-shaped base.

4. Isle Royale of the Present is the largest of the three tanks and has samples of every kind of fish living in Lake Superior today. The base of this tank is approximately 447.6 ft^2, and the tank has a water level of 23.33 ft. What is the volume of water in the tank?

5. The Isle Royale of the Past houses the fish that are native to the lake. The water level of the tank is 23.33 ft. Find the area of the base using the dimensions on the diagram, and then find the volume of water in the tank.

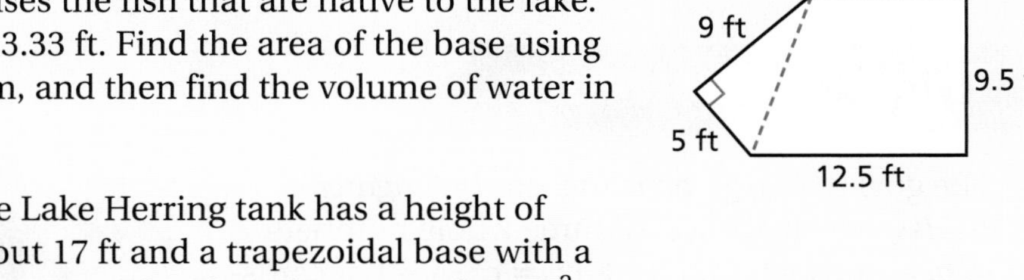

6. The Lake Herring tank has a height of about 17 ft and a trapezoidal base with a perimeter of 49 ft and an area of 294 ft^2. Find the area of the glass needed to construct the sides of this tank.

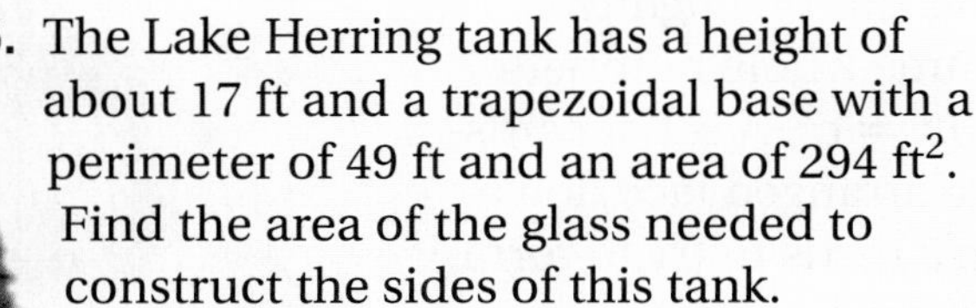

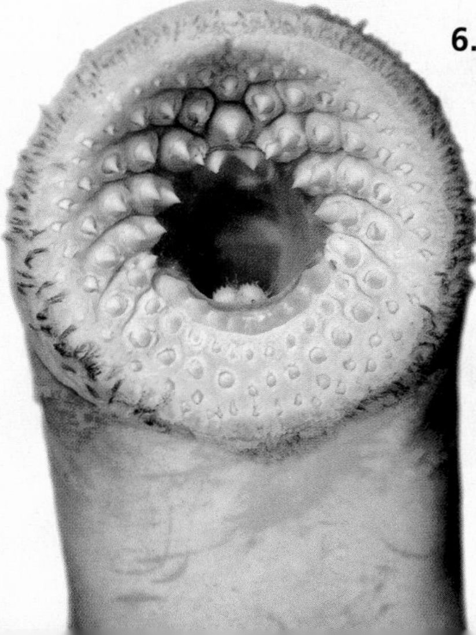

The sea lamprey is known as the "vampire of the Great Lakes," because of its blood-sucking method of eating fish.

MATH-ABLES

Planes in Space

Some three-dimensional figures can be generated by plane figures.

Experiment with a circle first. Move the circle around. See if you recognize any three-dimensional shapes.

If you rotate a circle around a diameter, you get a sphere.

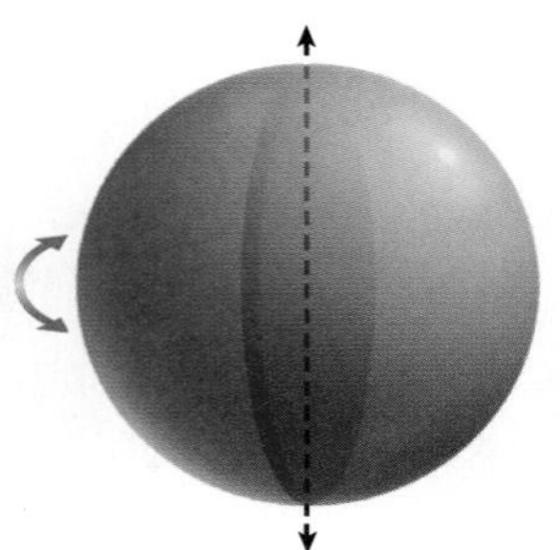

If you translate a circle up along a line perpendicular to the plane that the circle is in, you get a cylinder.

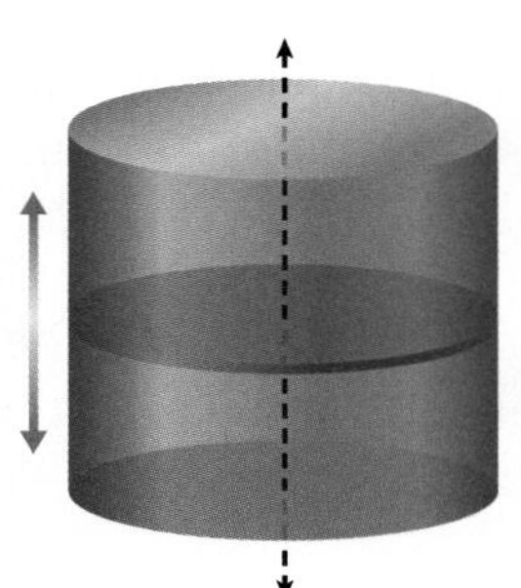

If you rotate a circle around a line outside the circle but in the same plane as the circle, you get a donut shape called a *torus*.

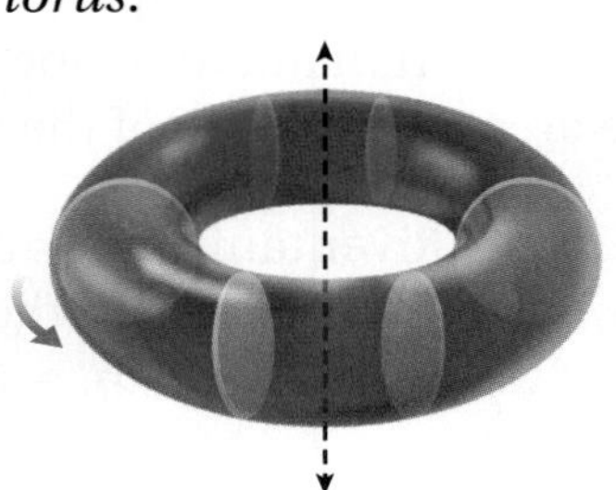

Draw or describe the three-dimensional figure generated by each plane figure.

1. a square translated along a line perpendicular to the plane it is in
2. a rectangle rotated around one of its edges
3. a right triangle rotated around one of its legs

Triple Concentration

The goal of this game is to form *Pythagorean triples*, which are sets of three whole numbers a, b, and c such that $a^2 + b^2 = c^2$. A set of cards with numbers on them are arranged face down. A turn consists of drawing 3 cards to try to form a Pythagorean triple. If the cards do not form a Pythagorean triple, they are replaced in their original positions.

internet connect
Go to ***go.hrw.com*** for a complete set of rules and cards.
KEYWORD: MP4 Game6

Chapter Test

Graph and find the area of each figure with the given vertices.

1. (4, 1), (−3, 1), (−3, −4), (4, −4)

2. (0, 4), (2, 3), (2, −3), (0, −2)

3. (−3, 0), (2, 0), (4, −2)

4. (2, 3), (6, −2), (−5, −2), (−2, 3)

5. Use the Pythagorean Theorem to find the height of rectangle *ABCD*.

6. Find the area of rectangle *ABCD*.

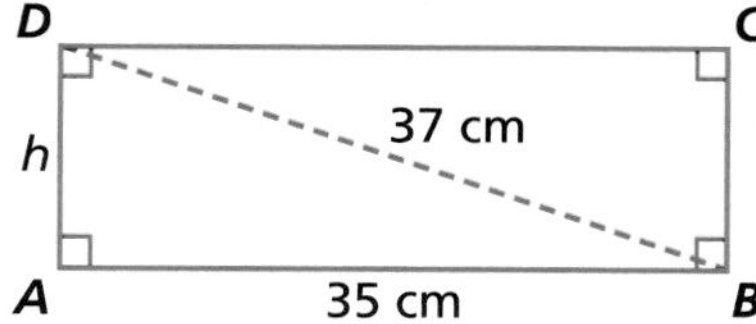

7. Use the Pythagorean Theorem to find the height of equilateral triangle *PQR* to the nearest hundredth.

8. Find the area of equilateral triangle *PQR* to the nearest tenth.

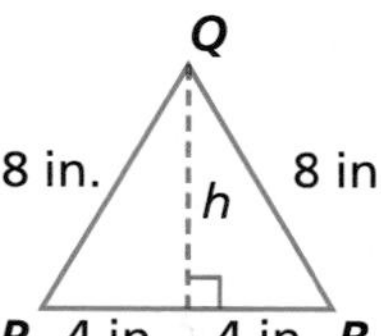

Find the area of the circle to the nearest tenth. Use 3.14 for π.

9. radius = 11 in.

10. diameter = 26 cm

Find the volume of each figure.

11. a sphere of radius 8 cm

12. a cylinder of height 10 in. and radius 6 in.

13. a pyramid with a 3 ft by 3 ft square base and height 5 ft

14. a cone of diameter 12 in. and height 18 in.

Find the surface area of each figure.

15.

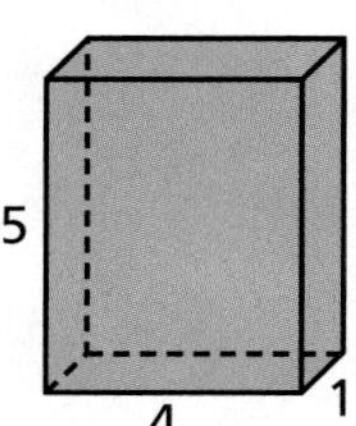

16.

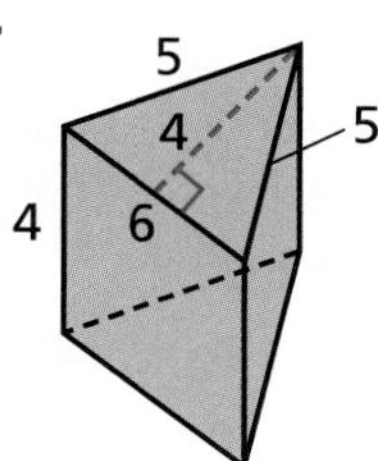

17.

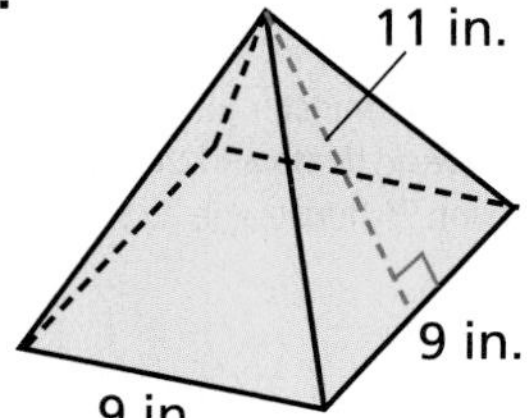

18.

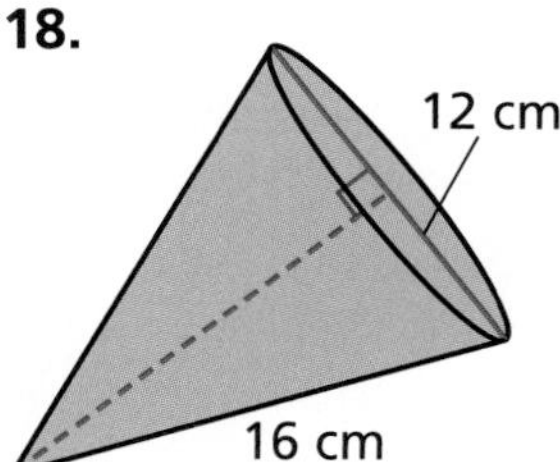

Chapter Test

Chapter 6

Performance Assessment

Show What You Know

Create a portfolio of your work from this chapter. Complete this page and include it with your four best pieces of work from Chapter 6. Choose from your homework or lab assignments, mid-chapter quiz, or any journal entries you have done. Put them together using any design you want. Make your portfolio represent what you consider your best work.

Short Response

Trace each figure, and then locate the vanishing point or horizon line.

1. Draw a rectangle with base length 7 cm and height 4 cm. Then draw a rectangle with base length 14 cm and height 1 cm. Which rectangle has the larger area? Which rectangle has the larger perimeter? Show your work or explain in words how you determined your answers.

2. A cylinder with a height of 6 in. and a diameter of 4 in. is filled with water. A cone with a height of 6 in. and a diameter of 2 in. is placed in the cylinder, point down, with its base even with the top of the cylinder. Draw a diagram to illustrate the situation described, and then determine how much water is left in the cylinder. Show your work.

Extended Problem Solving

3. A *geodesic dome* is constructed of triangles. The surface is approximately spherical.
   a. A pattern for a geodesic dome that approximates a hemisphere uses 30 triangles with base 8 ft and height 5.63 ft and 75 triangles with base 8 ft and height 7.13 ft. Find the surface area of the dome.
   b. The base of the dome is approximately a circle with diameter 41 ft. Use a hemisphere with this diameter to estimate the surface area of the dome.
   c. Compare your answer from part **a** to your estimate from part **b.** Explain the difference.

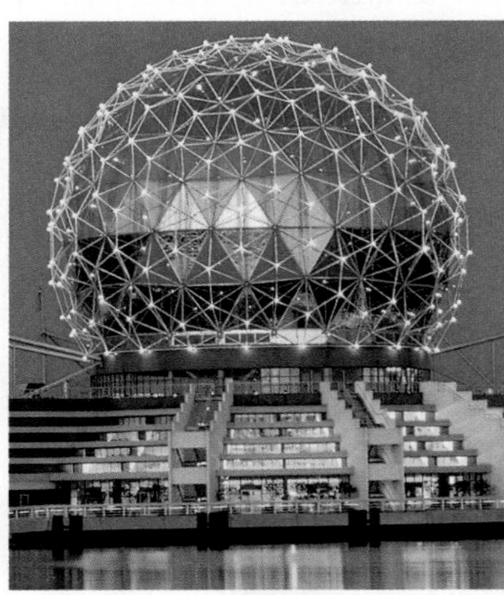

Richard Buckminster Fuller created the *geodesic dome* and designed the Dymaxion™ house, car, and map.

internet connect
State-Specific Test Practice Online
go.hrw.com Keyword: MP4 TestPrep

Standardized Test Prep

Chapter 6

Cumulative Assessment, Chapters 1–6

1. The shaded figure below is a net that can be used to form a rectangular prism. What is the surface area of the prism?

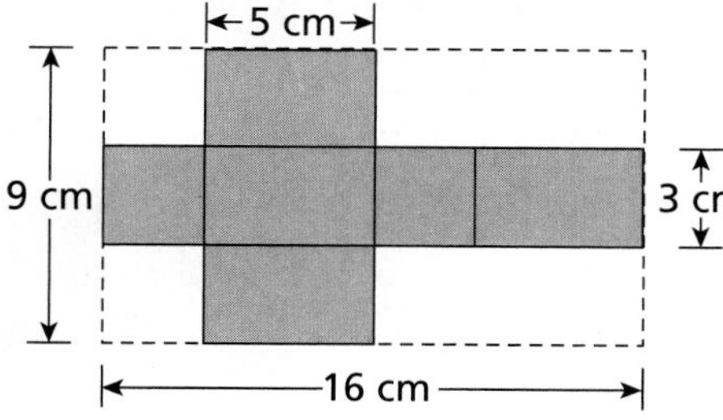

Ⓐ 15 cm^2
Ⓑ 144 cm^2
Ⓒ 78 cm^2
Ⓓ 180 cm^2

2. What is the value of x in the table below?

Number of Inches	5	10	x
Number of Centimeters	12.7	25.4	50.8

Ⓕ 15
Ⓖ 18
Ⓗ 20
Ⓙ 22

3. The quantity (3×8^{12}) is how many times the quantity (3×8^5)?

Ⓐ 7
Ⓑ 8
Ⓒ 21
Ⓓ 8^7

4. The arithmetic mean of 3 numbers is 60. If two of the numbers are 50 and 60, what is the third number?

Ⓕ 55
Ⓖ 60
Ⓗ 65
Ⓙ 70

5. What is the value of $26 - 24 \cdot 2^3$?

Ⓐ 18
Ⓑ 16
Ⓒ −118
Ⓓ −166

6. If $p = 3$, what is $4r(3 - 2p)$ in terms of r?

Ⓕ $-12r$
Ⓖ $-8r$
Ⓗ $-7r$
Ⓙ $12r - 6$

7. Point A' is formed by reflecting $A(-9, -8)$ across the y-axis. Find the coordinates of A'.

Ⓐ (9, 8)
Ⓑ (9, −8)
Ⓒ (−9, 8)
Ⓓ (−8, −9)

TEST TAKING TIP!

Look for a pattern in the data set to help you find the answer.

8. In the cylinder, point A lies on the top edge and point B on the bottom edge. If the radius of the cylinder is 2 units and the height is 5 units, what is the greatest straight-line distance between A and B?

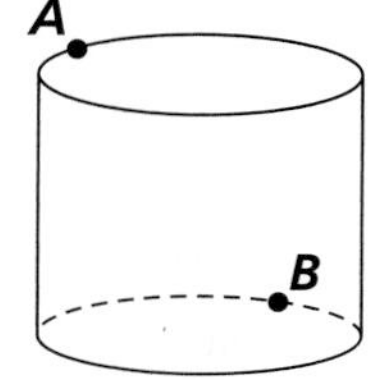

Ⓕ 5
Ⓖ 7
Ⓗ $\sqrt{29}$
Ⓙ $\sqrt{41}$

9. ***SHORT RESPONSE*** On a number line, point A has the coordinate −3 and point B has the coordinate 12. Point P is $\frac{2}{3}$ of the way from A to B. Draw and label the three points on a number line.

10. ***SHORT RESPONSE*** The tip of a blade on an electric fan is 1.5 feet from the axis of rotation. If the fan spins at a full rate of 1760 revolutions per minute, how many miles will a point at the tip of a blade travel in one hour? (1 mile = 5280 feet) Show your work.

Chapter 7

Ratios and Similarity

TABLE OF CONTENTS

Tree	Natural Height (ft)	Bonsai Height (in.)
Chinese elm	60	10
Brush cherry	50	8
Juniper	10	6
Pitch pine	200	14
Eastern hemlock	80	18

Career *Horticulturist*

Chances are that a horticulturist helped create many of the varieties of plants at your local nursery. Horticulturists work in vegetable development, fruit growing, flower growing, and landscape design. Horticulturists who are also scientists work to develop new types of plants or ways to control plant diseases.

The art of *bonsai,* or making miniature plants, began in China and became popular in Japan. Now bonsai is practiced all over the world.

internet connect

Chapter Opener Online
go.hrw.com
KEYWORD: MP4 Ch7

ARE YOU READY?

Choose the best term from the list to complete each sentence.

1. To solve an equation, you use __?__ to isolate the variable. So to solve the __?__ $3x = 18$, divide both sides by 3.
2. In the fractions $\frac{2}{3}$ and $\frac{1}{6}$, 18 is a __?__, but 6 is the __?__.
3. If two polygons are congruent, all of their __?__ sides and angles are congruent.

common denominator

corresponding

inverse operations

least common denominator

multiplication equation

Complete these exercises to review skills you will need for this chapter.

✔ Simplify Fractions

Write each fraction in simplest form.

4. $\frac{8}{24}$ **5.** $\frac{15}{50}$ **6.** $\frac{18}{72}$ **7.** $\frac{25}{125}$

✔ Use a Least Common Denominator

Find the least common denominator for each set of fractions.

8. $\frac{2}{3}$ and $\frac{1}{5}$ **9.** $\frac{3}{4}$ and $\frac{1}{8}$ **10.** $\frac{5}{7}$, $\frac{3}{7}$, and $\frac{1}{14}$ **11.** $\frac{1}{2}$, $\frac{2}{3}$, and $\frac{3}{5}$

✔ Order Decimals

Write each set of decimals in order from least to greatest.

12. 4.2, 2.24, 2.4, 0.242 **13.** 1.1, 0.1, 0.01, 1.11 **14.** 1.4, 2.53, $1.\overline{3}$, $0.\overline{9}$

✔ Solve Multiplication Equations

Solve.

15. $5x = 60$ **16.** $0.2y = 14$ **17.** $\frac{1}{2}t = 10$ **18.** $\frac{2}{3}z = 9$

✔ Identify Corresponding Parts of Congruent Figures

If $\triangle ABC \cong \triangle JRW$, complete each congruence statement.

19. $\overline{AB} \cong$ __?__ **20.** $\angle R \cong$ __?__ **21.** $\overline{AC} \cong$ __?__ **22.** $\angle C \cong$ __?__

7-1 Ratios and Proportions

Learn to find equivalent ratios to create proportions.

Vocabulary

ratio

equivalent ratio

proportion

Relative density is the ratio of the density of a substance to the density of water at 4°C. The relative density of silver is 10.5. This means that silver is 10.5 times as heavy as an equal volume of water.

The comparisons of water to silver in the table are *ratios* that are all equivalent.

Comparisons of Mass of Equal Volumes of Water and Silver				
Water	1 g	2 g	3 g	4 g
Silver	10.5 g	21 g	31.5 g	42 g

Mexico and Peru are the world's largest silver producers.

Reading Math

Ratios can be written in several ways. A colon is often used. 90:3 and $\frac{90}{3}$ name the same ratio.

A **ratio** is a comparison of two quantities by division. In one rectangle, the ratio of shaded squares to unshaded squares is 7:5. In the other rectangle, the ratio is 28:20. Both rectangles have equivalent shaded areas. Ratios that make the same comparison are **equivalent ratios**.

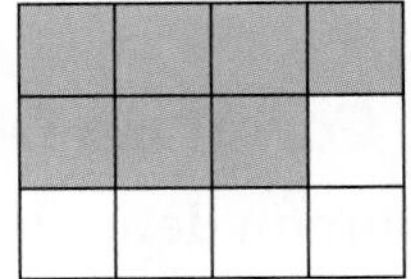

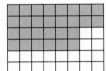

EXAMPLE 1 Finding Equivalent Ratios

Find two ratios that are equivalent to each given ratio.

A $\frac{6}{8}$

$\frac{6}{8} = \frac{6 \cdot 2}{8 \cdot 2} = \frac{12}{16}$

$\frac{6}{8} = \frac{6 \div 2}{8 \div 2} = \frac{3}{4}$

Multiply or divide the numerator and denominator by the same nonzero number.

Two ratios equivalent to $\frac{6}{8}$ are $\frac{12}{16}$ and $\frac{3}{4}$.

B $\frac{48}{27}$

$\frac{48}{27} = \frac{48 \cdot 2}{27 \cdot 2} = \frac{96}{54}$

$\frac{48}{27} = \frac{48 \div 3}{27 \div 3} = \frac{16}{9}$

Two ratios equivalent to $\frac{48}{27}$ are $\frac{96}{54}$ and $\frac{16}{9}$.

Ratios that are equivalent are said to be *proportional*, or in **proportion**. Equivalent ratios are identical when they are written in simplest form.

EXAMPLE 2 Determining Whether Two Ratios are in Proportion

Simplify to tell whether the ratios form a proportion.

A $\frac{7}{21}$ and $\frac{2}{6}$

$\frac{7}{21} = \frac{7 \div 7}{21 \div 7} = \frac{1}{3}$

$\frac{2}{6} = \frac{2 \div 2}{6 \div 2} = \frac{1}{3}$

Since $\frac{1}{3} = \frac{1}{3}$, the ratios are in proportion.

B $\frac{9}{12}$ and $\frac{16}{24}$

$\frac{9}{12} = \frac{9 \div 3}{12 \div 3} = \frac{3}{4}$

$\frac{16}{24} = \frac{16 \div 8}{24 \div 8} = \frac{2}{3}$

Since $\frac{3}{4} \neq \frac{2}{3}$, the ratios are *not* in proportion.

EXAMPLE 3 *Earth Science Application*

Silver is a rare mineral usually mined along with lead, copper, and zinc.

At 4°C, two cubic feet of silver has the same mass as 21 cubic feet of water. At 4°C, would 126 cubic feet of water have the same mass as 6 cubic feet of silver?

$\frac{2}{21} \stackrel{?}{=} \frac{6}{126}$

$\frac{2}{21} \stackrel{?}{=} \frac{6 \div 6}{126 \div 6}$ *Simplify.*

$\frac{2}{21} \neq \frac{1}{21}$

Since $\frac{2}{21}$ is not equal to $\frac{1}{21}$, 126 cubic feet of water would not have the same mass at 4°C as 6 cubic feet of silver.

Think and Discuss

1. **Describe** how two ratios can form a proportion.
2. **Give** three ratios equivalent to 12:24.
3. **Explain** why the ratios 2:4 and 6:10 do not form a proportion.
4. **Give an example** of two ratios that are proportional and have numerators with different signs.

7-1 Exercises

FOR EXTRA PRACTICE
see page 744

internet connect
Homework Help Online
go.hrw.com Keyword: MP4 7-1

GUIDED PRACTICE

See Example 1
Find two ratios that are equivalent to each given ratio.

1. $\frac{4}{10}$ **2.** $\frac{3}{9}$ **3.** $\frac{21}{7}$ **4.** $\frac{40}{32}$

See Example 2
Simplify to tell whether the ratios form a proportion.

5. $\frac{6}{30}$ and $\frac{3}{15}$ **6.** $\frac{6}{9}$ and $\frac{10}{18}$ **7.** $\frac{35}{21}$ and $\frac{20}{12}$

See Example 3
8. A recipe calls for 1.5 cups of mix to make 8 pancakes. Mike wants to make 12 pancakes and uses 2 cups of mix. Does Mike have the correct ratio for the recipe? Explain.

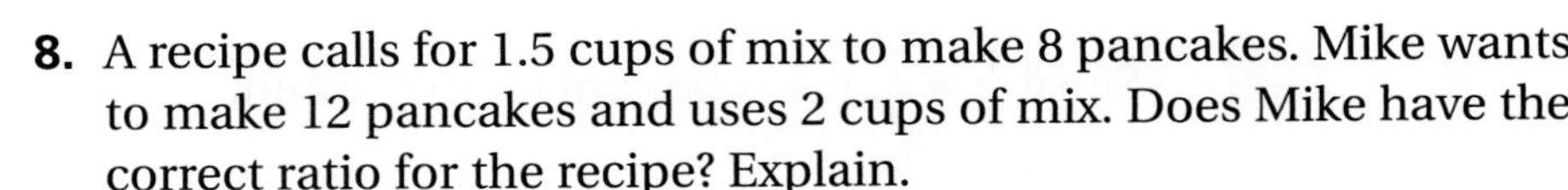

INDEPENDENT PRACTICE

See Example 1
Find two ratios that are equivalent to each given ratio.

9. $\frac{1}{7}$ **10.** $\frac{5}{11}$ **11.** $\frac{16}{14}$ **12.** $\frac{65}{15}$

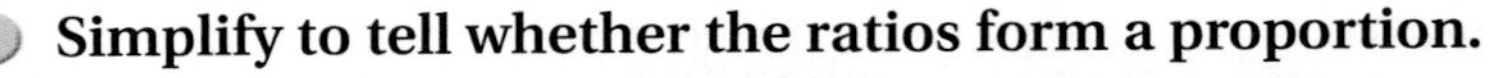

See Example 2
Simplify to tell whether the ratios form a proportion.

13. $\frac{7}{14}$ and $\frac{13}{28}$ **14.** $\frac{80}{100}$ and $\frac{4}{5}$ **15.** $\frac{1}{3}$ and $\frac{15}{45}$

See Example 3
16. A molecule of carbonic acid contains 3 atoms of oxygen for every 2 atoms of hydrogen. Could a compound containing 81 hydrogen atoms and 54 oxygen atoms be carbonic acid? Explain.

PRACTICE AND PROBLEM SOLVING

Tell whether the ratios form a proportion. If not, find a ratio that would form a proportion with the first ratio.

17. $\frac{8}{14}$ and $\frac{6}{21}$ **18.** $\frac{7}{9}$ and $\frac{140}{180}$ **19.** $\frac{4}{7}$ and $\frac{12}{49}$

20. $\frac{30}{36}$ and $\frac{15}{16}$ **21.** $\frac{13}{12}$ and $\frac{39}{36}$ **22.** $\frac{11}{20}$ and $\frac{22}{40}$

23. $\frac{16}{84}$ and $\frac{6}{62}$ **24.** $\frac{24}{10}$ and $\frac{44}{18}$ **25.** $\frac{11}{121}$ and $\frac{33}{363}$

26. ***BUSINESS*** Cal pays his employees weekly. He would like to start paying them four times the weekly amount on a monthly basis. Is a month equivalent to four weeks? Explain.

27. ***TRANSPORTATION*** Aaron's truck has a 12-gallon gas tank. He just put 3 gallons of gas into the tank. Is this equivalent to a third of a tank? If not, what amount of gas is equivalent to a third of a tank?

28. ***ENTERTAINMENT*** The table lists prices for movie tickets.

a. Are the ticket prices proportional?

b. How much do 6 movie tickets cost?

c. If Suzie paid $57.75 for movie tickets, how many did she buy?

Movie Ticket Prices			
Number of Tickets	1	2	3
Price	$8.25	$16.50	$24.75

29. ***HOBBIES*** A bicycle chain moves between two sprockets when you shift gears. The number of teeth on the front sprocket and the number of teeth on the rear sprocket form a ratio. Equivalent ratios provide equal pedaling power. Find a ratio equivalent to the ratio shown, $\frac{52}{24}$.

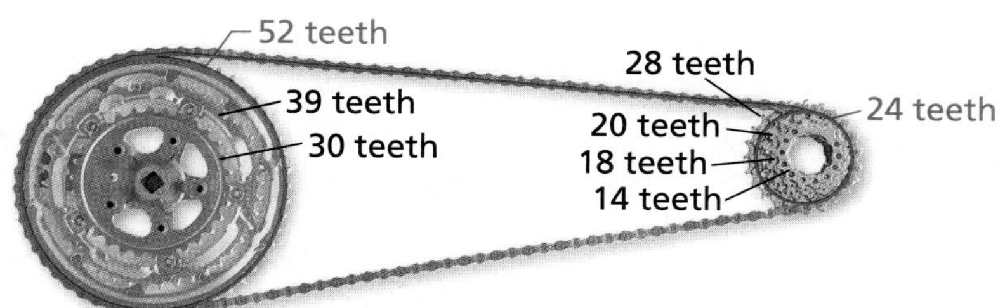

30. ***COMPUTERS*** While a file downloads, a computer displays the total number of kilobytes downloaded and the number of seconds that have passed. If the display shows 42 kilobytes after 7 seconds, is the file downloading at about 6 kilobytes per second? Explain.

31. ***WRITE A PROBLEM*** The ratio of the number of bones in the human skull to the number of bones in the ears is 11:3. There are 22 bones in the skull and 6 in the ears. Use this information to write a problem using equivalent ratios. Explain your solution.

32. ***WRITE ABOUT IT*** Describe at least two ways, given a ratio, to create an equivalent ratio.

33. ***CHALLENGE*** Write all possible proportions using each of the numbers 2, 4, 8, and 16 once.

Spiral Review

Add or subtract. (Lesson 3-5)

34. $\frac{5}{7} + \frac{2}{3}$ **35.** $\frac{4}{9} + \left(-1\frac{3}{4}\right)$ **36.** $\frac{3}{5} - \frac{7}{10}$ **37.** $2\frac{7}{9} - 1\frac{8}{11}$

Find the two square roots of each number. (Lesson 3-8)

38. 49 **39.** 9 **40.** 81 **41.** 169

42. TEST PREP Name the two integers that $-\sqrt{74}$ lies between. (Lesson 3-9)

A -7 and -6 **B** -9 and -8 **C** -10 and -11 **D** -8 and -7

7-2 Ratios, Rates, and Unit Rates

Learn to work with rates and ratios.

Vocabulary

rate

unit rate

unit price

Movie and television screens range in shape from almost perfect squares to wide rectangles. An *aspect ratio* describes a screen by comparing its width to its height. Common aspect ratios are 4:3, 37:20, 16:9, and 47:20.

Most high-definition TV screens have an aspect ratio of 16:9.

EXAMPLE 1 ***Entertainment Application***

By design, movies can be viewed on screens with varying aspect ratios. The most common ones are 4:3, 37:20, 16:9, and 47:20.

A **Order the width-to-height ratios from least (standard TV) to greatest (wide-screen).**

$4:3 = \frac{4}{3} = 1.\overline{3}$ *Divide.* $\frac{4}{3} = \frac{1.\overline{3}}{1}$

$37:20 = \frac{37}{20} = 1.85$

$16:9 = \frac{16}{9} = 1.\overline{7}$

$47:20 = \frac{47}{20} = 2.35$

The decimals in order are $1.\overline{3}$, $1.\overline{7}$, 1.85, and 2.35.
The width-to-height ratios in order from least to greatest are 4:3, 16:9, 37:20, and 47:20.

B **A wide-screen television has screen width 32 in. and height 18 in. What is the aspect ratio of this screen?**

The ratio of the width to the height is 32:18.

The ratio $\frac{32}{18}$ can be simplified: $\frac{32}{18} = \frac{2(16)}{2(9)} = \frac{16}{9}$.

The screen has the aspect ratio 16:9.

A ratio is a comparison of two quantities. A **rate** is a comparison of two quantities that have different units.

ratio: $\frac{90}{3}$ rate: $\frac{90 \text{ miles}}{3 \text{ hours}}$ ← *Read as "90 miles per 3 hours."*

Unit rates are rates in which the second quantity is 1. The ratio $\frac{90}{3}$ can be simplified by dividing: $\frac{90}{3} = \frac{30}{1}$.

unit rate: $\frac{30 \text{ miles}}{1 \text{ hour}}$, or 30 mi/h

EXAMPLE 2 Using a Bar Graph to Determine Rates

The number of acres destroyed by wildfires in 2000 is shown for the states with the highest totals. Use the bar graph to find the number of acres, to the nearest acre, destroyed in each state per day.

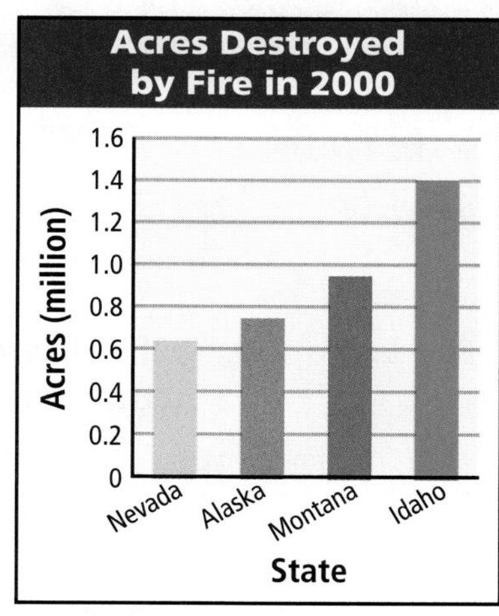

Source: National Interagency Fire Center

$$\text{Nevada} = \frac{640{,}000 \text{ acres}}{366 \text{ days}} \approx \frac{1749 \text{ acres}}{1 \text{ day}}$$

$$\text{Alaska} = \frac{750{,}000 \text{ acres}}{366 \text{ days}} \approx \frac{2049 \text{ acres}}{1 \text{ day}}$$

$$\text{Montana} = \frac{950{,}000 \text{ acres}}{366 \text{ days}} \approx \frac{2596 \text{ acres}}{1 \text{ day}}$$

$$\text{Idaho} = \frac{1{,}400{,}000 \text{ acres}}{366 \text{ days}} \approx \frac{3825 \text{ acres}}{1 \text{ day}}$$

Nevada: 1749 acres/day; Alaska: 2049 acres/day; Montana: 2596 acres/day; Idaho: 3825 acres/day

Unit price is a unit rate used to compare costs per item.

EXAMPLE 3 Finding Unit Prices to Compare Costs

A **Blank videotapes can be purchased in packages of 3 for \$4.99, or 10 for \$15.49. Which is the better buy?**

$$\frac{\text{price for package}}{\text{number of videotapes}} = \frac{\$4.99}{3} \approx \$1.66$$

$$\frac{\text{price for package}}{\text{number of videotapes}} = \frac{\$15.49}{10} \approx \$1.55$$

Divide the price by the number of tapes.

The better buy is the package of 10 for \$15.49.

B **Leron can buy a 64 oz carton of orange juice for \$2.49 or a 96 oz carton for \$3.99. Which is the better buy?**

$$\frac{\text{price for carton}}{\text{number of ounces}} = \frac{\$2.49}{64} \approx \$0.0389$$

$$\frac{\text{price for carton}}{\text{number of ounces}} = \frac{\$3.99}{96} \approx \$0.0416$$

Divide the price by the number of ounces.

The better buy is the 64 oz carton for \$2.49.

Think and Discuss

1. **Choose** the quantity that has a lower unit price: 6 oz for \$1.29 or 15 oz for \$3.00. Explain your answer.
2. **Explain** why an aspect ratio is not considered a rate.
3. **Determine** two different units of measurement for speed.

7-2 Exercises

FOR EXTRA PRACTICE

see page 744

GUIDED PRACTICE

See Example 

1. The height of a bridge is 68 ft, and its length is 340 ft. Find the ratio of its height to its length in simplest form.

See Example 2

For Exercises 2 and 3, use the bar graph to find each unit rate.

2. Ellen's words per minute
3. Yoshiko's words per minute

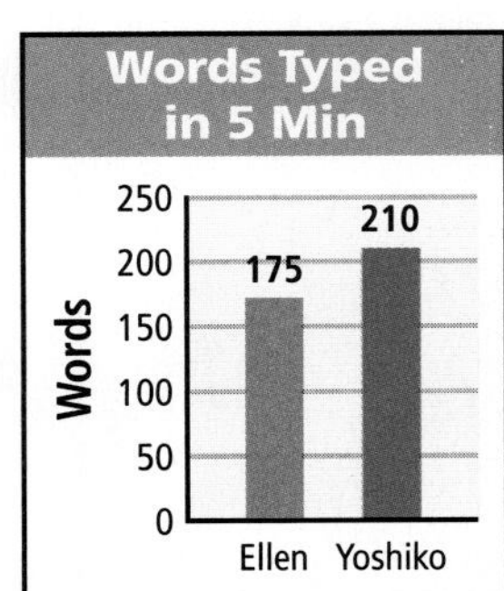

See Example 3

Determine the better buy.

4. a 15 oz can of corn for \$1.39 or a 22 oz can for \$1.85
5. a dozen golf balls for \$22.99 or 20 golf balls for \$39.50

INDEPENDENT PRACTICE

See Example 

6. A child's basketball hoop is 6 ft tall. Find the ratio of its height to the height of a regulation basketball hoop, which is 10 ft tall. Express the ratio in simplest form.

See Example 2

For Exercises 7 and 8, use the bar graph to find each unit rate.

7. gallons per hour for machine A
8. gallons per hour for machine B

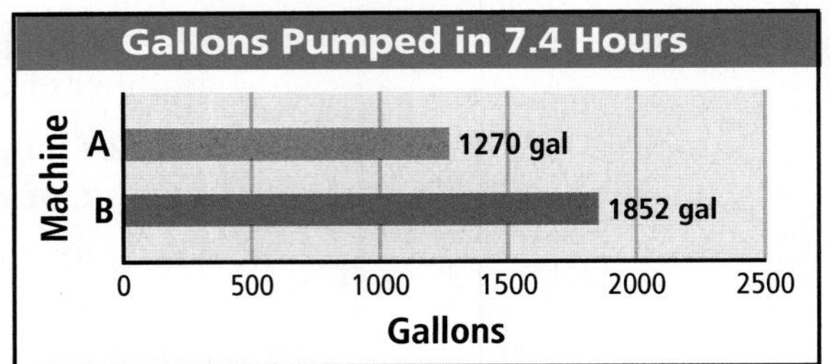

See Example 3

Determine the better buy.

9. 4 boxes of cereal for \$9.56; 2 boxes of cereal for \$4.98
10. 8 oz jar of soup for \$2.39; 10 oz jar of soup for \$2.69

PRACTICE AND PROBLEM SOLVING

Find each unit rate.

11. \$525 for 20 hours of work
12. 96 chairs in 8 rows
13. 12 slices of pizza for \$9.25
14. 64 beats in 4 measures of music

Find each unit price and tell which is the better buy.

15. \$7.47 for 3 yards of fabric; \$11.29 for 5 yards of fabric
16. A $\frac{1}{2}$-pound hamburger for \$3.50; a $\frac{1}{3}$-pound hamburger for \$3.25
17. 10 gallons of gasoline for \$13.70; 12.5 gallons of gasoline for \$17.75
18. \$1.65 for 5 pounds of bananas; \$3.15 for 10 pounds of bananas

19. ***COMMUNICATIONS*** Super-Cell offers a wireless phone plan that includes 250 base minutes for \$24.99 a month. Easy-Phone has a plan that includes 325 base minutes for \$34.99.

   a. Find the unit rate for the base minutes for each plan.

   b. Which company offers a lower rate for base minutes?

20. ***BUSINESS*** A cereal company pays \$59,969 to have its new cereal placed in a grocery store display for one week. Find the daily rate for this display.

21. ***ENTERTAINMENT*** Tom, Cherise, and Tina work as film animators. The circle graph shows the number of frames they each rendered in an 8-hour day.

   a. Find the hourly unit rendering rate for each employee.

   b. Who was the most efficient employee?

   c. How many more frames per hour did Cherise render than Tom?

   d. How many more frames per hour did Tom and Cherise together render than Tina?

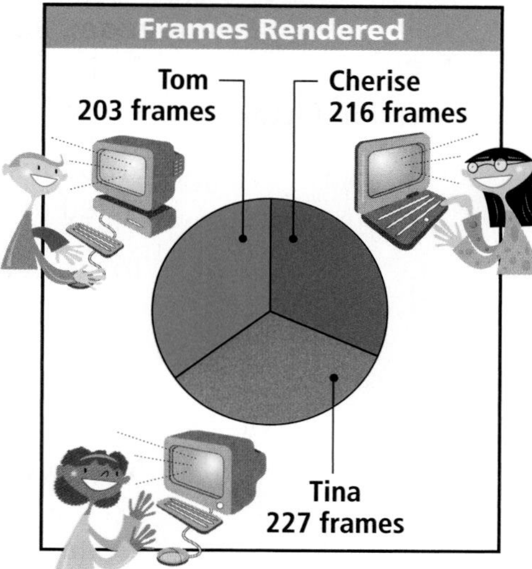

22. ***WHAT'S THE ERROR?*** A clothing store charges \$30 for 12 pairs of socks. A student says that the unit price is \$0.40 per pair. What is the error? What is the correct unit price?

23. ***WRITE ABOUT IT*** Explain how to find unit rates. Give an example and explain how consumers can use unit rates to save money.

24. ***CHALLENGE*** The size of a television (13 in., 25 in., 32 in., and so on) represents the length of the diagonal of the television screen. A 25 in. television has an aspect ratio of 4:3. What is the width and height of the screen?

Spiral Review

Evaluate each expression for the given value of the variable. (Lesson 2-1)

25. $c + 4$ for $c = -8$ **26.** $m - 2$ for $m = 13$ **27.** $5 + d$ for $d = -10$

Evaluate each expression for the given value of the variable. (Lesson 3-2)

28. $45.6 + x$ for $x = -11.1$ **29.** $17.9 - b$ for $b = 22.3$ **30.** $r + (-4.9)$ for $r = 31.8$

31. TEST PREP How much fencing, to the nearest foot, is needed to enclose a square lot with an area of 350 ft^2? (Lesson 3-9)

A 74 ft **B** 65 ft **C** 68 ft **D** 75 ft

7-3 Analyze Units

Problem Solving Skill

Learn to use one or more conversion factors to solve rate problems.

Vocabulary

conversion factor

You can measure the speed of an object using a strobe lamp and a camera in a dark room. Each time the lamp flashes, the camera records the object's position.

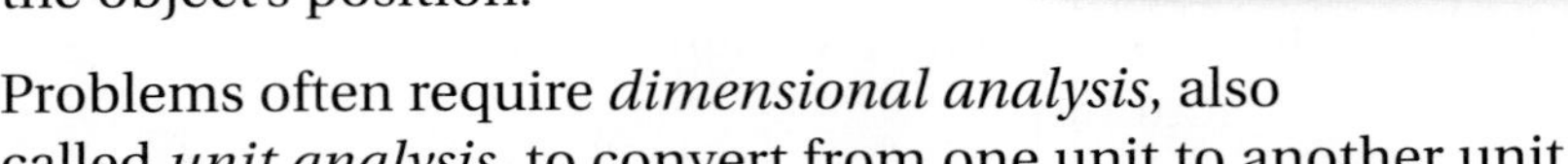

Problems often require *dimensional analysis,* also called *unit analysis,* to convert from one unit to another unit.

To convert units, multiply by one or more ratios of equal quantities called **conversion factors**.

For example, to convert inches to feet you would use the ratio at right as a conversion factor.

$$\frac{1\text{ ft}}{12\text{ in.}}$$

Multiplying by a conversion factor is like multiplying by a fraction that reduces to 1, such as $\frac{5}{5}$.

$$\frac{1\text{ ft}}{12\text{ in.}} = \frac{12\text{ in.}}{12\text{ in.}},\text{ or }\frac{1\text{ ft}}{1\text{ ft}}, = 1$$

EXAMPLE 1 Finding Conversion Factors

Helpful Hint

The conversion factor
- must introduce the unit desired in the answer and
- must cancel the original unit so that the unit desired is all that remains.

Find the appropriate factor for each conversion.

A quarts to gallons

There are 4 quarts in 1 gallon. To convert quarts to gallons, multiply the number of quarts by $\frac{1\text{ gal}}{4\text{ qt}}$.

B meters to centimeters

There are 100 centimeters in 1 meter. To convert meters to centimeters, multiply the number of meters by $\frac{100\text{ cm}}{1\text{ m}}$.

EXAMPLE 2 Using Conversion Factors to Solve Problems

The average American eats 23 pounds of pizza per year. Find the number of ounces of pizza the average American eats per year.

The problem gives the ratio 23 *pounds* to 1 year and asks for an answer in *ounces* per year.

$\frac{23\text{ lb}}{1\text{ yr}} \cdot \frac{16\text{ oz}}{1\text{ lb}}$ — *Multiply the ratio by the conversion factor.*

$= \frac{23 \cdot 16\text{ oz}}{1\text{ yr}}$ — *Cancel lb units.* $\frac{\cancel{lb}}{yr} \cdot \frac{oz}{\cancel{lb}} = \frac{oz}{yr}$

$= 368$ oz per year — *Multiply 23 by 16 oz.*

The average American eats 368 ounces of pizza per year.

EXAMPLE 3

PROBLEM SOLVING APPLICATION

A car traveled 990 feet down a road in 15 seconds. How many miles per hour was the car traveling?

1 Understand the Problem

The problem is stated in units of feet and seconds. The question asks for the **answer** in units of miles and hours. You will need to use several conversion factors.

List the important information:

- Feet to miles ⟶ $\frac{1 \text{ mi}}{5280 \text{ ft}}$
- Seconds to minutes ⟶ $\frac{60 \text{ s}}{1 \text{ min}}$; minutes to hours ⟶ $\frac{60 \text{ min}}{1 \text{ h}}$

 Make a Plan

Multiply by each conversion factor separately, or **simplify the problem** and multiply by several conversion factors at once.

3 Solve

First, convert 990 feet in 15 seconds into a unit rate.

$$\frac{990 \text{ ft}}{15 \text{ s}} = \frac{(990 \div 15) \text{ ft}}{(15 \div 15) \text{ s}} = \frac{66 \text{ ft}}{1 \text{ s}}$$

Create a single conversion factor to convert seconds directly to hours:

seconds to minutes ⟶ $\frac{60 \text{ s}}{1 \text{ min}}$; minutes to hours ⟶ $\frac{60 \text{ min}}{1 \text{ h}}$

seconds to hours $= \frac{60 \text{ s}}{1 \cancel{\text{min}}} \cdot \frac{60 \cancel{\text{min}}}{1 \text{ h}} = \frac{3600 \text{ s}}{1 \text{ h}}$

$\frac{66 \text{ ft}}{1 \text{ s}} \cdot \frac{1 \text{ mi}}{5280 \text{ ft}} \cdot \frac{3600 \text{ s}}{1 \text{ h}}$ *Set up the conversion factors.*

Do not include the numbers yet. Notice what happens to the units.

$\frac{\cancel{\text{ft}}}{\cancel{\text{s}}} \cdot \frac{\text{mi}}{\cancel{\text{ft}}} \cdot \frac{\cancel{\text{s}}}{\text{h}}$ *Simplify. Only $\frac{mi}{h}$ remain.*

$\frac{66 \text{ ft}}{1 \text{ s}} \cdot \frac{1 \text{ mi}}{5280 \text{ ft}} \cdot \frac{3600 \text{ s}}{1 \text{ h}}$ *Multiply.*

$$\frac{66 \cdot 1 \text{ mi} \cdot 3600}{1 \cdot 5280 \cdot 1 \text{ h}} = \frac{237{,}600 \text{ mi}}{5280 \text{ h}} = \frac{45 \text{ mi}}{1 \text{ h}}$$

The car was traveling 45 miles per hour.

A rate of 45 mi/h is less than 1 mi/min. 15 seconds is $\frac{1}{4}$ min. A car traveling 45 mi/h would go less than $\frac{1}{4}$ of 5280 ft in 15 seconds. It goes 990 ft, so 45 mi/h is a reasonable speed.

EXAMPLE 4 Physical Science Application

Physical Science LINK

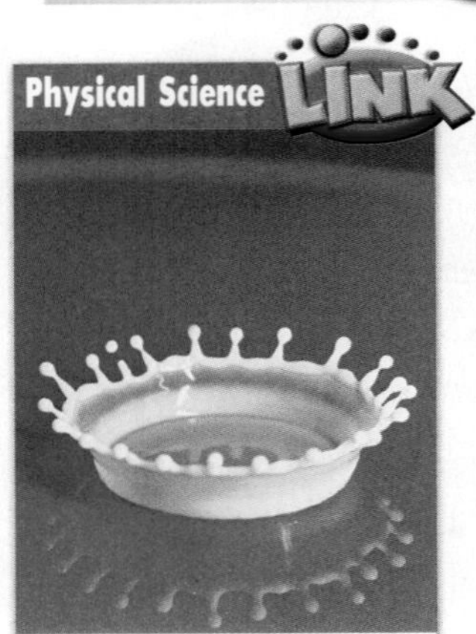

A strobe light flashing on dripping liquid can make droplets appear to stand still or even move upward.

A strobe lamp can be used to measure the speed of an object. The lamp flashes every $\frac{1}{1000}$ s. A camera records the object moving 7.5 cm between flashes. How fast is the object moving in m/s?

$$\frac{7.5 \text{ cm}}{\frac{1}{1000} \text{ s}}$$ *Use rate = $\frac{\text{distance}}{\text{time}}$.*

It may help to eliminate the fraction $\frac{1}{1000}$ first.

$$\frac{7.5 \text{ cm}}{\frac{1}{1000} \text{ s}} = \frac{1000 \cdot 7.5 \text{ cm}}{1000 \cdot \frac{1}{1000} \text{ s}}$$ *Multiply top and bottom by 1000.*

$$= \frac{7500 \text{ cm}}{1 \text{ s}}$$

Now convert centimeters to meters.

$$\frac{7500 \text{ cm}}{1 \text{ s}}$$

$$= \frac{7500 \text{ cm}}{1 \text{ s}} \cdot \frac{1 \text{ m}}{100 \text{ cm}}$$ *Multiply by the conversion factor.*

$$= \frac{7500 \text{ m}}{100 \text{ s}} = \frac{75 \text{ m}}{1 \text{ s}}$$

The object is traveling 75 m/s.

EXAMPLE 5 Transportation Application

The rate of one knot equals one nautical mile per hour. One nautical mile is 1852 meters. What is the speed in meters per second of a ship traveling at 20 knots?

20 knots = 20 nautical mi/h

Set up the units to obtain m/s in your answer.

$$\frac{\cancel{\text{nautical mi}}}{\cancel{\text{h}}} \cdot \frac{\text{m}}{\cancel{\text{nautical mi}}} \cdot \frac{\cancel{\text{h}}}{\text{s}}$$ *Examine the units.*

$$\frac{20 \text{ nautical mi}}{\text{h}} \cdot \frac{1852 \text{ m}}{\text{nautical mi}} \cdot \frac{1 \text{ h}}{3600 \text{ s}}$$

$$\frac{20 \cdot 1852}{3600} \approx 10.3$$

The ship is traveling about 10.3 m/s.

Think and Discuss

1. **Give** the conversion factor for converting $\frac{\text{lb}}{\text{yr}}$ to $\frac{\text{lb}}{\text{mo}}$.
2. **Explain** how to find whether 10 miles per hour is faster than 15 feet per second.
3. **Give an example** of a conversion between units that includes ounces as a unit in the conversion.

7-3 Exercises

FOR EXTRA PRACTICE

see page 744

GUIDED PRACTICE

See Example 1 **Find the appropriate factor for each conversion.**

1. feet to inches **2.** gallons to pints **3.** centimeters to meters

See Example 2 **4.** Aihua drinks 4 cups of water a day. Find the total number of gallons of water she drinks in a year.

See Example 3 **5.** A model airplane flies 22 feet in 2 seconds. What is the airplane's speed in miles per hour?

See Example 4 **6.** If a fish swims 0.09 centimeter every hundredth of a second, how fast in meters per second is it swimming?

See Example 5 **7.** There are about 400 cocoa beans in a pound. There are 2.2 pounds in a kilogram. About how many grams does a cocoa bean weigh?

INDEPENDENT PRACTICE

See Example 1 **Find the appropriate factor for each conversion.**

8. kilometers to meters **9.** inches to yards **10.** days to weeks

See Example 2 **11.** A theme park sells 71,175 yards of licorice each year. How many feet per day does the park sell?

See Example 3 **12.** A yellow jacket can fly 4.5 meters in 9 seconds. How fast in kilometers per hour can a yellow jacket fly?

See Example 4 **13.** Brilco Manufacturing produces 0.2 of a brick every tenth of a second. How many bricks can be produced in an 8-hour day?

See Example 5 **14.** Assume that one dollar is equal to 1.14 euros. If 500 g of an item is selling for 25 euros, what is its price in dollars per kg?

PRACTICE AND PROBLEM SOLVING

Use conversion factors to find each specified amount.

15. radios produced in 5 hours at a rate of 3 radios per minute

16. distance traveled (in feet) after 12 seconds at 87 miles per hour

17. hot dogs eaten in a month at a rate of 48 hot dogs eaten each year

18. umbrellas sold in a year at a rate of 5 umbrellas sold per day

19. miles jogged in 1 hour at an average rate of 7.3 feet per second

20. states visited in a two-week political campaign at a rate of 2 states per day

21. ***SPORTS*** Use the graph to find each world-record speed in miles per hour. (*Hint:* 1 mile ≈ 1609 m.)

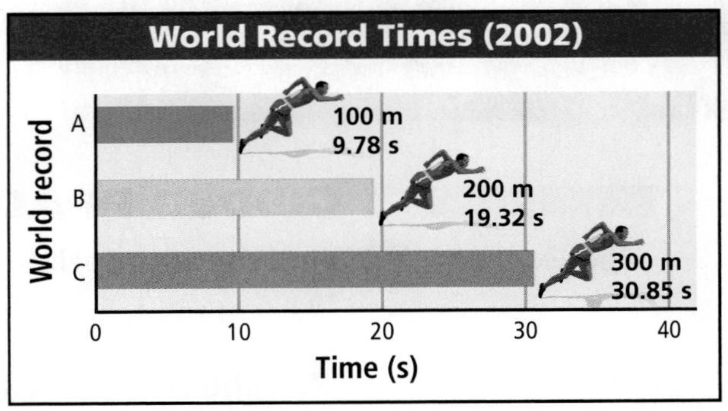

22. ***LIFE SCIENCE*** The Kelp Forest exhibit at the Monterey Bay Aquarium holds 335,000 gallons. How many days would it take to fill it at a rate of 1 gallon per second?

23. ***TRANSPORTATION*** An automobile engine is turning at 3000 revolutions per minute. During each revolution, each of the four spark plugs fires. How many times do the spark plugs fire in one second?

24. ***CHOOSE A STRATEGY*** The label on John's bottle of cough syrup says a person should take 3 teaspoons. Which spoon could John use to take the cough medicine? (*Hint:* 1 teaspoon = $\frac{1}{6}$ oz.)

A A 1.5 oz spoon

B A 0.5 oz spoon

C A 1 oz spoon

D None of these

25. ***WHAT'S THE ERROR?*** To convert 25 feet per second to miles per hour, a student wrote $\frac{25 \text{ ft}}{1 \text{ s}} \cdot \frac{1 \text{ mile}}{5280 \text{ ft}} \cdot \frac{60 \text{ s}}{1 \text{ h}} \approx 0.28$ mi/h. What error did the student make? What should the correct answer be?

26. ***WRITE ABOUT IT*** Describe the important role that conversion factors play in solving rate problems. Give an example.

27. ***CHALLENGE*** Anthony the anteater requires 1800 calories each day. He gets 1 calorie from every 50 ants that he eats. If he sticks his tongue out 150 times per minute and averages 2 ants per lick, how many hours will it take for him to get 1800 calories?

Spiral Review

Find the area of the quadrilateral with the given vertices. (Lesson 6-1)

28. (0, 0), (0, 9), (5, 9), (5, 0)

29. (–3, 1), (4, 1), (6, 3), (–1, 3)

Find the area of each circle to the nearest tenth. Use 3.14 for π. (Lesson 6-4)

30. circle with radius 7 ft

31. circle with diameter 17 in.

32. circle with radius 3.5 cm

33. circle with diameter 2.2 mi

34. **TEST PREP** A cylinder has radius 6 cm and height 14 cm. If the radius were cut in half, what would the volume of the cylinder be? Use 3.14 for π and round to the nearest tenth. (Lesson 6-6)

A 395.6 cm^3 **B** 791.3 cm^3 **C** 422.3 cm^3 **D** 393.5 cm^3

Model Proportions

Use with Lesson 7-4

WHAT YOU NEED:

- Ruler
- Pattern blocks

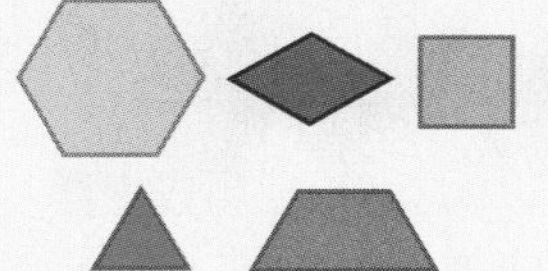

REMEMBER

- **Use the area formulas to find the area of each pattern block except the hexagon.**

To find the area of the hexagon, think of the pieces that can fit together to make the hexagon.

Activity

1. Measure each type of pattern block to the nearest eighth of an inch to determine its area. Use pattern blocks to find several area relationships that represent fractions equivalent to one-half. For example,

$= \frac{1}{2}$.

2. Above, you related area of pattern blocks to a ratio. Now make a proportion based upon area that uses only pattern blocks on both sides of the equal sign. Then write these proportions using numbers based on your measurements for area. Use cross products to check your work.

Think and Discuss

1. Which pattern-block area relationships equal $\frac{5}{6}$?
2. What area relationships can you make with a triangle and a trapezoid?
3. What area relationships can you make with only a triangle?

Try This

Use pattern blocks to complete each proportion based on area. Then write these proportions using numbers based on your measurements for area.

1.

= ____

2.

= ____

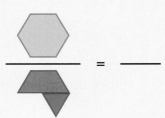

7-4 Solving Proportions

Learn to solve proportions.

Vocabulary

cross product

Unequal masses will not balance on a *fulcrum* if they are an equal distance from it; one side will go up and the other side will go down.

Unequal masses will balance when the following proportion is true:

$$\frac{\text{mass 1}}{\text{length 2}} = \frac{\text{mass 2}}{\text{length 1}}$$

Alexander Calder's sculpture *Totem* stands in Paris. Calder is known as the father of the mobile.

Mass 1
Mass 2
Length 1
Length 2
Fulcrum

One way to find whether ratios, such as those above, are equal is to find a common denominator. The ratios are equal if their numerators are equal after the fractions have been rewritten with a common denominator.

$$\frac{6}{8} = \frac{72}{96} \quad \frac{9}{12} = \frac{72}{96} \qquad \frac{6}{8} = \frac{9}{12}$$

Helpful Hint

The cross product represents the numerator of the fraction when a common denominator is found by multiplying the denominators.

CROSS PRODUCTS

Cross products in proportions are equal. If the ratios are *not* in proportion, the cross products are not equal.

Proportions		***Not*** **Proportions**	
$\frac{6}{8} = \frac{9}{12}$	$\frac{5}{2} = \frac{15}{6}$	$\frac{1}{6} \neq \frac{2}{7}$	$\frac{5}{12} \neq \frac{2}{5}$
$6 \cdot 12 = 8 \cdot 9$	$5 \cdot 6 = 2 \cdot 15$	$1 \cdot 7 \neq 6 \cdot 2$	$5 \cdot 5 \neq 12 \cdot 2$
$72 = 72$	$30 = 30$	$7 \neq 12$	$25 \neq 24$

EXAMPLE 1 Using Cross Products to Identify Proportions

Tell whether the ratios are proportional.

A $\frac{5}{6} \stackrel{?}{=} \frac{15}{21}$

$\frac{5}{6} \times \frac{15}{21}$ → 90, 105 *Find cross products.*

$105 \neq 90$

Since the cross products are not equal, the ratios are not proportional.

Focus on Problem Solving

Solve

- **Choose an operation: Multiplication or division**

When you are converting units, think about whether the number in the answer will be greater or less than the number given in the question. This will help you to decide whether to multiply or divide to convert the units.

For example, if you are converting feet to inches, you know that the number of inches will be greater than the number of feet because each foot is 12 inches. So you know that you should multiply by 12 to get a greater number.

In general, if you are converting to smaller units, the number of units will have to be greater to represent the same quantity.

For each problem, determine whether the number in the answer will be greater or less than the number given in the question. Use your answer to decide whether to multiply or divide by the conversion factor. Then solve the problem.

1. The speed a boat travels is usually measured in nautical miles, or knots. The Golden Gate–Sausalito ferry in California, which provides service between Sausalito and San Francisco, can travel at 20.5 knots. Find the speed in miles per hour. (*Hint:* 1 knot = 1.15 miles per hour)

2. When it is finished, the Crazy Horse Memorial in the Black Hills of South Dakota will be the world's largest sculpture. The sculpture's height will be 563 feet. Find the height in meters. (*Hint:* 1 meter = 3.28 feet)

3. The amounts of water typically used for common household tasks are given in the table below. Find the number of liters needed for each task. (*Hint:* 1 gallon = 3.79 liters)

Task	Water Used (gal)
Laundry (1 load)	40
5-minute shower	12.5
Washing hands	0.5
Flushing toilet	3.5

4. Lake Baikal, in Siberia, is so large that it would take all of the rivers on Earth combined an entire year to fill it. At 1.62 kilometers deep, it is the deepest lake in the world. Find the depth of Lake Baikal in miles. (1 mile = 1.61 kilometers)

7-5 Dilations

Learn to identify and create dilations of plane figures.

Vocabulary

dilation

scale factor

center of dilation

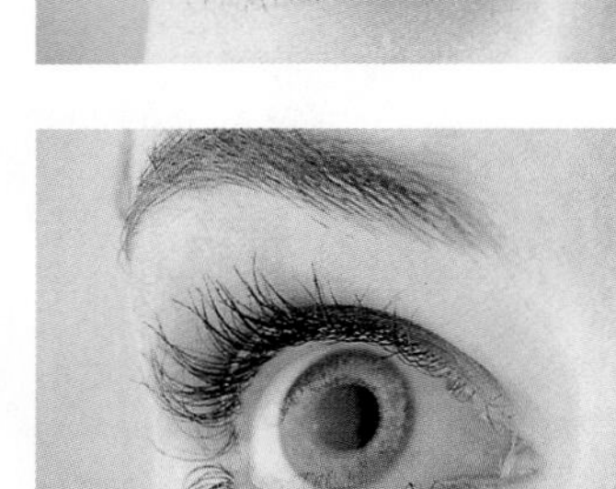

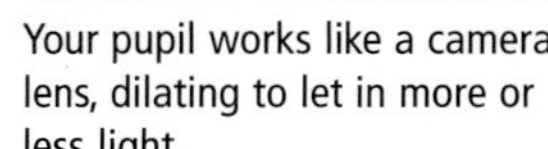

Your pupil works like a camera lens, dilating to let in more or less light.

Your pupils are the black areas in the center of your eyes. When you go to the eye doctor, the doctor may *dilate* your pupils, which makes them larger.

Translations, reflections, and rotations are transformations that do not change the size or shape of a figure. A **dilation** is a transformation that changes the size, but not the shape, of a figure. A dilation can enlarge or reduce a figure.

A **scale factor** describes how much a figure is enlarged or reduced. A scale factor can be expressed as a decimal, fraction, or percent. A 10% increase is a scale factor of 1.1, and a 10% decrease is a scale factor of 0.9.

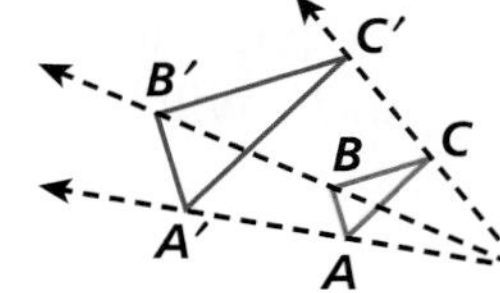

Helpful Hint

A scale factor between 0 and 1 reduces a figure. A scale factor greater than 1 enlarges it.

EXAMPLE 1 Identifying Dilations

Tell whether each transformation is a dilation.

A

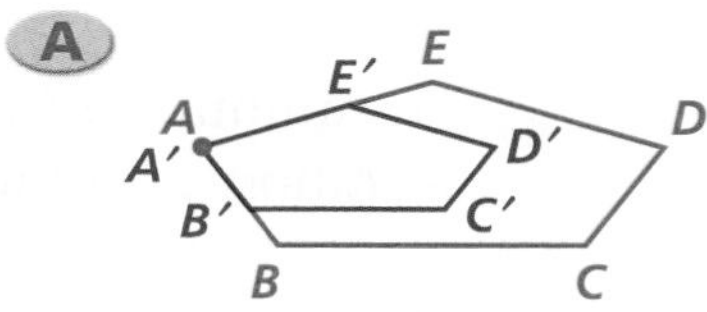

The transformation is a dilation.

B

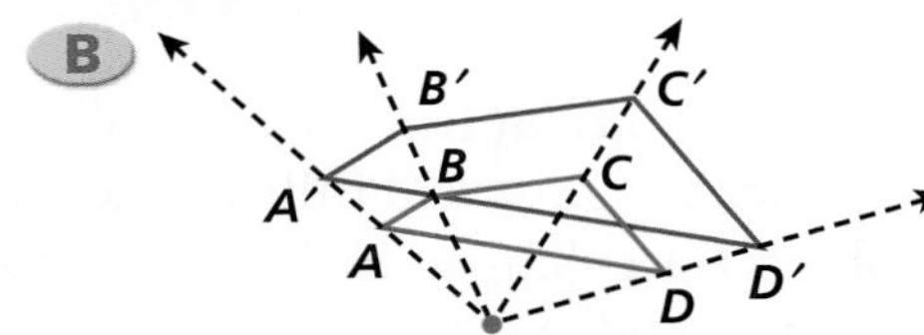

The transformation is a dilation.

C

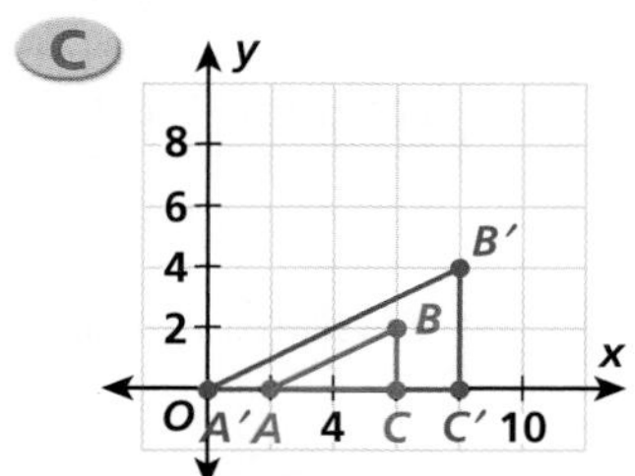

The transformation is a dilation.

D

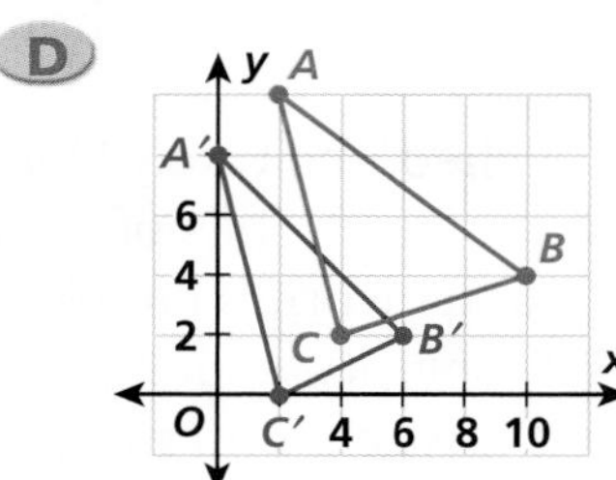

The transformation is *not* a dilation. The figure is distorted.

Every dilation has a fixed point that is the *center of dilation*. To find the center of dilation, draw a line that connects each pair of corresponding vertices. The lines intersect at one point. This point is the **center of dilation**.

EXAMPLE 2 Dilating a Figure

Dilate the figure by a scale factor of 0.4 with P as the center of dilation.

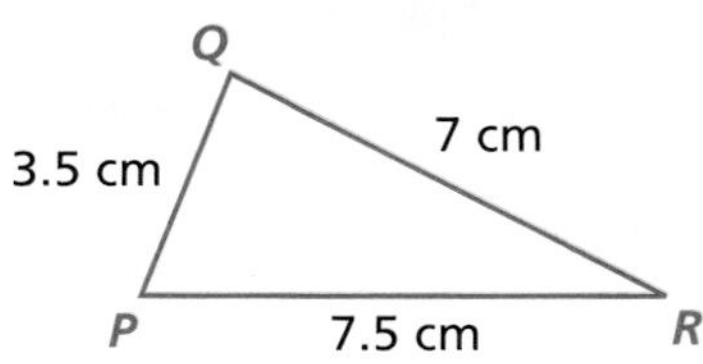

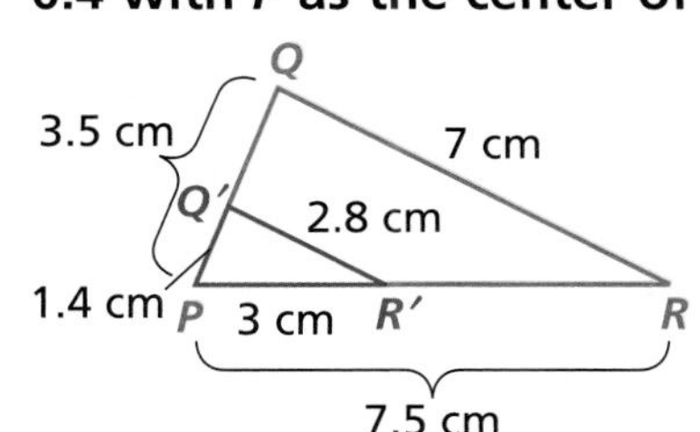

Multiply each side by 0.4.
P′ and P are the same point.

EXAMPLE 3 Using the Origin as the Center of Dilation

A **Dilate the figure by a scale factor of 1.5. What are the vertices of the image?**

Multiply the coordinates by 1.5 to find the vertices of the image.

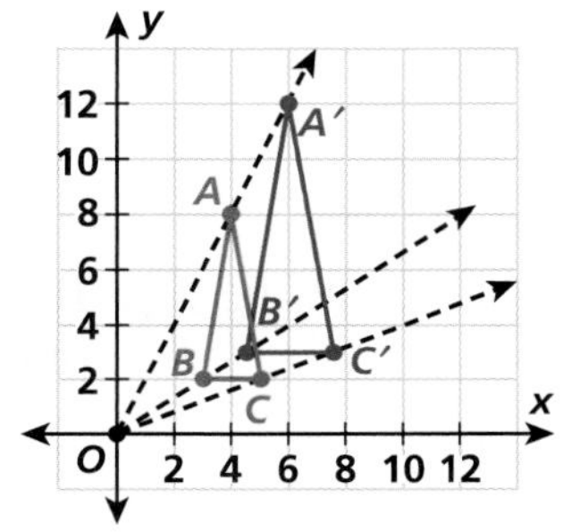

$\triangle ABC$		$\triangle A'B'C'$
$A(4, 8)$	$\longrightarrow A'(4 \cdot \mathbf{1.5}, 8 \cdot \mathbf{1.5}) \longrightarrow$	$A'(6, 12)$
$B(3, 2)$	$\longrightarrow B'(3 \cdot \mathbf{1.5}, 2 \cdot \mathbf{1.5}) \longrightarrow$	$B'(4.5, 3)$
$C(5, 2)$	$\longrightarrow C'(5 \cdot \mathbf{1.5}, 2 \cdot \mathbf{1.5}) \longrightarrow$	$C'(7.5, 3)$

The vertices of the image are $A'(6, 12)$, $B'(4.5, 3)$, and $C'(7.5, 3)$.

B **Dilate the figure by a scale factor of $\frac{2}{3}$. What are the vertices of the image?**

Multiply the coordinates by $\frac{2}{3}$ to find the vertices of the image.

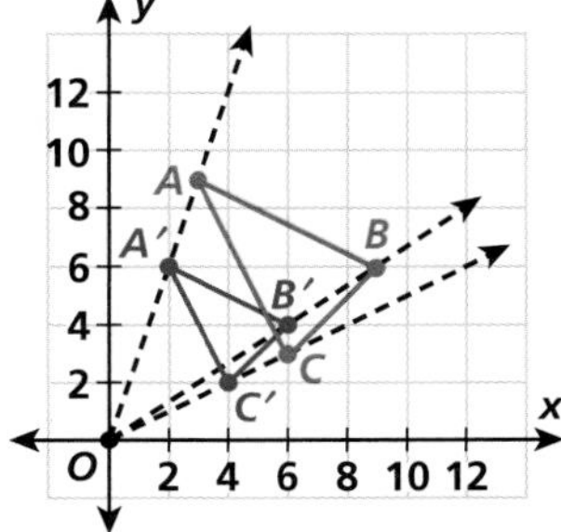

$\triangle ABC$		$\triangle A'B'C'$
$A(3, 9)$	$\longrightarrow A'\left(3 \cdot \frac{2}{3}, 9 \cdot \frac{2}{3}\right) \longrightarrow$	$A'(2, 6)$
$B(9, 6)$	$\longrightarrow B'\left(9 \cdot \frac{2}{3}, 6 \cdot \frac{2}{3}\right) \longrightarrow$	$B'(6, 4)$
$C(6, 3)$	$\longrightarrow C'\left(6 \cdot \frac{2}{3}, 3 \cdot \frac{2}{3}\right) \longrightarrow$	$C'(4, 2)$

The vertices of the image are $A'(2, 6)$, $B'(6, 4)$, and $C'(4, 2)$.

Think and Discuss

1. **Describe** the image of a dilation with a scale factor of 1.
2. **Compare** a dilation with the origin as the center of dilation to a dilation with a vertex of the figure as the center of dilation.

7-5 Exercises

FOR EXTRA PRACTICE

see page 745

internet connect
Homework Help Online
go.hrw.com Keyword: MP4 7-5

GUIDED PRACTICE

See Example 1 **Tell whether each transformation is a dilation.**

1. 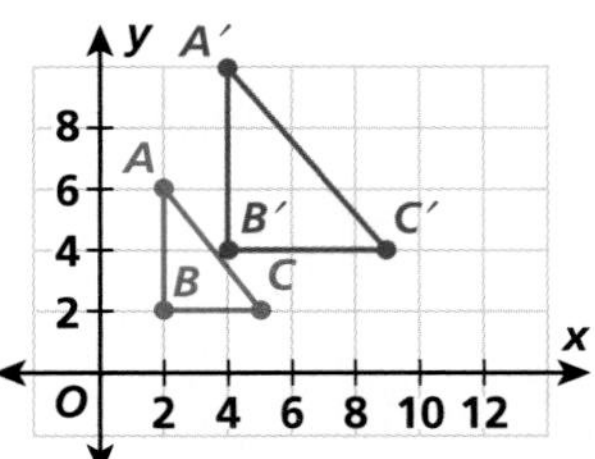

2. 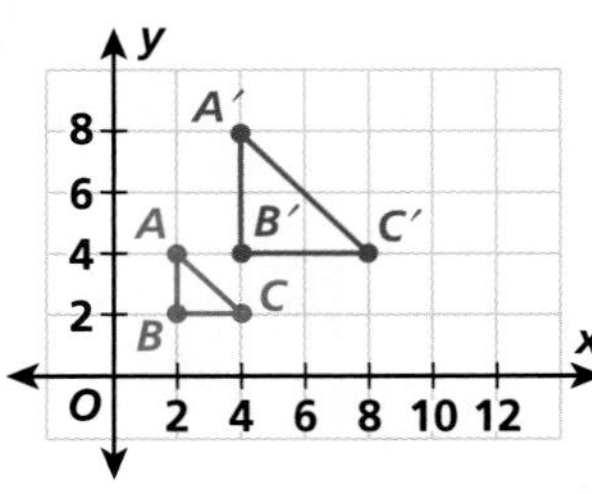

See Example 2 **Dilate each figure by the given scale factor with *P* as the center of dilation.**

3. 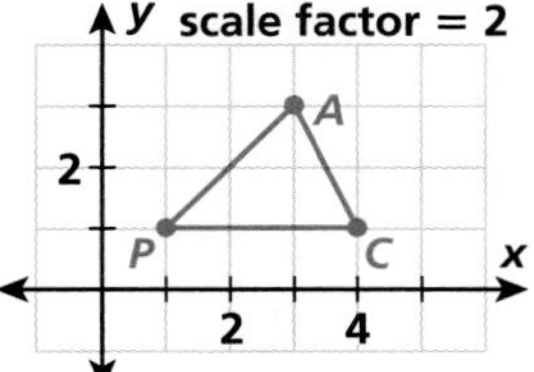

4. 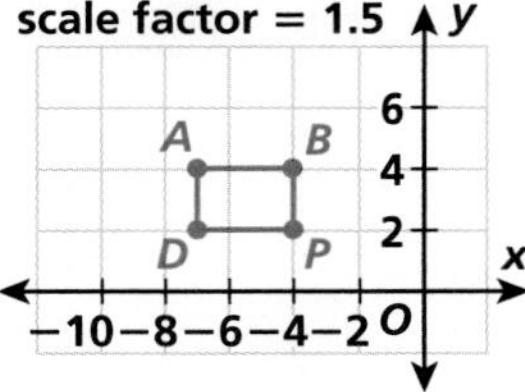

See Example 3 **Dilate each figure by the given scale factor with the origin as the center of dilation. What are the vertices of the image?**

5. 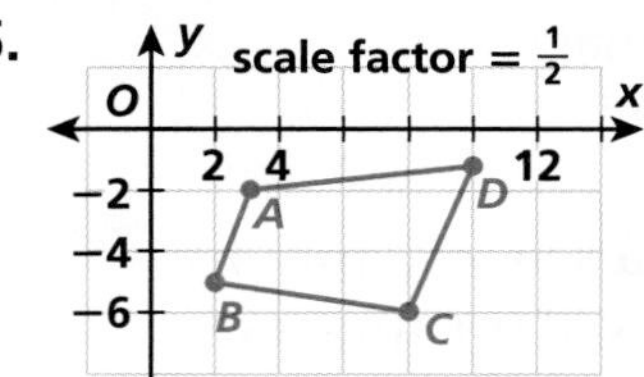

6. 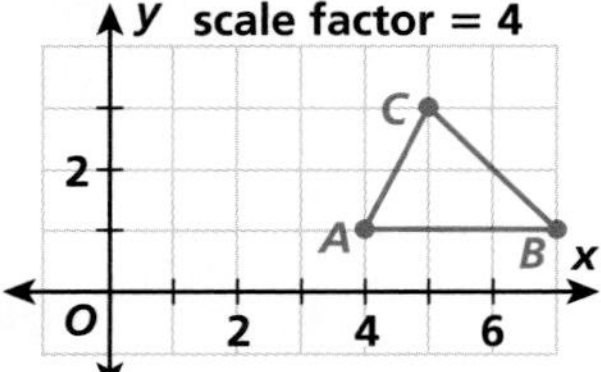

INDEPENDENT PRACTICE

See Example 1 **Tell whether each transformation is a dilation.**

7. 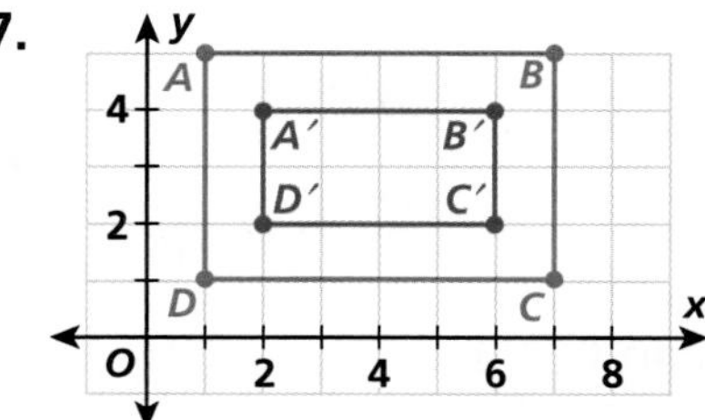

8. 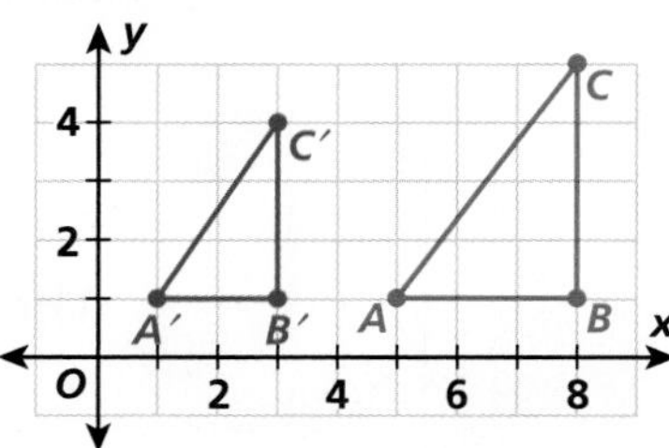

See Example 2 **Dilate each figure by the given scale factor with *P* as the center of dilation.**

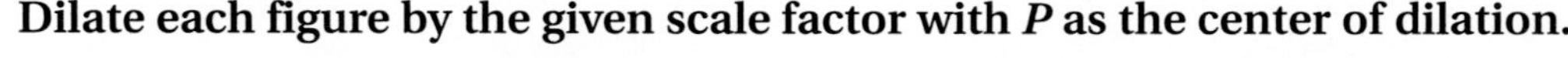

9. 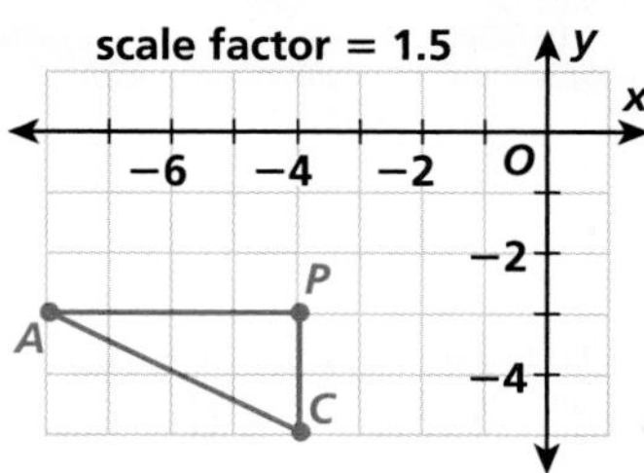

10. 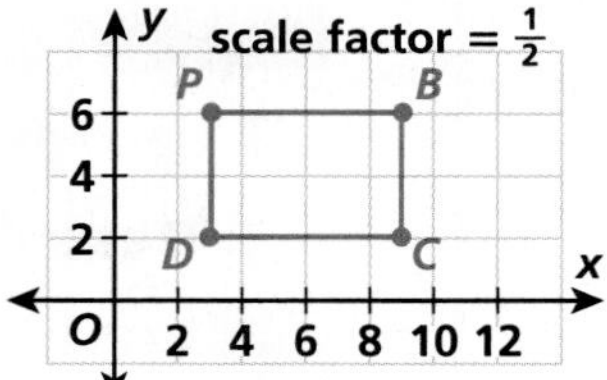

See Example 3 **Dilate each figure by the given scale factor with the origin as the center of dilation. What are the vertices of the image?**

11.

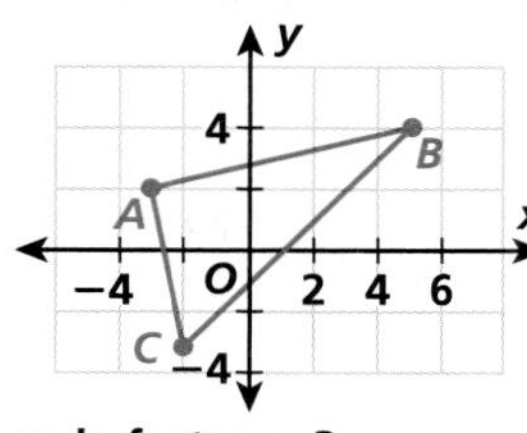

scale factor = 3

12.

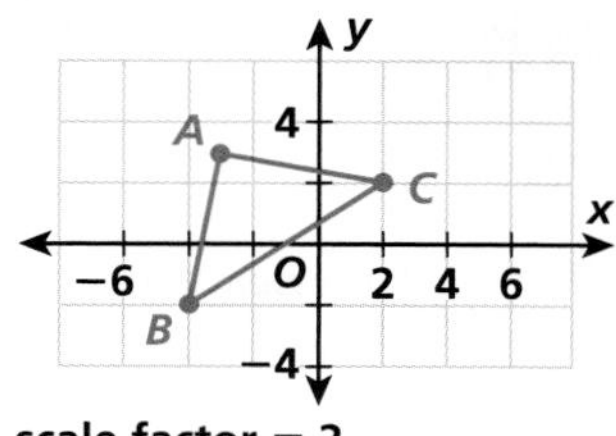

scale factor = 2

PRACTICE AND PROBLEM SOLVING

Identify the scale factor used in each dilation.

13.

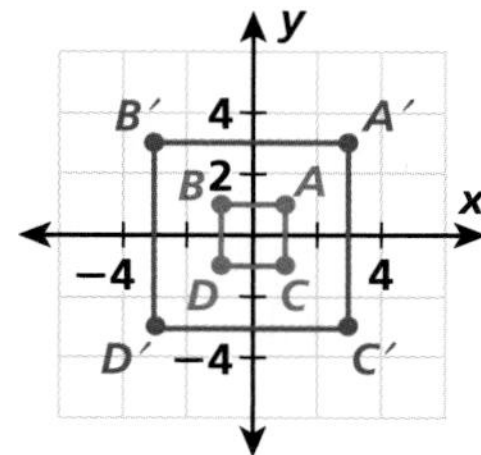

14.

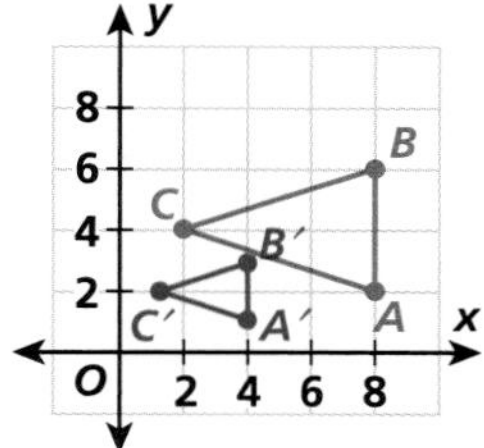

Photography LINK

In a camera lens, a larger aperture lets in more light than a smaller one.

15. ***PHOTOGRAPHY*** The *aperture* is the polygonal opening in a camera lens when a picture is taken. The aperture can be small or large. Is an aperture a dilation? Why or why not?

16. A rectangle has vertices $A(4, 4)$, $B(9, 4)$, $C(9, 0)$, and $D(4, 0)$. Give the coordinates after dilating from the origin by a scale factor of 2.5.

17. ***CHOOSE A STRATEGY*** The perimeter of an equilateral triangle is 48 cm. If the triangle is dilated by a scale factor of 0.25, what is the length of each side of the new triangle?

A 3 cm **B** 4 cm **C** 16 cm **D** 8 cm

18. ***WRITE ABOUT IT*** Explain how you can check the drawing of a dilation for accuracy.

19. ***CHALLENGE*** What scale factor was used in the dilation of a triangle with vertices $A(6, -2)$, $B(8, 3)$, and $C(-12, 10)$ to the triangle with vertices $A'\left(-2, \frac{2}{3}\right)$, $B'\left(-2\frac{2}{3}, -1\right)$, and $C'\left(4, -3\frac{1}{3}\right)$?

Spiral Review

Find the area of each figure with the given vertices. (Lesson 6-2)

20. (1, 0), (10, 0), (1, −6)

21. (5, 5), (2, 1), (11, 1), (8, 5)

22. (−8, −8), (8, −8), (4, 4), (−4, 4)

23. (−12, 4), (−6, 4), (−7, 11)

24. **TEST PREP** A pyramid has a rectangular base measuring 12 cm by 9 cm and height 15 cm. What is the volume of the pyramid? (Lesson 6-7)

A 540 cm^3 **B** 315 cm^3 **C** 270 cm^3 **D** 405 cm^3

Explore Similarity

Use with Lesson 7-6

WHAT YOU NEED:

- Two pieces of graph paper with different-sized boxes, such as 1 cm graph paper and $\frac{1}{4}$ in. graph paper
- Number cube
- Metric ruler
- Protractor

Triangles that have the same shape have some interesting relationships.

Activity

1 Follow the steps below to draw two triangles.

a. On a sheet of graph paper, plot a point below and to the left of the center of the paper. Label the point *A*. On the other sheet of paper, plot a point below and to the left of the center and label this point *D*.

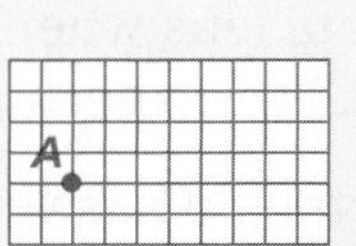

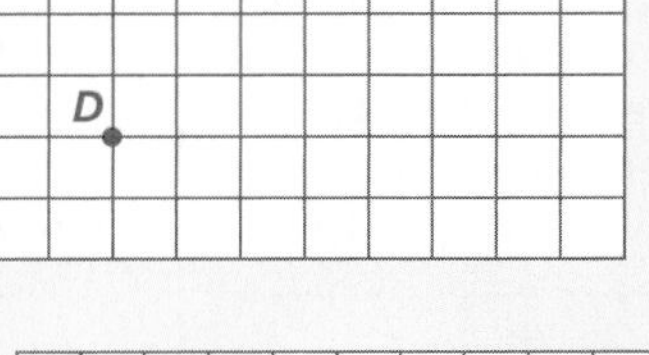

b. Roll a number cube twice. On each sheet of graph paper, move up the number on the first roll, move right the number on the second roll, and plot this location as point *B* on the first sheet and point *E* on the second sheet.

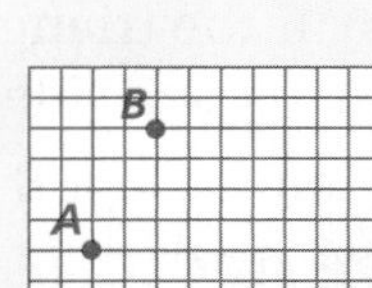

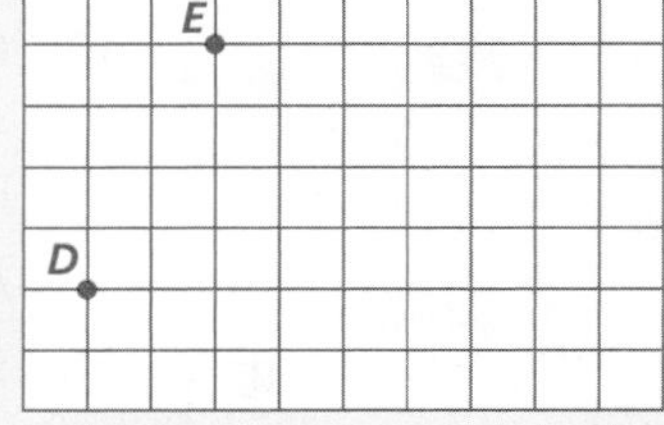

c. Roll the number cube twice again. On each sheet of graph paper, move down the number on the first roll, move right the number on the second roll, and plot point *C* on the first sheet and point *F* on the second sheet.

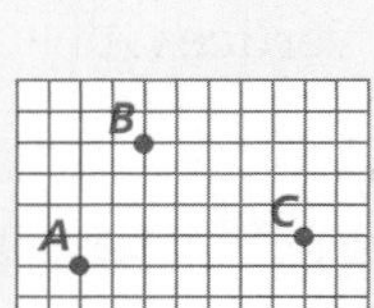
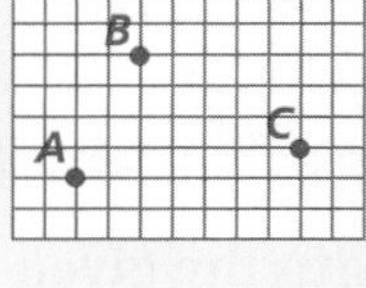

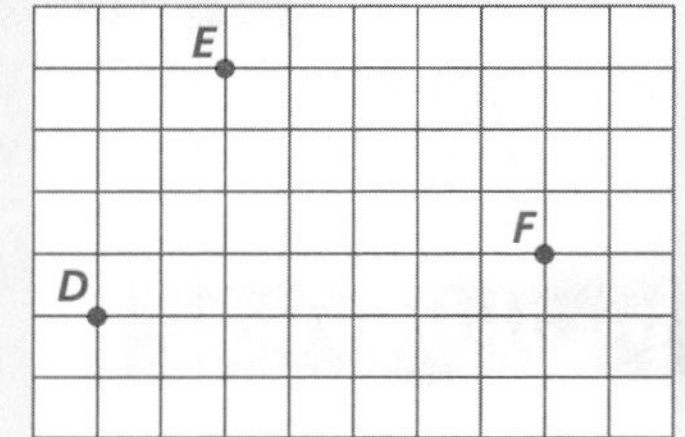

d. Connect the three points on each sheet of graph paper to form triangles *ABC* and *DEF*.

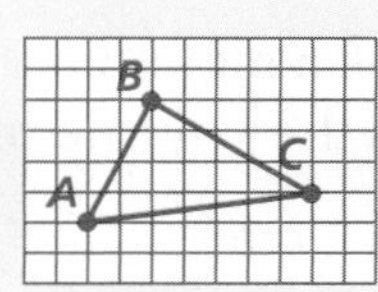

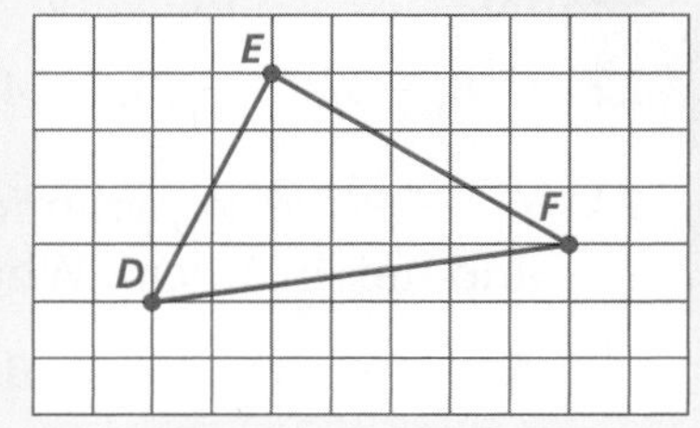

e. Measure the angles of each triangle. Measure the side lengths of each triangle to the nearest millimeter. Find the following:

$m\angle A$	$m\angle D$	$m\angle B$	$m\angle E$	$m\angle C$	$m\angle F$
AB	DE	$\frac{AB}{DE}$	BC	EF	$\frac{BC}{EF}$
AC	DF	$\frac{AC}{DF}$			

2 Follow the steps below to draw two triangles.

a. On one sheet of graph paper, plot a point below and to the left of the center of the paper. Label the point *A*.

b. Roll a number cube twice. Move up the number on the first roll, move right the number on the second roll, and plot this location as point *B*. From *B*, move up the number on the first roll, move right the number on the second roll, and label this point *D*.

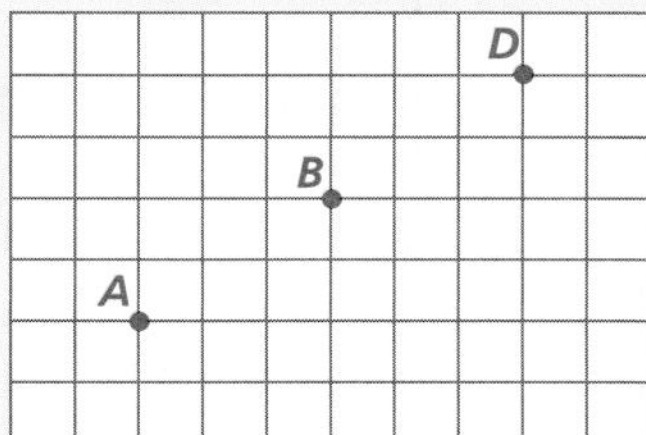

c. Roll a number cube twice. From *B*, move down the number on the first roll, move right the number on the second roll, and plot this location as point *C*.

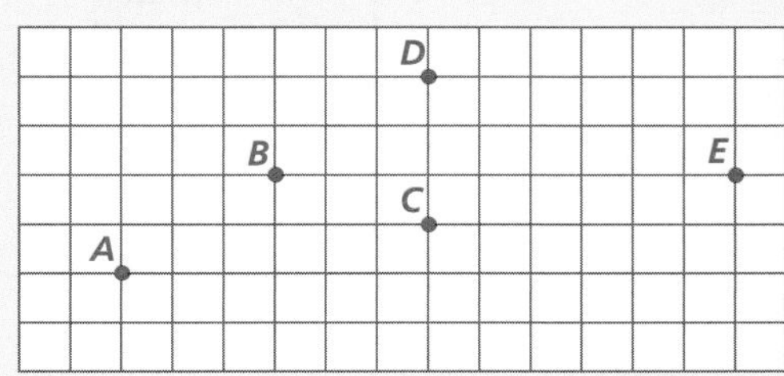

d. From *D*, move down twice the number on the first roll, move right twice the number on the second roll, and label this point *E*.

e. Connect points to form triangles *ABC* and *ADE*.

f. Measure the angles of each triangle. Measure the side lengths of each triangle to the nearest millimeter.

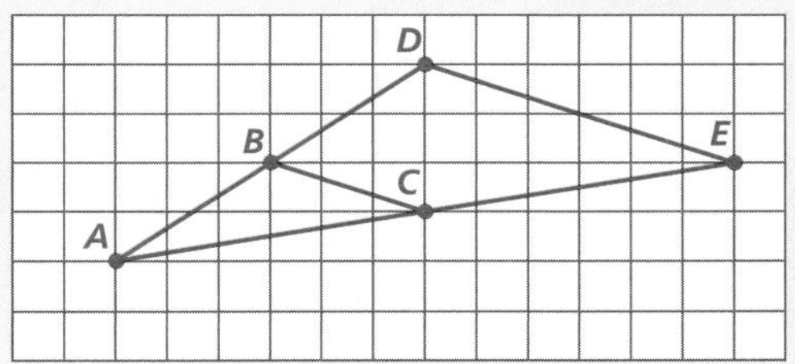

Think and Discuss

1. How do corresponding angles of triangles with the same shape compare?
2. How do corresponding side lengths of triangles with the same shape compare?
3. Suppose you enlarge a triangle on a copier machine. What measurements or values would be the same on the enlargement?

Try This

1. Make a small trapezoid on graph paper and triple the length of each side. Compare the angle measures and side lengths of the trapezoids.
2. Make a large polygon on graph paper. Use a copier to reduce the size of the polygon. Compare the angle measures and side lengths of the polygons.

7-6 Similar Figures

Learn to determine whether figures are similar, to use scale factors, and to find missing dimensions in similar figures.

Vocabulary

similar

The heights of letters in newspapers and on billboards are measured using *points* and *picas.* There are 12 points in 1 pica and 6 picas in one inch.

A letter 36 inches tall on a billboard would be 216 picas, or 2592 points. The first letter in this paragraph is 12 points.

12 points	24 points	48 points	72 points
1 pica	2 picas	4 picas	6 picas
A	A	A	A

Congruent figures have the same size and shape. **Similar** figures have the same shape, but not necessarily the same size. The *A*'s in the table are similar. They have the same shape, but they are not the same size.

For polygons to be similar,
• corresponding angles must be congruent, and • corresponding sides must have lengths that form equivalent ratios.

The ratio formed by the corresponding sides is the scale factor.

EXAMPLE  1

Using Scale Factors to Find Missing Dimensions

A picture 4 in. tall and 9 in. wide is to be scaled to 2.5 in. tall to be displayed on a Web page. How wide should the picture be on the Web page for the two pictures to be similar?

To find the scale factor, divide the known height of the scaled picture by the corresponding height of the original picture.

0.625 $\quad \frac{2.5}{4} = 0.625$

Then multiply the width of the original picture by the scale factor.

5.625 $\quad 9 \cdot 0.625$

The picture should be 5.625 in. wide.

EXAMPLE 2 Using Equivalent Ratios to Find Missing Dimensions

A company's logo is in the shape of an isosceles triangle with two sides that are each 2.4 in. long and one side that is 1.8 in. long. On a billboard, the triangle in the logo has two sides that are each 8 ft long. What is the length of the third side of the triangle on the billboard?

Set up a proportion.

$$\frac{2.4 \text{ in.}}{8 \text{ ft}} = \frac{1.8 \text{ in.}}{x \text{ ft}}$$

$2.4 \text{ in.} \cdot x \text{ ft} = 8 \text{ ft} \cdot 1.8 \text{ in.}$	*Find the cross products.*
$2.4 \cancel{\text{in.}} \cdot x \cancel{\text{ft}} = 8 \cancel{\text{ft}} \cdot 1.8 \cancel{\text{in.}}$	*in.· ft is on both sides*
$2.4x = 8 \cdot 1.8$	*Cancel the units.*
$2.4x = 14.4$	*Multiply.*
$x = \frac{14.4}{2.4} = 6$	*Solve for x.*

The third side of the triangle is 6 ft long.

EXAMPLE 3 Identifying Similar Figures

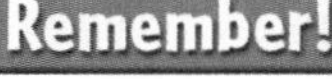

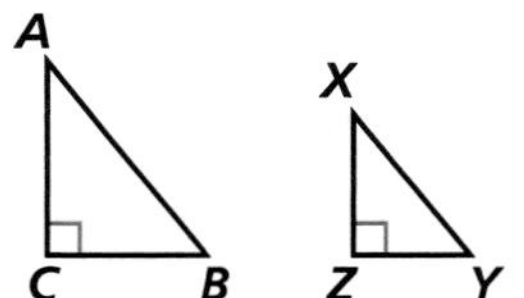

The following are matching, or corresponding:
$\angle A$ and $\angle X$
$\angle B$ and $\angle Y$
$\angle C$ and $\angle Z$
$\overline{AB}$ and $\overline{XY}$.
$\overline{BC}$ and $\overline{YZ}$.
$\overline{AC}$ and $\overline{XZ}$.

Which rectangles are similar?

A 2 in. 3 in.

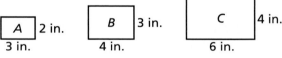

B 3 in. 4 in.

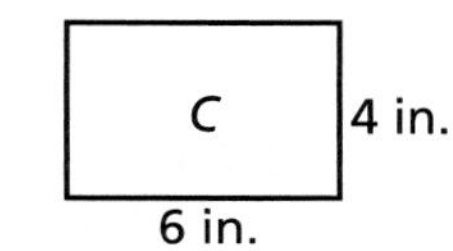

Since the three figures are all rectangles, all the angles are right angles. So the corresponding angles are congruent.

Compare the ratios of corresponding sides to see if they are equal.

$$\frac{\text{length of rectangle } A}{\text{length of rectangle } B} \rightarrow \frac{3}{4} \stackrel{?}{=} \frac{2}{3} \leftarrow \frac{\text{width of rectangle } A}{\text{width of rectangle } B}$$

$$9 \neq 8$$

The ratios are not equal. Rectangle *A* is not similar to rectangle *B*.

$$\frac{\text{length of rectangle } A}{\text{length of rectangle } C} \rightarrow \frac{3}{6} = \frac{2}{4} \leftarrow \frac{\text{width of rectangle } A}{\text{width of rectangle } C}$$

$$12 = 12$$

The ratios are equal. Rectangle *A* is similar to rectangle *C*. The notation $A \sim C$ shows similarity.

Think and Discuss

1. Compare an image formed by a scale factor greater than 1 to an image formed by a scale factor less than 1.

2. Describe one way for two figures not to be similar.

3. Explain whether two congruent figures are similar.

7-6 Exercises

FOR EXTRA PRACTICE
see page 745

GUIDED PRACTICE

See Example 1

1. Fran scans a document that is 8.5 in. wide by 11 in. long into her computer. If she scales the length down to 7 in., how wide should the similar document be?

See Example 2

2. An isosceles triangle has a base of 12 cm and legs measuring 18 cm. How wide is the base of a similar triangle with legs measuring 22 cm?

See Example 3

3. Which rectangles are similar?

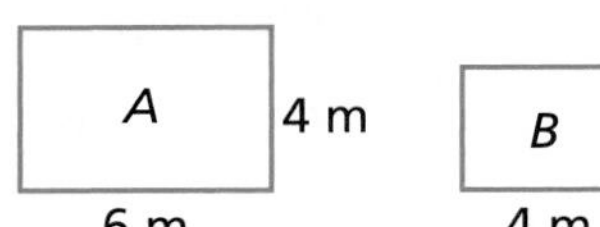

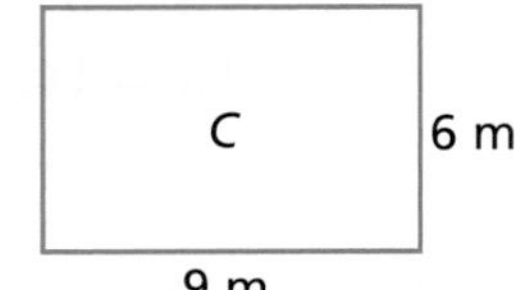

INDEPENDENT PRACTICE

See Example 1

4. A rectangular airfield measures 4.3 mi wide and 7.5 mi long. On a map, the width of the airfield is 3.75 in. How long is the airport on the map?

See Example 2

5. Rich drew a 7 in. wide by 4 in. tall picture that will be turned into a 40 ft wide billboard. How tall will the billboard be?

See Example 3

6. Which rectangles are similar?

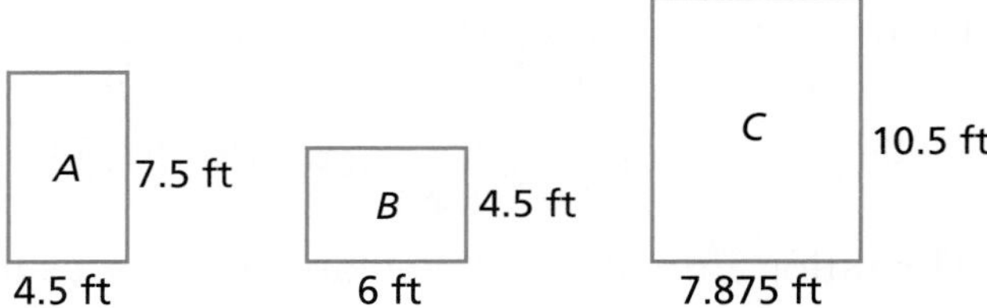

PRACTICE AND PROBLEM SOLVING

Tell whether the figures are similar. If they are not similar, explain.

7.

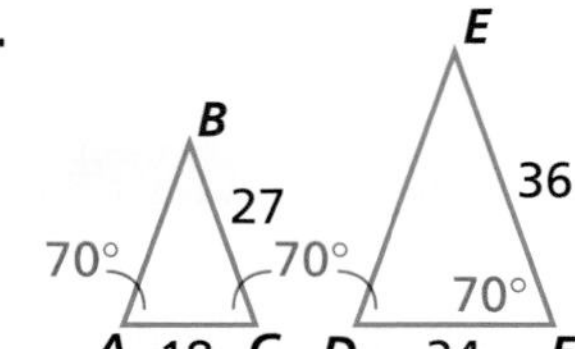

8.

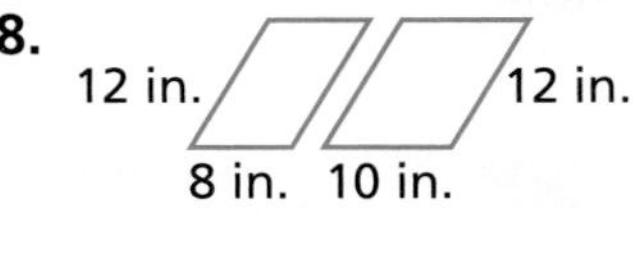

9.

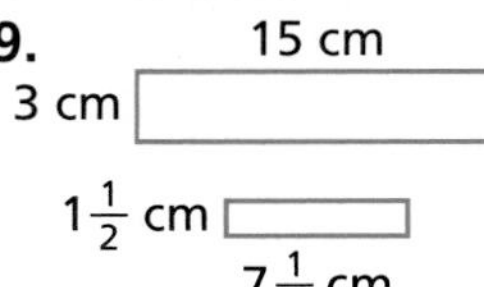

10. Draw a right triangle with vertices (0,0), (4,0), and (4,6) on a coordinate plane. Extend the hypotenuse to (6, 9), and form a new triangle with vertices (0, 0) and (6, 0). Are the triangles similar? Explain.

Many reproductions of artwork have been enlarged to fit unusual surfaces.

The figures in each pair are similar. Find the scale factor to solve for x.

11. 12 ft, 10 ft; x, 5 ft

12.

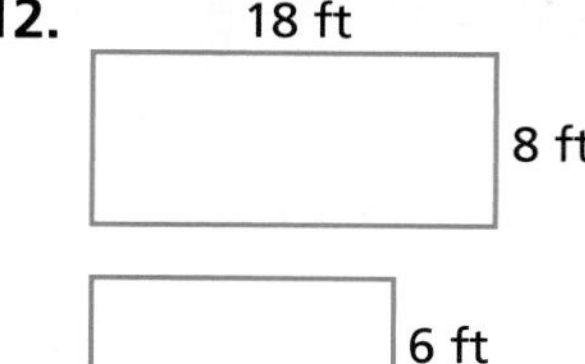

13.

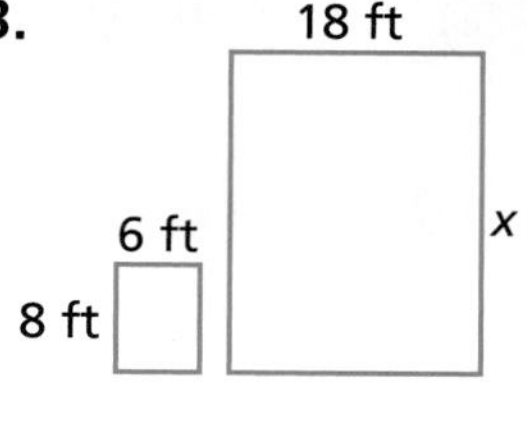

14. ***ART*** Helen is copying a printed reproduction of the *Mona Lisa.* The print is 24 in. wide and 36 in. tall. If Helen's canvas is 12 in. wide, how tall should her canvas be?

15. Ann's room is 10 ft by 12 ft 6 in. Her sketch of the room is 8 in. by 10 in. Is Ann's sketch a scale drawing? If so, what scale factor did she use?

16. A rectangle is 14 cm long and 9 cm wide. A similar rectangle is 4.5 cm wide and x cm long. Find x.

17. ***PHYSICAL SCIENCE*** Bill is 6 ft tall. He casts a 4 ft shadow at the same time that a tree casts a 16 ft shadow. Use similar triangles to find the height of the tree.

18. ***WRITE A PROBLEM*** A drawing on a sheet of graph paper shows a kite 8 cm wide and 10 cm long. The width of the kite is labeled 2 ft. Write and solve a problem about the kite.

19. ***WRITE ABOUT IT*** Consider the statement "All similar figures are congruent." Is this statement true or false? Explain.

20. ***CHALLENGE*** In right triangle ABC, $\angle B$ is the right angle, $AB =$ 21 cm, and $BC = 15$ cm. Right triangle ABC is similar to triangle DEF, which has length $DE = 7$ cm. Find the area of triangle DEF.

Spiral Review

Find the volume of each cone to the nearest tenth cubic unit. Use 3.14 for π. (Lesson 6-7)

21. radius 10 mm; height 12 mm

22. diameter 4 ft; height 5.7 ft

23. radius and height 12.5 cm

24. diameter 15 in.; height 35 in.

25. **TEST PREP** A data set contains 10 numbers in order. The median is ___?___. (Lesson 4-3)

A the fifth number

B the number occurring most often

C the average of the numbers

D the average of the fifth and sixth numbers

26. **TEST PREP** Which of the following describes how the volume of a sphere changes when the radius is doubled? (Lesson 6-10)

F The volume is tripled.

G The volume is 9 times greater.

H The volume is $\frac{1}{9}$ the original volume.

J The volume is 8 times greater.

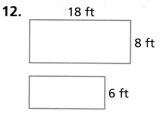

7-7 Scale Drawings

Learn to make comparisons between and find dimensions of scale drawings and actual objects.

Vocabulary

scale drawing

scale

reduction

enlargement

Stan Herd is a crop artist and farmer who has created works of art that are as large as 160 square acres. Herd first makes a *scale drawing* of each piece, and then he determines the actual lengths of the parts that make up the art piece.

To get an idea of scale, notice the red tractor at the lower right.

A **scale drawing** is a two-dimensional drawing that accurately represents an object. The scale drawing is mathematically similar to the object.

A **scale** gives the ratio of the dimensions in the drawing to the dimensions of the object. All dimensions are reduced or enlarged using the same scale. Scales can use the same units or different units.

Reading Math

The scale *a*:*b* is read "*a* to *b*." For example, the scale 1 cm:3 ft is read "one centimeter to three feet."

Scale	Interpretation
1:20	1 unit on the drawing is 20 units.
1 cm:1 m	1 cm on the drawing is 1 m.
$\frac{1}{4}$ in. = 1 ft	$\frac{1}{4}$ in. on the drawing is 1 ft.

EXAMPLE 1 Using Proportions to Find Unknown Scales or Lengths

A The length of an object on a scale drawing is 5 cm, and its actual length is 15 m. The scale is 1 cm:▢ m. What is the scale?

$\frac{1 \text{ cm}}{x \text{ m}} = \frac{5 \text{ cm}}{15 \text{ m}}$ *Set up proportion using* $\frac{\text{scale length}}{\text{actual length}}$.

$1 \cdot 15 = x \cdot 5$ *Find the cross products.*

$x = 3$ *Solve the proportion.*

The scale is 1 cm:3 m.

B The length of an object on a scale drawing is 3.5 in. The scale is 1 in:12 ft. What is the actual length of the object?

$\frac{1 \text{ in.}}{12 \text{ ft}} = \frac{3.5 \text{ in.}}{x \text{ ft}}$ *Set up proportion using* $\frac{\text{scale length}}{\text{actual length}}$.

$1 \cdot x = 3.5 \cdot 12$ *Find the cross products.*

$x = 42$ *Solve the proportion.*

The actual length is 42 ft.

A scale drawing that is smaller than the actual object is called a **reduction**. A scale drawing can also be larger than the object. In this case, the drawing is referred to as an **enlargement**.

EXAMPLE 2 *Life Science Application*

Under a 1000:1 microscope view, a paramecium appears to have length 39 mm. What is its actual length?

$\frac{1000}{1} = \frac{39 \text{ mm}}{x \text{ mm}}$ ← scale length / ← actual length

$1000 \cdot x = 1 \cdot 39$ *Find the cross products.*

$x = 0.039$ *Solve the proportion.*

The actual length of the paramecium is 0.039 mm.

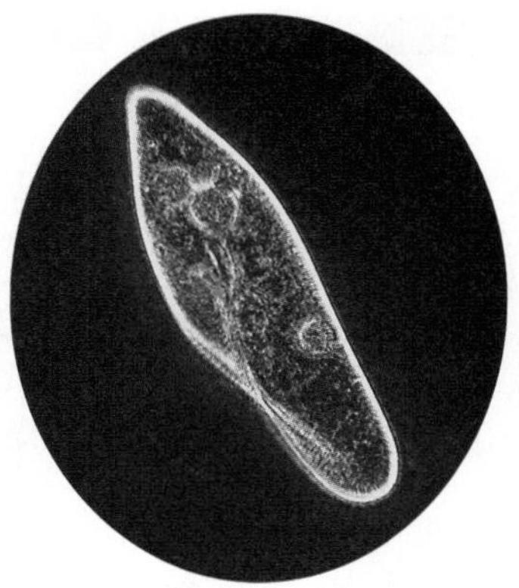

A paramecium is a cylindrical or foot-shaped microorganism.

A drawing that uses the scale $\frac{1}{4}$ in. = 1 ft is said to be in $\frac{1}{4}$ in. scale. Similarly, a drawing that uses the scale $\frac{1}{2}$ in. = 1 ft is in $\frac{1}{2}$ in. scale.

EXAMPLE 3 Using Scales and Scale Drawings to Find Heights

A **If a wall in a $\frac{1}{4}$ in. scale drawing is 3 in. tall, how tall is the actual wall?**

$\frac{0.25 \text{ in.}}{1 \text{ ft}} = \frac{3 \text{ in.}}{x \text{ ft}}$ ← scale length / ← actual length *Length ratios are equal.*

$0.25 \cdot x = 1 \cdot 3$ *Find the cross products.*

$x = 12$ *Solve the proportion.*

The wall is 12 ft tall.

B **How tall is the wall if a $\frac{1}{2}$ in. scale is used?**

$\frac{0.5 \text{ in.}}{1 \text{ ft}} = \frac{3 \text{ in.}}{x \text{ ft}}$ ← scale length / ← actual length *Length ratios are equal.*

$0.5 \cdot x = 1 \cdot 3$ *Cross multiply.*

$x = 6$ *Solve the proportion.*

The wall is 6 ft tall.

Think and Discuss

1. **Describe** which scale would produce the largest drawing of an object: 1:20, 1 in. = 1 ft, or $\frac{1}{4}$ in. = 1 ft.
2. **Describe** which scale would produce the smallest drawing of an object: 1:10, 1 cm = 10 cm, or 1 mm:1 m.

7-7 Exercises

FOR EXTRA PRACTICE

see page 745

internet connect

Homework Help Online
go.hrw.com Keyword: MP4 7-7

GUIDED PRACTICE

See Example 1

1. A 10 ft fence is 8 in. long on a scale drawing. What is the scale?
2. Using a scale of 2 cm:9 m, how long is an object that is 4.5 cm long in a drawing?

See Example 2

3. Under a 100:1 microscope view, a microorganism appears to have a length of 0.85 in. How long is the microorganism?
4. Using the microscope from Exercise 3, how long would a 0.075 mm microorganism appear to be under the microscope?

See Example 3

5. On a $\frac{1}{4}$ in. scale, a tree is 13 in. tall. How tall is the actual tree?
6. How high is a 54 ft bridge on a $\frac{1}{2}$ in. scale drawing?

INDEPENDENT PRACTICE

See Example 1

7. What is the scale of a drawing where a 6 m wall is 4 cm long?
8. If a scale of 2 in:10 ft is used, how long is an object that is 14 in. long in a drawing?

See Example 2

9. Using a 1000:1 magnification microscope, a paramecium has length 23 mm. What is the actual length of the paramecium?
10. If a 0.27 cm long crystal appears to be 13.5 cm long under a microscope, what is the power of the microscope?

See Example 

11. Using a $\frac{1}{2}$ in. scale, how tall would a 40 ft statue be in a drawing?
12. How wide is a 3 ft doorway in a $\frac{1}{4}$ in. scale drawing?

PRACTICE AND PROBLEM SOLVING

The scale of a map is 1 in. = 15 mi. Find each length on the map.

13. 30 mi
14. 45 mi
15. 7.5 mi
16. 153.75 mi

The scale of a drawing is 3 in. = 27 ft. Find each actual measurement.

17. 2 in.
18. 5 in.
19. 6.5 in.
20. 11.25 in.

21. Use the scale of the map and a ruler to find the distance in miles between Two Egg, Florida, and Gnaw Bone, Indiana.

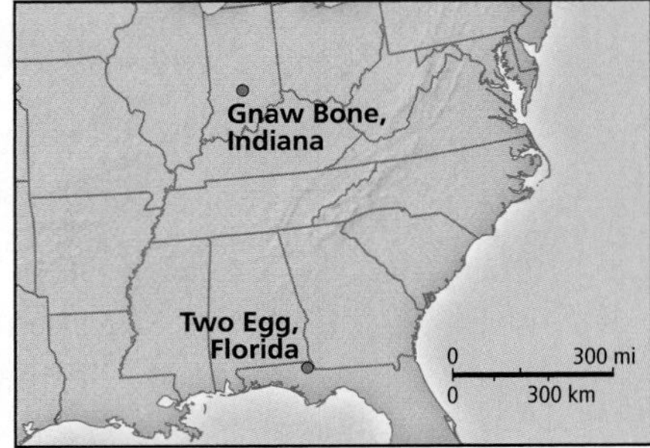

Architecture 

Use a metric ruler to measure the width of the 36-inch-wide door on the blueprint of the family room below.

For Exercises 22–28, indicate the scale that you used.

22. How wide are the pocket doors (shown by the red line)?

23. What is the distance *s* between two interior studs?

24. How long is the oak mantle? (The right side ends just above the *B* in the word *BRICK*.)

25. Could a 4 ft wide bookcase fit along the right-hand wall without blocking the pocket doors? Explain.

26. What is the area of the tiled hearth in in^2? in ft^2?

27. What is the area of the entire family room in ft^2?

28. Blueprint paper has a maximum width of 36 in., or about 91.4 cm. What does this width represent in the real world corresponding to the scale that you used?

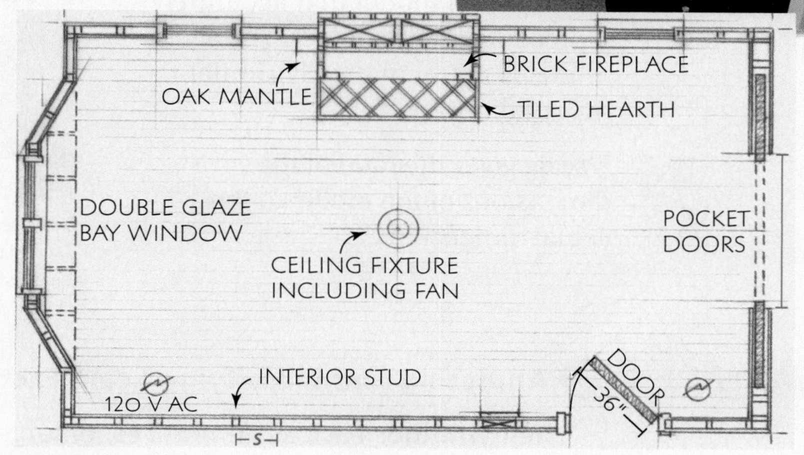

29. **CHALLENGE** Suppose the architect used a $\frac{1}{8}$ in. = 1 ft scale.

a. What would the dimensions of the family room be?

b. Use the result from part **a** to find the area of the family room.

c. If the carpet the Andersons want costs $4.99 per square foot, how much would it cost to carpet the family room?

go.hrw.com
Web Extra!
KEYWORD: MP4 Scale

Spiral Review

State whether the ratios in each pair are in proportion. (Lesson 7-1)

30. $\frac{3}{7}$ and $\frac{6}{14}$ **31.** $\frac{5}{8}$ and $\frac{10}{4}$ **32.** $\frac{13}{4}$ and $\frac{52}{16}$ **33.** $\frac{22}{7}$ and $\frac{11}{3}$

34. **TEST PREP** A tree was 3.5 ft tall after 2 years and 8.75 ft tall after 5 years. If the tree grew at a constant rate, how tall was it after 3 years? (Lesson 7-4)

A 5 ft **B** 5.25 ft **C** 6.5 ft **D** 5.75 ft

7-8 Scale Models

Learn to make comparisons between and find dimensions of scale models and actual objects.

Vocabulary

scale model

Mammoths weighing 4 to 6 tons roamed the earth from 3.75 million to 4000 years ago.

Very large and very small objects are often modeled. A **scale model** is a three-dimensional model that accurately represents a solid object. The scale model is mathematically similar to the solid object.

A scale gives the ratio of the dimensions of the model to the actual dimensions.

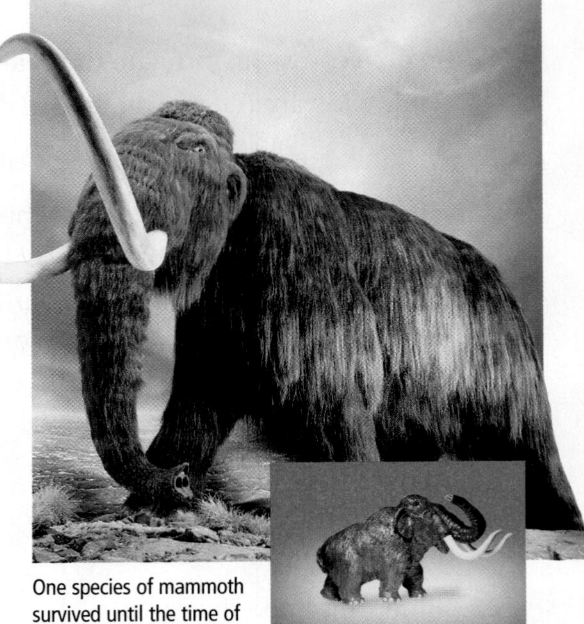

One species of mammoth survived until the time of the Egyptian pharaohs.

EXAMPLE 1 Analyzing and Classifying Scale Factors

Tell whether each scale reduces, enlarges, or preserves the size of the actual object.

A **1 yd:1 ft**

$\frac{1\text{ yd}}{1\text{ ft}} = \frac{3\text{ ft}}{1\text{ ft}} = 3$ *Convert: 1 yd = 3 ft. Simplify.*

The scale enlarges the size of the actual object 3 times.

B **100 cm:1 m**

$\frac{100\text{ cm}}{1\text{ m}} = \frac{1\text{m}}{1\text{m}} = 1$ *Convert: 100 cm = 1 m. Simplify.*

The scale preserves the size of the object since the scale factor is 1.

EXAMPLE 2 Finding Scale Factors

What scale factor relates a 20 in. scale model to an 80 ft apatosaurus?

20 in:80 ft *State the scale.*

$\frac{20\text{ in.}}{80\text{ ft}} = \frac{1\text{ in.}}{4\text{ ft}} = \frac{1\text{ in.}}{48\text{ in.}}$ *Write the scale as a ratio and simplify.*

The scale factor is $\frac{1}{48}$, or 1:48.

EXAMPLE 3 Finding Unknown Dimensions Given Scale Factors

A model of a 27 ft tall house was made using the scale 2 in:3 ft. What is the height of the model?

$\frac{2 \text{ in.}}{3 \text{ ft}} = \frac{2 \text{ in.}}{36 \text{ in.}} = \frac{1 \not{\text{in.}}}{18 \not{\text{in.}}}$ *First find the scale factor.*

The scale factor for the model is $\frac{1}{18}$. Now set up a proportion.

$\frac{1}{18} = \frac{h \text{ in.}}{324 \text{ in.}}$ *Convert: 27 ft = 324 in.*

$324 = 18h$ *Cross multiply.*

$h = 18$ *Solve for the height.*

The height of the model is 18 in.

EXAMPLE 4 *Life Science Application*

A DNA model was built using the scale 2 cm:0.0000001 mm. If the model of the DNA chain is 17 cm long, what is the length of the actual chain? Find the scale factor.

$$\frac{2 \text{ cm}}{0.0000001 \text{ mm}} = \frac{20 \text{ mm}}{0.0000001 \text{ mm}} = 200{,}000{,}000$$

The scale factor for the model is 200,000,000. This means the model is 200 million times larger than the actual chain.

$\frac{200{,}000{,}000}{1} = \frac{17 \text{ cm}}{x \text{ cm}}$ *Set up a proportion.*

$200{,}000{,}000x = 17(1)$ *Cross multiply.*

$x = 0.000000085$ *Solve for the length.*

The length of the DNA chain is 8.5×10^{-8} cm.

Think and Discuss

1. **Explain** how you would find the width of the model house in Example 3.
2. **Describe** how you would find the scale factor for a model of the Statue of Liberty. What information would you need to have?
3. **Explain** why comparing models with different scale factors, such as the apatosaurus in Example 2 and the house in Example 3, can be misleading.

7-8 Exercises

FOR EXTRA PRACTICE
see page 745

internet connect
Homework Help Online
go.hrw.com Keyword: MP4 7-8

GUIDED PRACTICE

See Example 1

Tell whether each scale reduces, enlarges, or preserves the size of the actual object.

1. 1 in:18 in. **2.** 4 ft:15 in. **3.** 1 m:1000 mm

4. 1 cm:10 mm **5.** 6 in:100 ft **6.** 80 ft:20 in.

See Example 

7. What scale factor relates a 15 in. tall model boat to a 30 ft tall yacht?

See Example 3

8. A model of a 42 ft tall shopping mall was built using the scale 1 in:3 ft. What is the height of the model?

See Example 4

9. A molecular model uses the scale 2.5 cm:0.00001 mm. If the model is 7 cm long, how long is the molecule?

INDEPENDENT PRACTICE

See Example 

Tell whether each scale reduces, enlarges, or preserves the size of the actual object.

10. 10 ft:24 in. **11.** 1 mi:5280 ft **12.** 6 in:100 ft

13. 0.25 in:1 ft **14.** 50 ft:1 in. **15.** 250 cm:1 km

See Example 

16. What scale factor was used to build a 55 ft wide billboard from a 25 in. wide model?

See Example 

17. A model of a house was built using the scale 5 in:25 ft. If a window in the model is 1.5 in. wide, how wide is the actual window?

See Example 

18. To create a model of an artery, a health teacher uses the scale 2.5 cm:0.75 mm. If the diameter of the artery is 2.7 mm, what is the diameter on the model?

PRACTICE AND PROBLEM SOLVING

Change both measurements to the same unit of measure, and find the scale factor.

19. 1 ft model of a 1 in. fossil **20.** 8 cm model of a 24 m rocket

21. 2 ft model of a 30 yd sports field **22.** 4 ft model of a 6 yd whale

23. 40 cm model of a 5 m tree **24.** 6 in. model of a 6 ft sofa

25. ***LIFE SCIENCE*** Wally has an 18 in. model of a 42 ft dinosaur, the *Tyrannosaurus rex*. What scale factor does this represent?

The Gateway Arch in St. Louis, Missouri, consists of 143 triangular sections, each about 12 feet tall. The sections decrease in cross section from 54 feet at the base to 17 feet at the top.

go.hrw.com
Web Extra!
KEYWORD: MP4 Arch

26. **BUSINESS** Engineers designed a theme park by creating a model using the scale 0.5 in:32 ft.
    a. If the dimensions of the model are 41.25 in. by 82.5 in., what are the dimensions of the park?
    b. What is the area of the park in square feet?
    c. If the builders estimate that it will cost $250 million to build the park, how much will it cost per square foot?

27. **ARCHITECTURE** Maurice is building a 2 ft high model of the Gateway Arch in St. Louis, Missouri. If he is using a 3 in:78.75 ft scale, how high is the actual arch?

28. **ENTERTAINMENT** At Tobu World Square, a theme park in Japan, there are more than 100 scale models of world-famous landmarks, $\frac{1}{25}$ the size of the originals. Using this scale factor,
    a. how tall in inches would a scale model of Big Ben's 320 ft clock tower be?
    b. how tall would a 5 ft tall person be in the model?

The models in Tobu World Square are often seen in movies and television.

29. **WHAT'S THE ERROR?** A student is asked to find the scale factor that relates a 10 in. scale model to a 45 ft building. She solves the problem by writing $\frac{10 \text{ in.}}{45 \text{ ft}} = \frac{2}{9} = \frac{1}{4.5}$. What error did the student make? What is the correct scale factor?

30. **WRITE ABOUT IT** Explain how you can tell whether a scale factor will make an enlarged scale model or a reduced scale model.

31. **CHALLENGE** A scientist wants to build a model, reduced 11,000,000 times, of the Moon revolving around Earth. Will the scale 48 ft:100,000 mi give the desired reduction?

Spiral Review

Find the surface area of each sphere. Use 3.14 for π. (Lesson 6-10)

32. radius 5 mm
33. radius 12.2 ft
34. diameter 4 in.
35. diameter 20 cm

Find each unit rate. (Lesson 7-2)

36. $90 for 8 hours of work
37. 5 apples for $0.85
38. 24 players on 2 teams

39. **TEST PREP** How long would it take to drain a 750-gallon hot tub at a rate of 12.5 gallons per minute? (Lesson 7-3)

    A 1 hour
    B 45 minutes
    C 80 minutes
    D 55 minutes

Make a Scale Model

Use with Lesson 7-9

WHAT YOU NEED
- Card stock
- Ruler
- Scissors
- Tape

REMEMBER
A scale such as 1 in. = 200 ft results in a smaller-scale model than a scale of 1 in. = 20 feet.

You can make a scale model of a solid object, such as a rectangular prism, in many ways; you can make a net and fold it, or you can cut card stock and tape the pieces together. The most important thing is to find a good scale.

Activity 1

The Trump Tower in New York City is a rectangular prism with these approximate dimensions: height, 880 feet; base length, 160 feet; base width, 80 feet.

1. Make a scale model of the Trump Tower.

   First determine the appropriate height for your model and find a good scale.

   To use $8\frac{1}{2}$ in. by 11 in. card stock, divide the longest dimension by 11 to find a scale.

   $\frac{880 \text{ ft}}{11 \text{ in.}} = \frac{80 \text{ ft}}{1 \text{ in.}}$

   Let 1 in. = 80 ft.

   The dimensions of the model using this scale are

   $\frac{880}{80} = 11$ in., $\frac{160}{80} = 2$ in., and $\frac{80}{80} = 1$ in.

   So you will need to cut the following:

   Two 11 in. × 2 in. rectangles

   Two 11 in. × 1 in. rectangles

   Two 2 in. × 1 in. rectangles

   Tape the pieces together to form the model.

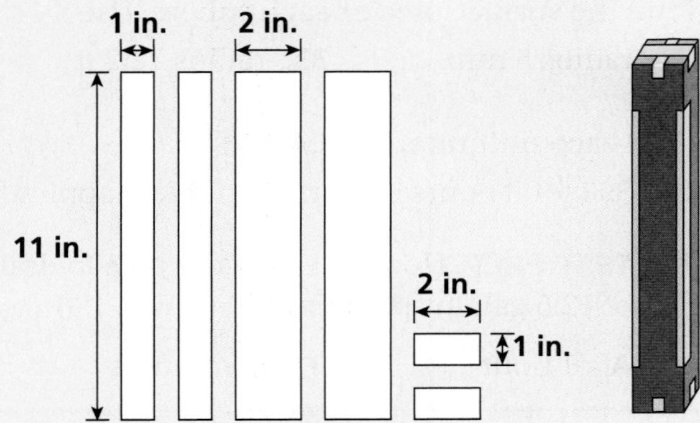

Kings Dominion

The 400-acre Kings Dominion theme park is located in Doswell and includes a 33-story replica of the Eiffel Tower, along with 50 rides located in eight different themed areas.

1. The 331 ft 6 in. Kings Dominion Eiffel Tower is built at about a 1:3 scale to the Eiffel Tower in Paris. Approximately how tall is the Eiffel Tower in Paris?

For 2–6, use the table.

Roller Coasters at Kings Dominion

Roller Coaster	Length (ft)	Height (ft)	Duration
Anaconda		128	1 min 50 s
HyperSonic XLC	1560		20 s
Rebel Yell	3368.5	85	2 min 15 s
Scooby-Doo's Ghoster Coaster	1385	35	

2. The height-to-length ratio of the Anaconda roller coaster at Kings Dominion is $\frac{32}{675}$. Approximately how long is the Anaconda?

3. The height-to-length ratio of the HyperSonic XLC roller coaster at Kings Dominion is $\frac{11}{104}$. Approximately how tall is the HyperSonic XLC?

4. The duration of the Hypersonic XLC has a ratio of 1:5 with the duration of Scooby-Doo's Ghoster Coaster. What is the duration of Scooby-Doo's Ghoster Coaster in minutes and seconds?

5. Convert the length of the Rebel Yell roller coaster to miles, and find the maximum number of rides the Rebel Yell could give in an hour.

6. A scale model of Scooby-Doo's Ghoster Coaster had a length of 277 feet and a height of 7 feet. What was the scale factor?

MATH-ABLES

Copy-Cat

You can use this method to copy a well-known work of art or any drawing. First, draw a grid over the work you want to copy, or draw a grid on tracing paper and tape it over the picture.

Next, on a separate sheet of paper draw a blank grid with the same number of squares. The squares do not have to be the same size. Copy each square from the original exactly onto the blank grid. Do not look at the overall picture as you copy. When you have copied all of the squares, the drawing on your finished grid should look just like the original work.

Suppose you are copying an image from a 12 in. by 18 in. print, and that you use 1-inch squares on the first grid.

1. If you use 3-inch squares on the blank grid, what size will your finished copy be?
2. If you want to make a copy that is 10 inches tall, what size should you make the squares on your blank grid? How wide will the copy be?
3. Choose a painting, drawing, or cartoon, and copy it using the method above.

Tic-Frac-Toe

Draw a large tic-tac-toe board. In each square, draw a blank proportion, $\frac{\square}{\square} = \frac{\square}{\square}$. Players take turns using a spinner with 12 sections or a 12-sided die. A player's turn consists of placing a number anywhere in one of the proportions. The player who correctly completes the proportion can claim that square. A square may also be blocked by filling in three parts of a proportion that cannot be completed with a number from 1 to 12. The first player to claim three squares in a row wins.

internet connect go.hrw.com

Go to ***go.hrw.com*** for a copy of the game board.
KEYWORD: MP4 Game7

Dilations of Geometric Figures

Use with Lesson 7-5

A **dilation** is a geometric transformation that changes the size but not the shape of a figure.

internet connect
Lab Resources Online
go.hrw.com
KEYWORD: MP4 TechLab7

Activity

1. Construct a triangle similar to the one shown below. Label the vertices *A, B,* and *C.*

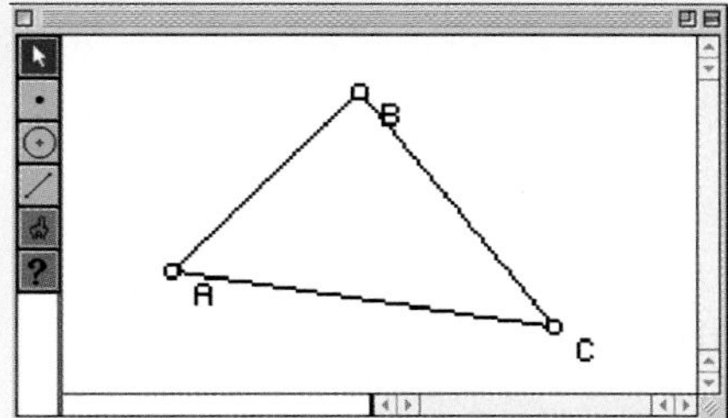

2. Next pick a center of dilation inside triangle *ABC* and label it point *D.*

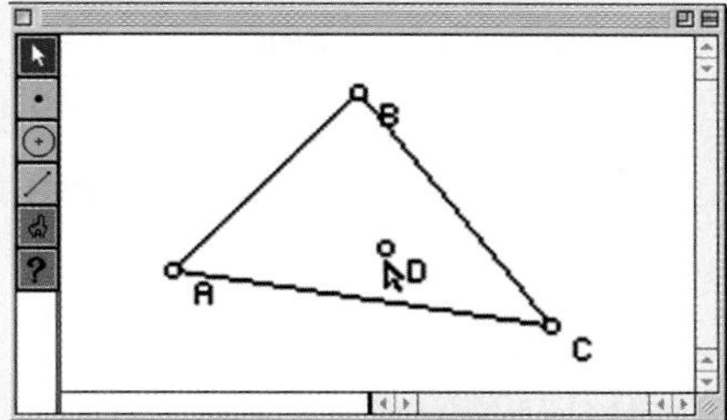

3. Use the dilation tool on your software to shrink the triangle by a ratio of 1 to 2.

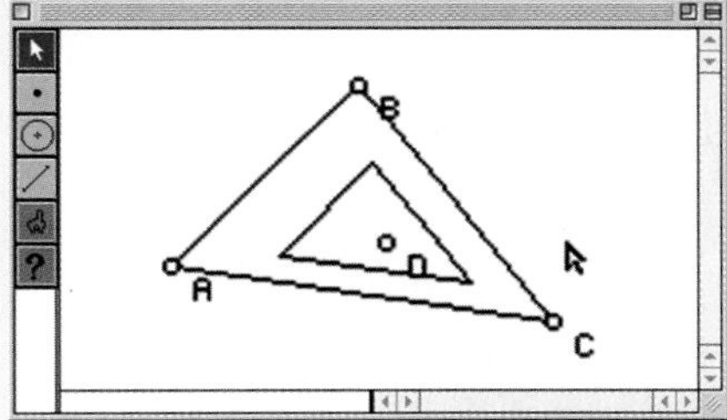

4. Use the dilation tool again to stretch the original triangle by a ratio of 4 to 3.

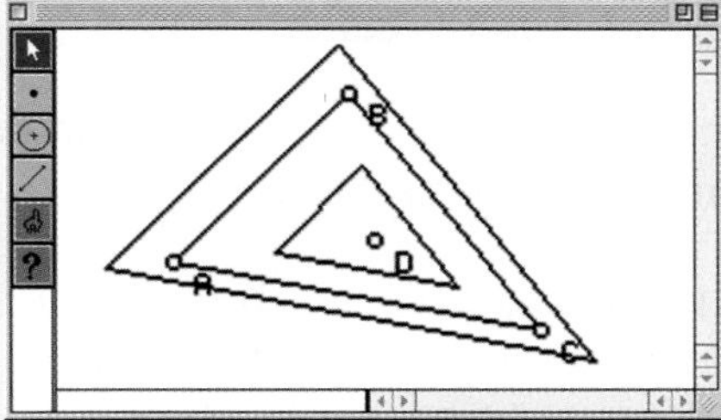

Notice that the dilations of triangle *ABC* are exactly the same *shape* as the original triangle, but they are different *sizes.*

Think and Discuss

1. Are all of the triangles shown in the last figure similar?
2. If the center of dilation is inside the triangle, and the dilated triangle is shrunk, is the smaller triangle always completely inside the original triangle?

Try This

1. Use geometry software to construct a quadrilateral *ABCD.*
   a. Choose a center of dilation inside *ABCD.* Shrink *ABCD* by a factor of 1 to 3.
   b. Choose a center of dilation outside *ABCD.* Stretch *ABCD* by a factor of 3 to 2.

Chapter 7

Study Guide and Review

Vocabulary

capacity	382	ratio	342
center of dilation	362	reduction	373
conversion factor	350	scale	372
cross product	356	scale drawing	372
dilation	362	scale factor	362
enlargement	373	scale model	376
equivalent ratio	342	similar	368
proportion	343	unit price	347
rate	346	unit rate	346

Complete the sentences below with vocabulary words from the list above. Words may be used more than once.

1. A __?__ is a comparison of two quantities by division. Two ratios that are equivalent are said to be in __?__.
2. A __?__ is a comparison of two quantities that have different units. A rate in which the second quantity is 1 is called a(n) __?__.
3. A scale drawing is mathematically __?__ to the actual object. All dimensions are reduced or enlarged using the same __?__.
4. A transformation that changes the size but not the shape of a figure is called a __?__. A scale factor greater than 1 results in a(n) __?__ of the figure, while a scale factor between 0 and 1 results in a(n) __?__ of the figure.

7-1 Ratios and Proportions (pp. 342–345)

EXAMPLE

- **Find two ratios that are equivalent to $\frac{4}{12}$.**

  $\frac{4 \cdot 2}{12 \cdot 2} = \frac{8}{24}$ $\qquad \frac{4 \div 2}{12 \div 2} = \frac{2}{6}$

  8:24 and 2:6 are equivalent to 4:12.

- **Simplify to tell whether $\frac{5}{15}$ and $\frac{6}{24}$ form a proportion.**

  $\frac{5 \div 5}{15 \div 5} = \frac{1}{3}$ $\qquad \frac{6 \div 6}{24 \div 6} = \frac{1}{4}$

  Since $\frac{1}{3} \neq \frac{1}{4}$, the ratios are not in proportion.

EXERCISES

Find two ratios that are equivalent to each given ratio.

5. $\frac{8}{16}$
6. $\frac{9}{18}$
7. $\frac{35}{60}$

Simplify to tell whether the ratios in each pair form a proportion.

8. $\frac{8}{24}$ and $\frac{2}{6}$
9. $\frac{3}{12}$ and $\frac{6}{18}$
10. $\frac{25}{125}$ and $\frac{5}{25}$
11. $\frac{6}{8}$ and $\frac{9}{16}$

internet connect
State-Specific Test Practice Online
go.hrw.com Keyword: MP4 TestPrep

Standardized Test Prep

Chapter 7

Cumulative Assessment, Chapters 1–7

1. Joan paid \$6.40 for 80 copies of a flyer. What is the unit rate?

Ⓐ 8 copies per dollar
Ⓑ 16 copies per dollar
Ⓒ \$0.80 per copy
Ⓓ \$0.08 per copy

2. A 9-inch model is made of a 15-foot boat. What is the scale factor?

Ⓕ 1:20 Ⓗ 3:5
Ⓖ 20:1 Ⓙ 5:3

3. If $x = yz$, which of the following must be equal to xy?

Ⓐ yz Ⓒ y^2z
Ⓑ yz^2 Ⓓ $\frac{z^2}{y}$

4. Each of these fractions is in its simplest form: $\frac{4}{n}$, $\frac{5}{n}$, $\frac{7}{n}$. Which of the following could be the value of n?

Ⓕ 28 Ⓗ 26
Ⓖ 27 Ⓙ 25

5. In the equation $A = \pi r^2$, if r is doubled, by what number is A multiplied?

Ⓐ 2 Ⓒ 4
Ⓑ $\frac{1}{2}$ Ⓓ $\frac{1}{4}$

6. Which of the following is true for the data set 20, 30, 50, 70, 80, 80, 90?

I. The mean is greater than 70.
II. The median is greater than 70.
III. The mode is greater than 70.

Ⓕ I and II only Ⓗ III only
Ⓖ II and III only Ⓙ I, II, and III

7. What is the next number in this sequence? −27, 9, −3, 1, ■, . . .

Ⓐ −3 Ⓒ 0
Ⓑ −1 Ⓓ $-\frac{1}{3}$

TIP!

TEST TAKING TIP!

Redraw a figure: Answers to geometry problems may become apparent as you redraw the figure.

8. How many edges are in the prism below?

Ⓕ 5 Ⓗ 10
Ⓖ 7 Ⓙ 15

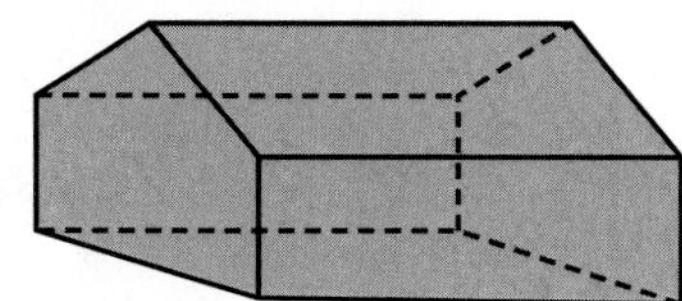

9. ***SHORT RESPONSE*** What is the value of $(-1 - 2)^3 + 2.5^1$? Use the order of operations, and show each step.

10. ***SHORT RESPONSE*** Use the map to estimate to the nearest 10 km the distance that the Steward family will travel as they sail from St. Petersburg to Pensacola, Florida. Explain in words how you determined your answer.

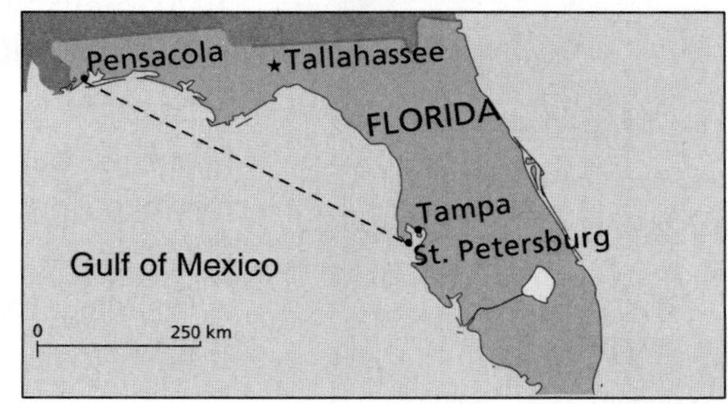

Standardized Test Prep

Chapter

8

Percents

TABLE OF CONTENTS

Player	Age	Home Runs	At Bats/Home Run
Barry Bonds	37	576	14.0
Sammy Sosa	33	450	14.4
Ken Griffey Jr.	32	460	14.6
Alex Rodriguez	26	241	15.6

Career Sports Statistician

Statisticians are mathematicians who work with data, creating statistics, graphs, and tables that describe and explain the real world. Sports statisticians combine their love of sports with their ability to use mathematics.

Statistics not only explain what has happened, but can help you predict what may happen in the future. The table describes the home run hitting of some active Major League baseball players.

Chapter Opener Online
go.hrw.com
KEYWORD: MP4 Ch8

21. ***PHYSICAL SCIENCE*** Of the 20 highest mountains in the United States, 17 are located in Alaska. What percent of the highest mountains in the United States are in Alaska?

22. ***LIFE SCIENCE*** When collecting plant specimens, it is a good idea to remove no more than 5% of a population of plants. A botanist wants to collect plants from an area with 60 plants. What is the greatest number of plants she should remove?

23. The graph shows the percents of the total U.S. land area taken up by the five largest states. The sixth section of the graph represents the area of the remaining 45 states.

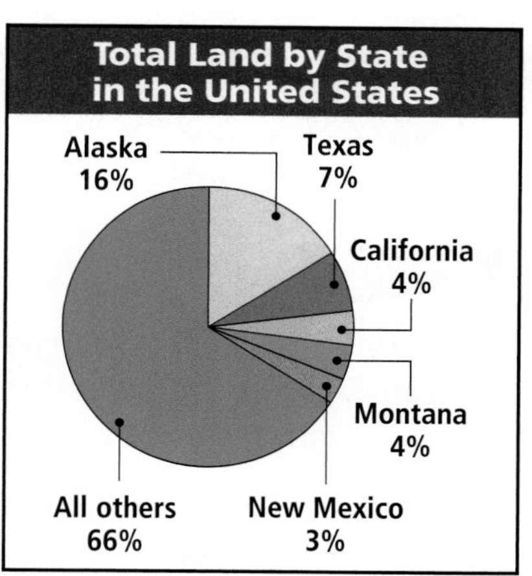

   a. Alaska is the largest state in total land area. Write Alaska's portion of the total U.S. land area as a fraction and as a decimal.

   b. What percent of the total U.S. land area is Alaska and Texas combined? How might you describe this percent?

24. ***WHAT'S THE ERROR?*** An analysis showed that 0.03% of the video games produced by one company were defective. Wynn says this is 3 out of every 100. What is Wynn's error?

25. ***WRITE ABOUT IT*** How can you find a fraction, decimal, or percent when you have only one form of a number?

26. ***CHALLENGE*** Luke and Lissa were asked to solve a percent problem using the numbers 17 and 45. Luke found 17% of 45, but Lissa found 45% of 17. Explain why they both got the same answer. Would this work for other numbers as well? Why or why not?

Spiral Review

Tell whether the two lines described in each exercise are parallel, perpendicular, or neither. (Lesson 5-5)

27. $\overleftrightarrow{PQ}$ has slope $\frac{3}{2}$. $\overleftrightarrow{EF}$ has slope $-\frac{2}{3}$.

28. $\overleftrightarrow{AB}$ has slope $\frac{9}{11}$. $\overleftrightarrow{CD}$ has slope $-\frac{3}{4}$.

29. $\overleftrightarrow{XY}$ has slope $\frac{13}{25}$. $\overleftrightarrow{QR}$ has slope $\frac{13}{25}$.

30. $\overleftrightarrow{MN}$ has slope $-\frac{1}{8}$. $\overleftrightarrow{OP}$ has slope 8.

31. **TEST PREP** A cone has diameter 12 cm and height 9 cm. Using 3.14 for π, find the volume of the cone to the nearest tenth. (Lesson 6-7)

   A 56.5 cm^3 **B** 118.3 cm^3 **C** 1356.5 cm^3 **D** 339.1 cm^3

32. **TEST PREP** Evaluate $Q - 1\frac{2}{3}$ for $Q = 4\frac{3}{4}$. (Lesson 3-5)

   F $3\frac{1}{12}$ **G** $5\frac{1}{12}$ **H** $1\frac{1}{6}$ **J** $3\frac{5}{12}$

Make a Circle Graph

Use with Lesson 8-1

WHAT YOU NEED:
- Compass
- Ruler
- Protractor
- Paper

REMEMBER
- A circle measures 360°.
- Percent compares a number to 100.

Lab Resources Online
go.hrw.com
KEYWORD: MP4 Lab8A

Activity

1 Skunks are legal pets in some states but not in most. Use the information from the table to make a circle graph showing the percents for each category.

Skunks as Pets by State

Legality	Number of States
Legal (no restrictions)	6
Legal with permit	12
Legal in some areas	2
Illegal	27
Other conditions	3

a. Use a compass to draw a large circle. Use a ruler to draw a vertical radius.

b. Extend the table to show the percent of states with each category of legality.

c. Use the percents to determine the angle measure of each sector of the graph.

d. Use a protractor to draw each angle clockwise from the radius.

e. Label the graph and each sector. Color the sectors.

Legality	Number of States	Percent of States	Angle of Section
Legal (no restrictions)	6	$\frac{6}{50} = 12\%$	$\frac{12}{100} \cdot 360 = 43.2°$
Legal with permit	12	$\frac{12}{50} = 24\%$	$\frac{24}{100} \cdot 360 = 86.4°$
Legal in some areas	2	$\frac{2}{50} = 4\%$	$\frac{4}{100} \cdot 360 = 14.4°$
Illegal	27	$\frac{27}{50} = 54\%$	$\frac{54}{100} \cdot 360 = 194.4°$
Other conditions	3	$\frac{3}{50} = 6\%$	$\frac{6}{100} \cdot 360 = 21.6°$

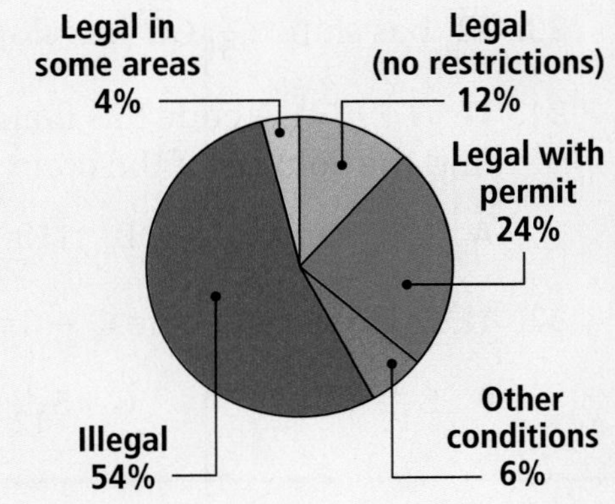

Think and Discuss

1. How many states would need to legalize skunks for the largest sector to be 180°?

Try This

1. Make a circle graph to show only the states where skunks are not illegal.

8-2 Finding Percents

Learn to find percents.

Relative humidity is a measure of the amount of water vapor in the air. When the relative humidity is 100%, the air has the maximum amount of water vapor. At this point, any additional water vapor would cause precipitation. To find the relative humidity on a given day, you would need to find a percent.

The rainy season in some parts of Indochina extends from March to November, and the average humidity is close to 90%.

EXAMPLE 1 Finding the Percent One Number Is of Another

A What percent of 162 is 90?

Method 1: Set up an equation to find the percent.

$p \cdot 162 = 90$ — *Set up an equation.*

$p = \frac{90}{162}$ — *Solve for p.*

$p = 0.\overline{5}$, or approximately 0.56. — *0.56 is 56%*

So 90 is approximately 56% of 162.

B Earth has a surface area of approximately 197 million square miles. About 58 million square miles of that surface area is land. Find the percent of Earth's surface area that is land.

Method 2: Set up a proportion to find the percent.

Think: What number is to 100 as 58 is to 197?

$\frac{\text{number}}{100} = \frac{\text{part}}{\text{whole}}$ — *Set up a proportion.*

$\frac{n}{100} = \frac{58}{197}$ — *Substitute.*

$n \cdot 197 = 100 \cdot 58$ — *Find the cross products.*

$197n = 5800$

$n = \frac{5800}{197}$ — *Solve for n.*

$n \approx 29.44$, or approximately 29.

$\frac{29}{100} \approx \frac{58}{197}$ — *The proportion is reasonable.*

So approximately 29% of Earth's surface area is land.

EXAMPLE 2 Finding a Percent of a Number

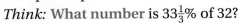

A **A domestic pig can run about $33\frac{1}{3}\%$ of the speed of a giraffe. A giraffe can run about 32 mi/h. To the nearest tenth, how fast can a domestic pig run?**

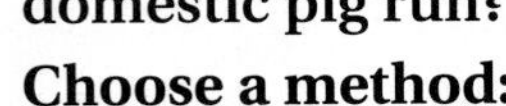

Choose a method: Set up an equation.

Think: **What number** is $33\frac{1}{3}\%$ of 32?

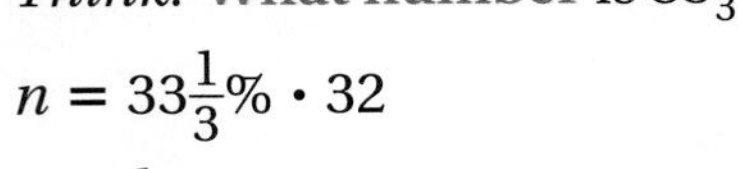

$n = 33\frac{1}{3}\% \cdot 32$ *Set up an equation.*

$n = \frac{1}{3} \cdot 32$ *$33\frac{1}{3}\%$ is equivalent to $\frac{1}{3}$.*

$n = \frac{32}{3} = 10\frac{2}{3} = 10.\overline{6}$

$n \approx 10.7$ *Round to the nearest tenth.*

A domestic pig can run about 10.7 miles per hour.

B **The Chrysler Building in New York City is about 1046 feet tall. The height of the Empire State Building is approximately 120% of the height of the Chrysler Building. To the nearest foot, find the height of the Empire State Building.**

Choose a method: Set up a proportion.

Think: 120 is to 100 as **what number** is to 1046?

$\frac{120}{100} = \frac{n}{1046}$ *Set up a proportion.*

$120 \cdot 1046 = 100 \cdot n$ *Find the cross products.*

$125{,}520 = 100n$

$1255.2 = n$ *Solve for n.*

$n \approx 1255$ *Round to the nearest whole number.*

The Empire State Building is about 1255 feet tall.

Helpful Hint

When solving a problem like this one, the number you are looking for will be greater than the number given, in this case, 1046.

Think and Discuss

1. **Show** why 5% of a number is less than $\frac{1}{10}$ of the number.
2. **Demonstrate** two ways to find 70% of a number.
3. **Give an example** of a situation in which one quantity is 300% of another quantity.
4. **Name** fractions in simplest form that are the same as 40% and as 250%.

8-2 Exercises

FOR EXTRA PRACTICE
see page 746

GUIDED PRACTICE

See Example 1 **Find each percent to the nearest tenth.**

1. What percent of 71 is 35?
2. What percent of 1130 is 225?
3. Of Earth's 197 million mi^2 of surface area, about 139 million mi^2 is water. Find the percent of Earth's surface that is covered by water.

See Example 2

4. Jay's term paper is 18 pages long. If Madison's paper is 175% of the length of Jay's paper, find the length of Madison's paper.

INDEPENDENT PRACTICE

See Example 1 **Find each percent to the nearest tenth.**

5. What percent of 74 is 222?
6. What percent of 150 is 25?
7. 12.5 is what percent of 1250?
8. 150 is what percent of 80?
9. About 600 mi^2 of the 700 mi^2 of the Okefenokee Swamp is located in Georgia. If Georgia is 57,906 mi^2, find the percent of that area that is part of the Okefenokee Swamp.

See Example 2

10. In Arkansas, the highest elevation is Mount Magazine, in west Arkansas, and the lowest is the Ouachita River, in the southeast corner of the state. Mount Magazine is 2753 ft above sea level, which is about 5098% of the elevation of the lowest portion of the state. Find the elevation of the Ouachita River area.

PRACTICE AND PROBLEM SOLVING

Find each number to the nearest tenth.

11. What number is $66\frac{2}{3}\%$ of 45?
12. What number is $22\frac{2}{3}\%$ of 320?
13. What number is 44% of 6?
14. What number is $2\frac{1}{2}\%$ of 11,960?
15. What number is 133% of 200?
16. What number is $66\frac{2}{3}\%$ of 750?

Complete each statement.

17. Since 9 is 15% of 60,
    - **a.** 18 is ▒% of 60.
    - **b.** 27 is ▒% of 60.
    - **c.** 90 is ▒% of 60.
18. Since 8 is 5% of 160,
    - **a.** 8 is ▒% of 80.
    - **b.** 8 is ▒% of 40.
    - **c.** 8 is ▒% of 20.
19. Since 20 is 200% of 10,
    - **a.** 20 is ▒% of 20.
    - **b.** 20 is ▒% of 40.
    - **c.** 20 is ▒% of 80.

20. ***LANGUAGE ARTS*** The Hawaiian words shown contain all of the letters of the Hawaiian alphabet. The ` is actually a consonant!

   a. What percent of the Hawaiian alphabet are vowels?

   b. To the nearest tenth, what percent of the letters in the English alphabet are also in the Hawaiian alphabet?

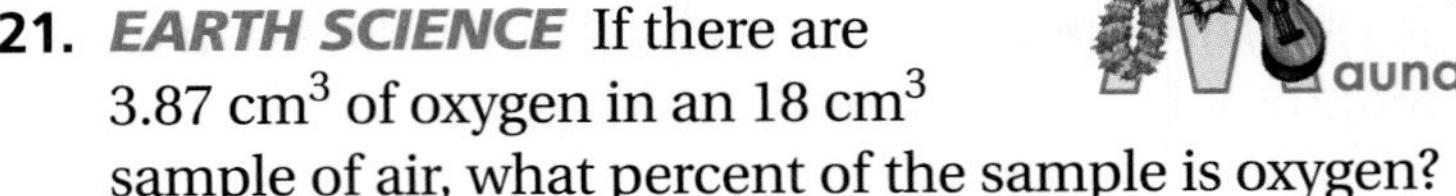

21. ***EARTH SCIENCE*** If there are 3.87 cm^3 of oxygen in an 18 cm^3 sample of air, what percent of the sample is oxygen?

22. ***SOCIAL STUDIES*** According to the 2000 U.S. Census, approximately 2.5 million Americans spend $12\frac{1}{2}$% of the 24-hour day commuting. How many hours a day does a person in this group spend commuting?

23. ***SOCIAL STUDIES*** Of the 50 states in the Union, 32% have names that begin with either M or N. How many states have names beginning with either M or N?

24. ***LIFE SCIENCE*** The General Sherman sequoia tree, in California, is thought to be the largest living thing on Earth by volume. It has a height of 275 ft. Its lowest large branch is at a height of 130 ft. What percent of the height of the tree would you need to climb to reach that branch?

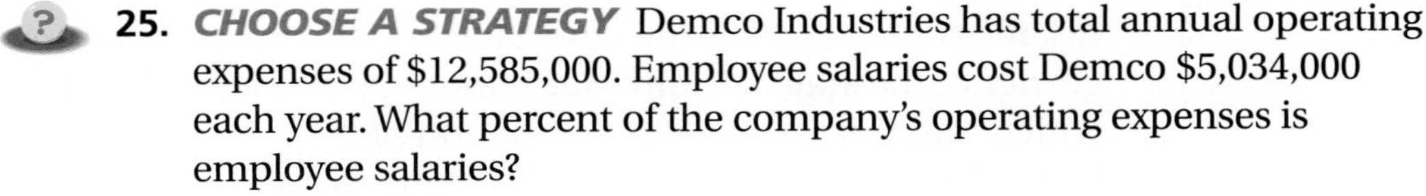

25. ***CHOOSE A STRATEGY*** Demco Industries has total annual operating expenses of $12,585,000. Employee salaries cost Demco $5,034,000 each year. What percent of the company's operating expenses is employee salaries?

   A 4% **B** 40% **C** 25% **D** 250%

26. ***WRITE ABOUT IT*** A question on a math quiz asks, "What is 150% of 88?" Mark calculates 13.2 as the answer. Is this a reasonable answer? Explain why or why not.

27. ***CHALLENGE*** Tani cut 2 ft 6 in. from a board measuring 3 yd 1 ft. What percent of the board's original length did Tani remove, and what is the length of the board that remains?

Spiral Review

State if each number is rational, irrational, or not a real number. (Lesson 3-10)

28. -14 **29.** $\sqrt{13}$ **30.** $\frac{127}{46,191}$ **31.** $\sqrt{-\frac{5}{6}}$

32. **TEST PREP** Each edge of a gift box is 4 in. long. How much wrapping paper would it take to cover the surface of the gift box? (Lesson 6-8)

   A 96 in^2 **B** 64 in^2 **C** 32 in^2 **D** 128 in^2

Find Percent Error

Use with Lesson 8-2

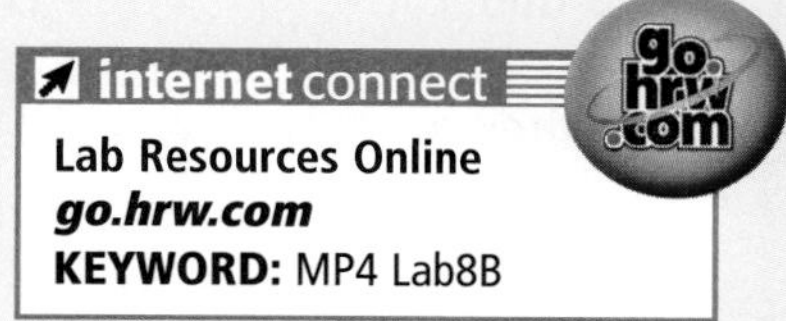

A measurement is only as precise as the device that is used to measure. There is often a difference between a measured value and an accepted or actual value. When the difference is given as a percent of the accepted value, this is called the *percent error*.

Percent error is always nonnegative, so use absolute value.

$$\text{percent error} = \frac{|\text{measured value} - \text{accepted value}|}{\text{accepted value}} \cdot 100$$

Activity

1. A student uses an 8 oz cup and finds the volume of a container to the nearest 8 oz as 64 oz. The actual volume of the container is 67.6 oz. Find the percent error of the measurement to the nearest tenth of a percent.

   a. Store the measured volume on your calculator as M and the actual volume as A. Type 64 STO▶ ALPHA M ENTER and 67.6 STO▶ ALPHA A ENTER.

   b. Find the percent error by using the following keystrokes:

   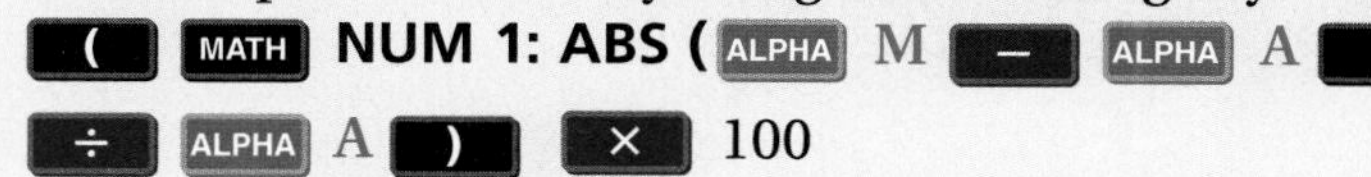

   To the nearest tenth of a percent, the percent error is 5.3%.

Think and Discuss

1. Can percent error exceed 100%? Explain.
2. Tell why one measurement that is 0.1 cm from an actual length may have a larger percent error than another measurement that is 25 cm from a different actual length.
3. Describe why a ruler with centimeter markings can only measure accurately to within $\frac{1}{2}$ cm of an actual length.

Try This

Find the percent error to the nearest tenth of a percent.

1. measured length 3 cm; actual length 3.4 cm
2. measured length 250 ft; actual length 246.9 ft

8-3 Finding a Number When the Percent Is Known

Learn to find a number when the percent is known.

The Pacific giant squid can grow to a weight of 2000 pounds. This is 1250% of the maximum weight of the Pacific giant octopus. When one number is known, and its relationship to another number is given by a percent, the other number can be found.

In studies, the Pacific giant octopus has been able to travel through mazes and unscrew jar lids for food.

EXAMPLE 1 Finding a Number When the Percent Is Known

36 is 4% of what number?

Set up an equation to find the number.

$36 = 4\% \cdot n$ *Set up an equation.*

$36 = 0.04n$ *$4\% = \frac{4}{100}$*

$\frac{36}{0.04} = \frac{0.04}{0.04}n$ *Divide both sides by 0.04.*

$900 = n$

36 is 4% of 900.

EXAMPLE 2 *Physical Science Application*

In a science lab, a sample of a compound contains 16.5 grams of sodium. If 82.5% of the sample is sodium, find the number of grams the entire sample weighs.

Choose a method: Set up a proportion to find the number.

Think: 82.5 is to 100 as 16.5 is to **what number?**

$\frac{82.5}{100} = \frac{16.5}{n}$ *Set up a proportion.*

$82.5 \cdot n = 100 \cdot 16.5$ *Find the cross products.*

$82.5n = 1650$ *Solve for n.*

$n = \frac{1650}{82.5}$

$n = 20$

The entire sample weighs 20 grams.

EXAMPLE 3 Life Science Application

A **The Pacific giant squid can grow to a weight of 2000 pounds. This is 1250% of the maximum weight of the Pacific giant octopus. To the nearest pound, find the maximum weight of the octopus.**

Choose a method: Set up an equation.

Think: 2000 is 1250% of what number?

$2000 = 1250\% \cdot n$ *Set up an equation.*

$2000 = 12.50 \cdot n$ *1250% = 12.50*

$\frac{2000}{12.50} = n$ *Solve for n.*

$160 = n$

The maximum weight of the Pacific giant octopus is about 160 lb.

B **The king cobra, the world's largest venomous snake, can reach a length of 18 feet. This is only about 60% of the length of the largest reticulated python. Find the length of the largest reticulated python.**

Choose a method: Set up a proportion.

Think: 60 is to 100 as 18 is to what number?

$\frac{60}{100} = \frac{18}{n}$ *Set up a proportion.*

$60 \cdot n = 100 \cdot 18$ *Find the cross products.*

$60n = 1800$

$n = \frac{1800}{60}$ *Solve for n.*

$n = 30$

The largest reticulated python is 30 feet long.

Life Science LINK

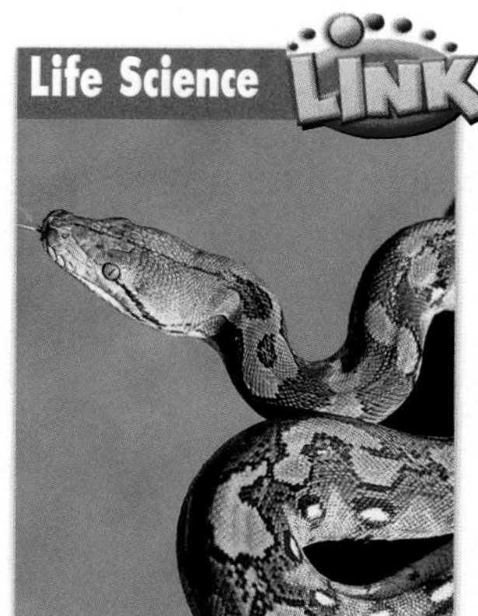

Reticulated means "net-like" or "forming a network." The reticulated python is named for the pattern on its skin.

You have now seen all three types of percent problems.

Three Types of Percent Problems	
1. Finding the percent of a number	15% of 120 = n
2. Finding the percent one number is of another	p% of 120 = 18
3. Finding a number when the percent is known	15% of n = 18

Think and Discuss

1. **Compare** finding a number when a percent is known to finding the percent one number is of another number.
2. **Explain** whether a number is greater than or less than 36 if 22% of the number is 36.

8-3 Exercises

FOR EXTRA PRACTICE

see page 746

internet connect

Homework Help Online
go.hrw.com Keyword: MP4 8-3

GUIDED PRACTICE

See Example 1

Find each number to the nearest tenth.

1. 4.3 is $12\frac{1}{2}\%$ of what number?

2. 56 is $33\frac{1}{3}\%$ of what number?

3. 18% of what number is 30?

4. 30% of what number is 96?

See Example 2

5. The only kind of rock that floats in water is pumice. Chalk, although denser, absorbs more water than pumice does. How much water can a 5.2 oz piece of chalk absorb if it can absorb 32% of its weight?

See Example 3

6. At 3 P.M., a chimney casts a shadow that is 135% of its actual height. If the shadow is 37.8 ft, what is the actual height of the chimney?

INDEPENDENT PRACTICE

See Example 1

Find each number to the nearest tenth.

7. 105 is $33\frac{1}{3}\%$ of what number?

8. 77 is 25% of what number?

9. 51 is 6% of what number?

10. 24 is 15% of what number?

11. 84% of what number is 14?

12. 56% of what number is 39.2?

13. 10% of what number is 57?

14. 180% of what number is 6?

See Example 2

15. Manuel sold 42 of his baseball cards at a collectors show. If this represented $12\frac{1}{2}\%$ of his total collection, how many baseball cards did Manuel have before the show?

See Example 3

16. When a tire is labeled "185/70/14," that means it is 185 mm wide, the sidewall height (from the rim to the road) is 70% of its width, and the wheel has a diameter of 14 in. What is the tire's sidewall height?

PRACTICE AND PROBLEM SOLVING

Complete each statement.

17. Since 1% of 600 is 6,

a. 2% of ▮ is 6.

b. 4% of ▮ is 6.

c. 8% of ▮ is 6.

18. Since 100% of 8 is 8,

a. 50% of ▮ is 8.

b. 25% of ▮ is 8.

c. 10% of ▮ is 8.

19. Since 5% of 80 is 4,

a. 10% of ▮ is 4.

b. 20% of ▮ is 4.

c. 40% of ▮ is 4.

20. In a poll of 225 students, 36 said that their favorite Thanksgiving food was turkey, and 56 said that their favorite was stuffing. Give the percent of students who said that each food was their favorite.

Social Studies LINK

The U.S. census collects information about state populations, economics, income and poverty levels, births and deaths, and so on. This information can be used to study trends and patterns. For Exercises 21–23, round answers to the nearest tenth.

2000 U.S. Census Data			
	Population	Male	Female
Alaska	626,932	324,112	302,820
New York	18,976,457	9,146,748	9,829,709
Age 34 and Under	139,328,990	71,053,554	68,275,436
Age 35 and Over	142,092,916	67,000,009	75,092,907
Total U.S.	281,421,906	138,053,563	143,368,343

The New York counties with the greatest populations are Kings (Brooklyn) and Queens.

21. What percent of New York's population is male?

22. What percent of the entire country's population, to the nearest tenth of a percent, is made up of people in New York?

23. Tell what percent of the U.S. population each represents.

a. people 34 and under **b.** people 35 and over

c. male **d.** female

24. American Indians and Native Alaskans make up about 15.6% of Alaska's population. What is their population, to the nearest thousand?

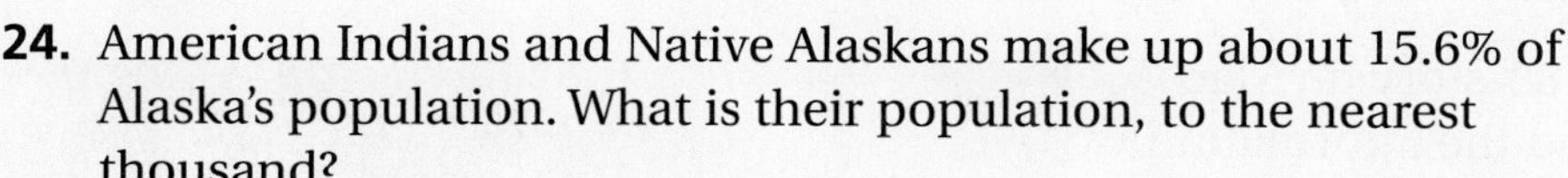

25. ***CHALLENGE*** About 71% of the U.S. population age 85 and over is female. Of the fractions that round to 71% when rounded to the nearest percent, which has the least denominator?

go.hrw.com
Web Extra!
KEYWORD: MP4 Census

Spiral Review

Find the range of each set of data. (Lesson 4-4)

26. 16, 32, 1, 54, 30, 28

27. 105, 969, 350, 87, 410

28. 0.2, 0.8, 0.65, 0.7, 1.6, 1.1

Find the first and third quartiles of the data set. (Lesson 4-4)

29. 55, 60, 40, 45, 70, 65, 35, 40, 75, 50, 60, 80, 45, 55

30. **TEST PREP** A triangle has vertices $A(4, 4)$, $B(6, -2)$, and $C(-4, -12)$. What are the vertices after dilating by a scale factor of 2 with the origin as the center of dilation? (Lesson 7-5)

A $A'(2, 2)$, $B'(3, -1)$, $C'(-2, -6)$

B $A'(-8, -8)$, $B'(-12, 4)$, $C'(8, 24)$

C $A'(8, 8)$, $B'(12, -4)$, $C'(-8, -24)$

D $A'(16, 16)$, $B'(36, 4)$, $C'(16, 144)$

Chapter 8

Mid-Chapter Quiz

LESSON 8-1 (pp. 400–403)

Find the equivalent value missing from the table for each value given on the circle graph.

Fraction	Decimal	Percent
$\frac{1}{8}$	1. ▒	2. ▒
3. ▒	0.25	4. ▒
5. ▒	6. ▒	$37\frac{1}{2}\%$
$\frac{1}{4}$	7. ▒	8. ▒

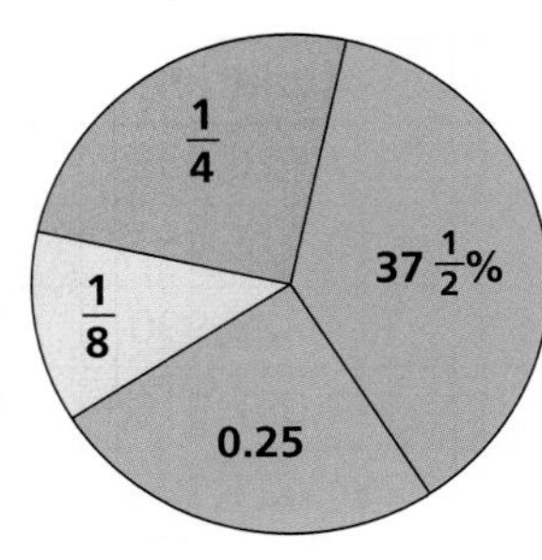

LESSON 8-2 (pp. 405–408)

9. What is 27% of 16?

10. 48 is what percent of 384?

11. In the November 2001 election, only 191,411 of the 509,719 voters registered in Westchester County, New York, cast a ballot. This was the lowest turnout in at least a century. To the nearest tenth, what percent of registered voters actually voted in the election?

12. Use the height of the 88-story Jin Mao Tower in Shanghai and the information shown at right to find the heights of the Eiffel Tower and Russia's Motherland Statue.

13. Of Canada's total area of 9,976,140 km^2, 755,170 km^2 is water. To the nearest tenth of a percent, what part of Canada is water?

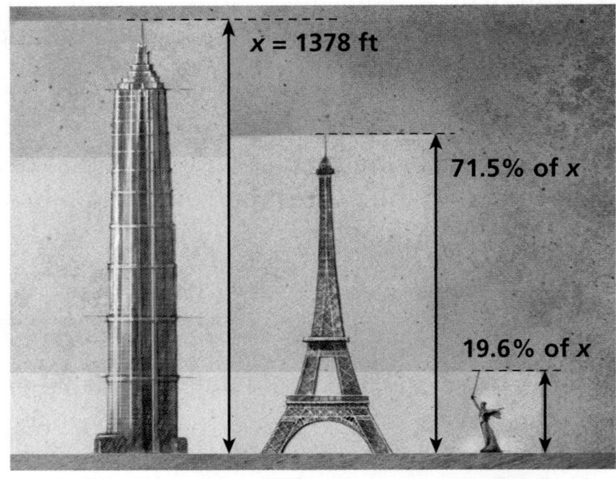

LESSON 8-3 (pp. 410–413)

14. 30 is 12.5% of what number?

15. 244 is 250% of what number?

16. The speed of sound in air at sea level at 32°F is 1088 ft/s. If that represents only 22.04% of the speed of sound in ice-cold water, what is the speed of sound in ice-cold water, to the nearest whole number?

17. In 2000, U.S. imports from Canada totaled $230,838.3 million. This was about 129% of the total dollar value of the U.S. exports to Canada. To the nearest ten million dollars, what was the value of U.S. exports to Canada?

Focus on Problem Solving

Make a Plan

• Do you need an estimate or an exact answer?

When you are solving a word problem, ask yourself whether you need an exact answer or whether an estimate is sufficient. For example, if the amounts given in the problem are approximate, only an approximate answer can be given. If an estimate is sufficient, you may wish to use estimation techniques to save time in your calculations.

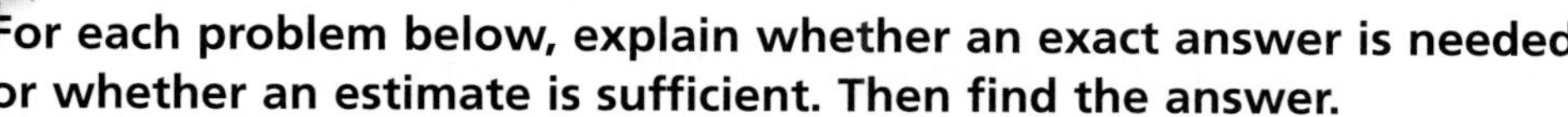

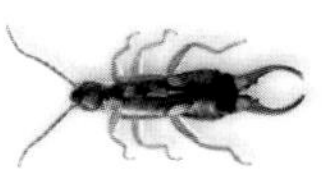

For each problem below, explain whether an exact answer is needed or whether an estimate is sufficient. Then find the answer.

1. In a poll of 3000 registered voters in a certain district, 1800 favored a proposed school bond package. What percent favored the bond package?

2. George needs to score 76% on his final exam to get a B in his math class. If the final is worth 200 points, how many points does he need?

3. Karou is trying to save about $3500 for a trip to Japan. If she has $1000 in an account that earns 8% interest and puts $100 per month in the account, will she have enough in 2 years?

4. Erik makes $7.60 per hour at his job. If he receives a 5% raise, how much will he be making per hour?

5. Jamie is planning to tile her kitchen floor. The room is 330 square feet. It is recommended that she buy enough tile for an area 15% greater than the actual kitchen floor in case of breakage. How many square feet of tile should she buy?

6. There are about 1,032,000 known species of animals on Earth. Of these, about 751,000 are insects. What percent of known species are insects?

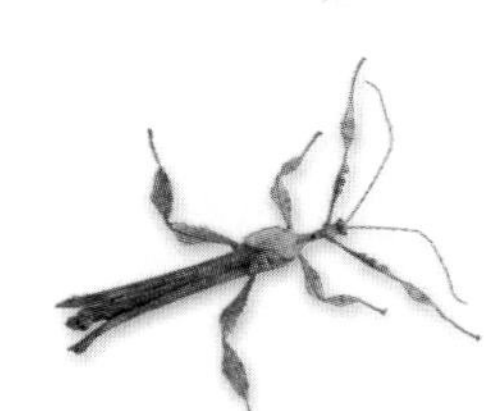

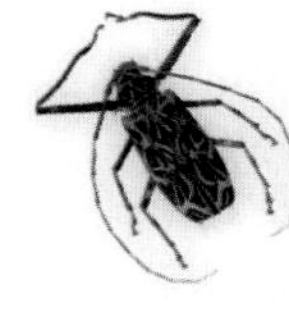

8-4 Percent Increase and Decrease

Learn to find percent increase and decrease.

Vocabulary

percent change

percent increase

percent decrease

Many animals hibernate during the winter to survive harsh conditions and food shortages. While they sleep, their body temperatures drop, their breathing rates decrease, and their heart rates slow. They may even appear to be dead.

"He hums in his sleep."

Percents can be used to describe a change. **Percent change** is the ratio of the *amount of change* to the *original amount.*

$$\text{percent change} = \frac{\text{amount of change}}{\text{original amount}}$$

Percent increase describes how much the original amount increases. **Percent decrease** describes how much the original amount decreases.

EXAMPLE 1 Finding Percent Increase or Decrease

Find the percent increase or decrease from 20 to 24.

This is percent increase.

$24 - 20 = 4$ — *First find the amount of change.*

Think: What percent is 4 of 20?

$\frac{\text{amount of increase}}{\text{original amount}} \rightarrow \frac{4}{20}$ — *Set up the ratio.*

$\frac{4}{20} = 0.2$ — *Find the decimal form.*

$= 20\%$ — *Write as a percent.*

From 20 to 24 is a 20% increase.

EXAMPLE 2 *Life Science Application*

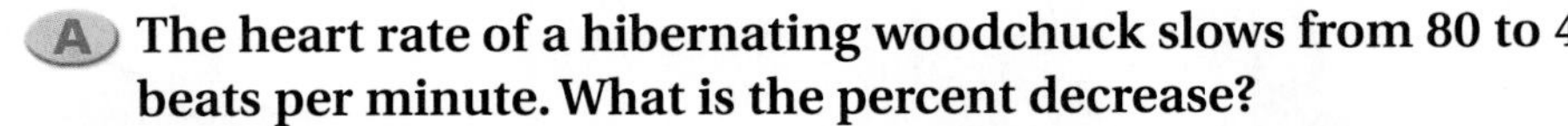

A The heart rate of a hibernating woodchuck slows from 80 to 4 beats per minute. What is the percent decrease?

$80 - 4 = 76$ — *First find the amount of change.*

Think: What percent is 76 of 80?

$\frac{\text{amount of decrease}}{\text{original amount}} \rightarrow \frac{76}{80}$ — *Set up the ratio.*

$\frac{76}{80} = 0.95$ — *Find the decimal form.*

$= 95\%$ — *76 is 95% of 80.*

The woodchuck's heart rate decreases by 95% during hibernation.

B **According to the U.S. Census Bureau, 69.9 million children lived in the United States in 1998. It is estimated that there will be 77.6 million children in 2020. What is the percent increase, to the nearest percent?**

$77.6 - 69.9 = 7.7$ *First find the amount of change.*

Think: What percent is 7.7 of 69.9?

$\frac{\text{amount of increase}}{\text{original amount}} = \frac{7.7}{69.9}$ *Set up the ratio.*

$\frac{7.7}{69.9} \approx 0.1102$ *Find the decimal form.*

$\approx 11.02\%$ *Write as a percent.*

The number of children in the United States is estimated to increase 11%.

EXAMPLE 3 Using Percent Increase or Decrease to Find Prices

A **Anthony bought an LCD monitor originally priced at $750 that was reduced in price by 35%. What was the reduced price?**

$\$750 \cdot 35\%$ *First find 35% of $750.*

$\$750 \cdot 0.35 = \$262.50$ *35% = 0.35*

The amount of decrease is $262.50.

Think: The reduced price is $262.50 *less than* $750.

$\$750 - \$262.50$ *Subtract the amount of decrease.*

$= \$487.50$

The reduced price of the monitor was $487.50.

B **Mr. Salazar received a shipment of sofas that cost him $366 each. He marks the price of each sofa up $33\frac{1}{3}\%$ to find the *retail price*. What is the retail price of each sofa?**

$\$366 \cdot 33\frac{1}{3}\%$ *First find $33\frac{1}{3}\%$ of $366.*

$\$366 \cdot \frac{1}{3} = \$122$ $33\frac{1}{3}\% = \frac{1}{3}$

The amount of increase is $122.

Think: The retail price is $122 *more than* $366.

$\$366 + \$122 = \$488$ *Add the amount of increase.*

The retail price of each sofa is $488.

Think and Discuss

1. **Explain** whether a 150% increase or a 150% decrease is possible.
2. **Compare** finding a 20% increase to finding 120% of a number.
3. **Explain** how you could find the percent of change if you knew the U.S. populations in 1990 and 2000.

8-4 Exercises

FOR EXTRA PRACTICE
see page 747

internet connect
Homework Help Online
go.hrw.com Keyword: MP4 8-4

GUIDED PRACTICE

See Example 1 **Find each percent increase or decrease to the nearest percent.**

1. from 40 to 55
2. from 85 to 30
3. from 75 to 150
4. from 55 to 90
5. from 110 to 82
6. from 82 to 110

See Example 2 

7. A population of geese rose from 234 to 460 over a period of two years. What is the percent increase, to the nearest tenth of a percent?

See Example 3

8. An automobile dealer agrees to cut 5% off the $10,288 sticker price of a new car for a customer. What is the price of the car for the customer?

INDEPENDENT PRACTICE

See Example 1 **Find each percent increase or decrease to the nearest percent.**

9. from 55 to 60
10. from 111 to 200
11. from 9 to 5
12. from 800 to 1500
13. from 0.84 to 0.67
14. from 45 to 20

See Example 2 

15. The boiling point of water is lower at higher altitudes. Water boils at 212°F at sea level and 193.7°F at 10,000 ft. What is the percent decrease in the temperatures, to the nearest tenth of a percent?

See Example 3

16. Mr. Simmons owns a hardware store and typically marks up merchandise by 28% over warehouse cost. How much would he charge for a hammer that costs him $13.50?

PRACTICE AND PROBLEM SOLVING

Find each percent increase or decrease to the nearest percent.

17. from $49.60 to $38.10
18. from $67 to $104
19. from $575 to $405
20. from $822 to $766
21. from $0.23 to $0.19
22. from $12.50 to $14.75

Find each missing number.

23. originally: $500
new price: ▇
20% increase
24. originally: 140
new amount: ▇
50% increase
25. originally: ▇
new amount: 230
15% increase
26. originally: ▇
new price: $4.20
5% decrease
27. originally: 32
new amount: 48
▇% increase
28. originally: $65
new price: $52
▇% decrease
29. Maria purchased a CD burner for $199. Six months later, the same burner was selling for $119. By what percent had the price decreased, to the nearest percent?

30. ***LIFE SCIENCE*** The *Carcharodon megaladon* shark of the Miocene era is believed to have been about 12 m long. The modern great white shark is about 6 m long. Write the change in length of these longest sharks over time as a percent increase or decrease.

31. A sale ad shows a \$240 winter coat discounted 35%.
    a. How much is the price decrease?
    b. What is the sale price of the coat?
    c. If the coat is reduced in price by an additional $33\frac{1}{3}$%, what will be the new sale price?
    d. What percent decrease does this final sale price represent?

32. Is the percent change the same when a blouse is marked up from \$15 to \$20 as when it is marked down from \$20 to \$15? Explain.

33. ***EARTH SCIENCE*** After the Mount St. Helens volcano erupted in 1980, the elevation of the mountain decreased by about 13.6%. Its elevation had been 9677 ft. What was its elevation after the eruption?

34. ***CHOOSE A STRATEGY*** A printer originally sold for \$199. Six months later, the price was reduced 45%. During a sale, the printer was discounted an additional 20% off the reduced price. What was the final price of the printer?

    A \$17.91 **B** \$87.56 **C** \$101.89 **D** \$98.97

35. ***WRITE ABOUT IT*** Describe how you can use mental math to find the percent increase from 80 to 100 and the percent decrease from 100 to 80.

36. ***CHALLENGE*** During a sale, the price of a computer game was decreased by 40%. By what percent must the sale price be increased to restore the original price?

Spiral Review

Find the surface area of each figure to the nearest tenth. Use 3.14 for π. (Lesson 6-9)

37. a square pyramid with base 13 m by 13 m and slant height 7.5 m

38. a cone with a diameter 90 cm and slant height 125 cm

39. a square pyramid with base length 6 yd and slant height 4 yd

40. **TEST PREP** A 1 lb 8 oz package of corn sells for \$5.76. What is the unit price? (Lesson 7-2)

    A \$0.34 per oz **B** \$0.32 per oz **C** \$0.24 per oz **D** \$0.64 per oz

8-5 Estimating with Percents

Learn to estimate with percents.

Vocabulary

estimate

compatible numbers

Waiters, waitresses, and other restaurant employees depend upon tips for much of their income. Typically, a tip is 15% to 20% of the bill. Tips do not have to be calculated exactly, so estimation is often used. When the sales tax is about 8%, doubling the tax gives a good estimate for a tip.

Some problems require only an **estimate**. Estimates involving percents and fractions can be found by using **compatible numbers**, numbers that go well together because they have common factors.

$\frac{13}{24}$ The numbers 13 and 24 are not compatible numbers.

Change 13 to 12. $\frac{13}{24}$ is nearly equivalent to $\frac{12}{24}$.

$\approx \frac{12}{24}$ 12 and 24 are compatible numbers. 12 is a common factor.

The fraction $\frac{12}{24}$ simplifies to $\frac{1}{2}$. *$\frac{13}{24} \approx \frac{1}{2}$*

EXAMPLE 1 Estimating with Percents

Helpful Hint

Methods of estimating:

1. Use compatible numbers.
2. Round to common percents. (10%, 25%, $33\frac{1}{3}$%)
3. Break percents into smaller parts. (1%, 5%, 10%)

Estimate.

A 26% of 48

Instead of computing the exact answer of 26% · 48, estimate.

$26\% = \frac{26}{100} \approx \frac{25}{100}$ *Use compatible numbers, 25 and 100.*

$\approx \frac{1}{4}$ *Simplify.*

$\frac{1}{4} \cdot 48 = 12$ *Use mental math: 48 ÷ 4.*

So 26% of 48 is about 12.

B 14% of 20

Instead of computing the exact answer of 14% · 20, estimate.

$14\% \approx 15\%$ *Round.*

$\approx 10\% + 5\%$ *Break down the percent into smaller parts.*

$15\% \cdot 20 = (10\% + 5\%) \cdot 20$ *Set up an equation.*

$= 10\% \cdot 20 + 5\% \cdot 20$ *Use Distributive Property.*

$= 2 + 1$ *10% of 20 is 2, so 5% of 20 is 1.*

So 14% of 20 is about 3.

EXAMPLE 2 PROBLEM SOLVING APPLICATION

Angel Falls, in Venezuela, is the tallest waterfall in the world. Horseshoe Falls, which makes up the large portion of Niagara Falls, has a height of only 173 ft. This is about 5.3% of the height of Angel Falls. Approximately how tall is Angel Falls?

Angel Falls has one section that drops uninterrupted for one-half mile.

1 Understand the Problem

The **answer** is the approximate height of Angel Falls.

List the **important information:**

- Horseshoe Falls is 173 ft tall.
- Horseshoe Falls is about 5.3% of the height of Angel Falls.

Let a represent the height of Angel Falls.

Height of Horseshoe Falls	≈	5.3%	•	Height of Angel Falls
173	≈	**5.3%**	•	a

2 Make a Plan

Think: The numbers 173 and 5.3% are difficult to work with.

Use compatible numbers: 173 is close to 170; 5.3% is close to 5%.

$5\% = \frac{5}{100} = \frac{1}{20}$ *Find an equivalent ratio for 5%.*

3 Solve

Think: 170 is $\frac{1}{20}$ of what number?

$20 \cdot 170 = a$

Angel Falls is approximately 3400 ft tall.

4 Look Back

5% of 3400 ft is $\frac{3400}{20}$, or 170 ft. This is the approximate height of Horseshoe Falls.

Think and Discuss

1. **Determine** the ratios that are nearly equivalent to each of the following percents: 23%, 53%, 65%, 12%, and 76%.
2. **Describe** how to find 35% of a number when you know 10% of the number.
3. **Explain** a method for estimating a 15%–20% tip on a $24.89 bill.

8-5 Exercises

FOR EXTRA PRACTICE
see page 747

internet connect
Homework Help Online
go.hrw.com Keyword: MP4 8-5

GUIDED PRACTICE

See Example 

Estimate.

1. 20% of 493
2. 15% of 162
3. 20 out of 81
4. 35% of 61
5. 5 out of 11
6. 60% of 1475

See Example 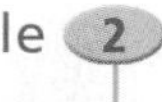

7. A restaurant bill is for a total of $29.84. Estimate the amount to leave as a 15% tip.

INDEPENDENT PRACTICE

See Example 

Estimate.

8. 25% of 494
9. 5021 out of 10,107
10. 63 out of 82
11. 55% of 810
12. 50% of 989
13. 103 out of 989

See Example 2

14. A low-flush toilet uses approximately 6 L water per flush while a standard toilet uses about 19 L water per flush. Estimate the percent of water that can be saved per flush with the more efficient toilet.

PRACTICE AND PROBLEM SOLVING

Choose the best estimate. Write A, B, or C.

15. 10% of 61.4
A 0.6
B 6
C 60

16. 50% of 29.85
A 3
B 12
C 15

17. 35.5% of 92
A 30
B 3
C 45

18. 75% of $238.99
A $150
B $180
C $230

19. 65% of $298.99
A $20
B $100
C $200

20. 105% of $776.50
A $80
B $900
C $800

Estimate each number or percent.

21. 50% of 297 is about what number?
22. About what percent of 42 is 31?
23. 48 is 20% of about what number?
24. 25% of 925 is about what number?
25. 795 is 50% of about what number?
26. 9.1 is about what percent of 21?
27. About what percent of 73 is 24?
28. 9.5% of 88 is about what number?
29. 98 is 26% of about what number?
30. 88 is about what percent of 180?

Freezing a light stick may make it glow longer, but not as brightly.

31. Yesterday, 294 books were checked out of the library. This is only 42% of the number usually checked out in a day. About how many books are usually checked out in a day?

32. A jury wants to give an award of about 5% of $788,116. What is a good estimate of the award?

33. ***PHYSICAL SCIENCE*** When you snap a light stick, you break a barrier between two chemical compounds. This causes a reaction that releases energy as light. If an improvement allows a 9 hr light stick to glow for 13 hr 4 min, about what percent increase is this?

34. ***EARTH SCIENCE*** Alaska is the largest state in the United States in total land area, and Rhode Island is the smallest.

Area and Population: 2000		
	Total Land (mi^2)	Population
Alaska	570,374	626,932
Rhode Island	1045	1,048,319

a. Rhode Island is about what percent of the size of Alaska?

b. Although much smaller than Alaska, Rhode Island has a larger population. About what percent of the population of Rhode Island is the population of Alaska?

c. Estimate the number of people per square mile in Alaska and in Rhode Island.

35. ***SPORTS*** In 2001, Barry Bonds reached base on 342 of 664 plate appearances. About what percent of the time did he reach base?

36. ***WRITE A PROBLEM*** Write a percent estimation problem using the following data: The diameter of Earth is about 12,756 km, and the diameter of the Moon is about 3475 km.

37. ***WRITE ABOUT IT*** Explain how you can estimate 1%, 10%, and 100% of 3051.

38. ***CHALLENGE*** How could you estimate the percent of words in the English language that begin with *Q*?

Spiral Review

Find the volume of each rectangular prism. (Lesson 6-6)

39. length 5 ft, width 3 ft, height 8 ft

40. length 2.5 m, width 3.5 m, height 7 m

41. length 11 in., width 6 in., height 2 in.

42. base 40 cm by 25 cm, height 10 cm

43. base 0.8 ft by 1.2 ft, height 0.5 ft

44. length 12 mm, width 24 mm, height 15 mm

45. **TEST PREP** A boat travels 110 feet in 5 seconds. What is the boat's speed in miles per hour? (Lesson 7-3)

A 22.5 mi/h **B** 20 mi/h **C** 11 mi/h **D** 15 mi/h

8-6 Applications of Percents

Learn to find commission, sales tax, and withholding tax.

Vocabulary

commission

commission rate

sales tax

withholding tax

Real estate agents often work for *commission.* A **commission** is a fee paid to a person who makes a sale. It is usually a percent of the selling price. This percent is called the **commission rate** .

Often agents are paid a commission plus a regular salary. The total pay is a percent of the sales they make plus a salary.

commission rate • sales = commission

EXAMPLE 1 Multiplying by Percents to Find Commission Amounts

A real-estate agent is paid a monthly salary of $1200 plus commissions. Last month she sold one house for $97,500, earning a 3% commission on the sale. How much was her commission? What was her total pay for last month?

First find her commission.

$3\% \cdot \$97{,}500 = c$ *commission rate · sales = commission.*

$0.03 \cdot 97{,}500 = c$ *Change the percent to a decimal.*

$2925 = c$ *Solve for c.*

She earned a commission of $2925 on the sale.

Now find her total pay for last month.

$\$2925 + \$1200 = \$4125$ *commission + salary = total pay.*

Her total pay for last month was $4125.

Sales tax is the tax on the sale of an item or service. It is a percent of the purchase price and is collected by the seller.

EXAMPLE 2 Multiplying by Percents to Find Sales Tax Amounts

If the sales tax rate is 8.25%, how much tax would Alexis pay if she bought one twin pack of black refill cartridges for her printer for $52.88 and two color refill cartridges for $34.79 each?

black refills: 1 at $52.88 → $52.88

color refills: 2 at $34.79 → $69.58

$122.46 *Total price*

$0.0825 \cdot 122.46 = 10.10295$ *Convert tax rate to a decimal and multiply by the total price.*

Alexis would pay $10.10 in sales tax.

A tax deducted from a person's earnings as an advance payment of income tax is called **withholding tax** .

EXAMPLE 3 Using Proportions to Find the Percent of Tax Withheld

Joseph earns $1070 monthly. Of that, $160.50 is withheld for taxes. What percent of Joseph's earnings is withheld?

Think: What percent of $1070 is $160.50?

Solve by proportion:

$$\frac{n}{100} = \frac{160.50}{1070}$$

$n \cdot 1070 = 100 \cdot 160.50$ *Find the cross products.*

$1070n = 16{,}050$

$n = \frac{16{,}050}{1070}$ *Divide both sides by 1070.*

$n = 15$

So 15% of Joseph's earnings is withheld.

EXAMPLE 4 Dividing by Percents to Find Total Sales

Students in Sele's class sell gift wrap to raise funds for class trips. The class earns 14% on all sales. If the class made $791.70 on sales of wrapping paper, how much were the total sales?

Think: 791.70 is 14% of what number?

Solve by equation:

$791.70 = 0.14 \cdot s$ *Let s = total sales.*

$\frac{791.70}{0.14} = s$ *Divide each side by 0.14.*

$5655 = s$

The total sales of gift wrap for Sele's class were $5655.

Think and Discuss

1. **Tell** how finding commission is similar to finding sales tax.
2. **Explain** whether adding 6% sales tax to a total gives the same result as finding 106% of the total.
3. **Explain** how to find the price of an item if you know the total cost after 5% sales tax.

8-6 Exercises

FOR EXTRA PRACTICE
see page 747

internet connect
Homework Help Online
go.hrw.com Keyword: MP4 8-6

GUIDED PRACTICE

See Example 1
1. Josh earns a weekly salary of $300 plus a 6% commission on sales. Last week, his sales totaled $3500. What was his total pay?

See Example 2
2. In a state with a sales tax rate of 7%, Hernando buys a radio for $59.99 and a CD for $13.99. How much is the sales tax?

See Example 3
3. Last year, Janell earned $33,095. From this amount, $7,446.38 was withheld for taxes. What percent of her income was withheld, to the nearest tenth of a percent?

See Example 4
4. Chuck works as a salesperson at an electronics store. If he earns $29.94 from a 6% commission on the sale of a video camera, what is the price of the camera?

INDEPENDENT PRACTICE

See Example 1
5. Marta earns a weekly salary of $110 plus a 6.5% commission on sales at a hobby store. How much would she make in a week if she sold $4300 worth of merchandise?

See Example 2
6. The sales tax rate in Lisa's town is 5.75%. If she purchases 4 chairs for $124.99 each and an area rug for $659.99, how much sales tax does she owe?

See Example 3
7. Jan typically earns $435 each week, of which $78.30 is withheld for taxes. What percent of Jan's earnings are withheld each week?

See Example 4
8. Heather works in a clothes shop where she earns a commission of 5% and no weekly salary. What will Heather's weekly sales have to be for her to earn $375?

PRACTICE AND PROBLEM SOLVING

Find each commission or sales tax to the nearest cent.

9. total sales: $12,000
commission rate: 2.75%

10. total sales: $125.50
sales tax rate: 6.25%

11. total sales: $26.98
sales tax rate: 8%

12. total sales: $895.75
commission rate: 4.25%

Find the total sales to the nearest cent.

13. commission: $78.55
commission rate: 4%

14. commission: $2842
commission rate: 3.5%

15. Elena can choose between a monthly salary of $2200 plus 5.5% of sales or $2800 plus 3% of sales. She expects sales between $10,000 and $20,000 a month. Which salary option should she choose?

Economics LINK

Tax brackets are used to determine how much income tax you pay. Depending upon your taxable income, your tax is given by the formula base tax + tax rate(amount over). "Amount over" refers only to the income above the amount listed. Refer to the table for Exercises 16–19.

2001 IRS Income Tax Brackets (Single)			
Taxable Income Range	Base Tax	Tax Rate	Amount Over
\$0–\$27,050	\$0	15%	\$0
\$27,050–\$65,550	\$4057.50	27.5%	\$27,050
\$65,550–\$136,750	\$14,645	30.5%	\$65,550
\$136,750–\$297,350	\$36,361	35.5%	\$136,750
\$297,350 and up	93,374	39.1%	\$297,350

Ellie's Flowers

Hours worked	24
Hourly rate	☐ per hour
Gross pay	\$162.50
Federal income tax (15%)	☐
Other federal taxes (7.65%)	☐
NET PAY	☐

16. Tina's pay stub is shown at right. Find the missing numbers.

17. Anna earned \$71,458 total in 2001. However, she was able to deduct \$7250 for job-related expenses. This amount is subtracted from her total income to determine her taxable income.

a. What was Anna's taxable income in 2001?

b. How much income tax did she owe?

c. What percent of Anna's total income did the tax represent?

d. What percent of her taxable income did the tax represent?

18. How much more tax would someone who made \$27,100 pay than someone who made \$27,000? What percent would they pay on the additional \$100 of income?

19. ***CHALLENGE*** Charlena paid \$10,050 in taxes in 2001. How much taxable income did she earn that year? (*Hint:* Which tax bracket must she have been in to have paid \$10,050 in taxes?)

Spiral Review

Find the scale factor that relates each model to the actual object. (Lesson 7-8)

20. 14 in. model, 70 in. object

21. 8 cm model, 6 mm object

22. 4 in. model, 6 ft 8 in. object

23. 0.25 m model, 0.0025 cm object

24. **TEST PREP** Of the 32 students in Mr. Smith's class, 14 have jobs during the summer. What percent of the students have a summer job? (Lesson 8-1)

A 43.75% **B** 68.56% **C** 56.25% **D** 35.65%

8-7 More Applications of Percents

Learn to compute simple interest.

Vocabulary

interest

simple interest

principal

rate of interest

When you borrow money from a bank, you pay **interest** for the use of the bank's money. When you deposit money into a savings account, you are paid interest. **Simple interest** is one type of fee paid for the use of money.

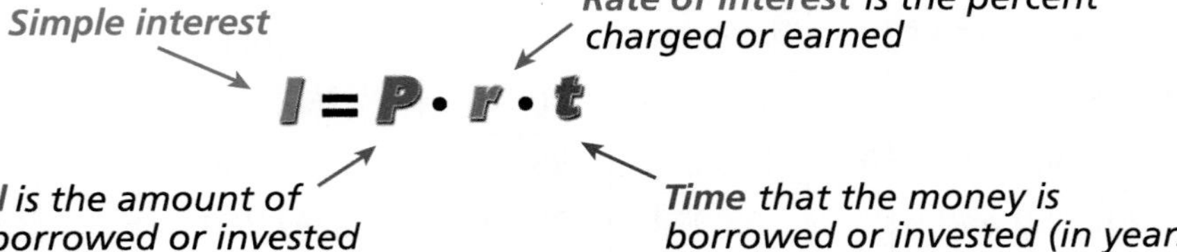
Simple interest
Rate of interest is the percent charged or earned
I = P • r • t
Principal is the amount of money borrowed or invested
Time that the money is borrowed or invested (in years)

EXAMPLE 1 Finding Interest and Total Payment on a Loan

Thurman borrowed $13,500 from his brother-in-law for 4 years at an annual simple interest rate of 6% to buy a car. How much interest will he pay if he pays the entire loan off at the end of the fourth year? What is the total amount he will repay?

First, find the interest he will pay.

$I = P \cdot r \cdot t$ — *Use the formula.*

$I = 13{,}500 \cdot 0.06 \cdot 4$ — *Substitute. Use 0.06 for 6%.*

$I = 3240$ — *Solve for I.*

Thurman will pay $3240 in interest.

You can find the total amount A to be repaid on a loan by adding the principal P to the interest I.

$P + I = A$ — *principal + interest = amount*

$13{,}500 + 3240 = A$ — *Substitute.*

$16{,}740 = A$ — *Solve for A.*

Thurman will repay a total of $16,740 on his loan.

EXAMPLE 2 Determining the Amount of Investment Time

Tony invested $3000 in a mutual fund at a yearly rate of 5%. He earned $525 in interest. How long was the money invested?

$I = P \cdot r \cdot t$ — *Use the formula.*

$525 = 3000 \cdot 0.05 \cdot t$ — *Substitute values into equation.*

$525 = 150t$ — *Solve for t.*

$3.5 = t$

The money was invested for 3.5 years, or 3 years and 6 months.

EXAMPLE 3 Computing Total Savings

Rebecca's grandmother deposited $2000 into a savings account as a college fund. How much will Rebecca have in this account after 3 years at a yearly simple interest rate of 2.5%?

$I = P \cdot r \cdot t$	*Use the formula.*
$I = 2000 \cdot 0.025 \cdot 3$	*Substitute. Use 0.025 for 2.5%.*
$I = 150$	*Solve for I.*

Now you can find the total.

$P + I = A$	*Use the formula.*
$2000 + 150 = A$	
$2150 = A$	

Rebecca will have $2150 in her savings account after three years.

EXAMPLE 4 Finding the Rate of Interest

Suzanne borrowed $5000 for 5 years at simple interest to pay for her college classes. If Suzanne repaid a total of $6187.50, at what interest rate did she borrow the money?

$P + I = A$	
$5000 + I = 6187.5$	*Find the amount of interest.*
$I = 6187.5 - 5000 = 1187.5$	

She paid $1187.50 in interest. Use the amount of interest to find the interest rate.

$I = P \cdot r \cdot t$	*Use the formula.*
$1187.5 = 5000 \cdot r \cdot 5$	*Substitute.*
$1187.5 = 25{,}000r$	*Multiply.*
$\frac{1187.5}{25{,}000} = r$	
$0.0475 = r$	

Suzanne borrowed the money at an annual rate of 4.75%, or $4\frac{3}{4}$%.

Think and Discuss

1. **Explain** the meaning of each variable in the interest formula.
2. **Tell** what value should be used for *t* when referring to 6 months.
3. **Name** the variables in the simple interest formula that represent dollar amounts.
4. **Demonstrate** that doubling the time while halving the interest rate results in the same amount of simple interest.

8-7 Exercises

FOR EXTRA PRACTICE
see page 747

internet connect
Homework Help Online
go.hrw.com Keyword: MP4 8-7

GUIDED PRACTICE

See Example 1
1. Leroy borrowed $8250 to be repaid after 3 years at an annual simple interest rate of 7.25%. How much interest will be due after 3 years? How much will Leroy have to repay?

See Example 2
2. Mr. Williams invested $4000 in a bond with a yearly interest rate of 4%. His total interest on the investment was $800. What was the length of the investment?

See Example 3
3. Kim deposited $1422 in a savings account. How much would she have in the account after 5 years at an annual simple interest rate of 3%?

See Example 4
4. Hank borrowed $25,000 for 3 years to remodel his house. At the end of the loan, he had repaid a total of $29,125. At what simple interest rate did he borrow the money?

INDEPENDENT PRACTICE

See Example 1
5. A bank offers an annual simple interest rate of 7% on home improvement loans. How much would Nick owe if he borrows $18,500 over a period of 3.5 years?

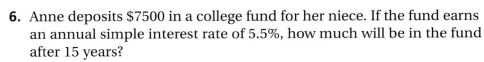

See Example 2
6. Anne deposits $7500 in a college fund for her niece. If the fund earns an annual simple interest rate of 5.5%, how much will be in the fund after 15 years?

See Example 3
7. Olivia gave a security deposit of $1500 to her landlord, Mr. Rey, 6 years ago. Mr. Rey will give her the deposit back with simple interest of 3.85%. How much will he return to her?

See Example 4
8. First Bank loaned a construction company $125,000 at an annual simple interest rate. After 3 years, the company repaid the bank $149,375. What was the loan's interest rate?

PRACTICE AND PROBLEM SOLVING

Find the interest and the total amount to the nearest cent.

9. $225 at 5% per year for 3 years

10. $775 at 8% per year for 1 year

11. $4250 at 7% per year for 1.5 years

12. $650 at 4.5% per year for 2 years

13. $397 at 5% per year for 9 months

14. $2975 at 6% per year for 5 years

15. $700 at 6.25% per year for 2 years

16. $500 at 9% per year for 3 months

17. Akule borrowed $1500 for 18 months at a 12% annual simple interest rate. How much interest will he have to repay? What is the total amount he will repay?

Many bank ATMs in Bangkok, Thailand, are located in sculptures to attract customers.

go.hrw.com
Web Extra!
KEYWORD: MP4 Money

18. Dena borrowed \$7500 to buy a used car. The credit union charged 9% simple interest per year. She paid \$2025 in interest. For what period of time did she borrow the money?

19. At Thrift Bank, if you keep \$675 in a savings account for 12 years, your money will earn \$486 in interest. What yearly interest rate does the account offer?

20. The Smiths will borrow \$35,500 from a bank to start a business. They have two loan options. Option A is a 5-year loan; option B is a 4-year loan. Use the graph to answer the following questions.

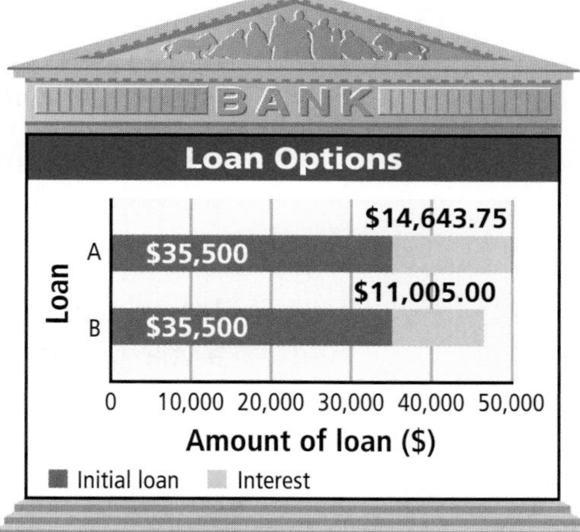

a. What is the total amount the Smiths would pay under each loan option?

b. What would be the interest rate under each loan option?

c. What would be the monthly payment under each loan option?

d. How much interest will the Smiths save by choosing loan option B?

21. ***WHAT'S THE ERROR?*** On a quiz, a student is asked to calculate the total interest owed on a \$4360 loan at a yearly rate of 4.5% over 3 years. The student's answer is \$4,948.60. What error has the student made, and what is the correct answer?

22. ***WRITE ABOUT IT*** Which loan would cost the borrower less: \$2000 at 8% for 3 years or \$2000 at 9.5% for 2 years? How much interest would the borrower save by taking the cheaper loan?

23. ***CHALLENGE*** How would the total payment on a 3-year loan at 6% annual simple interest compare with the total payment on a 3-year loan where one-twelfth of that simple interest, 0.5%, is calculated monthly? Give an example.

Spiral Review

Find each number or percent. (Lesson 8-2)

24. What percent of 82 is 20.5?

25. What is 15% of 96?

26. What is 146% of 12,500?

27. What percent of 750 is 125?

28. What percent of 0.26 is 0.0338?

29. What is 0.5% of 1000?

30. **TEST PREP** A washing machine that usually sells for \$459 goes on sale for \$379. What is the percent decrease, to the nearest tenth of a percent? (Lesson 8-4)

A 20.3% **B** 82.6% **C** 32.8% **D** 17.4%

EXTENSION

Compound Interest

Learn to compute compound interest.

Vocabulary

compound interest

After you deposit money in a savings account, the bank pays you interest. You will probably be paid *compound interest.* When you borrow money or use a credit card, the interest you pay is also *compounded.*

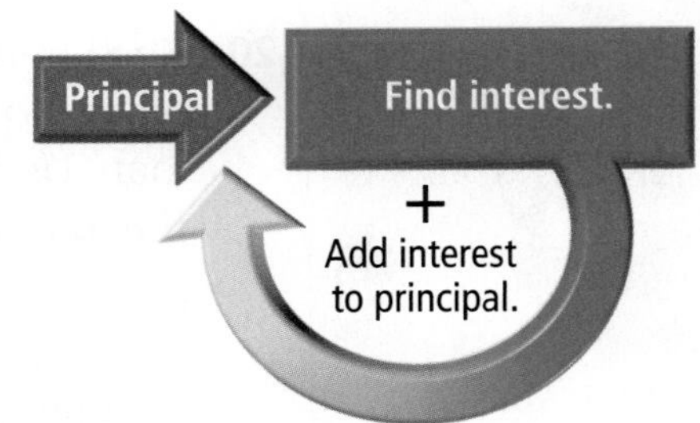

Compound interest is computed on the principal plus any interest already earned in a previous period.

Interest may compound *annually* (once a year), *semiannually* (twice a year), *quarterly* (four times a year), or *daily.*

EXAMPLE 1 Calculating Compound Interest Using a Spreadsheet

You deposit \$1000 in a saving account paying 5% interest, compounded annually. Use a spreadsheet or calculator to find how much money you would have after 3 years.

You can find the total after each year several different ways:

Method 1: Find the compound interest each year and add it to the total.

Year	Principal ($)	Compound Interest ($)	Total at End of Year ($)
1	1000	1000 × 0.05 = 50	1000 + 50 = 1050
2	1050	1050 × 0.05 = 52.50	1050 + 52.50 = 1102.50
3	1102.50	1102.50 × 0.05 = 55.125	1102.50 + 55.125 = 1157.625

You would have a total of \$1157.63 at the end of 3 years.

You can also use the Distributive Property to multiply quickly.

$1000 + 1000(0.05) = 1000(1) + 1000(0.05) = 1000(1.05)$

Method 2: Find the total for each year and add it to the previous total.

Year	Principal ($)	Total at End of Year ($)
1	1000	1000(1.05) = 1050
2	1050	1050(1.05) = 1102.50
3	1102.50	1102.50(1.05) = 1157.625

You would have a total of \$1157.63 at the end of 3 years.

You can calculate compound interest using a formula.

$A = P\left(1 + \frac{r}{k}\right)^{n \cdot k}$, where A = amount (new balance),

P = principal (original amount of account),

r = rate of annual interest,

n = number of years, and

k = number of compounding periods per year.

EXAMPLE 2 Calculating Compound Interest Using a Formula

Use the formula to find the amount after 3 years if $5000 is invested at 3% annual interest that is compounded semiannually.

$A = 5000\left(1 + \frac{0.03}{2}\right)^{3 \cdot 2}$ *Substitute $P = 5000$, $r = 0.03$, $k = 2$, $n = 3$.*

$A = 5000(1.015)^6$ *Evaluate in the parentheses and the exponent.*

$A = 5000(1.093443264)$ *Evaluate the power. Use a calculator.*

$A = \$5467.22$ *Evaluate the product, and round.*

There would be a total of $5467.22 at the end of 3 years.

EXTENSION Exercises

Use a spreadsheet or calculator to find the value of each investment after 3 years, compounded annually.

1. $10,000 at 8% annual interest
2. $1000 at 6% annual interest

Use the compound interest formula to find the value of each investment after 5 years, compounded semiannually.

3. $10,000 at 8% annual interest
4. $1000 at 6% annual interest

Use the compound interest formula to find the value of the investment.

5. $12,500 at 4% annual interest, compounded annually, for 5 years
6. $800 at $5\frac{1}{2}$% annual interest, compounded semiannually, for 7 years
7. $2000 at 7% annual interest, compounded quarterly, for 3 years
8. Determine the value of a $20,000 inheritance after 20 years if it is invested at a 4% annual rate of interest that is compounded annually, semiannually, and quarterly.
9. Determine the value of a $5000 savings account paying 6% interest, compounded monthly, over a 5-year period, assuming that no additional deposits or withdrawals are made during that time.
10. Explain whether money earns more compounded annually or quarterly.

Problem Solving on Location

PENNSYLVANIA

Punxsutawney Phil

Punxsutawney Phil is America's most famous groundhog. According to tradition, if he sees his shadow on Groundhog Day, there will be six more weeks of winter. If he doesn't see his shadow, there will be an early spring.

Groundhog Day began as Candlemas Day, which was around February 2. If the day was clear and sunny, people said it meant a longer winter. Because early German settlers in Pennsylvania found groundhogs in many parts of the state, the tradition gradually changed to include the groundhog. Today, tens of thousands of visitors trek to Punxsutawney, Pennsylvania, each year to await the famous groundhog's appearance.

The first official record of Groundhog Day in Punxsatawney was made in 1887. From 1887 to 2002, Phil saw his shadow 92 times and didn't see it 14 times. There are 10 years with no record.

1. Ignoring the years when there was no record, what percent of the time did Phil not see his shadow?
2. The table shows Punxsatawney Phil's shadow sightings for the years 1980–1998.What percent of the time did Phil see his shadow?
3. Compare the results from 1980 to 1998 with the results from 1887 to 2002.
4. According to records from the National Climatic Data Center in Asheville, North Carolina, Phil's accuracy rate from 1980 to1998 was about 59 percent. How many times did Phil correctly predict the length of winter during this time period?

Phil's Shadow sightings

1980	yes	1990	no
1981	yes	1991	yes
1982	yes	1992	yes
1983	no	1993	yes
1984	yes	1994	yes
1985	yes	1995	no
1986	no	1996	yes
1987	yes	1997	no
1988	no	1998	yes
1989	yes		

ARE YOU READY?

Choose the best term from the list to complete each sentence.

1. The term __?__ means "per hundred."
2. A __?__ is a comparison of two numbers.
3. In a set of data, the __?__ is the largest number minus the smallest number.
4. A __?__ is in simplest form when its numerator and denominator have no common factors other than 1.

fraction
percent
range
ratio

Complete these exercises to review skills you will need for this chapter.

✔ Simplify Ratios

Write each ratio in simplest form.

5. 5:50 **6.** 95 to 19 **7.** $\frac{20}{100}$ **8.** $\frac{192}{80}$

✔ Write Fractions as Decimals

Express each fraction as a decimal.

9. $\frac{52}{100}$ **10.** $\frac{7}{1000}$ **11.** $\frac{3}{5}$ **12.** $\frac{2}{9}$

✔ Write Fractions as Percents

Express each fraction as a percent.

13. $\frac{19}{100}$ **14.** $\frac{1}{8}$ **15.** $\frac{5}{2}$ **16.** $\frac{2}{3}$

17. $\frac{3}{4}$ **18.** $\frac{9}{20}$ **19.** $\frac{7}{10}$ **20.** $\frac{2}{5}$

✔ Operations with Fractions

Add. Write each answer in simplest form.

21. $\frac{3}{8} + \frac{1}{4} + \frac{1}{6}$ **22.** $\frac{1}{6} + \frac{2}{3} + \frac{1}{9}$ **23.** $\frac{1}{8} + \frac{1}{4} + \frac{1}{8} + \frac{1}{2}$ **24.** $\frac{1}{3} + \frac{1}{4} + \frac{2}{5}$

Multiply. Write each answer in simplest form.

25. $\frac{3}{8} \cdot \frac{1}{5}$ **26.** $\frac{2}{3} \cdot \frac{6}{7}$ **27.** $\frac{3}{7} \cdot \frac{14}{27}$ **28.** $\frac{13}{52} \cdot \frac{3}{51}$

29. $\frac{4}{5} \cdot \frac{11}{4}$ **30.** $\frac{5}{2} \cdot \frac{3}{4}$ **31.** $\frac{27}{8} \cdot \frac{4}{9}$ **32.** $\frac{1}{15} \cdot \frac{30}{9}$

9-1 Probability

Learn to find the probability of an event by using the definition of probability.

Vocabulary

experiment

trial

outcome

sample space

event

probability

impossible

certain

An **experiment** is an activity in which results are observed. Each observation is called a **trial**, and each result is called an **outcome**. The **sample space** is the set of all possible outcomes of an experiment.

Experiment	Sample space
• flipping a coin	• heads, tails
• rolling a number cube	• 1, 2, 3, 4, 5, 6
• guessing the number of jelly beans in a jar	• whole numbers

An **event** is any set of one or more outcomes. The **probability** of an event, written P(event), is a number from 0 (or 0%) to 1 (or 100%) that tells you how likely the event is to happen.

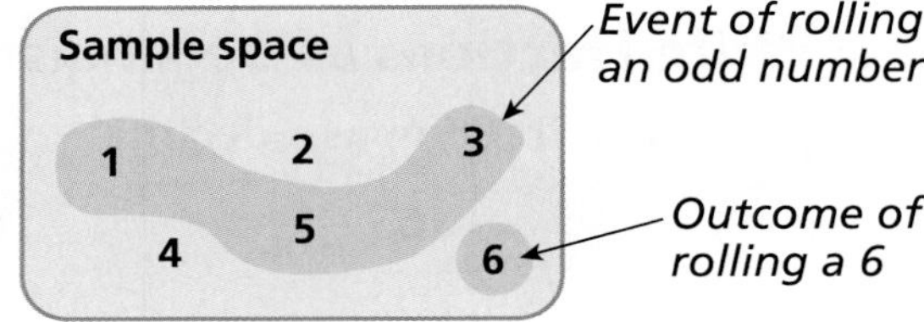

- A probability of 0 means the event is **impossible**, or can never happen.
- A probability of 1 means the event is **certain**, or has to happen.
- The probabilities of all the outcomes in the sample space add up to 1.

Never happens		Happens about half the time		Always happens
0	$\frac{1}{4}$	$\frac{1}{2}$	$\frac{3}{4}$	1
0	0.25	0.5	0.75	1
0%	25%	50%	75%	100%

EXAMPLE 1 Finding Probabilities of Outcomes in a Sample Space

Give the probability for each outcome.

A The weather forecast shows a 40% chance of rain.

Outcome	Rain	No rain
Probability		

The probability of rain is $P(\text{rain}) = 40\% = 0.4$. The probabilities must add to 1, so the probability of no rain is $P(\text{no rain}) = 1 - 0.4 = 0.6$, or 60%.

Give the probability for each outcome.

B

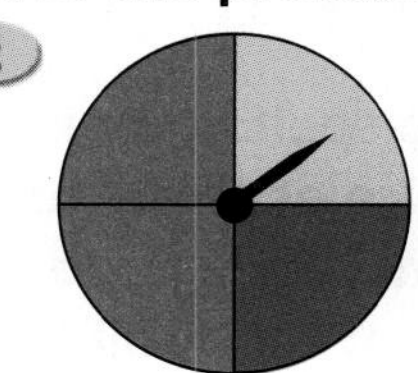

Outcome	Red	Yellow	Blue
Probability			

Half of the spinner is red, so a reasonable estimate of the probability that the spinner lands on red is $P(\text{red}) = \frac{1}{2}$.

One-fourth of the spinner is yellow, so a reasonable estimate of the probability that the spinner lands on yellow is $P(\text{yellow}) = \frac{1}{4}$.

One-fourth of the spinner is blue, so a reasonable estimate of the probability that the spinner lands on blue is $P(\text{blue}) = \frac{1}{4}$.

Check The probabilities of all the outcomes must add to 1.

$\frac{1}{2} + \frac{1}{4} + \frac{1}{4} = 1$ ✔

To find the probability of an event, add the probabilities of all the outcomes included in the event.

EXAMPLE  2 Finding Probabilities of Events

A quiz contains 5 multiple-choice questions. Suppose you guess randomly on every question. The table below gives the probability of each score.

Score	0	1	2	3	4	5
Probability	0.237	0.396	0.264	0.088	0.014	0.001

A **What is the probability of guessing one or more correct?**

The event "one or more correct" consists of the outcomes 1, 2, 3, 4, 5.

$$P(\text{one or more correct}) = 0.396 + 0.264 + 0.088 + 0.014 + 0.001$$
$$= 0.763, \text{ or } 76.3\%$$

B **What is the probability of guessing fewer than 2 correct?**

The event "fewer than 2 correct" consists of the outcomes 0 and 1.

$$P(\text{fewer than 2 correct}) = 0.237 + 0.396$$
$$= 0.633, \text{ or } 63.3\%$$

C **What is the probability of passing the quiz (getting 4 or 5 correct) by guessing?**

The event "passing the quiz" consists of the outcomes 4 and 5.

$$P(\text{passing the quiz}) = 0.014 + 0.001$$
$$= 0.015, \text{ or } 1.5\%$$

EXAMPLE 3 **PROBLEM SOLVING APPLICATION**

Six students remain in a spelling bee. Amy's probability of winning is $\frac{1}{3}$. Amy is twice as likely to win as Kim. Bob has the same chance as Kim. Pat, Ani, and Jo all have the same chance of winning. Create a table of probabilities for the sample space.

1 Understand the Problem

The **answer** will be a table of probabilities. Each probability will be a number from 0 to 1. The probabilities of all outcomes add to 1.

List the **important information:**

- $P(\text{Amy}) = \frac{1}{3}$
- $P(\text{Kim}) = \frac{1}{2} \cdot P(\text{Amy}) = \frac{1}{2} \cdot \frac{1}{3} = \frac{1}{6}$
- $P(\text{Kim}) = P(\text{Bob}) = \frac{1}{6}$
- $P(\text{Pat}) = P(\text{Ani}) = P(\text{Jo})$

2 Make a Plan

You know the probabilities add to 1, so use the strategy **write an equation**. Let p represent the probability for Pat, Ani, and Jo.

$$P(\text{Amy}) + P(\text{Kim}) + P(\text{Bob}) + P(\text{Pat}) + P(\text{Ani}) + P(\text{Jo}) = 1$$

$$\frac{1}{3} + \frac{1}{6} + \frac{1}{6} + p + p + p = 1$$

$$\frac{2}{3} + 3p = 1$$

3 Solve

$$\frac{2}{3} + 3p = 1$$

$$-\frac{2}{3} \qquad -\frac{2}{3}$$ *Subtract $\frac{2}{3}$ from both sides.*

$$3p = \frac{1}{3}$$

$$\frac{1}{3} \cdot 3p = \frac{1}{3} \cdot \frac{1}{3}$$ *Multiply both sides by $\frac{1}{3}$.*

$$p = \frac{1}{9}$$

Outcome	Amy	Kim	Bob	Pat	Ani	Jo
Probability	$\frac{1}{3}$	$\frac{1}{6}$	$\frac{1}{6}$	$\frac{1}{9}$	$\frac{1}{9}$	$\frac{1}{9}$

4 Look Back

Check that the probabilities add to 1.

$$\frac{1}{3} + \frac{1}{6} + \frac{1}{6} + \frac{1}{9} + \frac{1}{9} + \frac{1}{9} = 1 \checkmark$$

Think and Discuss

1. **Give** a probability for each of the following: usually, sometimes, always, never. Compare your values with the rest of your class.
2. **Explain** the difference between an outcome and an event.

9-1 Exercises

FOR EXTRA PRACTICE

see page 748

internet connect

Homework Help Online
go.hrw.com Keyword: MP4 9-1

GUIDED PRACTICE

See Example 

1. The weather forecast calls for a 55% chance of snow. Give the probability for each outcome.

Outcome	Snow	No snow
Probability		

See Example 2

An experiment consists of drawing 4 marbles from a bag and counting the number of blue marbles. The table gives the probability of each outcome.

Number of Blue Marbles	0	1	2	3	4
Probability	0.024	0.238	0.476	0.238	0.024

2. What is the probability of drawing at least 3 blue marbles?
3. What is the probability of drawing fewer than 3 blue marbles?

See Example 

4. There are 4 teams in a school tournament. Team A has a 25% chance of winning. Team B has the same chance as Team D. Team C has half the chance of winning as Team B. Create a table of probabilities for the sample space.

INDEPENDENT PRACTICE

See Example 

5. Give the probability for each outcome.

Outcome	Red	Blue	Yellow	Green
Probability				

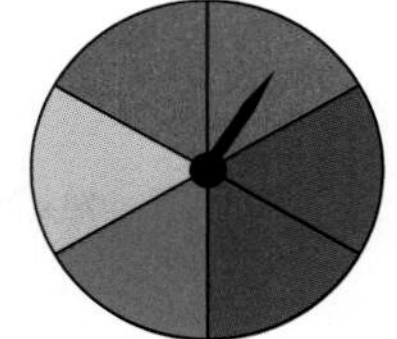

See Example 

Raul needs 3 more classes to graduate from college. He registers late, so he may not get all the classes he needs. The table gives the probabilities for the number of courses he will be able to register for.

Number of Classes Available	0	1	2	3
Probability	0.015	0.140	0.505	0.340

6. What is the probability that at least 1 of the classes will be available?
7. What is the probability that fewer than 2 of the classes will be available?

See Example 

8. There are 5 candidates for class president. Makyla and Jacob have the same chance of winning. Daniel has a 20% chance of winning, and Samantha and Maria are both half as likely to win as Daniel. Create a table of probabilities for the sample space.

PRACTICE AND PROBLEM SOLVING

Use the table to find the probability of each event.

Outcome	A	B	C	D	E
Probability	0.204	0.115	0	0.535	0.146

9. A, B, or C occurring

10. A or E occurring

11. A, B, D, or E occurring

12. C not occurring

13. D not occurring

14. C or D occurring

15. Jamal has a 10% chance of winning a contest, Elroy has the same chance as Tina and Mel, and Gina is three times as likely as Jamal to win. Create a table of probabilities for the sample space.

16. ***BUSINESS*** Community planners have decided that a new strip mall has a 32% chance of being built in Zone A, 20% in Zone B, and 48% in Zone C. What is the probability that it will not be built in Zone C?

17. ***ENTERTAINMENT*** Contestants in a festival game have a 2% chance of winning \$5, a 7% chance of winning \$1, a 15% chance of winning \$0.50, and a 20% chance of winning \$0.25. What is the probability of not winning anything?

18. ***WHAT'S THE ERROR?*** Two people are playing a game. One of them says, "Either I will win or you will. The sample space contains two outcomes, so we each have a probability of one-half." What is the error?

19. ***WRITE ABOUT IT*** Suppose an event has a probability of p. What can you say about the value of p? What is the probability that the event will not occur? Explain.

20. ***CHALLENGE*** List all possible events in the sample space with outcomes A, B, and C.

Spiral Review

Find the surface area of each figure. Use 3.14 for π. (Lesson 6-8)

21. a rectangular prism with base 4 in. by 3 in. and height 2.5 in.

22. a cylinder with radius 10 cm and height 7 cm

23. a cylinder with diameter 7.5 yd and height 11.3 yd

24. a cube with side length 3.2 ft

25. **TEST PREP** The surface area of a sphere is 50.24 cm^2. What is its diameter? Use 3.14 for π. (Lesson 6-10)

A 2 cm **B** 4 cm **C** 1 cm **D** 2.5 cm

Generate Random Numbers

Use with Lesson 9-3

A spreadsheet can be used to generate random decimal numbers that are greater than or equal to 0 but less than 1. By using formulas, you can shift these numbers into a useful range.

> **internet connect**
> Lab Resources Online
> ***go.hrw.com***
> **KEYWORD:** MP4 Lab9A

Activity

1 Use a spreadsheet to generate five random decimal numbers that are between 0 and 1. Then convert these numbers to integers from 1 to 10.

a. Type **=RAND()** into cell A1 and press **ENTER**. A random decimal number appears.

	A
1	0.063515
2	

b. Click to highlight cell A1. Go to the **Edit** menu and **Copy** the contents of A1. Then click and drag to highlight cells A2 through A5. Go to the **Edit** menu and use **Paste** to fill cells A2 through A5.

	A
1	0.20589
2	0.837083
3	0.445334
4	0.939134
5	0.993354
6	

Notice that the random number in cell A1 changed when you filled the other cells.

RAND() gives a decimal number greater than or equal to 0, but less than 1. To generate random integers from 1 to 10, you need to do the following:

- Multiply **RAND()** by 10 (to give a number greater than or equal to 0 but less than 10).
- Use the **INT** function to drop the decimal part of the result (to give an integer from 0 to 9).
- Add 1 (to give an integer from 1 to 10).

c. Change the formula in A1 to **=INT(10*RAND()) + 1** and press **ENTER.** Repeat the process in part **b** to fill cells A2 through A5.

A2 = =INT(10*RAND()) + 1

	A	B	C	D
1	9			
2	1			
3	7			
4	7			
5	6			
6				

The formula **=INT(10*RAND()) + 1** generates random integers from 1 to 10.

Think and Discuss

1. Explain how **INT(10*RAND()) + 1** generates random integers from 1 to 10.

Try This

1. Use a spreadsheet to simulate three rolls of a number cube.

9-3 Use a Simulation

Problem Solving Strategy

Learn to use a simulation to estimate probability.

Vocabulary

simulation

random numbers

In basketball, free throws are worth only one point, but they can make a big difference. In a close game, the coach may put in players with good free-throw shooting records.

If a player shoots 78% from the free-throw line, he makes about 78 out of every 100 free throws. What is the probability that he will make at least 7 out of 10 free throws? A *simulation* can help you estimate this probability.

In the 2001–2002 season, Utah's Karl Malone had a free-throw percentage of 79.7%.

A **simulation** is a model of a real situation. In a set of **random numbers**, each number has the same probability of occurring as every other number, and no pattern can be used to predict the next number. Random numbers can be used to simulate random events in real situations. The table is a set of 280 random digits.

87244	11632	85815	61766	19579	28186	18533	42633
74681	65633	54238	32848	87649	85976	13355	46498
53736	21616	86318	77291	24794	31119	48193	44869
86585	27919	65264	93557	94425	13325	16635	28584
18394	73266	67899	38783	94228	23426	76679	41256
39917	16373	59733	18588	22545	61378	33563	65161
96916	46278	78210	13906	82794	01136	60848	98713

EXAMPLE 1 **PROBLEM SOLVING APPLICATION**

A player has a free-throw rate of 78%. Estimate the probability that he will make at least 7 out of his next 10 shots.

1 Understand the Problem

The **answer** will be the probability that he will make at least 7 out of his next 10 free throws. It must be a number between 0 and 1.

List the **important information:**

- The probability that the player will make a free throw is 0.78.

Focus on Problem Solving

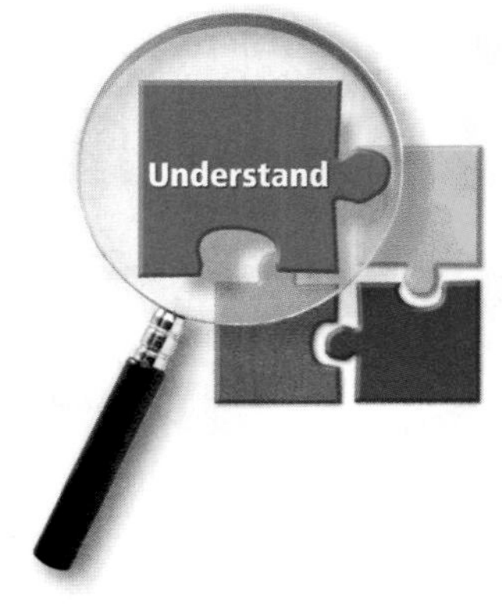

Understand the Problem

• **Understand the words in the problem**

Words that you don't understand can make a simple problem seem difficult. Before you try to solve a problem, you will need to know the meaning of the words in it.

If a problem gives a name of a person, place, or thing that is difficult to understand, such as *Eulalia*, you can use another name or a pronoun in its place. You could replace *Eulalia* with *she*.

Read the problems so that you can hear yourself saying the words.

Copy each problem, and circle any words that you do not understand. Look up each word and write its definition, or use context clues to replace the word with a similar word that is easier to understand.

1. A point in the circle is chosen randomly. What is the probability that the point is in the inscribed triangle?

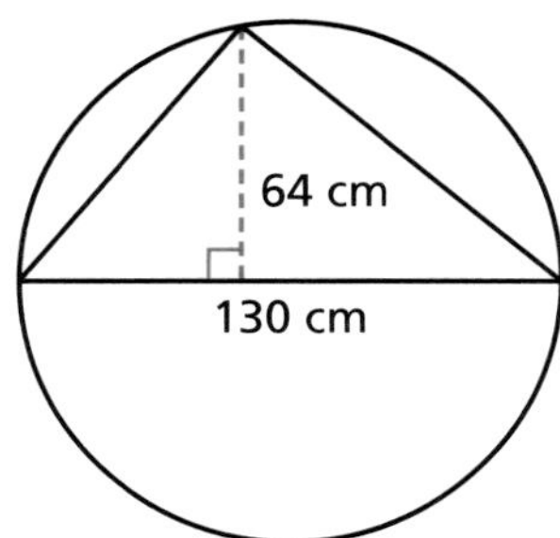

2. A chef has observed the number of people ordering each entrée from the evening's specials. Estimate the probability that the next customer will order Boeuf Bourguignon.

Entrée	Boeuf Bourguignon	Chateaubriand	Rabbit Provençal
Number Ordered	23	15	12

3. Eulalia and Nunzio play cribbage 5 times a week. Eulalia skunked Nunzio 3 times in the last 12 weeks. Estimate the probability that Eulalia will skunk Nunzio the next time they play cribbage.

4. A pula has a coat of arms on the obverse and a running zebra on the reverse. If a pula is tossed 150 times and lands with the coat of arms facing up 70 times, estimate the probability of its landing with the zebra facing up.

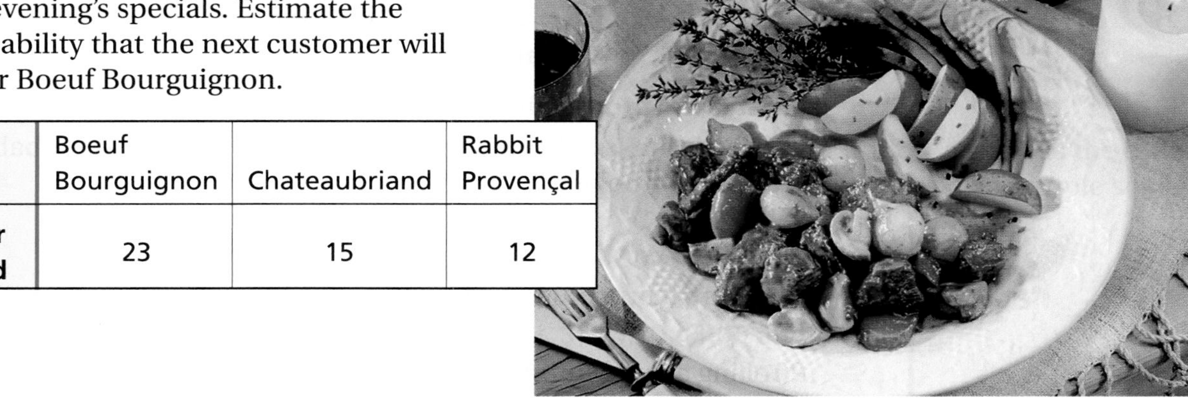

$P(\text{total} = 10) = \frac{3}{36} = \frac{1}{12}$

D What is the probability that the total shown is less than 5?

There are 6 outcomes in the event "a total less than 5": (1, 1), (1, 2), (1, 3), (2, 1), (2, 2), and (3, 1).

$P(\text{total} < 5) = \frac{6}{36} = \frac{1}{6}$

9-4 Theoretical Probability

Learn to estimate

In the game of Monopoly®, you can

Two events are **mutually exclusive** if they cannot both occur in the same trial of an experiment. Suppose A and B are two mutually exclusive events.

- P(both A *and* B will occur) $= 0$
- P(either A *or* B will occur) $= P(A) + P(B)$

Examples 2C and 2D are mutually exclusive, because the total cannot be less than 5 and equal to 10 at the same time. Examples 2B and 2C are *not* mutually exclusive, because the outcome (5, 5) is a double *and* has a sum of 10.

EXAMPLE 3 Finding the Probability of Mutually Exclusive Events

Suppose you are playing a game of Monopoly and have just rolled doubles two times in a row. If you roll doubles again, you will go to jail. You will also go to jail if you roll a total of 3, because you are 3 spaces away from the "Go to Jail" square. What is the probability that you will go to jail?

It is impossible to roll a total of 3 and doubles at the same time, so the events are mutually exclusive. Add the probabilities to find the probability of going to jail on the next roll.

The event "total = 3" consists of two outcomes, (1, 2) and (2, 1), so $P(\text{total of } 3) = \frac{2}{36}$. From Example 2B, $P(\text{doubles}) = \frac{6}{36}$.

$$P(\text{going to jail}) = P(\text{doubles}) + P(\text{total} = 3)$$
$$= \frac{6}{36} + \frac{2}{36}$$
$$= \frac{8}{36}$$

The probability of going to jail is $\frac{8}{36} = \frac{2}{9}$, or about 22.2%.

Think and Discuss

1. **Describe** a sample space for tossing two coins that has all outcomes equally likely.
2. **Give an example** of an experiment in which it would not be reasonable to assume that all outcomes are equally likely.

9-4 Exercises

FOR EXTRA PRACTICE
see page 749

internet connect
Homework Help Online
go.hrw.com Keyword: MP4 9-4

GUIDED PRACTICE

See Example 1

An experiment consists of rolling a fair die.

1. What is the probability of rolling an even number?
2. What is the probability of rolling a 3 or a 5?

See Example 2

An experiment consists of rolling two fair dice. Find each probability.

3. P(total shown = 7)
4. P(rolling two 5's)
5. P(rolling two even numbers)
6. P(total shown > 8)

See Example 3

7. Suppose you are playing a game in which two fair dice are rolled. To make the first move, you need to roll doubles or a sum of 3 or 11. What is the probability that you will be able to make the first move?

INDEPENDENT PRACTICE

See Example 1

An experiment consists of rolling a fair die.

8. What is the probability of rolling a 7?
9. What is the probability of not rolling a 6?
10. What is the probability of rolling a number greater than 2?

See Example 2

An experiment consists of rolling two fair dice. Find each probability.

11. P(total shown = 12)
12. P(not rolling doubles)
13. P(total shown > 0)
14. P(total shown < 4)

See Example 3

15. Suppose you are playing a game in which two fair dice are rolled. You need 7 to land on the finish by an exact count, or 4 to land on a "roll again" space. What is the probability of landing on the finish or rolling again?

PRACTICE AND PROBLEM SOLVING

Three fair coins are tossed: a penny, a dime, and a quarter. The table shows a sample space with all outcomes equally likely. Find each probability.

16. P(HTT)
17. P(THT)
18. P(TTT)
19. P(2 heads)
20. P(0 tails)
21. P(at least 1 head)
22. P(1 tail)
23. P(all the same)

Penny	Dime	Quarter	Outcome
H	H	H	HHH
H	H	T	HHT
H	T	H	HTH
H	T	T	HTT
T	H	H	THH
T	H	T	THT
T	T	H	TTH
T	T	T	TTT

Life Science 

What color are your eyes? Can you roll your tongue? These traits are determined by the genes you inherited from your parents before you were born. A *Punnett square* shows all possible gene combinations for two parents whose genes are known.

To make a Punnett square, draw a two-by-two grid. Write the genes of one parent above the top row, and the other parent along the side. Then fill in the grid as shown.

	B	*b*
b	*Bb*	*bb*
b	*Bb*	*bb*

24. In the Punnett square above, one parent has the gene combination *Bb*, which represents one gene for brown eyes and one gene for blue eyes. The other parent has the gene combination *bb*, which represents two genes for blue eyes. If all outcomes in the Punnett square are equally likely, what is the probability of a child with the gene combination *bb*?

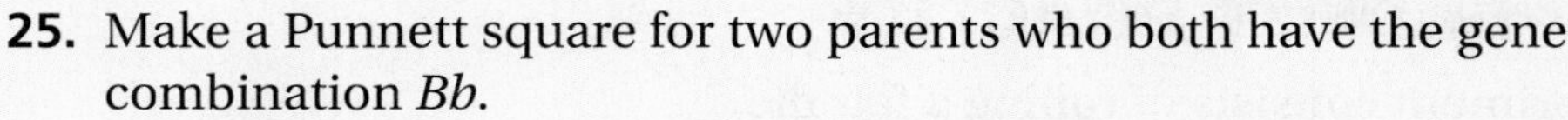

25. Make a Punnett square for two parents who both have the gene combination *Bb*.

a. If all outcomes in the Punnett square are equally likely, what is the probability of a child with the gene combination *BB*?

b. The gene combinations *BB* and *Bb* will result in brown eyes, and the gene combination *bb* will result in blue eyes. What is the probability that the couple will have a child with brown eyes?

26. ***CHALLENGE*** The combinations *Tt* and *TT* represent the ability to roll your tongue, and the combination *tt* means you cannot roll your tongue. Draw a Punnett square that results in a probability of $\frac{1}{2}$ that the child can roll his or her tongue. What can you say about whether the parents can roll their tongues?

Spiral Review

Write each value as indicated. (Lesson 8-1)

27. $\frac{9}{10}$ as a percent

28. 46% as a fraction

29. $\frac{3}{8}$ as a decimal

30. $\frac{7}{14}$ as a decimal

31. 0.78 as a fraction

32. 52.5% as a decimal

33. **TEST PREP** Last year, a factory produced 1,235,600 parts. If the company expects a 12% increase in production this year, how many parts will the factory produce? (Lesson 8-4)

A 1,383,872 **B** 14,827,200 **C** 12,625,400 **D** 1,482,720

34. **TEST PREP** Angles 1 and 2 are supplementary, and $m\angle 1 = 50°$. Find $m\angle 2$. (Lesson 5-1)

F 40° **G** 50° **H** 130° **J** 140°

9-5 The Fundamental Counting Principle

Learn to find the number of possible outcomes in an experiment.

Vocabulary

Fundamental Counting Principle

tree diagram

Computers can generate random passwords that are hard to guess because of the many possible arrangements of letters, numbers, and symbols.

If you tried to guess another person's password, you might have to try over one billion different codes!

"Your logon password is XB#2D940. Write it down and don't lose it again."

THE FUNDAMENTAL COUNTING PRINCIPLE

If there are m ways to choose a first item and n ways to choose a second item after the first item has been chosen, then there are $m \cdot n$ ways to choose all the items.

EXAMPLE 1 Using the Fundamental Counting Principle

A computer randomly generates a 5-character password of 2 letters followed by 3 digits. All passwords are equally likely.

A Find the number of possible passwords.

Use the Fundamental Counting Principle.

first letter	second letter	first digit	second digit	third digit
?	?	?	?	?
26 choices	26 choices	10 choices	10 choices	10 choices

$26 \cdot 26 \cdot 10 \cdot 10 \cdot 10 = 676{,}000$

The number of possible 2-letter, 3-digit passwords is 676,000.

B Find the probability of being assigned the password MQ836.

$$P(\text{MQ836}) = \frac{1}{\text{number of possible passwords}} = \frac{1}{676{,}000} \approx 0.0000015$$

C Find the probability of a password that does not contain an *A*.

First use the Fundamental Counting Principle to find the number of passwords that do not contain an *A*.

$25 \cdot 25 \cdot 10 \cdot 10 \cdot 10 = 625{,}000$ possible passwords without an *A*

There are 25 choices for any letter except A.

$$P(\text{no A}) = \frac{625{,}000}{676{,}000} = \frac{625}{676} \approx 0.925$$

A computer randomly generates a 5-character password of 2 letters followed by 3 digits. All passwords are equally likely.

D **Find the probability that a password contains exactly one 4.**

Only one of the digits can be a 4. The other two can be any of the 9 other digits. The 4 could be in one of three positions.

One digit must be a 4. *Other digits can be any digit but 4.*

$26 \cdot 26 \cdot 1 \cdot 9 \cdot 9 =$ 54,756 possible passwords with 4 as 1st digit
$26 \cdot 26 \cdot 9 \cdot 1 \cdot 9 =$ 54,756 possible passwords with 4 as 2nd digit
$26 \cdot 26 \cdot 9 \cdot 9 \cdot 1 =$ 54,756 possible passwords with 4 as 3rd digit
164,268 containing exactly one 4

$$P(\text{exactly one 4}) = \frac{164{,}268}{676{,}000} = \frac{243}{1000} = 0.243$$

The Fundamental Counting Principle tells you only the *number* of outcomes in some experiments, not what the outcomes are. A **tree diagram** is a way to show all of the possible outcomes.

EXAMPLE 2 Using a Tree Diagram

You pack 2 pairs of pants, 3 shirts, and 2 sweaters for your vacation. Describe all of the outfits you can make if each outfit consists of a pair of pants, a shirt, and a sweater.

You can find all of the possible outcomes by making a tree diagram. There should be $2 \cdot 3 \cdot 2 = 12$ different outfits.

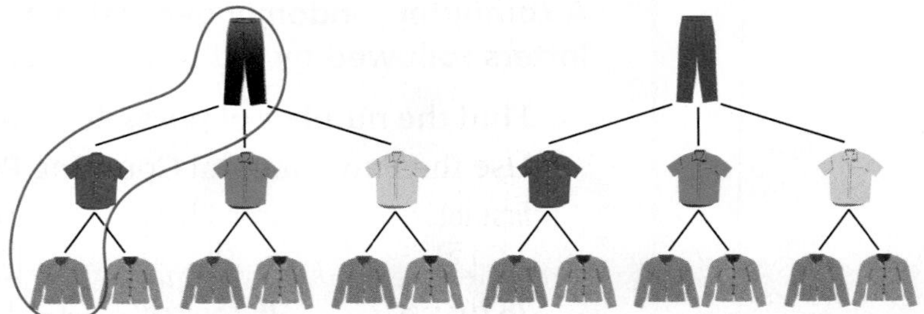

Each "branch" of the tree diagram represents a different outfit. The outfit shown in the circled branch could be written as (black, red, gray). The other outfits are as follows:
(black, red, tan), (black, green, gray), (black, green, tan),
(black, yellow, gray), (black, yellow, tan),
(blue, red, gray), (blue, red, tan), (blue, green, gray),
(blue, green, tan), (blue, yellow, gray), (blue, yellow, tan)

Think and Discuss

1. **Suppose** in Example 2 you could pack one more item. Which would you bring, another shirt or another pair of pants? Explain.

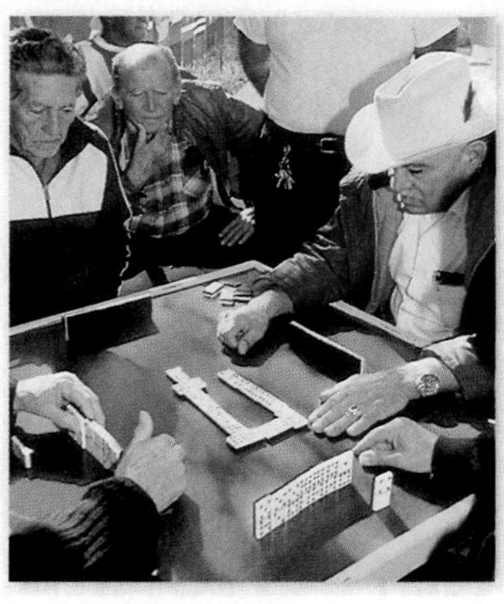

19. Ruben and Manuel play dominoes twice a week. Over the last 12 weeks, Ruben has won 16 times. Estimate the odds in favor of Manuel winning the next match.

20. The probability that Ann's city will be selected to host the Winter Olympics is $\frac{1}{12}$. What are the odds in favor of her city being selected?

21. The odds against pulling a pure silver dollar from a jar of coins are 1274:1. What is the probability of pulling a silver dollar from the jar?

22. ***BUSINESS*** To promote sales, a software company is putting scratch-off game pieces on 1200 of its software boxes. Of these pieces, 25 win a free mouse cover, and 35 win a free mouse pad.
   a. What are the odds in favor of winning a free mouse cover?
   b. What is the probability of winning a prize in the contest?
   c. What are the odds against winning a prize in the contest?

23. ***FUNDRAISING*** An organization sold 714 raffle tickets for 3 cruises.
   a. What are the odds against winning one of the cruises?
   b. What is the probability of not winning one of the cruises?

24. ***WHAT'S THE ERROR?*** A company receives 6 applications for one job. All of the candidates are equally likely to be selected for the job. One of the candidates says, "The odds in favor of my being selected are 1:6." What error has the candidate made?

25. ***WRITE ABOUT IT*** A computer randomly selects a digit from 0 to 9. Describe how to determine the odds that the number selected will be less than 4.

26. ***CHALLENGE*** A sample space has 3 outcomes, A, B, and C. B and C are equally likely, and A is twice as likely to occur as B or C. Find the odds in favor of A occurring.

Spiral Review

A jar contains 9 blue marbles, 8 red marbles, 13 green marbles, and 5 clear marbles. One marble is randomly selected from the jar. Find each probability. (Lesson 9-4)

27. P(clear)
28. P(red or green)
29. P(black or yellow)
30. P(not clear)
31. P(blue, red, or clear)
32. P(blue, green, or clear)

33. **TEST PREP** In how many ways can 8 students form a single file line if each student's place in line must be considered? (Lesson 9-6)

A 40,320 **B** 8 **C** 1 **D** 5040

Problem Solving on Location

Ohio

Rutherford B. Hayes Presidential Center

Rutherford B. Hayes was the nineteenth president of the United States. His home in Fremont, Ohio, is located on a 25-acre park called Spiegel Grove. In 1916, Spiegel Grove became the location of the first presidential library.

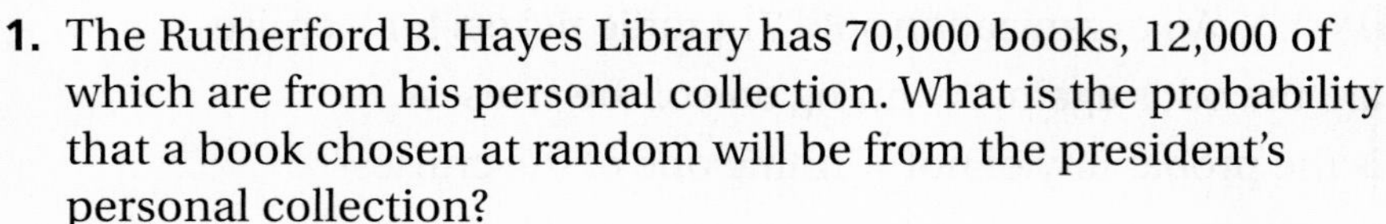

1. The Rutherford B. Hayes Library has 70,000 books, 12,000 of which are from his personal collection. What is the probability that a book chosen at random will be from the president's personal collection?

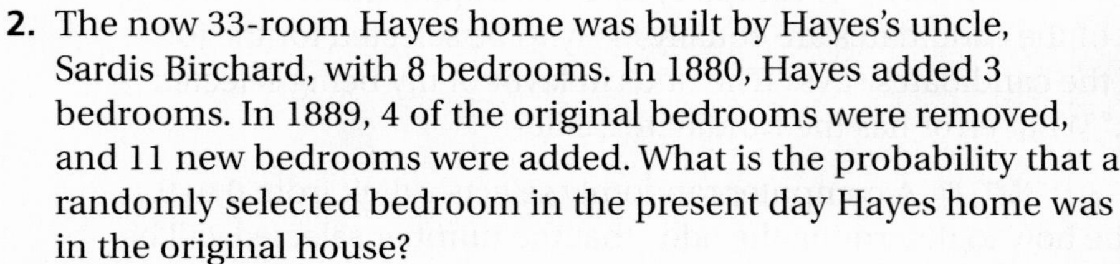

2. The now 33-room Hayes home was built by Hayes's uncle, Sardis Birchard, with 8 bedrooms. In 1880, Hayes added 3 bedrooms. In 1889, 4 of the original bedrooms were removed, and 11 new bedrooms were added. What is the probability that a randomly selected bedroom in the present day Hayes home was in the original house?

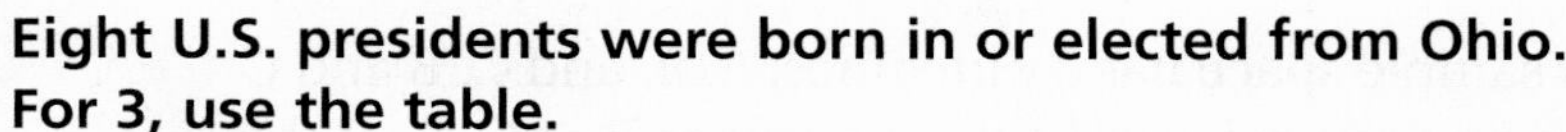

Eight U.S. presidents were born in or elected from Ohio. For 3, use the table.

3. If you randomly choose one of the presidents in the table, what is the probability that he could have served at least 4 years in office? What is the probability that he served as Ohio governor?

Presidents Born in or Living in Ohio When Elected

President	Ohio Governor	Inaugurated	Died
William H. Harrison	No	1841	1841
Ulysses S. Grant	No	1869	1885
Rutherford B. Hayes	Yes	1877	1893
James A. Garfield	No	1881	1881
Benjamin Harrison	No	1889	1901
William McKinley	Yes	1897	1901
William H. Taft	No	1909	1930
Warren G. Harding	No	1921	1923

A 1912 cartoon shows Teddy Roosevelt attempting to pull Ohio's voters away from William Howard Taft in Taft's home state.

ARE YOU READY?

Choose the best term from the list to complete each sentence.

1. A letter that represents a value that can change is called a(n) __?__.

2. A(n) __?__ has one or more variables.

3. The algebraic expression $5x^2 - 3y + 4x^2 + 7$ has four __?__. Since they have the same variable raised to the same power, $5x^2$ and $4x^2$ are __?__.

4. When you individually multiply the numbers inside parentheses by the factor outside the parentheses, you are applying the __?__.

algebraic expression
Distributive Property
like terms
terms
variable

Complete these exercises to review skills you will need for this chapter.

✔ Distribute Multiplication

Replace each ▇ with a number so that each equation illustrates the Distributive Property.

5. $6 \cdot (11 + 8) = 6 \cdot 11 + 6 \cdot$ ▇

6. $7 \cdot (14 + 12) =$ ▇ $\cdot 14 +$ ▇ $\cdot 12$

7. $9 \cdot (6 -$ ▇ $) = 9 \cdot 6 - 9 \cdot 2$

8. $14 \cdot ($ ▇ $- 7) = 14 \cdot 20 - 14 \cdot 7$

✔ Simplify Algebraic Expressions

Simplify each expression by applying the Distributive Property and combining like terms.

9. $3(x + 2) + 7x$

10. $4(y - 3) + 8y$

11. $2(z - 1) - 3z$

12. $-4(t - 6) - t$

13. $-(r - 3) - 8r$

14. $-5(4 - 2m) + 7$

✔ Connect Words and Equations

Write an equation to represent each situation.

15. The perimeter P of a rectangle is the sum of twice the length ℓ and twice the width w.

16. The volume V of a rectangular prism is the product of its three dimensions: length ℓ, width w, and height h.

17. The surface area S of a sphere is the product of 4π and the square of the radius r.

18. The cost c of a telegram of 18 words is the cost f of the first 10 words plus the cost a of each additional word.

10-1 Solving Two-Step Equations

Learn to solve two-step equations.

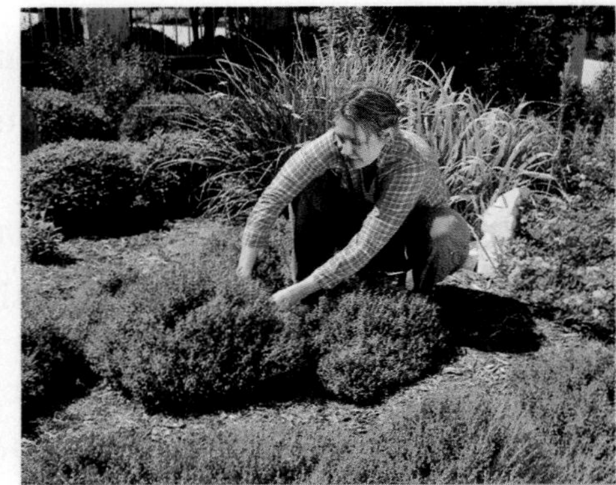

Sometimes more than one inverse operation is needed to solve an equation. Before solving, ask yourself, "What is being done to the variable, and in what order?" Then work backward to undo the operations.

Landscapers charge an hourly rate for labor, plus the cost of the plants. The number of hours a landscaper worked can be found by solving a two-step equation.

EXAMPLE 1 PROBLEM SOLVING APPLICATION

Chris's landscaping bill is \$380. The plants cost \$212, and the labor cost \$48 per hour. How many hours did the landscaper work?

1 Understand the Problem

The **answer** is the number of hours the landscaper worked on the yard. List the **important information:** The plants cost \$212, the labor cost \$48 per hour, and the total bill is \$380.

Let h represent the hours the landscaper worked.

Total bill	=	Plants	+	Labor
380	=	212	+	$48h$

2 Make a Plan

Think: First the variable is multiplied by 48, and then 212 is added to the result. Work backward to solve the equation. Undo the operations in reverse order: First subtract 212 from both sides of the equation, and then divide both sides of the new equation by 48.

3 Solve

$$\begin{aligned} 380 &= 212 + 48h \\ -212 &\quad -212 \\ 168 &= 48h \end{aligned}$$ *Subtract to undo addition.*

$$\frac{168}{48} = \frac{48h}{48}$$ *Divide to undo multiplication.*

$$3.5 = h$$

The landscaper worked 3.5 hours.

4 Look Back

If the landscaper worked 3.5 hours, the labor would be $\$48(3.5) = \$168$. The sum of the plants and the labor would be $\$212 + \$168 = \$380$.

EXAMPLE 2 Solving Two-Step Equations

Solve.

A $\frac{p}{4} + 5 = 13$

Think: First the variable is **divided by 4,** and then **5 is added.** To isolate the variable, **subtract 5,** and then **multiply by 4.**

$$\begin{aligned} \frac{p}{4} + 5 &= 13 \\ -5 &\quad -5 \end{aligned}$$ *Subtract to undo addition.*

$$\frac{p}{4} = 8$$

$$4 \cdot \frac{p}{4} = 4 \cdot 8$$ *Multiply to undo division.*

$$p = 32$$

Check $\frac{p}{4} + 5 \stackrel{?}{=} 13$

$\frac{32}{4} + 5 \stackrel{?}{=} 13$ *Substitute 32 into the original equation.*

$8 + 5 \stackrel{?}{=} 13$ ✔

B $1.8 = -2.5m - 1.7$

Think: First the variable is **multiplied by −2.5,** and then **1.7 is subtracted.** To isolate the variable, **add 1.7,** and then **divide by −2.5.**

$$\begin{aligned} 1.8 &= -2.5m - 1.7 \\ +1.7 &\qquad\quad +1.7 \end{aligned}$$ *Add to undo subtraction.*

$$3.5 = -2.5m$$

$$\frac{3.5}{-2.5} = \frac{-2.5m}{-2.5}$$ *Divide to undo multiplication.*

$$-1.4 = m$$

C $\frac{k+4}{9} = 6$

Think: First **4 is added** to the variable, and then the result is **divided by 9.** To isolate the variable, **multiply by 9,** and then **subtract 4.**

$$\frac{k+4}{9} = 6$$

$$9 \cdot \frac{k+4}{9} = 9 \cdot 6$$ *Multiply to undo division.*

$$\begin{aligned} k + 4 &= 54 \\ -4 &\quad -4 \end{aligned}$$ *Subtract to undo addition.*

$$k = 50$$

Think and Discuss

1. Describe how you would solve $4(x - 2) = 16$.

10-1 Exercises

FOR EXTRA PRACTICE

see page 750

internet connect

Homework Help Online
go.hrw.com Keyword: MP4 10-1

GUIDED PRACTICE

See Example  1

1. Joe is paid a weekly salary of \$520. He is paid an additional \$21 for every hour of overtime he works. This week his total pay, including regular salary and overtime pay, was \$604. How many hours of overtime did Joe work this week?

See Example 2 

Solve.

2. $9t + 12 = 75$
3. $-2.4 = -1.2x + 1.8$
4. $\frac{r}{7} + 11 = 25$
5. $\frac{b + 24}{2} = 13$
6. $14q - 17 = 39$
7. $\frac{a - 3}{28} = 3$

INDEPENDENT PRACTICE

See Example  1

8. The cost of a family membership at a health club is \$58 per month plus a one-time \$129 start-up fee. If a family spent \$651, how many months is their membership?

See Example 2 

Solve.

9. $\frac{m}{-3} - 2 = 8$
10. $\frac{c - 1}{2} = 12$
11. $15g - 4 = 46$
12. $\frac{h + 19}{19} = 2$
13. $6y + 3 = -27$
14. $9.2 = 4.4z - 4$

PRACTICE AND PROBLEM SOLVING

Solve.

15. $5w + 3.8 = 16.3$
16. $15 - 3x = -6$
17. $\frac{m}{5} + 6 = 9$
18. $2.3a + 8.6 = -5.2$
19. $\frac{q + 4}{7} = 1$
20. $9 = -5g - 23$
21. $6z - 2 = 0$
22. $\frac{5}{2}d - \frac{3}{2} = -\frac{1}{2}$
23. $47k + 83 = 318$
24. $8 = 6 + \frac{p}{4}$
25. $46 - 3n = -23$
26. $\frac{7 + s}{5} = -4$
27. $9y - 7.2 = 4.5$
28. $\frac{2}{3} - 6h = -\frac{11}{6}$
29. $-1 = \frac{3}{5}b + \frac{1}{5}$

Write an equation for each sentence, and then solve it.

30. The quotient of a number and 2, minus 9, is 14.
31. A number increased by 5 and then divided by 7 is 12.
32. The sum of 10 and 5 times a number is 25.

Life Science LINK

About 20% of the more than 2500 species of snakes are venomous. The United States has 20 domestic venomous snake species, including coral snakes, rattlesnakes, copperheads, and cottonmouths.

Venom is collected from snakes and injected into horses, which develop antibodies. The horses' blood is sterilized to make antivenom.

33. The inland taipan of central Australia is the world's most toxic venomous snake. Just 1 mg of its venom is enough to kill 1000 mice. One bite contains up to 110 mg of venom. About how many mice could be killed with the venom contained in just one inland taipan bite?

34. A rattlesnake grows a new rattle segment each time it sheds its skin. Rattlesnakes shed their skin an average of three times per year. However, segments often break off. If a rattlesnake had 44 rattle segments break off in its lifetime and it had 10 rattles when it died, approximately how many years did the rattlesnake live?

35. All snakes shed their skin as they grow. The shed skin of a snake is an average of 10% longer than the actual snake. If the shed skin of a coral snake is 27.5 inches long, estimate the length of the coral snake.

36. ***CHALLENGE*** Black mambas feed mainly on small rodents and birds. Suppose a black mamba is 100 feet away from an animal that is running at 8 mi/h. About how long will it take for the mamba to catch the animal? (*Hint*: 1 mile = 5280 feet)

go.hrw.com
Web Extra!
KEYWORD: MP4 Snakes

Records of World's Most Venomous Snakes

Category	Record	Type of Snake
Fastest	12 mi/h	Black mamba
Longest	18 ft 9 in.	King cobra
Heaviest	34 lb	Eastern diamondback rattlesnake
Longest fangs	2 in.	Gaboon viper

Spiral Review

Simplify. (Lesson 1-6)

37. $x + 4x + 3 + 7x$ **38.** $-2m + 4 + 2m$ **39.** $w - 17 + 2$ **40.** $5s + 3r + s - 5r$

41. **TEST PREP** Find the area of the parallelogram. (Lesson 6-1)

24 cm
14 cm
12 cm

A 38 cm^2 **B** 76 cm^2 **C** 288 cm^2 **D** 336 cm^2

10-2 Solving Multistep Equations

Learn to solve multistep equations.

To solve a complicated equation, you may have to simplify the equation first by combining like terms.

EXAMPLE 1 Solving Equations That Contain Like Terms

Solve.

$$\mathbf{2x + 4 + 5x - 8 = 24}$$

$$\begin{aligned} 2x + 4 + 5x - 8 &= 24 \\ 7x - 4 &= 24 && \textit{Combine like terms.} \\ +4 \quad &\;\; +4 && \textit{Add to undo subtraction.} \\ 7x &= 28 \\ \frac{7x}{7} &= \frac{28}{7} && \textit{Divide to undo multiplication.} \\ x &= 4 \end{aligned}$$

Check

$$\begin{aligned} 2x + 4 + 5x - 8 &= 24 \\ 2(4) + 4 + 5(4) - 8 &\stackrel{?}{=} 24 && \textit{Substitute 4 for x.} \\ 8 + 4 + 20 - 8 &\stackrel{?}{=} 24 \\ 24 &\stackrel{?}{=} 24 \checkmark \end{aligned}$$

If an equation contains fractions, it may help to multiply both sides of the equation by the least common denominator (LCD) to clear the fractions before you isolate the variable.

EXAMPLE 2 Solving Equations That Contain Fractions

Solve.

A $\frac{3y}{7} + \frac{5}{7} = -\frac{1}{7}$

Multiply both sides by 7 to clear fractions, and then solve.

$$\begin{aligned} 7\left(\frac{3y}{7} + \frac{5}{7}\right) &= 7\left(-\frac{1}{7}\right) \\ 7\left(\frac{3y}{7}\right) + 7\left(\frac{5}{7}\right) &= 7\left(-\frac{1}{7}\right) && \textit{Distributive Property} \\ 3y + 5 &= -1 \\ -5 \quad &\;\; -5 && \textit{Subtract to undo addition.} \\ 3y &= -6 \\ \frac{3y}{3} &= \frac{-6}{3} && \textit{Divide to undo multiplication.} \\ y &= -2 \end{aligned}$$

Solve.

B $\frac{2p}{3} + \frac{p}{4} - \frac{1}{6} = \frac{7}{2}$

The LCD is 12.

$$12\left(\frac{2p}{3} + \frac{p}{4} - \frac{1}{6}\right) = 12\left(\frac{7}{2}\right)$$ *Multiply both sides by the LCD.*

$$12\left(\frac{2p}{3}\right) + 12\left(\frac{p}{4}\right) - 12\left(\frac{1}{6}\right) = 12\left(\frac{7}{2}\right)$$ *Distributive Property*

$$8p + 3p - 2 = 42$$

$$11p - 2 = 42$$ *Combine like terms.*

$$\underline{\quad + 2 \quad + 2}$$ *Add to undo subtraction.*

$$11p = 44$$

$$\frac{11p}{11} = \frac{44}{11}$$ *Divide to undo multiplication.*

$$p = 4$$

Check

$$\frac{2p}{3} + \frac{p}{4} - \frac{1}{6} = \frac{7}{2}$$

$$\frac{2(4)}{3} + \frac{4}{4} - \frac{1}{6} \stackrel{?}{=} \frac{7}{2}$$ *Substitute 4 for p.*

$$\frac{8}{3} + 1 - \frac{1}{6} \stackrel{?}{=} \frac{7}{2}$$

$$\frac{16}{6} + \frac{6}{6} - \frac{1}{6} \stackrel{?}{=} \frac{21}{6}$$ *The LCD is 6.*

$$\frac{21}{6} \stackrel{?}{=} \frac{21}{6} \checkmark$$

Remember!

The least common denominator (LCD) is the smallest number that each of the denominators will divide into.

EXAMPLE  3 *Money Application*

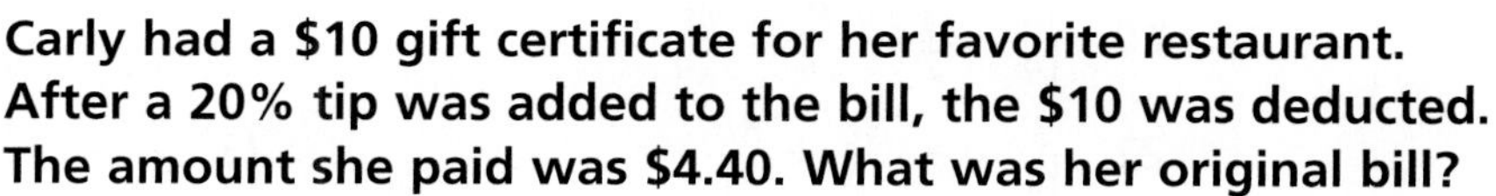

Carly had a $10 gift certificate for her favorite restaurant. After a 20% tip was added to the bill, the $10 was deducted. The amount she paid was $4.40. What was her original bill?

Let b represent the amount of the original bill.

$$b + 0.20b - 10 = 4.40$$ *bill + tip − gift certificate = amount paid*

$$1.20b - 10 = 4.40$$ *Combine like terms.*

$$\underline{\quad + 10 \quad + 10}$$ *Add 10 to both sides.*

$$1.20b = 14.40$$

$$\frac{1.20b}{1.20} = \frac{14.40}{1.20}$$ *Divide both sides by 1.20.*

$$b = 12$$ Her original bill was $12.

Think and Discuss

1. **List** the steps required to solve $3x - 4 + 2x = 7$.
2. **Tell** how you would clear the fractions in the equation $\frac{3x}{4} - \frac{2x}{3} + \frac{5}{8} = 1$.

10-2 Exercises

FOR EXTRA PRACTICE

see page 750

internet connect

Homework Help Online
go.hrw.com Keyword: MP4 10-2

GUIDED PRACTICE

See Example 1 **Solve.**

1. $8d - 11 + 3d + 2 = 13$
2. $2y + 5y + 4 = 25$
3. $10e - 2e - 9 = 39$
4. $3c - 7 + 12c = 53$
5. $4h + 8 + 7h - 2h = 89$
6. $8x - 3x + 2 = -33$

See Example 2

7. $\frac{5x}{11} + \frac{4}{11} = -\frac{1}{11}$
8. $\frac{y}{2} - \frac{3y}{8} + \frac{1}{4} = \frac{1}{2}$
9. $\frac{4}{5} - \frac{2p}{5} = \frac{6}{5}$
10. $\frac{9}{4}z + \frac{1}{2} = 2$

See Example 3

11. Joley used a $20 gift certificate to help pay for dinner for herself and a friend. After an 18% tip was added to the bill, the $20 was deducted. The amount she paid was $8.90. What was the original bill?

INDEPENDENT PRACTICE

See Example 1 **Solve.**

12. $6n + 4n - n + 5 = 23$
13. $-83 = 6k + 17 + 4k$
14. $36 - 4c - 3c = 22$
15. $10 + 4w - 3w = 13$
16. $28 = 10a - 5a - 2$
17. $30 = 7y - 35 + 6y$

See Example 2

18. $\frac{3}{8} + \frac{p}{8} = 3\frac{1}{8}$
19. $\frac{9h}{10} - \frac{3h}{10} = \frac{18}{10}$
20. $\frac{4g}{14} - \frac{3}{7} - \frac{g}{14} = \frac{3}{14}$
21. $\frac{5}{18} = \frac{4m}{9} - \frac{m}{3} + \frac{1}{2}$
22. $\frac{5}{11} = -\frac{3b}{11} + \frac{8b}{22}$
23. $\frac{3x}{4} - \frac{11x}{24} = -1\frac{1}{6}$

See Example 3

24. Pat bought 6 shirts that were all the same price. He used a traveler's check for $25, and then paid the difference of $86. What was the price of each shirt?

PRACTICE AND PROBLEM SOLVING

Solve and check.

25. $\frac{5n}{6} - \frac{1}{4} = \frac{3}{8}$
26. $5n + 12 - 9n = -16$
27. $6b - 1 - 10b = 51$
28. $\frac{x}{2} + \frac{2}{3} = \frac{5}{6}$
29. $-2x - 7 + 3x = 10$
30. $\frac{3r}{4} - \frac{2}{3} = \frac{5}{6}$
31. $5y - 2 - 8y = 31$
32. $7n - 10 - 9n = -13$
33. $\frac{h}{6} + \frac{h}{8} = 1\frac{1}{6}$
34. $2a + 7 + 3a = 32$
35. $\frac{b}{6} + \frac{3b}{8} = \frac{5}{12}$
36. $-10 = 9m - 13 - 7m$

You can estimate the weight in pounds of a fish that is L inches long and G inches around at the thickest part by using the formula $W \approx \frac{LG^2}{800}$.

37. Gina is paid 1.5 times her normal hourly rate for each hour she works over 40 hours in a week. Last week she worked 48 hours and earned \$634.40. What is her normal hourly rate?

38. ***SPORTS*** The average weight of the top 5 fish at a fishing tournament was 12.3 pounds. The weights of the second-, third-, fourth-, and fifth-place fish are shown in the table. What was the weight of the heaviest fish?

Winning Entries

Caught By	Weight (lb)
Wayne S.	■
Carla P.	12.8
Deb N.	12.6
Virgil W.	11.8
Brian B.	9.7

39. ***PHYSICAL SCIENCE*** The formula $C = \frac{5}{9}(F - 32)$ is used to convert a temperature from degrees Fahrenheit to degrees Celsius. Water boils at 100°C. Use the formula to find the boiling point of water in degrees Fahrenheit.

40. At a bulk food store, Kerry bought $\frac{2}{3}$ lb of coffee that cost \$4.50/lb, $\frac{3}{4}$ lb of coffee that cost \$5.20/lb, and $\frac{1}{5}$ lb of coffee that did not have a price marked. If her total cost was \$8.18, what was the price per pound of the third type of coffee?

41. ***WHAT'S THE ERROR?*** A student's work in solving an equation is shown. What error has the student made, and what is the correct answer?

$$\frac{1}{3}x + 3x = 7$$
$$x + 3x = 21$$
$$4x = 21$$
$$x = \frac{21}{4}$$

42. ***WRITE ABOUT IT*** Compare the steps you would use to solve the following equations.

$4x - 8 = 16$ $\qquad$ $4(x - 2) = 16$

43. ***CHALLENGE*** List the steps you would use to solve the following equation.

$$\frac{5\left(\frac{1}{2}x - \frac{1}{3}\right) + \frac{7}{6}x}{2} + 2 = 3$$

Spiral Review

Evaluate each expression for the given value of the variable. (Lesson 3-2)

44. $19.4 - x$ for $x = -5.6$
45. $11 - r$ for $r = 13.5$
46. $p + 65.1$ for $p = -42.3$
47. $-\frac{3}{7} - t$ for $t = 1\frac{5}{7}$
48. $3\frac{5}{11} + y$ for $y = -2\frac{4}{11}$
49. $-\frac{1}{19} + g$ for $g = \frac{18}{19}$

50. **TEST PREP** $\overleftrightarrow{AB}$ has a slope of $\frac{2}{5}$. What is the slope of a line perpendicular to $\overleftrightarrow{AB}$? (Lesson 5-5)

A $-\frac{2}{5}$ **B** $\frac{5}{2}$ **C** $-\frac{5}{2}$ **D** $\frac{7}{5}$

Hands-On
LAB
10A

Model Equations with Variables on Both Sides

Use with Lesson 10-3

KEY

Algebra tiles

[+ long tile] $= x$ [− long tile] $= -x$

[+ small tile] $= 1$ [− small tile] $= -1$

REMEMBER

It will not change the value of an expression if you add or remove zero.

[+ long tile] + [− long tile] = 0 [+ small tile] + [− small tile] = 0

internet connect
Lab Resources Online
go.hrw.com
KEYWORD: MP4 Lab10A
go.hrw.com

To solve an equation with the same variable on both sides of the equal sign, you must first add or subtract to eliminate the variable term from one side of the equation.

Activity

1 Model and solve the equation $-x + 2 = 2x - 4$.

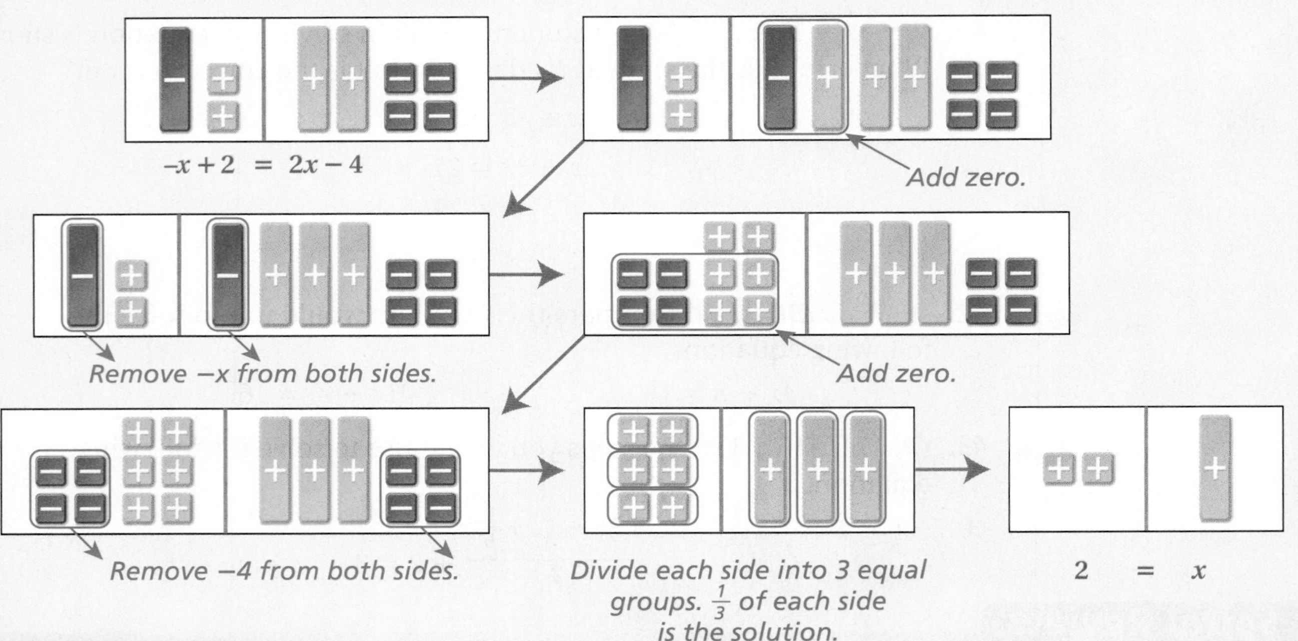
−x + 2 = 2x − 4
Add zero.
Remove −x from both sides.
Add zero.
Remove −4 from both sides.
Divide each side into 3 equal groups. 1/3 of each side is the solution.
2 = x

Think and Discuss

1. How would you check the solution to $-x + 2 = 2x - 4$ using algebra tiles?
2. Why must you isolate the variable terms by having them on only one side of the equation?

Try This

Model and solve each equation.

1. $x + 1 = -x - 1$
2. $3x = -3x + 18$
3. $4 - 2x = -5x + 7$
4. $2x + 2x + 1 = x + 10$

10-3 Solving Equations with Variables on Both Sides

Learn to solve equations with variables on both sides of the equal sign.

Some problems produce equations that have variables on both sides of the equal sign. For instance, Elaine runs the same distance each day. On Mondays, Fridays, and Saturdays, she runs 3 laps on the track and an additional 5 miles off the track. On Tuesdays and Thursdays, she runs 4 laps on the track and 2.5 miles off the track.

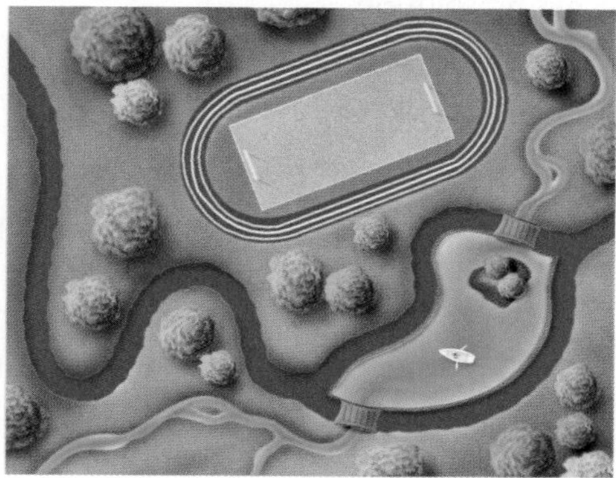

Expression for Mondays, Fridays, and Saturdays $\underbrace{3x+5}$ $\underbrace{4x+2.5}$ *Expression for Tuesdays and Thursdays*

$$3x + 5 = 4x + 2.5$$

The variable x in these expressions is the length of one lap of the track. Since the total distance each day is the same, the two expressions are equal.

Solving an equation with variables on both sides is similar to solving an equation with a variable on only one side. You can add or subtract a term containing a variable on both sides of an equation.

EXAMPLE 1 Solving Equations with Variables on Both Sides

Solve.

A $2a + 3 = 3a$

$$2a + 3 = 3a$$
$$\underline{-2a} \qquad \underline{-2a}$$ *Subtract 2a from both sides.*
$$3 = a$$

B $4v - 7 = 5 + 7v$

$$4v - 7 = 5 + 7v$$
$$\underline{-4v} \qquad \underline{-4v}$$ *Subtract 4v from both sides.*
$$-7 = 5 + 3v$$
$$\underline{-5} \qquad \underline{-5}$$ *Subtract 5 from both sides.*
$$-12 = 3v$$
$$\frac{-12}{3} = \frac{3v}{3}$$ *Divide both sides by 3.*
$$-4 = v$$

Helpful Hint

If the variables in an equation are eliminated and the resulting statement is false, the equation has no solution.

Solve.

C $g + 5 = g - 2$

$$\begin{aligned} g + 5 &= g - 2 \\ \underline{-g} \quad & \quad \underline{-g} \qquad \text{Subtract } g \text{ from both sides.} \\ 5 &\neq -2 \end{aligned}$$

No solution. There is no number that can be substituted for the variable g to make the equation true.

To solve multistep equations with variables on both sides, first combine like terms and clear fractions. Then add or subtract variable terms to both sides so that the variable occurs on only one side of the equation. Then use properties of equality to isolate the variable.

EXAMPLE 2 Solving Multistep Equations with Variables on Both Sides

Solve.

A $2c + 4 - 3c = -9 + c + 5$

$$\begin{aligned} 2c + 4 - 3c &= -9 + c + 5 \\ -c + 4 &= -4 + c && \text{Combine like terms.} \\ \underline{+c} \quad & \quad \underline{+c} && \text{Add } c \text{ to both sides.} \\ 4 &= -4 + 2c \\ \underline{+4} \quad & \underline{+4} && \text{Add to undo subtraction.} \\ 8 &= 2c \\ \frac{8}{2} &= \frac{2c}{2} && \text{Divide to undo multiplication.} \\ 4 &= c \end{aligned}$$

B $\frac{w}{2} - \frac{3w}{4} + \frac{1}{3} = w + \frac{7}{6}$

$$\begin{aligned} \frac{w}{2} - \frac{3w}{4} + \frac{1}{3} &= w + \frac{7}{6} \\ 12\left(\frac{w}{2} - \frac{3w}{4} + \frac{1}{3}\right) &= 12\left(w + \frac{7}{6}\right) && \text{Multiply by LCD, 12.} \\ 12\left(\frac{w}{2}\right) - 12\left(\frac{3w}{4}\right) + 12\left(\frac{1}{3}\right) &= 12(w) + 12\left(\frac{7}{6}\right) \\ 6w - 9w + 4 &= 12w + 14 \\ -3w + 4 &= 12w + 14 && \text{Combine like terms.} \\ \underline{+3w} \quad & \quad \underline{+3w} && \text{Add } 3w \text{ to both sides.} \\ 4 &= 15w + 14 \\ \underline{-14} \quad & \quad \underline{-14} && \text{Subtract 14 from both sides.} \\ -10 &= 15w \\ \frac{-10}{15} &= \frac{15w}{15} && \text{Divide both sides by 15.} \\ -\frac{2}{3} &= w \end{aligned}$$

Focus on Problem Solving

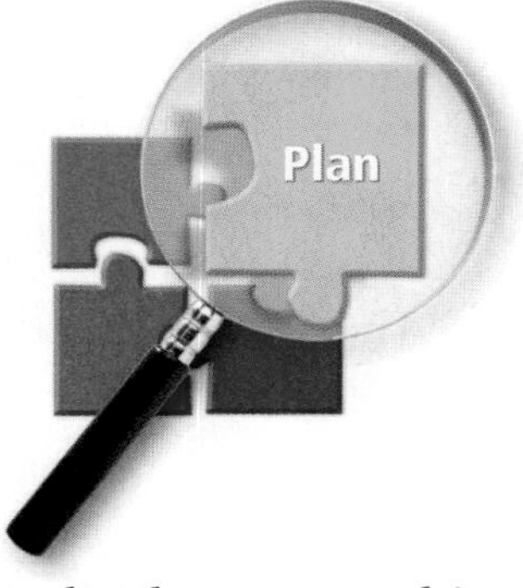

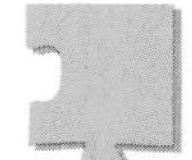

Make a Plan

- **Write an equation**

Several steps may be needed to solve a problem. It often helps to write an equation that represents the steps.

Example:

Juan's first 3 exam scores are 85, 93, and 87. What does he need to score on his next exam to average 90 for the 4 exams?

Let x be the score on his next exam. The average of the exam scores is the sum of the 4 scores, divided by 4. This amount must equal 90.

$$\text{Average of exam scores} = 90$$
$$\frac{85 + 93 + 87 + x}{4} = 90$$
$$\frac{265 + x}{4} = 90$$
$$4\left(\frac{265 + x}{4}\right) = 4(90)$$
$$265 + x = 360$$
$$\underline{-265} \qquad \underline{-265}$$
$$x = 95$$

Juan needs a 95 on his next exam.

Read each problem and write an equation that could be used to solve it.

1. The average of two numbers is 27. The first number is twice the second number. What are the two numbers?

2. Nancy spends $\frac{1}{3}$ of her monthly salary on rent, $\frac{1}{10}$ on her car payment, $\frac{1}{12}$ on food, $\frac{1}{5}$ on other bills, and has $680 left for other expenses. What is Nancy's monthly salary?

3. A vendor at a concert sells caps and T-shirts. The T-shirts cost 1.5 times as much as the caps. If 5 caps and 7 T-shirts cost $248, what is the price of each item?

4. Amanda and Rick have the same amount to spend on school supplies. Amanda buys 4 notebooks and has $8.60 left. Rick buys 7 notebooks and has $7.55 left. How much does each notebook cost?

10-4 Solving Multistep Inequalities

Learn to solve two-step inequalities and graph the solutions of an inequality on a number line.

The student council is making silk-screened T-shirts with the school logo on them for a fund-raiser. The cost of making the shirts has two parts.

1. fixed costs (silk screen equipment, etc.)
2. unit costs (shirts, ink, etc.)

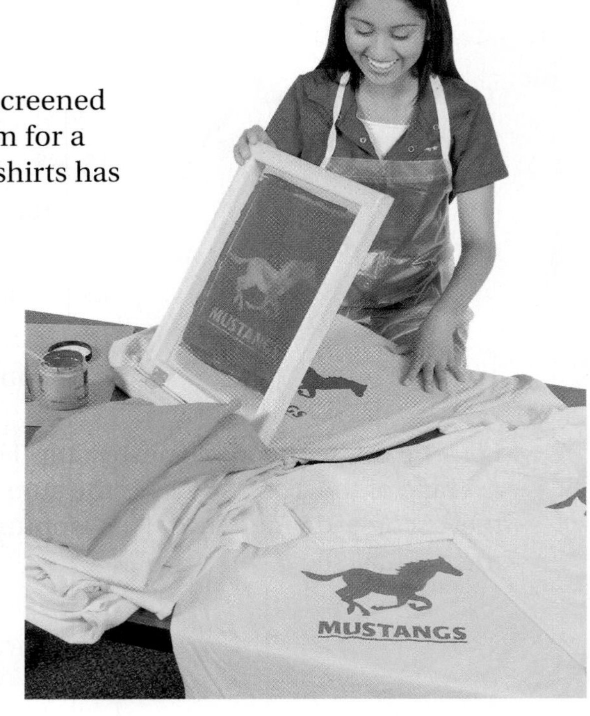

Revenue is the price each unit is sold for multiplied by the number of units sold. The student council makes a profit when the revenue is greater than the cost. To find out how many units they need to sell for the revenue to be greater than the cost you can write and solve a multistep inequality.

Solving a multistep inequality uses the same inverse operations as solving a multistep equation. Multiplying or dividing the inequality by a negative number reverses the inequality symbol.

EXAMPLE 1 Solving Two-Step Inequalities

Solve and graph.

A $2x - 3 > 5$

$2x - 3 > 5$

$\underline{\quad +3} \quad \underline{+3}$ *Add 3 to both sides.*

$2x > 8$

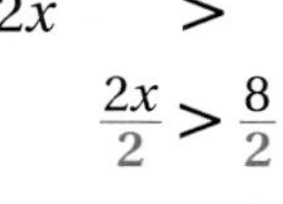

$\frac{2x}{2} > \frac{8}{2}$ *Divide both sides by 2.*

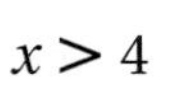

$x > 4$

B $-10 < 3x + 2$

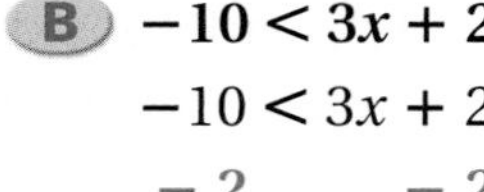

$-10 < 3x + 2$

$\underline{-2} \quad \underline{\quad -2}$ *Subtract 2 from both sides.*

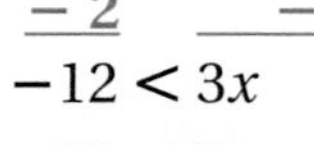

$-12 < 3x$

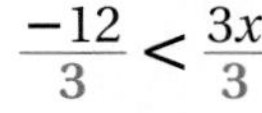

$\frac{-12}{3} < \frac{3x}{3}$ *Divide both sides by 3.*

$-4 < x$

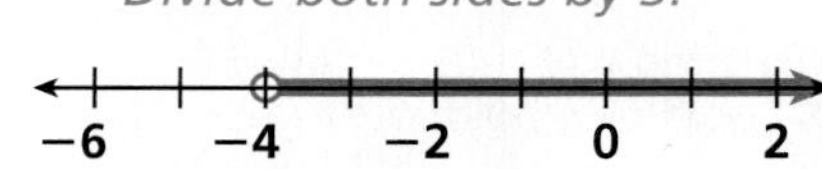

Solve and graph.

C $-2x + 4 \le 3$

$$\begin{aligned} -2x + 4 &\le 3 \\ \underline{\quad -4} &\quad \underline{-4} \\ -2x &\le -1 \end{aligned}$$ *Subtract 4 from both sides.*

$$\frac{-2x}{-2} \ge \frac{-1}{-2}$$ *Divide each side by −2; change ≤ to ≥.*

$$x \ge \frac{1}{2}$$

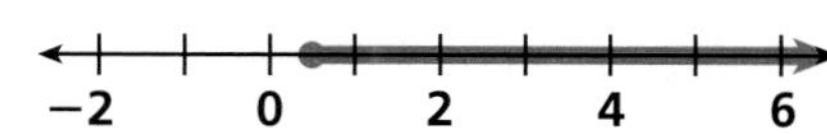

EXAMPLE 2 Solving Multistep Inequalities

Solve and graph.

A $3x - 2 - 4x > 5$

$$3x - 2 - 4x > 5$$

$$-1x - 2 > 5$$ *Combine like terms.*

$$\begin{aligned} \underline{\quad +2} &\quad \underline{+2} \\ -1x &> 7 \end{aligned}$$ *Add 2 to both sides.*

$$\frac{-1x}{-1} < \frac{7}{-1}$$ *Divide both sides by −1; change > to <.*

$$x < -7$$

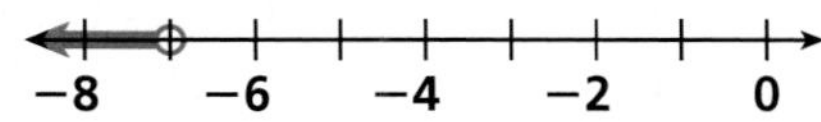

B $\frac{2x}{3} + \frac{1}{2} \le \frac{5}{6}$

$$\frac{2x}{3} + \frac{1}{2} \le \frac{5}{6}$$

$$6\left(\frac{2x}{3} + \frac{1}{2}\right) \le 6\left(\frac{5}{6}\right)$$ *Multiply by LCD, 6.*

$$6\left(\frac{2x}{3}\right) + 6\left(\frac{1}{2}\right) \le 6\left(\frac{5}{6}\right)$$

$$4x + 3 \le 5$$

$$\begin{aligned} \underline{\quad -3} &\quad \underline{-3} \\ 4x &\le 2 \end{aligned}$$ *Subtract 3 from both sides.*

$$\frac{4x}{4} \le \frac{2}{4}$$ *Divide both sides by 4.*

$$x \le \frac{1}{2}$$

−2 0 2 4 6

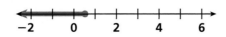

Solve and graph.

C $2x + 3 > 5x - 6$

$$\begin{aligned} 2x + 3 &> 5x - 6 \\ \underline{-2x} \quad &\quad \underline{-2x} \\ 3 &> 3x - 6 \\ \underline{+6} \quad &\quad \underline{+6} \\ 9 &> 3x \\ \frac{9}{3} &> \frac{3x}{3} \\ 3 &> x \end{aligned}$$

Subtract 2x from both sides.

Add 6 to both sides.

Divide both sides by 3.

−2 0 2 4 6

EXAMPLE 3 Business Application

The student council sells T-shirts with the school logo on them. The unit cost is \$10.50 for the shirt and the ink. They have a fixed cost of \$60 for silk screen equipment. If they sell the shirts for \$12 each, how many must they sell to make a profit?

Let R represent the revenue and C represent the cost. In order for the student council to make a profit, the revenue must be greater than the cost.

$$R > C$$

The revenue from selling x shirts at \$12 each is $12x$. The cost of producing x shirts is the fixed cost plus the unit cost times the number of shirts produced, or $60 + 10.50x$. Substitute the expressions for R and C.

$$\begin{aligned} 12x &> 60 + 10.50x \\ \underline{-10.50x} \quad &\quad \underline{-10.50x} \\ 1.5x &> 60 \\ \frac{1.5x}{1.5} &> \frac{60}{1.5} \\ x &> 40 \end{aligned}$$

Let x represent the number of shirts sold.

Subtract 10.50x from both sides.

Divide both sides by 1.5.

The student council must sell more than 40 shirts to make a profit.

Think and Discuss

1. **Compare** solving a multistep equation with solving a multistep inequality.
2. **Describe** two situations in which you would have to reverse the inequality symbol when solving a multistep inequality.

10-4 Exercises

FOR EXTRA PRACTICE

see page 750

internet connect

Homework Help Online

go.hrw.com Keyword: MP4 10-4

GUIDED PRACTICE

See Example 1

Solve and graph.

1. $2k + 4 > 10$
2. $\frac{1}{2}z - 5.5 \le 4.5$
3. $5y + 10 < -25$
4. $-4x + 6 \ge 14$
5. $4y + 1.5 \ge 13.5$
6. $3k - 2 > 13$

See Example 2

7. $4x - 3 + x < 12$
8. $\frac{4b}{5} + \frac{7}{10} \ge \frac{1}{2}$
9. $4 + 9h - 7 \le 3h + 3$
10. $14c + 2 - 3c > 8 + 8c$
11. $\frac{1}{9} + \frac{d}{3} < \frac{1}{2} - \frac{2d}{3}$
12. $\frac{5}{6} \ge \frac{4m}{9} - \frac{1}{3} + \frac{2m}{9}$

See Example 3

13. A school's Spanish club is selling printed caps to raise money for a trip. The printer charges \$150 in advance plus \$3 for every cap ordered. If the club sells caps for \$12.50 each, at least how many caps do they need to sell to make a profit?

INDEPENDENT PRACTICE

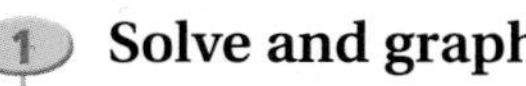

See Example 1

Solve and graph.

14. $6k - 8 > 22$
15. $10x + 2 > 42$
16. $5p - 5 \le 45$
17. $14 \ge 13q - 12$
18. $3.6 + 7.2n < 25.2$
19. $-8x - 12 \ge 52$

See Example 2

20. $7p + 5 < 6p - 12$
21. $11 + 17a \ge 13a - 1$
22. $\frac{11}{13} + \frac{n}{2} > \frac{25}{26}$
23. $\frac{2}{3} \le \frac{1}{2}k - \frac{5}{6}$
24. $\frac{n}{7} + \frac{11}{14} \le -\frac{17}{14}$
25. $3r - 16 + 7r < 14$

See Example 3

26. Josef is on the planning committee for the eighth-grade holiday party. The food, decoration, and entertainment costs total \$350. The committee has \$75 in the treasury. If the committee expects to sell the tickets for \$5 each, at least how many tickets must be sold to cover the remaining cost of the party?

PRACTICE AND PROBLEM SOLVING

Solve and graph.

27. $3p - 3 \le 19$
28. $12n + 26 > -10$
29. $4 - 9w < 13$
30. $-8x - 18 \ge 14$
31. $16a + 3 > 11$
32. $-2y + 1 \ge 8$
33. $3q - 5q > -12$
34. $\frac{3m}{4} + \frac{2}{3} > \frac{m}{2} + \frac{7}{8}$
35. $7b - 4.6 < 3b + 6.2$
36. $6k + 4 - 3k \ge 2$
37. $26 - \frac{33}{4} \le -\frac{2}{3}f - \frac{1}{4}$
38. $\frac{7}{9}v + \frac{5}{12} - \frac{3}{18}v \ge \frac{3}{4}v + \frac{1}{3}$

39. ***ENTERTAINMENT*** A concert is being held in a gymnasium that can hold no more than 550 people. A permanent bleacher will seat 30 people. The event organizers are setting up 20 rows of chairs. At most, how many chairs can be in each row?

40. Katie and April are making a string of pi beads for pi day (March 14). They use 10 colors of beads that represent the digits 0–9, and the beads are strung in the order of the digits of π. The string already has 70 beads. If they have 30 days to string the beads, and they want to string 1000 beads by π day, at least how many beads do they have to string each day?

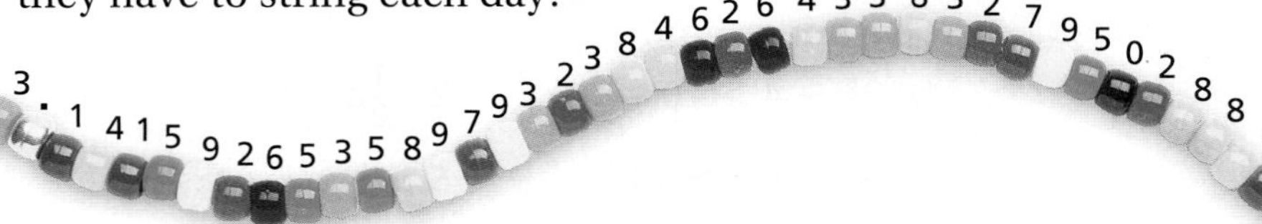

41. ***SPORTS*** The Cubs have won 44 baseball games and have lost 65 games. They have 53 games remaining. At least how many of the remaining 53 games must the Cubs win to have a winning season? (A winning season means they win more than 50% of their games.)

42. ***ECONOMICS*** Satellite TV customers can either purchase a dish and receiver for \$249 or pay a \$50 fee and rent the equipment for \$12 a month.

a. How much would it cost to rent the equipment for 9 months?

b. How many months would it take for the rental charges to exceed the purchase price?

43. ***WRITE A PROBLEM*** Write and solve an inequality using the following shipping rates for orders from a mail-order catalog.

Mail-Order Shipping Rates				
Merchandise Amount	\$0.01–\$20	\$20.01–\$30	\$30.01–\$45	\$45.01–\$60
Shipping Cost	\$4.95	\$5.95	\$7.95	\$8.95

44. ***WRITE ABOUT IT*** Describe two ways to solve the inequality below. In one way, you must reverse the inequality symbol, but in the other way, you do not need to reverse the symbol.

$$-2x - 3 < x + 4$$

45. ***CHALLENGE*** Solve the inequality $\frac{x-1}{5} - \frac{x+2}{6} \geq \frac{7}{15}$.

Spiral Review

Find each number. (Lesson 8-3)

46. 19 is 20% of what number?

47. 74% of what number is 481?

48. 32% of what number is 58.88?

49. 0.7488 is 52% of what number?

50. **TEST PREP** What is the probability of rolling an odd number on a fair number cube? (Lesson 9-4)

A $\frac{1}{2}$ **B** $\frac{2}{3}$ **C** $\frac{1}{6}$ **D** $\frac{1}{3}$

10-6 Systems of Equations

Learn to solve systems of equations.

Vocabulary

system of equations

solution of a system of equations

Tickets for a concert are \$40 for main-floor seats and \$25 for upper-level seats. A total of 2000 concert tickets were sold. The total ticket sales were \$62,000. How many main-floor tickets were sold and how many upper-level tickets were sold? You can solve this problem using two equations.

A **system of equations** is a set of two or more equations that contain two or more variables. A **solution of a system of equations** is a set of values that are solutions of all of the equations. If the system has two variables, the solutions can be written as ordered pairs.

EXAMPLE 1 Identifying Solutions of a System of Equations

Determine if each ordered pair is a solution of the system of equations below.

$$\mathbf{2x + 3y = 8}$$
$$\mathbf{x - 4y = 15}$$

A (−2, 4)

$$2x + 3y = 8 \qquad x - 4y = 15$$
$$2(-2) + 3(4) \stackrel{?}{=} 8 \qquad -2 - 4(4) \stackrel{?}{=} 15 \qquad \textit{Substitute for x and y.}$$
$$8 = 8 \checkmark \qquad -18 \neq 15 \times$$

The ordered pair (−2, 4) is not a solution of the system of equations.

B (7, −2)

$$2x + 3y = 8 \qquad x - 4y = 15$$
$$2(7) + 3(-2) \stackrel{?}{=} 8 \qquad 7 - 4(-2) \stackrel{?}{=} 15 \qquad \textit{Substitute for x and y.}$$
$$8 = 8 \checkmark \qquad 15 = 15 \checkmark$$

The ordered pair (7, −2) is a solution of the system of equations.

C (11, −1)

$$2x + 3y = 8 \qquad x - 4y = 15$$
$$2(11) + 3(-1) \stackrel{?}{=} 8 \qquad 11 - 4(-1) \stackrel{?}{=} 15 \qquad \textit{Substitute for x and y.}$$
$$19 \neq 8 \times \qquad 15 = 15 \checkmark$$

The ordered pair (11, −1) is not a solution of the system of equations.

EXAMPLE 2 Solving Systems of Equations

Solve the system of equations. $y = x + 3$
$y = 2x + 5$

The expressions $x + 3$ and $2x + 5$ both equal y, so they equal each other.

$y = y$

$y = x + 3$ $y = 2x + 5$

$x + 3 = 2x + 5$

Solve the equation to find x.

$$\begin{aligned} x + 3 &= 2x + 5 \\ -x \quad & \quad -x & \text{Subtract } x \text{ from both sides.} \\ 3 &= x + 5 \\ -5 \quad & \quad -5 & \text{Subtract 5 from both sides.} \\ -2 &= x \end{aligned}$$

Subtract x from both sides.

Subtract 5 from both sides.

Helpful Hint

When solving systems of equations, remember to find values for all of the variables.

To find y, substitute -2 for x in one of the original equations.

$y = x + 3 = -2 + 3 = 1$

The solution is $(-2, 1)$.

Check: Substitute -2 for x and 1 for y in each equation.

$y = x + 3$	$y = 2x + 5$
$1 \stackrel{?}{=} -2 + 3$	$1 \stackrel{?}{=} 2(-2) + 5$
$1 = 1$ ✔	$1 = 1$ ✔

To solve a general system of two equations with two variables, you can solve both equations for x or both for y.

EXAMPLE 3 Solving Systems of Equations

Solve the system of equations.

A $x + y = 5$
$x - 2y = -4$

Solve both equations for x.

$$\begin{aligned} x + y &= 5 \\ -y \quad & \quad -y \\ x \quad &= 5 - y \end{aligned} \qquad \begin{aligned} x - 2y &= -4 \\ +2y \quad & \quad +2y \\ x \quad &= -4 + 2y \end{aligned}$$

$$\begin{aligned} 5 - y &= -4 + 2y \\ +y \quad & \quad +y & \text{Add } y \text{ to both sides.} \\ 5 &= -4 + 3y \\ +4 \quad & \quad +4 & \text{Add 4 to both sides.} \\ 9 &= 3y \\ 3 &= y & \text{Divide both sides by 3.} \end{aligned}$$

Add y to both sides.

Add 4 to both sides.

Divide both sides by 3.

$$\begin{aligned} x &= 5 - y \\ &= 5 - 3 = 2 \end{aligned}$$

Substitute 3 for y.

The solution is $(2, 3)$.

Solve the system of equations.

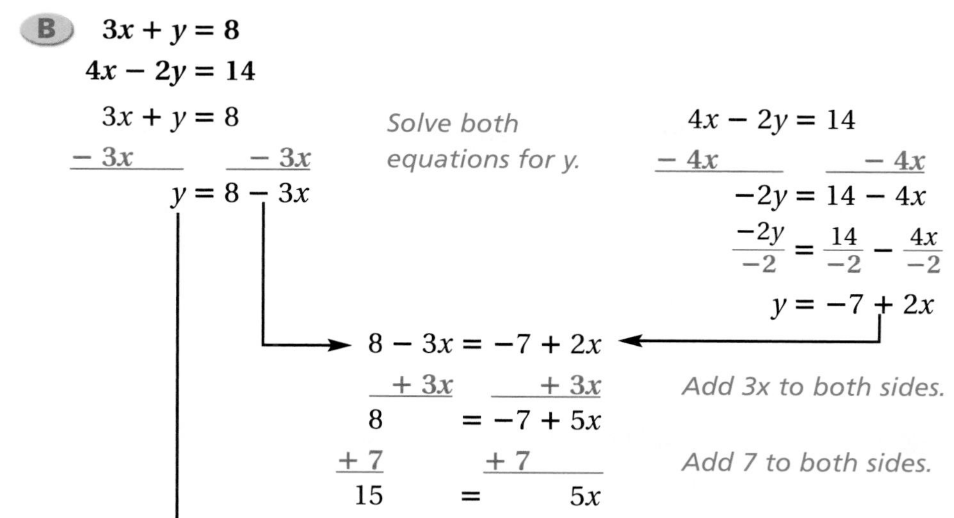

B $3x + y = 8$
$4x - 2y = 14$

Solve both equations for *y*.

$$\begin{aligned} 3x + y &= 8 \\ -3x \quad & \quad -3x \\ y &= 8 - 3x \end{aligned}$$

$$\begin{aligned} 4x - 2y &= 14 \\ -4x \quad & \quad -4x \\ -2y &= 14 - 4x \\ \frac{-2y}{-2} &= \frac{14}{-2} - \frac{4x}{-2} \\ y &= -7 + 2x \end{aligned}$$

$$\begin{aligned} 8 - 3x &= -7 + 2x \\ +3x \quad & \quad +3x && \textit{Add 3x to both sides.} \\ 8 &= -7 + 5x \\ +7 \quad & \quad +7 && \textit{Add 7 to both sides.} \\ 15 &= 5x \\ 3 &= x && \textit{Divide both sides by 5.} \end{aligned}$$

$$\begin{aligned} y &= 8 - 3x \\ &= 8 - 3(3) = -1 && \textit{Substitute 3 for x.} \end{aligned}$$

The solution is $(3, -1)$.

You can choose either variable to solve for. It is usually easiest to solve for a variable that has a coefficient of 1.

Think and Discuss

1. **Compare** an equation to a system of equations.
2. **Describe** how you would know whether $(-1, 0)$ is a solution of the system of equations below.

$$\begin{aligned} x + 2y &= -1 \\ -3x + 4y &= 3 \end{aligned}$$

10-6 Exercises

FOR EXTRA PRACTICE
see page 751

internet connect
Homework Help Online
go.hrw.com Keyword: MP4 10-6

GUIDED PRACTICE

See Example 1

Determine if the ordered pair is a solution of each system of equations.

1. (2, 3) $y = 2x - 1$, $y = x + 1$

2. (2, 7) $y = 5x - 3$, $y = 3x + 1$

3. (2, 4) $y = 4x - 4$, $y = 2x$

4. (2, 2) $y = 2x + 1$, $y = 3x - 2$

See Example 2 **Solve each system of equations.**

5. $y = x + 1$
$y = 2x - 1$

6. $y = -3x + 2$
$y = 4x - 5$

7. $y = 5x - 3$
$y = 2x + 6$

8. $y = 4x - 3$
$y = 2x + 5$

9. $y = -2x + 6$
$y = 3x - 9$

10. $y = 5x + 7$
$y = -3x + 7$

See Example 3

11. $x + y = 8$
$x + 3y = 14$

12. $x + y = 20$
$x = y - 4$

13. $2x + y = 12$
$3x - y = 13$

14. $4x - 3y = 33$
$x = -4y - 25$

15. $5x - 2y = 4$
$11x + 4y = -8$

16. $x = -3y$
$7x - 2y = -69$

INDEPENDENT PRACTICE

See Example 1 **Determine if the ordered pair is a solution of the system of equations.**

17. $(0, 1)$ $\quad y = -2x - 1$
$y = 2x + 1$

18. $(5, 11)$ $\quad y = 3x - 4$
$y = 2x + 1$

19. $(-1, 5)$ $\quad y = 4x + 1$
$y = 3x$

20. $(-6, -9)$ $\quad y = x - 3$
$y = 2x + 3$

See Example 2 **Solve each system of equations.**

21. $y = -x - 2$
$y = 3x + 2$

22. $y = 3x - 6$
$y = x + 2$

23. $y = -3x + 5$
$y = x - 3$

24. $y = 2x - 3$
$y = 4x - 3$

25. $y = x + 6$
$y = -2x - 12$

26. $y = 3x - 1$
$y = -2x + 9$

See Example 3

27. $x + y = 5$
$x - 2y = -4$

28. $x + 2y = 4$
$2x - y = 3$

29. $y = 5x - 2$
$4x + 3y = 13$

30. $2x + 3y = 1$
$4x - 3y = -7$

31. $5x - 9y = 11$
$3x + 7y = 19$

32. $12x + 18y = 30$
$4x - 13y = 67$

PRACTICE AND PROBLEM SOLVING

Solve each system of equations.

33. $y = 3x - 2$
$y = x + 2$

34. $y = 5x - 11$
$y = -2x + 10$

35. $x + y = -1$
$x - y = 5$

36. $y = 2x + 7$
$x + y = 4$

37. $4x - 3y = 0$
$-7x + 9y = 0$

38. $10x + 15y = 74$
$30x - 5y = -68$

39. $3x - y = 5$
$x - 4y = -2$

40. $x = 9y - 100$
$x = -5y + 54$

41. $2x + 6y = 1$
$4x - 3y = 0$

42. $3x - 4y = -5$
$x + 6y = 35$

43. $\frac{1}{3}x + \frac{1}{4}y = 6$
$-\frac{1}{2}x + y = 2$

44. $y = 2x - 2$
$y = -2$

45. $9.7x - 1.5y = 62.7$
$-2.3x - 7.4y = 8.4$

46. $-1.2x + 2.7y = 9.9$
$4.2x + 6.8y = 40.1$

47. $\frac{5}{6}x - 4y = -\frac{5}{2}$
$\frac{10}{3}x + \frac{1}{4}y = \frac{5}{6}$

The Metropolitan Opera House in New York has 6 levels and 3500 seats.

go.hrw.com
Web Extra!
KEYWORD: MP4 Music

Write and solve a system of equations for Exercises 48–50.

48. Two numbers have a sum of 23 and a difference of 9. Find the two numbers.

49. Two numbers have a sum of 18. The first number is 2 more than 3 times the second number. Find the two numbers.

50. Two numbers have a difference of 6. The first number is 9 more than 2 times the second number. Find the two numbers.

51. ***ENTERTAINMENT*** Tickets for a concert are \$40 for main-floor seats and \$25 for upper-level seats. A total of 2000 concert tickets were sold. The ticket sales were \$62,000. Let m represent the number of main-floor tickets and u the number of upper-level tickets.

a. Write an equation about the total number of tickets sold.

b. Write an equation about the total ticket sales.

c. Solve the system of equations to find how many main-floor tickets were sold and how many upper-level tickets were sold.

52. ***CHOOSE A STRATEGY*** Jan invested some money at 7% interest and \$500 more than that at 9% interest. The total interest earned in 1 year was \$141. How much did she invest at each rate?

A \$350 at 7%, \$850 at 9%
B \$800 at 7%, \$1300 at 9%
C \$575 at 7%, \$1075 at 9%
D \$600 at 7%, \$1100 at 9%

53. ***WRITE ABOUT IT*** List the steps you would use to solve the system of equations below. Explain which variable you would solve for and why.

$$x + 2y = 7$$
$$2x + y = 8$$

54. ***CHALLENGE*** Solve the following system of equations.

$$\frac{x-2}{4} + \frac{y+3}{8} = 1$$
$$\frac{2x-1}{12} + \frac{y+3}{6} = \frac{5}{4}$$

Spiral Review

Use the Fundamental Counting Principle to find the number of possible outcomes. (Lesson 9-5)

55. toppings: mayo, onion, lettuce, tomato
sandwich: burger, fish, chicken

56. stain: oak, redwood, pine, amber, rosewood
finish: glossy, matte, clear

57. distances: 50 m, 100 m, 400 m
races: freestyle, backstroke, butterfly

58. snacks: nachos, candy, hot dog, pizza
drinks: water, soda

59. **TEST PREP** If A and B are independent events such that $P(A) = 0.14$ and $P(B) = 0.28$, what is the probability that both A and B will occur? (Lesson 9-7)

A 0.42 **B** 0.24 **C** 0.0784 **D** 0.0392

Problem Solving on Location

North Carolina

The Blue Ridge Parkway

The 469-mile Blue Ridge Parkway is a recreational highway connecting Great Smoky Mountains National Park and Shenandoah National Park. The parkway's construction began in September 1935 and was finished in September 1987 with the completion of the 7.5-mile missing link. The completion of the missing link included the difficult construction of the Linn Cove Viaduct.

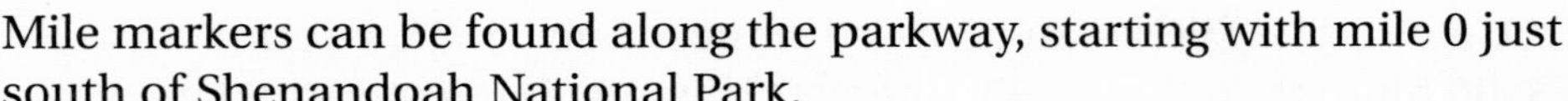

Mile markers can be found along the parkway, starting with mile 0 just south of Shenandoah National Park.

For 1–3, use the formula $d = rt$ (distance = rate × time) and the table.

1. A tourist drove from Cumberland Knob to the Linn Cove Viaduct in 2.5 hours. Solve the distance formula for r and then find the average rate (speed) to the nearest mile per hour that the tourist traveled.

2. The Perez family traveled from the Virginia–North Carolina state line to Brinegar Cabin at an average speed of 27 mi/h. In the same amount of time, the Lewis family traveled from Hare Mill Pond to Alligator Back parking overlook. At what speed in miles per hour did the Lewis family travel?

3. Solve the distance formula $d = rt$ for t, and then find the time it takes to travel at an average speed of 35 mi/h from Brinegar Cabin to the Daniel Boone Wilderness Trail.

Points of Interest Along the Blue Ridge Parkway

Mile Marker	Point of Interest
216.9	Virginia–North Carolina state line
217.5	Cumberland Knob
225.2	Hare Mill Pond
238.5	Brinegar Cabin
242.4	Alligator Back parking overlook
261.2	Horse Gap
285.1	Daniel Boone Wilderness Trail
304.4	Linn Cove Viaduct

ARE YOU READY?

Choose the best term from the list to complete each sentence.

1. The expression $4 - 3$ is an example of a(n) ___?___ expression.
2. When you divide both sides of the equation $2x = 20$ by 2, you are ___?___.
3. An example of a(n) ___?___ is $3x > 12$.
4. The expression $7 - 6$ can be rewritten as the ___?___ expression $7 + (-6)$.

addition
inequality in one variable
solving for the variable
subtraction

Complete these exercises to review skills you will need for this chapter.

✔ Operations with Integers

Simplify.

5. $\frac{7-5}{-2}$ **6.** $\frac{-3-5}{-2-3}$ **7.** $\frac{-8+2}{-2+8}$

8. $\frac{-16}{-2}$ **9.** $\frac{-22}{2}$ **10.** $-12 + 9$

✔ Equations

Solve.

11. $3p - 4 = 8$ **12.** $2(a + 3) = 4$ **13.** $9 = -2k + 27$

14. $3s - 4 = 1 - 3s$ **15.** $7x + 1 = x$ **16.** $4m - 5(m + 2) = 1$

Determine whether each ordered pair is a solution to $-\frac{1}{2}x + 3 = y$.

17. $(4, 1)$ **18.** $\left(-\frac{8}{2}, 2\right)$ **19.** $(0, 5)$ **20.** $(-4, 5)$

21. $(8, 1)$ **22.** $(2, 2)$ **23.** $(-2, 4)$ **24.** $(0, 1)$

✔ Solve for One Variable

Solve each equation for the indicated variable.

25. Solve for x: $5y - x = 4$. **26.** Solve for y: $3y + 9 = 2x$.

27. Solve for y: $2y + 3x = 6$. **28.** Solve for x: $ax + by = c$.

✔ Solve Inequalities in One Variable

Solve and graph each inequality.

29. $x + 4 > 2$ **30.** $-3x < 9$ **31.** $x - 1 \leq -5$

11-1 Graphing Linear Equations

Learn to identify and graph linear equations.

Vocabulary

linear equation

In most bowling leagues, bowlers have a handicap added to their scores to make the game more competitive. For some leagues, the *linear equation* $h = 160 - 0.8s$ expresses the handicap h of a bowler who has an average score of s.

A **linear equation** is an equation whose solutions fall on a line on the coordinate plane. All solutions of a particular linear equation fall on the line, and all the points on the line are solutions of the equation. To find a solution that lies between two points (x_1, y_1) and (x_2, y_2), choose an x-value between x_1 and x_2 and find the corresponding y-value.

Reading Math

Read x_1 as "x sub one" or "x one."

If an equation is linear, a constant change in the x-value corresponds to a constant change in the y-value. The graph shows an example where each time the x-value increases by 3, the y-value increases by 2.

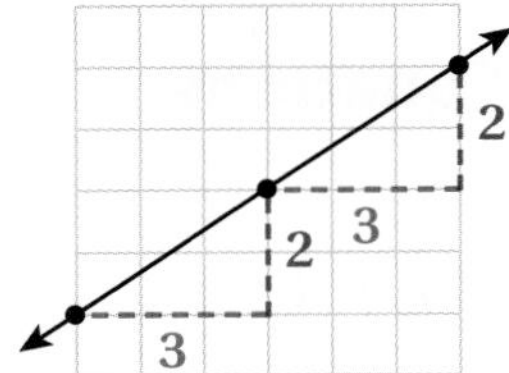

EXAMPLE 1 Graphing Equations

Graph each equation and tell whether it is linear.

A $y = 2x - 3$

x	$2x - 3$	y	(x, y)
−2	2(−2) − 3	−7	(−2, −7)
−1	2(−1) − 3	−5	(−1, −5)
0	2(0) − 3	−3	(0, −3)
1	2(1) − 3	−1	(1, −1)
2	2(2) − 3	1	(2, 1)
3	2(3) − 3	3	(3, 3)

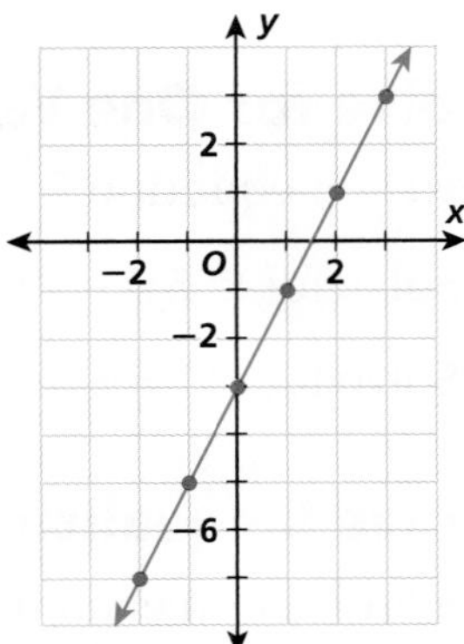

The equation $y = 2x - 3$ is a linear equation because it is the graph of a straight line and each time x increases by 1 unit, y increases by 2 units.

Graph each equation and tell whether it is linear.

B $y = x^2$

x	x^2	y	(x, y)
−2	$(-2)^2$	4	(−2, 4)
−1	$(-1)^2$	1	(−1, 1)
0	$(0)^2$	0	(0, 0)
1	$(1)^2$	1	(1, 1)
2	$(2)^2$	4	(2, 4)

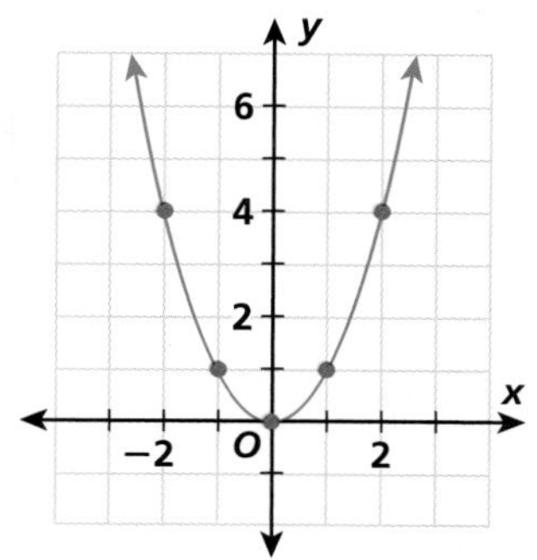

The equation $y = x^2$ is not a linear equation because its graph is not a straight line. Also notice that as x increases by a constant of 1, the change in y is not constant.

x	−2	−1	0	1	2
y	4	1	0	1	4

−3 −1 +1 +3

C $y = \frac{2x}{3}$

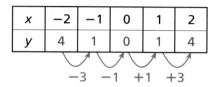

x	$\frac{2x}{3}$	y	(x, y)
−2	$\frac{2(-2)}{3}$	$-\frac{4}{3}$	$(-2, -\frac{4}{3})$
−1	$\frac{2(-1)}{3}$	$-\frac{2}{3}$	$(-1, -\frac{2}{3})$
0	$\frac{2(0)}{3}$	0	(0, 0)
1	$\frac{2(1)}{3}$	$\frac{2}{3}$	$(1, \frac{2}{3})$
2	$\frac{2(2)}{3}$	$\frac{4}{3}$	$(2, \frac{4}{3})$

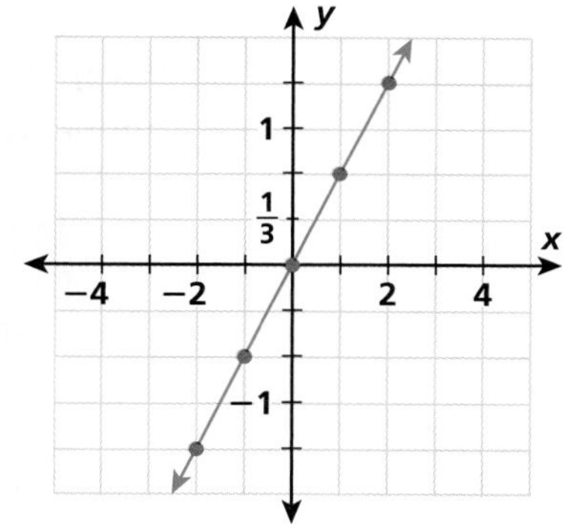

The equation $y = \frac{2x}{3}$ is a linear equation because the points form a straight line. Each time the value of x increases by 1, the value of y increases by $\frac{2}{3}$, or y increases by 2 each time x increases by 3.

D $y = -3$

x	−3	y	(x, y)
−2	−3	−3	(−2, −3)
−1	−3	−3	(−1, −3)
0	−3	−3	(0, −3)
1	−3	−3	(1, −3)
2	−3	−3	(2, −3)

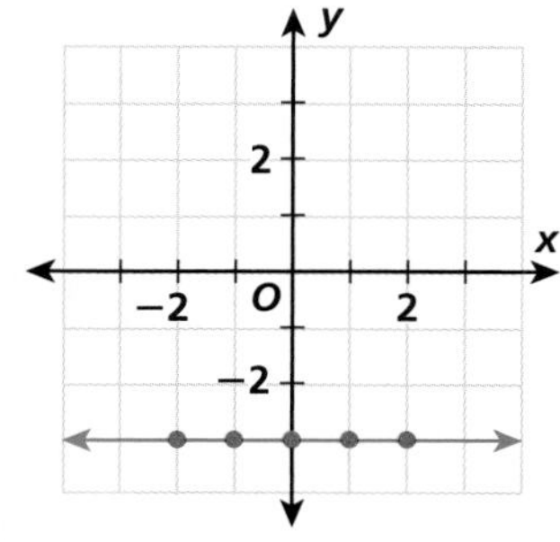

For any value of x, y = −3.

The equation $y = -3$ is a linear equation because the points form a straight line. As the value of x increases, the value of y has a constant change of 0.

EXAMPLE 2 *Sports Application*

In bowling, the equation $h = 160 - 0.8s$ represents the handicap h calculated for a bowler with average score s. How much will the handicap be for each bowler listed in the table? Draw a graph that represents the relationship between the average score and the handicap.

Bowler	Average Score
Sandi	145
Dominic	125
Leo	160
Sheila	140
Tawana	175

s	$h = 160 - 0.8s$	h	(s, h)
145	$h = 160 - 0.8(145)$	44	(145, 44)
125	$h = 160 - 0.8(125)$	60	(125, 60)
160	$h = 160 - 0.8(160)$	32	(160, 32)
140	$h = 160 - 0.8(140)$	48	(140, 48)
175	$h = 160 - 0.8(175)$	20	(175, 20)

The handicaps are: Sandi, 44 pins; Dominic, 60 pins; Leo, 32 pins; Sheila, 48 pins; and Tawana, 20 pins. This is a linear equation because when s increases by 10 units, h decreases by 8 units. Note that a bowler with an average score of over 200 is given a handicap of 0.

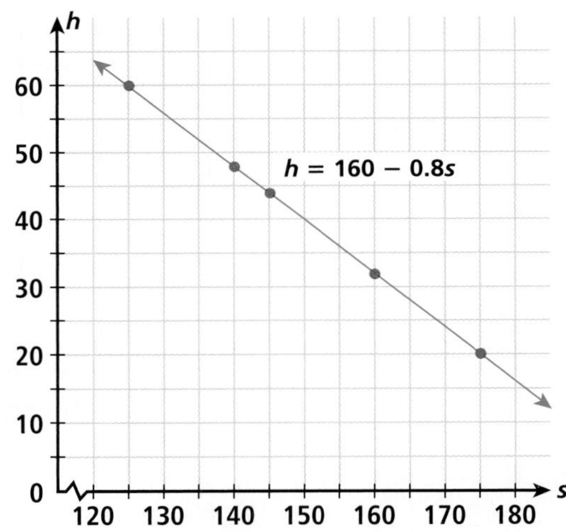

Think and Discuss

1. Explain whether an equation is linear if three ordered-pair solutions lie on a straight line but a fourth does not.

2. Compare the equations $y = 3x + 2$ and $y = 3x^2$. Without graphing, explain why one of the equations is not linear.

3. Describe why the ordered pair for a bowler with an average score of 210 would not fall on the line in Example 2.

11-1 Exercises

FOR EXTRA PRACTICE
see page 752

internet connect
Homework Help Online
go.hrw.com Keyword: MP4 11-1

GUIDED PRACTICE

See Example 1

Graph each equation and tell whether it is linear.

1. $y = x + 2$ **2.** $y = -2x$ **3.** $y = x^3$

See Example 2

4. Kelp is one of the fastest-growing plants in the world. It grows about 2 ft every day. If you found a kelp plant that was 124 ft long, the equation $\ell = 2d + 124$ would represent the length ℓ of the plant d days later. How long would the plant be after 3 days? after 4.5 days? after 6 days? Graph the equation. Is this a linear equation?

INDEPENDENT PRACTICE

See Example 1

Graph each equation and tell whether it is linear.

5. $y = \frac{1}{3}x - 2$ **6.** $y = -6$ **7.** $y = \frac{1}{2}x^2$

8. $x = 3$ **9.** $y = x^2 - 12$ **10.** $y = 2x + 1$

See Example 2

11. A catering service charges a $150 setup fee plus $7.50 for each guest at a reception. This is represented by the equation $C = 7.5g + 150$, where C is the total cost based on g guests. Find the total cost of catering for the following numbers of guests: 100, 150, 200, 250, 300. Is this a linear equation? Draw a graph that represents the relationship between the total cost and the number of guests.

PRACTICE AND PROBLEM SOLVING

Evaluate each equation for $x = -1$, 0, and 1. Then graph the equation.

12. $y = 4x$ **13.** $y = 2x + 5$ **14.** $y = 6x - 3$

15. $y = x - 10$ **16.** $y = 4x - 2$ **17.** $y = 4x + 3$

18. $y = 2x - 4$ **19.** $y = x + 7$ **20.** $y = 3x + 2.5$

21. ***PHYSICAL SCIENCE*** The force exerted on an object by Earth's gravity is given by the formula $F = 9.8m$, where F is the force in newtons and m is the mass of the object in kilograms. How many newtons of gravitational force are exerted on a student with mass 52 kg?

22. At a rate of $0.08 per kilowatt-hour, the equation $C = 0.08t$ gives the cost of a customer's electric bill for using t kilowatt-hours of energy. Complete the table of values and graph the energy cost equation for t ranging from 0 to 1000.

Kilowatt-hours (t)	540	580	620	660	700	740
Cost in Dollars (C)						

23. The minute hand of a clock moves $\frac{1}{10}$ degree every second. If you look at the clock when the minute hand is 10 degrees past the 12, you can use the equation $y = \frac{1}{10}x + 10$ to find how many degrees past the 12 the minute hand is after x seconds. Graph the equation and tell whether it is linear.

24. ***ENTERTAINMENT*** A bowling alley charges $4 for shoe rental plus $1.75 per game bowled. Write an equation that shows the total cost of bowling g games. Graph the equation. Is it linear?

25. ***BUSINESS*** A car wash pays d dollars an hour. The table shows how much employees make based on the number of hours they work.

Car Wash Wages				
Hours Worked (*h*)	20	25	30	40
Earnings (*E*)	$150.00	$187.50	$225.00	$300.00

a. Write and solve an equation to find the hourly wage.

b. Write an equation that gives an employee's earnings E for h hours of work.

c. Graph the equation for h between 0 and 50 hours.

d. Is the equation linear?

26. ***WHAT'S THE QUESTION?*** The equation $C = 9.5n + 1350$ gives the total cost of producing n trailer hitches. If the answer is $10,850, what is the question?

27. ***WRITE ABOUT IT*** Explain how you could show that $y = 5x + 1$ is a linear equation.

28. ***CHALLENGE*** Three solutions of an equation are (1, 1), (3, 3), and (5, 5). Draw one possible graph that would show that the equation is not a linear equation.

Spiral Review

Two fair dice are rolled. Find each probability. (Lessons 9-4 and 9-7)

29. rolling two odd numbers

30. rolling a two and a prime number

31. rolling a pair of ones

32. rolling a six and a seven

33. **TEST PREP** The probability of winning a raffle is $\frac{1}{1200}$. What are the odds in favor of winning the raffle? (Lesson 9-8)

A 1:1200

B 1:1199

C 1199:1

D 1200:1

34. **TEST PREP** A bag of 9 marbles has 3 red marbles and 6 blue marbles in it. What is the probability of drawing a red marble? (Lesson 9-4)

F 1

G $\frac{2}{3}$

H $\frac{1}{3}$

J $\frac{1}{2}$

11-2 Slope of a Line

Learn to find the slope of a line and use slope to understand and draw graphs.

Remember!

You looked at slope on the coordinate plane in Lesson 5-5 (p. 244).

In skiing, the term *slope* refers to a slanted mountainside. The steeper a slope is, the higher its difficulty rating will be. In math, slope defines the "slant" of a line. The larger the absolute value of the slope of a line is, the "steeper," or more vertical, the line will be.

Linear equations have constant slope.
For a line on the coordinate plane, slope is the following ratio:

$$\frac{\text{vertical change}}{\text{horizontal change}} = \frac{\text{change in } y}{\text{change in } x}$$

This ratio is often referred to as $\frac{\text{rise}}{\text{run}}$, or "rise over run," where *rise* indicates the number of units moved up or down and *run* indicates the number of units moved to the left or right. Slope can be positive, negative, zero, or undefined. A line with positive slope goes up from left to right. A line with negative slope goes down from left to right.

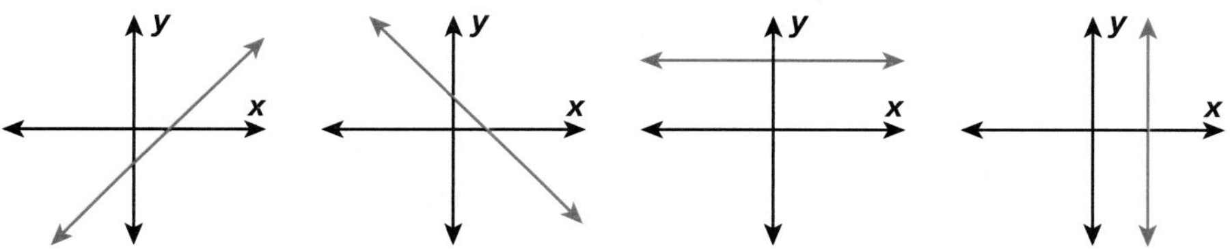

Positive slope **Negative slope** **Zero slope** **Undefined slope**

If you know any two points on a line, or two solutions of a linear equation, you can find the slope of the line without graphing.
The slope of a line through the points (x_1, y_1) and (x_2, y_2) is as follows:

$$\frac{y_2 - y_1}{x_2 - x_1}$$

EXAMPLE 1 Finding Slope, Given Two Points

Find the slope of the line that passes through (2, 5) and (8, 1).

Let (x_1, y_1) be (2, 5) and (x_2, y_2) be (8, 1).

$$\frac{y_2 - y_1}{x_2 - x_1} = \frac{1 - 5}{8 - 2}$$ *Substitute 1 for y_2, 5 for y_1, 8 for x_2, and 2 for x_1.*

$$= \frac{-4}{6} = -\frac{2}{3}$$

The slope of the line that passes through (2, 5) and (8, 1) is $-\frac{2}{3}$.

When choosing two points to evaluate the slope of a line, you can choose any two points on the line because slope is constant.

Below are two graphs of the same line.

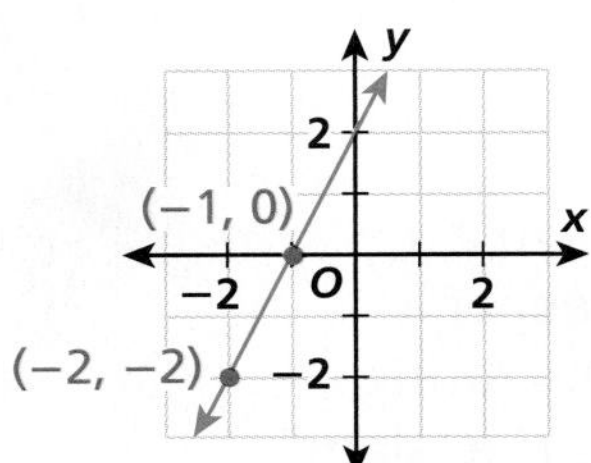

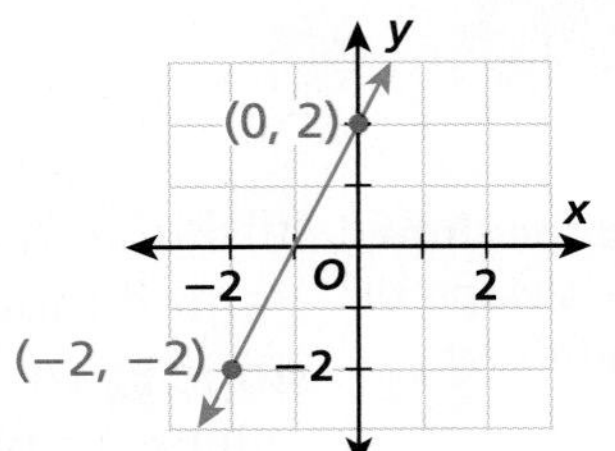

$$\frac{y_2 - y_1}{x_2 - x_1} = \frac{0 - (-2)}{-1 - (-2)} = \frac{2}{1} = 2$$

$$\frac{y_2 - y_1}{x_2 - x_1} = \frac{2 - (-2)}{0 - (-2)} = \frac{4}{2} = \frac{2}{1} = 2$$

The slope of the line is 2. Notice that although different points were chosen in each case, the slope formula still results in the same slope for the line.

EXAMPLE 2 Finding Slope from a Graph

Use the graph of the line to determine its slope.

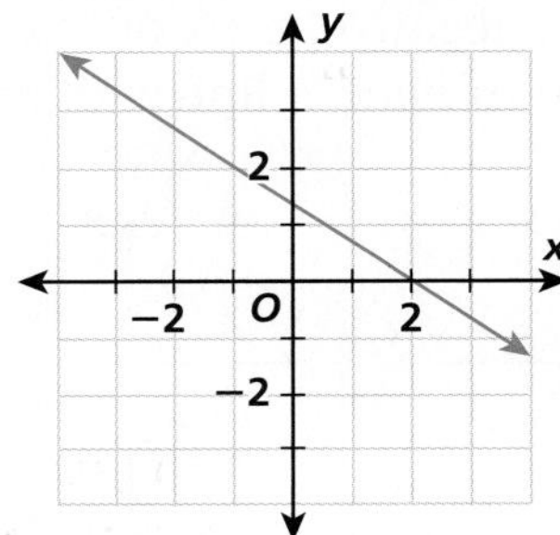

Choose two points on the line: $(-1, 2)$ and $(2, 0)$.

Guess by looking at the graph:

$$\frac{\text{rise}}{\text{run}} = \frac{-2}{3} = -\frac{2}{3}$$

Use the slope formula.

Let $(2, 0)$ be (x_1, y_1) and $(-1, 2)$ be (x_2, y_2).

$$\frac{y_2 - y_1}{x_2 - x_1} = \frac{2 - 0}{-1 - 2} = \frac{2}{-3} = -\frac{2}{3}$$

Notice that if you switch (x_1, y_1) and (x_2, y_2), you get the same slope:

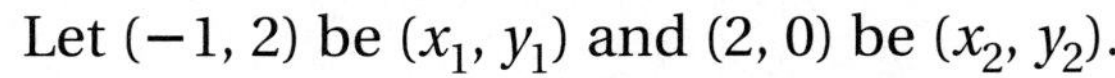

Let $(-1, 2)$ be (x_1, y_1) and $(2, 0)$ be (x_2, y_2).

$$\frac{y_2 - y_1}{x_2 - x_1} = \frac{0 - 2}{2 - (-1)} = \frac{-2}{3} = -\frac{2}{3}$$

The slope of the given line is $-\frac{2}{3}$.

Helpful Hint

It does not matter which point is chosen as (x_1, y_1) and which point is chosen as (x_2, y_2).

Recall that two parallel lines have the same slope. The slopes of two perpendicular lines are negative reciprocals of each other.

EXAMPLE 3 Identifying Parallel and Perpendicular Lines by Slope

Tell whether the lines passing through the given points are parallel or perpendicular.

A line 1: (1, 9) and (−1, 5); line 2: (−3, −5) and (4, 9)

$$\text{slope of line 1: } \frac{y_2 - y_1}{x_2 - x_1} = \frac{5 - 9}{-1 - 1} = \frac{-4}{-2} = 2$$

$$\text{slope of line 2: } \frac{y_2 - y_1}{x_2 - x_1} = \frac{9 - (-5)}{4 - (-3)} = \frac{14}{7} = 2$$

Both lines have a slope equal to 2, so the lines are parallel.

Remember!

The product of the slopes of perpendicular lines is −1.

B line 1: (−10, 0) and (20, 6); line 2: (−1, 4) and (2, −11)

$$\text{slope of line 1: } \frac{y_2 - y_1}{x_2 - x_1} = \frac{6 - 0}{20 - (-10)} = \frac{6}{30} = \frac{1}{5}$$

$$\text{slope of line 2: } \frac{y_2 - y_1}{x_2 - x_1} = \frac{-11 - 4}{2 - (-1)} = \frac{-15}{3} = -5$$

Line 1 has a slope equal to $\frac{1}{5}$ and line 2 has a slope equal to −5. $\frac{1}{5}$ and −5 are negative reciprocals of each other, so the lines are perpendicular.

You can graph a line if you know one point on the line and the slope.

EXAMPLE 4 Graphing a Line Using a Point and the Slope

Graph the line passing through (1, 1) with slope $-\frac{1}{3}$.

The slope is $-\frac{1}{3}$. So for every 1 unit down, you will move 3 units to the right, and for every 1 unit up, you will move 3 units to the left.

Plot the point (1, 1). Then move 1 unit down, and right 3 units and plot the point (4, 0). Use a straightedge to connect the two points.

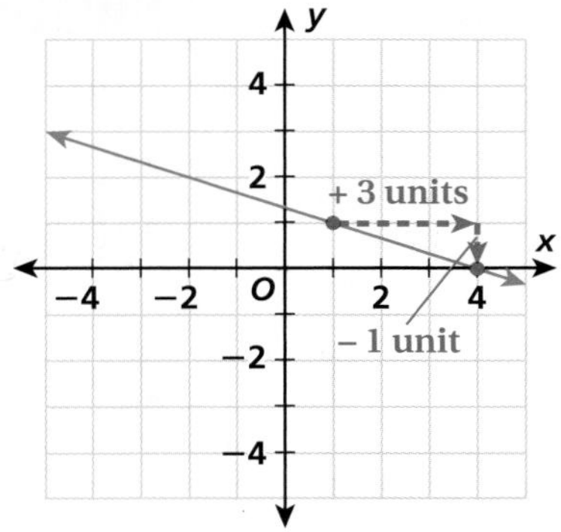

Think and Discuss

1. **Explain** why it does not matter which point you choose as (x_1, y_1) and which point you choose as (x_2, y_2) when finding slope.
2. **Give an example** of two pairs of points from each of two parallel lines.

11-2 Exercises

FOR EXTRA PRACTICE

see page 752

internet connect

Homework Help Online

go.hrw.com Keyword: MP4 11-2

GUIDED PRACTICE

See Example 1 Find the slope of the line that passes through each pair of points.

1. (1, 3) and (2, 4) **2.** (2, 6) and (0, 2) **3.** (−1, 2) and (5, 5)

See Example 2 Use the graph of each line to determine its slope.

4.

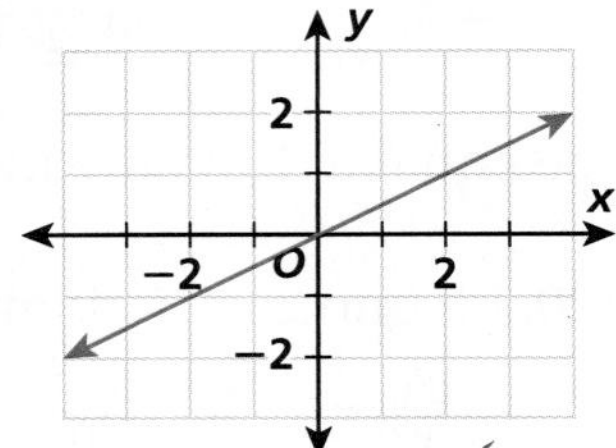

5.

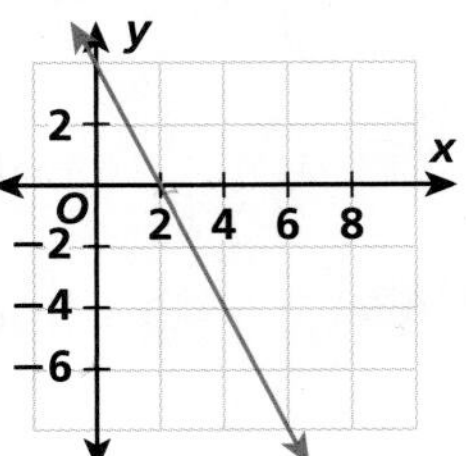

See Example 3 Tell whether the lines passing through the given points are parallel or perpendicular.

6. line 1: (2, 3) and (4, 7)
line 2: (5, 2) and (9, 0)

7. line 1: (−4, 1) and (0, 29)
line 2: (3, 3) and (5, 17)

See Example 4

8. Graph the line passing through (0, 2) with slope $-\frac{1}{2}$.

9. Graph the line passing through (−2, 0) with slope $\frac{2}{3}$.

INDEPENDENT PRACTICE

See Example 1 Find the slope of the line that passes through each pair of points.

10. (−1, −1) and (−3, 2) **11.** (0, 0) and (6, −3) **12.** (2, −5) and (1, −2)

13. (3, 1) and (0, 3) **14.** (−2, −3) and (2, 4) **15.** (0, −2) and (−6, 3)

See Example 2 Use the graph of each line to determine its slope.

16.

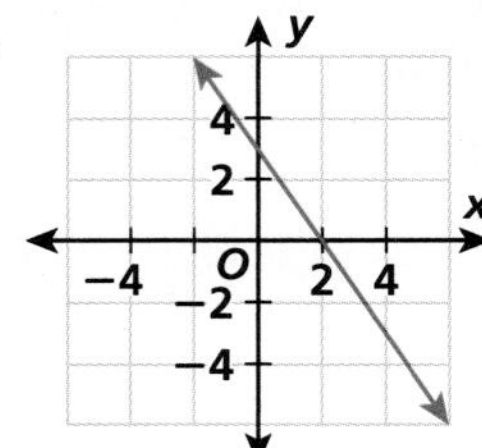

17.

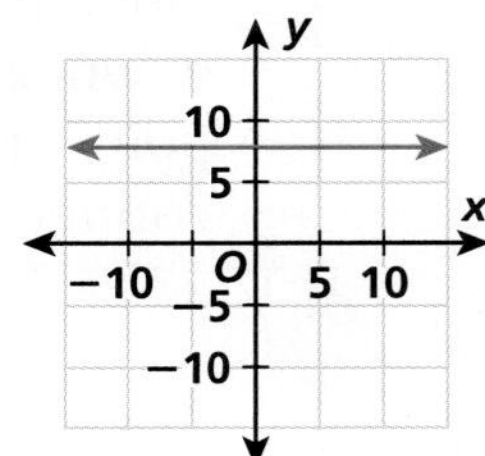

See Example 3 Tell whether the lines passing through the given points are parallel or perpendicular.

18. line 1: (1, 4) and (6, 6)
line 2: (−1, −6) and (4, −4)

19. line 1: (−1, −1) and (−3, 2)
line 2: (7, −3) and (13, 1)

See Example 4

20. Graph the line passing through (−1, 3) with slope $\frac{1}{4}$.

21. Graph the line passing through (4, 2) with slope $-\frac{4}{5}$.

PRACTICE AND PROBLEM SOLVING

22. ***SAFETY*** To accommodate a 2.5 foot vertical rise, a wheelchair ramp extends horizontally for 30 feet. Find the slope of the ramp.

For Exercises 23–26, find the slopes of each pair of lines. Use the slopes to determine whether the lines are perpendicular, parallel, or neither.

23. 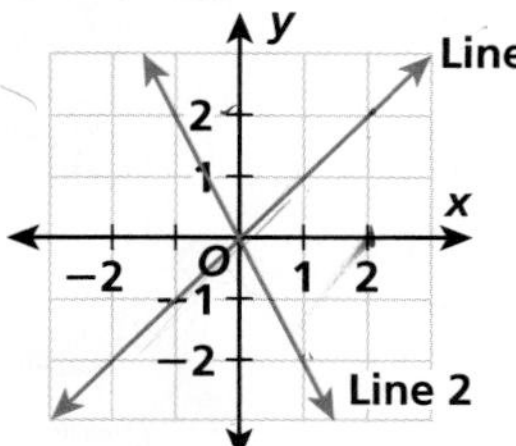

24. 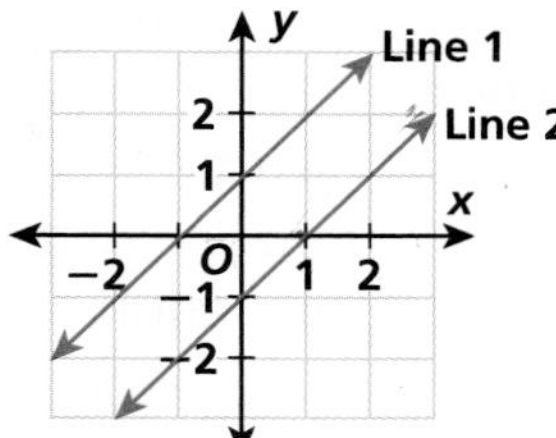

25. 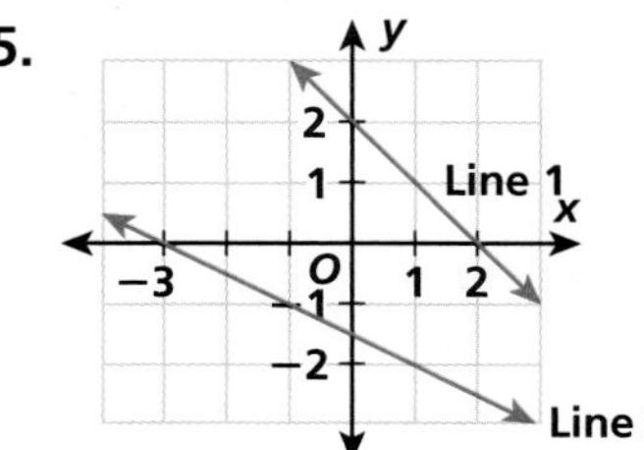

26. 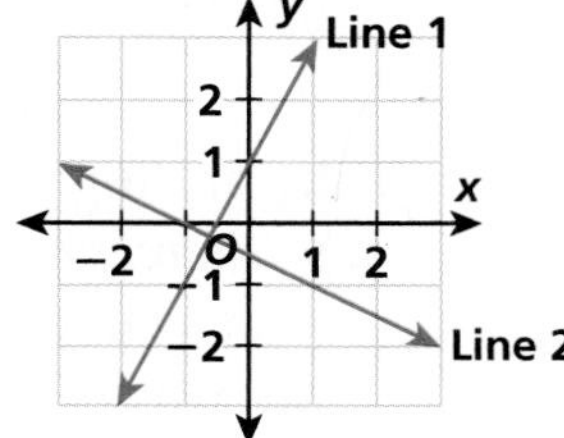

27. The Luxor Hotel in Las Vegas, Nevada, has a 350 ft tall glass pyramid. The elevator of the pyramid moves at an incline, which has a slope of $-\frac{4}{5}$. Graph the line that describes the path it travels along. (*Hint:* The point (0, 350) is the top of the pyramid.)

28. ***WHAT'S THE ERROR?*** The slope of the line through the points (1, 4) and (−1, −4) is $\frac{1-(-1)}{4-(-4)} = \frac{1}{4}$. What is the error in this statement?

29. ***WRITE ABOUT IT*** The equation of a vertical line is $x = a$ where a is any number. Explain why the slope of a vertical line is undefined, using a specific vertical line.

30. ***CHALLENGE*** Graph the equations $y = 2x - 3$, $y = -\frac{1}{2}x$ and $y = 2x + 4$ on one coordinate plane. Find the slope of each line and determine whether each combination of two lines is parallel, perpendicular, or neither. Explain how to tell whether two lines are parallel, perpendicular, or neither by their equations.

Spiral Review

Find the area of each figure with the given dimensions. (Lesson 6-2)

31. triangle: $b = 4$, $h = 6$

32. triangle: $b = 3$, $h = 14$

33. trapezoid: $b_1 = 9$, $b_2 = 11$, $h = 12$

34. trapezoid: $b_1 = 3.4$, $b_2 = 6.6$, $h = 1.8$

35. **TEST PREP** A circular flower bed has radius 22 in. What is the circumference of the bed to the nearest tenth of an inch? Use 3.14 for π. (Lesson 6-4)

A 1519.8 in. **B** 69.1 in. **C** 103.7 in. **D** 138.2 in.

11-3 Using Slopes and Intercepts

Learn to use slopes and intercepts to graph linear equations.

Vocabulary

x-intercept

y-intercept

slope-intercept form

At an arcade, you buy a game card with 50 credit points on it. Each game of Skittle-ball reduces the number of points on your card by 3.5 points. The linear equation $y = -3.5x + 50$ relates the number of points y remaining on your card to the number of games x that you have played.

You can graph a linear equation easily by finding the *x-intercept* and the *y-intercept*. The **x-intercept** of a line is the value of x where the line crosses the x-axis (where $y = 0$). The **y-intercept** of a line is the value of y where the line crosses the y-axis (where $x = 0$).

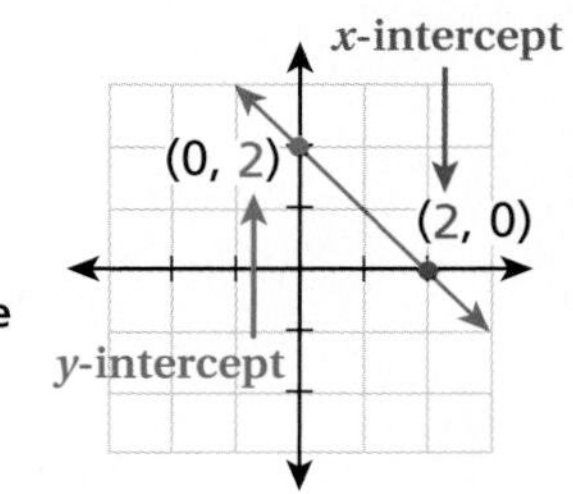

Graph of the line $y = -x + 2$

EXAMPLE 1 Finding x-intercepts and y-intercepts to Graph Linear Equations

Find the x-intercept and y-intercept of the line $2x + 3y = 6$. Use the intercepts to graph the equation.

Find the x-intercept ($y = 0$).

$$2x + 3y = 6$$
$$2x + 3(0) = 6$$
$$2x = 6$$
$$\frac{2x}{2} = \frac{6}{2}$$
$$x = 3$$

The x-intercept is 3.

Find the y-intercept ($x = 0$).

$$2x + 3y = 6$$
$$2(0) + 3y = 6$$
$$3y = 6$$
$$\frac{3y}{3} = \frac{6}{3}$$
$$y = 2$$

The y-intercept is 2.

The graph of $2x + 3y = 6$ is the line that crosses the x-axis at the point (3, 0) and the y-axis at the point (0, 2).

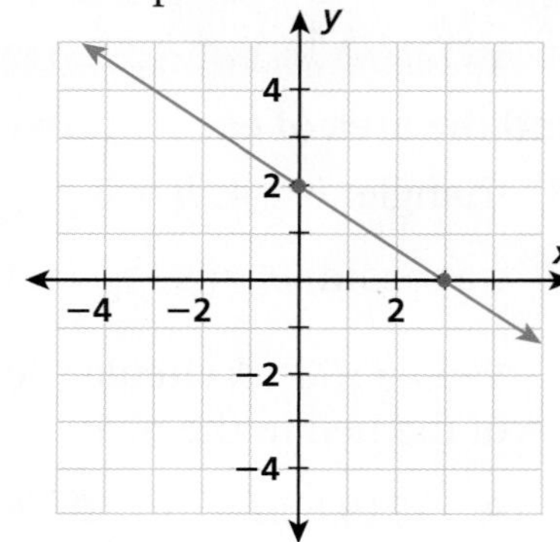

In an equation written in **slope-intercept form**, $y = mx + b$, m is the slope and b is the y-intercept.

EXAMPLE 2 Using Slope-Intercept Form to Find Slopes and y-intercepts

Helpful Hint

For an equation such as $y = x - 6$, write it as $y = x + (-6)$ to read the y-intercept, -6.

Write each equation in slope-intercept form, and then find the slope and y-intercept.

A $y = x$

$y = x$

$y = 1x + 0$ *Rewrite the equation to show each part.*

$m = 1$ $b = 0$

The slope of the line $y = x$ is 1, and the y-intercept of the line is 0.

B $7x = 3y$

$7x = 3y$

$3y = 7x$ *Reverse the expressions.*

$\frac{3y}{3} = \frac{7x}{3}$ *Divide both sides by 3 to solve for y.*

$y = \frac{7}{3}x + 0$ *The equation is in slope-intercept form.*

$m = \frac{7}{3}$ $b = 0$

The slope of the line $7x = 3y$ is $\frac{7}{3}$, and the y-intercept is 0.

C $2x + 5y = 8$

$2x + 5y = 8$

$\underline{-2x \qquad\quad -2x}$ *Subtract 2x from both sides.*

$5y = 8 - 2x$

Rewrite to match slope-intercept form.

$5y = -2x + 8$

$\frac{5y}{5} = \frac{-2x}{5} + \frac{8}{5}$ *Divide both sides by 5.*

$y = -\frac{2}{5}x + \frac{8}{5}$ *The equation is in slope-intercept form.*

$m = -\frac{2}{5}$ $b = \frac{8}{5}$

The slope of the line $2x + 5y = 8$ is $-\frac{2}{5}$, and the y-intercept is $\frac{8}{5}$.

EXAMPLE 3 *Entertainment Application*

Helpful Hint

The y-intercept represents the initial number of points (50). The slope represents the rate of change (−3.5 points per game).

An arcade deducts 3.5 points from your 50-point game card for each Skittle-ball game you play. The linear equation $y = -3.5x + 50$ represents the number of points y on your card after x games. Graph the equation using the slope and y-intercept.

$y = -3.5x + 50$ *The equation is in slope-intercept form.*

$m = -3.5 \qquad b = 50$

The slope of the line is −3.5, and the y-intercept is 50. The line crosses the y-axis at the point (0, 50) and moves down 3.5 units for every 1 unit it moves to the right.

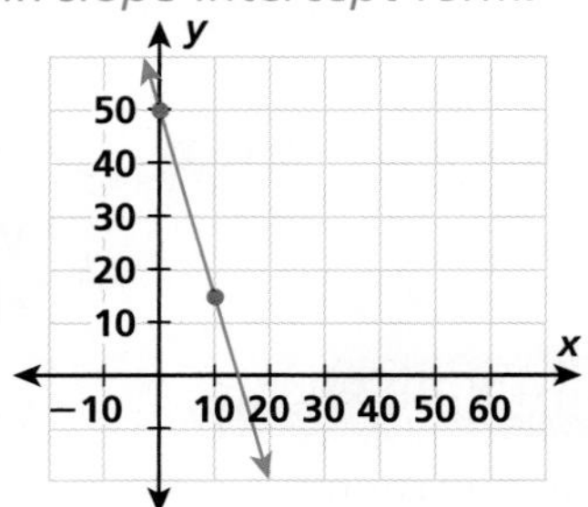

EXAMPLE 4 Writing Slope-Intercept Form

Write the equation of the line that passes through (−3, 1) and (2, −1) in slope-intercept form.

Find the slope.

$$\frac{y_2 - y_1}{x_2 - x_1} = \frac{-1 - 1}{2-(-3)} = \frac{-2}{5} = -\frac{2}{5}$$ *The slope is $-\frac{2}{5}$.*

Choose either point and substitute it along with the slope into the slope-intercept form.

$$y = mx + b$$

$$-1 = -\frac{2}{5}(2) + b$$ *Substitute 2 for x, −1 for y, and $-\frac{2}{5}$ for m.*

$$-1 = -\frac{4}{5} + b$$ *Simplify.*

Solve for b.

$$-1 = -\frac{4}{5} + b$$

$$\underline{+\frac{4}{5} \qquad +\frac{4}{5}}$$ *Add $\frac{4}{5}$ to both sides.*

$$-\frac{1}{5} = b$$

Write the equation of the line, using $-\frac{2}{5}$ for m and $-\frac{1}{5}$ for b.

$$y = -\frac{2}{5}x + \left(-\frac{1}{5}\right), \text{ or } y = -\frac{2}{5}x - \frac{1}{5}$$

Think and Discuss

1. **Describe** the line represented by the equation $y = -5x + 3$.
2. **Give** a real-life example with a graph that has a slope of 5 and a y-intercept of 30.

11-3 Exercises

FOR EXTRA PRACTICE
see page 752

internet connect
Homework Help Online
go.hrw.com Keyword: MP4 11-3

GUIDED PRACTICE

See Example 1

Find the x-intercept and y-intercept of each line. Use the intercepts to graph the equation.

1. $x - y = 5$ **2.** $2x + 3y = 12$ **3.** $3x + 5y = -15$ **4.** $-5x + 2y = -10$

See Example 2

Write each equation in slope-intercept form, and then find the slope and y-intercept.

5. $2x = 4y$ **6.** $3x - y = 14$ **7.** $3x - 9y = 27$ **8.** $x + 2y = 8$

See Example 3

9. A freight company charges \$22 plus \$3.50 per pound to ship an item that weighs n pounds. The total shipping charges are given by the equation $C = 3.5n + 22$. Identify the slope and y-intercept, and use them to graph the equation for n between 0 and 100 pounds.

See Example 4

Write the equation of the line that passes through each pair of points in slope-intercept form.

10. $(-1, -6)$ and $(2, 6)$ **11.** $(0, 5)$ and $(3, -1)$ **12.** $(3, 5)$ and $(6, 6)$

INDEPENDENT PRACTICE

See Example 1

Find the x-intercept and y-intercept of each line. Use the intercepts to graph the equation.

13. $2y = 20 - 4x$ **14.** $4x = 12 + 3y$ **15.** $-y = 18 - 6x$ **16.** $2x + y = 7$

See Example 2

Write each equation in slope-intercept form, and then find the slope and y-intercept.

17. $-y = 2x$ **18.** $5y + 2x = 15$ **19.** $-4y - 8x = 8$ **20.** $2y + 6x = -14$

See Example 3

21. A salesperson receives a weekly salary of \$300 plus a commission of \$15 for each TV sold. Total weekly pay is given by the equation $P = 15n + 300$. Identify the slope and y-intercept, and use them to graph the equation for n between 0 and 40 TVs.

See Example 4

Write the equation of the line that passes through each pair of points in slope-intercept form.

22. $(0, -7)$ and $(4, 25)$ **23.** $(-1, 1)$ and $(3, -3)$ **24.** $(-6, -3)$ and $(12, 0)$

PRACTICE AND PROBLEM SOLVING

Use the x-intercept and y-intercept of each line to graph the equation.

25. $y = 2x - 10$ **26.** $y = \frac{1}{3}x + 2$ **27.** $y = 4x - 2.5$ **28.** $y = -\frac{4}{5}x + 15$

Life Science LINK

Often people will get sick at high altitudes because there is less oxygen and lower atmospheric pressure.

Acute Mountain Sickness (AMS) occurs if you ascend in altitude too quickly without giving your body time to adjust. It usually occurs at altitudes over 10,000 feet above sea level. To prevent AMS you should not ascend more than 1000 feet per day. And every time you climb a total of 3000 feet, your body needs two nights to adjust.

29. The map shows a team's plan for climbing Long's Peak in Rocky Mountain National Park.

a. Make a graph of the team's plan of ascent and find the slope of the line. (Day number should be your x-value, and altitude should be your y-value.)

b. Find the y-intercept and explain what it means.

c. Write the equation of the line in slope-intercept form.

d. Does the team run a high risk of getting AMS?

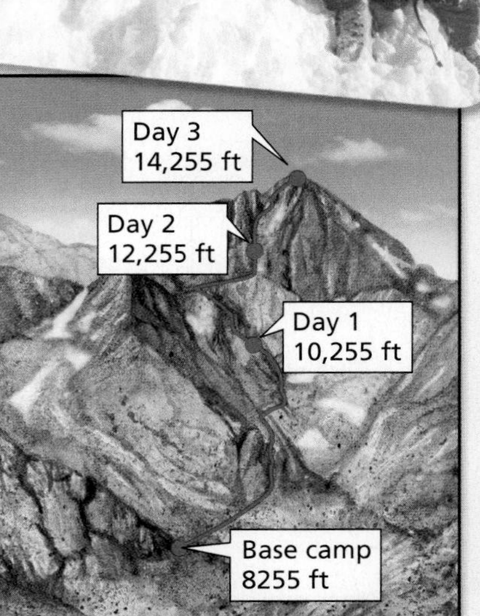

30. An expedition starts at an altitude of 9056 ft and climbs at an average rate of 544 ft of elevation a day. Write an equation in slope-intercept form that describes the expedition's climb. Are the climbers likely to suffer from AMS at their present climbing rate? On what day of their climb will they be at risk?

31. The equation that describes a mountain climber's ascent up Mount McKinley in Alaska is $y = 955x + 16{,}500$, where x is the day number and y is the altitude at the end of the day. What are the slope and y-intercept? What do they mean in terms of the climb?

32. ***CHALLENGE*** Make a graph of the ascent of a team that follows the rules to avoid AMS exactly and spends the minimum number of days climbing from base camp (17,600 ft) to the summit of Mount Everest (29,035 ft). Can you write a linear equation describing this trip? Explain your answer.

Spiral Review

Estimate the number or percent. (Lesson 8-5)

33. 25% of 398 is about what number?

34. 202 is about 50% of what number?

35. About what percent of 99 is 39?

36. About what percent of 989 is 746?

37. **TEST PREP** Carlos has $3.35 in dimes and quarters. If he has a total of 23 coins, how many dimes does he have? (Lesson 10-6)

A 16 **B** 11 **C** 18 **D** 9

Graph Equations in Slope-Intercept Form

Use with Lesson 11-4

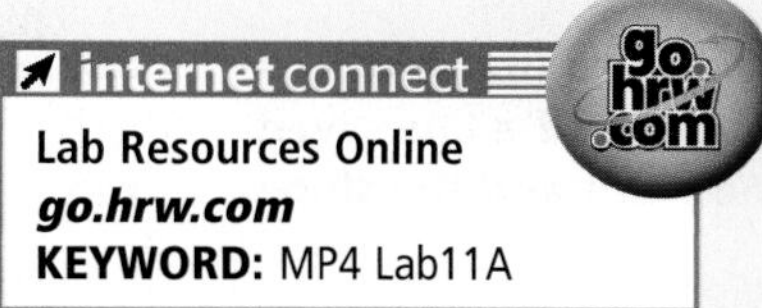

To graph $y = x + 1$, a linear equation in slope-intercept form, in the standard graphing calculator window, press Y= ; enter the right side of the equation, X,T,θ,n + 1; and press ZOOM **6:ZStandard.**

From the slope-intercept equation, you know that the slope of the line is 1. Notice that the standard window distorts the screen, and the line does not appear to have a great enough slope.

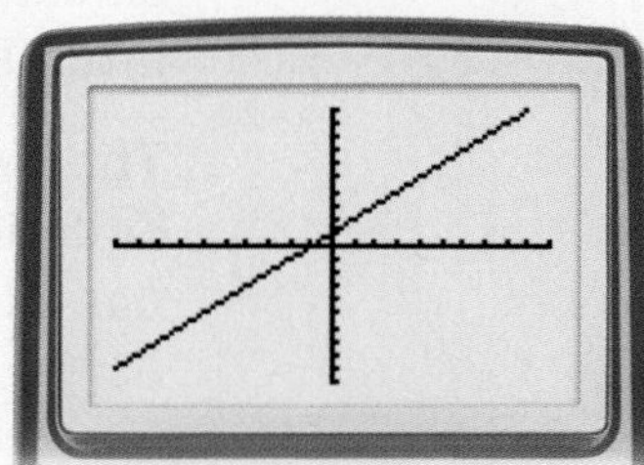

Press ZOOM **5:ZSquare**. This changes the scale for x from -10 to 10 to -15.16 to 15.16. The graph is shown at right. Or press ZOOM **8:ZInteger** ENTER . This changes the scale for x to -47 to 47 and the scale for y to -31 to 31.

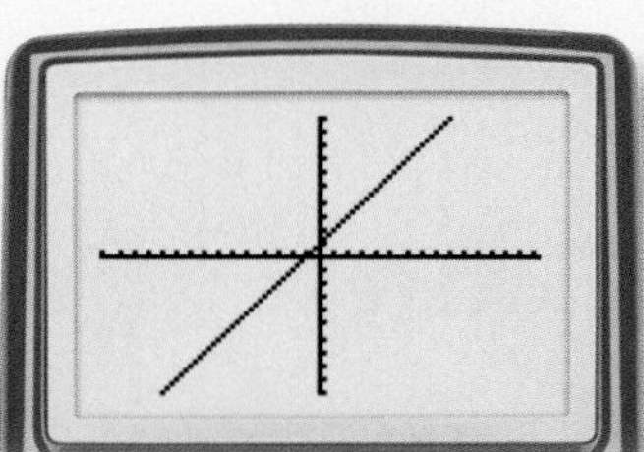

Activity

1. Graph $2x + 3y = 36$ in the integer window. Find the x- and y-intercepts of the graph.

   First solve $3y = -2x + 36$ for y.

   $y = \frac{-2x + 36}{3}$, so $y = \frac{-2}{3}x + 12$.

   Press Y= ; enter the right side of the equation, ((–) 2 ÷ 3) X,T,θ,n + 12; and press ZOOM **8:ZInteger** ENTER .

   Press TRACE to see the equation of the line and the y-intercept. The graph in the **ZInteger** window is shown.

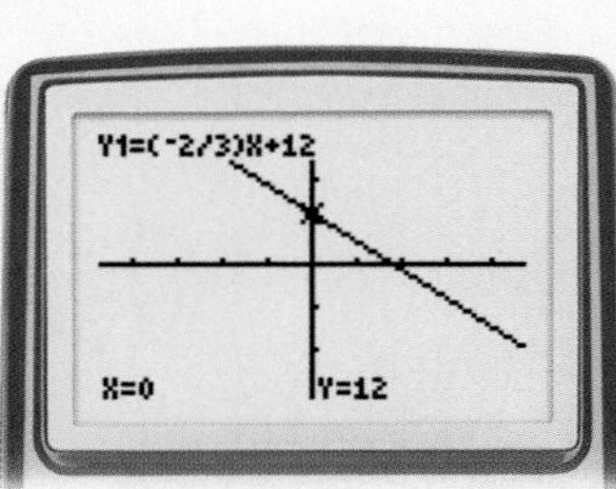

Think and Discuss

1. How do the ratios of the range of y to the range of x in the **ZSquare** and **ZInteger** windows compare?

Try This

Graph each equation in a square window.

1. $y = 2x$
2. $2y = x$
3. $2y - 4x = 12$
4. $2x + 5y = 40$

11-4 Point-Slope Form

Learn to find the equation of a line given one point and the slope.

Vocabulary

point-slope form

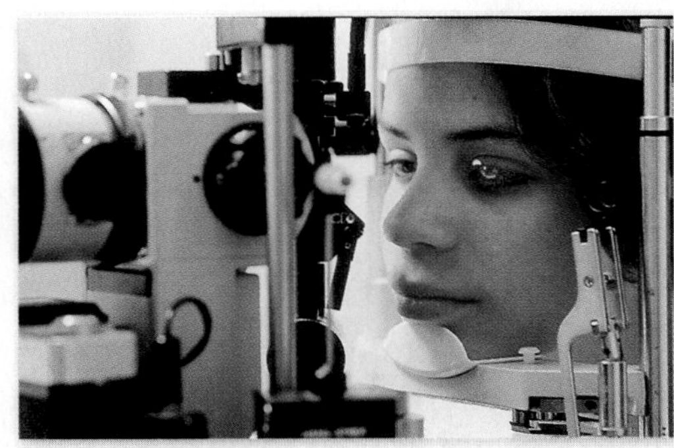

Lasers aim light along a straight path. If you know the destination of the light beam (a point on the line) and the slant of the beam (the slope), you can write an equation in *point-slope form* to calculate the height at which the laser is positioned.

The **point-slope form** of an equation of a line with slope m passing through (x_1, y_1) is $y - y_1 = m(x - x_1)$.

Point on the line	Point-slope form
(x_1, y_1)	$y - y_1 = m(x - x_1)$ (Slope: m)

EXAMPLE 1 Using Point-Slope Form to Identify Information About a Line

Use the point-slope form of each equation to identify a point the line passes through and the slope of the line.

A $y - 9 = -\frac{2}{3}(x - 21)$

$y - y_1 = m(x - x_1)$

$y - 9 = -\frac{2}{3}(x - 21)$ *The equation is in point-slope form.*

$m = -\frac{2}{3}$ *Read the value of m from the equation.*

$(x_1, y_1) = (21, 9)$ *Read the point from the equation.*

The line defined by $y - 9 = -\frac{2}{3}(x - 21)$ has slope $-\frac{2}{3}$, and passes through the point (21, 9).

B $y - 3 = 4(x + 7)$

$y - y_1 = m(x - x_1)$

$y - 3 = 4(x + 7)$

$y - 3 = 4[x - (-7)]$ *Rewrite using subtraction instead of addition.*

$m = 4$

$(x_1, y_1) = (-7, 3)$

The line defined by $y - 3 = 4(x + 7)$ has slope 4, and passes through the point $(-7, 3)$.

Focus on Problem Solving

Understand the Problem

- **Identify important details in the problem**

When you are solving word problems, you need to find the information that is important to the problem.

You can write the equation of a line if you know the slope and one point on the line or if you know two points on the line.

Example:

A school bus carrying 40 students is traveling toward the school at **30 mi/hr**. After **15 minutes**, it has **20 miles to go**. How far away from the school was the bus when it started?

You can write the equation of the line in point-slope form.

$$y - y_1 = m(x - x_1)$$

$$y - (-20) = 30(x - 0.25)$$ *The slope is the rate of change, or 30.*

15 minutes = 0.25 hours

$$y + 20 = 30x - 7.5$$ *(0.25, −20) is a point on the line.*

$$\underline{\quad - 20 \qquad\qquad - 20}$$

$$y = 30x - 27.5$$

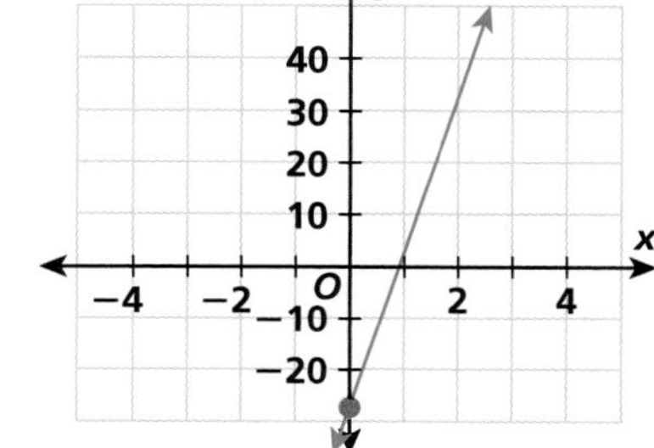

The y-intercept of the line is −27.5. At 0 minutes, the bus had 27.5 miles to go.

Read each problem, and identify the information needed to write the equation of a line. Give the slope and one point on the line, or give two points on the line.

1. At sea level, water boils at 212°F. At an altitude of 2000 ft, water boils at 208°F. If the relationship is linear, estimate the temperature that water would boil at an altitude of 5000 ft.

2. Don earns a weekly salary of $480, plus a commission of 5% of his total sales. How many dollars in merchandise does he have to sell to make $500 in one week?

3. An environmental group has a goal of planting 10,000 trees. On Arbor Day, volunteers planted 4500 trees. If the group can plant 500 trees per week, how long will it take them to plant the remaining trees to reach their goal?

4. Kayla rents a booth at a craft fair. If she sells 50 bracelets, her profit is $25. If she sells 80 bracelets, her profit is $85. What would her profit be if she sold 100 bracelets?

11-5 Direct Variation

Learn to recognize direct variation by graphing tables of data and checking for constant ratios.

Vocabulary

direct variation

constant of proportionality

A satellite in orbit travels 8 miles in 1 second, 16 miles in 2 seconds, 24 miles in 3 seconds, and so on.

The ratio of distance to time is constant. The satellite travels 8 miles every 1 second.

$$\frac{\text{distance}}{\text{time}} = \frac{8 \text{ mi}}{1 \text{ s}} = \frac{16 \text{ mi}}{2 \text{ s}} = \frac{24 \text{ mi}}{3 \text{ s}}$$

DIRECT VARIATION		
Words	**Numbers**	**Algebra**
For **direct variation**, two variable quantities are related proportionally by a constant positive ratio. The ratio is called the **constant of proportionality**.	$8 = k$ $16 = 2k$ $24 = 3k$	$y = kx$ $k = \frac{y}{x}$

The distance the satellite travels *varies directly* with time and is represented by the equation $y = kx$. The constant ratio k is 8.

EXAMPLE 1 Determining Whether a Data Set Varies Directly

Determine whether the data set shows direct variation.

Helpful Hint

The graph of a direct-variation equation is always linear *and* always contains the point (0, 0). The variables x and y either increase together or decrease together.

A

Shoe Sizes					
U.S. Size	7	8	9	10	11
European Size	39	41	43	44	45

Make a graph that shows the relationship between the U.S. sizes and the European sizes. The graph is not linear.

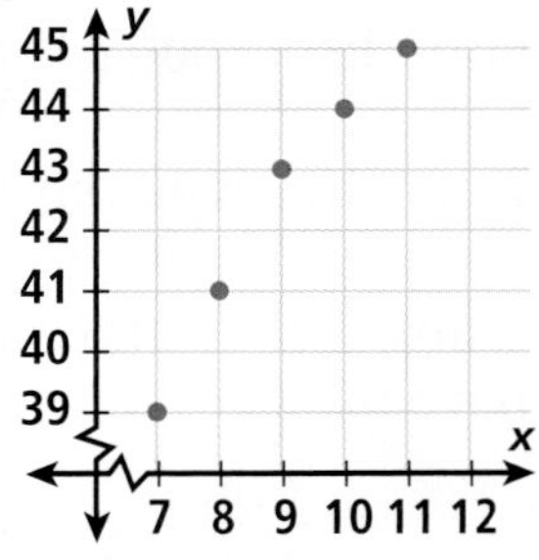

You can also compare ratios to see if a direct variation occurs.

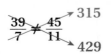

$\frac{39}{7} \neq \frac{45}{11}$ → 315, 429

315 ≠ 429
The ratios are not proportional.

Determine whether the data set shows direct variation.

B

Distance Sound Travels at 20°C (m)					
Time (s)	0	1	2	3	4
Distance (m)	0	350	700	1050	1400

Make a graph that shows the relationship between the number of seconds and the distance sound travels.

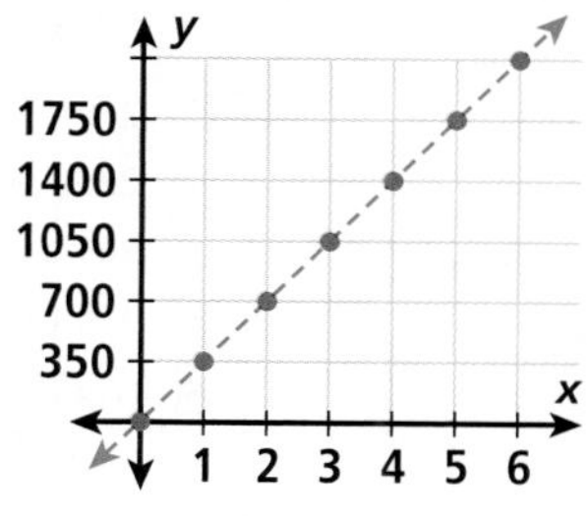

Plot the points.

The points lie in a straight line.

(0, 0) is included.

You can also compare ratios to see if a direct variation occurs.

$\frac{350}{1} = \frac{700}{2} = \frac{1050}{3} = \frac{1400}{4}$ *Compare ratios. The ratio is constant.*

The ratios are proportional. The relationship is a direct variation.

EXAMPLE 2 Finding Equations of Direct Variation

Find each equation of direct variation, given that y varies directly with x.

A y **is 52 when** x **is 4**

$y = kx$	*y varies directly with x.*
$52 = k \cdot 4$	*Substitute for x and y.*
$13 = k$	*Solve for k.*
$y = 13x$	*Substitute 13 for k in the original equation.*

B x **is 10 when** y **is 15**

$y = kx$	*y varies directly with x.*
$15 = k \cdot 10$	*Substitute for x and y.*
$\frac{3}{2} = k$	*Solve for k.*
$y = \frac{3}{2}x$	*Substitute $\frac{3}{2}$ for k in the original equation.*

C y **is 5 when** x **is 2**

$y = kx$	*y varies directly with x.*
$5 = k \cdot 2$	*Substitute for x and y.*
$\frac{5}{2} = k$	*Solve for k.*
$y = \frac{5}{2}x$	*Substitute $\frac{5}{2}$ for k in the original equation.*

EXAMPLE 3 *Physical Science Application*

When a driver applies the brakes, a car's total stopping distance is the sum of the reaction distance and the braking distance. The reaction distance is the distance the car travels before the driver presses the brake pedal. The braking distance is the distance the car travels after the brakes have been applied.

Determine whether there is a direct variation between either data set and speed. If so, find the equation of direct variation.

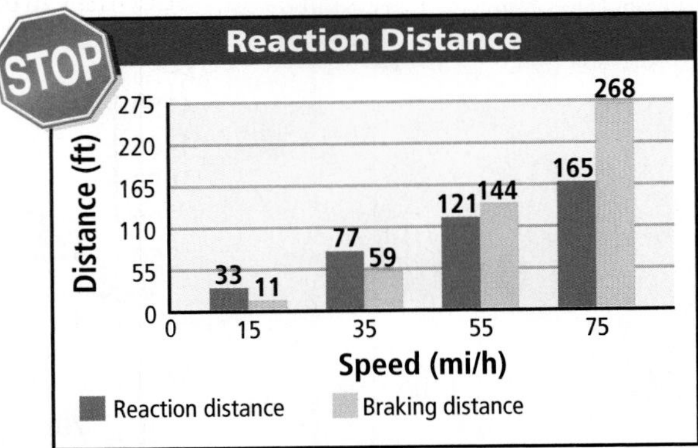

A **reaction distance and speed**

$\frac{\text{reaction distance}}{\text{speed}} = \frac{33}{15} = 2.2$ $\qquad$ $\frac{\text{reaction distance}}{\text{speed}} = \frac{77}{35} = 2.2$

The first two pairs of data result in a common ratio. In fact, all of the reaction distance to speed ratios are equivalent to 2.2.

$$\frac{\text{reaction distance}}{\text{speed}} = \frac{33}{15} = \frac{77}{35} = \frac{121}{55} = \frac{165}{75} = 2.2$$

The variables are related by a constant ratio of 2.2 to 1, and (0, 0) is included. The equation of direct variation is $y = 2.2x$, where x is the speed, y is the reaction distance, and 2.2 is the constant of proportionality.

B **braking distance and speed**

$\frac{\text{braking distance}}{\text{speed}} = \frac{11}{15} = 0.7\overline{3}$ $\qquad$ $\frac{\text{braking distance}}{\text{speed}} = \frac{59}{35} = 1.69$

$0.7\overline{3} \neq 1.69$

If any of the ratios are not equal, then there is no direct variation. It is not necessary to compute additional ratios or to determine whether (0, 0) is included.

Think and Discuss

1. **Describe** the slope and the y-intercept of a direct variation equation.
2. **Tell** whether two variables that do not vary directly can result in a linear graph.

11-5 Exercises

FOR EXTRA PRACTICE

see page 753

internet connect

Homework Help Online
go.hrw.com Keyword: MP4 11-5

GUIDED PRACTICE

See Example 1 **Make a graph to determine whether the data sets show direct variation.**

1. The table shows an employee's pay per number of hours worked.

Hours Worked	0	1	2	3	4	5	6
Pay ($)	0	8.50	17.00	25.50	34.00	42.50	51.00

See Example 2 **Find each equation of direct variation, given that y varies directly with x.**

2. y is 10 when x is 2

3. y is 16 when x is 4

4. y is 12 when x is 15

5. y is 3 when x is 6

6. y is 220 when x is 2

7. y is 5 when x is 40

See Example 3 **8.** The following table shows how many hours it takes to travel 300 miles, depending on your speed in miles per hour. Determine whether there is direct variation between the two data sets. If so, find the equation of direct variation.

Speed (mi/h)	5	6	7.5	10	15	30	60
Time (hr)	60	50	40	30	20	10	5

INDEPENDENT PRACTICE

See Example 1 **Make a graph to determine whether the data sets show direct variation.**

9. The table shows the amount of current flowing through a 12-volt circuit with various resistances.

Resistance (ohms)	48	24	12	6	4	3	2
Current (amps)	0.25	0.5	1	2	3	4	6

See Example 2 **Find each equation of direct variation, given that y varies directly with x.**

10. y is 2.5 when x is 2.5

11. y is 2 when x is 8

12. y is 93 when x is 3

13. y is 8 when x is 22

14. y is 52 when x is 4

15. y is 10 when x is 100

See Example 3 **16.** The following table shows how many hours it takes to drive certain distances at a speed of 60 miles per hour. Determine whether there is direct variation between the two data sets. If so, find the equation of direct variation.

Distance (mi)	15	30	60	90	120	150	180
Time (hr)	0.25	0.5	1	1.5	2	2.5	3

PRACTICE AND PROBLEM SOLVING

Tell whether each equation represents direct variation between x and y.

17. $y = 133x$ **18.** $y = -4x^2$ **19.** $y = \frac{k}{x}$ **20.** $y = 2\pi x$

Most reptiles have a thick, scaly skin, which prevents them from drying out. As they grow, the outermost layer of this skin is shed. Although snakes shed their skins all in one piece, most reptiles shed their skins in much smaller pieces.

21. ***LIFE SCIENCE*** The weight of a person's skin is related to body weight by the equation $s = \frac{1}{16}w$, where s is skin weight and w is body weight.

a. Does this equation show direct variation between body weight and skin weight?

b. If a person calculates skin weight as $9\frac{3}{4}$ lb, what is the person's body weight?

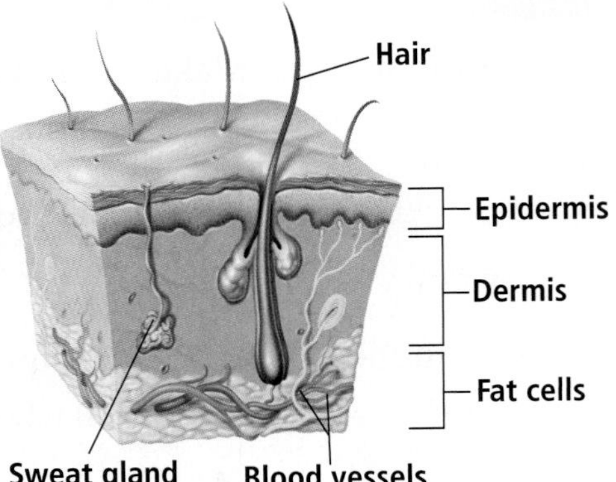

22. ***PHYSICAL SCIENCE*** Boyle's law states that for a fixed amount at a constant temperature, the volume of a gas increases as its pressure decreases. Explain whether the relationship between volume and pressure described by Boyle's law is a direct variation.

23. ***COOKING*** A waffle recipe calls for different amounts of mix, depending on the number of servings. Graph the data set and determine whether it shows direct variation.

Number of Servings	2	4	6	8	10	12	14
Waffle Mix (c)	1.5	3	4.5	6	7.5	9	10.5

24. ***WRITE A PROBLEM*** In physical science, Charles's law states that for a fixed amount at a constant pressure, the volume of a gas increases as the temperature increases. Write a direct variation problem about Charles's law.

25. ***WRITE ABOUT IT*** Describe how the constant of proportionality k affects the appearance of the graph of a direct variation equation.

26. ***CHALLENGE*** Bananas are sold at 39¢ a pound. Determine what condition would need to be satisfied if the price paid and the number of bananas purchased represented a direct variation.

Spiral Review

Solve. (Lesson 10-1)

27. $5x + 2 = -18$ **28.** $\frac{b}{-6} + 12 = 5$ **29.** $\frac{a + 4}{11} = -3$ **30.** $\frac{1}{3}x - \frac{1}{4} = \frac{5}{12}$

31. **TEST PREP** The area of a trapezoid is given by the formula $A = \frac{1}{2}(b_1 + b_2)h$. Find b_1 if $A = 60\text{ m}^2$, $b_2 = 5$ m, and $h = 6$ m. (Lesson 10-5)

A 7 m **B** 15 m **C** 14.5 m **D** 12 m

11-6 Graphing Inequalities in Two Variables

Learn to graph inequalities on the coordinate plane.

Vocabulary

boundary line

linear inequality

Graphing can help you visualize the relationship between the maximum distance a Mars rover can travel and the number of Martian days.

A graph of a linear equation separates the coordinate plane into three parts: the points on one side of the line, the points on the **boundary line**, and the points on the other side of the line.

Solar-powered rovers landing on Mars in 2004 will have a range of up to 330 feet per Martian day.

Each point in the coordinate plane makes one of these three statements true:

Equality → $y = x + 2$

Inequality → $y > x + 2$, $y < x + 2$

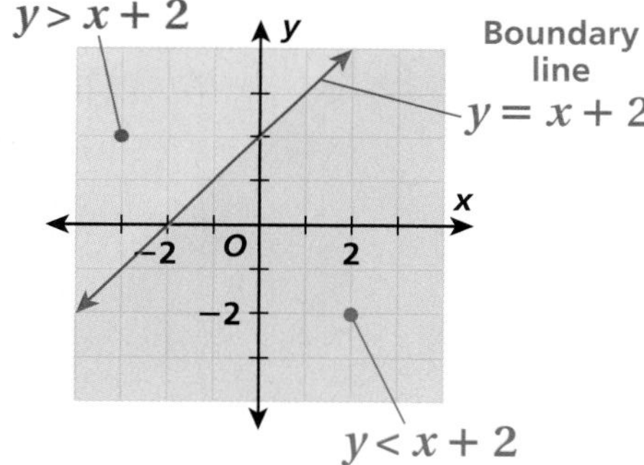

When the equality symbol is replaced in a linear equation by an inequality symbol, the statement is a **linear inequality**. Any ordered pair that makes the linear inequality true is a solution.

EXAMPLE 1 Graphing Inequalities

Graph each inequality.

A $y > x + 1$

First graph the boundary line $y = x + 1$. Since no points that are on the line are solutions of $y > x + 1$, make the line *dashed*. Then determine on which side of the line the solutions lie.

$(0, 0)$ *Test a point not on the line.*

$y > x + 1$

$0 \overset{?}{>} 0 + 1$ *Substitute 0 for x and 0 for y.*

$0 \overset{?}{>} 1$

Since $0 > 1$ is not true, $(0, 0)$ is not a solution of $y > x + 1$. Shade the side of the line that does not include $(0, 0)$.

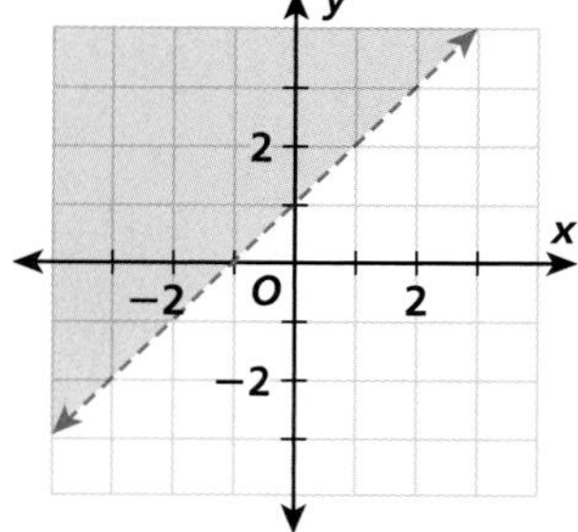

Helpful Hint

Any point on the line $y = x + 1$ is not a solution of $y > x + 1$ because the inequality symbol $>$ means only "greater than" and does not include "equal to."

Helpful Hint

Any point on the line $y = x + 1$ is a solution of $y \leq x + 1$. This is because the inequality symbol $\leq$ means "less than *or equal to.*"

Graph each inequality.

B $y \leq x + 1$

First graph the boundary line $y = x + 1$. Since points that are on the line are solutions of $y \leq x + 1$, make the line ***solid.***

Then shade the part of the coordinate plane in which the rest of the solutions of $y \leq x + 1$ lie.

$(2, 1)$ *Choose any point not on the line.*

$y \leq x + 1$

$1 \overset{?}{\leq} 2 + 1$ *Substitute 2 for x and 1 for y.*

$1 \overset{?}{\leq} 3$

Since $1 \leq 3$ is true, $(2, 1)$ is a solution of $y \leq x + 1$. Shade the side of the line that includes the point $(2, 1)$.

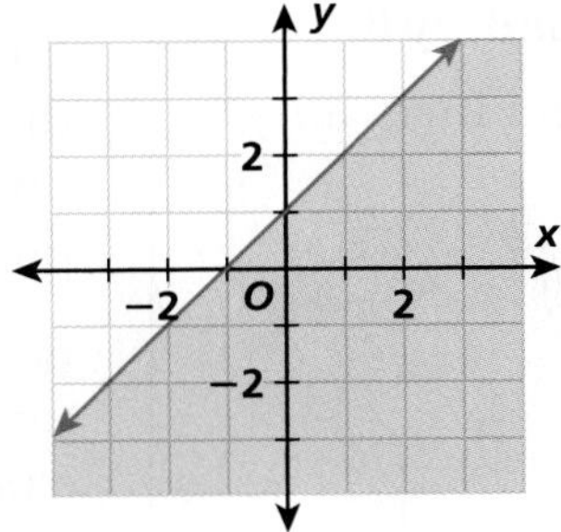

C $3y + 4x \leq 12$

First write the equation in slope-intercept form.

$3y + 4x \leq 12$

$3y \leq -4x + 12$ *Subtract 4x from both sides.*

$y \leq -\frac{4}{3}x + 4$ *Divide both sides by 3.*

Then graph the line $y = -\frac{4}{3}x + 4$. Since points that are on the line are solutions of $y \leq -\frac{4}{3}x + 4$, make the line solid. Then shade the part of the coordinate plane in which the rest of the solutions of $y \leq -\frac{4}{3}x + 4$ lie.

$(0, 0)$ *Choose any point not on the line.*

$y \leq -\frac{4}{3}x + 4$

$0 \overset{?}{\leq} 0 + 4$ *Substitute 0 for x and 0 for y.*

$0 \overset{?}{\leq} 4$

Since $0 \leq 4$ is true, $(0, 0)$ is a solution of $y \leq -\frac{4}{3}x + 1$. Shade the side of the line that includes the point $(0, 0)$.

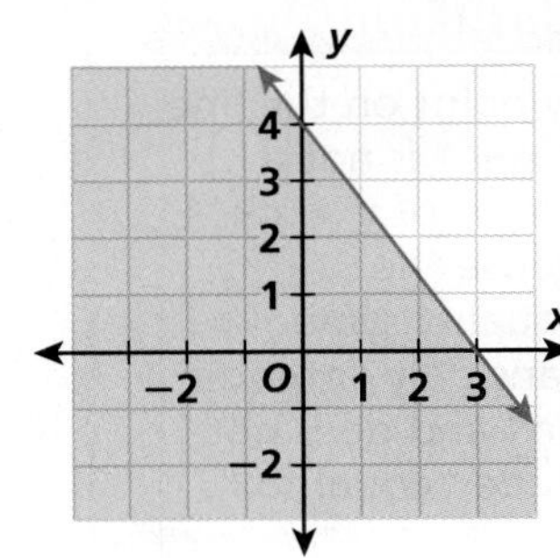

EXAMPLE 2 Science Application

Helpful Hint

The phrase "up to 330 ft" can be translated as "less than or equal to 330 ft."

Solar-powered rovers landing on Mars in 2004 will have a range of up to 330 feet per Martian day. Graph the relationship between the distance a rover can travel and the number of Martian days. Can a rover travel 3000 feet in 8 days?

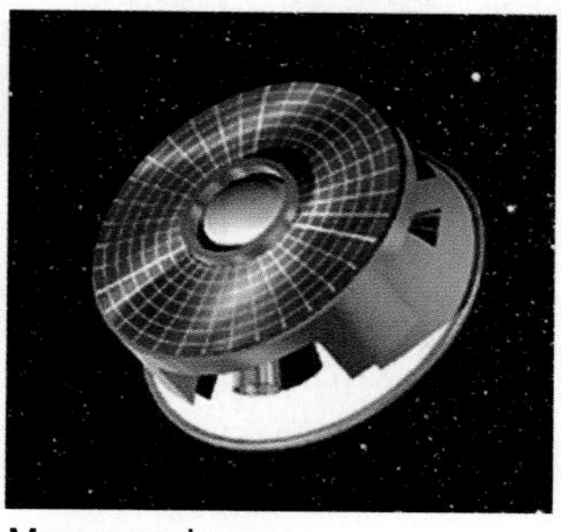
Mars rover in space.

First find the equation of the line that corresponds to the inequality.

In 0 days the rover travels 0 feet. ⟶ point (0, 0)

In 1 day the rover can travel up to 330 feet. ⟶ point (1, 330)

$m = \frac{330 - 0}{1 - 0} = \frac{330}{1} = 330$ *With two known points, find the slope.*

$y = 330x + 0$ *The y-intercept is 0.*

Graph the boundary line $y = 330x$. Since points on the line are solutions of $y \leq 330x$, make the line solid.

Shade the part of the coordinate plane in which the rest of the solutions of $y \leq 330x$ lie.

(5, 0) *Choose any point not on the line.*

$y \leq 330x$

$0 \leq 330 \cdot 5$ *Substitute 5 for x and 0 for y.*

$0 \leq 1650$

Since $0 \leq 1650$ is true, (5, 0) is a solution of $y \leq 330x$. Shade the part on the side of the line that includes point (5, 0).

The point (8, 3000) is not included in the shaded area, so the rover cannot travel 3000 feet in 8 days.

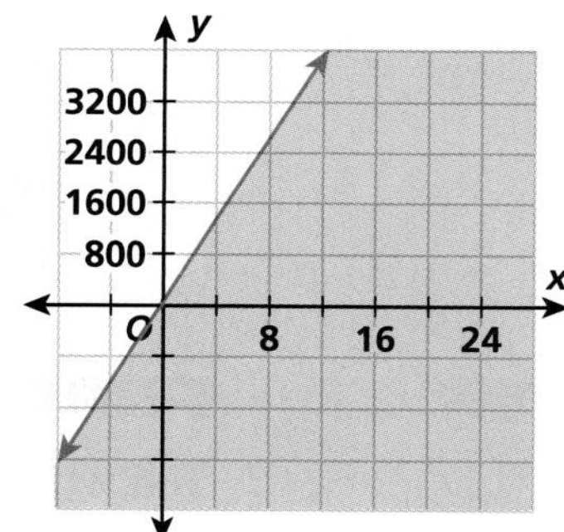

Think and Discuss

1. **Describe** the graph of $5x + y < 15$. Tell how it would change if $<$ were changed to $\geq$.
2. **Compare and contrast** the use of an open circle, a closed circle, a dashed line, and a solid line when graphing inequalities.
3. **Explain** how you can tell if a point on the line is a solution of the inequality.
4. **Name** a linear inequality for which the graph is a horizontal dashed line and all points below it.

11-6 Exercises

FOR EXTRA PRACTICE

see page 753

internet connect

Homework Help Online

go.hrw.com Keyword: MP4 11-6

GUIDED PRACTICE

See Example 1

Graph each inequality.

1. $y < x + 3$

2. $y \geq 2x - 1$

3. $y > -3x + 2$

4. $4x + y \leq 1$

5. $y \leq \frac{2}{3}x + 3$

6. $\frac{1}{2}x - \frac{1}{4}y < -1$

See Example 2

7. a. The organizers of a golf outing have a prize budget of $150 to buy golf gloves and hats for the players. They can buy golf gloves for $10 each and hats for $12 each. Write and graph an inequality showing the different ways the organizers can spend their prize budget.

b. Can the organizers of the golf outing purchase 7 hats and 6 golf gloves and still be within their prize budget?

INDEPENDENT PRACTICE

See Example 1

Graph each inequality.

8. $y \leq -\frac{1}{2}x - 4$

9. $y < -1.5x + 2.5$

10. $-4(2x + y) \geq -8$

11. $3x - \frac{3}{4}y > -2$

12. $6x - 9y > 15$

13. $3\left(\frac{2}{3}x + \frac{1}{3}y\right) \leq -3$

See Example 2

14. a. To avoid suffering from the bends, a diver should ascend no faster than 30 feet per minute. Write and graph an inequality showing the relationship between the depth of a diver and the time required to ascend to the surface.

b. If a diver initially at a depth of 77 ft ascends to the surface in 2.6 minutes, is the diver in danger of developing the bends?

PRACTICE AND PROBLEM SOLVING

Tell whether the given ordered pair is a solution of each inequality shown.

15. $y \leq 2x + 4$, (2, 1)

16. $y > -6x + 1$, (−3, 19)

17. $y \geq 3x - 3$, (5, 14)

18. $y > -x + 12$, (0, 14)

19. $y \geq 3.4x + 1.9$, (4, 22)

20. $y \leq 7(x - 3)$, (3, 3)

21. a. Graph the inequality $y \geq x + 5$.

b. Name an ordered pair that is a solution of the inequality.

c. Is (3, 5) a solution of $y \geq x + 5$? Explain how to check your answer.

d. Which side of the line $y = x + 5$ is shaded?

e. Name an ordered pair that is a solution of $y < x + 5$.

22. ***FOOD*** The school cafeteria needs to buy no more than 30 pounds of potatoes. A supermarket sells 3-pound and 5-pound bags of potatoes. Write and graph an inequality showing the number of 3-pound and 5-pound bags of potatoes the cafeteria can buy.

23. ***SPORTS*** A basketball player scored 18 points in a game. Some of her points may have been from free throws, so her points from 2-point and 3-point field goals could be at most 18. Write and graph an inequality showing the possible numbers of 2-point and 3-point field goals she scored.

24. ***BUSINESS*** It costs a manufacturing company \$35 an hour to operate machine A and \$25 an hour to operate machine B. The total cost of operating both machines can be no more than \$250 each day.
   a. Write and graph an inequality showing the number of hours each machine can be used each day.
   b. If machine A is used for 4 hours, for how many hours can machine B be used without going over \$250?

25. ***EARTH SCIENCE*** A weather balloon can ascend at a rate of up to 800 feet per minute.
   a. Write an inequality showing the relationship between the distance the balloon can ascend and the number of minutes.
   b. Graph the inequality for time between 0 and 30 minutes.
   c. Can the balloon ascend to a height of 2 miles within 15 minutes? (One mile is equal to 5280 feet.)

26. ***CHOOSE A STRATEGY*** Which of the following ordered pairs is NOT a solution of the inequality $4x + 9y \leq 108$?
   A (0, 0) **B** (−6, 15) **C** (−4, −12) **D** (7, 8)

27. ***WRITE ABOUT IT*** When you graph a linear inequality that is solved for y, when do you shade above the boundary line and when do you shade below it? When do you use a dashed line?

28. ***CHALLENGE*** Graph the region that satisfies all three inequalities: $x \geq -2$, $y \geq 4$, and $y < -\frac{1}{2}x + 6$.

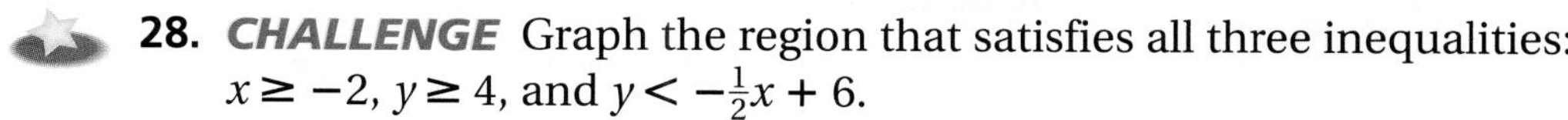

Spiral Review

Solve for the indicated variable. (Lesson 10-5)

29. Solve $A = \frac{1}{2}bh$ for h.
30. Solve $2a + 2b + 2c = 2d$ for b.
31. Solve $A = \frac{1}{2}(b_1 + b_2)h$ for b_2.
32. Solve $W = X - 2Y + 4Z$ for Y.

33. **TEST PREP** What is the equation of the line that passes through points (1, 6) and (−1, −2) in slope-intercept form. (Lesson 11-3)
   A $y = 4x + 2$ **B** $y = -3x + 6$ **C** $y = 4x - 2$ **D** $y = 2x + 4$

11-7 Lines of Best Fit

Learn to recognize relationships in data and find the equation of a line of best fit.

The graph shows the winning times for the women's 3000 meter Olympic speed skating event. As is the case with many Olympic sports, the athletes keep improving and setting new records, so there is a correlation between the year and the winning time.

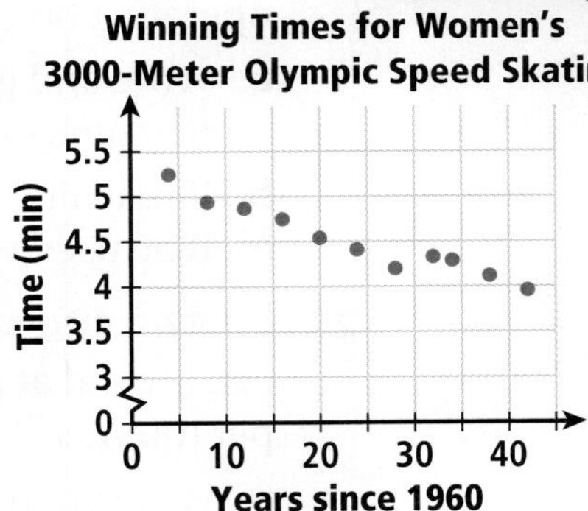

When data show a correlation, you can estimate and draw a *line of best fit* that approximates a trend for a set of data and use it to make predictions.

To estimate the equation of a line of best fit:

- calculate the means of the x-coordinates and y-coordinates: (x_m, y_m).
- draw the line through (x_m, y_m) that appears to best fit the data.
- estimate the coordinates of another point on the line.
- find the equation of the line.

EXAMPLE 1 Finding a Line of Best Fit

Plot the data and find a line of best fit.

x	2	4	5	1	3	8	6	7
y	4	8	7	3	4	8	5	9

Plot the data points and find the mean of the x- and y-coordinates.

$x_m = \frac{2+4+5+1+3+8+6+7}{8} = 4.5 \qquad y_m = \frac{4+8+7+3+4+8+5+9}{8} = 6$

$(x_m, y_m) = (4.5, 6)$

Draw a line through (4.5, 6) that best represents the data.

Estimate and plot the coordinates of another point on that line, such as (7, 8). Find the equation of the line.

$m = \frac{8-6}{7-4.5} = \frac{2}{2.5} = 0.8$ *Find the slope.*

$y - y_1 = m(x - x_1)$ *Use point-slope form.*

$y - 6 = 0.8(x - 4.5)$ *Substitute.*

$y - 6 = 0.8x - 3.6$

$y = 0.8x + 2.4$

The equation of a line of best fit is $y = 0.8x + 2.4$.

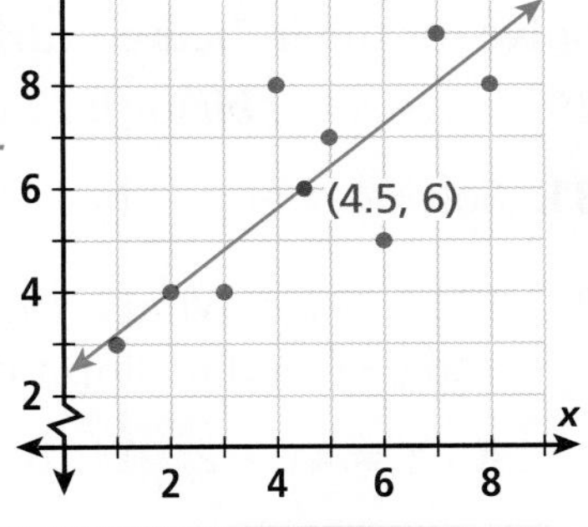

Remember!

The line of best fit is the line that comes closest to all the points on a scatter plot. Try to draw the line so that about the same number of points are above the line as below the line.

EXAMPLE 2 *Sports Application*

Find a line of best fit for the women's 3000-meter speed skating. Use the equation of the line to predict the winning time in 2006.

Year	1964	1968	1972	1976	1980	1984	1988	1992	1994	1998	2002
Winning Time (min)	5.25	4.94	4.87	4.75	4.54	4.41	4.20	4.33	4.29	4.12	3.96

Let 1960 represent year 0. The first point is then (4, 5.25), and the last point is (42, 3.96).

Plot the data points and find the mean of the x- and y-coordinates.

$$x_m = \frac{4 + 8 + 12 + 16 + 20 + 24 + 28 + 32 + 34 + 38 + 42}{11} \approx 23.5$$

$$y_m = \frac{5.25 + 4.94 + 4.87 + 4.75 + 4.54 + 4.41 + 4.20 + 4.33 + 4.29 + 4.12 + 3.96}{11} \approx 4.5$$

$$(x_m, y_m) = (23.5, 4.5)$$

Draw a line through (23.5, 4.5) that best represents the data.

Estimate and plot the coordinates of another point on that line, (8, 5).

Find the equation of that line.

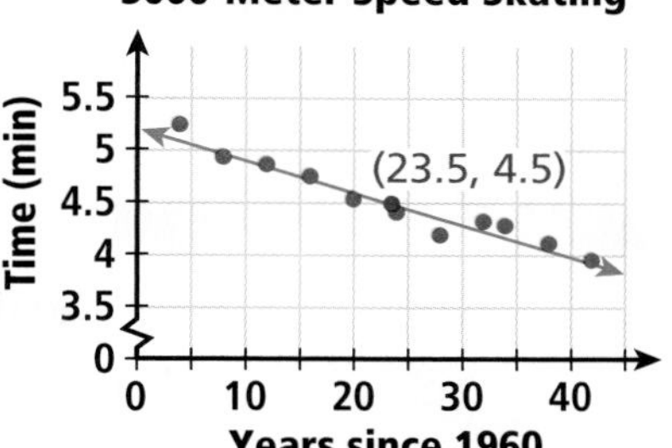

$$m = \frac{5 - 4.5}{8 - 23.5} = \frac{0.5}{-15.5} \approx -0.03$$

$$y - y_1 = m(x - x_1)$$

$$y - 4.5 = -0.03(x - 23.5)$$

$$y - 4.5 = -0.03x + 0.7 \quad \textit{Round 0.705 to 0.7.}$$

$$y = -0.03x + 5.2$$

The equation of a line of best fit is $y = -0.03x + 5.2$.

Since 1960 represents year 0, 2006 represents year 46.

$y = -0.03(46) + 5.2$ *Substitute.*

$y = -1.38 + 5.2$

$y = 3.82$

The equation predicts a winning time of 3.82 minutes for the year 2006.

Helpful Hint

If you substitute 2006 instead of 46 for the year, you get a negative value for y. The answer would not be reasonable.

Think and Discuss

1. **Explain** why selecting a different second point may result in a different equation.
2. **Describe** what a line of best fit can tell you.
3. **Tell** whether a line of best fit must include one or more points in the data.

11-7 Exercises

FOR EXTRA PRACTICE
see page 753

internet connect
Homework Help Online
go.hrw.com Keyword: MP4 11-7

GUIDED PRACTICE

See Example 1 **Plot the data and find a line of best fit.**

1.

x	2	7	3	4	6	1	9	5
y	4	13	7	8	11	2	17	10

2.

x	22	32	28	20	26	30	24	34
y	11	7	9	12	10	8	10	6

See Example 2

3. Ten students each did a different number of jumping jacks and then recorded their heart rates. Find and graph a line of best fit for the data. How is heart rate related to exercise?

Jumping Jacks	0	5	10	15	20	25	30	35	40	45
Heart Rate (beats/min)	78	76	84	86	93	90	96	92	100	107

INDEPENDENT PRACTICE

See Example 1 **Plot the data and find a line of best fit.**

4.

x	10	25	5	40	30	20	15	35
y	25	62	13	100	75	48	39	88

5.

x	0.4	0.5	0.3	0.7	0.2	0.8	0.1	0.6
y	5	5	6	2	8	1	8	3

See Example 2

6. Find a line of best fit for the price of a retailer's stock. Use the equation of the line to predict the stock price in 2003.

Year	1994	1995	1996	1997	1998	1999	2000
Stock Price	11.70	11.95	12.28	12.54	12.77	13.00	13.26

PRACTICE AND PROBLEM SOLVING

Tell whether a line of best fit for each scatter plot would have a positive or negative slope. If a line of best fit would not be appropriate for the data, write *neither.*

7. 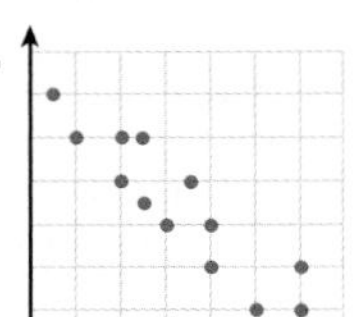

8. 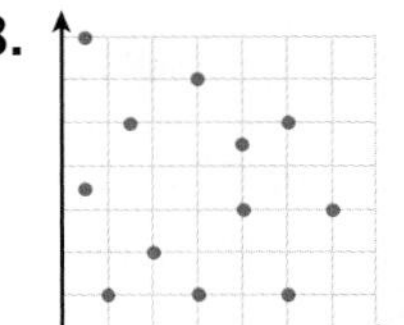

9. 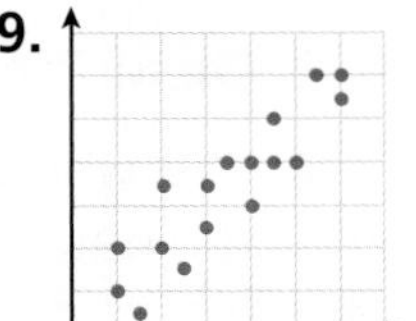

10. 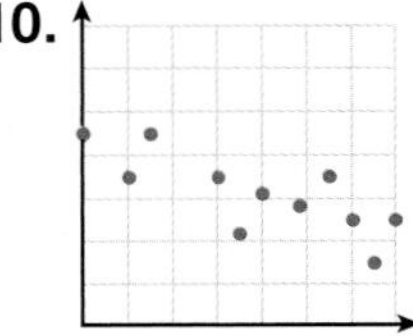

Economics LINK

Economic analysts study trends in data dealing with consumer purchases and ownership. Analysts often make predictions about future markets based on these economic trends. The table shows data on how many American households owned a computer during the past several years.

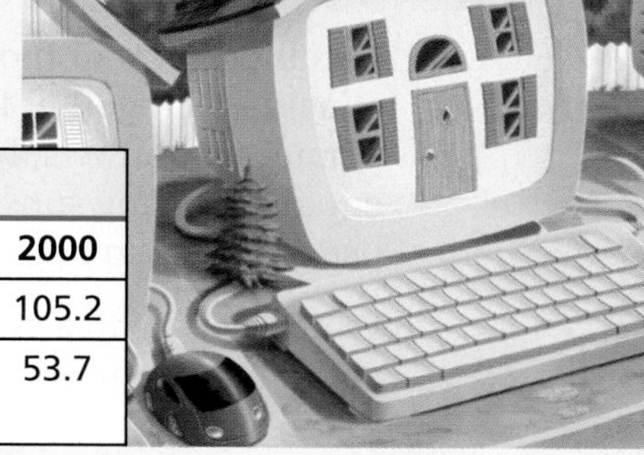

Computer Ownership in the U.S. (1989–2000)				
Year	**1989**	**1993**	**1997**	**2000**
Total U.S. Households (millions)	94.1	99.1	102.2	105.2
U.S. Households Owning a Computer (millions)	13.7	22.6	37.4	53.7

Source: U.S. Census

11. Let 1989 represent year 0 along the x-axis.

a. What is the mean number of years for the data shown?

b. Find the *percent* of U.S. households owning a computer for each year shown in the table, to the nearest tenth. Then find the mean.

12. Let y represent the percent of U.S. households that owned a computer between 1989 and 2000. Find a line of best fit, and plot it on the same graph as the data points. Use the point (6, 32) to write the equation of the line of best fit.

13. In 1998 about 42.1% of U.S. households owned a computer. What percent of households owned a computer in 1998 according to the line of best fit?

14. Use the equation of the line of best fit to predict the percent of U.S. households owning a computer in the year 2005. Do you think the actual value will be higher or lower than the predicted value?

15. ***CHALLENGE*** What information does the slope of the line of best fit give you? What would it mean to an economic analyst if the slope were negative?

Spiral Review

Tell whether the lines passing through the given points are parallel, perpendicular, or neither. (Lesson 11-2)

16. l: (2, 3), (4, 8)
m: (2, 3), (7, 1)

17. l: (3, −1), (7, 4)
m: (5, 5), (0, 9)

18. l: (−6, 1), (−7, 7)
m: (−3,−3), (−4, 3)

19. l: (5, 4), (−11, 0)
m: (1, −2), (0, 6)

20. **TEST PREP** Given that y varies directly with x, find the equation of direct variation if y is 16 when x is 20. (Lesson 11-5)

A $y = 1\frac{1}{5}x$ **B** $y = \frac{5}{4}x$ **C** $y = \frac{4}{5}x$ **D** $y = 0.6x$

EXTENSION Systems of Equations

Learn to solve a system of equations by graphing.

Recall that two or more equations considered together form a system of equations. You've solved systems of equations using substitution. You can also use graphing to help you solve a system.

When you graph a system of linear equations in the same coordinate plane, their point of intersection is the solution of the system.

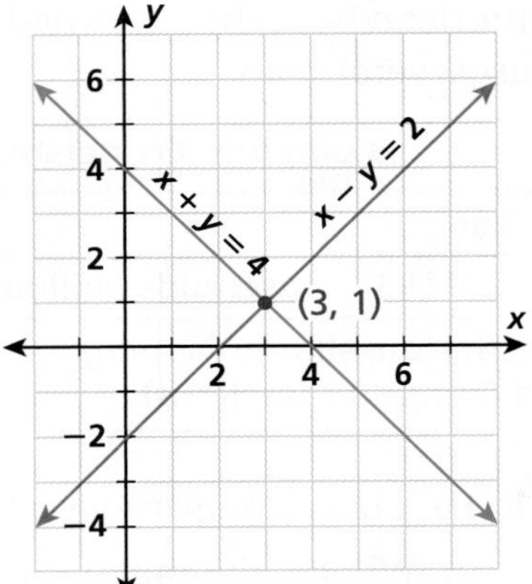

EXAMPLE 1 **Using a Graph to Solve a System of Linear Equations**

Solve the system graphically, and check your answer algebraically.

$$2x + y = 8$$
$$y - x = 2$$

Write each equation in slope-intercept form.

$2x + y = 8$

$y = -2x + 8$

slope = -2, y-intercept = 8

$y - x = 2$

$y = x + 2$

slope = 1, y-intercept = 2

Use each slope and y-intercept to graph. The point of intersection of the graphs, (2, 4), appears to be the solution of the system.

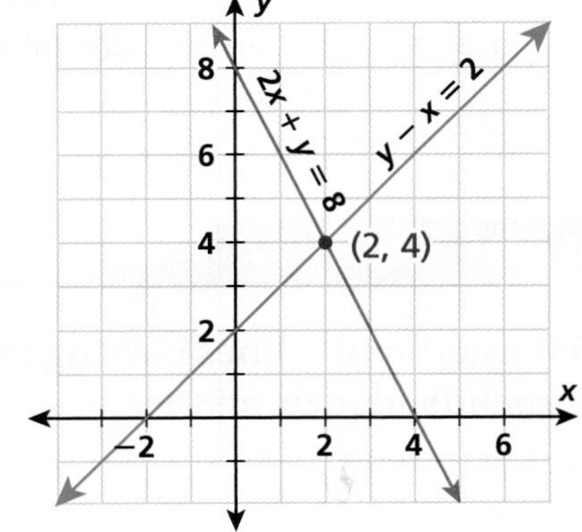

Check by substituting $x = 2$ and $y = 4$ into each of the *original* equations in the system.

Check

$2x + y = 8$
$2(2) + 4 \stackrel{?}{=} 8$
$4 + 4 \stackrel{?}{=} 8$
$8 \stackrel{?}{=} 8$ ✔

$y - x = 2$
$4 - 2 \stackrel{?}{=} 2$
$2 \stackrel{?}{=} 2$ ✔

The ordered pair (2, 4) checks in the original system of equations, so (2, 4) is the solution.

EXAMPLE 2 Graphing a System of Linear Equations to Solve a Problem

A plane left Los Angeles at 525 mi/h on a trans-Pacific flight. After the plane had traveled 1500 miles, a second plane started along the same route, flying at 600 mi/h. How many hours after the second plane leaves Los Angeles will it catch up with the first plane?

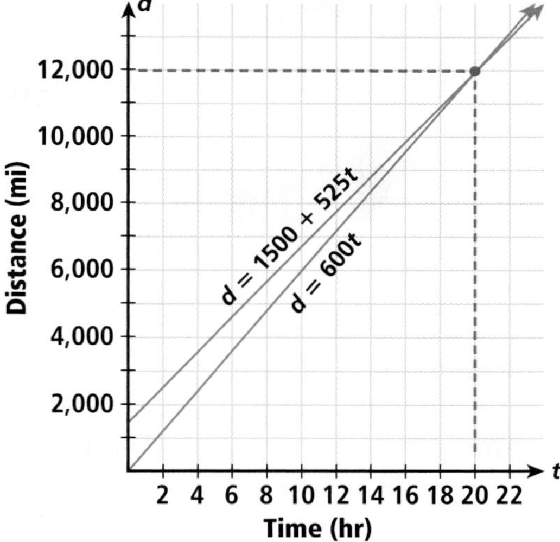

Let $t =$ the number of hours and $d =$ the distance in miles.

For plane 1, $d = 1500 + 525t$.
For plane 2, $d = 600t$.

Graph each equation. The point of intersection is (20, 12,000).

Check

$12{,}000 = 1500 + 525(20)$ $\quad$ $12{,}000 = 600(20)$

$12{,}000 = 12{,}000$ ✔ $\quad$ $12{,}000 = 12{,}000$ ✔

Plane 2 will catch up with plane 1 after 20 hours in flight, 12,000 miles from Los Angeles.

EXTENSION Exercises

Tell whether the ordered pair is the solution of each given system.

1. (5, 11) $\begin{array}{l} y = 3x - 4 \\ y = 2x + 1 \end{array}$
2. (0, 1) $\begin{array}{l} y = 4x + 1 \\ y = 3x \end{array}$
3. (2, −5) $\begin{array}{l} 3x + y = 1 \\ -5x + y = -7 \end{array}$

Solve each system graphically, and check your answer algebraically.

4. $\begin{array}{l} y = 2x \\ y = 3x - 3 \end{array}$
5. $\begin{array}{l} y = -2x + 3 \\ y = \frac{1}{2}x + 3 \end{array}$
6. $\begin{array}{l} y - x = -2 \\ x - 2y = 4 \end{array}$
7. A lion cub is running toward the rim of a deep gorge. The gorge is 1800 meters from his mother. The cub is running at 480 meters per minute, and the lioness races after him at 660 meters per minute. If the cub had a 450-meter head start, will his mother catch him in time?
8. Lillian has a choice of two long-distance telephone plans. The first plan has a monthly fee of \$3.95 plus 5 cents per minute. The second plan has no monthly fee, but charges 7 cents per minute. If Lillian averages about 300 minutes of long-distance calls per month, which plan is better for her?

Problem Solving on Location

Missouri

The Pony Express

A monument in St. Joseph, Missouri, marks the founding site of the Pony Express. "Mail in ten days" by horseback was promised for delivery of mail along the 1966-mile route from St. Joseph, Missouri, to Sacramento, California. The first run of the Pony Express was on April 3, 1860. Mail-carrying riders left from both ends of the route, met in the middle to trade mail, and then returned to the cities where they began.

1. The cost of mailing a letter by Pony Express was calculated per $\frac{1}{2}$ ounce. In the beginning, it cost \$10 to send a 1-ounce letter and \$25 to send a $2\frac{1}{2}$-ounce letter. Find the slope of the line that describes the cost of mailing a letter by Pony Express. What does the slope of the line represent?

2. Write the equation of the line in point-slope form that describes the cost of mailing a letter by Pony Express.

3. Write the equation of the line in slope-intercept form that describes the cost of mailing a letter by Pony Express. What is the y-intercept of this equation?

4. By the time the Pony Express stopped delivering mail, the cost of mailing a letter was \$1 per $\frac{1}{2}$ ounce. Write an equation in slope-intercept form to find the cost of mailing a letter by Pony Express at the final rate.

5. Riders for the Pony Express would change horses every 10 to 15 miles. Write two inequalities—one that represents the maximum number of stops to change horses for a trip of x miles and one that represents the minimum number of stops. Graph each inequality.

Mark Twain's Childhood Home

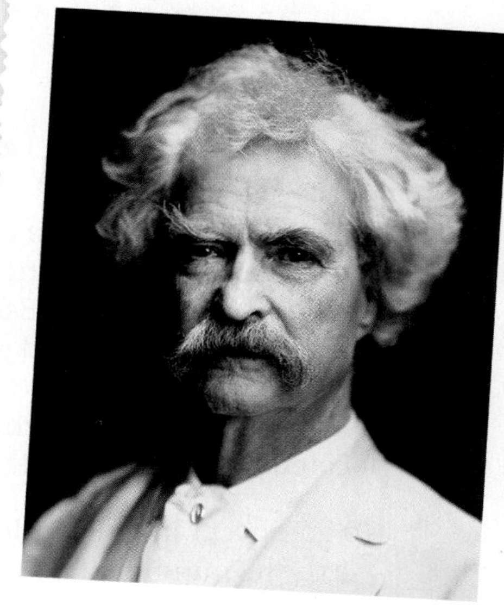

Samuel Clemens—known to the world as Mark Twain, author of the famous children's stories *The Adventures of Huckleberry Finn* and *The Adventures of Tom Sawyer*—was raised in Hannibal, Missouri. Many of the homes and landmarks in Hannibal were described in his books. Today, the town pays tribute to Twain, the elements of life that he wrote about, and the characters in his books.

1. Samuel Clemens chose a phrase used by riverboat crews on the Mississippi River as his pen name. When the crews measured river depth, they would yell out "mark twain!" each time a depth of 1 twain (2 fathoms) was measured.
   a. The number of fathoms varies directly with the number of feet, and 7 fathoms equal 42 feet. Find the direct variation equation.
   b. Write the direct variation equation that can be used to convert fathoms to inches. What is the constant of proportionality? How many inches equal one twain?

2. The *Mark Twain*, a riverboat, has a maximum capacity of 400 people. Write and graph an inequality to express that the number of children x plus the number of adults y cannot exceed the maximum. What is the equation of the boundary line? Is the boundary line solid or dashed?

3. The price of a one-hour boat tour on the *Mark Twain* is \$9 for adults and \$6 for children. Write the equation of the line that gives you the possible numbers of children's tickets and adult tickets purchased for a boat tour in which \$3615 worth of tickets was sold. Graph your equation on the same coordinate plane as your inequality from problem 2. Is it possible that the boat sold \$3615 worth of tickets for a single boat ride? Explain.

MATH-ABLES

Graphing in Space

You can graph a point in two dimensions using a coordinate plane with an x- and a y-axis. Each point is located using an ordered pair (x, y). In three dimensions, you need three coordinate axes, and each point is located using an ordered triple (x, y, z).

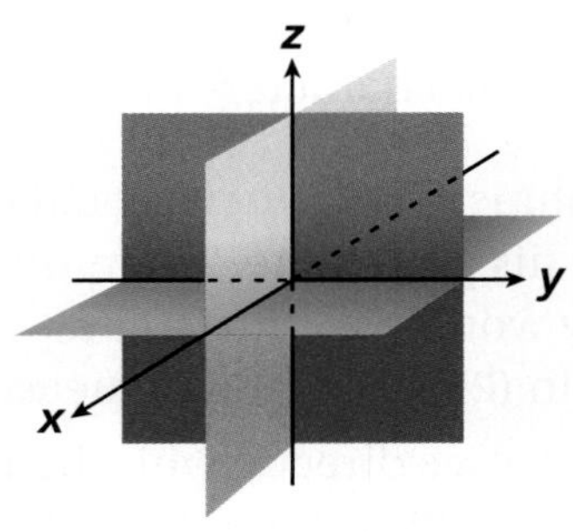

To graph a point, move along the x-axis the number of units of the x-coordinate. Then move left or right the number of units of the y-coordinate. Then move up or down the number of units of the z-coordinate.

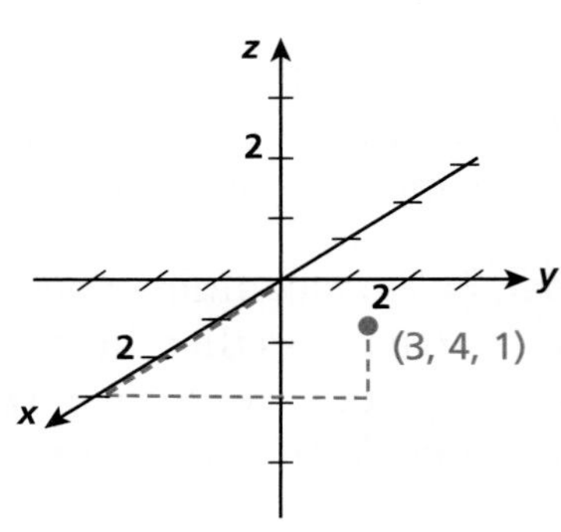

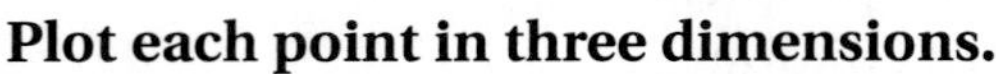

Plot each point in three dimensions.

1. (1, 2, 5) **2.** (−2, 3, −2)

3. (4, 0, 2)

The graph of the equation $y = 2$ in three dimensions is a plane that is perpendicular to the y-axis and is two units to the right of the origin.

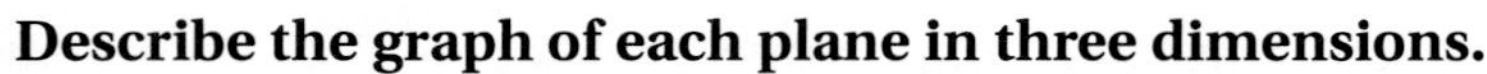

Describe the graph of each plane in three dimensions.

4. $x = 3$ **5.** $z = 1$ **6.** $y = -1$

Line Solitaire

Use a red and a blue number cube and a coordinate plane. Roll the number cubes to generate the coordinates of points on the coordinate plane. The x-coordinate of each point is the number on the red cube, and the y-coordinate is the number on the blue cube. Generate seven ordered pairs and plot the points on the coordinate plane. Then try to write the equations of three lines that divide the plane into seven regions so that each point is in a different region.

internet connect
State-Specific Test Practice Online
go.hrw.com Keyword: MP4 TestPrep

Standardized Test Prep

Chapter 11

Cumulative Assessment, Chapters 1–11

1. A savings plan requires \$1000 to start plus a monthly deposit, as shown on the graph.

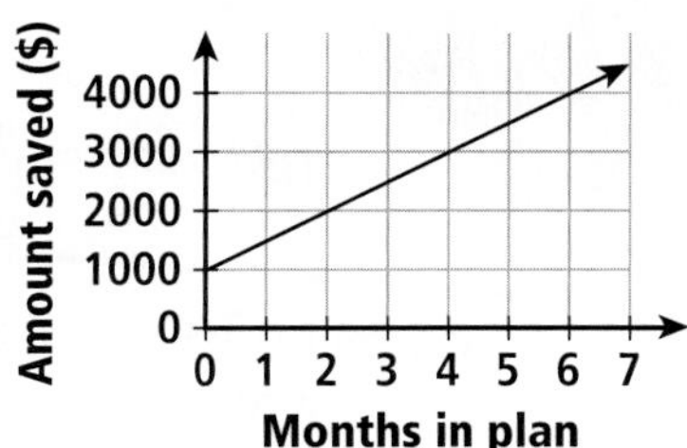

What does the slope of the line joining these points represent?

(A) The plan is for 500 weeks.
(B) Members will make 500 deposits.
(C) Each successive deposit is \$500 more.
(D) The monthly deposit is \$500.

2. Find the value of k so that the slope of the line joining the points $(k, -3)$ and $(4, 2)$ is $\frac{1}{2}$.

(F) 6 (H) 14
(G) −6 (J) −14

3. If 75% of a group of 96 graduates are older than 25 and, of those over 25, $\frac{1}{3}$ are business majors, how many are business majors?

(A) 72 (C) 48
(B) 64 (D) 24

4. What is the volume of the cube whose surface area is $150e^2$?

(F) $25e^3$ (H) $125e^3$
(G) $50e^3$ (J) $625e^3$

5. Which of the following is not a real number?

(A) $-\sqrt{5}$ (C) $\sqrt{-5}$
(B) $\sqrt[3]{-8}$ (D) −8

6. Playing with blocks, a child named Luke places the letters *K, U, E,* and *L* together at random. What is the probability that they spell his name?

(F) $\frac{1}{4}$ (H) $\frac{1}{12}$
(G) $\frac{1}{8}$ (J) $\frac{1}{24}$

7. One can of paint covers an area of 10 ft by 50 ft. Which is an expression for the number of cans of paint needed to paint an area l ft by w ft?

(A) $\frac{500}{lw}$ (C) $\frac{lw}{500}$
(B) $\frac{l+w}{500}$ (D) $500lw$

8. If $x \star y$ means $x^2 < y^2$, then which of the following statements is true?

(F) $\frac{1}{4} \star \frac{1}{3}$ (H) $-2 \star \frac{1}{2}$
(G) $-3 \star 2$ (J) $-4 \star -2$

TEST TAKING TIP!
Read the requirement for the problem: Be sure you know what you have to find.

9. ***SHORT RESPONSE*** If $7 + x + y = 50$ and $x + y = c$, what is the value of $50 - c$? Show your work.

10. ***SHORT RESPONSE*** A factory recycled 5 of every 25 machine parts earmarked for scrap. What was the ratio of nonrecycled parts to recycled parts? Explain in words how you determined your answer.

Chapter 12

Sequences and Functions

TABLE OF CONTENTS

internet connect

Chapter Opener Online
go.hrw.com
KEYWORD: MP4 Ch12

Growth Rates of *E. coli* Bacteria	
Conditions	**Doubling Time (min)**
Optimum temperature (30°C) and growth medium	20
Low temperature (below 30°C)	40
Low nutrient growth medium	60
Low temperature and low nutrient growth medium	120

Career *Bacteriologist*

Bacteriologists study the growth and characteristics of microorganisms. They generally work in the fields of medicine and public health.

Bacteria colonies grow very quickly. The rate at which bacteria multiply depends upon temperature, nutrient supply, and other factors. The table shows growth rates of an *E. coli* bacteria colony under different conditions.

ARE YOU READY?

Choose the best term from the list to complete each sentence.

linear equation
point-slope form
slope
***x*-intercept**
***y*-intercept**

1. An equation whose solutions fall on a line on a coordinate plane is called a(n) __?__.
2. When the equation of a line is written in the form $y = mx + b$, m represents the __?__ and b represents the __?__.
3. To write an equation of the line that passes through (1, 3) and has slope 2, you might use the __?__ of the equation of a line.

Complete these exercises to review skills you will need for this chapter.

✔ Number Patterns

Find the next three numbers in the pattern.

4. $\frac{1}{-3}, \frac{3}{-4}, \frac{5}{-5}, \ldots$
5. 2, 3, 6, 11, 18, . . .
6. −11, −8, −5, . . .
7. $4, 2\frac{1}{2}, 1, \ldots$

✔ Evaluate Expressions

Evaluate each expression for the given values of the variables.

8. $a + (b - 1)c$ for $a = 6$, $b = 3$, $c = -4$
9. $a \cdot b^c$ for $a = -2$, $b = 4$, $c = 2$
10. $(ab)^c$ for $a = 3$, $b = -2$, $c = 2$
11. $-(a + b) + c$ for $a = -1$, $b = -4$, $c = -10$

✔ Graph Linear Equations

Use the slope and the *y*-intercept to graph each line.

12. $y = \frac{2}{3}x + 4$
13. $y = -\frac{1}{2}x - 2$
14. $y = 3x + 1$
15. $2y = 3x - 8$
16. $3y + 2x = 6$
17. $x - 5y = 5$

✔ Simplify Ratios

Write each ratio in simplest form.

18. $\frac{3}{9}$
19. $\frac{21}{5}$
20. $\frac{-12}{4}$
21. $\frac{27}{45}$
22. $\frac{3}{-45}$
23. $\frac{20}{-8}$

12-1 Arithmetic Sequences

Learn to find terms in an arithmetic sequence.

Vocabulary

sequence

term

arithmetic sequence

common difference

Joaquín received 5000 bonus miles for joining a frequent-flier program. Each time he flies to visit his grandparents, he earns 1250 miles.

The number of miles Joaquín has in his account is 6250 after 1 trip, 7500 after 2 trips, 8750 after 3 trips, and so on.

After 1 trip	After 2 trips	After 3 trips	After 4 trips
6250	7500	8750	10,000

Difference $7500 - 6250 = 1250$

Difference $8750 - 7500 = 1250$

Difference $10{,}000 - 8750 = 1250$

A **sequence** is a list of numbers or objects, called **terms**, in a certain order. In an **arithmetic sequence**, the difference between one term and the next is always the same. This difference is called the **common difference**. The common difference is added to each term to get the next term.

EXAMPLE 1 Identifying Arithmetic Sequences

Determine if each sequence could be arithmetic. If so, give the common difference.

Helpful Hint

You cannot tell if a sequence is arithmetic by looking at a finite number of terms, because the next term might not fit the pattern.

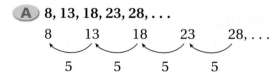

A **8, 13, 18, 23, 28, . . .**

8 13 18 23 28, . . .

5 5 5 5

Find the difference of each term and the term before it.

The sequence could be arithmetic with a common difference of 5.

B **1, 2, 4, 8, 16, . . .**

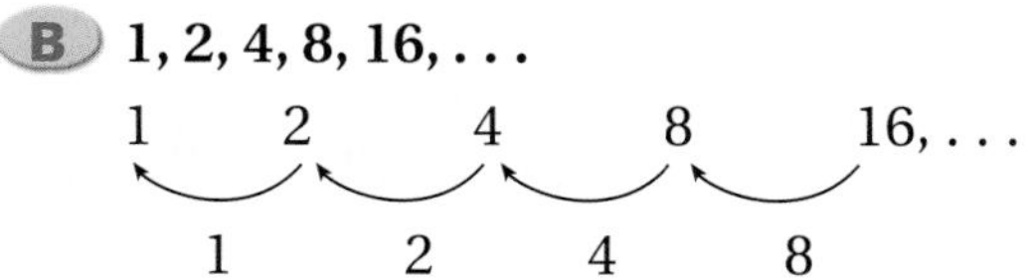

Find the difference of each term and the term before it.

The sequence is not arithmetic.

Determine if each sequence could be arithmetic. If so, give the common difference.

C **100, 93, 86, 79, 72, . . .**

100 93 86 79 72, . . .

−7 −7 −7 −7

Find the difference of each term and the term before it.

The sequence could be arithmetic with a common difference of −7.

D $1, \frac{3}{2}, 2, \frac{5}{2}, 3, \frac{7}{2}, 4, \ldots$

$1 \quad \frac{3}{2} \quad 2 \quad \frac{5}{2} \quad 3 \quad \frac{7}{2} \quad 4, \ldots$

$\frac{1}{2} \quad \frac{1}{2} \quad \frac{1}{2} \quad \frac{1}{2} \quad \frac{1}{2} \quad \frac{1}{2}$

Find the difference of each term and the term before it.

The sequence could be arithmetic with a common difference of $\frac{1}{2}$.

E **5, 1, −3, −7, −11, . . .**

5 1 −3 −7 −11, . . .

−4 −4 −4 −4

Find the difference of each term and the term before it.

The sequence could be arithmetic with a common difference of −4.

Writing Math

Subscripts are used to show the positions of terms in the sequence. The first term is a_1, the second is a_2, and so on.

Suppose you wanted to know the 100th term of the arithmetic sequence 5, 7, 9, 11, 13, ... If you do not want to find the first 99 terms, you could look for a pattern in the terms of the sequence.

Term Name	a_1	a_2	a_3	a_4	a_5	a_6
Term	5	7	9	11	13	15
Pattern	5 + 0(2)	5 + 1(2)	5 + 2(2)	5 + 3(2)	5 + 4(2)	5 + 5(2)

The common difference d is 2. For the 2nd term, one 2 is added to a_1. For the 3rd term, two 2's are added to a_1. The pattern shows that for each term, the **number of 2's added** is one less than the **term number**, or $(n - 1)$. The 100th term is the first term, 5, plus 99 times the common difference, 2.

$$a_{100} = 5 + 99(2) = 5 + 198 = 203$$

FINDING THE *n*th TERM OF AN ARITHMETIC SEQUENCE

The nth term a_n of an arithmetic sequence with common difference d is

$$a_n = a_1 + (n - 1)d.$$

EXAMPLE 2 Finding a Given Term of an Arithmetic Sequence

Find the given term in each arithmetic sequence.

A **15th term: 5, 7, 9, 11, . . .**

$a_n = a_1 + (n - 1)d$

$a_{15} = 5 + (15 - 1)2$

$a_{15} = 33$

B **23rd term: 25, 21, 17, 13, . . .**

$a_n = a_1 + (n - 1)d$

$a_{23} = 25 + (23 - 1)(-4)$

$a_{23} = -63$

C **12th term: −9, −5, −1, 3, . . .**

$a_n = a_1 + (n - 1)d$

$a_{12} = -9 + (12 - 1)4$

$a_{12} = 35$

D **20th term: $a_1 = 3$, $d = 15$**

$a_n = a_1 + (n - 1)d$

$a_{20} = 3 + (20 - 1)15$

$a_{20} = 288$

You can use the formula for the *n*th term of an arithmetic sequence to solve for other variables.

EXAMPLE 3 *Travel Application*

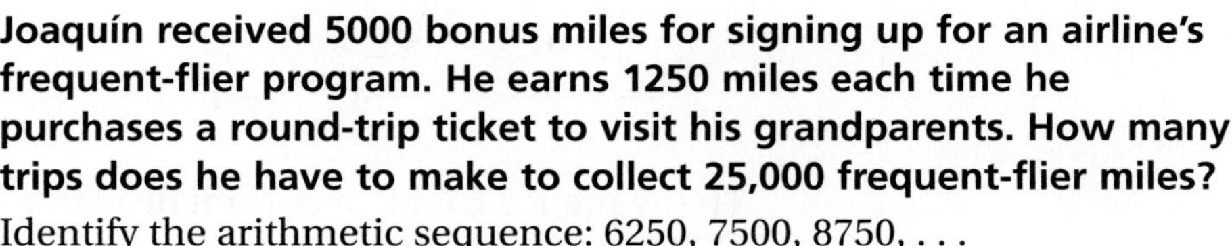

Joaquín received 5000 bonus miles for signing up for an airline's frequent-flier program. He earns 1250 miles each time he purchases a round-trip ticket to visit his grandparents. How many trips does he have to make to collect 25,000 frequent-flier miles?

Identify the arithmetic sequence: 6250, 7500, 8750, . . .

$a_1 = 6250$ *Let $a_1 = 6250$ = frequent flier miles after first trip.*

$d = 1250$

$a_n = 25{,}000$

Let *n* represent the trip number in which Joaquín will have earned a total of 25,000 miles. Use the formula for arithmetic sequences.

$a_n = a_1 + (n - 1)d$	*Solve for n.*
$25{,}000 = 6250 + (n - 1)1250$	*Distributive Property*
$25{,}000 = 6250 + 1250n - 1250$	*Combine like terms.*
$25{,}000 = 5000 + 1250n$	*Subtract 5000 from both sides.*
$20{,}000 = 1250n$	*Divide both sides by 1250.*
$16 = n$	

After 16 trips, Joaquín will have collected 25,000 frequent-flier miles.

Think and Discuss

1. **Explain** how to determine if a sequence might be an arithmetic sequence.
2. **Compare** your answers for the 10th term of the arithmetic sequence 5, 7, 9, 11, 13, . . . by finding all of the first 10 terms and by using the formula.

12-1 Exercises

FOR EXTRA PRACTICE
see page 754

internet connect
Homework Help Online
go.hrw.com Keyword: MP4 12-1

GUIDED PRACTICE

See Example 1
Determine if each sequence could be arithmetic. If so, give the common difference.

1. 4, 6, 8, 10, 12, . . .
2. 14, 12, 11, 9, 8, . . .
3. $\frac{2}{9}, \frac{1}{3}, \frac{4}{9}, \frac{5}{9}, \frac{2}{3}, \ldots$
4. 99, 92, 85, 78, 71, . . .
5. $\frac{1}{2}, \frac{1}{4}, \frac{1}{8}, \frac{1}{16}, \frac{1}{32}, \ldots$
6. 9, 6, 3, 0, −3, . . .

See Example 2
Find the given term in each arithmetic sequence.

7. 17th term: 5, 7, 9, 11, . . .
8. 24th term: 2, 6, 10, 14, . . .
9. 21st term: −4, −8, −12, −16, . . .
10. 30th term: $a_1 = 11, d = 5$

See Example 3
11. Postage for a first-class letter costs $0.37 for the first ounce and $0.23 for each additional ounce. If a letter costs $1.52 to mail, how many ounces is it?

INDEPENDENT PRACTICE

See Example 1
Determine if each sequence could be arithmetic. If so, give the common difference.

12. $\frac{1}{2}, 1, 1\frac{1}{2}, 2, 2\frac{1}{2}, \ldots$
13. 3, 2, 1, 0, −1, . . .
14. $\frac{1}{8}, \frac{3}{8}, \frac{7}{8}, 1\frac{1}{8}, 1\frac{5}{8}, \ldots$
15. 6, 29, 52, 75, 98, . . .
16. $\frac{4}{5}, 1\frac{1}{5}, 1\frac{3}{5}, 2, 2\frac{1}{5}, \ldots$
17. 0.1, 0.4, 0.7, 1, 1.3, . . .

See Example 2
Find the given term in each arithmetic sequence.

18. 11th term: 5, 3, 1, −1, . . .
19. 23rd term: 0.1, 0.15, 0.2, 0.25
20. 50th term: $a_1 = 1, d = 2$
21. 18th term: $a_1 = 44.5, d = -3.5$

See Example 3
22. Mariano received a bonus of $50 for working the day after Thanksgiving, plus his regular wage of $9.45 an hour. If his total wages for the day were $135.05, how many hours did he work?

PRACTICE AND PROBLEM SOLVING

Write the next three terms of each arithmetic sequence.

23. 11, 14, 17, 20, . . .
24. −14, −8, −2, 4, . . .
25. 101, 90, 79, 68, . . .
26. $\frac{1}{2}, \frac{5}{8}, \frac{3}{4}, \frac{7}{8}, \ldots$
27. −6, −18, −30, −42, . . .
28. 0.5, 0.4, 0.3, 0.2, . . .

Write the first five terms of each arithmetic sequence.

29. $a_1 = 1, d = 1$
30. $a_1 = 3, d = 7$
31. $a_1 = 0, d = 0.25$
32. $a_1 = 100, d = -5$
33. $a_1 = 32, d = 1\frac{4}{5}$
34. $a_1 = 6, d = -4$

35. The 5th term of an arithmetic sequence is 134. The common difference is 14. What are the first four terms of the arithmetic sequence?

36. The 1st term of an arithmetic sequence is 9. The common difference is 11. What position in the sequence is the term 163?

37. Julia's watch loses 5 minutes each day. At noon on Sunday, her watch read 11:55. Write the first four terms of an arithmetic sequence modeling the situation. (Assume $a_1 = 11{:}55$.)

38. ***RECREATION*** The rates for a mini grand-prix course are shown in the flyer.

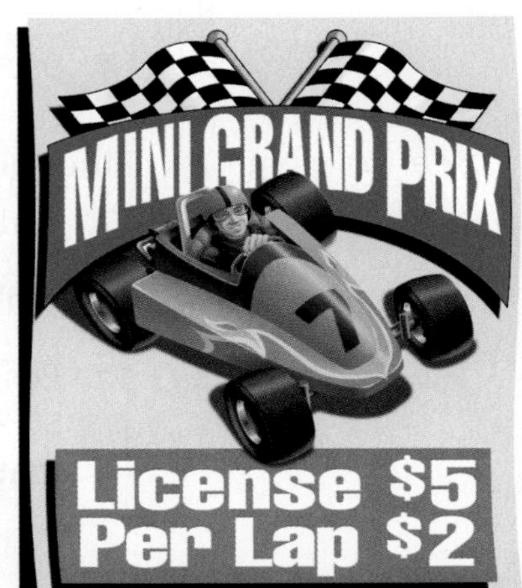

a. What are the first 5 terms of the arithmetic sequence that represents the fees for the course?

b. What would the rate be for 9 laps around the course?

c. If the cost of a license plus n laps is $11, find n.

39. ***BUSINESS*** A law firm charges an administrative fee of $75, plus a $52.50 fee for each half hour of consultation.

a. What are the first 4 terms of an arithmetic sequence that represents the rates of the law firm?

b. How long was a consultation if the total bill came to $390?

40. ***WRITE ABOUT IT*** Explain how to find the common difference of an arithmetic sequence. What can you say about the terms of a sequence if the common difference is positive? if the common difference is negative?

41. ***WRITE A PROBLEM*** Write an arithmetic sequence problem using $a_7 = -15$ and $d = 6.5$.

42. ***CHALLENGE*** The 1st term of an arithmetic sequence is 4, and the common difference is 5. Find two consecutive terms of the sequence that have a sum of 103. What positions are the terms in the sequence?

Spiral Review

Solve each inequality. (Lesson 10-4)

43. $12x - 4 > 3x + 14$

44. $6p + 11 < 10 + 5p$

45. $5 + 4p \geq 18 + 2p$

46. $0.5x - 1 \leq 0.25x + 4$

47. $19c - 11 > 14c + 14$

48. $10.5d - 1.5 < 9.5d$

49. **TEST PREP** A right triangle has vertices at (0, 0), (4, 0), and (4, 10). What is the slope of the hypotenuse? (Lesson 5-5)

A 2.5 **B** 0.4 **C** 2 **D** 1.8

12-2 Geometric Sequences

Learn to find terms in a geometric sequence.

Vocabulary

geometric sequence

common ratio

Joey mows his family's yard every week. His mother offers him a choice of \$10 per week, or 1¢ the first week, 2¢ the second week, 4¢ the third week, and so on.

Week 1	Week 2	Week 3	Week 4
1¢	2¢	4¢	8¢

Ratio $\frac{2}{1} = 2$ Ratio $\frac{2}{1} = 2$ Ratio $\frac{2}{1} = 2$

The weekly amounts Joey would get paid in this plan form a geometric sequence. In a **geometric sequence**, the ratio of one term to the next is always the same. This ratio is called the **common ratio**. The common ratio is multipied by each term to get the next term.

EXAMPLE 1 Identifying Geometric Sequences

Determine if each sequence could be geometric. If so, give the common ratio.

A **96, 48, 24, 12, 6, . . .**

96   48   24   12   6, . . .

$\frac{1}{2}$ $\frac{1}{2}$ $\frac{1}{2}$ $\frac{1}{2}$

Divide each term by the term before it.

The sequence could be geometric with a common ratio of $\frac{1}{2}$.

B **5, −5, 5, −5, 5, . . .**

5   −5   5   −5   5, . . .

−1   −1   −1   −1

Divide each term by the term before it.

The sequence could be geometric with a common ratio of −1.

C **5, 7, 9, 11, . . .**

5   7   9   11, . . .

$\frac{7}{5}$ $\frac{9}{7}$ $\frac{11}{9}$

Divide each term by the term before it.

The sequence is not geometric.

Determine if each sequence could be geometric. If so, give the common ratio.

D **4, −6, 9, −13.5, 20.25, . . .**

4 −6 9 −13.5 20.25, . . .

−1.5 −1.5 −1.5 −1.5

Divide each term by the term before it.

The sequence could be geometric with a common ratio of −1.5.

Suppose you wanted to find the 15th term of the geometric sequence 2, 6, 18, 54, 162, ... If you do not want to find the first 14 terms, you could look for a pattern in the terms of the sequence.

Term Name	a_1	a_2	a_3	a_4	a_5	a_6
Term	2	6	18	54	162	486
Pattern	$2(3)^0$	$2(3)^1$	$2(3)^2$	$2(3)^3$	$2(3)^4$	$2(3)^5$

The common ratio r is 3. For the 2nd term, a_1 is multiplied by 3 once. For the 3rd term, a_1 is multiplied by 3 twice. The pattern shows that for each term, the **number of times 3 is multiplied** is one less than the **term number**, or $(n - 1)$. The 15th term is the first term, 2, times the common ratio, 3, raised to the 14th power.

$$a_{15} = 2(3)^{14} = 2(4{,}782{,}969) = 9{,}565{,}938$$

FINDING THE *n*th TERM OF A GEOMETRIC SEQUENCE

The nth term a_n of a geometric sequence with common ratio r is

$$a_n = a_1 r^{n-1}.$$

EXAMPLE 2 Finding a Given Term of a Geometric Sequence

Find the given term in each geometric sequence.

A **12th term: 6, 18, 54, 162, . . .**

$r = \frac{18}{6} = 3$

$a_{12} = 6(3)^{11} = 1{,}062{,}882$

B **57th term: 1, −1, 1, −1, 1, . . .**

$r = \frac{-1}{1} = -1$

$a_{57} = 1(-1)^{56} = 1$

C **10th term: 5, $\frac{5}{2}$, $\frac{5}{4}$, $\frac{5}{8}$, $\frac{5}{16}$, . . .**

$r = \frac{\frac{5}{2}}{5} = \frac{1}{2}$

$a_{10} = 5\left(\frac{1}{2}\right)^9 = \frac{5}{512}$

D **20th term: 625, 500, 400, 320, . . .**

$r = \frac{500}{625} = 0.8$

$a_{20} = 625(0.8)^{19} \approx 9.01$

EXAMPLE 3 *Money Application*

For mowing his family's yard every week, Joey has two options for payment: (1) \$10 per week or (2) 1¢ the first week, 2¢ the second week, 4¢ the third week, and so on, where he makes twice as much each week as he made the week before. If Joey will mow the yard for 15 weeks, which option should he choose?

If Joey chooses \$10 per week, he will get a total of 15(\$10) = \$150.

If Joey chooses the second option, his payment for just the 15th week will be more than the total of all the payments in option 1.

$$a_{15} = (\$0.01)(2)^{14} = (\$0.01)(16{,}384) = \$163.84$$

Option 1 gives Joey more money in the beginning, but option 2 gives him a larger total amount.

Think and Discuss

1. **Compare** arithmetic sequences with geometric sequences.
2. **Describe** how you find the common ratio in a geometric sequence.

12-2 Exercises

FOR EXTRA PRACTICE
see page 754

internet connect
Homework Help Online
go.hrw.com Keyword: MP4 12-2

GUIDED PRACTICE

See Example 1

Determine if each sequence could be geometric. If so, give the common ratio.

1. $-4, -2, 0, 2, 4, \ldots$
2. $2, 6, 18, 54, 162, \ldots$
3. $\frac{2}{3}, -\frac{2}{3}, \frac{2}{3}, -\frac{2}{3}, \frac{2}{3}, \ldots$
4. $1, 1.5, 2.25, 3.375, \ldots$
5. $\frac{3}{16}, \frac{3}{8}, \frac{3}{4}, \frac{3}{2}, \ldots$
6. $-2, -4, -8, -16, \ldots$

See Example 2

Find the given term in each geometric sequence.

7. 12th term: $3, 6, 12, 24, 48, \ldots$
8. 101st term: $\frac{1}{3}, -\frac{1}{3}, \frac{1}{3}, -\frac{1}{3}, \frac{1}{3}, \ldots$
9. 22nd term: $a_1 = 262{,}144$, $r = \frac{1}{2}$
10. 8th term: $1, 4, 16, 64, 256, \ldots$

See Example 3

11. Heather makes \$6.50 per hour. Every three months, she is eligible for a 2% raise. How much will she make after 2 years if she gets a raise every time she is eligible?

INDEPENDENT PRACTICE

See Example 1 **Determine if each sequence could be geometric. If so, give the common ratio.**

12. 16, 8, 4, 2, 1, ...

13. $\frac{1}{2}, \frac{1}{8}, \frac{1}{4}, \frac{1}{16}, \ldots$

14. 3, 6, 9, 12, ...

15. 768, 384, 192, 96, ...

16. 1, −3, 9, −27, 81, ...

17. $6, 2, \frac{2}{3}, \frac{2}{9}, \ldots$

See Example 2 **Find the given term in each geometric sequence.**

18. 6th term: $\frac{1}{2}, 1, 2, 4, \ldots$

19. 5th term: $a_1 = 4096$, $r = \frac{7}{8}$

20. 5th term: $a_1 = 12$, $r = -\frac{1}{2}$

21. 7th term: 3, 6, 12, 24, ...

22. 22nd term: $\frac{1}{36}, \frac{1}{18}, \frac{1}{9}, \frac{2}{9}, \ldots$

23. 6th term: 1, 1.5, 2.25, 3.375, ...

See Example 3 **24.** A tank contains 54,000 gallons of water. One-third of the water remaining in the tank is removed each day. How much water is left in the tank on the 15th day?

PRACTICE AND PROBLEM SOLVING

Find the next three terms of each geometric sequence.

25. $a_1 = 24$, common ratio $= \frac{1}{2}$

26. $a_1 = 4$, common ratio $= 2$

27. $a_1 = \frac{1}{81}$, common ratio $= -3$

28. $a_1 = 3$, common ratio $= 2.5$

Find the first five terms of each geometric sequence.

29. $a_1 = 1, r = 1$

30. $a_1 = 5, r = -3$

31. $a_1 = 100, r = 1.1$

32. $a_1 = 64, r = \frac{3}{2}$

33. $a_1 = 10, r = 0.25$

34. $a_1 = 64, r = -4$

35. Find the 1st term of the geometric sequence with 6th term $\frac{64}{5}$ and common ratio 2.

36. Find the 3rd term of the geometric sequence with 7th term 256 and common ratio −4.

37. Find the 1st term of the geometric sequence with 5th term $\frac{125}{432}$ and common ratio $\frac{5}{6}$.

38. Find the 1st term of a geometric sequence with 4th term 28 and common ratio 2.

39. Find the 5th term of a geometric sequence with 3rd term 8 and 4th term 12.

40. Find the 3rd term of a geometric sequence with 4th term 5400 and 6th term 7776.

41. Find the 1st term of a geometric sequence with 3rd term 72 and 5th term 32.

42. ***ECONOMICS*** A car that was originally valued at $16,000 depreciates at 15% per year. This means that after each year, the car is worth 85% of its worth the previous year. What is the value of the car after 6 years? Round to the nearest dollar.

43. ***LIFE SCIENCE*** Under controlled conditions, a culture of bacteria doubles in size every 2 days. How many cells of the bacteria are in the culture after 2 weeks if there were originally 32 cells?

44. ***PHYSICAL SCIENCE*** A rubber ball is dropped from a height of 256 ft. After each bounce the height of the ball is recorded.

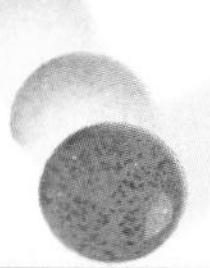

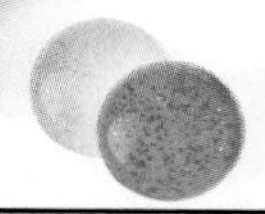

Height of Bouncing Ball					
Number of Bounces	1	2	3	4	5
Height (ft)	192	144	108	81	60.75

a. Could the heights in the table form a geometric sequence? If so, what is the common ratio?

b. Estimate the height of the ball after the 8th bounce. Round your answer to the nearest foot.

45. ***WRITE ABOUT IT*** Compare a geometric sequence with $a_1 = 2$ and $r = 3$ with a geometric sequence with $a_1 = 3$ and $r = 2$.

46. ***WHAT'S THE ERROR?*** A student is asked to find the next three terms of the geometric sequence with $a_1 = 10$ and common ratio 5. His answer is 2, $\frac{2}{5}$, $\frac{2}{25}$. What error has the student made, and what is the correct answer?

47. ***CHALLENGE*** The 5th term in a geometric sequence is 768. The 10th term is 786,432. Find the 7th term.

Spiral Review

Find the appropriate conversion factor. (Lesson 7-3)

48. meters to millimeters
49. quarts to gallons
50. gallons to pints
51. grams to centigrams
52. kilograms to grams
53. yards to inches

54. **TEST PREP** On a blueprint, a window is 2.5 inches wide. If the actual window is 85 inches wide, what scale factor was used to create the blueprint? (Lesson 7-7)

A $\frac{1}{28}$ **B** $\frac{1}{17}$ **C** $\frac{1}{24}$ **D** $\frac{1}{34}$

Fibonacci Sequence

Use with Lesson 12-3

internet connect
Lab Resources Online
go.hrw.com
KEYWORD: MP4 Lab12A

WHAT YOU NEED:
Square tiles

Activity

1. Use square tiles to model the following numbers:

   1 1 2 3 5 8 13 21

   1 1 2 3 5 8 13 21

2. Place the first stack of tiles on top of the second stack of tiles. What do you notice?

The first two stacks added together are equal in height to the third stack.

3. Place the second stack of tiles on top of the third stack of tiles. What do you notice?

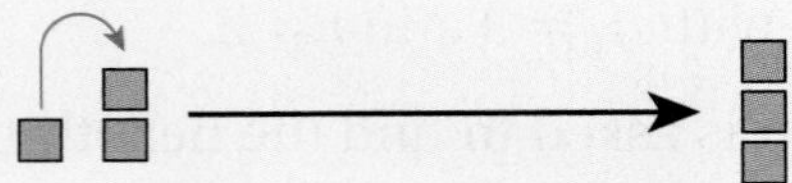

The second stack and the third stack added together are equal in height to the fourth stack.

This sequence is called the **Fibonacci sequence.** By adding two successive numbers you get the next number in the sequence. The sequence will go on forever.

Think and Discuss

1. If there were a term before the 1 in the sequence, what would it be? Explain your answer.
2. Could the numbers 144, 233, 377 be part of the Fibonacci sequence? Explain.

Try This

1. Use your square tiles to find the next two numbers in the sequence. What are they?
2. The 18th and 19th terms of the Fibonacci sequence are 2584 and 4181. What is the 20th term?

Music LINK

Pitch is the frequency of a musical note, measured in units called *hertz* (Hz). The lower the frequency of a pitch, the lower it sounds, and the higher the frequency of a pitch, the higher it sounds. A pitch is named by its octave. A_4 is in the 4th octave on the piano keyboard and is often called middle A.

55 Hz A_1
110 Hz A_2
165 Hz E_2
220 Hz A_3
$C\#_3$ 275 Hz
? Hz E_3
440 Hz A_4
? Hz A_5
A_6
A_7
A_8

27. What kind of sequence is represented by the frequencies of A_1, A_2, A_3, A_4, . . . ? Write a rule to calculate these frequencies.

28. What is the frequency of the note A_5, which is one octave higher than A_4?

When a string of an instrument is played, its vibrations create many different frequencies at the same time. These varying frequencies are called *harmonics.*

Frequencies of Harmonics on A_1					
Harmonic	Fundamental (1st)	2nd	3rd	4th	5th
Note	A_1	A_2	E_2	A_3	$C^{\#}_3$

29. What kind of sequence is represented by the frequencies of different harmonics? Write a rule to calculate these frequencies.

30. What is the frequency of the note E_3 if it is the 6th harmonic on A_1?

31. **CHALLENGE** In music an important interval is a *fifth.* As you progress around the circle of fifths, the pitch frequencies are approximately as shown (rounded to the nearest tenth). What type of sequence do the frequencies form in clockwise order from C? Write the rule for the sequence. If the rule holds all the way around the circle, what would the frequency of the note F be?

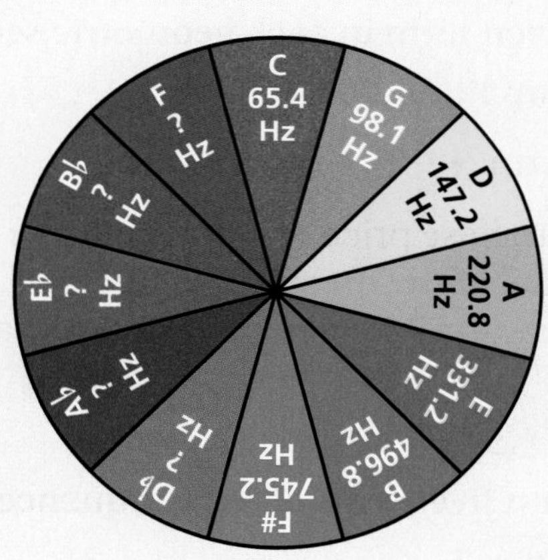

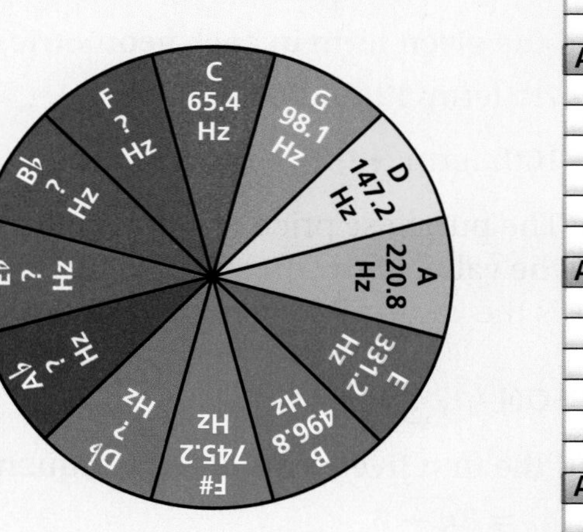

Spiral Review

Find the x-intercept and y-intercept of each line. (Lesson 11-3)

32. $3x - 8y = 48$ **33.** $5y - 15x = -45$ **34.** $13x + 2y = 26$ **35.** $9x + 27y = 81$

36. **TEST PREP** If y varies directly with x and $y = 25$ when $x = 15$, find the equation of direct variation. (Lesson 11-5)

A $y = \frac{3}{5}x$ **B** $y = \frac{5}{3}x$ **C** $y = 15x$ **D** $y = 25x$

Chapter 12

Mid-Chapter Quiz

LESSON 12-1 (pp. 590–594)

Determine if each sequence could be arithmetic. If so, give the common difference.

1. 10, 11, 13, 16, ...
2. 27, 24, 21, 18, ...
3. 11, 22, 33, 44, ...
4. 17, 60, 103, 177, ...

Find the given term in each arithmetic sequence.

5. 8th term: 5, 8, 11, 14, ...
6. 11th term: 7, 6.9, 6.8, ...
7. 14th term: 9, $9\frac{1}{4}$, $9\frac{1}{2}$, ...
8. 6th term: 28, 15, 2, –11, ...
9. Frank deposited $25 in an account the first week. Each week, he deposits $5 more than the previous week. In which week will he deposit $100?

LESSON 12-2 (pp. 595–599)

Determine if each sequence could be geometric. If so, give the common ratio.

10. 1, −5, 25, −125, ...
11. 2, −5, −12, −19, ...
12. 81, 27, 9, 3, ...
13. 60, 18, 5.4, 1.62, ...

Find the given term in each geometric sequence.

14. 7th term: 12, 36, 108, ...
15. 9th term: 36, 12, 4, ...
16. 10th term: $-\frac{3}{2}$, 3, −6, ...
17. 15th term: 1000, 100, 10, ...
18. The purchase price of a machine at a factory was $500,000. Each year, the value of the machine depreciates by 5%. To the nearest dollar, what is the value of the machine after 6 years?

LESSON 12-3 (pp. 601–605)

Find the first five terms of each sequence, given its rule.

19. $a_n = 3n - 5$
20. $a_n = 2^{n-1}$
21. $a_n = (-1)^n \cdot 3n$
22. $a_n = (n + 1)^2 - 1$

Use first and second differences to find the next three terms in each sequence.

23. 9, 9, 11, 15, 21, ...
24. 3, 10, 21, 36, 55, ...
25. −6, −11, −13, −12, −8, ...
26. 0, 4, 11, 22, 38, 60, ...

Give the next three terms in each sequence using the simplest rule you can find.

27. $\frac{1}{2}, \frac{3}{4}, \frac{5}{6}, \frac{7}{8}$...
28. 1, 8, 27, 64, ...

Focus on Problem Solving

Solve

- **Eliminate answer choices**

When answering a multiple-choice question, you may be able to eliminate some of the choices. If the question is a word problem, check whether any answers do not make sense in the problem.

Example:

Gabrielle has a savings account with $125 in it. Each week, she deposits $5 in the account. How much will she have in 12 weeks?

A $65 **B** $185 **C** $142 **D** $190

The following sequence represents the weekly balance in dollars:

125, 130, 135, 140, 145, ...

The amount will be greater than $125, so it cannot be **A.** It will also be a multiple of 5, so it cannot be **C.**

Read each question and decide whether you can eliminate any answer choices before choosing an answer. Explain your reasoning.

1. An art gallery has 400 paintings. Each year, the curator acquires 15 new paintings. How many paintings will the gallery have in 7 years?

   A 450 **C** 505
   B 6000 **D** 295

2. There are 360 deer in a forest. The population increases each year by 10% over the previous year. How many deer will there be after 9 years?

   A 849 **C** 324
   B 450 **D** 684

3. Donna is in a book club. She has read 24 books so far, and she thinks she can read 3 books a week during the summer. How many weeks will it take for her to read a total of 60 books?

   A 20 weeks **C** 3 weeks
   B 12 weeks **D** 60 weeks

4. Oliver has $230.00 in a savings account that earns 6% interest each year. How much will he have in 12 years?

   A $230.00 **C** $395.60
   B $109.46 **D** $462.81

12-4 Functions

Domain

Input

Function

Output

Range

Learn to represent functions with tables, graphs, or equations.

Vocabulary

function

input

output

domain

range

function notation

A **function** is a rule that relates two quantities so that each **input** value corresponds to exactly one **output** value.

The **domain** is the set of all possible input values, and the **range** is the set of all possible output values.

Function
One input gives one output.

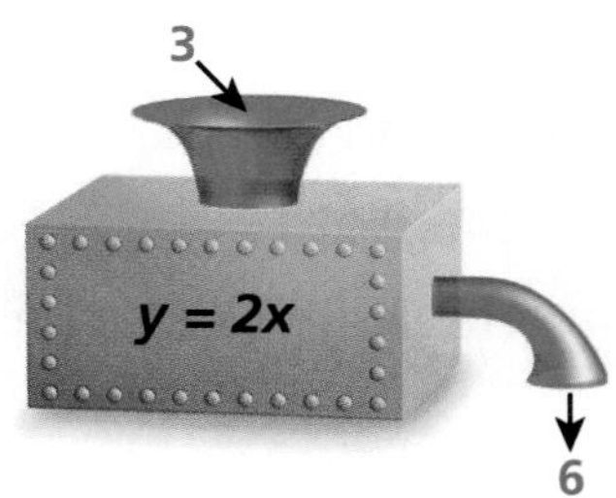

Example: The output is 2 times the input.

Not a Function
One input gives more than one output.

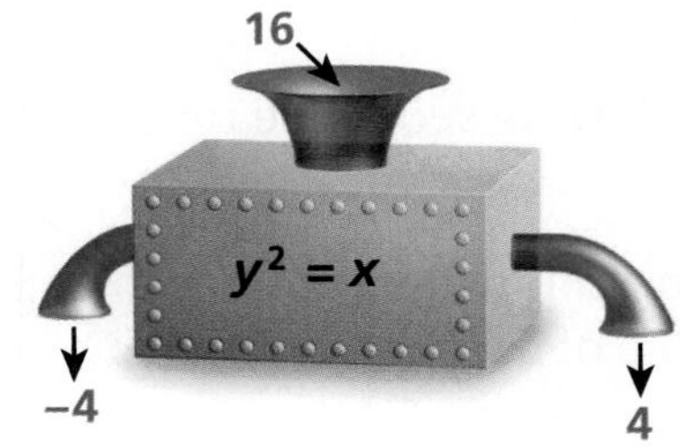

Example: The outputs are the square roots of the input.

Functions can be represented in many ways, including tables, graphs, and equations. If the domain of a function has infinitely many values, it is impossible to represent them all in a table, but a table can be used to show some of the values and to help in creating a graph.

EXAMPLE 1 Finding Different Representations of a Function

Make a table and a graph of $y = x^2 + 1$.

Make a table of inputs and outputs. Use the table to make a graph.

x	$x^2 + 1$	y
−2	$(-2)^2 + 1$	5
−1	$(-1)^2 + 1$	2
0	$(0)^2 + 1$	1
1	$(1)^2 + 1$	2
2	$(2)^2 + 1$	5

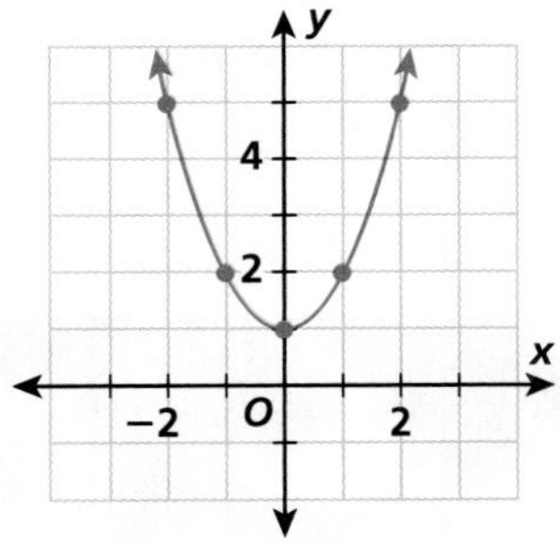

To determine if a relationship is a function, verify that each input has exactly one output.

12-5 Linear Functions

Learn to identify linear functions.

Vocabulary

linear function

Elephant seals weigh about 100 pounds at birth. The mother's milk is so rich—about 50% fat—that the pup gains about 8 pounds per day while nursing.

Elephant seals are the largest seals. Adult males weigh an average of about 5000 pounds, and adult females weigh an average of about 1100 pounds.

Weight of Elephant Seal Pup					
Day	0	1	2	3	4
Weight (lb)	100	108	116	124	132

Notice that the weights form an arithmetic sequence with a common difference of 8. Also, the data can be plotted on a coordinate plane as a line with slope 8 and y-intercept 100.

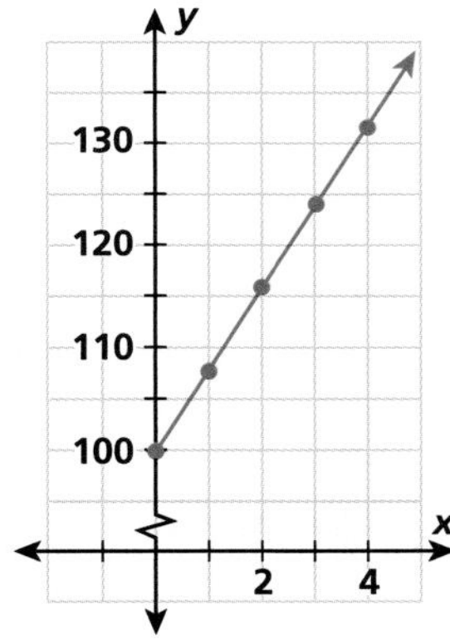

The graph of a **linear function** is a line. The linear function $f(x) = mx + b$ has a slope of m and a y-intercept of b. You can use the equation $f(x) = mx + b$ to write the equation of a linear function from a graph or table.

EXAMPLE 1 Writing the Equation for a Linear Function from a Graph

Write the rule for the linear function.

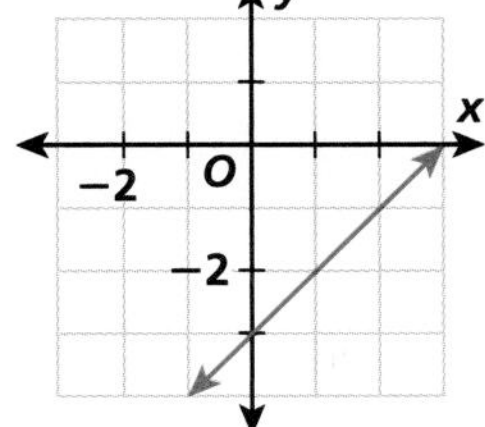

Use the equation $f(x) = mx + b$. To find b, identify the y-intercept from the graph.

$b = -3$

$f(x) = mx + (-3)$

$f(x) = mx - 3$

Locate another point on the graph, such as $(1, -2)$. Substitute the x- and y-values of the point into the equation, and solve for m.

$f(x) = mx - 3$

$-2 = m(1) - 3$ *(x, y) = (1, −2)*

$-2 = m - 3$

$\underline{+3} \quad \underline{\quad +3}$

$1 = m$

The rule is $f(x) = 1x + -3$, or $f(x) = x - 3$.

EXAMPLE 2 Writing the Equation for a Linear Function from a Table

Write the rule for each linear function.

A

x	y
−2	9
−1	8
0	7
1	6

The y-intercept can be identified from the table as $b = f(0) = 7$. Substitute the x- and y-values of the point (1, 6) into the equation $f(x) = mx + 7$, and solve for m.

$$f(x) = mx + 7$$
$$6 = m(1) + 7$$
$$6 = m + 7$$
$$\underline{-7 \qquad -7}$$
$$-1 = m$$

The rule is $f(x) = -1x + 7$, or $f(x) = -x + 7$.

B

x	y
−2	−16
−1	−13
1	−7
2	−4

Use two points, such as (1, −7) and (2, −4), to find the slope.

$$m = \frac{y_2 - y_1}{x_2 - x_1} = \frac{-4 - (-7)}{2 - 1} = \frac{3}{1} = 3$$

Substitute the x- and y-values of the point (1, −7) into $f(x) = 3x + b$, and solve for b.

$$f(x) = 3x + b$$
$$-7 = 3(1) + b \qquad \textit{(x, y) = (1, −7)}$$
$$-7 = 3 + b$$
$$\underline{-3 \qquad -3}$$
$$-10 = b$$

The rule is $f(x) = 3x + (-10)$, or $f(x) = 3x - 10$.

EXAMPLE 3 *Life Science Application*

An elephant seal weighs 100 pounds at birth and gains 8 pounds each day while nursing. Find a rule for the linear function that describes the growth of the pup, and use it to find out how much the pup will weigh after 23 days, when it will be weaned.

$$f(x) = mx + 100 \qquad \textit{The y-intercept is the birth weight, 100 pounds.}$$
$$108 = m(1) + 100 \qquad \textit{At 1 day old, the pup will weigh 108 pounds.}$$
$$108 = m + 100$$
$$\underline{-100 \qquad -100}$$
$$8 = m$$

The rule for the function is $f(x) = 8x + 100$. After 23 days, the pup's weight will be $f(23) = 8(23) + 100 = 184 + 100 = 284$ pounds.

Think and Discuss

1. Describe how to use a graph to find the equation of a linear function.

32. ***PHYSICAL SCIENCE*** The height of a toy rocket launched straight up with an initial velocity of 48 feet per second is given by the function $f(t) = 48t - 16t^2$. The time t is in seconds.

   a. Graph the function for $t = 0, 0.5, 1, 1.5, 2, 2.5$, and 3.

   b. When is the rocket at its highest point? What is its height?

   c. How many seconds does it take for the rocket to land?

33. ***BUSINESS*** A store owner can sell 30 digital cameras a week at a price of $150 each. For every $5 drop in price, she can sell 2 more cameras a week. If x is the number of $5 price reductions, the weekly sales function is $f(x) = (30 + 2x)(150 - 5x)$.

   a. Find $f(x)$ for $x = 3, 4, 5, 6$, and 7. How many $5 price reductions will result in the highest weekly sales?

   b. What will the price of a camera be in part **a**?

Predicted Sales			
Price	$150	$145	$140
Number Sold	30	32	34
Weekly Sales	$4500	$4640	$4760

34. ***HOBBIES*** The height of a model airplane launched from the top of a 24 ft hill is given by the function $f(t) = -0.08t^2 + 2.6t + 24$. Find $f(40)$. What does this tell you about $t = 40$ seconds?

35. ***WRITE ABOUT IT*** Which will grow faster as x gets larger, $f(x) = x^2$ or $f(x) = 2^x$? Check by testing each function for several values of x.

36. ***CHOOSE A STRATEGY*** Suppose the function $f(x) = -4x^2 + 200x + 1150$ gives a company's profit for producing x items. How many items should be produced to maximize profit?

   A 20 **B** 25 **C** 30 **D** 35

37. ***CHALLENGE*** Create a table of values for the quadratic function $f(x) = -2(x^2 + 1)$, and then graph it. What are the x-intercepts of the function?

Spiral Review

Write the slope and y-intercept of each equation. (Lesson 11-3)

38. $y = 4x - 2$ **39.** $y = -2x + 12$ **40.** $y = -0.25x$ **41.** $y = -x - 4$

42. $x - 3y = 12$ **43.** $y + 4x = 1$ **44.** $5x + 5y = 25$ **45.** $4 - y = 2x$

46. **TEST PREP** The 4th term of an arithmetic sequence is 10. The common difference is 5. What is the 1st term of the sequence? (Lesson 12-1)

   A -5 **B** -15 **C** 0 **D** 5

47. **TEST PREP** The 4th term of a geometric sequence is 10.125. The common ratio is 1.5. What is the 1st term of the sequence? (Lesson 12-2)

   F 1.5 **G** 5.625 **H** 3 **J** 34.171875

Technology LAB 12B

Explore Cubic Functions

Use with Lesson 12-7

internet connect
Lab Resources Online
go.hrw.com
KEYWORD: MP4 Lab12B

You can use your graphing calculator to explore cubic functions. To graph the cubic equation $y = x^3$ in the standard graphing calculator window, press Y= ; enter the right side of the equation, X,T,θ,n ^ 3; and press ZOOM **6:ZStandard.** Notice that the graph goes from the lower left to the upper right and crosses the x-axis once, at $x = 0$.

Activity 1

1 Graph $y = -x^3$. Describe the graph.

Press Y= , and enter the right side of the equation, (−) X,T,θ,n ^ 3.

The graph goes from the upper left to the lower right and crosses the x-axis once.

2 Graph $y = x^3 + 3x^2 - 2$. Describe the graph.

Press Y= ; enter the right side of the equation, X,T,θ,n ^ 3 + 3 X,T,θ,n x^2 − 2; and press ZOOM **6:ZStandard.** The graph goes from the lower left to the upper right and crosses the x-axis three times.

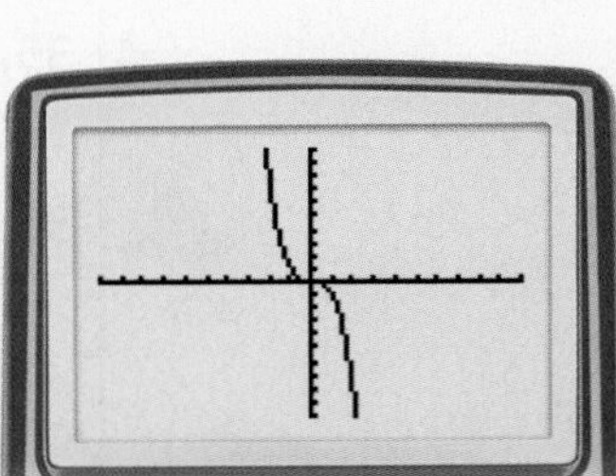

Think and Discuss

1. How does the sign of the x^3 term affect the graph of a cubic function?

2. How could you find the value of 7^3 from the graph of $y = x^3$?

Try This

Graph each function and describe the graph.

1. $y = x^3 - 2$ **2.** $y = x^3 + 3x^2 - 2$ **3.** $y = (x - 2)^3$ **4.** $y = 5 - x^3$

Activity 2

1 Compare the graphs of $y = x^3$ and $y = x^3 + 3$.

Graph **Y₁=X^3** and **Y₂=X^3+3** on the same screen, as shown. Use the TRACE button and the ◀ and ▶ buttons to trace to any integer value of x. Then use the ▲ and ▼ keys to move from one function to the other to compare the values of y for both functions for the value of x. You can also press 2nd GRAPH (TABLE) to see a table of values for both functions.

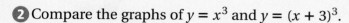

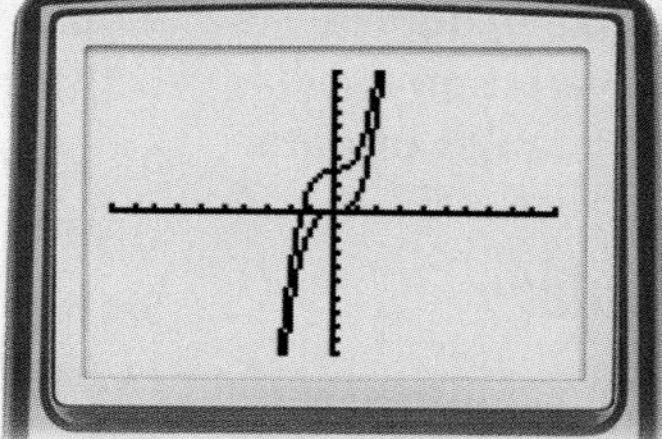

The graph of $y = x^3 + 3$ is translated up 3 units from the graph of $y = x^3$.

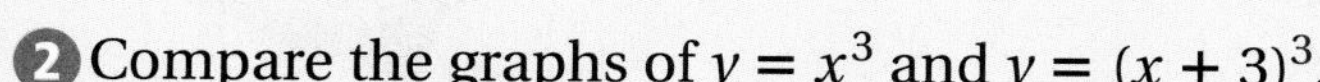

2 Compare the graphs of $y = x^3$ and $y = (x + 3)^3$.

Graph **Y₁=X^3** and **Y₂=(X+3)^3** on the same screen. Notice that the graph of $y = (x + 3)^3$ is the graph of $y = x^3$ moved left 3 units. Press 2nd GRAPH (TABLE) to see a table of values. The graph of $y = (x + 3)^3$ is translated left 3 units from the graph of $y = x^3$.

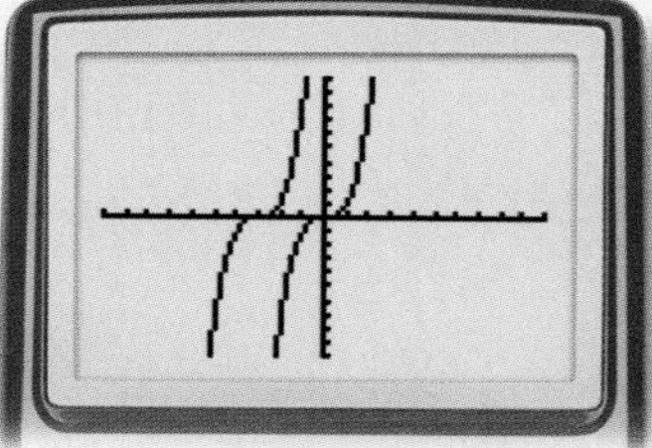

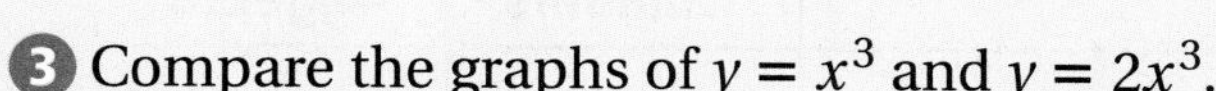

3 Compare the graphs of $y = x^3$ and $y = 2x^3$.

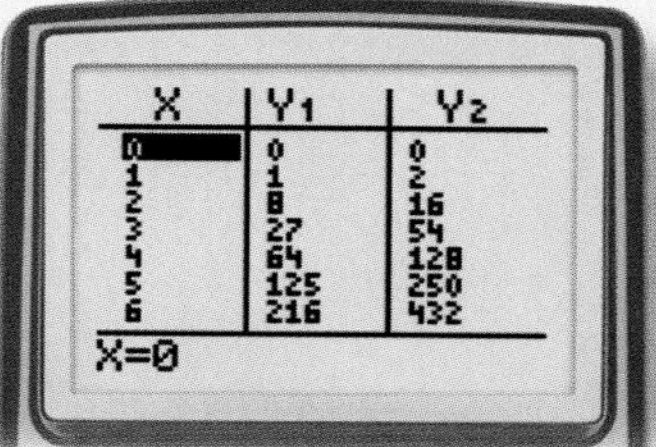

Graph **Y₁=X^3** and **Y₂=2X^3** on the same screen. Use the TRACE button and the arrow keys to see the values of y for any value of x. Press 2nd GRAPH (TABLE) to see a table of values.

The graph of $y = 2x^3$ is stretched upward from the graph of $y = x^3$. The y-value for $y = 2x^3$ increases twice as fast as it does for $y = x^3$. The table of values is shown.

Think and Discuss

1. What function would translate $y = x^3$ right 6 units?
2. Do you think that the methods shown of translating a cubic function would have the same result on a quadratic function? Explain.

Try This

Compare the graph of $y = x^3$ to the graph of each function.

1. $y = x^3 - 2$
2. $y = (x - 7)^3$
3. $y = \left(\frac{1}{2}\right)x^3$
4. $y = 5 - x^3$

12-8 Inverse Variation

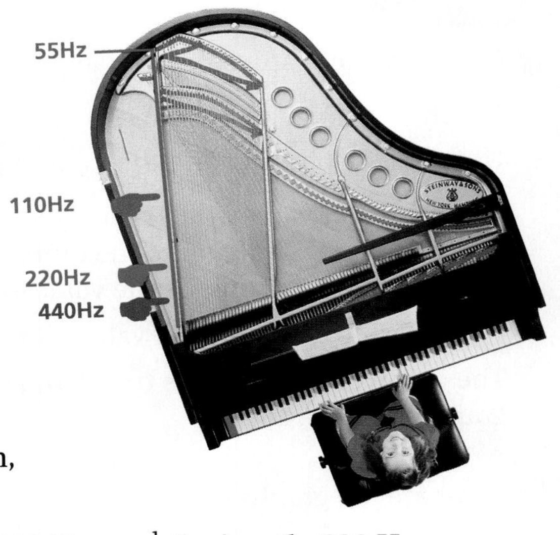

Learn to recognize inverse variation by graphing tables of data.

Vocabulary

inverse variation

The frequency of a piano string is related to its length. You can double a string's frequency by placing your finger at the halfway point of the string. The lowest note on the piano is A_1. As you place your finger at various fractions of the string's length, the frequency will *vary inversely*.

Full length: 55 Hz $\quad \frac{1}{2}$ the length: 110 Hz $\quad \frac{1}{4}$ the length: 220 Hz

The fraction of the string length times the frequency is always 55.

INVERSE VARIATION

Words	Numbers	Algebra
An **inverse variation** is a relationship in which one variable quantity increases as another variable quantity decreases. The product of the variables is a constant.	$y = \frac{120}{x}$ $xy = 120$	$y = \frac{k}{x}$ $xy = k$

EXAMPLE 1 Identifying Inverse Variation

Tell whether each relationship is an inverse variation.

Helpful Hint

To determine if a relationship is an inverse variation, check if the product of x and y is always the same number.

A **The table shows the number of days needed to construct a building based on the size of the work crew.**

Crew Size	2	3	5	10	20
Days of Construction	90	60	36	18	9

$20(9) = 180$; $10(18) = 180$; $5(36) = 180$; $3(60) = 180$; $2(90) = 180$

$xy = 180$ *The product is always the same.*

The relationship is an inverse variation: $y = \frac{180}{x}$.

B **The table shows the number of chips produced in a given time.**

Chips Produced	36	60	84	108	120	144
Time (min)	3	5	7	9	10	12

$36(3) = 108$; $60(5) = 300$ *The product is not always the same.*

The relationship is not an inverse variation.

In the inverse variation relationship $y = \frac{k}{x}$, where $k \neq 0$, y is a function of x. The function is not defined for $x = 0$, so the domain is all real numbers except 0.

EXAMPLE 2 Graphing Inverse Variations

Graph each inverse variation function.

A $f(x) = \frac{1}{x}$

x	y
-3	$-\frac{1}{3}$
-2	$-\frac{1}{2}$
-1	-1
$-\frac{1}{2}$	-2
$\frac{1}{2}$	2
1	1
2	$\frac{1}{2}$
3	$\frac{1}{3}$

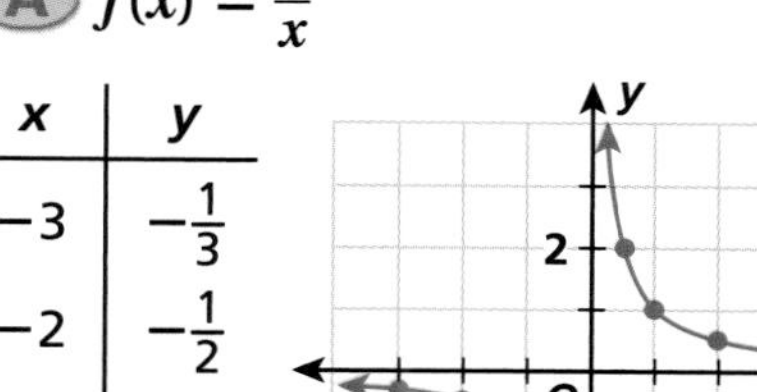

B $f(x) = \frac{-2}{x}$

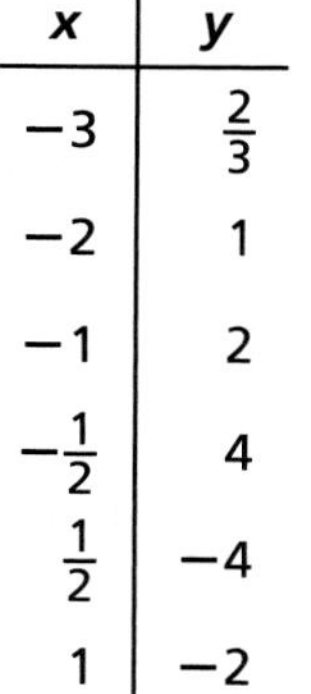

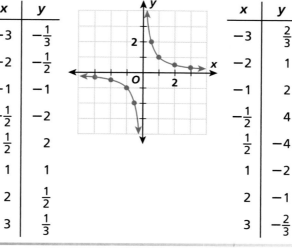

x	y
-3	$\frac{2}{3}$
-2	1
-1	2
$-\frac{1}{2}$	4
$\frac{1}{2}$	-4
1	-2
2	-1
3	$-\frac{2}{3}$

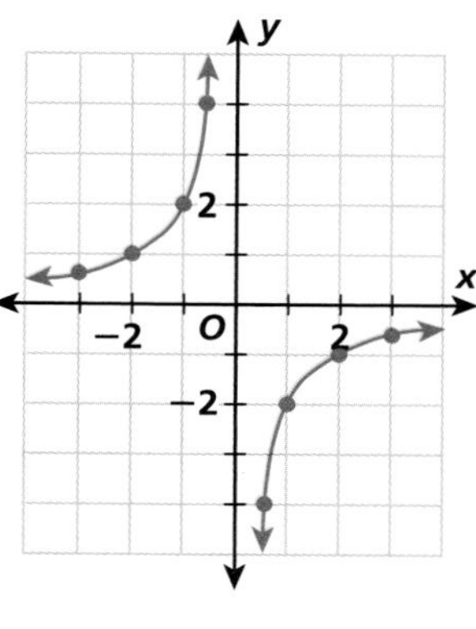

EXAMPLE 3 *Music Application*

The frequency of a piano string changes according to the fraction of its length that is allowed to vibrate. Find the inverse variation function, and use it to find the resulting frequency when $\frac{1}{16}$ of the string A_1 is allowed to vibrate.

Frequency of A_1 by Fraction of the Original String Length				
Frequency (Hz)	55	110	220	440
Fraction of the Length	1	$\frac{1}{2}$	$\frac{1}{4}$	$\frac{1}{8}$

You can see from the table that $xy = 55(1) = 55$, so $y = \frac{55}{x}$.
If the string is reduced to $\frac{1}{16}$ of its length, then its frequency will be $y = 55 \div \left(\frac{1}{16}\right) = 16 \cdot 55 = 880$ Hz.

Think and Discuss

1. **Identify** k in the inverse variation $y = \frac{3}{x}$.
2. **Describe** how you know if a relationship is an inverse variation.

12-8 Exercises

FOR EXTRA PRACTICE
see page 755

internet connect
Homework Help Online
go.hrw.com Keyword: MP4 12-8

GUIDED PRACTICE

See Example 1

Tell whether each relationship is an inverse variation.

1. The table shows the number of CDs produced in a given time.

CDs Produced	45	120	135	165	210
Time (min)	3	8	9	11	14

2. The table shows the construction time of a wall based on the number of workers.

Construction Time (hr)	5	9	15	22.5	45
Number of Workers	9	5	3	2	1

See Example 2

Graph each inverse variation function.

3. $f(x) = \frac{3}{x}$ **4.** $f(x) = \frac{2}{x}$ **5.** $f(x) = \frac{1}{2x}$

See Example 3

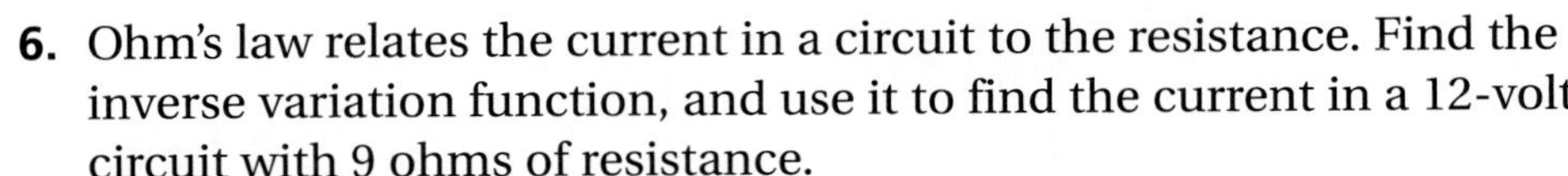

6. Ohm's law relates the current in a circuit to the resistance. Find the inverse variation function, and use it to find the current in a 12-volt circuit with 9 ohms of resistance.

Current (amps)	0.25	0.5	1	2	4
Resistance (ohms)	48	24	12	6	3

INDEPENDENT PRACTICE

See Example 1

Tell whether each relationship is an inverse variation.

7. The table shows the time it takes to throw a baseball from home plate to first base depending on the speed of the throw.

Speed of Throw (ft/s)	30	36	45	60	90
Time (s)	3	2.5	2	1.5	1

8. The table shows the number of miles jogged in a given time.

Miles Jogged	1	1.5	3	4	5
Time (min)	8	12	24	32	40

See Example 2

Graph each inverse variation function.

9. $f(x) = -\frac{1}{x}$ **10.** $f(x) = \frac{1}{3x}$ **11.** $f(x) = -\frac{1}{2x}$

See Example 3

12. According to Boyle's law, when the volume of a gas decreases, the pressure increases. Find the inverse variation function, and use it to find the pressure of the gas if the volume is decreased to 4 liters.

Volume (L)	8	10	20	40	80
Pressure (atm)	5	4	2	1	0.5

PRACTICE AND PROBLEM SOLVING

Find the inverse variation equation, given that x and y vary inversely.

13. $y = 2$ when $x = 2$ **14.** $y = 10$ when $x = 2$ **15.** $y = 8$ when $x = 4$

16. If y varies inversely with x and $y = 27$ when $x = 3$, find the constant of variation.

17. The height of a triangle with area 50 cm^2 varies inversely with the length of its base. If $b = 25$ cm when $h = 4$ cm, find b when $h = 10$ cm.

18. ***PHYSICAL SCIENCE*** If a constant force of 30 N is applied to an object, the mass of the object varies inversely with its acceleration. The table contains data for several objects of different sizes.

Mass (kg)	3	6	30	10	5
Acceleration (m/s^2)	10	5	1	3	6

a. Use the table to write an inverse variation function.

b. What is the mass of an object if its acceleration is 15 m/s^2?

19. ***FINANCE*** Mr. Anderson wants to earn $125 in interest over a 2-year period from a savings account. The principal he must deposit varies inversely with the interest rate of the account. If the interest rate is 6.25%, he must deposit $1000. If the interest rate is 5%, how much must he deposit?

20. ***WRITE ABOUT IT*** Explain the difference between direct variation and inverse variation.

21. ***WRITE A PROBLEM*** Write a problem that can be solved using inverse variation. Use facts and formulas from your science book.

22. ***CHALLENGE*** The resistance of a 100 ft piece of wire varies inversely with the square of its diameter. If the diameter of the wire is 3 in., it has a resistance of 3 ohms. What is the resistance of a wire with a diameter of 1 in.?

Spiral Review

For each function, find $f(-1)$, $f(0)$, and $f(1)$. (Lesson 12-4)

23. $f(x) = 3x^2 - 5x + 1$ **24.** $f(x) = x^2 + 15x - 4$ **25.** $f(x) = 3(x - 9)^2$

26. $f(x) = 2x^3 - 6x - 2$ **27.** $f(x) = (x - 5)(x + 7)$ **28.** $f(x) = -144x^2 - 64x$

29. **TEST PREP** The half-life of a particular radioactive isotope of thorium is 8 minutes. If 160 grams of the isotope are initially present, how many grams will remain after 40 minutes? (Lesson 12-6)

A 10 grams **B** 2.5 grams **C** 5 grams **D** 1.25 grams

Problem Solving on Location

Alabama

NASA Marshall Space Flight Center

At NASA's Marshall Space Flight Center in Huntsville, Alabama, scientists work on the development of the International Space Station. One area of research that scientists at the Marshall Center specialize in is microgravity. Microgravity researchers try to minimize the effects of gravity in order to simulate the zero gravity of space.

To find the distance d in meters that a free-falling object travels in t seconds with no air resistance, you would use the function $d = \frac{1}{2}gt^2$. In this distance function, g is the gravitational constant. On Earth, this constant is $g = 9.8$ m/s².

1. What is the domain of the function $d = \frac{1}{2}gt^2$? What is the range?
2. Graph $d = \frac{1}{2}gt^2$.
3. In a microgravity experiment, NASA scientists recorded that it took 4.5 seconds for an object to fall 100 meters. Find the gravitational constant g in the experiment.

NASA's KC-135 aircraft, referred to as the Weightless Wonder or the Vomit Comet, is used to create a microgravity environment.

4. While the KC-135 is climbing at a 45° angle, the equation of its path is $y = x$. While it is descending at a 45° angle, the equation of its path is $y = -x$. Are these linear or quadratic functions?
5. While the KC-135 is in a microgravity environment, the equation of its path is $y = -x^2$. Is this function linear or quadratic?

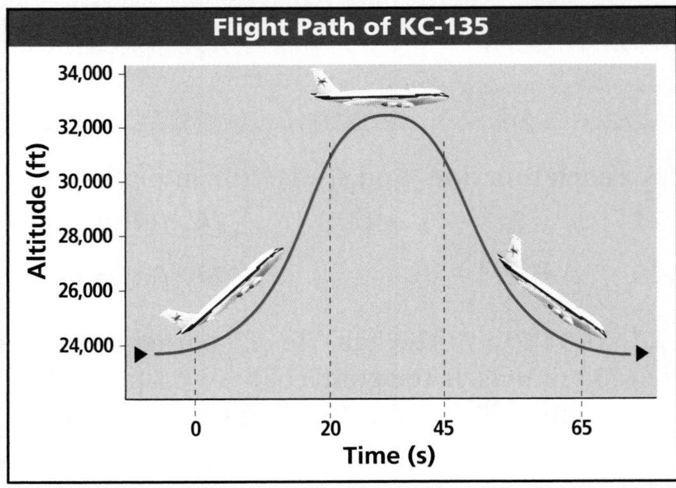

internet connect
State-Specific Test Practice Online
go.hrw.com Keyword: MP4 TestPrep

Standardized Test Prep

Chapter **12**

Cumulative Assessment, Chapters 1–12

1. What is the next term in the sequence? 1, 2, 4, 7, 11, . . .

Ⓐ 13 Ⓒ 15
Ⓑ 14 Ⓓ 16

2. A sequence is formed by doubling the preceding number: 2, 4, 8, 16, 32, ... What is the remainder when the 15th term of the sequence is divided by 6?

Ⓕ 0 Ⓗ 2
Ⓖ 1 Ⓙ 4

3. Which equation describes the relationship shown in the graph?

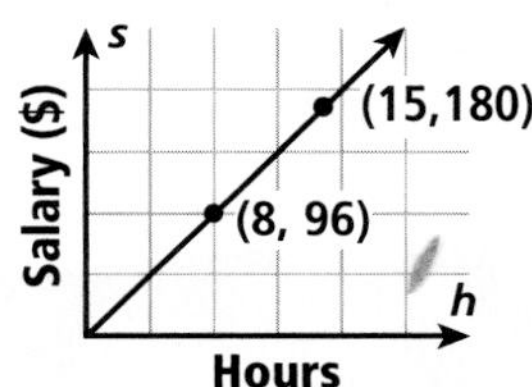

Ⓐ $h = 12s$ Ⓒ $h = s + 88$
Ⓑ $s = 12h$ Ⓓ $s = h + 88$

4. Which of the following is a solution of the system shown?

$x > 3$
$x + y < 2$

Ⓕ (4, −1) Ⓗ (5, 1)
Ⓖ (4, −3) Ⓙ (−5, 4)

5. If $r = \frac{t}{5}$ and $10r = 32$, find the value of t.

Ⓐ 64 Ⓒ 16
Ⓑ 32 Ⓓ 8

6. If $a = 3$ and $b = 4$, evaluate $b - ab^a$.

Ⓕ 64 Ⓗ −188
Ⓖ 8 Ⓙ −1724

7. In parallelogram $JKLM$, $\overline{KP}$ is perpendicular to diagonal $\overline{JL}$. Which of the following is true?

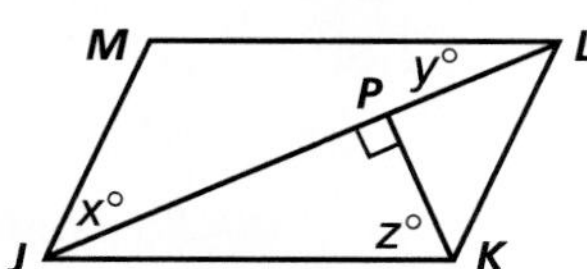

Ⓐ $x + y + z = 180$
Ⓑ $x + z = 90$
Ⓒ $y + z = 90$
Ⓓ $x + y = 90$

TEST TAKING TIP!

Reworking the given choices: It is sometimes useful to look at a choice in a form different from the given form.

8. If $2^{3x-1} = 8$, then what is the value of x?

Ⓕ $\frac{2}{3}$ Ⓗ $1\frac{1}{3}$
Ⓖ 2 Ⓙ $2\frac{1}{3}$

9. ***SHORT RESPONSE*** The length of a rectangle is 8 ft less than twice its width w. Draw a diagram of the rectangle, and label each side length. What is the perimeter of the rectangle expressed in terms of w?

10. ***SHORT RESPONSE*** If two different numbers are selected at random from the set {1, 2, 3, 4, 5, 6}, what is the probability that their product will be 12? Show your work or explain in words how you determined your answer.

Chapter 13

Polynomials

TABLE OF CONTENTS

Chapter Opener Online
go.hrw.com
KEYWORD: MP4 Ch13

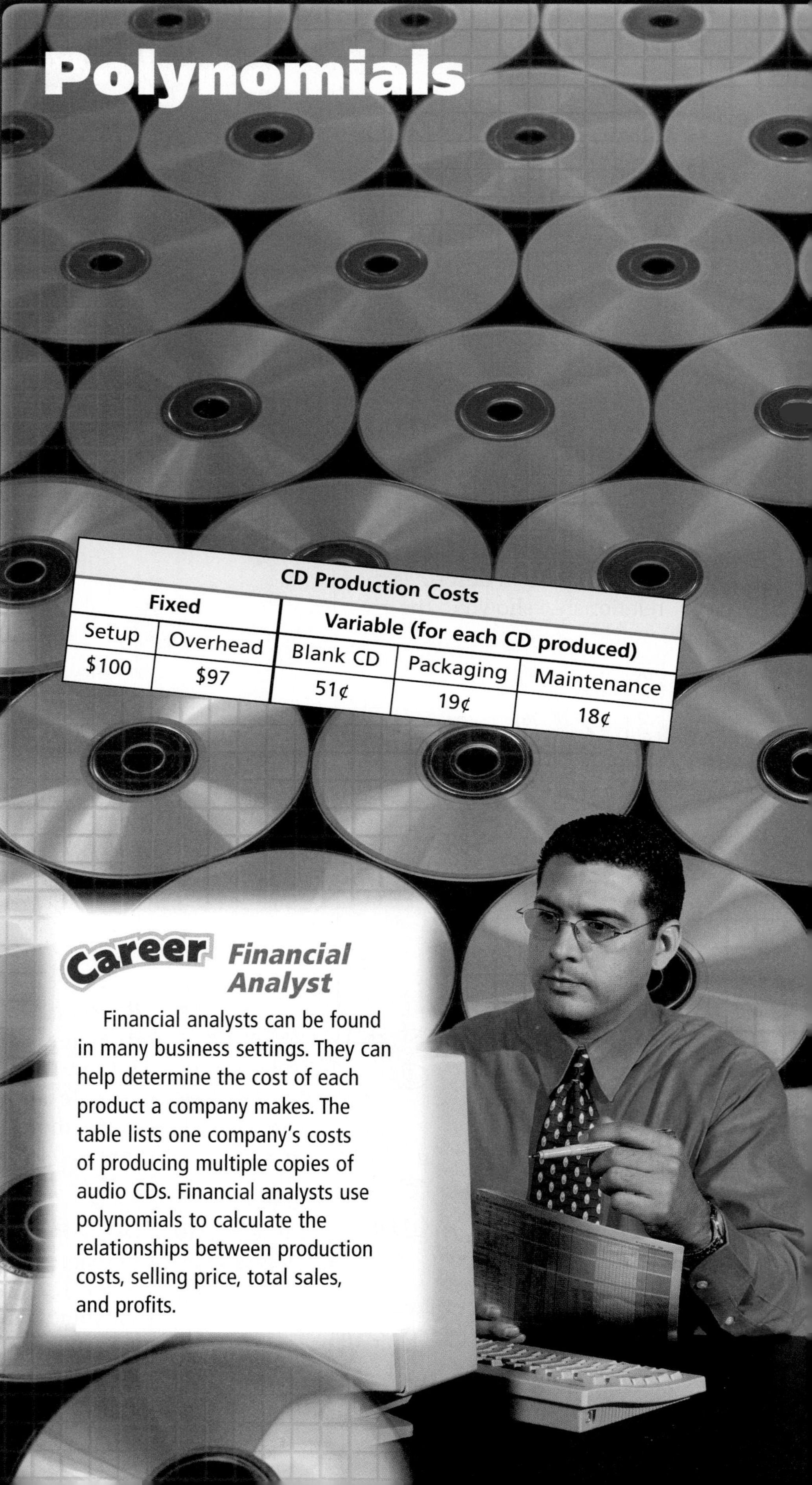

CD Production Costs

Fixed		Variable (for each CD produced)		
Setup	Overhead	Blank CD	Packaging	Maintenance
\$100	\$97	51¢	19¢	18¢

Career *Financial Analyst*

Financial analysts can be found in many business settings. They can help determine the cost of each product a company makes. The table lists one company's costs of producing multiple copies of audio CDs. Financial analysts use polynomials to calculate the relationships between production costs, selling price, total sales, and profits.

ARE YOU READY?

Choose the best term from the list to complete each sentence.

1. __?__ have the same variables raised to the same powers.
2. In the expression $4x^2$, 4 is the __?__.
3. $5 + (4 + 3) = (5 + 4) + 3$ by the __?__.
4. $3 \cdot 2 + 3 \cdot 4 = 3(2 + 4)$ by the __?__.

Associative Property
coefficient
Distributive Property
like terms

Complete these exercises to review skills you will need for this chapter.

✔ Subtract Integers

Subtract.

5. $12 - 4$
6. $8 - 10$
7. $14 - (-4)$
8. $-9 - 5$
9. $-9 - (-5)$
10. $9 - (-5)$

✔ Exponents

Multiply. Write each product as one power.

11. $3^4 \cdot 3^6$
12. $10^2 \cdot 10^3$
13. $x \cdot x^5$
14. $5^5 \cdot 5^5$
15. $y^2 \cdot y^6$
16. $z^3 \cdot z^3$
17. $a^2 \cdot a$
18. $b \cdot b$

✔ Distributive Property

Rewrite using the Distributive Property.

19. $5(7 + 8)$
20. $3(x + y)$
21. $(a + b)6$
22. $(r + s)4$

✔ Area

Find the area of the shaded portion in each figure.

23.
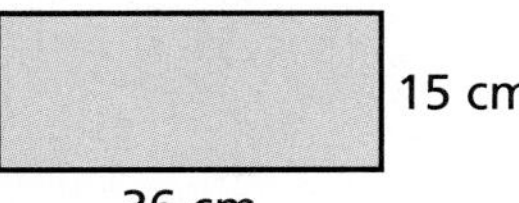

24.
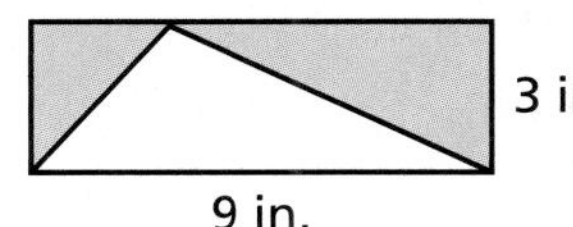

25.
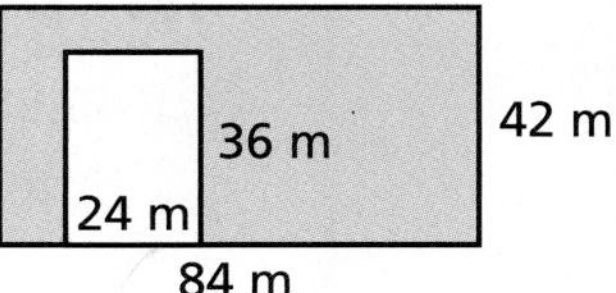

26.
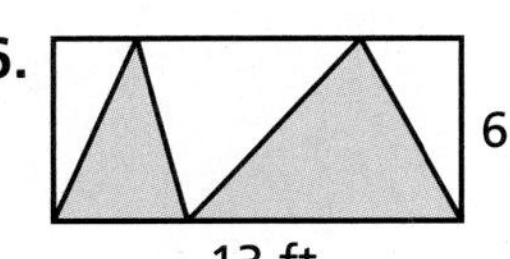

27.
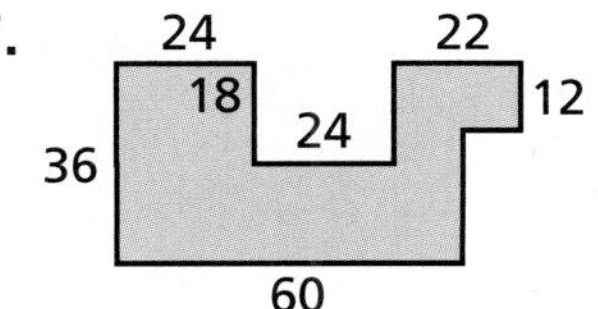

28.
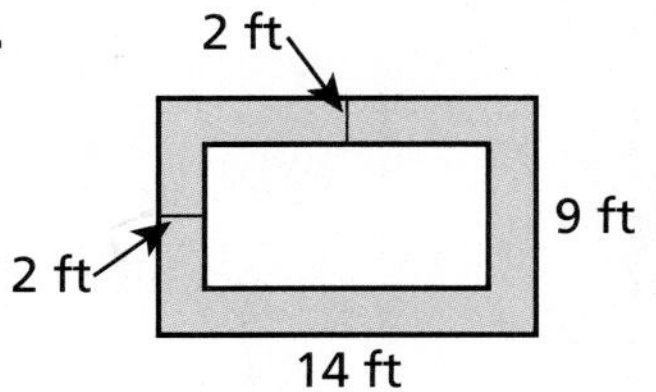

13-1 Polynomials

Learn to classify polynomials by degree and by the number of terms.

Vocabulary

monomial

polynomial

binomial

trinomial

degree of a polynomial

Some fireworks shows are synchronized to music for dramatic effect. *Polynomials* are used to compute the exact height of each firework when it explodes.

The simplest type of polynomial is called a *monomial*. A **monomial** is a number or a product of numbers and variables with exponents that are whole numbers.

Monomials	$2n$, x^3, $4a^4b^3$, 7
Not monomials	$p^{2.4}$, 2^x, $\sqrt{x}$, $\frac{5}{g^2}$

EXAMPLE 1 Identifying Monomials

Determine whether each expression is a monomial.

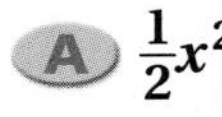

A $\frac{1}{2}x^2y^5$

monomial

2 and 5 are whole numbers.

B $12xy^{0.4}$

not a monomial

0.4 is not a whole number.

A **polynomial** is one monomial or the sum or difference of monomials. Polynomials can be classified by the number of terms. A monomial has 1 term, a **binomial** has 2 terms, and a **trinomial** has 3 terms.

EXAMPLE 2 Classifying Polynomials by the Number of Terms

Classify each expression as a monomial, a binomial, a trinomial, or not a polynomial.

A $49.99h + 24.99g$

binomial *Polynomial with 2 terms*

B $-3x^4y$

monomial *Polynomial with 1 term*

C $4x^2 - 2xy + \frac{3}{x}$

not a polynomial *A variable is in the denominator.*

D $5mn + 2m - 3n$

trinomial *Polynomial with 3 terms*

A polynomial can also be classified by its degree. The **degree of a polynomial** is the degree of the term with the greatest degree.

$$\underbrace{\underbrace{4x^2}_{\text{Degree 2}} + \underbrace{2x^5}_{\text{Degree 5}} + \underbrace{x}_{\text{Degree 1}} + \underbrace{5}_{\text{Degree 0}}}_{\text{Degree 5}}$$

EXAMPLE 3 Classifying Polynomials by Their Degrees

Find the degree of each polynomial.

A $5x^2 + 2x + 3$

$5x^2$	+	$2x$	+	3
Degree 2		*Degree 1*		*Degree 0*

The degree of $5x^2 + 2x + 3$ is 2.

B $5 + 2m^3 + 3m^6$

5	+	$2m^3$	+	$3m^6$
Degree 0		*Degree 3*		*Degree 6*

The degree of $5 + 2m^3 + 3m^6$ is 6.

C $h + 2h^3 + h^2$

h	+	$2h^3$	+	h^2
Degree 1		*Degree 3*		*Degree 2*

The degree of $h + 2h^3 + h^2$ is 3.

EXAMPLE 4 *Physics Application*

The height in feet of a firework launched straight up into the air from *s* feet off the ground at velocity *v* after *t* seconds is given by the polynomial $-16t^2 + vt + s$. Find the height of a firework launched from a 10 ft platform at 200 ft/s after 5 seconds.

$-16t^2 + vt + s$ *Write the polynomial expression for height.*

$-16(5)^2 + 200(5) + 10$ *Substitute 5 for t, 200 for v, and 10 for s.*

$-400 + 1000 + 10$ *Simplify.*

610

The firework is 610 ft high 5 seconds after launching.

Social Studies LINK

These colorfully decorated fireworks are part of a traditional Chinese New Year celebration.

Think and Discuss

1. **Describe** two ways you can classify a polynomial. Give a polynomial with three terms, and classify it two ways.
2. **Explain** why $-5x^2 - 3$ is a polynomial but $-5x^{-2} - 3$ is not.

13-1 Exercises

FOR EXTRA PRACTICE
see page 756

internet connect
Homework Help Online
go.hrw.com Keyword: MP4 13-1

GUIDED PRACTICE

See Example 1
Determine whether each expression is a monomial.

1. $-2x^2y$
2. $\frac{3}{2x}$
3. $4a^{2.4}b^{3.2}$
4. $3m^2n^2$

See Example 2
Classify each expression as a monomial, a binomial, a trinomial, or not a polynomial.

5. $3x^2 - 4x$
6. $5r - 3r^2 + 6$
7. $\frac{5}{x^2} + 3x$
8. 3

See Example 3
Find the degree of each polynomial.

9. $-5m^4 + 2m^7$
10. $9w^3 + 4$
11. $-4b^4 + 5b^6 - 2b$
12. $x^3 + 2x^2 - 18$

See Example 4
13. The trinomial $-16t^2 + 20t + 50$ describes the height in feet of a ball thrown straight up from a 50 ft platform with a velocity of 20 ft/s after t seconds. What is the ball's height after 2 seconds?

INDEPENDENT PRACTICE

See Example 1
Determine whether each expression is a monomial.

14. $6.7x^4$
15. $-2x^{-4}$
16. $\frac{4y^3}{5x}$
17. $\frac{4}{7}x^4y^2$

See Example 2
Classify each expression as a monomial, a binomial, a trinomial, or not a polynomial.

18. $-8m^3n^5$
19. $4g^{\frac{1}{2}}h^3$
20. $4x^3 + 2x^5 + 3$
21. $-a + 2$

See Example 3
Find the degree of each polynomial.

22. $2x^2 - 7x + 1$
23. $-5m^3 + 6m^4 - 3$
24. $-1 + 2x + 3x^3$
25. $5p^4 + 7p^3$

See Example 4
26. The volume of a box with height x, length $x + 1$, and width $2x - 4$ is given by the trinomial $2x^3 - 2x^2 - 4x$. What is the volume of the box if its height is 3 inches?

PRACTICE AND PROBLEM SOLVING

Classify each expression as a monomial, a binomial, a trinomial, or not a polynomial. If it is a polynomial, give its degree.

27. $3x^2$

28. $5x^{0.5} + 2x$

29. $-\frac{4}{5}x + \frac{2}{3}x^2$

30. $5y^2 - 4y$

31. $3f^4 + 6f^6 - f$

32. $6 - \frac{4}{x}$

33. $5x + 3\sqrt{x}$

34. $5x^{-3}$

35. $2b^2 - 7b - 6b^3$

36. $3 + 4x$

37. $3x^{\frac{2}{3}} - 4x^3 + 6$

38. 8

39. ***TRANSPORTATION*** Gas mileage at speed s can be estimated using the given polynomials. Evaluate the polynomials to complete the table.

		Gas Mileage (mi/gal)		
		40 mi/h	50 mi/h	60 mi/h
Compact	$-0.025s^2 + 2.45s - 30$			
Midsize	$-0.015s^2 + 1.45s - 13$			
Van	$-0.03s^2 + 2.9s - 53$			

40. ***TRANSPORTATION*** The distance in feet required for a car traveling at r mi/h to come to a stop can be approximated by the binomial $\frac{r^2}{20} + r$. About how many feet will be required for a car to stop if it is traveling at 60 mi/h?

41. ***WHAT'S THE QUESTION?*** For the polynomial $4b^5 - 7b^9 + 6b$, the answer is 9. What is the question?

42. ***WRITE ABOUT IT*** Give some examples of words that start with *mono-*, *bi-*, *tri-*, and *poly-*, and relate the meaning of each to polynomials.

43. ***CHALLENGE*** The base of a triangle is described by the binomial $x + 2$, and its height is described by the trinomial $2x^2 + 3x - 7$. What is the area of the triangle if $x = 5$?

Spiral Review

Write each number or product in scientific notation. (Lesson 2-9)

44. 3,400,000,000

45. 0.00000045

46. $(3.2 \times 10^4) \times (2 \times 10^{-5})$

Simplify. (Lesson 3-8)

47. $\sqrt{144}$

48. $\sqrt{64}$

49. $\sqrt{169}$

50. $\sqrt{225}$

51. **TEST PREP** The length of the base of an isosceles triangle is half the length of a leg. Which expression shows the perimeter of the triangle if the length of the base is x? (Lesson 6-2)

A $\frac{5}{2}x$ **B** $5x$ **C** $6x$ **D** $\frac{3}{2}x$

Model Polynomials

Use with Lesson 13-1

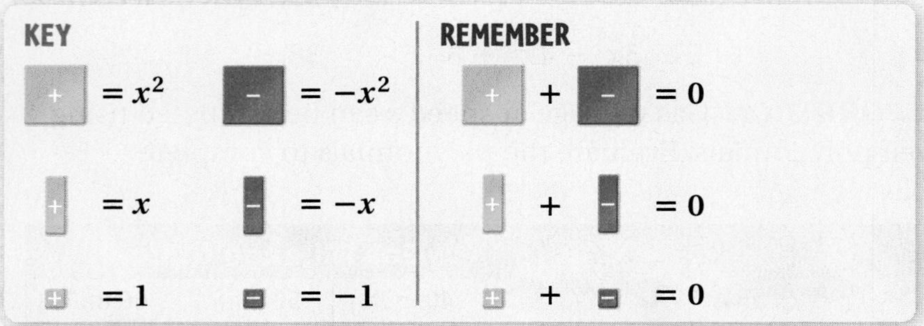

You can use algebra tiles to model polynomials. To model the polynomial $4x^2 + x - 3$, you need four x^2-tiles, one x-tile, and three -1-tiles.

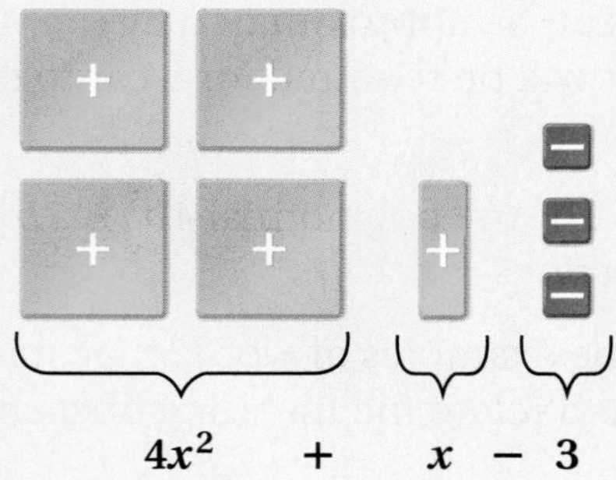

Activity 1

1. Use algebra tiles to model the polynomial $2x^2 + 4x + 6$.

   All signs are positive, so use all yellow tiles.

$2x^2$ + $4x$ + 6

2 Use algebra tiles to model the polynomial $-x^2 + 6x - 4$.

Modeling $-x^2 + 6x - 4$ is similar to modeling $2x^2 + 4x + 6$. Remember to use red tiles for negative values.

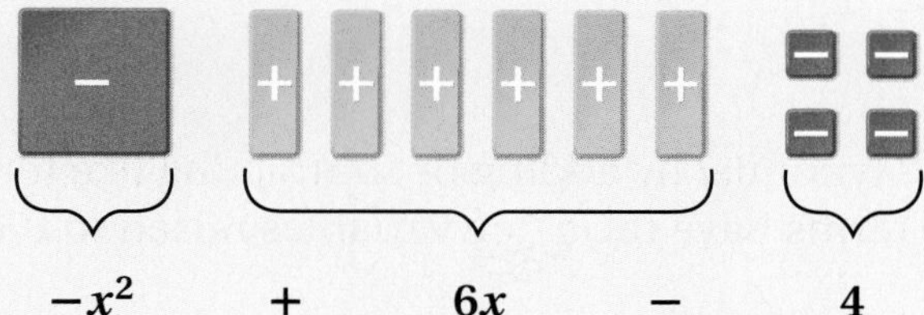

$-x^2 \quad + \quad 6x \quad - \quad 4$

Think and Discuss

1. How do you know when to use red tiles?

Try This

Use algebra tiles to model each polynomial.

1. $3x^2 + 2x - 4$
2. $-5x^2 + 4x - 1$
3. $4x^2 - x + 7$

Activity 2

1 Write the polynomial modeled by the tiles below.

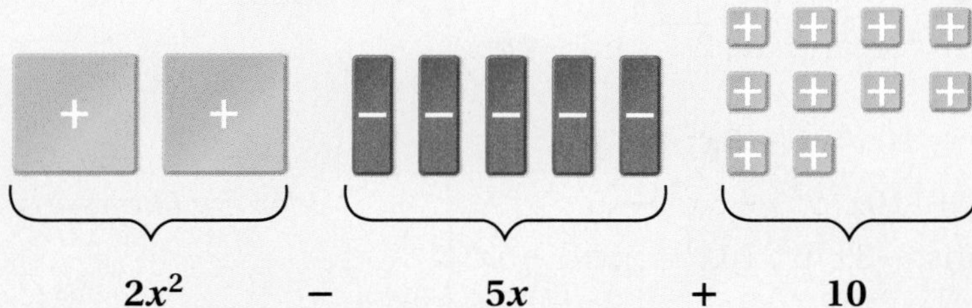

$2x^2 \quad - \quad 5x \quad + \quad 10$

The polynomial modeled by the tiles is $2x^2 - 5x + 10$.

Think and Discuss

1. How do you know the coefficient of the x^2 term in Activity 2?

Try This

Write a polynomial modeled by each group of algebra tiles.

1.  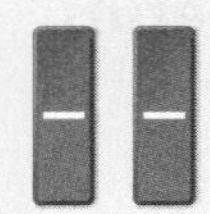

2.  

3. 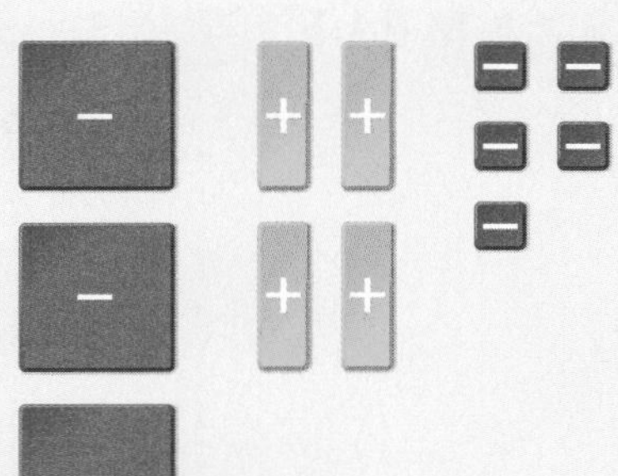

13-2 Simplifying Polynomials

Learn to simplify polynomials.

You can simplify a polynomial by adding or subtracting like terms. Remember that like terms have the same variables raised to the same powers.

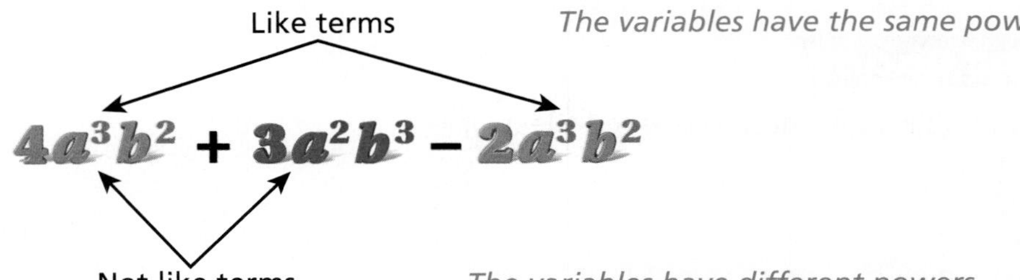

Like terms
The variables have the same powers.
$4a^3b^2 + 3a^2b^3 - 2a^3b^2$
Not like terms
The variables have different powers.

EXAMPLE 1 Identifying Like Terms

Identify the like terms in each polynomial.

A $3a + 2a^2 - 3 + 6a - 4a^2$

$3a + 2a^2 - 3 + 6a - 4a^2$ *Identify like terms.*

Like terms: $3a$ and $6a$, $2a^2$ and $-4a^2$

B $-3x^4y^2 + 10x^4y^2 - 3x^2 - 5x^4y^2$

$-3x^4y^2 + 10x^4y^2 - 3x^2 - 5x^4y^2$ *Identify like terms.*

Like terms: $-3x^4y^2$, $10x^4y^2$, and $-5x^4y^2$

C $4m^2 - 2mn + 3m$

$4m^2 - 2mn + 3m$ *Identify like terms.*

There are no like terms.

To simplify a polynomial, combine like terms. It may be easier to arrange the terms in *descending* order (highest degree to lowest degree) before combining like terms.

EXAMPLE 2 Simplifying Polynomials by Combining Like Terms

Simplify.

A $x^2 + 6x^4 - 8 + 9x^2 + 2x^4 - 6x^2$

$x^2 + 6x^4 - 8 + 9x^2 + 2x^4 - 6x^2$

$6x^4 + 2x^4 + x^2 + 9x^2 - 6x^2 - 8$ *Arrange in descending order.*

$6x^4 + 2x^4 + x^2 + 9x^2 - 6x^2 - 8$ *Identify like terms.*

$8x^4 + 4x^2 - 8$ *Combine coefficients: $6 + 2 = 8$ and $1 + 9 - 6 = 4$*

Simplify.

B $-4a^2b + 10ab^2 - 3a^2b - ab^2 + 2ab$

$-4a^2b + 10ab^2 - 3a^2b - ab^2 + 2ab$ *Identify like terms.*

$-7a^2b + 9ab^2 + 2ab$ *Combine coefficients: $-4 - 3 = -7$ and $10 - 1 = 9$*

Sometimes you may need to use the Distributive Property to simplify a polynomial.

EXAMPLE 3 Simplifying Polynomials by Using the Distributive Property

Simplify.

A $5(2x^2 + 6x)$

$5(2x^2 + 6x)$ *Distributive Property*

$5 \cdot 2x^2 + 5 \cdot 6x$

$10x^2 + 30x$

B $2(3ab^2 - 6b) + 2ab^2 + 5$

$2(3ab^2 - 6b) + 2ab^2 + 5$ *Distributive Property*

$2 \cdot 3ab^2 - 2 \cdot 6b + 2ab^2 + 5$

$6ab^2 - 12b + 2ab^2 + 5$

$8ab^2 - 12b + 5$ *Combine like terms.*

EXAMPLE 4 *Business Application*

A *board foot* is 1 ft by 1 ft by 1 in. of lumber. The amount of lumber that can be harvested from a tree with diameter d in. is approximately $20 + 0.005(d^3 - 30d^2 + 300d - 1000)$ board feet. Use the Distributive Property to write an equivalent expression.

$$20 + 0.005(d^3 - 30d^2 + 300d - 1000) = 20 + 0.005d^3 - 0.15d^2 + 1.5d - 5$$
$$= 15 + 0.005d^3 - 0.15d^2 + 1.5d$$

Think and Discuss

1. **Tell** how you know when you can combine like terms.
2. **Give** an example of an expression that you could simplify by using the Distributive Property and an expression that you could simplify by combining like terms.

13-2 Exercises

FOR EXTRA PRACTICE

see page 756

internet connect

Homework Help Online
go.hrw.com Keyword: MP4 13-2

GUIDED PRACTICE

See Example 1 **Identify the like terms in each polynomial.**

1. $-2b^2 + 4b + 3b^2 - b + 8$
2. $5mn - 4m^2n^2 + 6m^2n + 3m^2n^2$

See Example 2 **Simplify.**

3. $3x^2 - 4x + 6x^2 + 8x - 6$
4. $7 - 4b + 2b^4 - 6b^2 + 8 + 5b - 4b^2$

See Example 3

5. $3(2x - 7)$
6. $6(4a^2 - 7a) + 3a^2 + 5a$

See Example 4

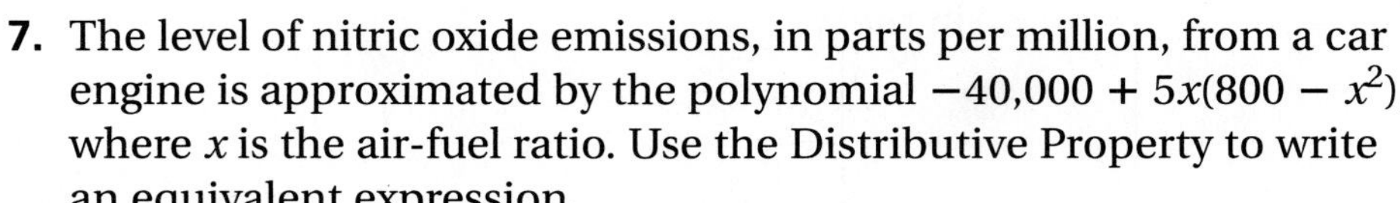

7. The level of nitric oxide emissions, in parts per million, from a car engine is approximated by the polynomial $-40{,}000 + 5x(800 - x^2)$, where x is the air-fuel ratio. Use the Distributive Property to write an equivalent expression.

INDEPENDENT PRACTICE

See Example  **Identify the like terms in each polynomial.**

8. $-t + 5t^2 - 6t^2 + 6t - 3$
9. $9rs - 2r^2s^2 + 4r^2s^2 + 3rs - 7$

See Example 2 **Simplify.**

10. $3p - 4p^2 + 6p + 10p^2$
11. $2fg + f^2g - fg^2 - 2fg + 3f^2g + 5fg^2$

See Example 3

12. $4(x^2 - 4x) + 3x^2 - 6x$
13. $3(b - 4) + 6b - 4b^2$

See Example 4

14. The concentration of a certain medication in an average person's bloodstream h hours after injection can be estimated using the expression $7(0.04h - 0.003h^2 - 0.02h^3)$. Use the Distributive Property to write an equivalent expression.

PRACTICE AND PROBLEM SOLVING

Simplify.

15. $3s^2 - 4s + 12s^2 + 6s - 2$
16. $4gh^2 + 2g^2h + 3g^2h - g^2h$
17. $3(x^2 - 4x + 3) - 2x + 6$
18. $4(x - x^5 + x^3) - 2x$
19. $2(3m - 4m^2) + 6(2m^2 - 5m)$
20. $8b^4 + 3b^2 + 2(b^2 - 8)$
21. $7mn - 4m^3n^2 + 4(m^3n^2 + 2mn)$
22. $4(x + 2y) + 3(2x - 3y)$
23. ***LIFE SCIENCE*** The rate of flow in cm/s of blood in an artery at d cm from the center is given by the polynomial $1000(0.04 - d^2)$. Use the Distributive Property to write an equivalent expression.

internet connect
State-Specific Test Practice Online
go.hrw.com Keyword: MP4 TestPrep

Standardized Test Prep

Chapter 13

Cumulative Assessment, Chapters 1–13

1. The solution of $12x = -24$ is ___?___.

Ⓐ $x = -288$
Ⓑ $x = -2$
Ⓒ $x = 2$
Ⓓ $x = 288$

2. If the product of five integers is positive, then at most how many of the five integers could be negative?

Ⓕ Two
Ⓖ Three
Ⓗ Four
Ⓙ Five

TEST TAKING TIP!

If a problem involves decimals, you may be able to eliminate answer choices that do not have the correct number of places after the decimal point.

3. Find the product of 1.8×0.541.

Ⓐ 0.9738
Ⓑ 9.738
Ⓒ 97.3800
Ⓓ 9.738×10^4

4. The simplest form of the product of the binomials $(x + 2)$ and $(x - 3)$ is which type of polynomial?

Ⓕ Monomial
Ⓖ Binomial
Ⓗ Trinomial
Ⓙ Polynomial with four terms

5. Which number is equivalent to 2^{-3}?

Ⓐ $-\frac{1}{6}$
Ⓑ $-\frac{1}{8}$
Ⓒ $\frac{1}{8}$
Ⓓ $\frac{1}{6}$

6. What is the length of the diagonal of a rectangle with a length of 4 in. and width of 3 in.?

Ⓕ 5 in.
Ⓖ 7 in.
Ⓗ 12 in.
Ⓙ 14 in.

7. For which set of data are the mean and mode equal?

Ⓐ 1, 1, 1, 2
Ⓑ 1, 2, 2, 3
Ⓒ 2, 3, 4, 5
Ⓓ 2, 3, 3, 5

8. Point R' is formed by reflecting $R(-3, -2)$ across the y-axis. What are the coordinates of R'?

Ⓕ (3, 2)
Ⓖ (3, −2)
Ⓗ (−3, 2)
Ⓙ (−2, −3)

9. ***SHORT RESPONSE*** A fair number cube is rolled twice. What is the probability that the outcomes of the two rolls will have a sum of 4? Explain.

10. ***SHORT RESPONSE*** What is the area of the shaded region in the figure below? Give your answer in terms of π. Show or explain how you got your answer.

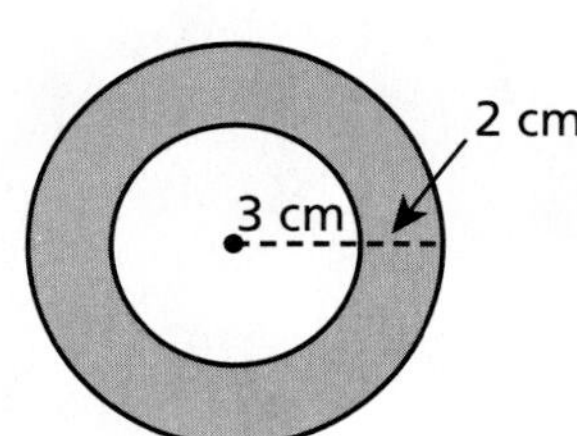

Chapter 14

Set Theory and Discrete Math

TABLE OF CONTENTS

"And" Circuit Table

Gate				Information Flow	
A	Status	*B*	Status	*A and B*	Flow?
0	Closed	0	Closed	0	No
1	Open	0	Closed	0	No
0	Closed	1	Open	0	No
1	Open	1	Open	1	Yes

Career *Computer Chip Designer*

Chip designers take on a task that is a lot like putting the United States highway system on a dime. These integrated-circuit developers enjoy decision making and problem solving. They rely on logic to create intricate chip and circuit designs. Binary notation can be used to describe whether the logic gates they design to control information flow are open or closed.

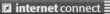

internet connect

Chapter Opener Online
go.hrw.com
KEYWORD: MP4 Ch14

ARE YOU READY?

Choose the best term from the list to complete each sentence.

1. Numbers divisible by only themselves and 1 are ___?___.
2. The set of whole numbers consists of the set of ___?___ and 0.
3. Numbers that cannot be written as decimals that terminate or repeat are called ___?___.
4. The set $\ldots -4, -3, -2, -1, 0, 1, 2, 3, 4, \ldots$ is the set of ___?___.

counting numbers
integers
irrational numbers
prime numbers
rational numbers
real numbers

Complete these exercises to review skills you will need for this chapter.

✔ Composite Numbers

List the factors of each number. Tell whether the number is composite.

5. 37 **6.** 57 **7.** 63

8. 83 **9.** 103 **10.** 155

✔ Identify Sets of Numbers

State whether each number is rational, irrational, or not a real number.

11. $\frac{0}{3}$ **12.** $\sqrt{12}$ **13.** $\frac{3}{0}$ **14.** $\sqrt{2}$

15. $\sqrt{-5}$ **16.** $-\sqrt{9}$ **17.** $\sqrt{81}$ **18.** π

✔ Identify Polygons

Give all of the names that apply to each figure.

19.

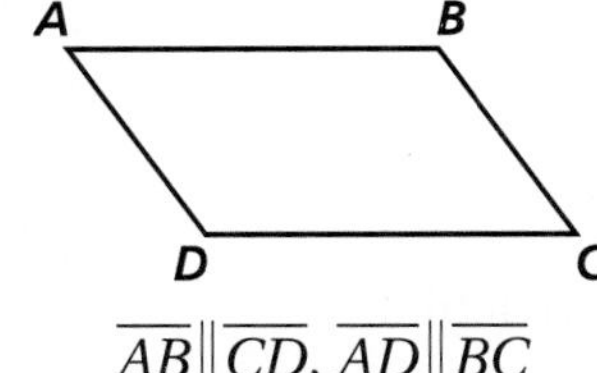

$\overline{AB} \parallel \overline{CD}, \overline{AD} \parallel \overline{BC}$

20.

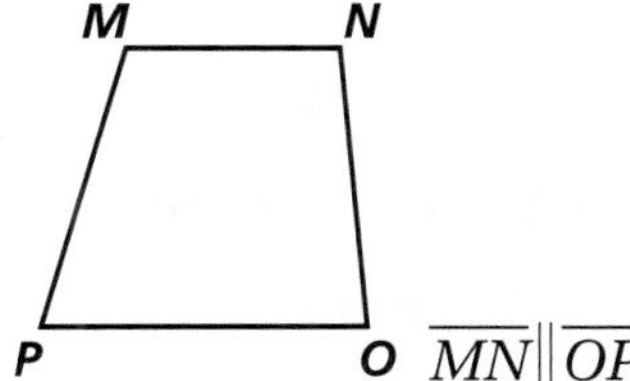

$\overline{MN} \parallel \overline{OP}$

21.

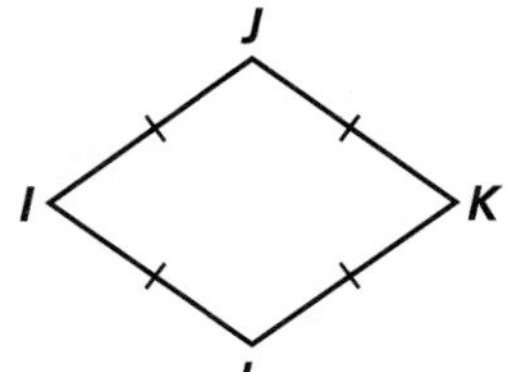

22.

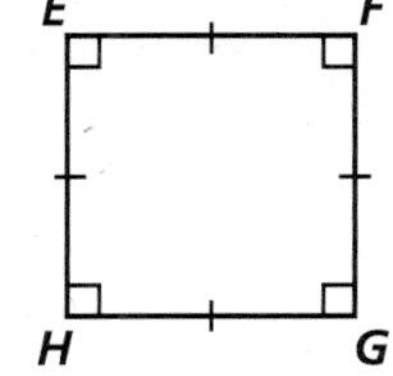

14-1 Sets

Learn to understand mathematical sets and set notation.

Vocabulary

set
element
subset
finite set
infinite set

Shana and Robert are collectors. Shana collects seashells and shell-related objects, and Robert collects owl-related objects.

A **set** is a collection of objects, called **elements**. Elements of a set can be described in two ways: *roster notation* and *set-builder notation.* An owl made from seashells may be a member of Shana's or Robert's sets.

Set	Roster Notation	Set-Builder Notation
Even counting numbers	{2, 4, 6, 8, 10, ...}	{x|x is an even counting number} *Read as "the set of all x such that x is an even counting number."*
Great Lakes	{Huron, Ontario, Michigan, Erie, Superior}	{x|x is one of the Great Lakes}

Helpful Hint

Think of the element symbol ∈ as the letter *e*.

The symbol ∈ is read as "is an element of." Read the statement 3 ∈ {odd numbers} as "3 is an element of the set of odd numbers." The symbol ∉ is read as "is *not* an element of." Read the statement 2 ∉ {odd numbers} as "2 is *not* an element of the set of odd numbers."

EXAMPLE 1 Identifying Elements of a Set

Insert ∈ or ∉ to make each statement true.

A **1 ■ {numbers that are their own reciprocals}**

1 ∈ {numbers that are their own reciprocals} *1 is equivalent to $\frac{1}{1}$.*

B **broccoli ■ {red vegetables}**

broccoli ∉ {red vegetables} *Broccoli is not a red vegetable.*

C **◗ ■ {polygons}**

◗ ∉ {polygons} *A semicircle is not a polygon.*

Set A is a **subset** of set B if every element in A is also in B. The symbol $\subset$ is read as "is a subset of," and the symbol $\not\subset$ is read as "is *not* a subset of."

EXAMPLE 2 Identifying Subsets

Determine whether the first set is a subset of the second set. Use the correct symbol.

A **Q = {rational numbers}** **R = {real numbers}**

Yes, $Q \subset R$. *Every rational number is a real number.*

B **T = {0, 1, 2, 3}** **N = {counting numbers}**

No, $T \not\subset N$. *0 is not a counting number.*

C **H = {rhombuses}** **G = {rectangles}**

No, $H \not\subset G$. *Some rhombuses are not rectangles.*

A **finite set** contains a finite number of elements. An **infinite set** contains an infinite number of elements.

EXAMPLE 3 Identifying Finite and Infinite Sets

Tell whether each set is finite or infinite.

A **{letters of the alphabet}**

finite *There are exactly 26 elements in the set.*

B **{rational numbers between 99 and 100}**

infinite *There are an infinite number of rational numbers between any two rational numbers.*

C **{integers with absolute value less than 3}**

finite *Only −2, −1, 0, 1, and 2 have absolute values less than 3.*

Think and Discuss

1. **Describe** the set of whole numbers that are not counting numbers.
2. **Name** three different sets that have {apricots} as a subset.
3. **Give** two examples of finite sets that have 20 as an element. Give two examples of infinite sets that have 20 as an element.

14-1 Exercises

FOR EXTRA PRACTICE
see page 758

internet connect
Homework Help Online
go.hrw.com Keyword: MP4 14-1

GUIDED PRACTICE

See Example 1

Insert $\in$ or $\notin$ to make each statement true.

1. oak tree ■ {living things}
2. $x^2 - \frac{4}{x} + 2$ ■ {trinomials}

See Example 2

Determine whether the first set is a subset of the second set. Use the correct symbol.

3. E = {even numbers}
   R = {real numbers}
4. P = {parallelograms}
   S = {squares}

See Example 3

Tell whether each set is finite or infinite.

5. {letters that are vowels}
6. {number of radii in a circle}

INDEPENDENT PRACTICE

See Example 1

Insert $\in$ or $\notin$ to make each statement true.

7. Spanish ■ {world languages}
8. $2\frac{3}{7}$ ■ {rational numbers}

See Example 2

Determine whether the first set is a subset of the second set. Use the correct symbol.

9. F = {football players}
   T = {team athletes}
10. C = {counting numbers}
    P = {prime numbers}
11. P = {prime numbers}
    O = {odd numbers}
12. S = {squares}
    P = {parallelograms}

See Example 3

Tell whether each set is finite or infinite.

13. {composite numbers}
14. {rational numbers less than 0}
15. {seconds in a year}
16. {past U.S. presidents}

PRACTICE AND PROBLEM SOLVING

Choose the symbol that best completes each statement. Use the symbols $\subset$, $\not\subset$, $\in$, and $\notin$.

17.  ■ {cats}
18. ■ {shapes that tessellate}
19. 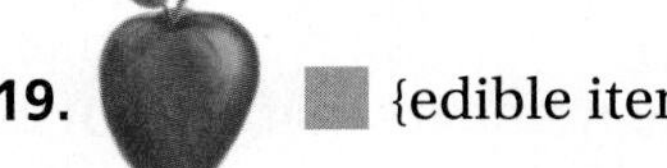 ■ {edible items}
20.  ■ {flags of South America}
21. 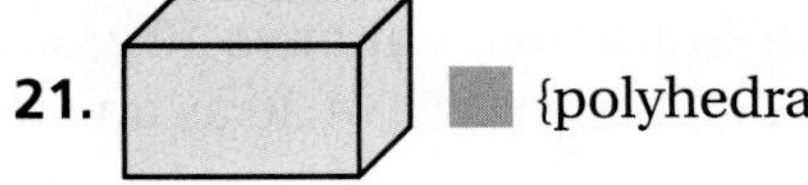 ■ {polyhedra}
22.  ■ {U.S. currency}

Determine whether each set is finite or infinite.

23. {people on Earth}

24. {counting numbers}

25. {trinomials}

26. {integers between 0 and 2}

27. {whole number factors of 20}

28. {solutions of $x < 0$}

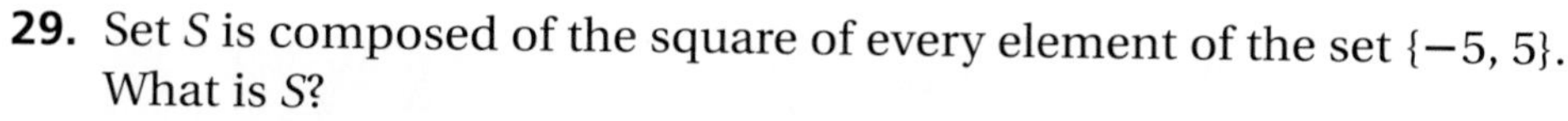

29. Set S is composed of the square of every element of the set $\{-5, 5\}$. What is S?

Music LINK

The first percussion instruments to be used in orchestras were the *timpani,* or kettle drums, in the 1600's.

30. The *closure property* states that a set is *closed* under an operation if performing that operation on any elements of the set always results in an element of the set. The set of integers is closed under multiplication because multiplying integers always results in an integer. Tell whether each set is closed under the given operation.

a. {0, 1}; multiplication

b. {positive numbers}; subtraction

c. {counting numbers}; division

d. {even numbers}; addition

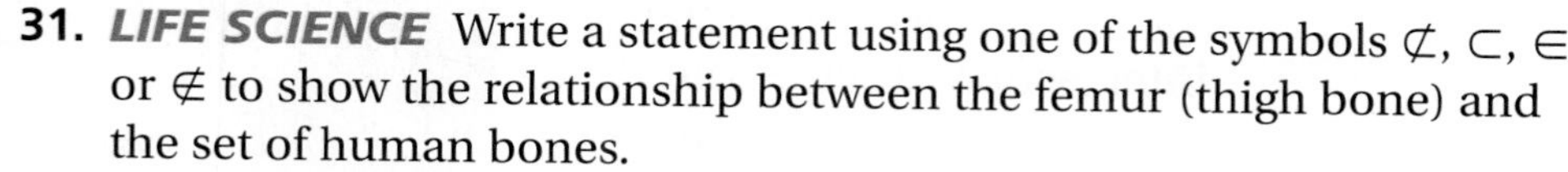

31. ***LIFE SCIENCE*** Write a statement using one of the symbols $\not\subset$, $\subset$, $\in$, or $\notin$ to show the relationship between the femur (thigh bone) and the set of human bones.

32. ***MUSIC*** Write a statement using one of the symbols $\not\subset$, $\subset$, $\in$, or $\notin$ to show the relationship between the set of percussion instruments and the set of string instruments.

33. ***SOCIAL STUDIES*** Write a statement using one of the symbols $\not\subset$, $\subset$, $\in$, or $\notin$ to show the relationship between the city of Miami, Florida, and the set of state capitals.

34. ***WRITE A PROBLEM*** Using facts you find in your social studies or science textbook, show that one set is a subset of another set.

35. ***WRITE ABOUT IT*** Compare the meanings of the symbols $\subset$ and $\in$. How are they alike? How are they different?

36. ***CHALLENGE*** If $P = \{2, 4, 6, 8\}$ and $Q =$ {even integers between 0 and 10}, is P a subset of Q? Explain.

Spiral Review

Simplify. (Lesson 13-2)

37. $-4(m^2 - 3m + 6)$

38. $3(a^2b - 4a + 3ab) - 2ab$

39. $x^2y + 4(xy^2 - 3x^2y + 4xy)$

40. **TEST PREP** Which polynomial shows the result of using the FOIL method to find $(x - 2)(x + 6)$? (Lesson 13-6)

A $x^2 - 12$ **B** $x^2 + 6x - 2x - 12$ **C** $2x - 2x - 12$ **D** $x^2 + 4$

41. **TEST PREP** Which is equivalent to $x^2 - 16$? (Lesson 13-6)

F $(x - 4)(x + 4)$ **G** $(x - 4)^2$ **H** $(x + 4)^2$ **J** $(x)(x - 16)$

14-2 Intersection and Union

Learn to describe the intersection and union of sets.

Vocabulary

intersection

empty set

union

The Caspian Sea, surrounded by the countries Azerbaijan, Iran, Kazakhstan, Russia, and Turkmenistan, is one of the world's largest lakes as well as one of the world's deepest.

The **intersection** of sets A and B is the set of all elements that are in both A *and* B. In other words, the intersection of sets A and B is the set of all elements that are common to both A and B.

To indicate the intersection of sets A and B, write $A \cap B$.

If A is the set of the world's five largest lakes by area, then A = {Caspian Sea, Lake Superior, Lake Victoria, Lake Huron, Lake Michigan}.

If B is the set of the world's five deepest lakes, then B = {Lake Baikal, Lake Tanganyika, Caspian Sea, Lake Nyasa, Issyk Kul}.

Reading Math

The empty set may also be represented by empty brackets, { }.

$A \cap B$ = {Caspian Sea} because the Caspian Sea is the only lake in both sets.

The set with no elements is called the **empty set**, or *null set*. The symbol for the empty set is $\varnothing$.

EXAMPLE 1 Finding the Intersection of Two Sets

Find the intersection of the sets.

A $Z = \{0, 1, 2, 3\}$ $\quad$ $T = \{2, 4, 6, 8\}$

The only element that appears in both Z and T is 2.

$Z \cap T = \{2\}$

B Q = {rational numbers} $\quad$ I = {irrational numbers}

There are no numbers that are both rational and irrational.

$Q \cap I = \{\ \}$ or $\varnothing$

Find the intersection of the sets.

C $L = \{x|x < 10\}$ $G = \{x|x > 5\}$

$L \cap G = \{x \mid 5 < x < 10\}$

4 5 6 7 8 9 10 11

The **union** of sets Q and R is the set of all elements that are in either Q *or* R. To show the union of sets Q and R, write $Q \cup R$.

If $Q = \{-4, 2, 6, 10\}$ and $R = \{-2, 2, 6\}$, then $Q \cup R = \{-4, -2, 2, 6, 10\}$. If an element appears in both sets, represent it only once in the union.

EXAMPLE 2 Finding the Union of Two Sets

Find the union of the sets.

A $Q =$ **{rational numbers}** $I =$ **{irrational numbers}**

Every real number is either rational or irrational.

$Q \cup I =$ {real numbers}

B $Z = \{0, 1, 2, 3\}$ $T = \{2, 3, 4, 5\}$

$Z \cup T = \{0, 1, 2, 3, 4, 5\}$

C $N =$ **{negative integers}** $W =$ **{whole numbers}**

The negative integers are $\{\ldots, -3, -2, -1\}$. The whole numbers are $\{0, 1, 2, 3, \ldots\}$.

$N \cup W =$ {integers}

D $T = \{2, 4, 8, 16\}$ $E =$ **{even integers}**

T is a subset of E, so the union of T and E is E.

$T \cup E =$ {even integers}

E $L = \{x|x < 10\}$ $G = \{x|x > 5\}$

Every real number can be found in either set L or set G.

$L \cup G =$ {real numbers}

4 5 6 7 8 9 10 11

Think and Discuss

1. **Describe** two sets whose intersection is $\{7, 8, 9, 10\}$.
2. **Describe** two sets whose union is $\{7, 8, 9, 10\}$.
3. **Give** an example of two sets whose intersection is the empty set.

14-2 Exercises

FOR EXTRA PRACTICE
see page 758

internet connect
Homework Help Online
go.hrw.com Keyword: MP4 14-2

GUIDED PRACTICE

See Example 1 **Find the intersection of the sets.**

1. $B = \{-2, 0, 2, 4, 6\}$
   $D = \{2, 4, 6, 8, 10\}$
2. $A = \{10, 11, 12, 13, 14\}$
   $E = \{\text{even numbers}\}$
3. $G = \{x \mid x \geq 2\}$
   $H = \{x \mid x \leq 5\}$
4. $M = \{x \mid x \leq 7\}$
   $N = \{x \mid x \geq 0\}$

See Example 2 **Find the union of the sets.**

5. $R = \{2, 4, 6, 8, 10, 12\}$
   $S = \{1, 2, 3, 4, 5\}$
6. $B = \{x \mid 0 < x < 10\}$
   $C = \{x \mid x \geq 2\}$
7. $Q = \{\text{negative integers}\}$
   $W = \{\text{whole numbers}\}$
8. $Q = \{\text{rational numbers}\}$
   $I = \{\text{integers}\}$

INDEPENDENT PRACTICE

See Example 1 **Find the intersection of the sets.**

9. $R = \{-10, -8, -6, -4\}$
   $T = \{-4, -2, 0, 2, 4\}$
10. $L = \{\text{negative integers}\}$
    $N = \{\text{natural numbers}\}$
11. $O = \{\text{positive odd integers}\}$
    $X = \{x \mid -10 \leq x \leq 5\}$
12. $K = \{x \mid x < 5\}$
    $R = \{x \mid x < 2\}$

See Example 2 **Find the union of the sets.**

13. $G = \{-12, -10, -8, -6, -4\}$
    $H = \{-12, -8, -4, 0\}$
14. $D = \{1, 2, 3, 4, 5\}$
    $F = \{2, 4, 6\}$
15. $Y = \{x \mid x \leq 0\}$
    $W = \{x \mid x > 0\}$
16. $K = \{\text{positive integers}\}$
    $T = \{\text{rational numbers}\}$

PRACTICE AND PROBLEM SOLVING

Find the union and the intersection of the sets.

17. $F = \{-2, -1, 0, 1, 2\}$
    $G = \{-2, 0, 2\}$
18. $W = \{2, 3, 4, 5, 6, 7\}$
    $R = \{\text{even integers}\}$
19. $R = \{x \mid x \geq 7\}$
    $M = \{x \mid x < 6\}$
20. $T = \{x \mid 0 \leq x \leq 10\}$
    $P = \{x \mid 5 < x \leq 15\}$
21. $A = \{\text{even integers}\}$
    $B = \{\text{odd integers}\}$
22. $Q = \{x \mid x < 5\}$
    $T = \{x \mid x > 3\}$
23. $P = \{\text{positive multiples of 2}\}$
    $M = \{\text{even integers}\}$
24. $J = \{\text{reciprocals of 1, 2, 3, and 4}\}$
    $R = \{\text{squares of 1, 2, 3, and 4}\}$

Life Science 

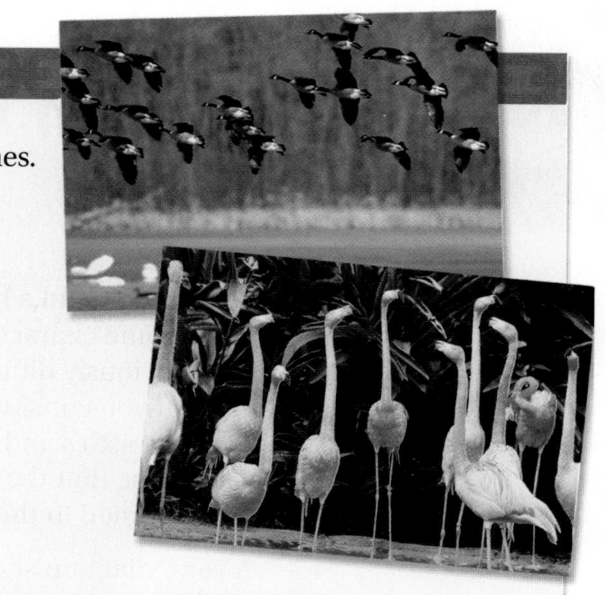

Groups of birds of a species may be known by several names.

Bird	Group Names
Chickens	{flock, run, brood, clutch}
Crows	{clan, murder, hover}
Ducks	{bed, brace, flock, flight, paddling, raft}
Flamingos	{stand, flamboyance}
Geese	{covert, flock, gaggle, plump, skein}
Peacocks	{pride, muster, ostentation}
Pheasants	{nye, brood, nide}
Pigeons	{flock, flight}
Starlings	{chattering, murmeration}
Swans	{bank, bevy, herd, team, wedge}

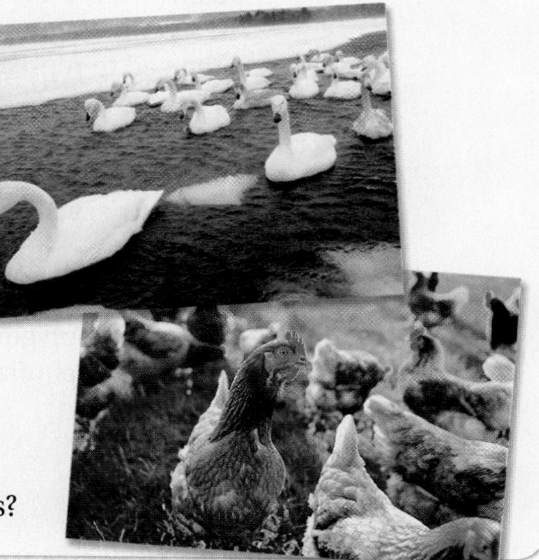

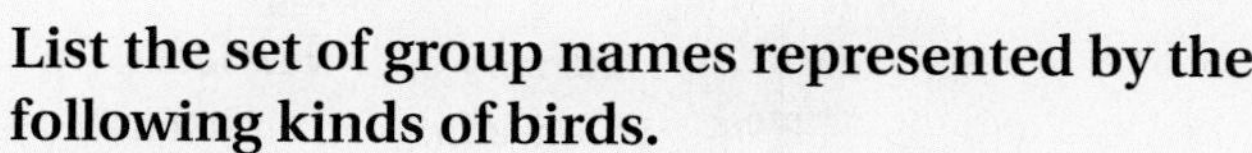

List the set of group names represented by the following kinds of birds.

25. Find {swans} ∪ {geese}.

26. Find {pheasants} ∩ {chickens}.

27. Find two sets whose intersection is the empty set.

28. Find two sets whose intersection is one of the sets.

29. ***CHALLENGE*** {Quails} ∩ {swans} = {bevy} and {quails} ∪ {swans} = {bank, bevy, herd, covey, team, wedge}. What are all of the names for a group of quails?

Spiral Review

Simplify each expression. (Lesson 3-8)

30. $\sqrt{121} + \sqrt{25}$ **31.** $(4 + 3)^2$ **32.** $\frac{\sqrt{441}}{\sqrt{144}}$ **33.** $\sqrt{5^2 + 12^2}$

34. TEST PREP Which figure has the fewest lines of symmetry? (Lesson 5-8)

A 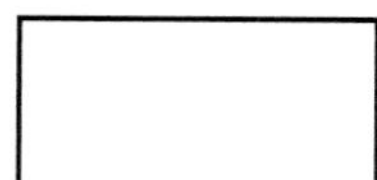 **B** 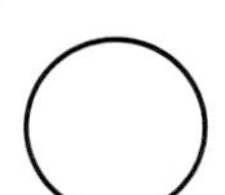 **C** 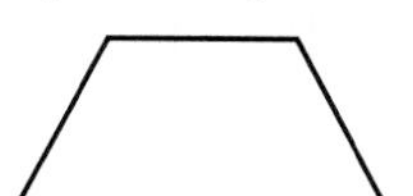 **D** 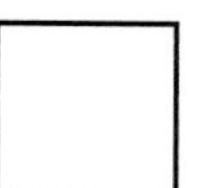

35. TEST PREP The lengths of the sides of a rectangle are whole numbers. If the rectangle's perimeter is 24 units, which of the following could **not** be the rectangle's area? (Lesson 6-1)

F 27 square units **G** 20 square units **H** 24 square units **J** 11 square units

14-3 Venn Diagrams

Learn to make and use Venn diagrams.

A computer and a human brain share some characteristics, but they obviously differ in many ways. If you consider their characteristics and abilities as sets, those that they share would be contained in their intersection.

A Venn diagram shows relationships among sets. In a Venn diagram, circles are used to represent sets. When two circles overlap, the region shared by both circles represents the intersection of the two sets.

The intersection of the set of all triangles and the set of all regular polygons for example, is the set of equilateral triangles.

Computer: Nonliving, Must be programmed, Unemotional, Analyzes all possible outcomes, Hard, Dry

Computer and Brain: Memory, Stores info, Can be damaged, Multitask, Math and logic, Needs energy, Chess

Brain: Living, New ideas, Dreams, Creates, Has emotions, Fatigue, Sleeps, Soft, Moist

EXAMPLE 1 Drawing Venn Diagrams

Draw a Venn diagram to show the relationship between the sets.

A **Vowels: {*A, E, I, O, U*}**
Letters used to represent musical notes: {*A, B, C, D, E, F, G*}

To draw the Venn diagram, first determine what is in the intersection of the sets.

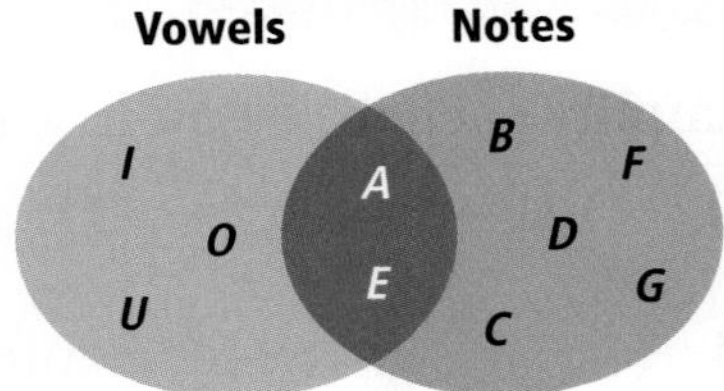

The intersection of the sets is {*A, E*}.

B **Factors of 28: {1, 2, 4, 7, 14, 28}**
Factors of 32: {1, 2, 4, 8, 16, 32}

The intersection of the sets is {1, 2, 4}.

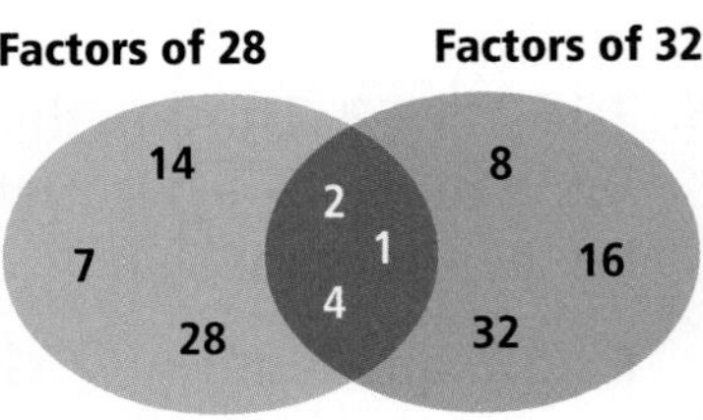

EXAMPLE 2 Analyzing Venn Diagrams

Use each Venn diagram to identify intersections, unions, and subsets.

A

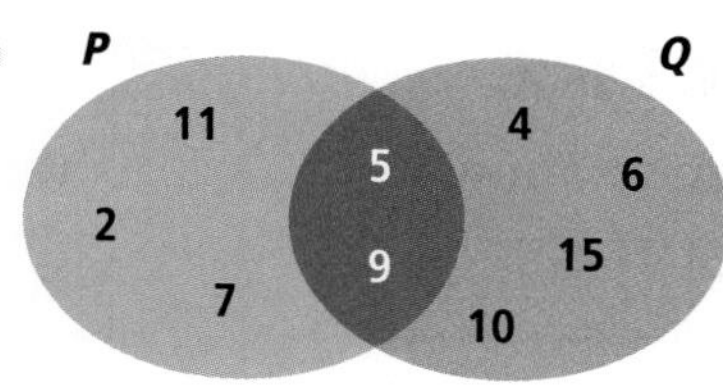

Intersection: $P \cap Q = \{5, 9\}$

Union: $P \cup Q = \{2, 4, 5, 6, 7, 9, 10, 11, 15\}$

Subsets: none

B

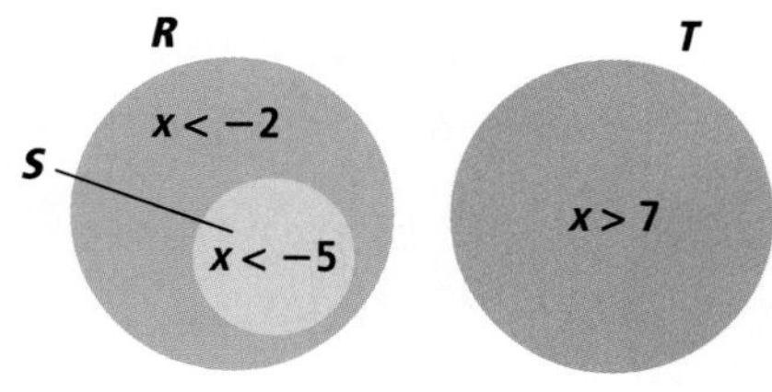

Intersections: $R \cap S = S$, $R \cap T = \varnothing$, $S \cap T = \varnothing$

Unions: $R \cup S = R$, $R \cup T = \{x \mid x < -2 \text{ or } x > 7\}$, and
$S \cup T = \{x \mid x < -5 \text{ or } x > 7\}$

Subsets: $S \subset R$

Remember!

S is a subset of *R* if every element of *S* is also an element of *R*.

The symbol ∴ means "therefore," and it symbolizes the conclusion of a logical argument.

EXAMPLE 3 Using Venn Diagrams

Use a Venn diagram to show the following logical argument.

All frogs are amphibians.
No opossums are amphibians.
∴ No opossums are frogs.

Amphibians
Frogs
Opossums

Think and Discuss

1. **Describe** how a subset is shown in a Venn diagram.
2. **Give** an example of a Venn diagram in which the intersection is the empty set.

14-3 Exercises

FOR EXTRA PRACTICE
see page 758

internet connect
Homework Help Online
go.hrw.com Keyword: MP4 14-3

GUIDED PRACTICE

See Example 1 Draw a Venn diagram to show the relationship between the sets.

1.

Set	Elements
Ron's favorite TV channels	2, 4, 5, 6, 7, 8
Eve's favorite TV channels	4, 6, 7, 9, 10, 14

2.

Set	Elements
First ten multiples of 4	4, 8, 12, 16, 20, 24, 28, 32, 36, 40
First ten multiples of 6	6, 12, 18, 24, 30, 36, 42, 48, 54, 60

See Example 2 Use each Venn diagram to identify intersections, unions, and subsets.

3.

A B
5 8 12
C 10 3
15
6
4 9 2

4.

M N
$x|x > 5$ $x|x \leq 7$

See Example 3 Use a Venn diagram to show the following logical argument.

5. All squares are rectangles. All rectangles are parallelograms.
∴ All squares are parallelograms.

INDEPENDENT PRACTICE

See Example 1 Draw a Venn diagram to show the relationship between the sets.

6.

Set	Elements
Faces on U.S. bills	{Washington, Lincoln, Hamilton, Jackson, Grant, Franklin}
Faces on U.S. coins	{Lincoln, F.D.R., Kennedy, Jefferson, Washington, Sacagawea}

7.

Set	Elements
Integers from −3 to 5	{−3, −2, −1, 0, 1, 2, 3, 4, 5}
Integers from −6 to 0	{−6, −5, −4, −3, −2, −1, 0}

See Example 2 Use each Venn diagram to identify intersections, unions, and subsets.

8.

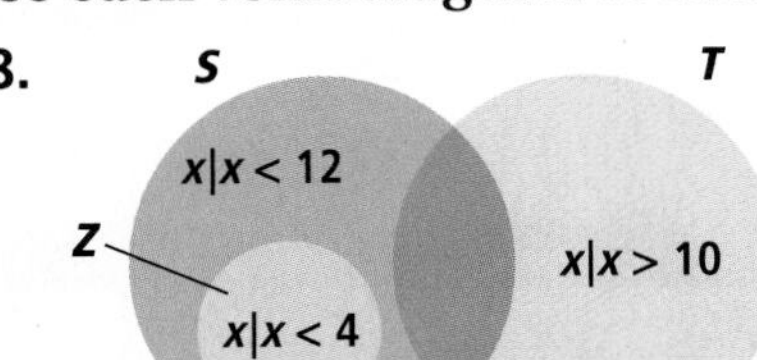

9.

Q
8 14
T 3
12
4 16

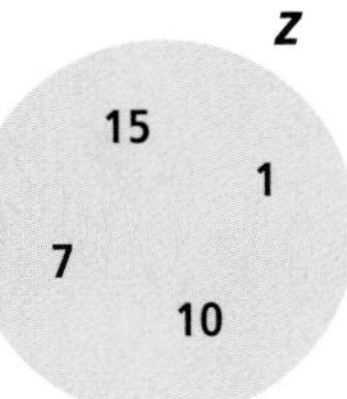

See Example 3 Use a Venn diagram to show the following logical argument.

10. All quadrilaterals are polygons. No circles are polygons.
∴ No circles are quadrilaterals.

PRACTICE AND PROBLEM SOLVING

Socrates (469–399 B.C.) was an ancient Greek philosopher who taught people to question accepted truths.

go.hrw.com
Web Extra!
KEYWORD: MP4 Socrates

11. All prime numbers except 2 are odd. Use a Venn diagram to display the statement.

12. ***HISTORY*** A well-known argument states:

    "All men are mortal. Socrates was a man.
    Therefore, Socrates was mortal."

    Use a Venn diagram to show the argument.

13. ***MUSIC*** All reed instruments are woodwinds. Some reed instruments are double-reed instruments. Therefore, all double-reed instruments are woodwinds. Use a Venn diagram to show the argument.

14. ***ENTERTAINMENT*** Use the information shown to write inequalities to show the age limits. Then make a Venn diagram for the situation. Identify the union and intersection of the sets.

15. ***CHOOSE A STRATEGY*** The following uniform numbers have been retired by the New York Yankees: 1, 3, 4, 5, 7, 8, 9, 10, 15, 16, 23, 32, 37, 42, and 44. The Los Angeles Dodgers have retired 1, 2, 4, 19, 20, 24, 32, 39, 42, and 53. How many uniform numbers from 0–99 are available to be worn by players on either team?

16. ***WRITE ABOUT IT*** Describe how Venn diagrams are useful for finding the union and intersection of two sets.

17. ***CHALLENGE*** In a class, 22 students have been on a plane, 28 on a train, 23 on a boat, 15 on a plane and train, 20 on a train and boat, 14 on a plane and boat, 12 on all three, and 1 on none of them. How many students are in the class?

Spiral Review

Find the volume of each figure. Use 3.14 for π. (Lessons 6-6, 6-7)

18. a 3 ft by 5 ft by 11 ft rectangular prism

19. a cylinder with radius 3 in. and height 8 in.

20. a cone with diameter 7 in. and height 12 in.

21. a square pyramid with base length 5 cm and height 10 cm

22. **TEST PREP** Rachel reached into a bag containing 7 malt energy bars and 4 berry energy bars and pulled out 2 bars. What is the probability that Rachel chose 2 berry bars? (Lesson 9-7)

    A $\frac{2}{11}$ **B** $\frac{12}{121}$ **C** $\frac{21}{55}$ **D** $\frac{6}{55}$

Chapter 14

Mid-Chapter Quiz

LESSON 14-1 (pp. 688–691)

Insert $\in$ or $\notin$ to make each statement true.

1. Nevada ■ {U.S. states}

2. Mexico ■ {continents}

Determine whether the first set is a subset of the second set. Use the correct symbol.

3. K = {pyramids}
J = {prisms}

4. $H = \{1, 2, 3, 4, 5\}$
S = {rational numbers}

Tell whether each set is finite or infinite.

5. {integers less than 200}

6. {factors of 1500}

LESSON 14-2 (pp. 692–695)

Find the intersection of the sets.

7. $R = \{10, 20, 30, 40, 50\}$
$S = \{5, 10, 15, 20\}$

8. W = {integers}
X = {counting numbers}

Find the union of the sets.

9. $G = \{-3, -2, -1, 0\}$
$H = \{0, 1, 2, 3\}$

10. P = {positive integers}
R = {factors of 24}

LESSON 14-3 (pp. 696–699)

Draw a Venn diagram to show the relationships between the sets.

11.

Set	Elements
Factors of 30	{1, 2, 3, 5, 6, 10, 15, 30}
Factors of 18	{1, 2, 3, 6, 9, 18}

12.

Set	Elements
Integers greater than or equal to 7	{7, 8, 9, 10, ...}
Integers less than or equal to 5	{5, 4, 3, 2, ...}

Use the Venn diagrams to identify intersections, unions, and subsets.

13.

Whole numbers
Prime numbers
Composite numbers
1
0

14.

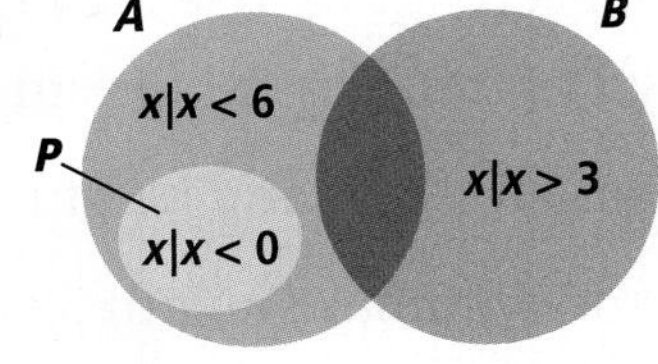

Use a Venn diagram to show each logical argument.

15. No circles are polygons.
All triangles are polygons.
$\therefore$ No triangles are circles.

16. All counting numbers are integers.
All integers are rational numbers.
$\therefore$ All counting numbers are rational numbers.

Illinois State Parks

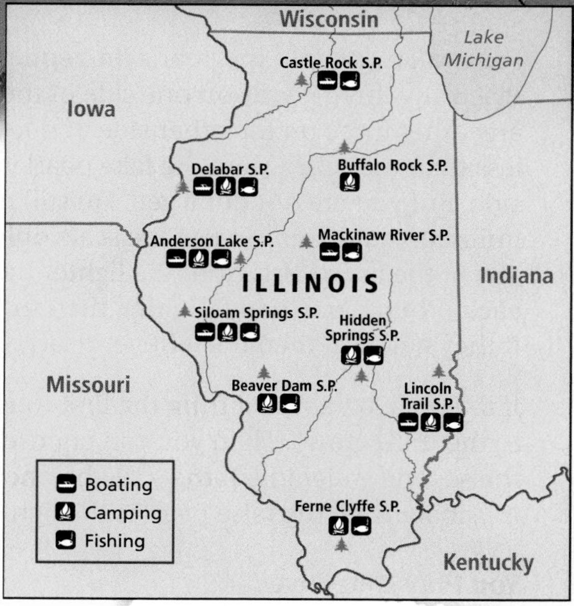

1. Of the ten state parks shown on the map, eight offer camping and six offer boating. Only four of the parks offer both.

   a. Draw a Venn diagram to show the parks that offer camping and the parks that offer boating and the intersection of the two sets.

   b. How many parks allow camping but not boating? How many allow boating but not camping?

2. Jim and José decide to visit four state parks on their vacation. The diagram shows the distances between each park. Can you find an Euler circuit in this diagram? Why or why not? Can you find a Hamiltonian circuit?

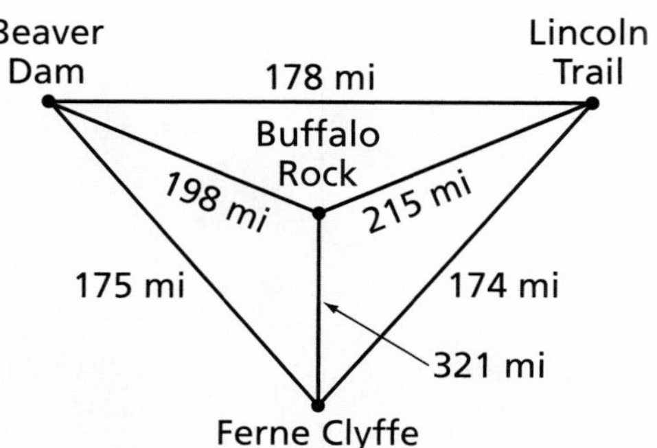

3. Find the shortest route that Jim and José can take if they begin and end their trip at Buffalo Rock State Park. How long is this route?

MATH-ABLES

Find the Phony!

Suppose you have nine identical-looking pearls. Eight are real, and one is fake. Using a balance scale that consists of two pans, you must find the bogus pearl. The real pearls weigh the same, and the fake weighs less. The scale can be used only twice. How can you find the phony?

First you must split the pearls into equal groups. Place any three pearls on one side of the scale and any other three on the other side. If one side weighs less than the other, then the fake pearl is on that side. But you are not done yet! You still need to find the imitation, and you can use the scale only once more. Take any of the two pearls from the lighter pan, and weigh them against each other. If one pan is lighter, then that pan contains the fake pearl. If they balance, then the leftover pearl of the group is the fake.

If the scale balances during the first weighing, then you know the fake is in the third group. Then you can choose two pearls from that group for the second weighing. If the scale balances, the fake is the one left. If it is unbalanced, the false pearl is the lighter one.

You Play Detective

Suppose you have 12 identical gold coins in front of you. One is counterfeit and weighs slightly more than the others. How can you identify the counterfeit in three weighings?

Sprouts

You and a partner play against each other to try to make the last move in the game. You start with three dots. Player one draws a path to join two dots or a path that starts and ends at the same dot. A new dot is then placed somewhere on that path. No dot can have more than three paths drawn from it, and no path can cross another. The last player to make a move is the winner!

internet connect

Go to ***go.hrw.com*** for a complete set of game rules.
KEYWORD: MP4 Game14

Student Handbook

Extra Practice ■ Chapter 1

1A Equations and Inequalities

LESSON 1-1

Evaluate each expression for the given value of the variable.

1. $2 + x$ for $x = 7$
2. $4m - 3$ for $m = 2$
3. $2(p + 3)$ for $p = 8$

Evaluate each expression for the given values of the variables.

4. $3x + y$ for $x = 2, y = 4$
5. $2y - x$ for $x = 2, y = 5$
6. $5x + 2y$ for $x = 1, y = 3$
7. $3x + 2.5y$ for $x = 1, y = 2$
8. $5.7x + 2y$ for $x = 2, y = 1$
9. $4.2x + 3y$ for $x = 2, y = 3$

LESSON 1-2

Write an algebraic expression for each word phrase.

10. seven less than a number b
11. eight more than the product of 7 and a
12. a quotient of 8 and a number m
13. five times the sum of c and 18

Solve.

14. The formula for converting a temperature in C degrees Celsius (°C) to degrees Fahrenheit (°F) is $F = 1.8C + 32$. Convert the temperature 28°C to degrees Fahrenheit.

LESSON 1-3

Solve.

15. $4 + x = 13$
16. $t - 3 = 8$
17. $17 = m + 11$
18. $5 + a = 7$
19. $p - 5 = 23$
20. $31 + y = 50$
21. $18 + k = 34$
22. $g - 16 = 23$

LESSON 1-4

Solve.

23. $5x = 30$
24. $\frac{m}{4} = 13$
25. $9a = 54$
26. $\frac{n}{7} = 7$
27. $3p = 96$
28. $\frac{s}{6} = 3$
29. $3k + 2 = 20$
30. $\frac{r}{4} - 5 = 3$
31. Four friends split the cost of a \$16.68 pizza. How much did each friend pay?

LESSON 1-5

Compare. Write < or >.

32. $15 - 8$ ▨ 6
33. $3(7)$ ▨ 23
34. $51 - 18$ ▨ 34
35. $4(16)$ ▨ 62

Solve and graph.

36. $x - 3.5 \geq 7$
37. $5p < 40$
38. $2 \leq \frac{a}{3}$
39. $h - 5 \leq 13$

LESSON 1-6

Combine like terms.

40. $3x + 2x + 5x$
41. $4x - 2x + 8 + 3x + 5$
42. $5a - 3b + 4 + 6b - 2a$

Solve.

43. $3x + 9 = 84$
44. $2a - 3 = 41$
45. $7b + 5 = 61$
46. $6h - 12 = 78$

Extra Practice

Extra Practice ■ Chapter 1

1B Graphing

LESSON 1-7

Determine whether each ordered pair is a solution of $3x + 5y = 25$.

1. (4, 3)
2. (5, 2)
3. (6, 1)
4. (3, 4)

Use the given values to make a table of solutions.

5. $y = x - 3$ for $x = -2, -1, 0, 1, 2$
6. $y = 2x + 1$ for $x = -2, -1, 0, 1, 2$
7. If sales tax is 6%, the equation for the total cost c of an item is $c = 1.06p$, where p is the price of the item before tax. What is the total cost of a $20 shirt, including sales tax?

LESSON 1-8

Graph each point on a coordinate plane.

8. (4, 3)
9. (3, 0)
10. (−1, 3)
11. (0, −5)
12. (−2, −4)
13. (4, −2)

Complete each table of ordered pairs. Graph each equation on a coordinate plane.

14. $x + 3 = y$

x	$x + 3$	y	(x, y)
1			
2			
3			
4			

15. $3x = y$

x	$3x$	y	(x, y)
2			
4			
6			
8			

LESSON 1-9

Match each situation to the correct graph.

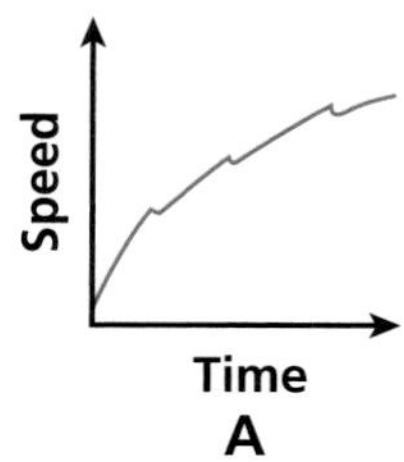

A

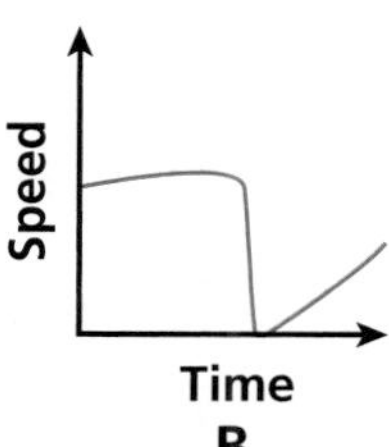

B

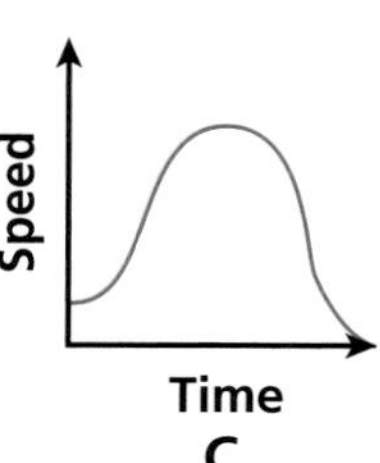

C

16. A skier increases speed going down a hill, and then comes to a stop.
17. A skier travels cross-country, stopping only to rest for a minute before going up a hill.
18. A skier accelerates going downhill, decreases speed slightly before sharp turns, and then accelerates again.

Extra Practice

Extra Practice ■ Chapter 2

2A Integers

LESSON 2-1

Add.

1. $-4 + 6$
2. $3 + (-8)$
3. $-6 + (-2)$
4. $7 + (-11)$
5. $-6 + 3$
6. $7 + (-2)$
7. $-4 + (-1)$
8. $9 + (-5)$

Evaluate each expression for the given value of the variable.

9. $x + 9$ for $x = -8$
10. $x + 3$ for $x = -3$
11. $x + 5$ for $x = -7$
12. $x + 1$ for $x = -5$
13. $x + 6$ for $x = -9$
14. $x + 2$ for $x = -8$

LESSON 2-2

Subtract.

15. $-5 - 3$
16. $4 - (-1)$
17. $-9 - (-4)$
18. $-4 - 7$
19. $-2 - 5$
20. $3 - (-8)$
21. $-6 - (-12)$
22. $-1 - 6$
23. An elevator rises to 281 feet above ground level and then drops 314 feet to the basement. What is the position of the elevator relative to ground level?

Evaluate each expression for the given value of the variable.

24. $4 - x$ for $x = -7$
25. $-7 - s$ for $s = -5$
26. $-5 - b$ for $b = 9$
27. $12 - y$ for $y = -8$
28. $-13 - f$ for $f = -8$
29. $-2 - c$ for $c = 5$

LESSON 2-3

Multiply or divide.

30. $5(-8)$
31. $\frac{-81}{9}$
32. $-6(-4)$
33. $\frac{24}{-3}$
34. $7(-3)$
35. $\frac{-36}{6}$
36. $-8(-4)$
37. $\frac{48}{-8}$
38. $-9(-12)$
39. $\frac{-54}{9}$
40. $13(-5)$
41. $\frac{96}{-12}$

LESSON 2-4

Solve.

42. $x + 13 = 8$
43. $-7 + t = -15$
44. $h = -8 + 17$
45. $g + 15 = 3$
46. $-8 + p = -20$
47. $n = -4 + 31$
48. $m + 4 = 9$
49. $d = -8 + 2$
50. $\frac{a}{-4} = -2$
51. $-49 = 7d$
52. $\frac{c}{-2} = -8$
53. $-57 = 3p$

LESSON 2-5

Solve and graph.

54. $w - 1 < -4$
55. $x - 3 \geq -2$
56. $h - 2 \leq -5$
57. $g - 6 > -1$
58. $k - 3 > -9$
59. $m - 5 > -8$
60. $f - 9 < -2$
61. $m - 2 \leq -1$
62. $-3a > 15$
63. $\frac{x}{-4} < 6$
64. $-5b \leq 65$
65. $\frac{a}{-8} \geq 4$

Extra Practice ■ Chapter 2

2B Exponents and Scientific Notation

LESSON 2-6

Write using exponents.

1. $2 \times 2 \times 2 \times 2$
2. $5 \times 5 \times 5 \times 5 \times 5 \times 5 \times 5$
3. $4 \cdot 4 \cdot 4 \cdot 4 \cdot 4$
4. $9 \cdot 9 \cdot 9 \cdot 9 \cdot 9 \cdot 9 \cdot 9 \cdot 9$
5. $a \cdot a \cdot a \cdot a \cdot a \cdot a \cdot a$
6. p

Evaluate.

7. 2^4
8. 3^3
9. $(-5)^2$
10. $(-3)^5$
11. 8^3
12. 6^5
13. $(-2)^8$
14. $(-4)^3$

Simplify.

15. $20 + 3(2^3)$
16. $14 + 5(3^4)$
17. $19 + 3(2 \cdot 4^2)$
18. $22 + 5(8 + 2^4)$
19. $8 + 2(3 \cdot 4^3)$
20. $17 + 2(4 + 5^3)$
21. $32 + 4(5 + 2^5)$
22. $58 + 3(9 + 6^3)$

LESSON 2-7

Multiply or divide. Write as one power.

23. $5^4 \cdot 5^3$
24. $2^6 \cdot 2^3$
25. $4^4 \cdot 4^8$
26. $7^3 \cdot 7^9$
27. $12^8 \cdot 12^5$
28. $a^8 \cdot a^5$
29. $b^6 \cdot b^{12}$
30. $w^7 \cdot w^7$
31. $\frac{16^4}{16^2}$
32. $\frac{8^9}{8^3}$
33. $\frac{7^{12}}{7^5}$
34. $\frac{15^{12}}{15^{11}}$
35. $\frac{a^7}{a^4}$
36. $\frac{w^{11}}{w^4}$
37. $\frac{c^6}{c^2}$
38. $\frac{z^{16}}{z^9}$

LESSON 2-8

Evaluate each power of 10.

39. 10^{-2}
40. 10^{-3}
41. 10^{-4}
42. 10^{-5}
43. 10^{-6}
44. 10^{-7}
45. 10^{-8}
46. 10^{-9}

Evaluate.

47. $(-3)^{-2}$
48. 4^{-3}
49. $(-6)^{-4}$
50. 7^{-3}
51. $10^4 \cdot 10^{-2}$
52. $\frac{3^2}{3^4}$
53. $2^5 \cdot 2^{-2}$
54. $\frac{4^3}{4^5}$

LESSON 2-9

Write each number in standard notation.

55. 3.6×10^3
56. 5.62×10^5
57. 7.13×10^{-4}
58. 8.39×10^{-7}
59. 1.6×10^2
60. 3.12×10^7
61. 1.13×10^{-5}
62. 5.92×10^{-8}

Write each number in scientific notation.

63. 0.000483
64. 5,410,000,000
65. 0.00328
66. 12,600,000
67. 0.0000000000912
68. 432,000,000,000,000

Extra Practice

Extra Practice ■ Chapter 3

3A Rational Numbers and Operations

LESSON 3-1

Write each decimal as a fraction in simplest form.

1. 0.4 **2.** 0.05 **3.** 0.12 **4.** 0.625

Write each fraction as a decimal.

5. $\frac{3}{8}$ **6.** $\frac{1}{4}$ **7.** $\frac{9}{4}$ **8.** $\frac{3}{5}$

LESSON 3-2

Add or subtract.

9. $\frac{2}{3} - \frac{5}{3}$ **10.** $\frac{17}{4} + \frac{13}{4}$ **11.** $\frac{5}{8} - \frac{15}{8}$ **12.** $-\frac{8}{3} + \frac{11}{3}$

13. $\frac{9}{2} - \frac{15}{2}$ **14.** $\frac{19}{3} + \frac{27}{3}$ **15.** $\frac{9}{4} - \frac{22}{4}$ **16.** $-\frac{31}{5} + \frac{24}{5}$

Evaluate each expression for the given value of the variable.

17. $32.9 + x$ for $x = -15.8$ **18.** $21.3 + a$ for $a = -37.6$ **19.** $-\frac{3}{5} + z$ for $z = 3\frac{1}{5}$

LESSON 3-3

Multiply. Write each answer in simplest form.

20. $-\frac{2}{3}\left(-\frac{5}{8}\right)$ **21.** $\frac{7}{10}\left(-\frac{2}{3}\right)$ **22.** $-\frac{4}{5}\left(-\frac{9}{10}\right)$ **23.** $-\frac{5}{8}\left(\frac{11}{12}\right)$

24. $-3.9(-9)$ **25.** $-4.1(8.6)$ **26.** $-0.08(3.1)$ **27.** $-0.004(-1.9)$

LESSON 3-4

Divide. Write each answer in simplest form.

28. $3\frac{2}{3} \div \frac{1}{4}$ **29.** $5\frac{1}{5} \div \frac{7}{8}$ **30.** $6\frac{5}{8} \div \frac{2}{3}$ **31.** $4\frac{1}{9} \div \frac{3}{7}$

32. $5.68 \div 0.2$ **33.** $9.45 \div 0.05$ **34.** $2.31 \div 0.7$ **35.** $0.522 \div 6$

LESSON 3-5

Add or subtract.

36. $\frac{9}{10} + \frac{3}{8}$ **37.** $\frac{2}{7} - \frac{3}{4}$ **38.** $\frac{3}{4} + \frac{1}{9}$ **39.** $\frac{5}{8} - \frac{3}{10}$

40. $5\frac{1}{3} + \left(-2\frac{1}{8}\right)$ **41.** $3\frac{2}{3} + \left(-1\frac{7}{8}\right)$ **42.** $4\frac{1}{8} + \left(-1\frac{3}{5}\right)$ **43.** $9\frac{1}{9} + \left(-5\frac{2}{11}\right)$

LESSON 3-6

Solve.

44. $x - 3.2 = 5.1$ **45.** $-3.1p = 15.5$ **46.** $\frac{a}{-2.3} = 7.9$ **47.** $-4.3x = 34.4$

48. $m - \frac{1}{3} = \frac{5}{8}$ **49.** $x - \frac{3}{7} = \frac{1}{9}$ **50.** $\frac{4}{5}w = \frac{2}{3}$ **51.** $\frac{9}{10}z = \frac{5}{8}$

LESSON 3-7

Solve.

52. $1.2x > 7.2$ **53.** $a - 3.8 < 5.4$ **54.** $3.8b \geq 26.6$ **55.** $d - 5.3 \leq 7.9$

56. $w + \frac{2}{3} > \frac{2}{5}$ **57.** $-2\frac{1}{4}b < 9$ **58.** $b + \frac{3}{8} \geq \frac{9}{10}$ **59.** $4\frac{2}{5}z \leq 39\frac{3}{5}$

Extra Practice

Extra Practice ■ Chapter 3

3B Real Numbers

LESSON 3-8

Find the two square roots of each number.

1. 25
2. 81
3. 144
4. 169
5. 100
6. 225
7. 36
8. 400

Evaluate each expression.

9. $3\sqrt{9}$
10. $5\sqrt{36}$
11. $7\sqrt{16}$
12. $3\sqrt{49}$
13. $\sqrt{97 + 24}$
14. $\sqrt{111 + 85}$
15. $\sqrt{231 + 253}$
16. $\sqrt{45 - 9}$

Solve.

17. The area of a square room is 729 square feet. What are the dimensions of the room?
18. The area of a square garden is 1,444 square feet. What are the dimensions of the garden?

LESSON 3-9

Each square root is between two integers. Name the integers.

19. $\sqrt{29}$
20. $\sqrt{51}$
21. $\sqrt{93}$
22. $\sqrt{74}$
23. $\sqrt{32}$
24. $\sqrt{12}$
25. $\sqrt{48}$
26. $\sqrt{128}$

Use a calculator to find the square root of each number. Round to the nearest tenth.

27. $\sqrt{212}$
28. $\sqrt{186}$
29. $\sqrt{542}$
30. $\sqrt{219}$
31. $\sqrt{384}$
32. $\sqrt{410}$
33. $\sqrt{334}$
34. $\sqrt{96}$
35. $\sqrt{54}$
36. $\sqrt{683}$
37. $\sqrt{614}$
38. $\sqrt{304}$

LESSON 3-10

Write the names that apply to each number.

39. $\sqrt{7}$
40. -61.2
41. $\frac{\sqrt{16}}{2}$
42. -8
43. 4.168
44. $\frac{\sqrt{25}}{\sqrt{1}}$
45. $\sqrt{11}$
46. $\sqrt{13}$

State whether the number is rational, irrational, or not a real number.

47. $\sqrt{\frac{9}{16}}$
48. $\sqrt{-4}$
49. $\sqrt{19}$
50. $\sqrt{-13}$
51. 12
52. $\frac{8}{0}$
53. $\sqrt{\frac{36}{49}}$
54. $\frac{13}{0}$

Find a real number between the two given numbers.

55. $5\frac{1}{8}$ and $5\frac{2}{8}$
56. $2\frac{1}{3}$ and $2\frac{2}{3}$
57. $4\frac{4}{9}$ and $4\frac{5}{9}$
58. $1\frac{5}{7}$ and $1\frac{6}{7}$
59. $3\frac{1}{8}$ and $3\frac{1}{4}$
60. $9\frac{4}{7}$ and $9\frac{5}{7}$

Extra Practice ■ Chapter 4

4A Collecting and Describing Data

LESSON 4-1

Identify the population and the sample. Give a reason why the sample could be biased.

1. A company chooses 2000 veterinarians who belong to the same veterinary association for a survey on their opinion about a new dog medicine.

Identify the sampling method used.

2. In a nationwide survey, 7 states are chosen at random, and 150 people are chosen from each state.
3. A questionnaire is distributed to every fifth adult shopper at a grocery store.

LESSON 4-2

4. **Use the given data to make a stem-and-leaf plot.**

Number of Floors in Selected Major Buildings					
Promenade	40	One Park Tower	32	Commerce Plaza	31
One Financial Center	46	One Post Office Square	40	Water Tower Place	74
Park Tower Condos	54	City Plaza	40	Harbour Point	54
Park Millennium	53	Energy Plaza	49	San Felipe Plaza	45
The Spires	41	Santa Maria	51	Cityspire	72

5. **Use the given data to make a back-to-back stem-and-leaf plot.**

World Series Win/Loss Records of Selected Teams (through 2001)							
Team	Yankees	Pirates	Giants	Tigers	Cardinals	Dodgers	Orioles
Wins	26	5	5	4	9	6	3
Losses	12	2	11	5	6	12	4

LESSON 4-3

Find the mean, median, and mode of each data set.

6. 8, 3, 9, 10, 8, 4, 5, 7, 6, 7, 8, 5
7. 31, 28, 25, 41, 52, 40, 38, 24, 43, 27, 24, 35

LESSON 4-4

Find the range and first and third quartiles for each data set.

8. 18, 20, 15, 13, 13, 20, 17, 20, 15, 13, 18, 20, 19, 17, 19
9. 82, 77, 74, 71, 85, 89, 81, 85, 80, 91, 72, 81, 88, 86, 75

Use the given data to make a box-and-whisker plot.

10. 3, 12, 17, 9, 8, 4, 13, 24, 17, 19, 5
11. 57, 53, 52, 31, 48, 59, 64, 86, 56, 54, 55

Extra Practice ■ Chapter 12

12B Functions

LESSON 12-4

Determine whether each relationship represents a function.

1.

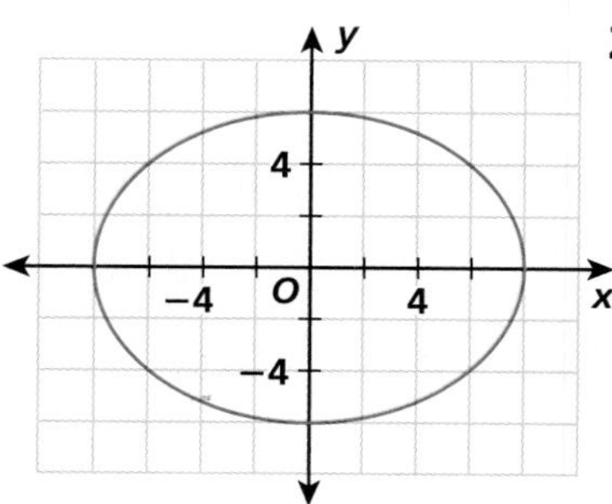

2.

x	y
−3	1
−1	−1
0	−2
2	0
4	2

3.

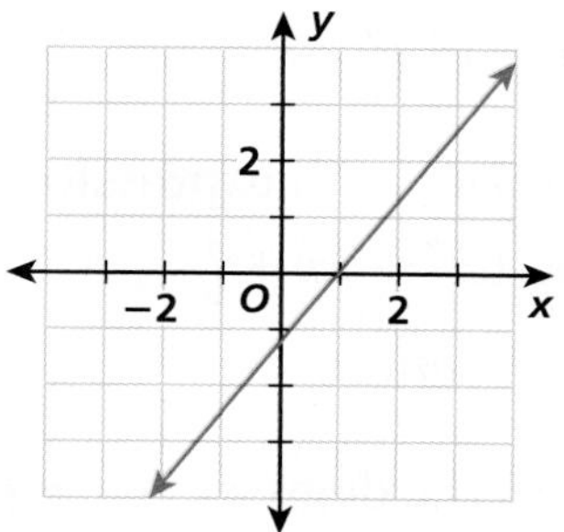

For each function, find $f(-1)$, $f(1)$, and $f(3)$.

4. $f(x) = x^2 + 1$ **5.** $f(x) = |x| - 2$ **6.** $f(x) = 3x + 1$ **7.** $f(x) = \frac{x^2}{x - 2}$

LESSON 12-5

Write the rule for each linear function.

8.

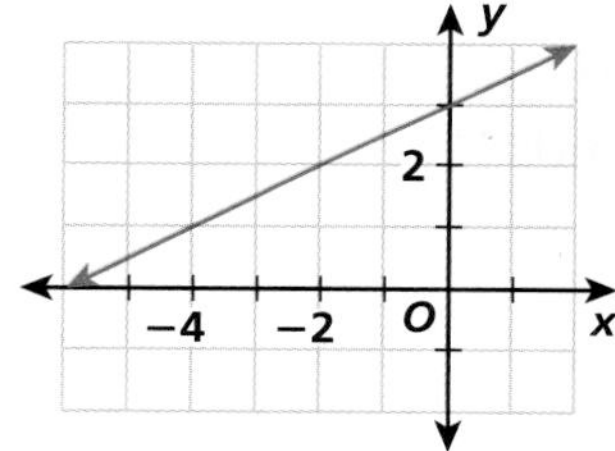

9.

x	y
−2	−7
−1	−5
0	−3
1	−1
2	1

10.

x	y
−2	3
−1	2
0	1
1	0
2	−1

LESSON 12-6

Create a table for each exponential function, and use it to graph the function.

11. $f(x) = 3 \cdot 4^x$ **12.** $f(x) = \frac{1}{2} \cdot 3^x$ **13.** $f(x) = 0.75 \cdot 2^x$ **14.** $f(x) = 2 \cdot 10^x$

15. The isotope cobalt-60, found in radioactive waste, has a half-life of 5 years. How much of a 150 g sample of cobalt-60 would remain after 35 years?

LESSON 12-7

Create a table for each quadratic function, and use it to make a graph.

16. $f(x) = x^2 - 3$ **17.** $f(x) = x^2 - x + 6$ **18.** $f(x) = (x - 1)(x + 2)$

LESSON 12-8

Tell whether the relationship is an inverse variation.

19.

Outdoor Temperature (°F)	40°	25°	20°	10°	5°
Cups of Coffee Sold	200	320	400	800	1600

Graph each inverse variation function.

20. $f(x) = \frac{3}{x}$ **21.** $f(x) = \frac{-0.5}{x}$ **22.** $f(x) = \frac{3}{2x}$

Extra Practice ▪ Chapter 13

13A Introduction to Polynomials

LESSON 13-1

Determine whether each expression is a monomial.

1. $\frac{2}{3}r^2st^3$
2. $-4p^5q$
3. 5^xy^2
4. $\frac{4m^2}{n^4}$

Classify each expression as a monomial, a binomial, a trinomial, or not a polynomial.

5. $6x^2 + 3x + \frac{1}{2}$
6. $-3a^4bc^4$
7. $\frac{3}{4}m^3n^2 + m^2$
8. $5f + 3f^{\frac{1}{2}}g^2$
9. $-mn^5 - 109$
10. $-\frac{2}{z^3}$
11. $-9h^3 + h^2 - 2$
12. $3xy^2$

Find the degree of each polynomial.

13. $2x^2 + 3x^4 + 7$
14. $8r + r^3 + 3r^2$
15. $-10y^4 + 4 + 5y^5$
16. $6m^3 + 11m^4 - 3m$
17. The trinomial $-16t^2 + vt + 3$ describes the height in feet of a model rocket launched straight up from a 3-foot platform with a velocity of v ft/s after t seconds. Find the height of the rocket after 4 seconds if $v = 70$ ft/s.
18. The trinomial $-16t^2 + vt + 10$ describes the height in feet of a model rocket launched straight up from a 10-foot platform with a velocity of v ft/s after t seconds. Find the height of the rocket after 3 seconds if $v = 50$ ft/s.

LESSON 13-2

Identify the like terms in each polynomial.

19. $5s - 2rs^2 + 3rs^2 + 2rs - s$
20. $-2x^3y^2 + 2x^2y^2 - x^3y + 4x^3y^2$
21. $6b + 4b^2 - 3b^3 + 5b - b^2$

Simplify.

22. $8r^3 - 2r + 6(r^2 - 3r)$
23. $5(a^2b^2 + 3ab) + 3(ab^2 - 5ab)$
24. $7x - 3x^3 + 4x + 12x^2$
25. $2s^2t^2 + st^2 + 5s^2t^2 - 7s^2t - 3st^2 + s^2t$
26. A rectangle has a width of 13 cm and a length of $(4x^2 + 18)$ cm. The area is given by the expression $13(4x^2 + 18)$ cm^2. Use the Distributive Property to write an equivalent expression.
27. A parallelogam has a base of $(3x^2 - 4)$ in. and a height of 4 in. The area is given by the expression $4(3x^2 - 4)$ in^2. Use the Distributive Property to write an equivalent expression.

Extra Practice ■ Chapter 13

13B Polynomial Operations

LESSON 13-3

Add.

1. $(5x^2y^2 - 3xy^2 + 2y^2) + (3x^2y^2 + 5y^2)$
2. $(4a^2 + 3ab^2) + (2ab^2 + b^2) + (-5a^2 - 2b^2)$
3. $(m^3 + 3m^2n^2 + 4) + (6m^2n^2 - 9)$
4. $(10r^3s^2 - 7r^2s + 4r) + (-4r^3s^2 + 3r)$
5. A rectangle has a width of $(x + 5)$ in. and a length of $(4x - 3)$ in. A square has sides of length $(x^2 + 2x - 3)$ in. Write an expression for the sum of the perimeter of the rectangle and the perimeter of the square.

LESSON 13-4

Find the opposite of each polynomial.

6. $-6xy - 2y^3$
7. $5a^2b^2 + 3ab - 2$
8. $-4x^4 - 5x + x^3$
9. $9m^3 + mn^2$

Subtract.

10. $(5x^2 + 2xy - 3y^2) - (3x^2 + 2y^2 - 8)$
11. $12a - (4a^3 - 2a + 7)$
12. $(8r^2s^2 + 4r^2s + rs) - (-2r^2s - 6rs + 3r^2)$
13. $(12y^3 - 6xy + 1) - (8xy - 2x + 1)$
14. The area of the larger rectangle is $15x^2 + 11x - 14$ cm^2. The area of the smaller rectangle is $6x^2 + 8x$ cm^2. What is the area of the shaded region?

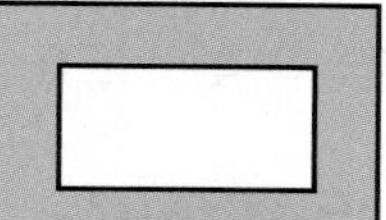

LESSON 13-5

Multiply.

15. $(3x^2y^2)(4x^3y)$
16. $(2a^2bc^2)(-5a^3b^2)$
17. $(6m^3n^4)(2mn)$
18. $3s(5t - 8s)$
19. $-p(3p^2 + 2pq - 9)$
20. $2x^2y(3x^2y^3 + 5x^2y - xy + 12y)$
21. A rectangle has a width of $3x^2y$ ft and a length of $2x^2 + 4xy + 7$ ft. Write and simplify an expression for the area of the rectangle. Then find the area of the rectangle if $x = 2$ and $y = 3$.

LESSON 13-6

Multiply.

22. $(y + 5)(y - 3)$
23. $(t + 1)(t - 6)$
24. $(3m + 2)(4m - 3)$
25. $(y + 2)^2$
26. $(a - 4)^2$
27. $(c - 2)(c + 2)$

Extra Practice ■ Chapter 14

14A Set Theory

LESSON 14-1

Insert the correct symbol to make each statement true.

1. pear ■ {fruit}
2. $\sqrt{4}$ ■ {prime numbers}

Determine whether the first set is a subset of the second set. Use the correct symbol.

3. T = {trapezoids}
   P = {parallelograms}
4. $N = \{(x + 3), x^2y^2, \frac{1}{2}x\}$
   P = {polynomials}

Tell whether each set is finite or infinite.

5. {points on a line}
6. {prime numbers less than 100}

LESSON 14-2

Find the intersection of the sets.

7. $A = \{-3, -1, 3, 5, 7\}$
   $B = \{1, 3, 5, 7, 9\}$
8. $N = \{-2, \frac{1}{3}, 0, 1.5, 2\frac{1}{3}, 8\}$
   I = {integers}
9. P = {prime numbers}
   E = {even numbers}

Find the union of the sets.

10. $E = \{0, 2, 4, 6, 8\}$
    $F = \{-4, -2, 0, 2\}$
11. O = {odd numbers}
    $M = \{1, 3, 7, 11\}$
12. $X = \{-3, -2, 0, 2, 3\}$
    $Y = \{0, 1, 2, 3\}$

LESSON 14-3

Draw a Venn diagram to show the relationship between the sets.

13.

Set	Elements
First 10 multiples of 3	{3, 6, 9, 12, 15, 18 21, 24, 27, 30}
Factors of 24	{1, 2, 3, 4, 6, 8, 12, 24}

14.

Set	Elements
Students in the science club	{Mark, Tina, Maria, Jacob, Patty, Lucas, Vivian, Bob, Missy, Ariana, Cindy, Dan}
Students in the jazz band	{Nick, Jacob, Rob, Missy, Cathy, Natalie, Cindy}

Use each Venn diagram to identify intersections, unions, and subsets.

15.

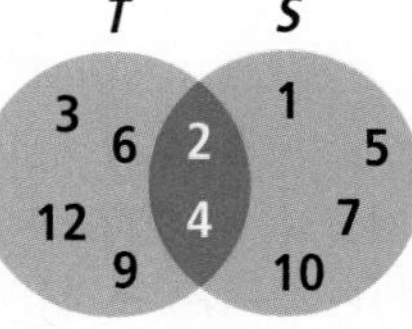

16.

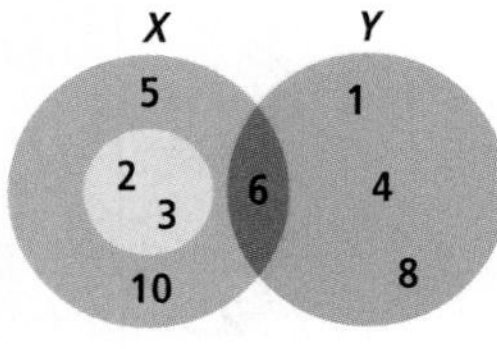

Use a Venn diagram to show the following logical argument.

17. All squares are rhombuses.
    All rhombuses are quadrilaterals.
    ∴ All squares are quadrilaterals.

Extra Practice ■ Chapter 14

14B Logic and Discrete Math

LESSON 14-4

Make a truth table for *P and Q*.

1. *P:* Greg is in eighth grade.
   Q: Greg has a GPA greater than 3.0.

Make a truth table for *P or Q*.

2. *P:* The number x is a multiple of 5.
   Q: The number x is even.

LESSON 14-5

Identify the hypothesis and the conclusion in each conditional.

3. The baseball games are canceled when it rains.
4. If $x + 4 = 10$, then $x = 6$.
5. If a polygon has four sides, it is a quadrilateral.

Make a conclusion, if possible, from each deductive argument.

6. A polygon with eight sides is an octagon. Figure D is a polygon with eight sides.
7. If x is a multiple of 8, it is a multiple of 4. $x = 4^2 + (3)(7)$
8. If a triangle has a base of 8 cm and a height of 5 cm, it has an area of 20 cm^2. Triangle ABC has an area of 20 cm^2.

LESSON 14-6

Find the degree of each vertex, and determine whether the graph is connected.

9. 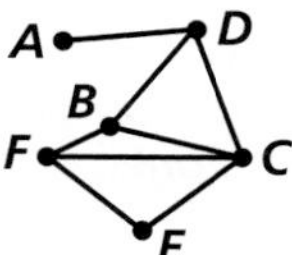

10. 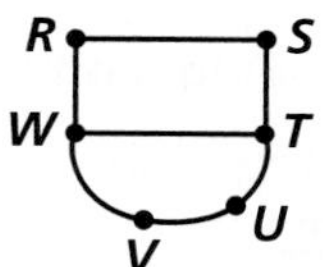

Determine whether each graph above can be traversed through an Euler circuit. If your answer is yes, describe an Euler circuit in the graph.

11. The graph in Exercise 9.
12. The graph in Exercise 10.

LESSON 14-7

Find a Hamiltonian circuit in each graph.

13. 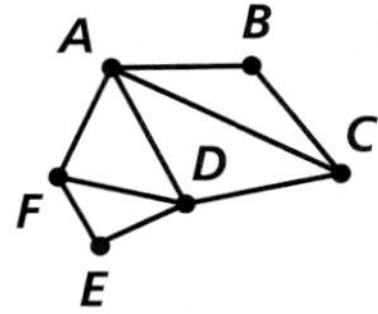

14. 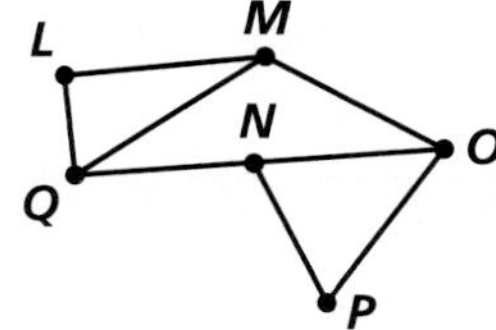

Determine the shortest Hamiltonian circuit beginning at *A*.

15. 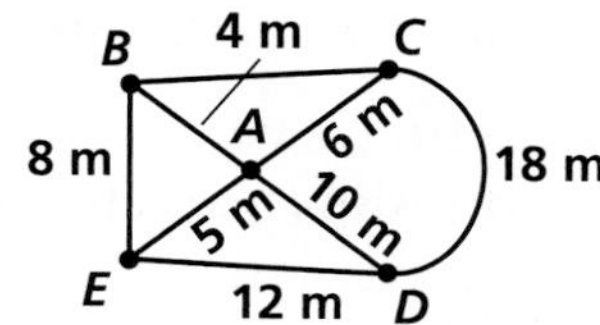

Extra Practice

Draw a Diagram

When problems involve objects, distances, or places, drawing a diagram can make the problem clearer. You can **draw a diagram** to help understand the problem and to solve the problem.

Problem Solving Strategies

Draw a Diagram	Make a Table
Make a Model	Solve a Simpler Problem
Guess and Test	Use Logical Reasoning
Work Backward	Use a Venn Diagram
Find a Pattern	Make an Organized List

June is moving her cat, dog, and goldfish to her new apartment. She can only take 1 pet with her on each trip. She cannot leave the cat and the dog or the cat and the goldfish alone together. How can she get all of her pets safely to her new apartment?

Understand the Problem The answer will be the description of the trips to her new apartment. At no time can the cat be alone with the dog or the goldfish.

Make a Plan **Draw a diagram** to represent each trip to and from the apartment.

Solve In the beginning, the cat, dog, and goldfish are all at her old apartment.

Old Apartment		New Apartment	
June, Cat, Dog, Fish	June, Cat →	June, Cat	*Trip 1: She takes the cat and returns alone.*
June, Dog, Fish	← June	Cat	
June, Dog, Fish	June, Dog →	June, Dog, Cat	*Trip 2: She takes the dog and returns with the cat.*
June, Cat, Fish	← June, Cat	Dog	
June, Cat, Fish	June, Fish →	June, Dog, Fish	*Trip 3: She takes the fish and returns alone.*
June, Cat	← June	Dog, Fish	
June, Cat	June, Cat →	June, Cat, Dog, Fish	*Trip 4: She takes the cat.*

Look Back Check to make sure that the cat is never alone with either the fish or the dog.

PRACTICE

1. There are 8 flags evenly spaced around a circular track. It takes Ling 15 s to run from the first flag to the third flag. At this pace, how long will it take her to run around the track twice?

2. A frog is climbing a 22-foot tree. Every 5 minutes, it climbs up 3 feet, but slips back down 1 foot. How long will it take it to climb the tree?

Make a Model

A problem that involves objects may be solved by making a model out of similar items. **Make a model** to help you understand the problem and find the solution.

Problem Solving Strategies

Draw a Diagram
Make a Model
Guess and Test
Work Backward
Find a Pattern
Make a Table
Solve a Simpler Problem
Use Logical Reasoning
Use a Venn Diagram
Make an Organized List

The volume of a rectangular prism can be found by using the formula $V = \ell wh$, where ℓ is the length, w is the width, and h is the height of the prism. Find all possible rectangular prisms with a volume of 16 cubic units and dimensions that are all whole numbers.

Understand the Problem You need to find the different possible prisms. The length, width, and height will be whole numbers whose product is 16.

Make a Plan You can use unit cubes to make a model of every possible rectangular prism. Work in a systematic way to find all possible answers.

Solve Begin with a $16 \times 1 \times 1$ prism.

$16 \times 1 \times 1$

Keeping the height of the prism the same, explore what happens to the length as you change the width. Then try a height of 2. Notice that an $8 \times 2 \times 1$ prism is the same as an $8 \times 1 \times 2$ prism turned on its side.

$8 \times 2 \times 1$

Not a rectangular prism

$4 \times 4 \times 1$

$4 \times 2 \times 2$

The possible dimensions are $16 \times 1 \times 1$, $8 \times 2 \times 1$, $4 \times 4 \times 1$, and $4 \times 2 \times 2$.

Look Back The product of the length, width, and height must be 16. Look at the prime factorization of the volume: $16 = 2 \cdot 2 \cdot 2 \cdot 2$. Possible dimensions:

$1 \cdot 1 \cdot (2 \cdot 2 \cdot 2 \cdot 2) = 1 \cdot 1 \cdot 16$ $\quad$ $1 \cdot 2 \cdot (2 \cdot 2 \cdot 2) = 1 \cdot 2 \cdot 8$

$1 \cdot (2 \cdot 2) \cdot (2 \cdot 2) = 1 \cdot 4 \cdot 4$ $\quad$ $2 \cdot 2 \cdot (2 \cdot 2) = 2 \cdot 2 \cdot 4$

PRACTICE

1. Four unit squares are arranged so that each square shares a side with another square. How many different arrangements are possible?

2. Four triangles are formed by cutting a rectangle along its diagonals. What possible shapes can be formed by arranging these triangles?

Guess and Test

When you think that guessing may help you solve a problem, you can use **guess and test.** Using clues to make guesses can narrow your choices for the solution. Test whether your guess solves the problem, and continue guessing until you find the solution.

Problem Solving Strategies

Draw a Diagram	Make a Table
Make a Model	Solve a Simpler Problem
Guess and Test	Use Logical Reasoning
Work Backward	Use a Venn Diagram
Find a Pattern	Make an Organized List

North Middle School is planning to raise $1200 by sponsoring a car wash. They are going to charge $4 for each car and $8 for each minivan. How many vehicles would have to be washed to raise $1200 if they plan to wash twice as many cars as minivans?

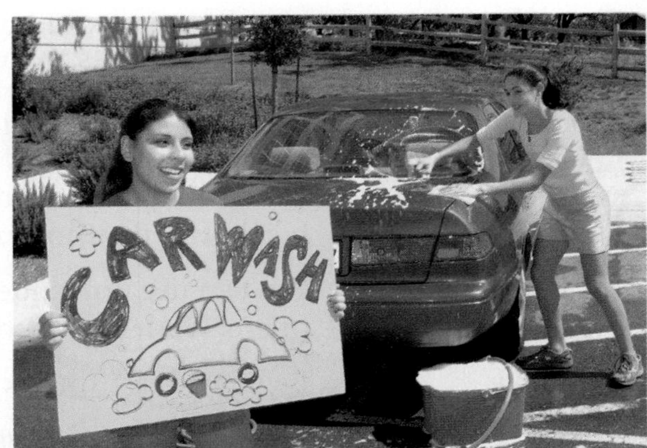

Understand the Problem You must determine the number of cars and the number of minivans that need to be washed to make $1200. You know the charge for each vehicle.

Make a Plan You can **guess and test** to find the number of cars and minivans. Guess the number of cars, and then divide it by 2 to find the number of minivans.

Solve You can organize your guesses in a table.

	Cars	Minivans	Money Raised	
First guess	200	100	$4(200) + $8(100) = $1600	*Too high*
Second guess	100	50	$4(100) + $8(50) = $800	*Too low*
Third guess	150	75	$4(150) + $8(75) = $1200	

They should wash 150 cars and 75 minivans, or 225 vehicles.

Look Back The total raised is $4(150) + $8(75) = $1200, and the number of cars is twice the number of minivans. The answer is reasonable.

PRACTICE

1. At a baseball game, adult tickets cost $15 and children's tickets cost $8. Twice as many children attended as adults, and the total ticket sales were $2480. How many people attended the game?

2. Angie is making friendship bracelets and pins. It takes her 6 minutes to make a bracelet and 4 minutes to make a pin. If she wants to make three times as many pins as bracelets, how many pins and bracelets can she make in 3 hours?

Work Backward

To solve a problem that asks for an initial value that follows a series of steps, you may want to **work backward**.

Problem Solving Strategies

Draw a Diagram	Make a Table
Make a Model	Solve a Simpler Problem
Guess and Test	Use Logical Reasoning
Work Backward	Use a Venn Diagram
Find a Pattern	Make an Organized List

Tyrone has two clocks and a watch. If the power goes off during the day, the following happens:

- **Clock A stops and then continues when the power comes back on.**
- **Clock B stops and then resets to 12:00 A.M. when the power comes back on.**

When Tyrone gets home, his watch reads 4:27 P.M., clock B reads 5:21 A.M., and clock A reads 3:39 P.M. What time did the power go off, and for how long was it off?

Understand the Problem You need to find the time that the power went off and how long it was off. You know how each clock works.

Make a Plan **Work backward** to the time that the power went off. Subtract from the correct time of 4:27, the time on Tyrone's watch.

Solve The difference between the correct time and the time on clock A is the length of time the power was off.

4:27 − 3:39 = 0:48 *The power was off for 48 minutes.*

Clock B reset to 12:00 when the power went on.

5:21 − 12:00 = 5:21 *The power came on 5 hours and 21 minutes ago.*

Subtract 5:21 from the correct time to find when the power came on.

4:27 − 5:21 = 11:06 *The power came on at 11:06 A.M.*

Subtract 48 minutes from 11:06 to find when the power went off.

11:06 − 0:48 = 10:18

The power went off at 10:18 A.M. and was off for 48 minutes.

Look Back If the power went off at about 10 A.M. for about an hour, it would come on at about 11 A.M., and each clock would run for about $5\frac{1}{2}$ hours.

PRACTICE

1. Jackie is 4 years younger than Roger. Roger is $2\frac{1}{2}$ years older than Jade. Jade is 14 years old. How old is Jackie?

2. Becca is directing a play that starts at 8:15 P.M. She wants the cast ready 10 minutes before the play starts. The cast needs 45 minutes to put on make-up, 15 minutes for a director's meeting, and then 35 minutes to get in costume. What time should the cast arrive?

Find a Pattern

If a problem involves numbers, shapes, or even codes, noticing a pattern can often help you solve it. To solve a problem that involves patterns, you need to use small steps that will help you **find a pattern**.

Problem Solving Strategies

Draw a Diagram	Make a Table
Make a Model	Solve a Simpler Problem
Guess and Test	Use Logical Reasoning
Work Backward	Use a Venn Diagram
Find a Pattern	Make an Organized List

Gil is trying to decode the following sentence, which may have been encoded using a pattern. What does the coded sentence say?

QEB NRFZH YOLTK CLU GRJMP LSBO QEB IXWV ALD.

Understand the Problem You need to find whether there was a pattern used to encode the sentence and then extend the pattern to decode the sentence.

Make a Plan **Find a pattern.** Try to decode one of the words first. Notice that *QEB* appears twice in the sentence.

Solve Gil thinks that *QEB* is probably the word *THE*. If *QEB* stands for *THE*, a pattern emerges with respect to the letters and their position in the alphabet.

Q: 17th letter	*T*: 20th letter	+ *3 letters*
E: 5th letter	*H*: 8th letter	+ *3 letters*
B: 2nd letter	*E*: 5th letter	+ *3 letters*

Continue the pattern. Although there is no 27th, 28th, or 29th letter of the alphabet, the remaining letters should be obvious (27 = 1 = *A*, 28 = 2 = *B*, and 29 = 3 = *C*).

```
QEB NRFZH YOLTK CLU GRJMP LSBO QEB IXWV ALD.
THE QUICK BROWN FOX JUMPS OVER THE LAZY DOG.
```

Look Back The sentence makes sense, so the pattern fits.

PRACTICE

Decode each sentence.

1. RFC DGTC ZMVGLE UGXYPBQ HSKN OSGAIJW.
(*RFC* = *THE*)

2. U PYLS VUX KOUWE GCABN DCHR TCJJS ZIQF.
(*U* = *A*)

Make a Table

To solve a problem that involves a relationship between two sets of numbers, you can **make a table.** A table can be used to organize data so that you can look at relationships and find the solution.

Problem Solving Strategies

Draw a Diagram	**Make a Table**
Make a Model	Solve a Simpler Problem
Guess and Test	Use Logical Reasoning
Work Backward	Use a Venn Diagram
Find a Pattern	Make an Organized List

Jill has 12 pieces of 2 ft long decorative edging. She wants to use the edging to enclose a garden with the greatest possible area against the back of her house. What is the largest garden she can make?

Understand the Problem You must determine the length and width of the edging.

Make a Plan **Make a table** of the possible widths and lengths. Begin with the least possible width and increase by multiples of 2 ft. Remember that the width is the same on two sides.

Solve Use the table to solve.

Width (ft)	Length (ft)	Garden Area (ft^2)
2	20	40
4	16	64
6	12	72
8	8	64
10	4	40

The maximum area that the garden can be is 72 ft^2, with a width of 6 ft and a length of 12 ft.

Look Back She can use 3 pieces of edging for the first side, 6 pieces for the second side, and another 3 pieces for the third side.

$3 + 6 + 3 = 12$ pieces
$6 \text{ ft} + 12 \text{ ft} + 6 \text{ ft} = 24 \text{ ft}$

PRACTICE

1. Suppose Jill decided not to use the house as one side of the garden. What is the greatest area that she could enclose?
2. A store sells batteries in packs of 3 for \$3.99 and 2 for \$2.99. Barry got 14 batteries total for \$18.95. How many of each package did he buy?

Solve a Simpler Problem

If a problem contains large numbers or requires many steps, try to **solve a simpler problem** first. Look for similarities between the problems, and use them to solve the original problem.

Problem Solving Strategies

Draw a Diagram	Make a Table
Make a Model	**Solve a Simpler Problem**
Guess and Test	Use Logical Reasoning
Work Backward	Use a Venn Diagram
Find a Pattern	Make an Organized List

Noemi heard that 10 computers in her school would be connected to each other. She thought that there would be a cable connecting each computer to every other computer. How many cables would be needed if this were true?

Understand the Problem You know that there are 10 computers and that each computer would require a separate cable to connect to every other computer. You need to find the total number of cables.

Make a Plan Start by **solving a simpler problem** with fewer computers.

Solve The simplest problem starts with 2 computers.

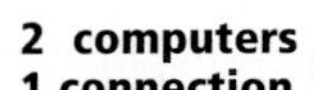

2 computers
1 connection

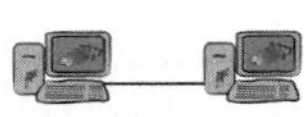

3 computers
3 connections

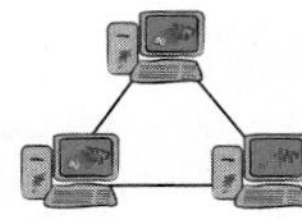

4 computers
6 connections

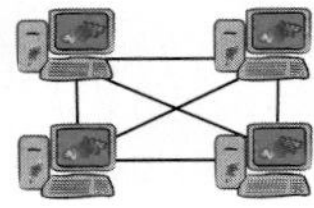

Organize the data in a table to help you find a pattern.

Number of Computers	Number of Connections
2	1
3	1 + 2 = 3
4	1 + 2 + 3 = 6
5	1 + 2 + 3 + 4 = 10
10	1 + 2 + 3 + 4 + 5 + 6 + 7 + 8 + 9 = 45

So if a separate cable were needed to connect each of 10 computers to every other one, 45 cables would be required.

Look Back Extend the number of computers to check that the pattern continues.

PRACTICE

1. A banquet table seats 2 people on each side and 1 at each end. If 6 tables are placed end to end, how many seats can there be?

2. How many diagonals are there in a dodecagon (a 12-sided polygon)?

Use Logical Reasoning

Sometimes a problem may provide clues and facts to help you find a solution. You can **use logical reasoning** to help solve this kind of problem.

Problem Solving Strategies

Draw a Diagram	Make a Table
Make a Model	Solve a Simpler Problem
Guess and Test	**Use Logical Reasoning**
Work Backward	Use a Venn Diagram
Find a Pattern	Make an Organized List

Kim, Lily, and Suki take ballet, tap, and jazz classes (but not in that order). Kim is the sister of the person who takes ballet. Lily takes tap.

Understand the Problem You want to determine which person is in which dance class. You know that there are three people and that each person takes only one dance class.

Make a Plan **Use logical reasoning** to make a table of the facts from the problem.

Solve List the types of dance and the people's names. Write *Yes* or *No* when you are sure of an answer. Lily takes tap.

	Ballet	Tap	Jazz
Kim		No	
Lily	No	Yes	No
Suki		No	

The person taking ballet is Kim's sister, so Kim does not take ballet. Suki must be the one taking ballet.

	Ballet	Tap	Jazz
Kim		No	
Lily	No	Yes	No
Suki	Yes	No	No

Kim must be the one taking jazz.

Kim takes jazz, Lily takes tap, and Suki takes ballet.

Look Back Make sure none of your conclusions conflict with the clues.

PRACTICE

1. Patrick, John, and Vanessa have a snake, a cat and a rabbit. Patrick's pet does not have fur. Vanessa does not have a cat. Match the owners with their pets.
2. Isabella, Keifer, Dylan, and Chrissy are in the sixth, seventh, eighth, and ninth grades. Isabella is not in seventh grade. The sixth-grader has band with Dylan and lunch with Isabella. Chrissy is in the ninth grade. Match the students with their grades.

Use a Venn Diagram

You can **use a Venn diagram** to display relationships among sets in a problem. Use ovals, circles, or other shapes to represent individual sets.

Problem Solving Strategies

Draw a Diagram	Make a Table
Make a Model	Solve a Simpler Problem
Guess and Test	Use Logical Reasoning
Work Backward	**Use a Venn Diagram**
Find a Pattern	Make an Organized List

Patricia took a poll of 100 students. She wrote down that 32 play basketball, 45 run track, and 19 do both. Mrs. Thornton wants to know how many of the students polled only play basketball.

Understand the Problem

You know that 100 students were polled, 32 play basketball, 45 run track, and 19 play basketball *and* run track.

The answer is the number of students who only play basketball.

Make a Plan

Use a Venn diagram to show the sets of students who play basketball, students who run track, and students who do both.

Solve

Draw and label two overlapping circles in a rectangle. Work from the inside out. Write 19 in the area where the two circles overlap. This represents the number of students who play basketball and run track.

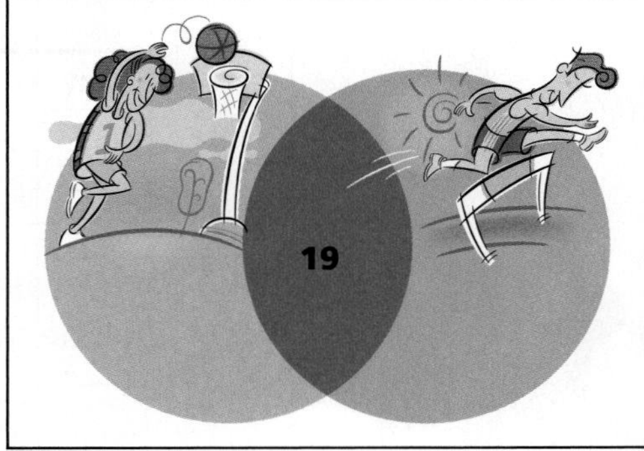

Use the information in the problem to complete the diagram. You know that 32 students play basketball, and 19 of those students run track.

So 13 students only play basketball.

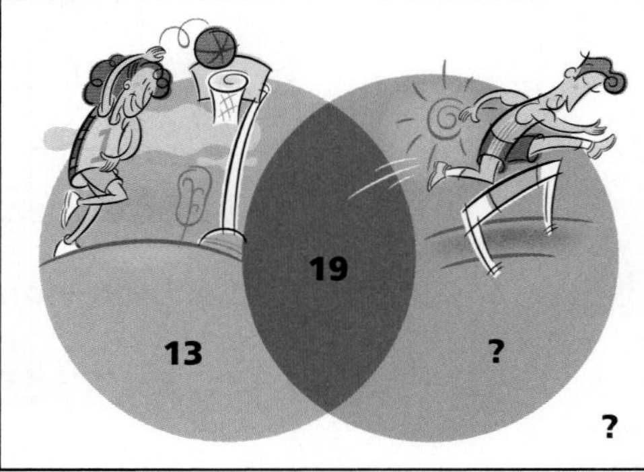

Look Back

When your Venn diagram is complete, check it carefully against the information in the problem to make sure it agrees with the facts given.

PRACTICE

1. How many of the students only run track?

2. How many of the students do not play basketball or run track?

Make an Organized List

Sometimes a problem involves many possible ways in which something can be done. To find a solution to this kind of problem, you need to **make an organized list.** This will help you to organize and count all the possible outcomes.

Problem Solving Strategies

Draw a Diagram	Make a Table
Make a Model	Solve a Simpler Problem
Guess and Test	Use Logical Reasoning
Work Backward	Use a Venn Diagram
Find a Pattern	**Make an Organized List**

What is the greatest amount of money you can have in coins (quarters, dimes, nickels, and pennies) without being able to make change for a dollar?

Understand the Problem You are looking for an amount of money. You cannot have any combinations of coins that make a dollar, such as 4 quarters or 3 quarters, 2 dimes, and a nickel.

Make a Plan **Make an organized list,** starting with the maximum possible number of each type of coin. Consider all the ways you can add other types of coins without making exactly one dollar.

Solve List the maximum number of each kind of coin you can have.

3 quarters = 75¢ 9 dimes = 90¢ 19 nickels = 95¢ 99 pennies = 99¢

Next, list all the possible combinations of two kinds of coins.

3 quarters and 4 dimes = 115¢	9 dimes and 1 quarter = 115¢
3 quarters and 4 nickels = 95¢	9 dimes and 1 nickel = 95¢
3 quarters and 24 pennies = 99¢	9 dimes and 9 pennies = 99¢

19 nickels and 4 pennies = 99¢

Look for any combinations from this list that you could add another kind of coin to without making exactly one dollar.

3 quarters, 4 dimes, and 4 pennies = 119¢
3 quarters, 4 nickels, and 4 pennies = 99¢
9 dimes, 1 quarter, and 4 pennies = 119¢
9 dimes, 1 nickel, and 4 pennies = 99¢

The largest amount you can have is 119¢, or \$1.19.

Look Back Try adding one of any type of coin to either combination that makes \$1.19, and then see if you could make change for a dollar.

PRACTICE

1. How can you arrange the numbers 2, 6, 7, and 12 with the symbols +, ×, and ÷ to create the expression with the greatest value?

2. How many ways are there to arrange 24 desks in 3 or more equal rows if each row must have at least 2 desks?

Skills Bank — Review Skills

Place Value to the Billions

A place-value chart can help you read and write numbers. The number 345,012,678,912.5784 (three hundred forty-five billion, twelve million, six hundred seventy-eight thousand, nine hundred twelve and five thousand seven hundred eighty-four ten-thousandths) is shown.

Billions	Millions	Thousands	Ones		Tenths	Hundredths	Thousandths	Ten-Thousandths
345,	012,	678,	912	.	5	7	8	4

EXAMPLE

Name the place value of the digit.

A the 7 in the thousands column
7 → *ten thousands place*

B the 0 in the millions column
0 → *hundred millions place*

C the 5 in the billions column
5 → *one billion, or billions, place*

D the 8 to the right of the decimal point
8 → *thousandths*

PRACTICE

Name the place value of the underlined digit.

1. 123,<u>4</u>56,789,123.0594
2. 1<u>2</u>3,456,789,123.0594
3. 123,456,789,123.05<u>9</u>4
4. 123,456,789,12<u>3</u>.0594
5. 123,456,789,123.<u>0</u>594
6. 123,45<u>6</u>,789,123.0594

Round Whole Numbers and Decimals

To round to a certain place, follow these steps.

1. Locate the digit in that place, and consider the next digit to the right.
2. If the digit to the right is 5 or greater, round up. Otherwise, round down.
3. Change each digit to the right of the rounding place to zero.

EXAMPLE

A **Round 125,439.378 to the nearest thousand.**
125,439.378 *Locate digit*
The digit to the right is less than 5, so round down.
125,000.000 = 125,000

B **Round 125,439.378 to the nearest tenth.**
125,439.378 *Locate digit.*
The digit to the right is greater than 5, so round up.
125,439.400 = 125,539.4

PRACTICE

Round 259,345.278 to the place indicated.

1. hundred thousand
2. ten thousand
3. thousand
4. hundred

Ways to Show Multiplication and Division

Multiplication and division can be shown in several ways.

EXAMPLE

1. Show the product of 7 and 8 in several ways.

7×8 $\quad$ $7 \cdot 8$ $\quad$ $7(8)$ $\quad$ $(7)(8)$

When a variable is used in an expression with multiplication, the multiplication sign is usually omitted. An expression such as $5 \times n$ can be written as $5n$.

2. Show the quotient 15 divided by 3 in several ways.

$15 \div 3$ $\quad$ $15/3$ $\quad$ $\frac{15}{3}$ $\quad$ $3\overline{)15}$

PRACTICE

Write each expression in two other ways.

1. 4×8 **2.** 9×10 **3.** $18 \div 3$ **4.** 2×11

5. $(9)(2)(5)$ **6.** $7 \div n$ **7.** $\frac{b}{2}$ **8.** $7 \cdot y$

9. $4(c)$ **10.** $(3)(b)(f)$ **11.** $24/6$ **12.** $11\overline{)55}$

Skills Bank

Long Division with Whole Numbers

You can use long division to divide large numbers.

EXAMPLE

Divide 8208 by 72.

114	
$72\overline{)8208}$	*Place the first number under the long division symbol.*
$\underline{72}$	*Subtract.*
100	*Bring down the next digit.*
$\underline{72}$	*Subtract.*
288	*Bring down the next digit.*
$\underline{288}$	*Subtract.*
0	

PRACTICE

Divide.

1. $125\overline{)4125}$ **2.** $158\overline{)20,698}$ **3.** $268\overline{)4556}$

4. $39\overline{)3471}$ **5.** $99\overline{)4653}$ **6.** $321\overline{)38,841}$

7. $120\overline{)5040}$ **8.** $108\overline{)10,476}$ **9.** $741\overline{)107,445}$

Factors and Multiples

When two numbers are multiplied to form a third, the two numbers are said to be **factors** of the third number. **Multiples** of a number can be found by multiplying the number by 1, 2, 3, 4, and so on.

EXAMPLE

 **List all the factors of 48.**

$1 \cdot 48 = 48, 2 \cdot 24 = 48, 3 \cdot 16 = 48,$
$4 \cdot 12 = 48$, and $6 \cdot 8 = 48$

So the factors of 48 are 1, 2, 3, 4, 6, 8, 12, 16, 24, and 48.

 **Find the first five multiples of 3.**

$3 \cdot 1 = 3, 3 \cdot 2 = 6, 3 \cdot 3 = 9,$
$3 \cdot 4 = 12$, and $3 \cdot 5 = 15$

So the first five multiples of 3 are 3, 6, 9, 12, and 15.

PRACTICE

List all the factors of each number.

1. 8 **2.** 20 **3.** 9 **4.** 51 **5.** 16 **6.** 27

Write the first five multiples of each number.

7. 9 **8.** 10 **9.** 20 **10.** 15 **11.** 7 **12.** 18

Divisibility Rules

A number is divisible by another number if the division results in a remainder of 0. Some divisibility rules are shown below.

A number is divisible by . . .	Divisible	Not Divisible
2 if the last digit is an even number.	11,994	2,175
3 if the sum of the digits is divisible by 3.	216	79
4 if the last two digits form a number divisible by 4.	1,028	621
5 if the last digit is 0 or 5.	15,195	10,007
6 if the number is even and divisible by 3.	1,332	44
8 if the last three digits form a number divisible by 8.	25,016	14,100
9 if the sum of the digits is divisible by 9.	144	33
10 if the last digit is 0.	2,790	9,325

PRACTICE

Determine which of these numbers each number is divisible by: 2, 3, 4, 5, 6, 8, 9, 10

1. 56 **2.** 200 **3.** 75 **4.** 324 **5.** 42 **6.** 812

7. 784 **8.** 501 **9.** 2345 **10.** 555,555 **11.** 3009 **12.** 2001

Prime and Composite Numbers

A **prime number** has exactly two factors, 1 and the number itself.

2	Factors: 1 and 2; prime
11	Factors: 1 and 11; prime
47	Factors: 1 and 47; prime

A **composite number** has more than two factors.

4	Factors: 1, 2, and 4; composite
12	Factors: 1, 2, 3, 4, 6, and 12; composite
63	Factors: 1, 3, 7, 9, 21, and 63; composite

EXAMPLE

Determine whether each number is prime or composite.

A 17

Factors
1, 17 ⟶ prime

B 16

Factors
1, 2, 4, 8, 16 ⟶ composite

C 51

Factors
1, 3, 17, 51 ⟶ composite

PRACTICE

Determine whether each number is prime or composite.

1. 5 **2.** 14 **3.** 18 **4.** 2 **5.** 23 **6.** 27

7. 13 **8.** 39 **9.** 72 **10.** 49 **11.** 9 **12.** 89

Prime Factorization (Factor Tree)

A composite number can be expressed as a product of prime numbers. This is the **prime factorization** of the number. To find the prime factorization of a number, you can use a factor tree.

EXAMPLE

Find the prime factorization of 24 by using a factor tree.

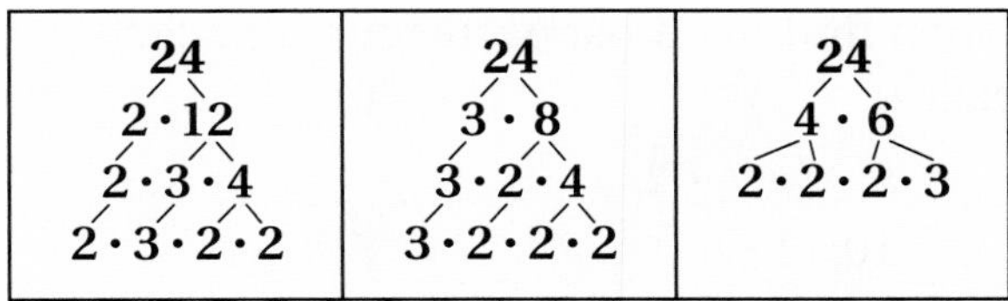

The prime factorization of 24 is $2 \cdot 2 \cdot 2 \cdot 3$, or $2^3 \cdot 3$.

PRACTICE

Find the prime factorization of each number by using a factor tree.

1. 25 **2.** 16 **3.** 56 **4.** 18 **5.** 72 **6.** 40

Skills Bank

Greatest Common Factor (GCF)

The **greatest common factor** (GCF) of two whole numbers is the greatest factor the numbers have in common.

EXAMPLE

Find the GCF of 24 and 32.

Method 1: List all the factors of both numbers.

Find all the common factors.

24: 1, 2, 3, 4, 6, 8, 12, 24
32: 1, 2, 4, 8, 16, 32

The common factors are 1, 2, 4, and 8.
So the GCF is 8.

Method 2: Find the prime factorizations.

Then find the common prime factors.

24: $2 \cdot 2 \cdot 2 \cdot 3$
32: $2 \cdot 2 \cdot 2 \cdot 2 \cdot 2$

The common prime factors are 2, 2, and 2.
The product of these is the GCF.
So the GCF is $2 \cdot 2 \cdot 2 = 8$.

PRACTICE

Find the GCF of each pair of numbers by either method.

1. 9, 15 **2.** 25, 75 **3.** 18, 30 **4.** 4, 10 **5.** 12, 17 **6.** 30, 96

7. 54, 72 **8.** 15, 20 **9.** 40, 60 **10.** 40, 50 **11.** 14, 21 **12.** 14, 28

Least Common Multiple (LCM)

The **least common multiple** (LCM) of two numbers is the smallest common multiple the numbers share.

EXAMPLE

Find the least common multiple of 8 and 10.

Method 1: List multiples of both numbers.

8: 8, 16, 24, 32, 40, 48, 56, 64, 72, 80
10: 10, 20, 30, 40, 50, 60, 70, 80, 90

The smallest common multiple is 40.

So the LCM is 40.

Method 2: Find the prime factorizations. Then find the most occurrences of each factor.

8: $2 \cdot 2 \cdot 2$
10: $2 \cdot 5$

The LCM is the product of the factors.

$2 \cdot 2 \cdot 2 \cdot 5 = 40$ So the LCM is 40.

PRACTICE

Find the LCM of each pair of numbers by either method.

1. 2, 4 **2.** 3, 15 **3.** 10, 25 **4.** 10, 15 **5.** 3, 7 **6.** 18, 27

7. 12, 21 **8.** 9, 21 **9.** 24, 30 **10.** 9, 18 **11.** 16, 24 **12.** 8, 36

Compatible Numbers

Compatible numbers are close to the numbers in a problem and divide without a remainder. You can use compatible numbers to estimate quotients.

EXAMPLE

Use compatible numbers to estimate each quotient.

A **6134 ÷ 32**

6134 ÷ 32

6000 ÷ 30 = 200 ← *Estimate*

↑ ↑ *Compatible numbers*

B **647 ÷ 7**

647 ÷ 7

630 ÷ 7 = 90 ← *Estimate*

↑ ↑ *Compatible numbers*

PRACTICE

Estimate the quotient by using compatible numbers.

1. 345 ÷ 5 **2.** 5474 ÷ 23 **3.** 46,170 ÷ 18 **4.** 749 ÷ 7

5. 861 ÷ 41 **6.** 1225 ÷ 2 **7.** 968 ÷ 47 **8.** 3456 ÷ 432

9. 5765 ÷ 26 **10.** 25,012 ÷ 64 **11.** 99,170 ÷ 105 **12.** 868 ÷ 8

Mixed Numbers and Fractions

Mixed numbers can be written as fractions greater than 1, and fractions greater than 1 can be written as mixed numbers.

EXAMPLE

A **Write $\frac{23}{5}$ as a mixed number.**

$\frac{23}{5}$ *Divide the numerator by the denominator.*

$$\begin{array}{r} 4 \\ 5\overline{)23} \\ \underline{20} \\ 3 \end{array} \longrightarrow 4\frac{3}{5}$$

← *Write the remainder as the numerator of a fraction.*

B **Write $6\frac{2}{7}$ as a fraction.**

Multiply the denominator by the whole number. *Add the product to the numerator.*

$6\frac{2}{7} \longrightarrow 7 \cdot 6 = 42 \longrightarrow 42 + 2 = 44$

Write the sum over the denominator. → $\frac{44}{7}$

PRACTICE

Write each mixed number as a fraction. Write each fraction as a mixed number.

1. $\frac{22}{5}$ **2.** $9\frac{1}{7}$ **3.** $\frac{41}{8}$ **4.** $5\frac{7}{9}$

5. $\frac{7}{3}$ **6.** $4\frac{9}{11}$ **7.** $\frac{47}{16}$ **8.** $3\frac{3}{8}$

9. $\frac{31}{9}$ **10.** $8\frac{2}{3}$ **11.** $\frac{33}{5}$ **12.** $12\frac{1}{9}$

Multiply and Divide Decimals by Powers of 10

Notice the pattern below.

$0.24 \cdot 10 = 2.4$
$0.24 \cdot 100 = 24$
$0.24 \cdot 1000 = 240$
$0.24 \cdot 10{,}000 = 2400$

*Think: When multiplying decimals by powers of 10, move the decimal point one place to the **right** for each power of 10, or for each zero.*

$10 = 10^1$
$100 = 10^2$
$1000 = 10^3$
$10{,}000 = 10^4$

Notice the pattern below.

$0.24 \div 10 = 0.024$
$0.24 \div 100 = 0.0024$
$0.24 \div 1000 = 0.00024$
$0.24 \div 10{,}000 = 0.000024$

*Think: When dividing decimals by powers of 10, move the decimal point one place to the **left** for each power of 10, or for each zero.*

PRACTICE

Find each product or quotient.

1. $10 \cdot 9.26$	**2.** $0.642 \cdot 100$	**3.** $10^3 \cdot 84.2$	**4.** $0.44 \cdot 10^4$
5. $69.7 \cdot 1000$	**6.** $11.32 \div 10$	**7.** $678 \cdot 10^8$	**8.** $1.276 \div 1000$
9. $536.5 \div 10^2$	**10.** $5.92 \div 10^3$	**11.** $25 \div 10{,}000$	**12.** $6.519 \cdot 10^2$

Multiply Decimals

When multiplying decimals, multiply as you would with whole numbers. The sum of the number of decimal places in the factors equals the number of decimal places in the product.

EXAMPLE

Find each product.

A **81.2 · 6.547**

```
     6.547 <— 3 decimal places
  ×   81.2 <— 1 decimal place
    1 3094
    6 5470
  523 7600
  531.6164 <— 4 decimal places
```

B **0.376 · 0.12**

```
    0.376 <— 3 decimal places
  ×  0.12 <— 2 decimal places
      752
     3760
  0.04512 <— 5 decimal places
```

PRACTICE

Find each product.

1. $6.8 \cdot 3.4$	**2.** $2.56 \cdot 4.6$	**3.** $6.787 \cdot 7.6$	**4.** $0.98 \cdot 4.6$
5. $0.97 \cdot 0.76$	**6.** $0.5 \cdot 3.761$	**7.** $42 \cdot 17.654$	**8.** $7.005 \cdot 32.1$
9. $9.76 \cdot 16.254$	**10.** $296.5 \cdot 2.4$	**11.** $7.7 \cdot 6.5$	**12.** $8.92 \cdot 2.8$
13. $3.65 \cdot 4.2$	**14.** $0.002 \cdot 8.1$	**15.** $0.03 \cdot 0.204$	**16.** $98.6 \cdot 4.9$

Divide Decimals

When dividing with decimals, set up the division as you would with whole numbers. Pay attention to the decimal places, as shown below.

EXAMPLE

Find each quotient.

A **89.6 ÷ 16**

$$\begin{array}{r} 5.6 \\ 16\overline{)89.6} \\ \underline{80} \\ 9\,6 \\ \underline{9\,6} \\ 0 \end{array}$$

Place decimal point.

B **3.4 ÷ 4**

$$\begin{array}{r} 0.85 \\ 4\overline{)3.40} \\ \underline{3\,2} \\ 20 \\ \underline{20} \\ 0 \end{array}$$

Place decimal point.
Insert zeros if necessary.

PRACTICE

Find each quotient.

1. 242.76 ÷ 68
2. 40.5 ÷ 18
3. 121.03 ÷ 98
4. 3.6 ÷ 4
5. 1.58 ÷ 5
6. 0.2835 ÷ 2.7
7. 8.1 ÷ 0.09
8. 0.42 ÷ 0.28
9. 480.48 ÷ 7.7
10. 36.9 ÷ 0.003
11. 0.784 ÷ 0.04
12. 15.12 ÷ 0.063

Terminating and Repeating Decimals

You can change a fraction to a decimal by dividing. If the resulting decimal has a finite number of digits, it is **terminating**. Otherwise, it is **repeating**.

EXAMPLE

Write $\frac{4}{5}$ and $\frac{2}{3}$ as decimals. Are the decimals terminating or repeating?

$\frac{4}{5} = 4 \div 5$

$$\begin{array}{r} 0.8 \\ 5\overline{)4.0} \\ \underline{4\,0} \\ 0 \end{array} \longrightarrow \frac{4}{5} = 0.8$$

$\frac{2}{3} = 2 \div 3$

$$\begin{array}{r} 0.6666 \\ 3\overline{)2.0000} \\ \underline{1\,8} \\ 20 \end{array} \longrightarrow \frac{2}{3} = 0.6666...$$

This pattern will repeat.

The number 0.8 is a terminating decimal. The number 0.6666 . . . is a repeating decimal.

PRACTICE

Write as a decimal. Is the decimal terminating or repeating?

1. $\frac{1}{5}$
2. $\frac{1}{3}$
3. $\frac{3}{11}$
4. $\frac{3}{8}$
5. $\frac{7}{9}$
6. $\frac{7}{15}$
7. $\frac{3}{4}$
8. $\frac{5}{6}$
9. $\frac{4}{11}$
10. $\frac{5}{10}$
11. $\frac{1}{9}$
12. $\frac{11}{12}$
13. $\frac{5}{9}$
14. $\frac{8}{11}$
15. $\frac{7}{8}$
16. $\frac{23}{25}$
17. $\frac{3}{20}$
18. $\frac{5}{11}$

Order of Operations

When simplifying expressions, follow the order of operations.

1. Simplify within parentheses.
2. Evaluate exponents and roots.
3. Multiply and divide from left to right.
4. Add and subtract from left to right.

EXAMPLE

A **Simplify the expression $3^2 \times (11 - 4)$.**

$3^2 \times (11 - 4)$	
$3^2 \times 7$	*Simplify within parentheses.*
9×7	*Evaluate the exponent.*
63	*Multiply.*

B **Use a calculator to simplify the expression $19 - 100 \div 5^2$.**

If your calculator follows the order of operations, enter the following keystrokes:

$19 - 100 \div 5$ x^2 ENTER The result is 15.

If your calculator does not follow the order of operations, insert parentheses so that the expression is simplified correctly.

$19 - (100 \div 5$  $)$ ENTER The result is 15.

PRACTICE

Simplify each expression.

1. $45 - 15 \div 3$

2. $51 + 48 \div 8$

3. $35 \div (15 - 8)$

4. $\sqrt{9} \times 5 - 15$

5. $24 \div 3 - 6 + 12$

6. $(6 \times 8) \div 2^2$

7. $20 - 3 \times 4 + 30 \div 6$

8. $3^2 - 10 \div 2 + 4 \times 2$

9. $27 \div (3 + 6) + 6^2$

10. $4 \div 2 + 8 \times 2^3 - 4$

11. $33 - \sqrt{64} \times 3 - 5$

12. $(8^2 \times 4) - 12 \times 13 + 5$

Use a calculator to simplify each expression.

13. $6 + 20 \div 4$

14. $37 - 21 \div 7$

15. $9^2 - 32 \div 8$

16. $10 \div 2 + 8 \times 2$

17. $\sqrt{25} + 4 \times 6$

18. $4 \times 12 - 4 + 8 \div 2$

19. $28 - 3^2 + 27 \div 3$

20. $9 + (50 - 16) \div 2$

21. $4^2 - (10 \times 8) \div 5$

22. $30 + 22 \div 11 - 7 - 3^2$

23. $3 + 7 \times 5 - 1$

24. $38 \div 2 + \sqrt{81} \times 4 - 31$

Properties

The following are basic properties of addition and multiplication when a, b, and c are real numbers.

Addition		Multiplication	
Closure:	$a + b$ is a real number.	**Closure:**	$a \cdot b$ is a real number.
Commutative:	$a + b = b + a$	**Commutative:**	$a \cdot b = b \cdot a$
Associative:	$(a + b) + c = a + (b + c)$	**Associative:**	$(a \cdot b) \cdot c = a \cdot (b \cdot c)$
Identity Property of Zero:	$a + 0 = a$ and $0 + a = a$	**Identity Property of One:**	$a \cdot 1 = a$ and $1 \cdot a = a$
		Multiplication Property of Zero:	$a \cdot 0 = 0$ and $0 \cdot a = 0$

The following properties are true when a, b, and c are real numbers.

Distributive: $a \cdot (b + c) = a \cdot b + a \cdot c$

Transitive: If $a = b$ and $b = c$, then $a = c$.

EXAMPLE

Name the property shown.

A $4 \cdot (7 \cdot 2) = (4 \cdot 7) \cdot 2$
Associative Property of Multiplication

B $4 \cdot (7 + 2) = (4 \cdot 7) + (4 \cdot 2)$
Distributive Property

PRACTICE

Give an example of each of the following properties, using real numbers.

1. Associative Property of Addition
2. Commutative Property of Multiplication
3. Closure Property of Multiplication
4. Distributive Property
5. Multiplication Property of Zero
6. Identity Property of Addition
7. Transitive Property
8. Closure Property of Addition

Name the property shown.

9. $4 + 0 = 4$
10. $(6 + 3) + 1 = 6 + (3 + 1)$
11. $7 \cdot 51 = 51 \cdot 7$
12. $5 \cdot 456 = 456 \cdot 5$
13. $17 \cdot (1 + 3) = 17 \cdot 1 + 17 \cdot 3$
14. $1 \cdot 5 = 5$
15. $(8 \cdot 2) \cdot 5 = 8 \cdot (2 \cdot 5)$
16. $72 + 1234 = 1234 + 72$
17. $0 \cdot 12 = 0$
18. $15.7 \cdot 1.3 = 1.3 \cdot 15.7$
19. $8.2 + (9.3 + 7) = (8.2 + 9.3) + 7$
20. $85.98 \cdot 0 = 0$
21. If $x = 3.5$ and $3.5 = y$, then $x = y$.
22. $12a \cdot 15b = 15b \cdot 12a$
23. $(2x + 3y) + 8z = 2x + (3y + 8z)$
24. $0 \cdot 6m^2n = 0$
25. $8j + 32k = 32k + 8j$
26. If $3 + 8 = 11$ and $11 = x$, then $3 + 8 = x$.

Compare and Order Rational Numbers

A number line is helpful when you compare and order rational numbers.

EXAMPLE

A **Compare. Write < or >.**

$-\frac{1}{2}$ ■ -2.5

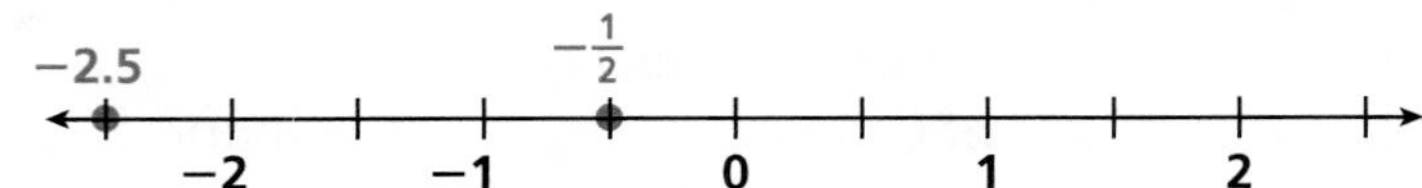

Graph both numbers on a number line.

$-\frac{1}{2}$ is to the right of −2.5.

$-\frac{1}{2} > -2.5$

B **Order 40%, 70%, and 10% in order from least to greatest. Use < between numbers.**

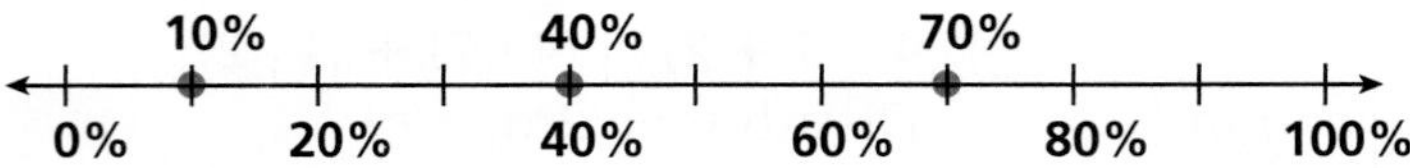

Graph all three percents on a number line.

10% is to the left of 40%, which is to the left of 70%.

10% < 40% < 70%

PRACTICE

Compare. Write < or >.

1. -0.3 ■ -0.1

2. $-\frac{3}{4}$ ■ $-\frac{5}{8}$

3. 35% ■ 6%

4. -8.65 ■ -9.97

5. 0.25 ■ $\frac{2}{5}$

6. 6.05 ■ 6.31

7. $-\frac{4}{5}$ ■ -0.5

8. 75% ■ 0.80

9. -0.07 ■ -0.7

10. 4.5 ■ 445%

11. 0.43 ■ 4.3%

12. $-9\frac{1}{3}$ ■ -9.03

Order the numbers from least to greatest. Use < between numbers.

13. 1.5, 0.15, 1.05

14. 34%, 76%, 9.8%

15. 0.4, $-\frac{3}{5}$, $-1\frac{1}{2}$

16. −2.6, −1.3, −6.3

17. −7.1, 0, −2.4

18. 2.5%, 105%, 53%

19. −0.25, $-\frac{2}{5}$, −1.2

20. 0.65, 61%, 3

21. 13%, 8.3%, 6.7%

22. $5\frac{3}{4}$, $5\frac{4}{25}$, $5\frac{2}{5}$

23. −0.1003, −0.018, −0.008

24. 2.7, $\frac{28}{100}$, 0.029

Absolute Value and Opposites

The **absolute value** of a number is the number's distance from zero on a number line. The symbol for absolute value is $|\ |$. Integers that are the same distance from 0 on a number line and are on opposite sides of 0 are **opposites.**

EXAMPLE

A **Name the opposite of 24.**

The opposite of 24 is -24.

B **Name the opposite of -8.**

The opposite of -8 is 8.

C **Evaluate $|-5|$ and $|3|$.**

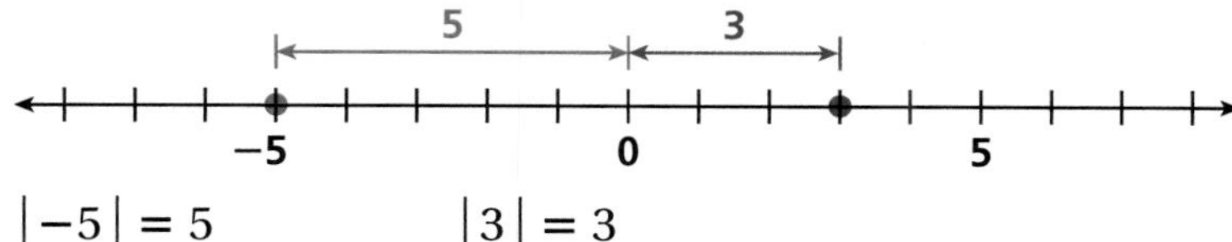

$|-5| = 5$ $\qquad$ $|3| = 3$

D **Evaluate $|-8 + 6|$.**

$|-2|$ *Simplify within the absolute value bars.*

2

PRACTICE

Name the opposite.

1. 13 **2.** 9 **3.** -28 **4.** -54

5. 85 **6.** 1 **7.** -16 **8.** -125

9. a **10.** $-2x$ **11.** $18x^2y$ **12.** $-20mn$

Evaluate.

13. $|-6|$ **14.** $|-12|$ **15.** $|2.5|$ **16.** $|18|$

17. $|-120|$ **18.** $|-4.4|$ **19.** $\left|\frac{1}{2}\right|$ **20.** $|0|$

21. $\left|-3\frac{2}{5}\right|$ **22.** $|-100{,}100|$ **23.** $|15.75|$ **24.** $|-52|$

25. $|8 + 6|$ **26.** $|19 - 3|$ **27.** $|2 - 6|$ **28.** $|-3 + 10|$

29. $|27 - 28|$ **30.** $|-107 + 120|$ **31.** $|-3| + |12|$ **32.** $|6| + |-4|$

33. $|-33| + |-17|$ **34.** $|25| - |30|$ **35.** $|15| - |-11|$ **36.** $|-7| + |7|$

Use $<$ or $>$ to compare.

37. $|-6| \ \blacksquare\ |5|$ **38.** $|-10| \ \blacksquare\ |-17|$ **39.** $|3.5| \ \blacksquare\ |-3.7|$ **40.** $\left|-\frac{1}{2}\right| \ \blacksquare\ \left|\frac{2}{3}\right|$

Skills Bank

Measure Angles

You can use a protractor to measure angles. To measure an angle, place the base of the protractor on one of the rays of the angle and center the base on the vertex. Look at the protractor scale that has zero on the first ray. Read the scale where the second ray crosses it. Extend the rays, if necessary.

EXAMPLE

A **Measure ∠*ABC*.**

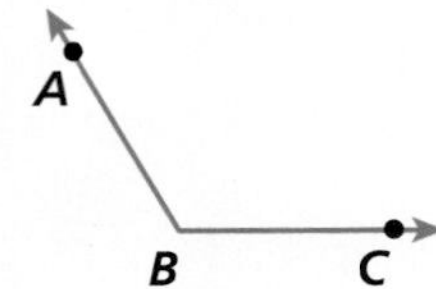

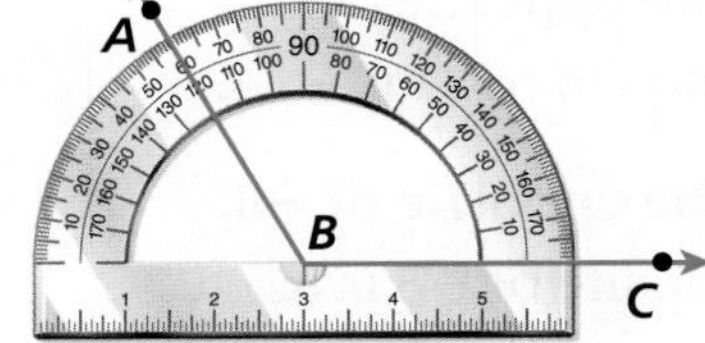

The measure of ∠*ABC*, or m∠*ABC*, equals 120°.

B **Measure ∠*XYZ*.**

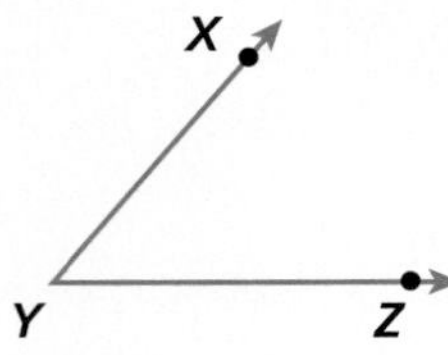

The measure of ∠*XYZ*, or m∠*XYZ*, equals 50°.

PRACTICE

Use a protractor to measure each angle.

1.

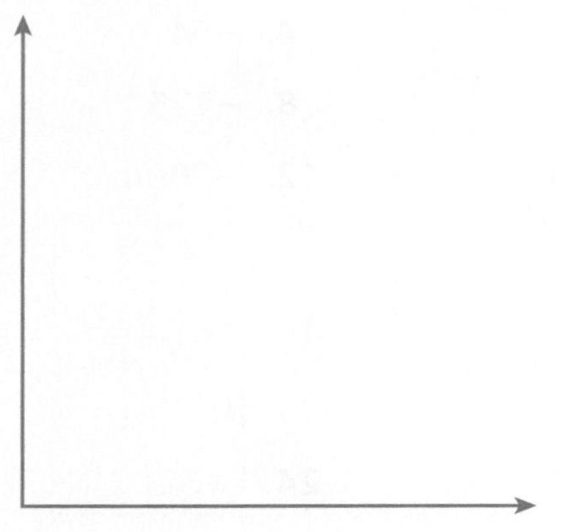

2.

3.

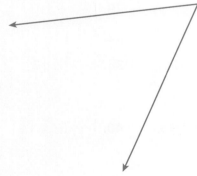

4.

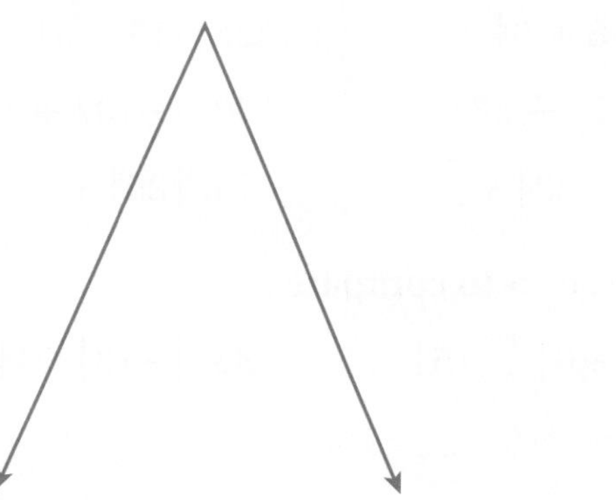

Informal Geometry Proofs

Inductive reasoning involves examining a set of data to determine a pattern and then making a conjecture about the data. In **deductive reasoning**, you reach a conclusion by using logical reasoning based on given statements or premises that you assume to be true.

EXAMPLE

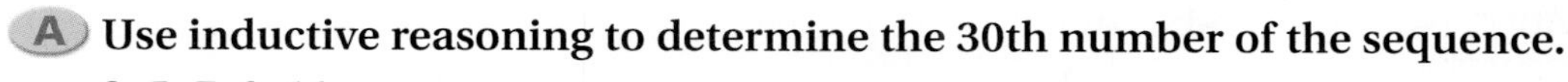

A **Use inductive reasoning to determine the 30th number of the sequence.**

3, 5, 7, 9, 11, . . .

Examine the pattern to determine the relationship between each term in the sequence and its value.

Term	1st	2nd	3rd	4th	5th
Value	3	5	7	9	11

$1 \cdot 2 + 1 = 2 + 1 = 3$

$2 \cdot 2 + 1 = 4 + 1 = 5$

$3 \cdot 2 + 1 = 6 + 1 = 7$

$4 \cdot 2 + 1 = 8 + 1 = 9$

$5 \cdot 2 + 1 = 10 + 1 = 11$

To obtain each value, multiply the term by 2 and add 1. So the 30th term is $30 \cdot 2 + 1 = 60 + 1 = 61$.

B **Use deductive reasoning to make a conclusion from the given premises.**

Premise: Makayla needs at least an 89 on her exam to get a B for the quarter in math class.

Premise: Makayla got a B for the quarter in math class.

Conclusion: Makayla got at least an 89 on her exam.

PRACTICE

Use inductive reasoning to determine the 100th number in each pattern.

1. $\frac{1}{2}, 1, 1\frac{1}{2}, 2, 2\frac{1}{2}, \ldots$

2. 1, 4, 9, 16, 25, . . .

3. 4, 6, 8, 10, 12, . . .

4. 0, 3, 6, 9, 12, 15, . . .

Use deductive reasoning to make a conclusion from the given premises.

5. Premise: If it is raining, then there must be a cloud in the sky.

Premise: It is raining.

6. Premise: A quadrilateral with four congruent sides and four right angles is a square.

Premise: Quadrilateral *ABCD* has four right angles.

Premise: Quadrilateral *ABCD* has four congruent sides.

7. Premise: Darnell is 3 years younger than half his father's age.

Premise: Darnell's father is 40 years old.

Iteration

An **iteration** is a step in the process of repeating something over and over again. You can show the steps of the process in an **iteration diagram**.

EXAMPLE

A **Use the iteration diagram below, and complete the process three times.**

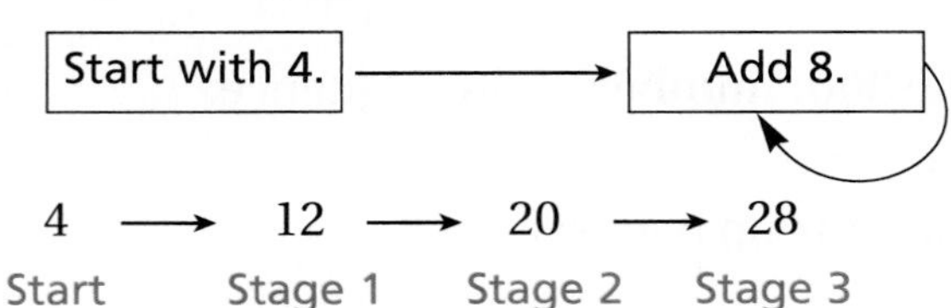

4 ⟶ 12 ⟶ 20 ⟶ 28

Start, Stage 1, Stage 2, Stage 3

B **For the pattern below, state the iteration and give the next three numbers in the pattern.**

1, 5, 25, 125, . . .

To get from one stage to the next, the iteration is to multiply by 5.

$125 \cdot 5 = 625$ $\qquad 625 \cdot 5 = 3125$ $\qquad 3125 \cdot 5 = 15{,}625$

The next three numbers in the pattern are 625, 3125, and 15,625.

PRACTICE

Use the diagram at right. Write the results of the first three iterations.

1. Start with 1.
2. Start with 8.
3. Start with 2.
4. Start with 25.
5. Start with −3.
6. Start with −7.

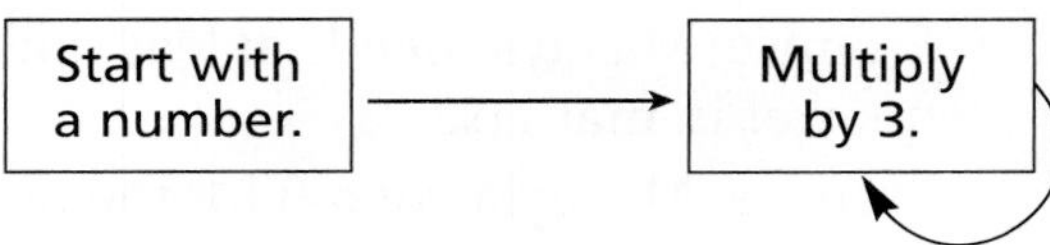

For each pattern, state the iteration and give the next three numbers in the pattern.

7. 11, 17, 23, 29, . . .
8. 5, 10, 20, 40, . . .
9. 345, 323, 301, 279, . . .
10. 30, 75, 120, 165, . . .
11. 15, 7, −1, −9, . . .
12. $1, 1\frac{2}{3}, 2\frac{1}{3}, 3, \ldots$

A **fractal** is a geometric pattern that is *self similar*, so each stage of the pattern is similar to a portion of another stage of the pattern. For example, the Koch snowflake is a fractal formed by beginning with a triangle and then adding an equilateral triangle to each segment of the triangle.

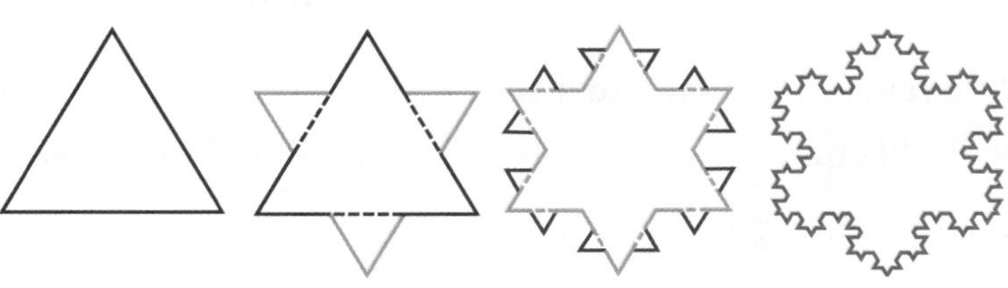

Draw the next two stages of each fractal.

13.

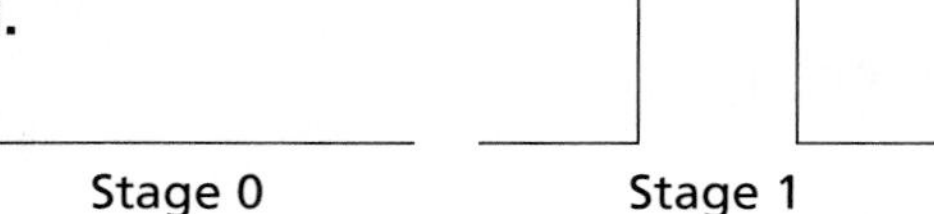

14.

Relative, Cumulative, and Relative Cumulative Frequency

A **frequency table** lists each value or range of values of the data set followed by its **frequency**, or number of times it occurs.

Relative frequency is the frequency of a value or range of values divided by the total number of data values.

Cumulative frequency is the frequency of all data values that are less than a given value.

Relative cumulative frequency is the cumulative frequency divided by the total number of values.

Test Score	Frequency
66–70	3
71–75	1
76–80	4
81–85	7
86–90	5
91–95	6
96–100	2

EXAMPLE

The frequency table above shows a range of test scores and the frequency, or the number of students who scored in that range.

A Find the relative frequency of test scores in the range 76–80.

$3 + 1 + 4 + 7 + 5 + 6 + 2 = 28$ *Find the total number of test scores.*

There are 4 test scores in the range 76–80. The relative frequency is $\frac{4}{28} \approx 0.14$.

B Find the cumulative frequency of test scores less than 86.

$7 + 4 + 1 + 3 = 15$ *Add the frequencies of all test scores less than 86.*

The cumulative frequency of test scores less than 86 is 15.

C Find the relative cumulative frequency of test scores less than 86.

$\frac{15}{28} \approx 0.54$ *Divide the cumulative frequency by the total number of values.*

The relative cumulative frequency of test scores less than 86 is 0.54.

PRACTICE

The frequency table shows the frequency of each range of heights among Mrs. Dawkin's students.

Height	Frequency
4 ft–4 ft 5 in.	2
4 ft 6 in–4 ft 11 in.	8
5 ft–5 ft 5 in.	10
5 ft 6 in–5 ft 11 in.	6
6 ft–6 ft 5 in.	1

1. What is the relative frequency of heights in the range 5 ft–5 ft 5 in.?
2. What is the relative frequency of heights in the range 4 ft–4 ft 5 in.?
3. What is the cumulative frequency of heights less than 6 ft?
4. What is the cumulative frequency of heights less than 5 ft?
5. What is the relative cumulative frequency of heights less than 5 ft 6 in.?
6. What is the relative cumulative frequency of heights less than 5 ft?

Frequency Polygons

A **histogram** is a common way to represent frequency tables. A histogram is a bar graph with no space between the bars. Each bar can represent a range of values of a data set.

A **frequency polygon** is made by connecting the midpoints of the tops of all of the bars of a histogram.

EXAMPLE

A The frequency table shows the frequency of the number of push-ups done by the students in a gym class. Draw a histogram and frequency polygon of the data.

Push-ups Done in 1 Minute	
Number of Push-ups	Frequency
0–9	3
10–19	6
20–29	11
30–39	10
40–49	4
50–59	2

Label the horizontal axis with the number of push-ups.

Label the vertical axis with the frequency.

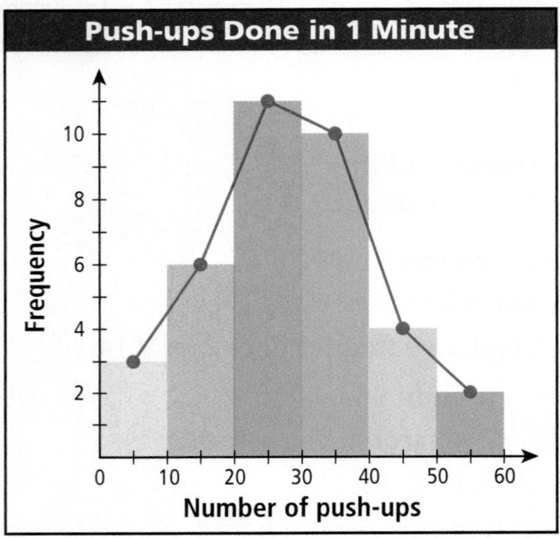

The frequency polygon is made up of the red points and red segments connecting the points.

PRACTICE

Use each frequency table to draw a histogram and frequency polygon of the data.

1.

Books Read over the Summer	
Number of Books	Frequency
0–2	5
3–5	8
6–8	12
9–11	6
12–14	4
15–17	2

2.

Miles Driven One Way to Work	
Number of Miles	Frequency
0–4	6
5–9	5
10–14	13
15–19	9
20–24	4
25–29	1

Exponential Growth and Quadratic Behavior

An **exponential growth function** is in the form $y = C(1 + r)^t$, where C is the starting amount, r is the percent increase, and t is the time.

EXAMPLE

A **Patrick invested \$2000 for 5 years at a 3% annual interest rate. Write an exponential growth function to represent this situation.**

C = starting amount = \$2000

r = percent increase = 3% = 0.03

t = time = 5 years

$y = 2000(1 + 0.03)^5$

$y = 2000(1.03)^5$

A function of the form $y = ax^2 + bx + c$ is called a **quadratic function**. The graph of a quadratic function is called a **parabola**. The most basic quadratic function is $y = x^2$. The graph of $y = x^2$ is shown at right. By examining the value of a in $y = ax^2$, you can determine the effect it will have on the graph of $y = x^2$.

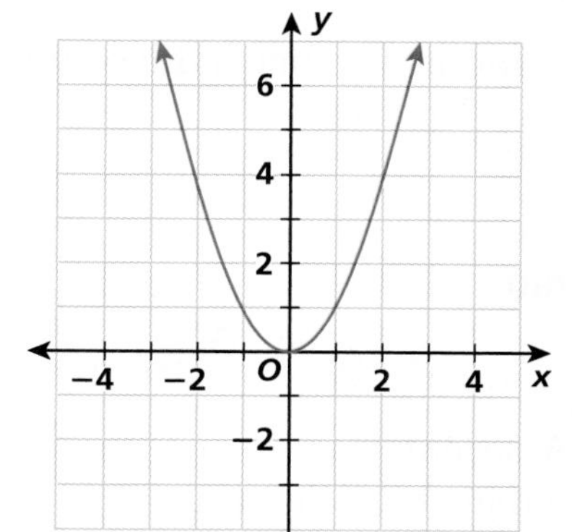

- If a is positive, the graph opens upward.
- If a is negative, the graph opens downward.
- If $|a| < 1$, the graph is wider than the graph of $y = x^2$.
- If $|a| > 1$, the graph is narrower than the graph of $y = x^2$.

EXAMPLE

B **Compare the graph of $y = -2x^2$ with the graph of $y = x^2$.**

Since a is negative, the graph will open downward. Since $|a| = 2(2 > 1)$, the graph will be narrower than the graph of $y = x^2$.

PRACTICE

Write an exponential growth function to represent each situation.

1. The population of a small town in 1997 was 25,500. Over a 5-year period, the population of the town increased at a rate of 2% each year.
2. Shante invested \$1800 at a 4.5% annual interest rate for 10 years.
3. Tyler took a job that paid \$30,000 annually with a 4% salary increase each year. He stayed at that job for 8 years.

Compare the graph of each quadratic function with the graph of $y = x^2$.

4. $y = -x^2$
5. $y = \frac{1}{2}x^2$
6. $y = 3x^2$
7. $y = -\frac{1}{4}x^2$
8. $y = -5x^2$
9. $y = 0.2x^2$
10. $y = -\frac{3}{2}x^2$
11. $6x^2 = y$

Circles

A circle can be named by its center, using the ⊙ symbol. A circle with a center labeled *C* would be named ⊙*C*. An unbroken part of a circle is called an **arc**. There are major arcs and minor arcs.

A **minor arc** of a circle is an arc that is shorter than half the circle and named by its endpoints. A **major arc** of a circle is an arc that is longer than half the circle and named by its endpoints and one other point on the arc.

$\overset{\frown}{AB}$ is a minor arc.

$\overset{\frown}{BAC}$ is a major arc.

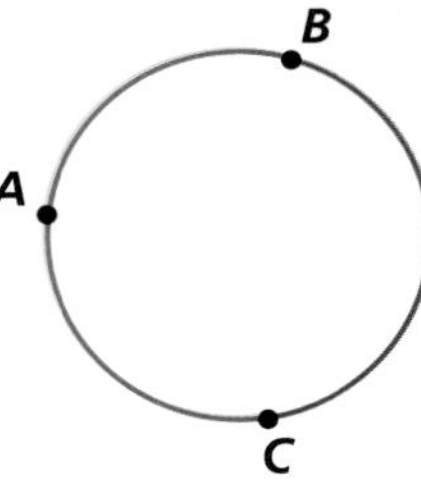

A **radius** connects the center with a point on a circle.

radius $\overline{CD}$

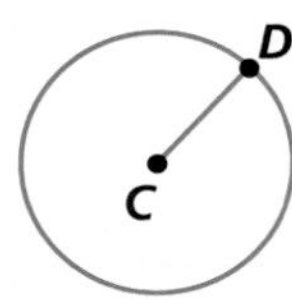

A **chord** connects two points point on a circle. A **diameter** is a chord that passes through the center of a circle.

chord $\overline{AB}$

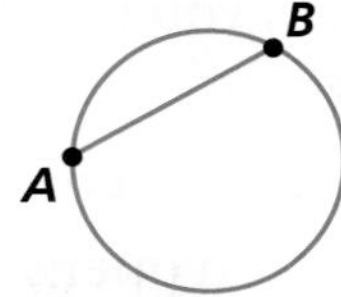

A **secant** is a line that intersects a circle at two points.

secant $\overleftrightarrow{EF}$

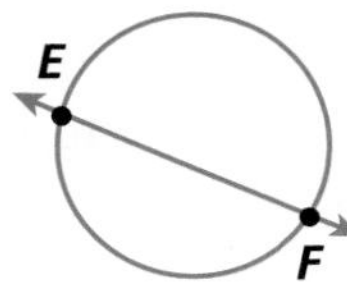

A **tangent** is a line that intersects a circle at one point.

tangent $\overleftrightarrow{GH}$

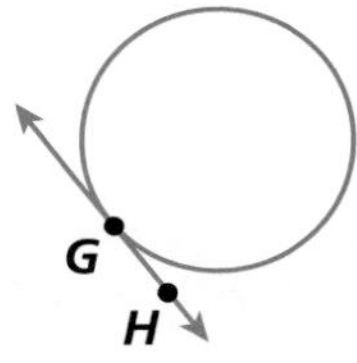

A **central angle** has its vertex at the center of the circle.

central angle
∠*JKL*

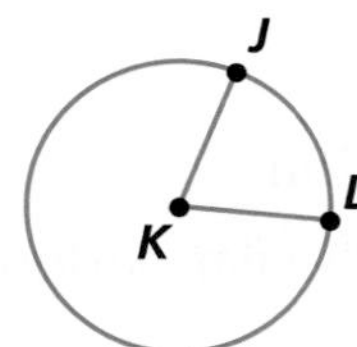

An **inscribed angle** has its vertex on the circle.

inscribed angle
∠*MNP*

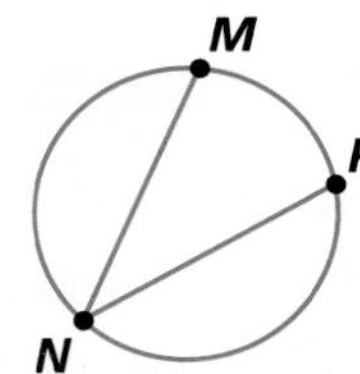

PRACTICE

Use the given diagram of ⊙*A* for exercises 1–6.

1. Name a radius.
2. What two chords make up the inscribed angle?
3. Name a secant.
4. Give the tangent line.
5. Name the central angle.
6. Name the inscribed angle.

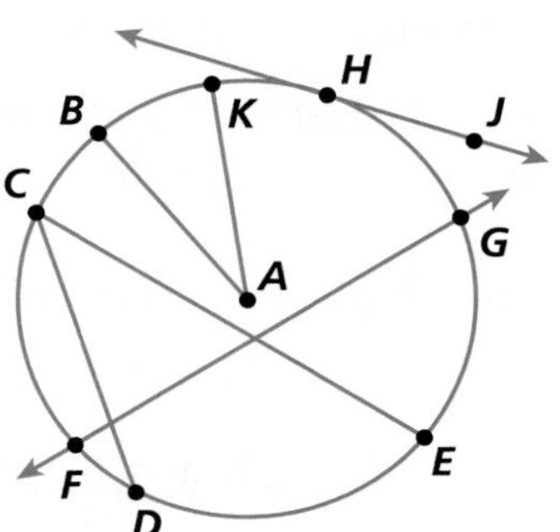

Matrices

A **matrix** is a rectangular arrangement of data enclosed in brackets. Matrices are used to list, organize, and sort data.

The **dimensions** of a matrix are given by the number of horizontal **rows** and vertical columns in the matrix. For example, Matrix A below is an example of a 3×2 ("3-by-2") matrix because it has 3 rows and 2 columns, for a total of 6 **elements.** The number of rows is always given first. So a 3×2 matrix is not the same as a 2×3 matrix.

$$A = \begin{bmatrix} 86 & 137 \\ 103 & 0 \\ 115 & 78 \end{bmatrix} \begin{matrix} \leftarrow \text{Row 1} \\ \leftarrow \text{Row 2} \\ \leftarrow \text{Row 3} \end{matrix}$$

$\uparrow$ Column 1 $\quad \uparrow$ Column 2

Each matrix element is identified by its row and column. The element in row 2 column 1 is 103. You can use the notation $a_{21} = 103$ to express this.

EXAMPLE

Use the data shown in the bar graph to create a matrix.

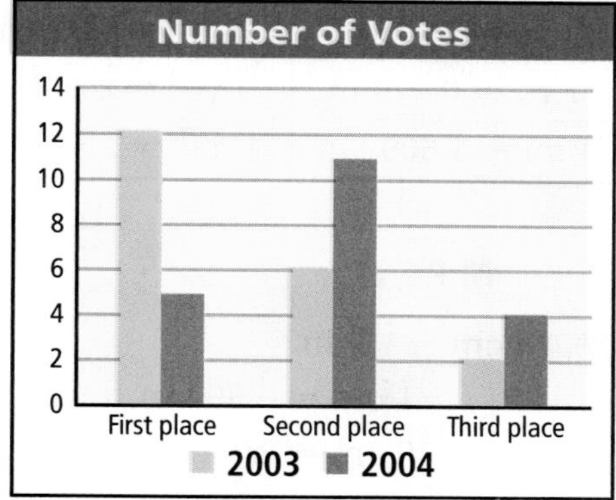

The matrix can be organized with the votes in each year as the columns:

$$\begin{bmatrix} 12 & 5 \\ 6 & 11 \\ 2 & 4 \end{bmatrix}$$

or with the votes in each year as the rows:

$$\begin{bmatrix} 12 & 6 & 2 \\ 5 & 11 & 4 \end{bmatrix}$$

PRACTICE

Use matrix B for Exercises 1–3.

1. B is a ▒ × ▒ matrix.
2. Name the element with a value of 5.
3. What is the value of b_{13}?
4. A football team scored 24, 13, and 35 points in three playoff games. Use this data to write a 3×1 matrix.
5. The greatest length and average weight of some whale species are as follows: finback whale—50 ft, 82 tons; humpback whale—33 ft, 49 tons; bowhead whale—50 ft, 59 tons; blue whale—84 ft, 98 tons; right whale—50 ft, 56 tons. Organize this data in a matrix.
6. The second matrix in the example is called the *transpose* of the first matrix. Write the transpose of matrix B above. What are its dimensions?

Skills Bank Science Skills

Conversion of Units in 1, 2, and 3 Dimensions

When converting between the metric and customary system, use **conversion factors**.

Common Metric to Customary Conversions		
Length	**Area**	**Volume**
1 cm ≈ 0.394 in.	1 cm^2 ≈ 0.155 in^2	1 cm^3 ≈ 0.061 in^3
1 m ≈ 3.281 ft	1 m^2 ≈ 10.764 ft^2	1 m^3 ≈ 35.315 ft^3
1 m ≈ 1.094 yd	1 m^2 ≈ 1.196 yd^2	1 m^3 ≈ 1.308 yd^3
1 km ≈ 0.621 mi	1 km^2 ≈ 0.386 mi^2	1 km^3 ≈ 0.239 mi^3

Common Customary to Metric Conversions		
Length	**Area**	**Volume**
1 in. ≈ 2.54 cm	1 in^2 ≈ 6.452 cm^2	1 in^3 ≈ 16.387 cm^3
1 ft ≈ 0.305 m	1 ft^2 ≈ 0.093 m^2	1 ft^3 ≈ 0.028 m^3
1 yd ≈ 0.914 m	1 yd^2 ≈ 0.836 m^2	1 yd^3 ≈ 0.765 m^3
1 mi ≈ 1.609 km	1 mi^2 ≈ 2.590 km^2	1 mi^3 ≈ 4.168 km^3

EXAMPLES

A **8 cm ≈ ▮ in.**

1 cm ≈ 0.394 in.
8 cm ≈ 8(0.394) in.
8 cm ≈ 3.152 in.

B **45 mi^2 ≈ ▮ km^2**

1 mi^2 ≈ 2.590 km^2
45 mi^2 ≈ 45(2.590) km^2
45 mi^2 ≈ 116.550 km^2

PRACTICE

Complete each conversion.

1. 2 in. ≈ ▮ cm

2. 3 km^3 ≈ ▮ mi^3

3. 4.2 m^2 ≈ ▮ ft^2

4. 5 ft^2 ≈ ▮ m^2

5. 10 mi ≈ ▮ km

6. 1.1 m^3 ≈ ▮ yd^3

7. 4 yd ≈ ▮ m

8. 15 in^2 ≈ ▮ cm^2

9. 12 yd ≈ ▮ m

10. 1 cm^3 ≈ ▮ in^3

11. 9 m^3 ≈ ▮ ft^3

12. 2 mi ≈ ▮ km

13. Approximately how many meters are in a mile?

Temperature Conversion

In the United States, the Fahrenheit (°F) temperature scale is the common scale used. For example, weather reports and body temperatures are given in degrees Fahrenheit. The metric temperature scale is Celsius (°C) and is commonly used in science applications. Temperatures given in one scale can be converted to the other system using one of the formulas below.

Formulas

Fahrenheit to Celsius (°F to °C)	$\frac{5}{9}(F - 32) = C$
Celsius to Fahrenheit (°C to °F)	$\frac{9}{5}C + 32 = F$

EXAMPLES

A **Convert 77°F to degrees Celsius.**

$$\frac{5}{9}(F - 32) = C$$
$$\frac{5}{9}(77 - 32) = C$$
$$\frac{5}{9}(45) = C$$
$$25 = C$$

B **Convert 103°C to degrees Fahrenheit.**

$$\frac{9}{5}C + 32 = F$$
$$\frac{9}{5}(103) + 32 = F$$
$$185.4 + 32 = F$$
$$217.4 = F$$

PRACTICE

Convert each temperature to degrees Celsius. Give the temperature to the nearest tenth of a degree.

1. 7°F
2. 0°F
3. 12°F
4. 40°F
5. 100°F
6. 32°F
7. 25°F
8. 212°F
9. −50°F
10. −8°F

Convert each temperature to degrees Fahrenheit. Give the temperature to the nearest tenth of a degree.

11. 0°C
12. 10°C
13. 22°C
14. 55°C
15. 212°C
16. 1°C
17. 100°C
18. 80°C
19. 95°C
20. 32°C
21. 31°C
22. 42°C
23. −6°C
24. −40°C

Customary and Metric Rulers

A metric ruler is divided into centimeter units, and each centimeter is divided into 10 millimeter units. A metric ruler that is 1 meter long is a *meter stick.*

1 m = 100 cm
1 cm = 10 mm

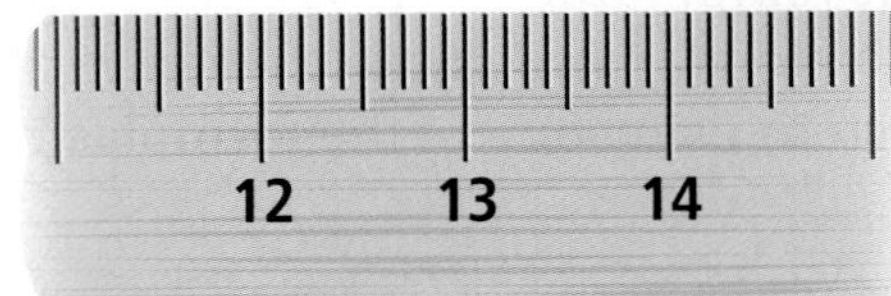

EXAMPLE

What is the length of the segment?

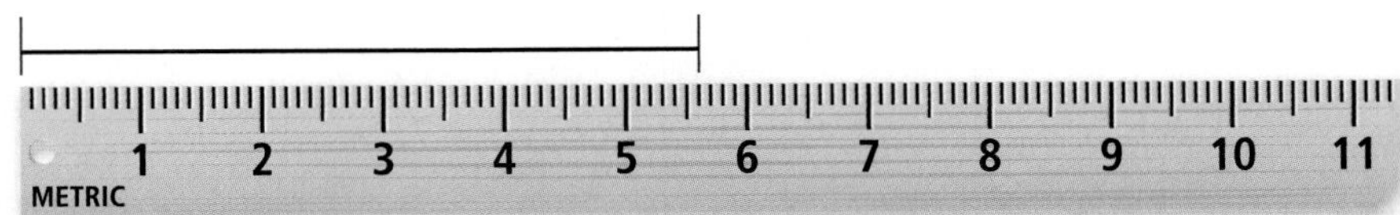

Since the segment is longer than 5 cm and shorter than 6 cm, its length is a decimal value between these measurements. The digit in the ones place is the number of centimeters and the digit in the tenths place is the number of millimeters. The length of the segment is 5.6 cm.

PRACTICE

Use a metric ruler to find the length of each segment.

1. |————|　　**2.** |————————|

A customary ruler is usually 12 inches long. The ruler is read in fractional units rather than in decimals. Each inch typically has a long mark at $\frac{1}{2}$ inch, shorter marks at $\frac{1}{4}$ and $\frac{3}{4}$ inch, even shorter marks at $\frac{1}{8}$, $\frac{3}{8}$, $\frac{5}{8}$, and $\frac{7}{8}$ inch, and the shortest marks at the remaining 16ths inches.

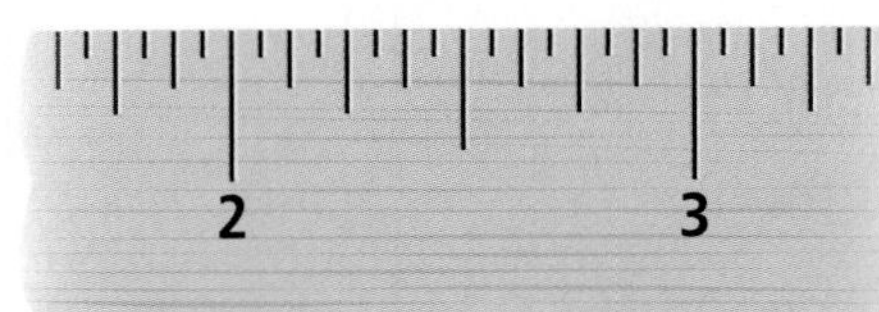

EXAMPLE

What is the length of the segment?

Since the segment is longer than 2 inches and shorter than 3 inches, its length is a mixed number with 2 as the whole number part. The fractional part is $\frac{11}{16}$. The length of the segment is $2\frac{11}{16}$ inches.

PRACTICE

Use a customary ruler to find the length of each segment.

3. |————————|　　**4.** |—————|

Precision and Significant Digits

In a measurement, all digits that are known with certainty are called **significant digits** . The more precise a measurement is, the more significant digits there are in the measurement. The table shows some rules for identifying significant digits.

Rule	Example	Number of Significant Digits
All nonzero digits	15.32	All 4
Zeros beween significant digits	43,001	All 5
Zeros after the last nonzero digit that are to the right of the decimal point	0.0070	2; 0.0070

Zeros at the end of a whole number are assumed to be nonsignificant. (Example: 500)

EXAMPLE

A **Which is a more precise measurement, 14 ft or 14.2 ft?**

Because 14.2 ft has three significant digits and 14 has only two, 14.2 ft is more precise. In the measurement 14.2 ft, each 0.1 ft is measured.

B **Determine the number of significant digits in 20.04 m, 200 m, and 200.0 m.**

20.04 All 4 digits are significant.
200 There is 1 significant digit.
200.0 All 4 digits are significant.

When calculating with measurements, the answer can only be as precise as the least precise measurement.

C **Multiply 16.3 m by 2.5 m. Use the correct number of significant digits in your answer.**

When muliplying or dividing, use the least number of significant digits of the numbers.

16.3 m · **2.5** m = 40.75

Round to 2 significant digits. ⟶ **41** m^2

D **Add 4500 in. and 70 in. Use the correct number of significant digits in your answer.**

When adding or subtracting, line up the numbers. Round the answer to the last significant digit that is farthest to the left.

4500 in. *5 is farthest left. Round to*
+ 70 in. *hundreds.*
4570 Round to the hundreds. ⟶ **4600** in.

PRACTICE

Tell which is more precise.

1. 31.8 g or 32 g
2. 496.5 mi or 496.50 mi
3. 3.0 ft or 3.001 ft

Determine the number of significant digits in each measurement.

4. 12 lb
5. 14.00 mm
6. 1.009 yd
7. 20.87 s

Perform the indicated operation. Use the correct number of significant digits in your answer.

8. 210 m + 43 m
9. 4.7 ft · 1.04 ft
10. 6.7 s − 0.08 s

Greatest Possible Error

The smaller the units used to measure something, the greater the precision of the measurement. The **greatest possible error** of a measurement is half the smallest unit. This is written as ± 0.5 unit, which is read as "plus or minus 0.5 unit."

EXAMPLES

A **Which is a more precise measurement, 292 cm or 3 m?**

The more precise measurement is 292 cm because its unit of measurement, 1 cm, is smaller than 1 m.

B **Find the greatest possible error for a measurement of 2.4 cm.**

The smallest unit is 0.1 cm.

$0.5 \times 0.1 = 0.05$

The greatest possible error is ± 0.05 cm.

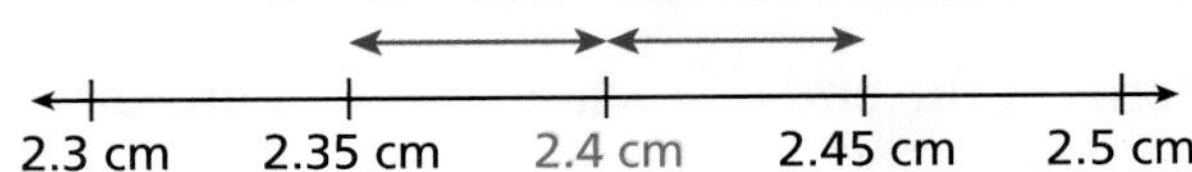

PRACTICE

Tell which is a more precise measurement.

1. 40 cm or 412 mm
2. 3.2 ft or 1 yd
3. 7 ft or 87 in.
4. 3116 m or 3 km
5. 1 mi or 5281 ft
6. 0.04 m or 4.2 cm

Find the greatest possible error of each measurement.

7. 5 ft
8. 22 mm
9. 12.5 mi
10. 60 km
11. 2.06 cm
12. 0.08 g

Skills Bank

pH (Logarithmic Scale)

pH is a measure of the concentration of hydrogen ions in a solution. pH ranges from 0 to 14. An *acid* has a pH below 7 and a *base* has a pH above 7. A pH of 7 is *neutral* and a hydrogen ion concentration of 1×10^{-7} mol/L. The exponent is the opposite of the pH.

0 Strong acids — Weak acids — 7 — Weak bases — Strong bases 14

EXAMPLES

A **Write the pH of the solution, given the hydrogen ion concentration.**

coffee: 1×10^{-5} mol/L

The coffee is acidic, with a pH of 5.

B **Write the hydrogen ion concentration of the solution in mol/L.**

antacid solution: pH = 10.0

1×10^{-10} mol/L in the antacid solution

PRACTICE

Write the pH of each solution, given the hydrogen ion concentration.

1. seawater: 1×10^{-8} mol/L
2. lye: 1×10^{-13} mol/L
3. borax: 1×10^{-9} mol/L

Write the hydrogen ion concentration in mol/L.

4. drain cleaner: pH = 14.0
5. lemon juice: pH = 2.0
6. milk: pH = 7.0

Richter Scale

An earthquake is classified according to its magnitude. The Richter scale is a mathematical system that compares the sizes and magnitudes of earthquakes.

The magnitude is related to the height, or *amplitude,* of seismic waves as recorded by a seismograph during an earthquake. The higher the number is on the Richter scale, the greater the amplitude of the earthquake's waves.

Earthquakes per Year	Magnitude on the Richter Scale	Severity
1	8.0 and higher	Great
18	7.0–7.9	Major
120	6.0–6.9	Strong
800	5.0–5.9	Moderate
6200	4.0–4.9	Light
49,000	3.0–3.9	Minor
≈ 3,300,000	below 3.0	Very minor

The Richter scale is a *logarithmic scale,* which means that the numbers in the scale measure factors of 10. An earthquake that measures 6.0 on the Richter scale is 10 times as great as one that measures 5.0.

The largest earthquake ever measured registered 8.9 on the Richter scale.

Skills Bank

EXAMPLE

How many times greater is an earthquake that measures 5.0 on the Richter scale than one that measures 3.0?

You can divide powers of 10, with the magnitudes as the exponents.

$$\frac{10^5}{10^3} = 10^2$$

A 5.0 quake is 100 times greater than a 3.0 quake.

PRACTICE

Describe the severity of an earthquake with each given Richter scale reading.

1. 7.6
2. 4.2
3. 5.0
4. 2.0
5. 3.6
6. 8.4

Each pair of numbers repesents two earthquake magnitudes on the Richter scale. How many times greater is the first earthquake in each pair? (Use a calculator for 10–12.)

7. 6.0 and 4.0
8. 8.0 and 5.0
9. 7.0 and 3.0
10. 7.5 and 5.5
11. 5.7 and 5.3
12. 8.6 and 7.1

Selected Answers

Chapter 1

1-1 Exercises

1. 17 **2.** 23 **3.** 3 **4.** 44 **5.** 1.8 **6.** 5 tbsp **7.** 8 tbsp **8.** 11.5 tbsp **9.** 17 tbsp **11.** 33 **13.** 67 **15.** 4 gal **17.** 2 gal **19.** 0 **21.** 22 **23.** 9 **25.** 6 **27.** 10 **29.** 16 **31.** 11 **33.** 20 **35.** 34 **37.** 12.6 **39.** 18 **41.** 105 **43.** 17 **45.** 30.5 **47.** 24 **49.** 0 **51.** Possible range: 204 to 208 beats per minute **53. b.** 165,600 frames **57.** 15, 21, 71 **59.** 49, 81 **61.** C

1-2 Exercises

1. $6 \div t$ **2.** $y - 25$ **3.** $7(m + 6)$ **4.** $7m + 6$ **5. a.** $8n$ **b.** $8(23) = \$184$ **6.** $\$15 + d$; \$17.50 **7.** $k + 34$ **9.** $5 + 5z$ **11. a.** $42 \div p$ **b.** 7 students **13.** $\$1.75n$; \$14.00 **15.** $6(4 + y)$ **17.** $\frac{1}{2}(m + 5)$ **19.** $13y - 6$ **21.** $2\left(\frac{m}{35}\right)$ **25.** $2(r - 1)$; $2(2.50 - 1) = \$3$

27.

24 + 4(2 − 2)	24
24 + 4(3 − 2)	28
24 + 4(4 − 2)	32
24 + 4(5 − 2)	36
24 + 4(6 − 2)	40

31. 202 **33.** 400 **35.** 200.2 **37.** 40 **39.** C

1-3 Exercises

1. 5 **2.** 21 **3.** $m = 32$ **4.** $t = 5$ **5.** $w = 17$ **6.** 15,635 feet **7.** 22 **9.** $w = 1$ **11.** $t = 12$ **13.** 20 **15.** 30 **17.** 7 **19.** 0 **21.** $t = 5$ **23.** $m = 24$ **25.** $h = 3$ **27.** $t = 2621$ **29.** $x = 110$ **31.** $n = 45$ **33.** $t = 0.5$ **35.** $w = 1.9$ **37. a.** $497 + m = 1696$; 1199 miles **b.** $1278 + m = 1696$; 418 miles **39. a.** $0.24 + c = 4.23$; \$3.99 **b.** $c - 3.82 = 0.53$; \$4.35 **43.** 22 **45.** 26

1-4 Exercises

1. $x = 7$ **2.** $t = 7$ **3.** $y = 14$ **4.** $w = 13$ **5.** $l = 60$ **6.** $k = 72$ **7.** $h = 57$ **8.** $m = 6$ **9.** $8n = 32$; $n = 4$ servings **10.** $\frac{1}{4}c = \$60$ or $\frac{c}{4} = \$60$; $c = \$240$ **11.** $x = 7$ **12.** $k = 40$ **13.** $y = 3$ **14.** $m = 36$ **15.** $d = 19$ **17.** $g = 10$ **19.** $n = 567$ **21.** $a = 612$ **23.** $10n = 80$; $n = 8$ mg **25.** $x = 2$ **27.** $y = 2$ **29.** $x = 7$ **31.** $y = 2$ **33.** $k = 56$ **35.** $b = 72$ **37.** $x = 17$ **39.** $y = 3$ **41.** $b = 48$ **43.** $n = 35$ **45.** $16m = 42{,}000$; $m = 2625$ miles **47.** $\frac{1}{6}m = 22$ or $\frac{m}{6} = 22$; $m = 132$ miles **49.** $x = 8$ **51.** $w = 2$ **53.** A

1-5 Exercises

1. $<$ **2.** $>$ **3.** $>$ **4.** $>$ **5.** $>$ **6.** $<$ **7.** $>$ **8.** $>$ **9.** $x < 1$ **10.** $b \geq 5$ **11.** $m \leq 32$ **12.** $15 > x$ **13.** $y \geq 17$ **14.** $f < 5$ **15.** $z > 21$ **16.** $14 \leq x$ **17.** $m > 40$; more than 40 members **19.** $<$ **21.** $>$ **23.** $<$ **25.** $<$ **27.** $x \geq 7$ **29.** $4 < t$ **31.** $x \geq 4$ **33.** $6 < a$ **35.** $x < 6$ **37.** $x > 4$ **39.** $x < 1$ **41.** $x \geq 5$ **43.** $50(50) > 2200$; $2500 > 2200$; no **45.** $x \geq 53$ **51.** 22; 19; 16; 13 **53.** 13; 21; 29; 37 **55.** 15; 13; 11; 9 **57.** H

1-6 Exercises

1. $4x$ **2.** $5z + 5$ **3.** $8f + 8$ **4.** $17g$ **5.** $4p - 8$ **6.** $4x + 12$ **7.** $3x + 5y$ **8.** $9x + y$ **9.** $5x + y$ **10.** $9p + 3z$ **11.** $7g + 5h - 12$ **12.** $10h$ **13.** $r + 6$ **14.** $10 + 8x$ **15.** $2t + 56$ **16.** $n = 42$ **17.** $y = 24$ **18.** $p = 17$ **19.** $13y$ **21.** $7a + 11$ **23.** $3x + 2$ **25.** $5p$ **27.** $9x + 3$ **29.** $5a + z$ **31.** $7x + 5q + 3$ **33.** $9a + 7c + 3$ **35.** $20y - 18$ **37.** $6y + 17$ **39.** $11x - 9$ **41.** $p = 5$ **43.** $y = 8$ **45.** $x = 14$ **47.** $8d + 1$ **49.** $x = 2$ **51.** $52g$; $41s$; $49b$ **57.** $x = 13$ **59.** $x = 8$ **61.** $x = 32$ **63.** $x = 16$ **65.** B

1-7 Exercises

1. no **2.** yes **3.** yes **4.** no

5.

x	y	(x, y)
1	2	(1, 2)
2	4	(2, 4)
3	6	(3, 6)
4	8	(4, 8)
5	10	(5, 10)
6	12	(6, 12)

6.

x	y	(x, y)
1	1	(1, 1)
2	4	(2, 4)
3	7	(3, 7)
4	10	(4, 10)
5	13	(5, 13)
6	16	(6, 16)

7. \$1.29 **9.** no **11.** no

13.

x	y	(x, y)
1	10	(1, 10)
2	12	(2, 12)
3	14	(3, 14)
4	16	(4, 16)
5	18	(5, 18)
6	20	(6, 20)

15.

x	y	(x, y)
2	2	(2, 2)
4	8	(4, 8)
6	14	(6, 14)
8	20	(8, 20)
10	26	(10, 26)

17. yes **19.** yes **21.** no **23.** yes

25.

x	y	(x, y)
1	1	(1, 1)
2	5	(2, 5)
3	9	(3, 9)
4	13	(4, 13)
5	17	(5, 17)
6	21	(6, 21)

27.

x	y	(x, y)
1	9	(1, 9)
2	10	(2, 10)
3	11	(3, 11)
4	12	(4, 12)
5	13	(5, 13)
6	14	(6, 14)

29.

x	y	(x, y)
2	8	(2, 8)
4	12	(4, 12)
6	16	(6, 16)
8	20	(8, 20)
10	24	(10, 24)

31. Possible answer: $x = y$ **33.** no; (13, 52) or (12.75, 51) **35. a.** (1980, 74) **b.** (2020, 81) **39.** 7 **41.** 4 **43.** 12 **45.** B

1-8 Exercises

1. (–2, 3) **2.** (3, 5) **3.** (2, –3) **4.** (5, –1) **5.** (5, 5) **6.** (–3, –4)

7–10.

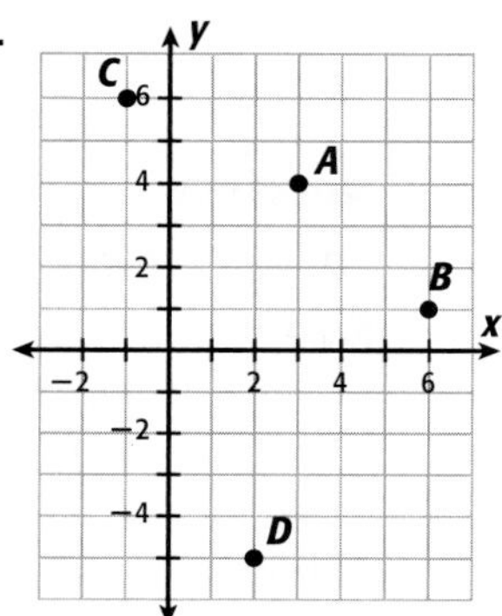

11.

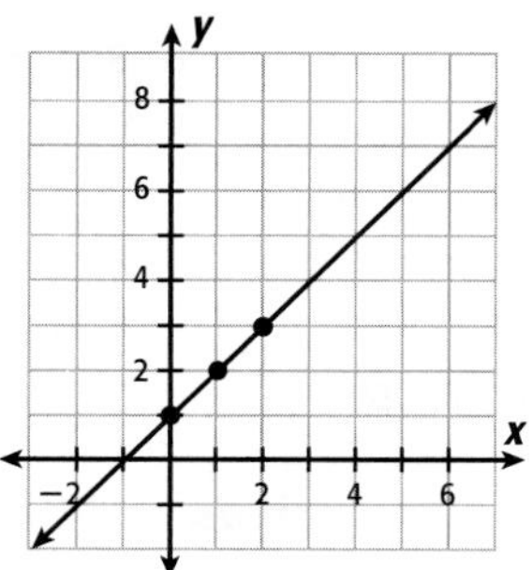

12.

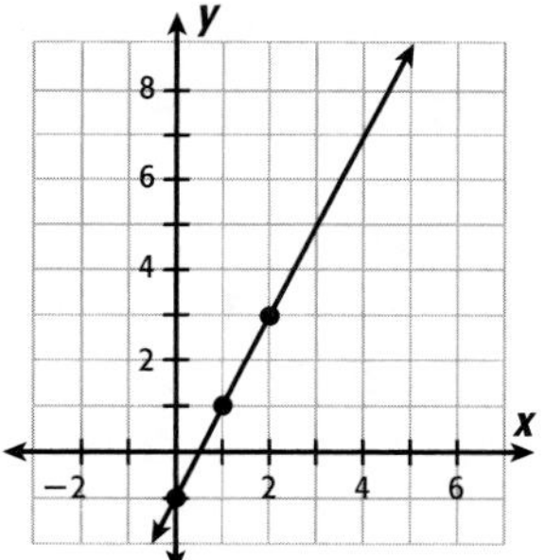

13. (0, 3) **15.** (2, −4) **17.** (−2, 5)

19–21.

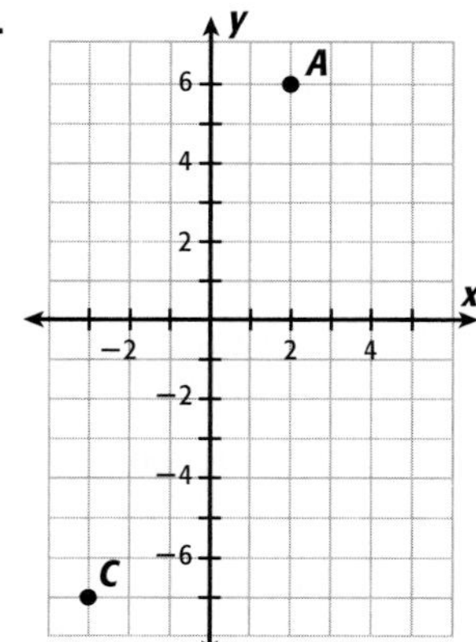

23.

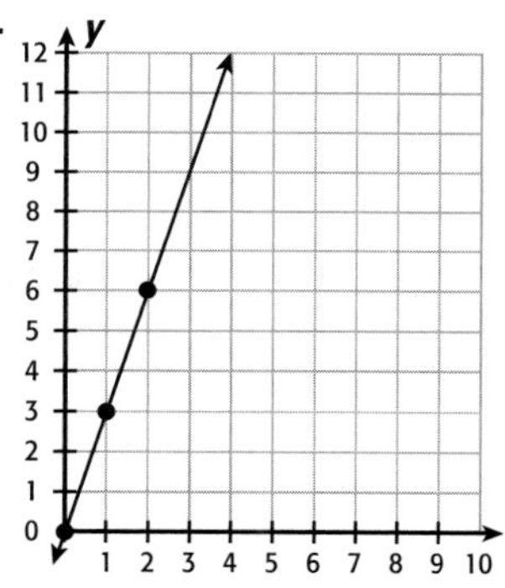

25–31. Possible answers given. **25.** (1, 0), (2, 0) **27.** (2, 7), (4, 7) **29.** (4, 3), (4, 5) **31.** (0, 4), (0, 5) **33.** 75 beats

35.

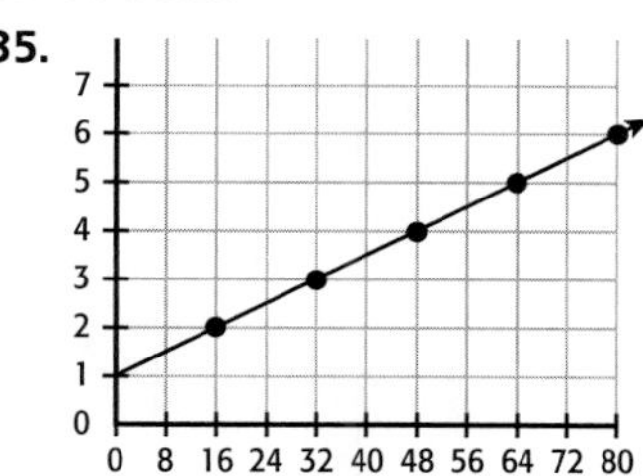

7 studs

39. $x - 13$ **41.** $x + 31$ **43.** C

1-9 Exercises

1. table 2 **2.** table 2; table 1; table 3; none

3.

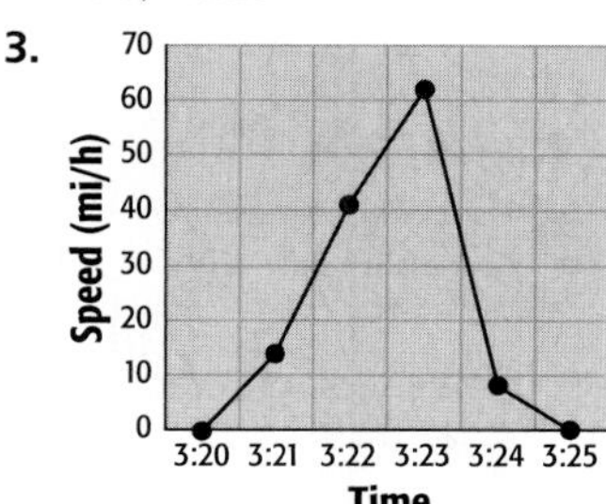

5. table 1; table 3; table 2

7.

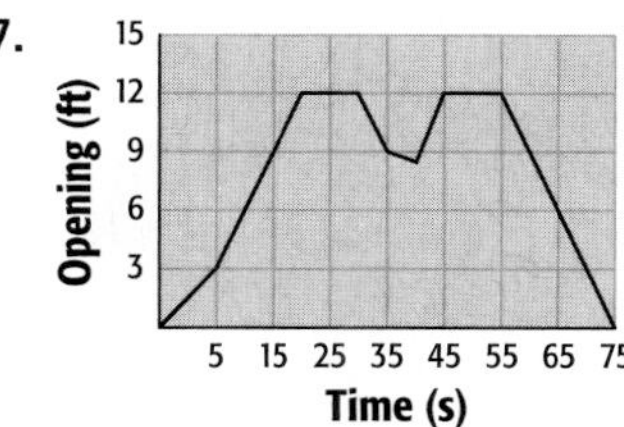

9. a. Old Faithful **b.** Riverside **11.** $x = 9$ **13.** $x = 11$ **15.** D

Chapter 1 Study Guide and Review

1. ordered pair; *x*-coordinate; *y*-coordinate **2.** solution set; inequality **3.** 147 **4.** 152 **5.** 278 **6.** $2(k + 4)$ **7.** $4t + 5$ **8.** $z = 23$ **9.** $t = 8$ **10.** $k = 15$ **11.** $x = 11$ **12.** 1300 lb. **13.** 3300 mi^2 **14.** $g = 8$ **15.** $k = 9$ **16.** $p = 80$ **17.** $w = 48$ **18.** $y = 40$ **19.** $z = 19.2$ **20.** 352.5 mi **21.** 24 months **22.** $h < 4$ **23.** $y > 7$ **24.** $x \geq 4$ **25.** $p < \frac{1}{2}$ **26.** $m > 2.3$ **27.** $q \leq 0$ **28.** $w \geq 8$ **29.** $x \leq 3$ **30.** $y > 16$ **31.** $x > 3$ **32.** $y > 6$ **33.** $x \leq 2$ **34.** $11m - 4$ **35.** $14w + 6$ **36.** $y = 5$ **37.** $z = 8$ **38.** yes **39.** no

40.

x	y	(x, y)
0	2	(0, 2)
1	5	(1, 5)
2	8	(2, 8)
3	11	(3, 11)
4	14	(4, 14)

41–46.

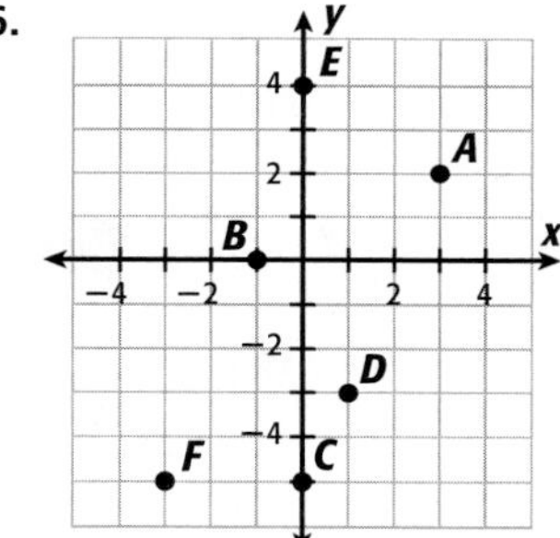

47. 5 **48.** 8 **49.** 20 **50.** Oven E

Chapter 2

2-1 Exercises

1. 5 **2.** 2 **3.** 4 **4.** −6 **5.** −8 **6.** 6 **7.** 3 **8.** –16 **9.** 11 **10.** 4 **11.** −8 **12.** \$297 **13.** −2 **15.** −3 **17.** 21 **19.** −18 **21.** 22 **23.** 9 **25.** $-6 + (-2) = -8$ **27.** −13 **29.** −18 **31.** −2 **33.** 43 **35.** 0 **37.** −19 **39.** 8 **41.** −20 **43.** −15 **45.** 5 **51.** $f = 6$ **53.** $q = 6$

2-2 Exercises

1. −15 **2.** −3 **3.** 14 **4.** −7 **5.** 13 **6.** −6 **7.** −15 **8.** 49°F **9.** −11 **11.** 17 **13.** 3 **15.** 4 **17.** 16 **19.** −17 **21.** −14 **23.** 40 m below sea level, or −40 m **25.** 5 − 8 = −3 **27.** 51 **29.** −62 **31.** −16 **33.** 13 **35.** 2 **37.** −42 **39.** Great Pyramid to Cleopatra; about 500 years **41.** Cleopatra takes throne and Napoleon invades Egypt. **45.** no like terms **47.** C

2-3 Exercises

1. −27 **2.** −8 **3.** 30 **4.** −4 **5.** 49 **6.** −77 **7.** −24 **8.** −72

9.

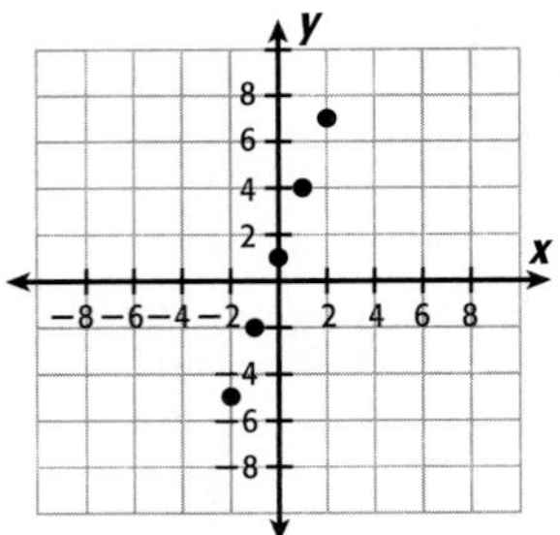

10.

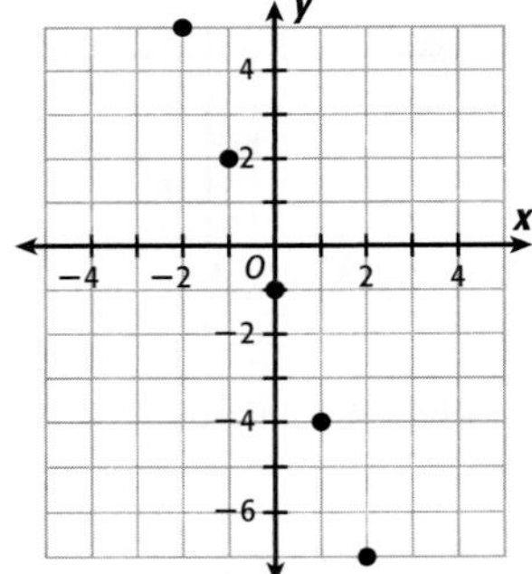

11.

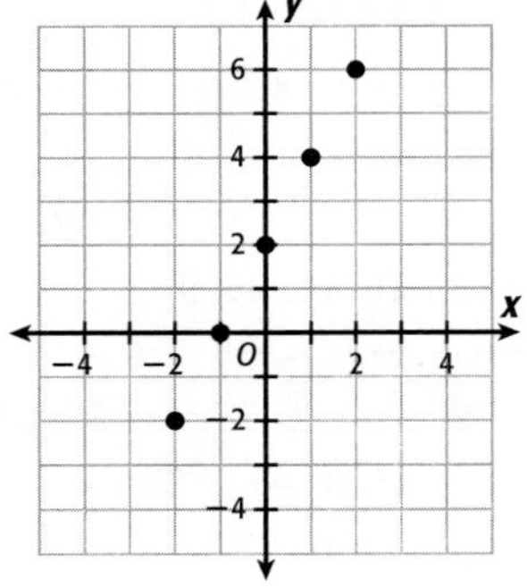

13. −11 **15.** −7 **17.** 130 **19.** −2

21.

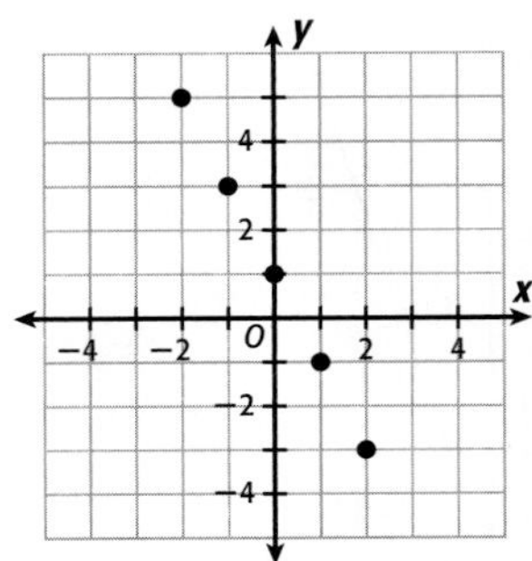

23. −45 **25.** 36 **27.** 24 **29.** −72 **31.** −80 **33.** 63 **35.** −19 **37.** 14 **39.** 3

41.

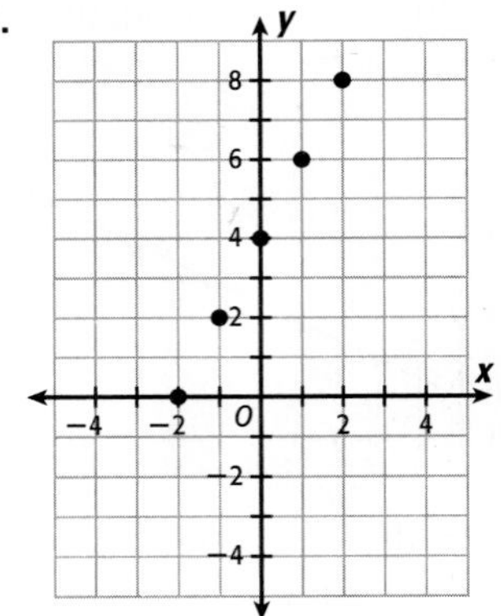

43.

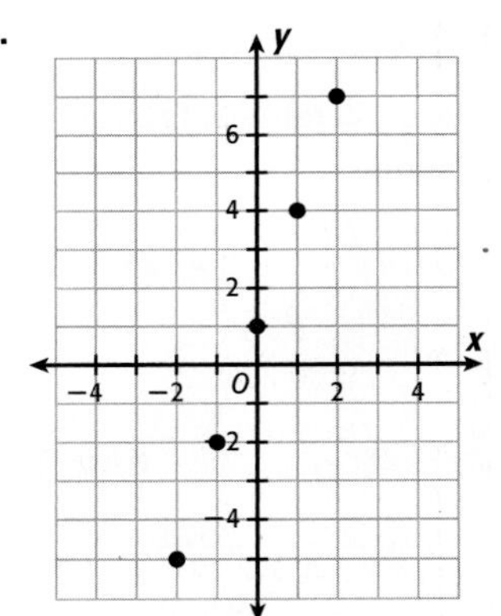

45. 32 days **51.** $w = 11$ **53.** $h = 0$ **55.** G

2-4 Exercises

1. $y = 6$ **2.** $d = 12$ **3.** $x = -11$ **4.** $b = -7$ **5.** $t = -16$ **6.** $g = -4$ **7.** $a = 12$ **8.** $f = -5$ **9.** 427°C **11.** $a = 13$ **13.** $b = -3$ **15.** $y = -37$ **17.** $h = -31$ **19.** $n = -39$ **21.** $c = 84$ **23.** $a = 45$ **25.** $r = -64$ **27.** $s = -11$ **29.** $x = 4$ **31.** $m = -27$ **33.** $z = 16$ **35.** $h = -4$ **37.** $y = -105$ **39.** $x = 24$ **41.** $p = -6$ **43. a.** $-4t = d$, t is time in minutes and d is depth. **b.** −68 m **c.** $-4t = -24$; $t = 6$ minutes **49.** $w = 2$ **51.** C

2-5 Exercises

1. $x \geq -5$ **2.** $y < 2$ **3.** $b \leq -7$ **4.** $h < 1$ **5.** $f > 4$ **6.** $k \leq 5$ **7.** $x < -3$ **8.** $y < -2$ **9.** $w \leq 3$ **10.** $x \geq -3$ **11.** $z > -8$ **12.** $n \leq 6$ **13.** $k > -3$ **15.** $x < -1$ **17.** $r \geq 2$ **19.** $n > 5$ **21.** $x \geq -4$ **23.** $x > -5$ **25.** $x > -2$ **27.** $k \geq 10$ **29.** $a \leq -12$ **31.** $r \leq -1$ **33.** $t = 2$ **35.** $b > 0$ **37.** $f = -18$ **39.** $c \leq 2$ **41.** $n < -6$ **43.** $g = 8$ **45.** $p = -9$ **47.** $3x + (-7x) > -12$; $x < 3$ **49.** $-1 + x < -7$; $x < -6$; less than 6 under par **55.** 9 **57.** −254 **59.** −16 **61.** 3 **63.** H

2-6 Exercises

1. 14^1 **2.** 15^2 **3.** b^4 **4.** $(-1)^3$ **5.** 81 **6.** 25 **7.** −243 **8.** 2401 **9.** −33 **10.** 90 **11.** −117 **12.** −47 **13.** 78 **15.** $(-7)^3$ **17.** c^5 **19.** 256 **21.** −512 **23.** 77 **25.** −360 **27.** $(-2)^3$ **29.** 4^4 **31.** 343 **33.** −1728 **35.** 729 **37.** 4 **39.** −116 **41.** −166 **43.** −4 **45.** −1 **47.** 216 **49.** 257 **51.** 2^{18} = 262,144 bacteria **59.** 9 **61.** 104 **63.** C

2-7 Exercises

1. 3^{11} **2.** 12^5 **3.** m^6 **4.** cannot combine **5.** 8^2 **6.** a^8 **7.** $12^0 = 1$ **8.** 7^{12} **9.** 10^2 plants **11.** 2^6 **13.** 16^4 **15.** cannot combine **17.** $10^0 = 1$ **19.** 6^3 **21.** a **23.** x^{10} **25.** 6^6 **27.** cannot combine **29.** $y^0 = 1$ **31.** x^8 **33.** 4^6 **35.** 10^{14} **37.** n^{16} **39.** 4^4 **41.** 6^9 **43.** 26^2, or 676 more ways **45.** 12^2; 12^1 **47.** 22^3 trips **51.** 3 **53.** −12 **55.** −16 **57.** −12 **59.** D

2-8 Exercises

1. 0.0000001 **2.** 0.001 **3.** 0.000001 **4.** 0.1 **5.** $\frac{1}{16}$ **6.** $\frac{1}{9}$ **7.** $\frac{1}{8}$ **8.** $-\frac{1}{32}$ **9.** 1000 **10.** $\frac{1}{9}$ **11.** 216 **12.** $\frac{1}{27}$ **13.** 0.01 **15.** 0.00001 **17.** $-\frac{1}{64}$ **19.** 0.0001 **21.** 10,000 **23.** 1 **25.** $\frac{1}{8}$ **27.** 0.001 **29.** 128 **31.** m^7 **33.** $\frac{1}{9}$ **35.** 1024 **37.** $\frac{1}{2}$ **39.** $\frac{1}{4}$ **41.** $\frac{1}{144}$ **43.** 4 **45.** 1 kilometer **47. a.** $10^{-5} \cdot 10^3 = 10^{-2}$ g **b.** $10^{-2} \cdot 10^7 = 10^5$ g **c.** $10^5 \div 10^1 = 10^{5-1} = 10^4$; 10^4 decagrams **51.** 30 **53.** 85

2-9 Exercises

1. 3150 **2.** 0.000000125 **3.** 410,000 **4.** 0.00039 **5.** 5.7×10^{-5} **6.** 3×10^{-4} **7.** 4.89×10^6 **8.** 1.4×10^{-7} **9.** (1.485×10^6)°C **11.** 0.00067 **13.** 63,700,000 **15.** 7.8×10^6 **17.** 3×10^{-8} **19.** 13,000 **21.** 56 **23.** 0.000000053 **25.** 8,580,000 **27.** 9,112,000 **29.** 0.00029 **31.** 4.67×10^{-3} **33.** 5.6×10^7 **35.** 7.6×10^{-3} **37.** 3.5×10^3 **39.** 9×10^2 **41.** 6×10^6 **43. a.** $\approx 2.21 \times 10^7$; $\approx 1.4 \times 10^4$ mi^2 **b.** 6.35×10^{-4} mi^2/person **45.** 0.000078 **51.** -20 **53.** 21 **55.** $t = -9$ **57.** $b = -27$

Chapter 2 Study Guide and Review

1. opposite **2.** scientific notation; power **3.** exponent; base **4.** -2 **5.** -12 **6.** -3 **7.** 1 **8.** -24 **9.** 8 **10.** -8 **11.** -16 **12.** 17 **13.** 3 **14.** 15 **15.** -22 **16.** -4 **17.** 16 **18.** -5 **19.** -35 **20.** -18 **21.** 52 **22.** 25 **23.** 120 **24.** 2 **25.** $p = 9$ **26.** $t = 3$ **27.** $k = 3$ **28.** $g = -6$ **29.** $w = -80$ **30.** $b = -20$ **31.** $a = -4$ **32.** $h = -91$ **33.** $S = 38$ **34.** $b < -2$ **35.** $r > 6$ **36.** $m \geq 3$ **37.** $p < -2$ **38.** $z < -5$ **39.** $q \geq 3$ **40.** $m \geq 4$ **41.** $x > -3$ **42.** $y < 4$ **43.** $x > -3$ **44.** $b \leq 0$ **45.** $y < 6$ **46.** 7^3 **47.** $(-3)^2$ **48.** K^4 **49.** 625 **50.** -32 **51.** -1 **52.** 4^7 **53.** 9^6 **54.** p^4 **55.** 8^3 **56.** 9^2 **57.** m^5 **58.** 5^3 **59.** y^5 **60.** k^0 **61.** $\frac{1}{125}$ **62.** $-\frac{1}{64}$ **63.** $\frac{1}{11}$ **64.** 1 **65.** 1 **66.** 1 **67.** $\frac{1}{8}$ **68.** $-\frac{1}{27}$ **69.** 1620 **70.** 0.00162 **71.** 910,000 **72.** 0.000091 **73.** 8.0×10^{-9} **74.** 7.3×10^7 **75.** 9.6×10^{-6} **76.** 5.64×10^{10}

Chapter 3

3-1 Exercises

1. $\frac{4}{5}$ **2.** $\frac{3}{5}$ **3.** $-\frac{2}{3}$ **4.** $\frac{11}{27}$ **5.** $\frac{19}{23}$ **6.** $-\frac{5}{6}$ **7.** $-\frac{7}{27}$ **8.** $\frac{7}{16}$ **9.** $\frac{3}{4}$ **10.** $1\frac{1}{8}$ **11.** $\frac{431}{1000}$ **12.** $\frac{4}{5}$ **13.** $-2\frac{1}{5}$ **14.** $\frac{5}{8}$ **15.** $3\frac{21}{100}$ **16.** $-\frac{1939}{5000}$ **17.** 0.875 **18.** 0.6 **19.** $0.41\overline{6}$ **20.** 0.75 **21.** 4.0 **22.** 0.125 **23.** 2.4 **24.** 2.25 **25.** $\frac{3}{4}$ **27.** $-\frac{1}{2}$ **29.** $\frac{13}{17}$ **31.** $\frac{16}{19}$ **33.** $\frac{2}{5}$ **35.** $\frac{71}{100}$ **37.** $1\frac{377}{1000}$ **39.** $-1\frac{2}{5}$ **41.** 0.375 **43.** 1.4 **45.** 0.68 **47.** 1.16 **49.** Possible answer: $\frac{25}{36}$ **51. a.** $\frac{3}{4}; \frac{1}{6}; \frac{5}{9}; \frac{17}{20}; \frac{13}{32}; \frac{11}{25}; \frac{19}{24}; \frac{8}{15}$ **b.** 2×2; 2×3; 3×3; $2 \times 2 \times 5$; $2 \times 2 \times 2 \times 2 \times 2$; 5×5; $2 \times 2 \times 2 \times 3$; 3×5 **c.** 0.75 terminating; $0.1\overline{6}$ repeating; $0.\overline{5}$ repeating; 0.85 terminating; 0.40625 terminating; 0.44 terminating; $0.791\overline{6}$ repeating; $0.5\overline{3}$ repeating **53.** GCF = 4; $\frac{12}{19}$; No **59.** 28; 48 **61.** 35; 14 **63.** H

3-2 Exercises

1. 9.693 seconds **2.** 1.4 **3.** -2 **4.** -0.4 **5.** $-2\frac{1}{2}$ **6.** -1.5 **7.** $-\frac{5}{9}$ **8.** -1.9 **9.** -3 **10.** $-\frac{1}{3}$ **11.** $-1\frac{1}{3}$ **12.** $\frac{4}{5}$ **13.** $\frac{2}{5}$ **14.** $\frac{1}{2}$ **15.** $\frac{5}{17}$ **16.** $4\frac{1}{5}$ **17.** $-2\frac{5}{9}$ **18.** 4.2 **19.** $\frac{2}{5}$ **20.** 21.4 **21.** $\frac{2}{5}$ **23.** -1.6 **25.** 1.6 **27.** 1.9 **29.** -2.7 **31.** $\frac{5}{11}$ **33.** $1\frac{8}{17}$ **35.** $-\frac{1}{2}$ **37.** $1\frac{2}{21}$ **39.** 28.7 **41.** -16.34 **43. a.** $\frac{29}{32}$ in. **b.** $1\frac{7}{32}$ in. **c.** $\frac{19}{32}$ in. **45. a.** 3.63 quadrillion Btu **b.** 2.717 quadrillion Btu **49.** $7x - 5y + 18$ **51.** $16x + 22y + 11$ **53.** A

3-3 Exercises

1. $1\frac{1}{3}$ **2.** $-14\frac{2}{5}$ **3.** $1\frac{7}{8}$ **4.** $-3\frac{4}{5}$ **5.** $3\frac{1}{9}$ **6.** $-8\frac{7}{11}$ **7.** $6\frac{3}{4}$ **8.** $6\frac{3}{8}$ **9.** $\frac{4}{21}$ **10.** $-\frac{21}{80}$ **11.** $3\frac{5}{9}$ **12.** $\frac{1}{4}$ **13.** $-\frac{25}{78}$ **14.** $2\frac{1}{32}$ **15.** $\frac{7}{12}$ **16.** $-\frac{55}{192}$ **17.** 12.4 **18.** 0.144 **19.** 36.5 **20.** -0.42 **21.** 41.3 **22.** 3.65 **23.** 14.1 **24.** -0.416 **25.** $13\frac{1}{7}$ **26.** $5\frac{3}{4}$ **27.** $-6\frac{4}{7}$ **28.** $-1\frac{20}{49}$ **29.** 23 **30.** $7\frac{2}{3}$ **31.** $-9\frac{6}{7}$ **32.** $-\frac{69}{70}$ **33.** $\frac{3}{5}$ **35.** $1\frac{1}{8}$ **37.** $8\frac{2}{5}$ **39.** 4 **41.** $\frac{5}{9}$ **43.** $\frac{38}{63}$ **45.** $-\frac{3}{10}$ **47.** $\frac{3}{32}$ **49.** 8.7 **51.** 43.4 **53.** 33.6 **55.** 28.8 **57.** $16\frac{1}{2}$ **59.** -11 **61.** $8\frac{1}{4}$ **63.** $-19\frac{1}{4}$ **65.** $72\frac{1}{2}$ ounces **67. a.** $1\frac{1}{4}$ tsp **b.** $1\frac{1}{2}$ tsp **c.** 2 tsp **73.** $x = 12$ **75.** $x = 34$ **77.** $x = 44$ **79.** F

3-4 Exercises

1. $\frac{4}{5}$ **2.** $\frac{45}{68}$ **3.** $-\frac{2}{7}$ **4.** $2\frac{11}{12}$ **5.** $1\frac{3}{14}$ **6.** $-\frac{5}{54}$ **7.** $1\frac{1}{2}$ **8.** $2\frac{9}{10}$ **9.** 12.4 **10.** 68 **11.** 15.3 **12.** 8.6 **13.** $3.8\overline{4}$ **14.** 17.6 **15.** 1310 **16.** 9.2 **17.** 22.5 **18.** 21 **19.** 45 **20.** 4 **21.** 13 **22.** 270 **23.** $\frac{6}{7}$ serving **25.** $1\frac{13}{15}$ **27.** $3\frac{3}{5}$ **29.** $-\frac{8}{21}$ **31.** $2\frac{1}{28}$ **33.** $\frac{1}{4}$ **35.** $-4\frac{1}{2}$ **37.** 97 **39.** 17.1 **41.** 27.4 **43.** 25.4 **45.** 32 **47.** 5.76 **49.** 13 **51.** 11 **53.** 370 **55.** 0.7 **57.** 6 chairs **59.** $2\frac{1}{2}$ tiles **61.** Yes **65.** $x = 6.5$ **67.** $x = 8$ **69.** $x = 4.5$ **71.** C

3-5 Exercises

1. $\frac{19}{24}$ **2.** $\frac{67}{112}$ **3.** $-\frac{4}{9}$ **4.** $\frac{7}{16}$ **5.** $-3\frac{7}{15}$ **6.** $-2\frac{11}{24}$ **7.** $\frac{47}{60}$ **8.** $1\frac{29}{40}$ **9.** $1\frac{19}{40}$ **10.** $-1\frac{8}{63}$ **11.** $\frac{5}{8}$ **12.** $-\frac{37}{48}$ **13.** $6\frac{5}{8}$ ft **15.** $\frac{44}{45}$ **17.** $1\frac{1}{4}$ **19.** $-\frac{11}{112}$ **21.** $1\frac{4}{45}$ **23.** $-\frac{5}{48}$ **25.** $-\frac{7}{60}$ **27.** $660\frac{779}{800}$ in. **29.** $18\frac{21}{50}$ in.

31. $47\frac{2}{25}$ meters **35.** −27 **37.** 88 **39.** 18 **41.** H

3-6 Exercises

1. $y = -75.4$ **2.** $f = -7$ **3.** $m = -19.2$ **4.** $r = 54.7$ **5.** $s = 68.692$ **6.** $g = 6.3$ **7.** $x = -\frac{4}{7}$ **8.** $k = -\frac{1}{3}$ **9.** $w = -\frac{7}{9}$ **10.** $m = 0$ **11.** $y = -9$ **12.** $t = 0$ **13.** $17\frac{24}{25}$ mm **15.** $m = -9$ **17.** $k = -2.4$ **19.** $c = 5.16$ **21.** $d = \frac{8}{15}$ **23.** $x = \frac{1}{2}$ **25.** $c = \frac{7}{20}$ **27.** $z = \frac{2}{3}$ **29.** $j = -32.4$ **31.** $g = 9$ **33.** $v = -30.25$ **35.** $y = -5.4$ **37.** $c = -\frac{1}{24}$ **39.** $y = 64.1$ **41.** $m = -2.8$ **43. a.** 15 tiles **b.** 9 tiles **c.** 5 boxes **49.** 21 **51.** 5.24×10^{-6} **53.** 6.4×10^{10}

3-7 Exercises

1. $x \geq 2$ **2.** $k > 9.3$ **3.** $g \leq 7$ **4.** $h < 0.79$ **5.** $w \leq 0.24$ **6.** $z > 0$ **7.** $k > \frac{3}{5}$ **8.** $y \geq 0$ **9.** $q \leq -\frac{1}{169}$ **10.** $x < 1\frac{2}{3}$ **11.** $f > \frac{4}{15}$ **12.** $m \geq 4$ **13.** between 6.7 and 8.1 hours **15.** $m \leq -.07$ **17.** $g \leq -24.3$ **19.** $w \leq -1.5$ **21.** $k \geq \frac{25}{36}$ **23.** $x \geq 4\frac{3}{5}$ **25.** $m \leq -1\frac{1}{7}$ **27.** $d \leq -3$ **29.** $g \geq -2$ **31.** $t > \frac{3}{13}$ **33.** $y \geq -8$ **35.** $w \leq -\frac{1}{3}$ **37.** $c > 3.1$ **39.** $c < 3\frac{1}{3}$ **41.** $t \leq 6$ **43.** at least 12.5 in., but not more than 3600 in. **47.** 0.3 **49.** −0.26 **51.** 16.8 **53.** −0.258 **55.** C

3-8 Exercises

1. ± 5 **2.** ±12 **3.** ±2 **4.** ±20 **5.** ±1 **6.** ±9 **7.** ±3 **8.** ±4 **9.** 16 ft **10.** 5 **11.** 2 **12.** −55 **13.** −1 **15.** ±15 **17.** ±13 **19.** ±21 **21.** ±19 **23.** −3 **25.** −20 **27.** ±7 **29.** ±17 **31.** ±30 **33.** ±23 **35.** $\pm\frac{1}{2}$ **37.** $\pm\frac{5}{2}$ **39.** $\pm\frac{3}{2}$ **41.** $\pm\frac{1}{10}$ **43.** 26 ft **45.** 327 **47. a.** 81; 1 **b.** 18 **51.** $t = 9$ **53.** $t = 22$ **55.** $\frac{1}{9}$ **57.** 1 **59.** D

3-9 Exercises

1. 6 and 7 **2.** −8 and −9 **3.** 14 and 15 **4.** −18 and −19 **5.** ≈ 13.27 ft **6.** 9.1 **7.** 6.5 **8.** 50 **9.** 13.8 **11.** 1 and 2 **13.** −31 and −32 **15.** 8.3 **17.** 25.5 **19.** B **21.** E **23.** F **25.** 7.14 **27.** 11.62 **29.** 42.85 **31.** −11.62 **33.** −32.83 **35.** ±5.20 **37.** ±317.02 **39.** 800 ft/s **43.** $y = -4.4$ **45.** $m = -25.6$ **47.** $x < 5\frac{2}{3}$ **49.** $m \geq 8$ **51.** 4 and −4 **53.** 10 and −10 **55.** D

3-10 Exercises

1. irrational, real **2.** whole, integer, rational, real **3.** rational, real **4.** rational, real **5.** rational **6.** rational **7.** irrational **8.** not real **9.** rational **10.** not real **11.** not real **12.** not real **13–15.** Possible answers given. **13.** $5\frac{1}{4}$ **14.** $\frac{2199}{700}$ **15.** $\frac{3}{16}$ **17.** rational, real **19.** integer, rational, real **21.** rational **23.** irrational **25.** irrational **27.** not real **29.** $-\frac{1}{200}$ **31.** whole, integer, rational, real **33.** irrational, real **35.** rational, real **37.** rational, real **39.** rational, real **41.** integer, rational, real **43–51.** Possible answers given. **43.** $-\sqrt{50}$ **45.** $\frac{11}{18}$ **47.** $\frac{3}{4}$ **49.** 3 **51.** −4.25 **53.** $x \geq 0$ **55.** $x \geq -3$ **57.** $x \geq -\frac{2}{5}$ **63.** 6.32 **65.** 7.75 **67.** −4.12 **69.** 3.46 **71.** 2.5×10^{6} **73.** 5.68×10^{15} **75.** J

Chapter 3 Study Guide and Review

1. rational number **2.** real numbers; irrational numbers **3.** relatively prime **4.** principal square root **5.** perfect square **6.** $\frac{3}{5}$ **7.** $\frac{1}{4}$ **8.** $\frac{21}{40}$ **9.** $\frac{2}{3}$ **10.** $\frac{2}{3}$ **11.** $\frac{3}{4}$ **12.** $\frac{-6}{13}$ **13.** $1\frac{2}{5}$ **14.** $\frac{5}{9}$ **15.** $\frac{1}{6}$ **16.** $-1\frac{1}{5}$ **17.** $7\frac{3}{5}$ **18.** $\frac{8}{15}$ **19.** −4 **20.** $2\frac{1}{4}$ **21.** $3\frac{1}{4}$ **22.** 6 **23.** $\frac{3}{8}$ **24.** $\frac{2}{9}$ **25.** −16 **26.** $1\frac{1}{4}$ **27.** 2 **28.** $1\frac{1}{6}$ **29.** $\frac{5}{18}$ **30.** $11\frac{3}{10}$ **31.** $4\frac{7}{20}$ **32.** $y = -21.8$ **33.** $z = -18$ **34.** $w = -\frac{5}{8}$ **35.** $p = 2$ **36.** $m > -\frac{1}{12}$ **37.** $t \geq -12$ **38.** $y \leq -3\frac{1}{4}$ **39.** $x > -\frac{1}{2}$ **40.** ±4 **41.** ±30 **42.** ±26 **43.** 5 **44.** $\frac{1}{2}$ **45.** 9 **46.** 89.4 in. **47.** 167.3 cm **48.** rational **49.** irrational **50.** not real **51.** irrational **52.** rational **53.** not real

Chapter 4

4-1 Exercises

1. Population: pet store customers; sample: 100 customers; possible bias: not all customers have dogs. **2.** systematic **3.** random **5.** systematic **7.** Population: students; sample: students who buy the entrée; possible bias: the students who buy the entrée may be the people who like the food in the cafeteria. **9.** Population: restaurant customers; sample: first four customers who order the cheese sauce; possible bias: if the customers ordered cheese sauce, then they probably like cheese. **11.** systematic **13.** stratified **15.** systematic **17 a.** Possible answer: Randomly select visitors leaving the zoo. **b.** Possible answer: Select every tenth visitor leaving the zoo. **c.** Possible answer: People visiting with children might visit the zoo only because they have children. **23.** $y = -7.2$ **25.** $c = -\frac{2}{7}$ **27.** $x > 25.6$

4-2 Exercises

1.

Nutrition in Potatoes			
	Baked Potato (100 g)	French Fries (100 g)	Potato Chips (100 g)
Fiber	2.4 g	3.2 g	4.5 g
Ca	10 mg	10 mg	24 mg
Mg	27 mg	22 mg	67 mg

2. 2, 3, 3, 7, 11, 13, 17, 17, 18, 20, 20, 27, 34, 34, 35, 35 **3.** 63, 66, 68, 73, 73, 75, 77, 80, 80, 81, 81, 90, 94, 95, 99

4.

Tens	Ones
0	1 6 7
1	8
2	0 2 6
3	5 6
4	7
5	3 6

Key: 1|8 means 18

5.

Democrats		Republicans
	3	2 6 7 8
6 6	4	1 2 3 4
8 7 6 4	5	3 4
8 4 1 1	6	

Key: |4|1 means 41; 6|4| means 46

7. 50, 51, 54, 58, 62, 66, 67, 71, 74, 75, 76, 76, 82

9.

Dollars	Cents
0.9	3 5 5
1.0	2 6
1.1	1 1 3 4 7
1.2	1 3 3 4
1.3	0 8

Key: 1.1|1 means $1.11

11.

Tens	Ones
4	3
5	7
6	5 8
7	2 2 3 5 6
8	1 2 4 8
9	1

Key: 5|7 means 57

13.

Energy Use in U.S.			
	1980	1990	2000
Fossil Fuels	89%	86%	85%
Nuclear Power	3%	7%	8%
Renewable Resources	7%	7%	7%

15.

Numbers		Time	
One	9	Night	12
Two	3	Day	4
Three	6	Supper-time	1
Ten	2	Bed-time	1
Twelve	1	Evening	1
Fourteen	1		

19. 5^{11} **21.** cannot combine **23.** population: students; sample: students on every other bus

4-3 Exercises

1. ≈ 34.43; 35; no mode **2.** 4.4; 4.4; 4.4 and 6.2 **3.** 5; 5; 5 **4.** ≈ 55.67; 56; no mode **5.** 2.39 million **6.** approximately 1.43 million **7.** 3.35 million **9.** 87.6; 88; 88 **11.** 5.85; 4.4; no mode **13.** approximately 74.33 million **15.** 25; 26; no mode; no outlier **17.** 11; 12; 10 and 13; 3 **19.** 4; 2; 2; 29 **21.** 1105 million miles; 484 million miles; no mode **29.** $14x - 45$ **31.** $x = 13$ **33.** $m = 100$ **35.** J

4-4 Exercises

1. 56; 42; 66 **2.** 6; 1.5; 4.5

3.

18 23.5 34 41.5 43

4.

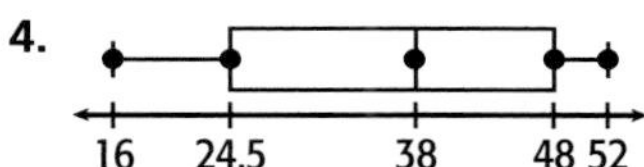

5. The medians are equal, but data set B has a much greater range. **6.** The range of the middle half of the data is greater for data set B. **7.** 30; 34.5; 46.5

9.

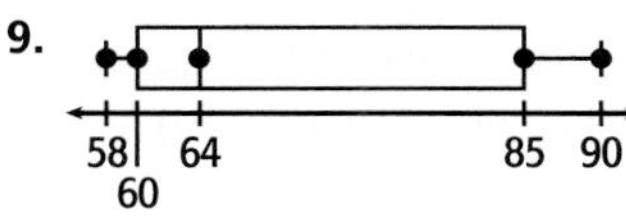

11. Data set Y has a greater median and range. **13.** 22; 78; 95 **15.** 38; 35; 57.5 **17.** 23; 9.5; 24.5

19.

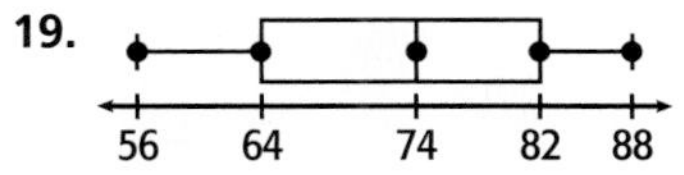

21.

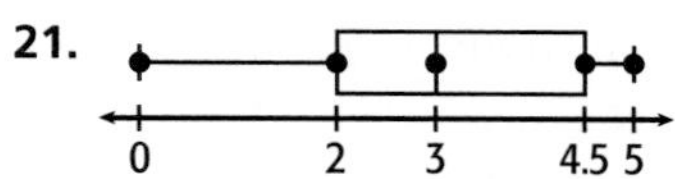

23.

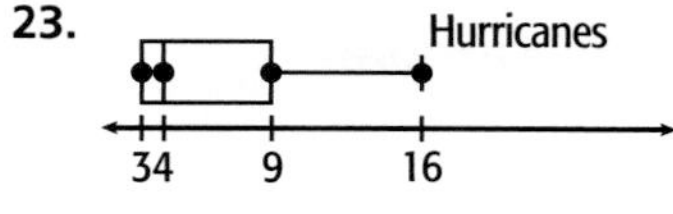

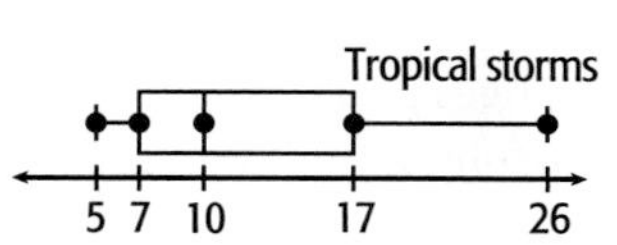

Possible answer: The median number of tropical storms is greater than the median number of hurricanes.

25. a. data set C **b.** data set A **c.** data set B **29.** −2 **31.** 10 **33.** graph B **35.** graph C

4-5 Exercises

1.

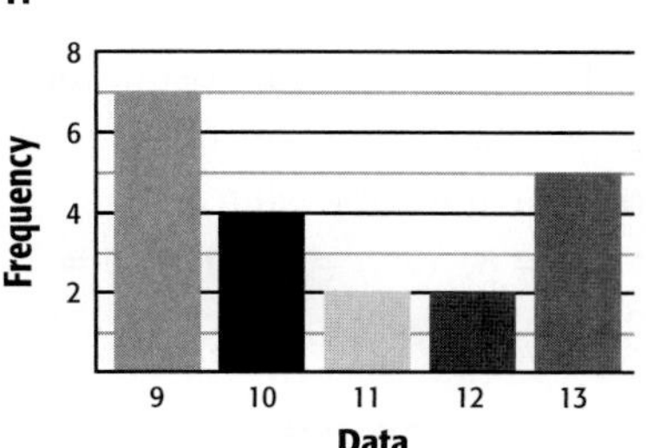

2.

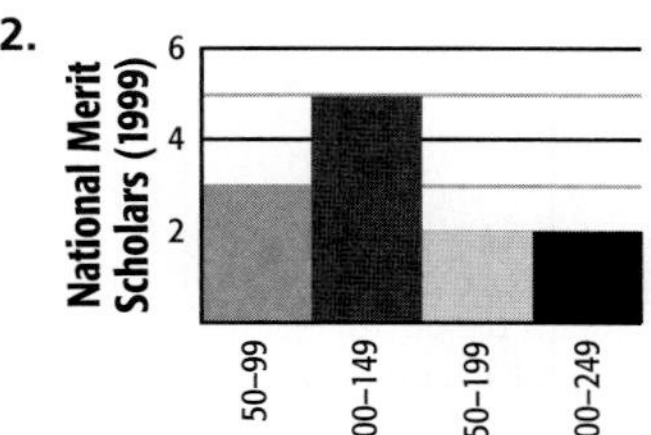

3. 74.1 years

5.

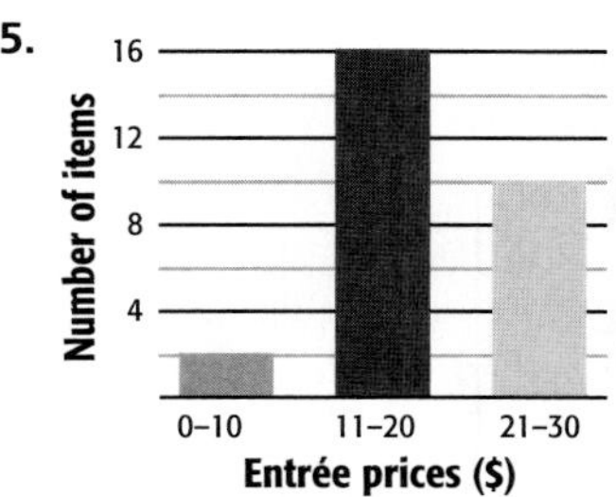

7.

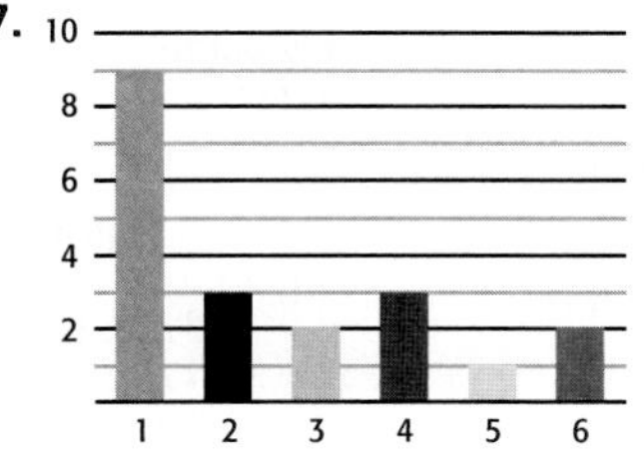

9. a. 34.9 hours **b.** $11.88
13. $x < 5$ **15.** $x \leq 2$ **17.** $x > 6$
19. $6 \geq x$ **21.** B

 4-6 Exercises

1–9. Possible answers given.
1. The scale does not start at zero, so changes appear exaggerated.
2. The intervals used in the histogram are not equal.
3. The fruits are all different sizes. A better comparison would be the same serving size of each fruit.
4. The sales are for different lengths of time. **5.** The graph has no scale, so it's impossible to compare the money earned.
7. The difference between the two groups' responses is only 3 people out of 1000. **9.** The areas of the sails distort the comparison. Your graph should use bars or pictures that are the same width.
15. $b = 6$ **17.** $a = 21$ **19.** $1.5 = h$
21. $f = 1.5$

 4-7 Exercises

1.

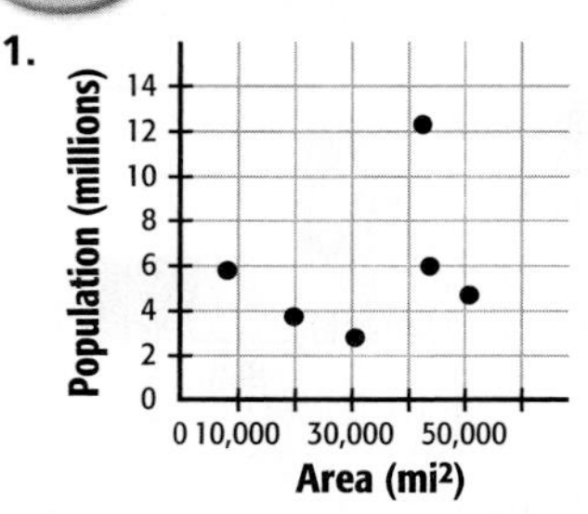

2. positive **3.** no correlation
4. 66°F
5.

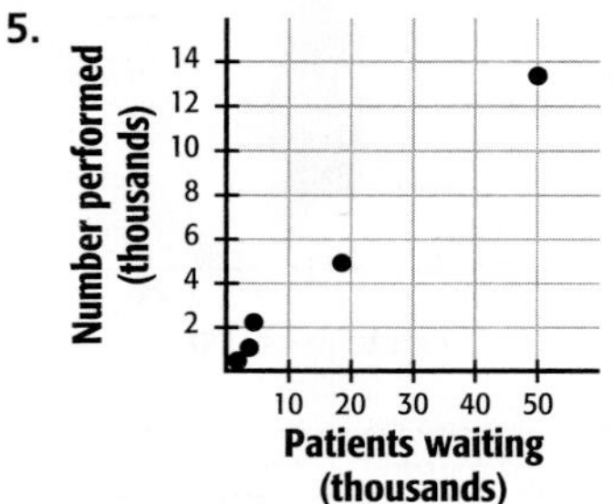

7. positive
9. There is a positive correlation between the pollen levels.
11. negative **15.** $x = 5$ **17.** $x = 6$
19. $x = 18$

Chapter 4 Extension

1. 2.4 **3.** 12.9 **5.** 2.3 **7.** 0 **9.** data set B **11. a.** week 1: 1.7; week 2: 3.1 **b.** week 2 **13.** Zero; the sum for the differences of the data values would be zero.

Chapter 4 Study Guide and Review

1. median; mode **2.** variability; variability; range **3.** line of best fit; scatter plot; correlation
4. population: moviegoers; sample: 25 people in line for a Star Wars movie; possible bias: people in line for Star Wars might have a preference for science fiction movies. **5.** population: community members; sample: 50 parents of middle-school-age children; possible bias: parents of middle-school-age children may support the field more than other community members.
6. population: constituents; sample: 75 constituents who visited the office; possible bias: constituents who visit the senator probably are strong supporters of the senator.
7.

Inaugural Age		Age at Death
3	4	6
7 7 2 1	5	6
	6	3 7
	7	
	8	3

Key: 3|4| means 43
|4|6 means 46

8. 760; 570; 500 **9.** 9.25; 9; 8, 9, and 10 **10.** 6; 6; 6 **11.** 3.1; 3.1; 3.1
12. 10; 80; 90 **13.** 32; 68; 99
14.

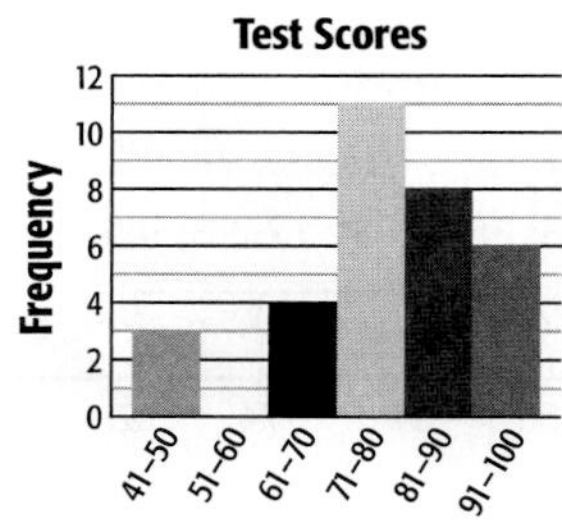

15.

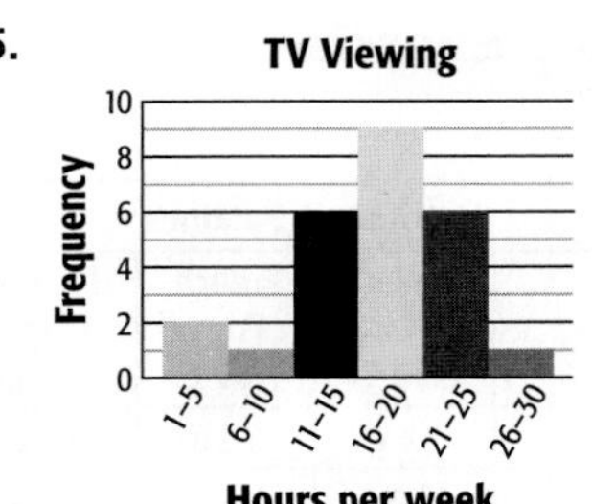

16. Possible answer: The symbols are different sizes even though they represent the same number of sightings. **17.** positive **18.** no correlation

Chapter 5

 5-1 Exercises

1. points A, B, C **2.** $\overleftrightarrow{BC}$
3. plane $\mathcal{Z}$ or plane ABC
4. $\overline{AB}$, $\overline{BC}$, $\overline{AC}$ **5.** $\overrightarrow{BA}$, $\overrightarrow{BC}$, $\overrightarrow{CB}$
7. $\angle LJM$, $\angle MJK$ **9.** $\angle LJM$ and $\angle MJK$ **11.** 115° **13.** points V, W, X, Y **15.** plane $\mathcal{N}$ or plane VWX
17. $\overrightarrow{WV}$, $\overrightarrow{VW}$, $\overrightarrow{WY}$, $\overrightarrow{YW}$, $\overrightarrow{WX}$
19. $\angle DEH$, $\angle GEF$ **21.** $\angle FEG$ and $\angle HED$ **23.** 117° **25.** False
27. False **29.** False **31.** False
33. False **35. a.** 145° **b.** They are supplementary angles.
41. 18; 18; 29 **43.** B

5-2 Exercises

1. $\angle 1 \cong \angle 4 \cong \angle 5 \cong \angle 8$ (45°); $\angle 2 \cong \angle 3 \cong \angle 6 \cong \angle 7$ (135°)
2. 59° **3.** 59° **4.** 121° **5.** 59°
7. 60° **9.** 120° **11.** $\angle 4$, $\angle 5$, $\angle 8$
13. Possible answers: $\angle 1$ and $\angle 2$, $\angle 1$ and $\angle 3$, $\angle 3$ and $\angle 4$.
15. 51° **17.** 90°
19. Possible answer:

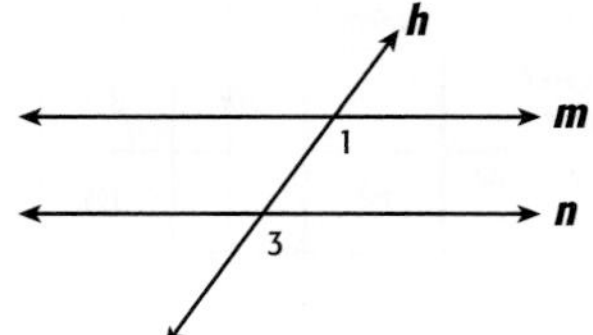

11. $26.25 per hour
13. $0.77 per slice **15.** $2.49/yard; $2.26/yard; 5 yards
17. $1.37/gal; $1.42/gal; 10 gal
19. a. Super-Cell: $0.10/min; Easy Phone: $0.11/min
b. Super-Cell offers a better rate.
21. a. Tom: $25\frac{3}{8}$ frames per hour; Cherise: 27 frames per hour; Tina: $28\frac{3}{8}$ frames per hour
b. Tina **c.** $1\frac{5}{8}$ **d.** 24 **25.** −4
27. −5 **29.** −4.4 **31.** D

7-3 Exercises

1. 12 in./1 ft **2.** 8 pt/1 gal
3. 1 m/100 cm **4.** 91.25 gal
5. 7.5 mi/h **6.** 0.09 m/s
7. ≈ 1.14 g **9.** 1 yd/36 in.
11. 585 ft **13.** 57,600 bricks
15. 900 radios **17.** 4 hot dogs
19. 4.98 mi **21.** A ≈ 22.88 mi/h; B ≈ 23.16 mi/h; C ≈ 21.76 mi/h
23. 200 times **29.** 14 units^2
31. 226.9 in^2 **33.** 3.8 mi^2

7-4 Exercises

1. yes **2.** yes **3.** no **4.** yes
5. no; $\frac{1}{8} \neq \frac{8}{56}$ **6.** $x = 1$ **7.** $n = 8$
8. $d = 2$ **9.** $h = 6$ **10.** $f = 9.75$
11. $t = 2$ **12.** $s = 9$ **13.** $q = 12.5$
14. ≈ 3.3 cm **15.** no **17.** no
19. yes; $\frac{18}{12} = \frac{15}{10}$ **21.** $b = 3$
23. $y = 6$ **25.** $n = 4$ **27.** $d = 0.5$
29. $\frac{6}{3}, \frac{18}{9}$ **31.** $\frac{66}{21}, \frac{22}{7}$ **33.** $\frac{0.25}{4}, \frac{1}{16}$
35. 12 molecules **37. a.** about 1.53:1 **b.** about 134.6 mm Hg
41. $-1\frac{1}{4}$ **43.** $11\frac{17}{100}$

7-5 Exercises

1. no **2.** yes
3.

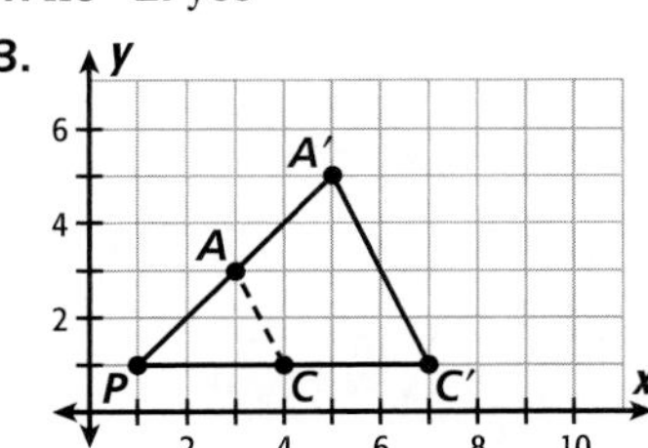

4.

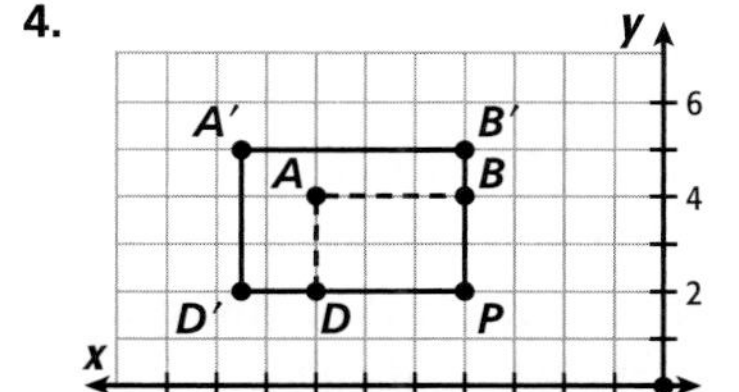

5. $A'(1.5, -1)$; $B'(1, -2.5)$; $C'(4, -3)$; $D'(5, -0.5)$ **6.** $A'(16, 4)$; $B'(28, 4)$; $C'(20, 12)$ **7.** no
9.

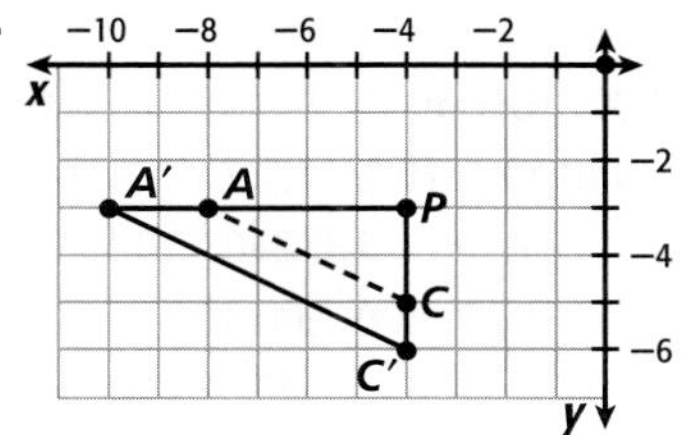

11. $A'(-9, 6)$; $B'(15, 12)$; $C'(-6, -9)$ **13.** 3 **15.** Yes
21. 24 units^2 **23.** 21 units^2

7-6 Exercises

1. ≈ 5.4 in. **2.** ≈ 14.7 cm **3.** *A* and *C* are similar. **5.** ≈ 22.9 ft
7. similar **9.** similar **11.** $x = 6$ ft
13. $x = 24$ ft **15.** yes; $\frac{1}{15}$ or $\frac{4 \text{ in.}}{5 \text{ ft}}$
17. 24 ft **21.** 1256 mm^3
23. 2044.3 cm^3 **25.** D

7-7 Exercises

1. 1 in:1.25 ft **2.** 20.25 m
3. 0.0085 in. **4.** 7.5 mm **5.** 52 ft
6. 27 in. **7.** 1 cm = 1.5 m
9. 0.023 mm **11.** 20 in. **13.** 2 in.
15. 0.5 in. **17.** 18 ft **19.** 58.5 ft
21. about 580 mi **23–27.** The scale is 1.2 cm:36 in. **23.** ≈ 18 in.
25. No; each wall is only ≈ 45 in. wide. **27.** ≈ 298 ft^2 **31.** no **33.** no

7-8 Exercises

1. reduces **2.** enlarges
3. preserves **4.** preserves
5. reduces **6.** enlarges **7.** $\frac{1}{24}$
8. 14 in. **9.** 0.000028 mm
11. preserves **13.** reduces
15. reduces **17.** 7.5 ft **19.** $\frac{12}{1}$
21. $\frac{1}{45}$ **23.** $\frac{1}{12.5}$ **25.** $\frac{1}{28}$ **27.** 630 ft
33. ≈ 1869.4 ft^2 **35.** 1256 cm^2
37. $0.17 per apple **39.** A

7-9 Exercises

1. 4:1 **2.** 16:1 **3.** 64:1 **4.** width: 30 in.; height: 10 in. **5.** 72 min
6. 7:1 **7.** 49:1 **9.** 32 cm **11.** 2 cm; 8 cubes **13.** 4 cm; 64 cubes
15. 5 cm; 125 cubes
17. 1,000,000 cm^3 **19.** 256,000
21. 14.58 oz **25.** Possible answers: $\frac{6}{10}, \frac{9}{15}$ **27.** Possible answers: $\frac{8}{22}, \frac{12}{33}$ **29.** 1.5 ft **31.** 18 ft **33.** D

Chapter 7 Extension

1. 0.777 **3.** 0.017 **5.** 45 ft
7. 16.7 m **9.** 137.7 m **11.** 11.7 yd
13. 10 ft **15.** 45°

Chapter 7 Study Guide and Review

1. ratio; proportion **2.** rate; unit rate **3.** similar; scale factor
4. dilation; enlargement; reduction **5–7.** Possible answers given. **5.** $\frac{1}{2}, \frac{2}{4}$ **6.** $\frac{3}{6}, \frac{4}{8}$ **7.** $\frac{7}{12}, \frac{14}{24}$
8. yes **9.** no **10.** yes **11.** no
12. $0.30 per disk; $0.29 per disk; 75 disks **13.** $3.75 per box; $3.75 per box; unit prices are the same.
14. $2.89 per divider; $4.00 per divider; 8-pack **15.** 90,000 m/h
16. 4500 ft/min **17.** $583\frac{1}{3}$ m/min
18. $80\frac{2}{3}$ ft/s **19.** 2160 m/h
20. $x = 15$ **21.** $h = 6$ **22.** $w = 21$
23. $y = 29\frac{1}{3}$
24.

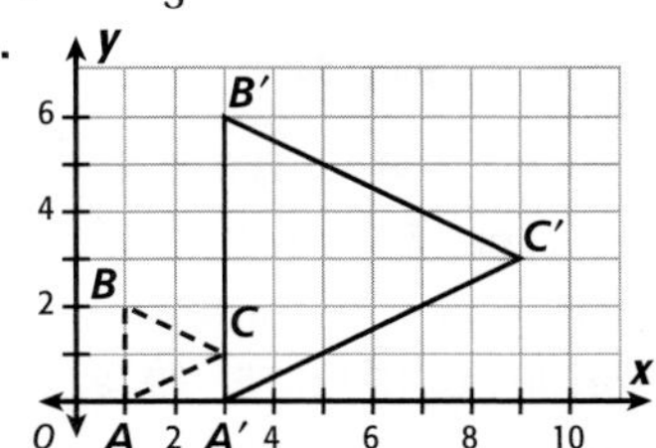

25.

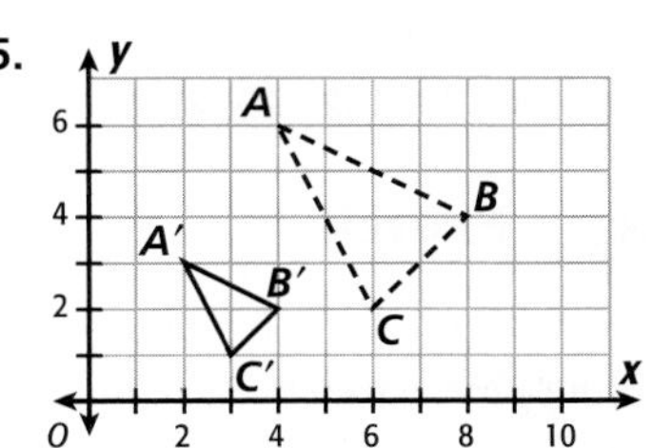

Selected Answers

26.

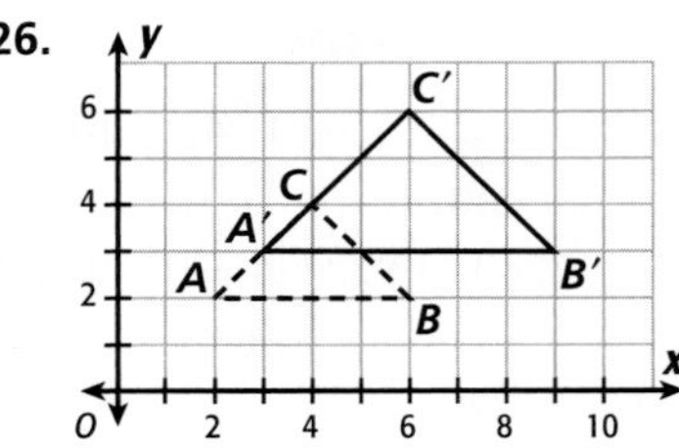

27. 12.5 in. **28.** 3.125 in. **29.** 64.8 m **30.** 6.6 in. **31.** $2.\overline{7}$:1; enlarges **32.** 2.5:1; enlarges **33.** 1:100; reduces **34.** 1:1; preserves **35.** 3:1 **36.** 9:1 **37.** 27:1

Chapter 8

8-1 Exercises

1. $\frac{3}{10}$ **2.** 46% **3.** 62.5% **4.** $\frac{17}{20}$ **5.** 40% **6.** $\frac{8}{25}$ **7.** 0.875 **8.** $33\frac{1}{3}$% **9.** 10% **11.** $\frac{3}{5}$ **13.** 0.32 **15.** $\frac{109}{200}$ **17.** 40%, 30%, 20%, 10% **19.** 40%, 30%, 25%, 5% **21.** 85% **23. a.** $\frac{4}{25}$; 0.16 **b.** 23% **27.** perpendicular **29.** parallel **31.** D

8-2 Exercises

1. 49.3% **2.** 19.9% **3.** 70.6% **4.** 31.5 pages **5.** 300% **7.** 1% **9.** 1.0% **11.** 30 **13.** 2.6 **15.** 266 **17. a.** 30 **b.** 45 **c.** 150 **19. a.** 100 **b.** 50 **c.** 25 **21.** 21.5% **23.** 16 **29.** irrational **31.** not real

8-3 Exercises

1. 34.4 **2.** 168 **3.** 166.7 **4.** 320 **5.** ≈ 1.7 oz **6.** 28 ft **7.** 315 **9.** 850 **11.** 16.7 **13.** 570 **15.** 336 **17. a.** 300 **b.** 150 **c.** 75 **19. a.** 40 **b.** 20 **c.** 10 **21.** 48.2% **23. a.** 49.5% **b.** 50.5% **c.** 49.1% **d.** 50.9% **27.** 882 **29.** 45, 65

8-4 Exercises

1. 38% increase **2.** 65% decrease **3.** 100% increase **4.** 64% increase **5.** 25% decrease **6.** 34% increase **7.** 96.6% increase **8.** \$9773.60 **9.** 9% increase **11.** 44% decrease **13.** 20% decrease **15.** ≈ 8.6% **17.** 23% decrease **19.** 30% decrease **21.** 17% decrease **23.** \$600 **25.** 200 **27.** 50 **29.** 40% **31. a.** \$84 **b.** \$156 **c.** \$104 **d.** $56\frac{2}{3}$% **33.** about 8361 ft **37.** 364 m^2 **39.** 84 yd^2

8-5 Exercises

Note: All answers are estimates.

1. 100 **2.** 24 **3.** 25% **4.** 21 **5.** 50% **6.** 900 **7.** \$4.50 **9.** 50% **11.** 440 **13.** 10% **15.** B **17.** A **19.** C **21.** 150 **23.** 250 **25.** 1600 **27.** 33% **29.** 400 **31.** 750 **33.** 50% **35.** 50% **39.** 120 ft^3 **41.** 132 in^3 **43.** 0.48 ft^3 **45.** D

8-6 Exercises

1. \$510 **2.** \$5.18 **3.** 22.5% **4.** \$499 **5.** \$389.50 **7.** 18% **9.** \$330 **11.** \$2.16 **13.** \$1963.75 **15.** \$2800 plus 3% of sales: \$3100 to \$3400 a month **17. a.** \$64,208 **b.** \$14,275.95 **c.** ≈ 20.0% **d.** ≈ 22.2% **21.** 40:3 **23.** 10,000:1

8-7 Exercises

1. \$1794.38; \$10,044.38 **2.** 5 years **3.** \$1635.30 **4.** 5.5% **5.** \$23,032.50 **7.** \$1846.50 **9.** \$33.75, \$258.75 **11.** \$446.25, \$4696.25 **13.** \$14.89, \$411.89 **15.** \$87.50, \$787.50 **17.** \$270, \$1770 **19.** 6% **25.** 14.4 **27.** $16\frac{2}{3}$% **29.** 5

Chapter 8 Extension

1. \$12,597.12 **3.** \$14,802.44 **5.** \$15,208.16 **7.** \$2462.88 **9.** \$6744.25

Chapter 8 Study Guide and Review

1. percent **2.** percent change **3.** commission **4.** simple interest; principal; rate of interest **5.** 0.4375 **6.** 43.75% **7.** $1\frac{1}{8}$ **8.** 112.5% **9.** $\frac{7}{10}$ **10.** 0.7 **11.** $\frac{1}{250}$ **12.** 0.4% **13.** 39% **14.** 4200 ft **15.** 3030 mi **16.** 5 lb 7 oz **17.** 20% **18.** 472,750% **19.** ≈ 12.38% **20.** ≈ 25% **21.** ≈ 25% **22.** ≈ 13 **23.** ≈ 16 **24.** ≈ 6 **25.** ≈ 4.5 **26.** \$10,990 **27.** \$3.04 **28.** \$1796.88 **29.** \$500 **30.** 7% **31.** $\frac{1}{2}$ yr, or 6 mo **32.** 2-year loan; \$50

Chapter 9

9-1 Exercises

1. 0.55; 0.45 **2.** 0.262 **3.** 0.738

4.

Team	A	B	C	D
Prob.	0.25	0.3	0.15	0.3

5. $\frac{1}{3}, \frac{1}{3}, \frac{1}{6}, \frac{1}{6}$ **7.** 0.155 **9.** 0.319 **11.** 1 **13.** 0.465

15.

Person	Probability
Jamal	0.1
Elroy	0.2
Tina	0.2
Mel	0.2
Gina	0.3

17. 0.56 **21.** 59 in^2 **23.** ≈ 354.43 yd^2 **25.** B

9-2 Exercises

1. 0.34 **2.** 0.11 **3.** ≈ 0.186; ≈ 0.281; more likely to listen to a rock station **5.** 0.433 **7.** 0.26 **9.** 0.06 **11.** 0.36 **13.** 0.308 **17.** $x = 2$ **19.** $b = 5$ **21.** D

9-3 Exercises

1–9. Possible answers are given.

1. 90% **2.** 50% **3.** 60% **5.** 30% **7.** 30% **9.** 50% **13.** 84 ft tall **15.** 42 ft tall **17.** B

9-4 Exercises

1. $\frac{1}{2}$ **2.** $\frac{1}{3}$ **3.** $\frac{1}{6}$ **4.** $\frac{1}{36}$ **5.** $\frac{1}{4}$ **6.** $\frac{5}{18}$ **7.** $\frac{5}{18}$ **9.** $\frac{5}{6}$ **11.** $\frac{1}{36}$ **13.** 1 **15.** $\frac{1}{4}$ **17.** $\frac{1}{8}$ **19.** $\frac{3}{8}$ **21.** $\frac{7}{8}$ **23.** $\frac{1}{4}$ **25. a.** $\frac{1}{4}$ **b.** $\frac{3}{4}$ **27.** 90% **29.** 0.375 **31.** $\frac{39}{50}$

11. $4f^2g + 4fg^2$ **13.** $9b - 12 - 4b^2$ **15.** $15s^2 + 2s - 2$ **17.** $3x^2 - 14x + 15$ **19.** $4m^2 - 24m$ **21.** $15mn$ **23.** $40 - 1000d^2$ **25.** $82xy + 82y$ in^2 **27.** -13 **29.** 30 **31.** $x \geq 5$ **33.** $x = \frac{40}{3}$

13-3 Exercises

1. $4x^3 + 3x + 5$ **2.** $32x - 12$ **3.** $9m^2n + 8mn$ **4.** $8b^2 + 2b + 1$ **5.** $11ab^2 + 3ab + ab^2 - 4$ **6.** $5h^4j + 2hj^3 - 4hj - 1$ **7.** $128 + 32w$ in. **9.** $5g^2 + g - 1$ **11.** $-h^6 + 9h^4 - h$ **13.** $11t^2 - 4t + 10$ **15.** $-w^2 - 6w - 3$ **17.** $3y^2 + xy$ **19.** $-3s^4t - 6st^3 + 4st^2 + 3st^4$ **21.** $8w^2y + wy^2 - 5wy$ **23.** $0.75n^2 + 8n + 16$ **25.** $4x^2 - 48x + 500$ miles **29.** 512 cm^3 **31.** 48 **33.** $\frac{90}{7}$ **35.** C

13-4 Exercises

1. $-4x^2y$ **2.** $4x - 3xy^4$ **3.** $-2x^2 + 7x - 4$ **4.** $6y^2 + 3y - 5$ **5.** $-2b^3 + 5b^2 - b + 4$ **6.** $-3b^2 + 4b + 10$ **7.** $6m^2n + 2mn^2 - 2mn$ **8.** $3x^2 - 8x - 2$ **9.** $-2x^2y - 5xy + 10x - 8$ **10.** $-6ab^2 - 7a^2b + 7ab - 6$ **11.** $-3x^3 + 7x^2 - 10x + 18$ in^3 **13.** $-2v + 4v^2$ **15.** $-4xy^2 - 2xy$ **17.** $6a - 5$ **19.** $3x^2 - x + 3$ **21.** $-5p^3 - 4p^2 - 2p^2t^2 + 8pt^2$ **23.** $3s^2 - 9s - 5$ **25.** $g^2h - 3gh$ **27.** $-3pq^2 - 11p^2q + 4pq$ **29.** $a^2 - 2a + 11$ cm^2 **31.** $25y + 16.25$ dollars **35.** $1\frac{1}{24}$ **37.** $4\frac{23}{40}$

13-5 Exercises

1. $-8s^3t^5$ **2.** $6x^6y^6$ **3.** $-24h^6j^{10}$ **4.** $15m^5$ **5.** $6hm - 8h^2$ **6.** $3a^3b^2 - 3a^2b^3$ **7.** $-2x^3 + 8x^2 - 24x$ **8.** $10c^3d^4 - 20c^5d^3 + 15c^3d^2$ **9.** $A = \frac{1}{2}b_1h + \frac{1}{2}b_2h$; 70 in^2 **11.** $3g^3h^8$ **13.** $-s^5t^4$ **15.** $8z^3 - 6z^2$ **17.** $-6c^4d^3 + 12c^2d^3$ **19.** $-20s^4t^3 - 24s^3t^3 + 8s^4t^4$ **21.** $-36b^6$ **23.** $6a^3b^6$ **25.** $-2m^5 + 12m^3$ **27.** $x^4 - x^5y^4$ **29.** $2f^2g^2 + f^3g^2 - f^2g^5$ **31.** $12m^4p^8 - 6m^3p^7 + 15m^4p^5$

33. a.

$220p - pa$	$226p - pa$
$205p - \frac{1}{2}pa$	$211p - \frac{1}{2}pa$

b. $-6p$

37. acute equilateral **39.** right scalene **41.** H

13-6 Exercises

1. $xy + 3x - 4y - 12$ **2.** $x^2 + 4x - 12$ **3.** $6m^2 + 4m - 32$ **4.** $2h^2 + 11h + 15$ **5.** $m^2 - 8m + 15$ **6.** $3b^2 + 7bc + 2c^2$ **7.** $200 - 60x + 4x^2$ ft^2 **8.** $x^2 + 6x + 9$ **9.** $b^2 - 16$ **10.** $x^2 - 10x + 25$ **11.** $x^2 + 3x - 10$ **13.** $w^2 + 8w + 15$ **15.** $6m^2 + 7m - 3$ **17.** $8t^2 + 2t - 1$ **19.** $6n^2 + 14bn - 12b^2$ **21.** $x^2 - 8x + 16$ **23.** $x^2 - 9$ **25.** $9x^2 - 6x + 1$ **27.** $m^2 - 25$ **29.** $q^2 + 9q + 20$ **31.** $g^2 - 9$ **33.** $10t^2 + 7t - 6$ **35.** $4a^2 + 20ab + 25b^2$ **37.** $w^2 - 25$ **39.** $15r^2 - 22rs + 8s^2$ **41.** $p^2 + 20p + 100$ **43.** $(M + \frac{1}{4}M)(V + b) = c$; $\frac{5}{4}MV + \frac{5}{4}Mb = c$ **47.** $\frac{2}{9}$ **49.** 0

Chapter 13 Extension

1. $3a^3$ **3.** $6a^2b$ **5.** $3ab^4c^4$ **7.** $2x^3 + 3x^2$ **9.** $p^4q^3 - 4p^5q$ **11.** $3a^3b^5 - 2a^9$ **13.** $2m^2n^2(3n^2 - 4m)$ **15.** $5z^3(3 + 5z^3)$ **17.** $6a^2(4 + 3a + a^5)$

Chapter 13 Study Guide and Review

1. polynomial; degree **2.** FOIL; binomials **3.** binomial; trinomial **4.** trinomial **5.** not a polynomial **6.** not a polynomial **7.** monomial **8.** not a polynomial **9.** binomial **10.** 8 **11.** 4 **12.** 3 **13.** 5 **14.** 6 **15.** $6t^2 - 2t + 1$ **16.** $11gh - 9g^2h$ **17.** $12mn - 6m$ **18.** $8a^2 - 10b$ **19.** $26st^2 - 15t$ **20.** $6x^2 - 2x + 5$ **21.** $4x^4 + x^2 - x + 7$ **22.** $3h^2 + 8h + 9$ **23.** $xy^2 - 2x^2y + 2xy$ **24.** $13n^2 + 12$ **25.** $5x^2 - 6$ **26.** $-w^2 - 12w + 14$ **27.** $-4x^2 + 14x - 12$ **28.** $4ab^2 - 11ab + 4a^2b$ **29.** $-p^3q^2 - 5p^2q^2 - 2pq^2$ **30.** $5s^2t^3 - 10s^2t^4 + 35st^3$ **31.** $12a^4b^3 + 30a^3b^3 - 36a^3b + 24a^2b^2$ **32.** $6m^3 - 15m^2 + 3m$ **33.** $-24gh^5 + 12g^3h^3 - 30h^2 + 12gh$ **34.** $2j^5k^3 - \frac{3}{2}j^4k^4 + j^6k^5$ **35.** $-8x^6y^{12} + 10x^7y^{14} - 14x^3y^6 + 6x^3y^7$ **36.** $p^2 - 8p + 15$ **37.** $b^2 + 10b + 24$ **38.** $4r^2 + 19r + 5$ **39.** $2a^2 - 5ab - 12b^2$ **40.** $m^2 - 16m + 64$ **41.** $4t^2 - 25$ **42.** $8b^2 + 4bt - 40t^2$ **43.** $100 - 4x^2$ **44.** $y^2 + 20y + 100$

Chapter 14

14-1 Exercises

1. $\in$ **2.** $\notin$ **3.** Yes, $E \subset R$. **4.** No, $P \not\subset S$. **5.** finite **6.** infinite **7.** $\in$ **9.** Yes, $F \subset T$. **11.** No, $P \not\subset O$. **13.** infinite **15.** finite **17.** $\in$ **19.** $\in$ **21.** $\in$ **23.** finite **25.** infinite **27.** finite **29.** {25} **31.** femur $\in$ {human bones} **33.** Miami $\in$ {state capitals} **37.** $-4m^2 + 12m - 24$ **39.** $-11x^2y + 4xy^2 + 16xy$ **41.** F

14-2 Exercises

1. {2, 4, 6} **2.** {10, 12, 14} **3.** $\{x|2 \leq x \leq 5\}$ **4.** $\{x|0 \leq x \leq 7\}$ **5.** {1, 2, 3, 4, 5, 6, 8, 10, 12} **6.** $\{x|x > 0\}$ **7.** {integers} **8.** {rational numbers} **9.** {−4} **11.** {1, 3, 5} **13.** {−12, −10, −8, −6, −4, 0} **15.** {real numbers} **17.** $F \cup G = \{-2, -1, 0, 1, 2\}$; $F \cap G = \{-2, 0, 2\}$ **19.** $R \cup M = \{x|x < 6 \text{ or } x \geq 7\}$; $R \cap M = \varnothing$ **21.** $A \cup B$ = {integers}; $A \cap B = \varnothing$ **23.** $P \cup M$ = {even integers}; $P \cap M$ = {positive multiples of 2} **25.** {covert, flock, gaggle, plump, skein, bank, bevy, herd, team, wedge} **27.** Possible answer: {crows} and {starlings} **31.** 49 **33.** 13 **35.** H

14-3 Exercises

1. Ron: 2, 5, 8; Ron and Eve: 4, 6, 7; Eve: 9, 10, 14

2.

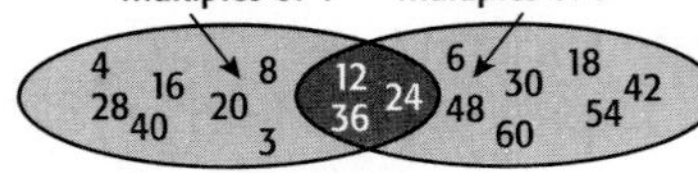

3. $A \cap C = C, A \cap B = \{3, 6\},$ $B \cap C = \varnothing; A \cup C = A,$ $A \cup B = \{2, 3, 4, 5, 6, 8, 9, 10, 12, 15\},$ $B \cup C = \{2, 3, 4, 6, 9, 12, 15\}; C \subset A$

4. $M \cap N = \{x | 5 < x \leq 7\};$ $A \cup B = \{\text{all real numbers}\}$; none

5.

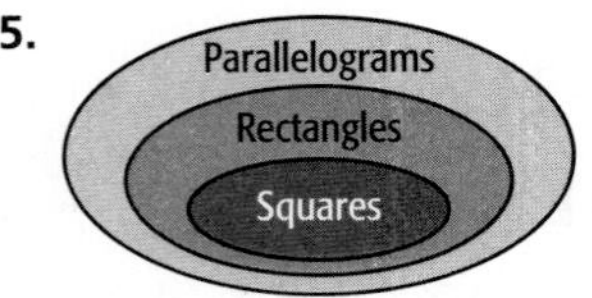

7. Integers from −3 to 5: 1, 2, 3, 4, 5; both: −3, −2, −1, 0; Integers from −6 to 0: −6, −5, −4

9. $Q \cap T = T, Q \cap Z = \varnothing,$ $Z \cap T = \varnothing; Q \cup T = Q, Q \cup Z =$ $\{1, 3, 4, 7, 8, 10, 12, 14, 15, 16\},$ $T \cup Z = \{1, 4, 7, 10, 15, 16\}; T \subset Q$

11.

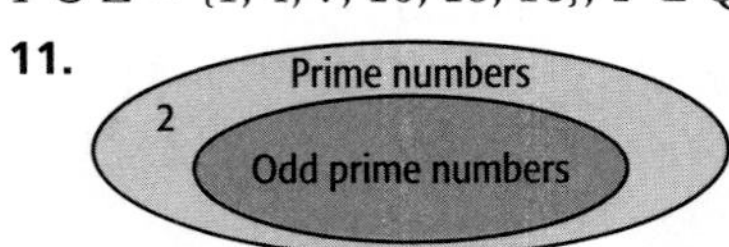

13.

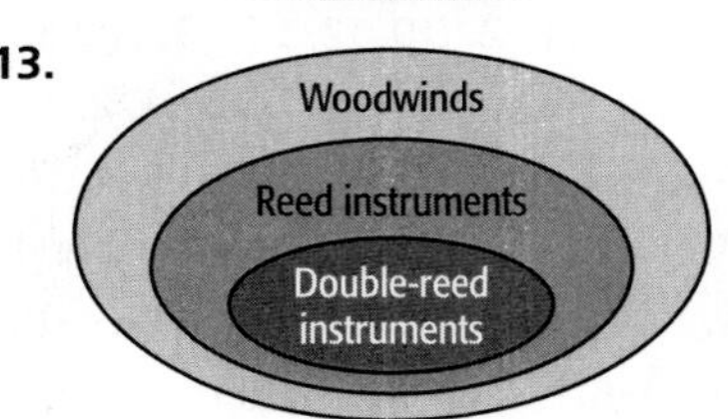

19. 226.08 in^3 **21.** $83\frac{1}{3}$ cm^3

14-4 Exercises

1–13. Possible examples given.

1.

Example	P	Q	P and Q
58 in. tall, 11 years old	T	T	T
40 in. tall, 7 years old	T	F	F
62 in. tall, 12 years old	F	T	F
63 in. tall, 8 years old	F	F	F

2.

Example	P	Q	P and Q
$x = 6$	T	T	T
$x = 8$	T	F	F
$x = 9$	F	T	F
$x = 7$	F	F	F

3.

Example	P	Q	P or Q
7 A.M., 65° outside	T	T	T
3 A.M., 82° outside	T	F	T
4 P.M., 30° outside	F	T	T
1 P.M., 90° outside	F	F	F

4.

Example	P	Q	P or Q
Live in AL, vacation in FL	T	T	T
Live in FL, are home	T	F	T
Live in TX, vacation in Mexico	F	T	T
Live in MI, are home	F	F	F

5.

Example	P	Q	P and Q
Blond hair, size 9	T	T	T
Blond hair, size 10	T	F	F
Red hair, size 9	F	T	F
Brown hair, size 11	F	F	F

7.

Example	P	Q	P and Q
ABCD is a rectangle, perimeter 25 cm	T	T	T
ABCD is a rectangle, perimeter 22 cm	T	F	F
ABCD is a trapezoid, perimeter 25 cm	F	T	F
ABCD is a trapezoid, perimeter 20 cm	F	F	F

9.

Example	P	Q	P or Q
10 A.M., math	T	T	T
10 A.M., science	T	F	T
3 P.M., math	F	T	T
5 P.M., at the movies	F	F	F

11.

Example	P	Q	P or Q
The word is *strong*.	T	T	T
The word is *wide*.	T	F	T
The word is *wisdom*.	F	T	T
The word is *smile*.	F	F	F

13.

Example	P	Q	P and Q	P or Q
20 yrs old, no drivers ed	T	F	F	T
14 yrs old, no drivers ed	F	F	F	F
16 yrs old, drivers ed	F	T	F	T
17 yrs old, drivers ed	T	T	T	T

15. Disjunction; if either condition is met, the warranty expires.
17. conjunction; possible answer:

Example	P	Q	P and Q
37 yrs old, lived in U.S. all his life	T	T	T
42 yrs old, lived in U.S. 12 yrs	T	F	F
21 yrs old, lived in U.S. 20 yrs	F	T	F
5 yrs old, lived in U.S. all his life	F	F	F

21. 0.625 **23.** 0.71 **25.** $\frac{11}{10}$, or $1\frac{1}{10}$
27. $\frac{6}{25}$ **29.** B

14-5 Exercises

1. Ron eats peanuts. Ron has an allergic reaction. **2.** A number is divisible by 4. The number is even. **3.** A pot is watched. The pot never boils. **4.** Figure *A* has 5 sides. **5.** $x + 2 = 9$ **6.** No conclusion can be made. **7.** $x - 1 = 6; x = 7$ **9.** It is the first Friday of the month. The garden club will hold a meeting. **11.** The expression $x^3 - 4x + 2$ is a trinomial. **13.** Quadrilateral *XYWZ* is a square. **25.** 60 **27.** D

14-6 Exercises

1. *A*: 2; *B*: 3; *C*: 2; *D*: 5; *E*: 2; *F*: 2; *G*: 0; no **2.** *A*: 2; *B*: 4; *C*: 2; yes **3.** no **4.** yes; possible answer: *A-B-C-B-A* **5.** *M*: 2; *R*: 2; *S*: 4; *T*: 2; yes **7.** yes; possible answer: *M-R-S-T-S-M* **9.** connected; *A*: 3; *B*: 2; *C*: 2; *D*: 3; *E*: 4; no **11.** land masses; bridges and tunnels **13.** 13 **15.** Yes; there is a path from each vertex to any other. **19.** $x = -1$ **21.** $z = \frac{11}{12}$ **23.** $x = 9$ **25.** $r = 3$ **27.** B

14-7 Exercises

1.–9. Possible answers given.

1. *A-B-C-D-A* **2.** *W-S-V-R-T-W* **3.** *A-C-B-D-A*; 24 mi **5.** *A-D-F-E-C-B-A* **7.** *B-T-N-M-R-B*; 43 mi **9.** *J-K-M-L-N-J*; 226 mi **11.** *S-A-C-B-S*; *S-A-B-C-S*; *S-B-C-A-S*; *S-B-A-C-S*; *S-C-A-B-S*; *S-C-B-A-S* **17.** $-3x^3y^2 - 2x^2y$ **19.** $18x^2 - 36x - 6$

Chapter 14 Study Guide Review

1. Euler circuit, vertex **2.** truth table **3.** Venn diagram; intersection **4.** empty set **5.** $\in$ **6.** $\notin$ **7.** $\subset$ **8.** finite **9.** infinite **10.** $P \cap Q = \{2, 4\}$; $P \cup Q = \{0, 1, 2, 3, 4, 5, 6\}$ **11.** $E \cap O = \varnothing$; $E \cup O = \{\text{integers}\}$ **12.** $H \cap R = \{x|3 < x < 7\}$; $H \cup R = \{\text{real numbers}\}$ **13.** intersection: {1, 2, 3, 6}; union: {1, 2, 3, 4, 6, 9, 12, 18}; subsets: none

14.

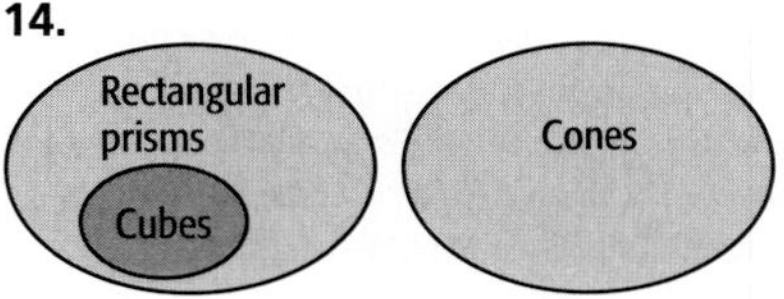

15.

Example	P	Q	P and Q
5 ft tall, 13 yrs old	T	T	T
5 ft tall, 10 yrs old	T	F	F
6 ft 2 in. tall, 13 yrs old	F	T	F
6 ft 1 in. tall, 10 yrs old	F	F	F

16.

Example	P	Q	P and Q
ABCD parallelogram, *EFGH* square	T	T	T
ABCD parallelogram, *EFGH* rhombus.	T	F	F
ABCD not a parallelogram, *EFGH* square	F	T	F
ABCD not a parallelogram, *EFGH* trapezoid	F	F	F

17.

Example	P	Q	P or Q
9-min mile, 50 sit-ups	T	T	T
9-min mile, 40 sit-ups	T	F	T
11-min mile, 50 sit-ups	F	T	T
12-min mile, 35 sit-ups	F	F	F

18.

Example	P	Q	P or Q
Graduated college, designs bridges	T	T	T
Graduated college, college professor	T	F	T
Graduated high school, designs bridges	F	T	T
Graduated high school, manager of a shoe store	F	F	F

19. No conclusion can be made. **20.** No conclusion can be made. **21.** Figure *ABCD* is a polygon. **22.** no **23.** *Y-X-Z-W-B-Y* or *Y-X-B-Z-W-Y*, (or reverses); 26 in.

Selected Answers

Photo

Cover (all), Pronk & Associates.; **Title Page** (all), Pronk & Associates.; ***Master Icons*** — teens (all), Sam Dudgeon/HRW.

Problem Solving Handbook: xix, Thomas Wiewandt/Visions of America, LLC/PictureQuest; xxi, xxii, xxiii, Victoria Smith/HRW; xxvi, xxvii, Sam Dudgeon/HRW; xxix, Digital Image ©2004 EyeWire.

All author photos by Sam Dudgeon/HRW. Jan Scheer photo by Ron Shipper.

Chapter One: 2-3 (bkgd), Peter Skinner/Photo Researchers, Inc.; 2 (b), Tom Tracy/Getty Images/FPG International; 4 (tl), Roy King/SuperStock; 4 (tr), Douglas Faulkner/Photo Researchers, Inc.; 7, The Kobal Collection; 8, Robert Landau/CORBIS; 10, ©(2002) PhotoDisc, Inc./HRW; 13, Robert Llewellyn/SuperStock; 15, Mark Lewis/Getty Images/Stone; 18 (tr), Danny Lehman/CORBIS; 18 (tc), Peter Van Steen/HRW; 19, ©2004 PhotoDisc, Inc./HRW; 27, Stephen Munday/Allsport/Getty Images; 33 (tr), Sam Dudgeon/HRW; 33 (tr), Sam Dudgeon/HRW; 34, Peter Van Steen/HRW; 37, Bettmann/CORBIS; 41, Laurence Fleury/Photo Researchers, Inc.; 43, Peter Van Steen/HRW; 47, Alec Pytlowany/Masterfile; 48 (c), Jack Olson; 48 (b), Jack Olson; 49 (t), Mark Segal/Getty Images/Stone; 49 (b), James Blank/Photophile; 50, Randall Hyman; 56, Peter Van Steen/HRW; **Chapter Two:** 58-59 (bkgrd), Science Photo Library/Photo Researchers, Inc.; 58 (b), Dean Conger/CORBIS; 60, Peter Van Steen/HRW; 63, Peter Van Steen/HRW; 64, Lloyd Sutton/Masterfile; 67 (tl), Steve Vidler/SuperStock; 67 (cl), Araldo de Luca/CORBIS; 67 (cr), The Art Archive/Napoleonic Museum Rome/Dagli Orti; 67 (tc), Bettmann/CORBIS; 68, Jeopardy Productions Inc.; 71, Peter David/Getty Images; 75, Sam Dudgeon/HRW; 78, Peter Van Steen/HRW; 81, Luke Frazza/AFP/CORBIS; 83 (b), Dean Conger/CORBIS; 87, S. Lowry/Univ.Ulster/Getty Images/Stone; 92, Courtesy Cornell University; 95 (tc), Francois Gohier/Photo Researchers, Inc.; 95 (bc), Flip Nicklin/Minden Pictures; 96, Sam Dudgeon/HRW; 97, Peter Van Steen/HRW; 99, Joe McDonald/CORBIS; 100 (br), Joseph Sohm; ChromoSohm Inc./CORBIS; 101 (tl), Sam Dudgeon/HRW; 101, John Belliveau; 102 (b), Randall Hyman; 108, Seth Carter/SuperStock; **Chapter Three:** 110-111 (bkgd), Bohemian Nomad Picturemakers/CORBIS; 110 (br), Sam Dudgeon/HRW; 112 (tr), Allsport/Getty Images; 117 (tr), AFP/CORBIS; 125 (tl), John Giustina/Bruce Coleman, Inc.; 130 (tr), Mark Tomalty/Masterfile; 131 (tr), Joe Viesti/Viesti Collection, Inc.; 132 (cl), Lindsay Hebberd/CORBIS; 134 (tr), Wofgang Kaehler/CORBIS; 134 (cr), Sam Dudgeon/HRW; 137 (cl), National Museum of Natural History © 2002 Smithsonian Institution; 140 (tr), Peter Van Steen/HRW Photo; 141, Bettmann/CORBIS; 141, Leonard de Selva/CORBIS;143 (cr), Stuart Westmorland/Getty Images/The Image Bank; 146 (tr), Roman Soumar/CORBIS; 147 (tr), Roberto Rivera; 149 (tr), Peter Van Steen/HRW Photo; 149 (tl), Uimonen Ilkka/CORBIS SYGMA; 150 (tr), Dave Bartruff/Index Stock Imagery, Inc.; 153 (tr), Chris Butler/Photo Researchers, Inc.; 156 (tr), John Garrett/CORBIS; 162 (b), Cosmo Condina/Getty Images/Stone; 163 (tr,br), Morton Beebe/CORBIS; 163 (t), Gail Mooney/CORBIS;164 (br), Jenny Thomas/HRW; 170 (br), Peter Van Steen/HRW; **Chapter Four:** 172-173 (bkgrd), David Joel/Getty Images/Stone; 172 (br), Sam Dudgeon/HRW; 179 (tr), Aaron Weithoff; 183 (tr), Richard Schultz; 185 (cl), Corbis Images; 188 (tr), Peter Van Steen/HRW/Kittens courtesy of Austin Humane Society/SPCA; 195 (br), Richard Cummins/CORBIS; 204 (tr), Custom Medical Stock Photo; 207 (c), Peter Van Steen/HRW; 210 (b), Bruce Schulman/Reuters/TimePix; 210 (cl), Michael Clevenger/AP/Wide World Photos; 211 (t), Layne Kennedy/CORBIS; 213 (br), ; 218 (cr), Michal Heron/Corbis Stock Market; **Chapter Five**: 220-211 (bkgrd), Richard T. Nowitz/CORBIS; 220 (br), Victoria Smith/HRW; 226 (tr), Stephen Dalton/Photo Researchers, Inc.; 226 (cr), Roberto Rivera; 228 (tr), Daryl Benson/Masterfile; 231 (tl), Hulton-Deutsch Collection/CORBIS; 243 (cl), Johnathan Blair/CORBIS; 244 , Lucasfilm, Ltd.; 250 (tr), Seth Kushner/Getty Images/Stone; 254 (tr), Angelo Cavalli/Getty Images/The Image Bank; 259 (butterfly), Bob Jensen/Bruce Coleman, Inc.; 259, Jeff Lepore/Photo Researchers, Inc.; 259, R.N. Mariscal/Bruce Coleman, Inc.; 259, Jeff Rotman/International Stock Photography; 259 (shells), SuperStock; 260 (tc) ; 260 (tr), Garry Black/Masterfile; 262 (tl), Grant V. Faint/Getty Images/The Image Bank; 263 (tr), SuperStock; 263 (cr), Adam Woolfitt/CORBIS; 267 (tr), Hand With Reflecting Sphere by M.C. Escher , Cordon Art - Baarn - Holland. All rights reserved.; 267 (cr), Reptiles by M.C. Escher. © 2004 Cordon Art - Baarn - Holland. All rights reserved; 268 (br), ©2004 EyeWire/Getty; 269 (t), Paul A. Souders/CORBIS; 269 (br), Mae Scanlan; 270 (br), Jenny Thomas/HRW; **Chapter Six:** 278-279 (bkgrd), UHB Trust/Getty Images/Stone; 278 (br), Rob Crandall/Alamy Photos; 280 (tr), Sam Dudgeon/HRW, Woodwork by Carl Childs; 288 (tr), Benelux/ZEFA/H. Armstrong Roberts; 290 (tr), Loukas Hapsis/On Location; 294 (tr), Michelle Bridwell/HRW Photo; 294 (tc), Peter Van Steen/HRW Photo; 297 (cl), Steve vidler/SuperStock; 299 (b), Dave G. Houser/Houserstock; 302 (tr, cr), Jeremy Boon; 306 (cr), Jeremy Boon; 306 (tl), Prat Thierry/Corbis/Sygma; 307 (tr), SuperStock; 309 (tr), Reuters/NewsCom; 311 (cr), Dallas and John Heaton/CORBIS; 311 (tl), G. Leavens/Photo Researchers, Inc.; 312 (tr), Steve Vidler/SuperStock; 313 (cr), Will & Deni McIntyre/Photo Researchers, Inc.; 315 (cl), Owen Franken/CORBIS; 315 (cr), Steve Vidler/SuperStock; 316 (tr), ©2004 Kelly Houle; 317 (cr), Peter Van Steen/HRW Photo; 319 (tr), Peter Van Steen/HRW; 319 (tl), Todd Patrick; 321 (cl), Robert & Linda Mitchell Photography; 322 (cr), Baldwin H. Ward & Kathryn C. Ward/CORBIS; 324 (tr), Imtek Imagineering/Masterfile; 327 (fossil eggs), Sinclair Stammers/Science Photo Library/Photo Researchers, Inc.; 327 (turtle eggs), Dwight Kuhn Photography; 327 (cr), Bob Gossington/Bruce Coleman, Inc.; 327 (c), Frank Lane Picture Agency/CORBIS; 327 (tr), Darryl Torckler/Getty Images/Stone; 328 (tl), Sam Dudgeon/HRW; 328 (tc), Art Stein/Photo Researchers, Inc.; 328 (tr), Neil Rabinowitz/CORBIS; 329 (br), John Elk III; 330 (br, cr), Waverly Traylor; 331 (tr), Courtesy of Great Lakes Aquarium; 331 (bl), Gary Meszaros/Photo Researchers, Inc.; 338 (br), Gunter Marx/CORBIS; **Chapter Seven:** 340-341 (bkgd), Galen Rowell/CORBIS; 340 (br), Michael S. Yamashita/CORBIS; 343 (cl), Biophoto Associates/Photo Researchers, Inc.; 345 (c), Sam Dudgeon/HRW; 346 (tr), Peter Van Steen/HRW Photo; 350 (tr), Stephen Dalton/Photo Researchers, Inc.; 352 (tl), Dr. Harold E. Edgerton/The Harold E. EdgertonTrust ©2004/courtesy Palm Press, Inc.; 356 (tr), Art on File/CORBIS; 359 (tr), Eyewire collection; 359 (tc), Andrew Syred / Microscopix Photolibrary; 359 (bc), Ed Reschke/PA; 361 (b), Nik Wheeler/CORBIS; 362 (tr), Phil Jude/Science Photo Library/Photo Researchers, Inc.; 365 (cl), Peter Van Steen/HRW; 368 (tr), Joseph Sohm; ChromoSohm Inc./CORBIS; 371 (tl), Layne Kennedy/CORBIS; 372 (tr), "Iowa Countryside Outside of Cedar Rapids Iowa" by Stan Herd, photo Jon Blumb; 373 (tr), Eric Grave/Photo Researchers, Inc.; 375 (c), Jeremy Boon, Sam Dudgeon/HRW Photo; 375 (tr), David Young-Wolff/PhotoEdit; 376 (tr), Jonathan Blair/CORBIS; 376 (cr), Peter Van Steen/HRW; 377 (cr), Digital Art/CORBIS; 379 (tl), SuperStock; 379 (cr), Michael S. Yamashita/CORBIS; 380 (cr), Lee Snider/CORBIS; 381 (cr), Peter Van Steen/HRW; 383 (tr), Gail Mooney/CORBIS; 385 (tr), Chris Lisle/CORBIS; 386 (br), Craig Aurness/CORBIS; 387 (tl), Bill Ross/CORBIS; 387 (tr), Robert Holmes/CORBIS; 388 (tr), Isaac Menashe/Zuma Press/NewsCom; 388 (br), AP/Wide World Photos; 388 (bc), William Manning/CORBIS; 389 (tr), Waverly Traylor; 389 (br), Lynda Richardson/CORBIS; 390 (br), Ken Karp/HRW; 390 (tr), Digital Image © 2004 PhotoDisc; 396 (cr), Bettmann/CORBIS; **Chapter Eight:** 398-399 (bkgrd), Photo File/TimePix; 398 (br), Clive Mason/Allsport/Getty Images; 400 (tr), SuperStock; 405 (tr), Ric Ergenbright/CORBIS; 410 (tr), Robert Jensen/Getty Images/Stone; 411 (cl), Hans Reinhard/Bruce Coleman, Inc.; 415 (insects), HRW Photo/Royalty Free; 420 (tr), John Langford/HRW; 421 (tr), Ken Fisher/Getty Images/Stone; 425 (cr), Peter Van Steen; 427, Sam Dudgeon/HRW; 431 (tl), AFP/CORBIS; 434 (cr), Reuters NewMedia Inc./Jacon Cohn/CORBIS; 435 (t), Bob Krist/CORBIS; 435 (br), © 2004 Conrad Gloos c/o MIRA; 436 (br), Victoria Smith/HRW; 442 (br), Sam Dudgeon/HRW; **Chapter Nine:** 444-445 (bkgrd), Erlendur Berg/SuperStock; 444 (br), Bettmann/CORBIS; 446 (tr), Peter Van Steen/HRW Photo; 446 (cr), Sam Dudgeon/HRW; 451 (tr), Joe Richard/AP/Wide World Photos; 454 (tc), Reuters NewMedia Inc./CORBIS; 454 (tr), David Weintraub/Photo Researchers, Inc.; 456 (tr), Duomo/CORBIS; 459 (tl), Raymond Gehman/CORBIS; 461 (br), Susan Marie Anderson/FoodPix; 462 (tr), Sam Dudgeon/HRW; 462 (tr), Sam Dudgeon/HRW; 462 (tr), Sam Dudgeon/HRW; 463 (bl), Peter Van Steen/HRW; 464 (cr), Peter Van Steen/HRW; 466 (tr), Sam Dudgeon/HRW; 467 (tr), ; 470 (tl), Steve Kahn/Getty Images/FPG International; 471 (tr), Peter Van Steen/HRW; 471 (tr), Peter Van Steen/HRW; 475 (tl), The Newark Museum/Art Resource, NY; 477 (tr), Jeffrey Cable/SuperStock; 481 (tl), Corbis/Sygma; 485 (tr), Jeff Greenberg/Photo Researchers, Inc.; 486 (br), From the U.S. Senate Collection, Center for Legislative Archives/Clifford Berryman/Cartoon A-24/May 21, 1912, Washington Evening Star, Washington, D.C.; 486 (cr), CORBIS; 487 (t), Bruce Burkhardt/CORBIS; 487 (br), Paul Sakuma/AP/Wide World Photos; 488 (br), Jenny Thomas/HRW; 494 (cl), Peter Van Steen/HRW Photo; 494 (cr), Peter Van Steen/HRW Photo; **Chapter Ten:** 496-497 (bkgrd), Tom Bean/Getty Images/Stone; 496 (br), David Edwards Photography; 498 (tr), Peter Van Steen; 501 (tr), Karl H. Switak/Photo Researchers, Inc.; 501 (cr), AFP/CORBIS; 503 (cl), Peter Van Steen/HRW; 503 (cl), Sam Dudgeon/HRW; 503 (cl), © 2004 EyeWire, Inc. All rights reserved.; 505 (tr), Peter Van Steen/HRW; 505 (tl), Buddy Mays/CORBIS; 511 (tl), Andrew Syred/Science Photo Library/Photo Researchers, Inc.; 513 (b), Sam Dudgeon/HRW; 514 (tr), Sam Dudgeon/HRW; 516 (cl), Sam Dudgeon/HRW; 518 (tc), Peter Van Steen/HRW; 523 (tr), Kelly-Mooney

Credits

Photography/CORBIS; 527 (tl), Rafael Macia/Photo Researchers, Inc.; 528 (b), Tony Arruza/CORBIS; 529 (t), Ric Ergenbright/CORBIS; 529 (br), Raymond Gehman/CORBIS; 529 (cr), Erwin Nielsen/Painet; 530 (br), Jenny Thomas; **Chapter Eleven:** 538-539 (bkgrd), Tom Stack/Painet; 538 (br), Gary Braasch; 540 (tr), Dick Reed/Corbis Stock Market; 540 (cr), Courtesy of Peabody Advertising; www.peabody-adv.com; 542 (cr), HRW Photo Research Library; 545 (tr), ; 554 (tr), (artist)/AlaskaStock Images; 556 (tr), John Greim/Science Photo Library/Photo Researchers, Inc.; 559 (tl), Art Wolfe/Getty Images/The Image Bank; 561 (b), Sam Dudgeon/HRW; 562 (tr), NASA/Science Photo Library/Photo Researchers, Inc.; 566 (tl), E.R. Degginger/Bruce Coleman, Inc.; 567 (tr), NASA/Science Photo Library/Photo Researchers, Inc.; 569 (tr), ; 572 (tr), Duomo/CORBIS; 578 (br), Craig Aurness/CORBIS; 578 (cr), Nat Farbman/TimePix; 579 (tr), Bettmann/CORBIS; 579 (b), Robert Holmes/CORBIS; 580 (br), Jenny Thomas; **Chapter Twelve:** 588-589 (bkgrd), C.N.R.I./Phototake; 588 (br), Stevie Grand/Science Photo Library/Photo Researchers, Inc.; 590 (tr), Getty Images/The Image Bank; 592 (cl), © 2004 PhotoDisc ; 599 (c), Peter Van Steen/HRW; 607 (bl), George McCarthy/CORBIS; 612 (tl), Schenectady Museum; Hall of Electrical History Foundation/CORBIS; 613 (tr), G. C. Kelley/Photo Researchers, Inc.; 616 (tl), Liz Hymans/CORBIS; 618 (bl), GJLP/Science Photo Library/Photo Researchers, Inc.; 620 (tr), John Langford/HRW; 621 (tr), Chip Simons Photography; 625 (tr), Sam Dudgeon/HRW; 628 (tr), Getty Images/Stone; 632 (cr), James A. Sugar/CORBIS; 633 (tr,b), Butch Dill; 633 (cr), Courtesy, New Deal Network; newdeal.feri.org; 634 (br), Randall Hyman; 640 (br), Sam Dudgeon/HRW. **Chapter Thirteen:** 642-643 (bkgd), © W. Cody/CORBIS; 642 (br), Victoria Smith/HRW; 644 © Otto Rogge/CORBIS; 645 © Dave G. Houser/CORBIS; 653 (b), © Paul Eekhoff/Masterfile; 653 (t), Private Collection/Bridgeman Art Library/© 2002 Fletcher Benton/Artists Rights Society (ARS), New York; 655 © Steve Gottlieb/ Stock Connection/ PictureQuest; 656 (l), Victoria Smith/HRW; 656 (r), Sam Dudgeon/HRW; 656 (frame), Victoria Smith/HRW; 657 Sam Dudgeon/HRW; 659 © Getty Images/The Image Bank; 660 Victoria Smith/HRW/Image of assembled plastic model kit used courtesy of Revell-Monogram, LLC © 2004; 661 Victoria Smith/HRW/Images of parts trees used courtesy of Revell-Monogram, LLC © 2004; 664 Sam Dudgeon/HRW; 665 Victoria Smith/HRW; 667 Sam Dudgeon/HRW; 670 © Robert Harding World Imagery/Alamy Photos; 673 (b), Sam Dudgeon/HRW; 676 (b), © RIchard Berenholtz/CORBIS; 677 (br), Bill Banaszewski/New England Stock Photos; 677 (t), © James Schwabel/Panoramic Images; 678 (b), Sam Dudgeon/HRW; 684 (t), Victoria Smith/HRW; 684 (b), Victoria Smith/HRW. **Chapter Fourteen:** 686 (br), Victoria Smith/HRW; 686-687 (bkgd), Corbis Images; 688 (tr, tc), Victoria Smith/HRW; 690 (br), Sam Dudgeon/HRW; 691 (tl), Tony Freeman/PhotoEdit; 692 (tr), © Jeremy Homer/CORBIS; 695 (flamingos), © Royalty-Free/CORBIS; 695 (swans), © Renee Lynn/CORBIS; 695 (geese), Paul J. Fusco/Photo Researchers, Inc.; 695 (chickens), Peter Cade/Getty Images/The Image Bank; 699 (tl), Silvio Fiore/SuperStock; 701 (b), Victoria Smith/HRW; 702 (tr), Lisette Le Bon/SuperStock; 708 (tr), Andrew Toos/CartoonResource.com; 712 (tr), Corbis Images; 715 (tr), © Owaki - Kulla/CORBIS; 716 (tr), Getty Images/The Image Bank; 717 (cl), Sam Dudgeon/HRW; 719 (r), © Roger Ressmeyer/CORBIS; 720 (br), © Sheldon Schafer/Lakeview Museum of Arts & Sciences 2002; 721 (t), © David Muench/CORBIS; 721 (br), AP Photo/The Daily Times, Tom Sistak; 722 (br), Victoria Smith/HRW.

Illustrations

All work, unless otherwise noted, contributed by Holt, Rinehart & Winston.

Table of Contents: Page xx (tr), Gary Otteson; xxv (tr), Rosie Sanders; xxvi (c), HRW; xxvi (c), HRW; xxvi (c), HRW; xxviii (cr), Cindy Jeftovic; xxiv (tr), Lori Bilter.

Chapter One: Page 4 (tl), Greg Geisler; 8 (cl), Greg Geisler; 8 (cl), Greg Geisler; 8 (cl), Greg Geisler; 8 (cl), Greg Geisler; 12 (c), Jeffrey Oh; 17 (t), Ortelius Design; 22 (tr), Mark Betcher; 23 (tr), Jeffrey Oh; 23 (c), Greg Geisler; 27 (tr), Ortelius Design; 28 (t), Jeffrey Oh; 28 (c), Greg Geisler; 31 (t), Argosy; 33 (tr), Argosy; 33 (t), Ortelius Design; 38 (tr), Mark Heine; 38 (c), Greg Geisler; 38 (c), Greg Geisler; 38 (c), Greg Geisler; 48 (tc), Ortelius Design; 50 (tr), Ted Williams. **Chapter Two:** Page 61 (br), Argosy; 65 (br), Argosy; 67 (t), Stephen Durke/Washington Artists; 71 (tr), Argosy; 77 (cr), Argosy; 77 (tr), Argosy; 81 (cr), Argosy; 84 (tr), Greg Geisler; 87 (cr), Argosy; 87 (cr), Stephen Durke/Washington Artists; 96 (c), Greg Geisler; 99 (tr), Argosy; 100 (tr), Ortelius Design; 100 (tr), Ortelius Design; 102 (tr), Jeffrey Oh; 108 (br), Stephen Durke/Washington Artists; 109 (br), Argosy. **Chapter Three:** Page 112 (tr), Greg Geisler; 113 (c), Argosy; 114 (t), Greg Geisler; 116 (cr), Argosy; 121 (tr), Kim Malek; 125 (tr), Argosy; 128 (tr), Mark Heine; 136 (tr), Jeffrey Oh; 139 (cr), Mark Heine; 143 (tr), Argosy; 145 (b), Argosy; 153 (cr), Argosy; 160 (tr), Robert Salinas; 162 (tr), Ortelius Design; 164 (tr), Nenad Jakesevic. **Chapter Four:** Page 174 (tr), Gary Otteson; 181 (c), Argosy; 182 (c), Ortelius Design; 186 (t), Ortelius Design; 187 (t), Argosy; 191 Argosy; 196 (tr), Jeffrey Oh; 196 (bc), Argosy; 197 (br), Argosy; 198 (b), Argosy; 199 (t), Argosy; 199 (br), Argosy; 200 (tr), Jeffrey Oh; 200 (c), Argosy; 200 (b), Argosy; 201 (t), Argosy; 202 (tl), Argosy; 202 (bl), Argosy; 202 (tr), Argosy; 202 (br), Argosy; 203 (tl), Argosy; 203 (tr), Argosy; 203 (br), Argosy; 206 (tr), Ortelius Design; 207 (l), Argosy; 207 (r), Argosy; 210 (tc), Ortelius Design; 216 (tl), Argosy; 216 (bl), Argosy; 216 (br), Argosy; 218 (br), Argosy. **Chapter Five:** Page 226 (t), Argosy; 228 (c), Argosy; 231 (tr), Jeffrey Oh; 234 (tr), Argosy; 238 (cr), Argosy; 239 (tr), Argosy; 243 (cr), Argosy; 260 (tl), Argosy; 262 (c), Argosy; 262 (c), Argosy; 262 (c), Argosy; 262 (c), Argosy; 262 (c), Argosy; 262 (c), Argosy; 262 (br), Argosy; 267 (cl), Argosy; 268 (cr), Argosy; 268 (tc), Ortelius Design; 276 (br) Jeffrey Oh. **Chapter Six:** Page 281 (t), Argosy; 284 (cr), Ortelius Design; 285 (t), Argosy; 288 (r), Argosy; 293 (cl), Argosy; 293 (br), Ortelius Design; 294 (cr), Greg Geisler; 297 (cr), Jeffrey Oh; 306 (tr), Mark Heine; 307 (tr), Ortelius Design; 310 (cr), Mark Heine; 310 (br), John White/The Neis Group; 311 (tr), Argosy; 321 (cr), Argosy; 323 (tr), Don Dixon; 324 (cr), Argosy; 328 (cr), Argosy; 329 (tl), Argosy; 329 (tc), Argosy; 329 (tr), Argosy; 329 (cl), Argosy; 329 (c), Argosy; 330 (tc), Ortelius Design; 332 (cl), Argosy; 332 (c), Argosy; 332 (cr), Argosy; 338 (cr), Argosy. **Chapter Seven:** Page 345 (tr), Argosy; 349 (cr), Argosy; 351 (tr), Argosy; 354 (tr), Argosy 374 (br), Ortelius Design; 375 (c), Mark Heine; 381 (tr), Argosy; 388 (tc), Ortelius Design; 397 (br), Ortelius Design. **Chapter Eight:** Page 403 (tr), Jane Sanders; 406 (tr), Gary Otteson; 408 (tr), Doug Bowles; 414 (br), Nenad Jakesevic; 419 (tr), John Bindon; 424 (t), Greg Geisler; 427 (cr), Stephen Durke/Washington Artists; 428 (t), Greg Geisler; 431 (cr), Argosy; 432 (tr), Greg Geisler; 434 (br), Jeffrey Oh; 434 (tc), Ortelius Design; 436 (tr), Gary Otteson. **Chapter Nine:** Page 453 (br), Argosy; 468 (b), Argosy; 470 (tr), Jeffrey Oh; 471 (tl), Greg Geisler; 478 (br), Jeffrey Oh; 482 (tr), Polly Powell; 482 (c), Greg Geisler; 486 (tr), Ortelius Design; 488 (tr), Gary Otteson; 494 (br), Bruno Paciulli. **Chapter Ten:** Page 507 (tc), Greg Geisler; 507 (tr), Mark Heine; 519 (tr), Nenad Jakesevic; 519 (tl), Greg Geisler; 522 (r), Gary Otteson; 528 (tr), Ortelius Design; 530 (tr), John Etheridge; 536 (br), John White/The Neis Group. **Chapter Eleven:** Page 540 (tr), HRW; 544 (c), Argosy; 545 (bc), Greg Geisler; 550 (tr), Cindy Jeftovic; 551 (tc), Greg Geisler; 554 (tr), Nenad Jakesevic; 559 (tr), Patrick Gnan; 559; 566 (tr), Christy Krames; 571 (cr), HRW; 575 (tr), Gary Otteson; 578 (tr), Ortelius Design; 580 (tc), Argosy; 580 (tr), Lance Lekander; 586 (br), Jeffrey Oh. **Chapter Twelve:** Page 594 (tr), Gary Otteson; 595 (tr), Fian Arroyo; 601 (t), HRW; 603 (cr), HRW; 605 (r), Argosy; 608 (tr), Jeffrey Oh; 608 (cl), Jeffrey Oh; 608 (cr), Jeffrey Oh; 617 (tr), Argosy; 623 (tl), Argosy; 632 (br), HRW; 632 (tr), Ortelius Design; 634 (tr), Gary Otteson; 682 (b), Argosy; 688 (b), Argosy; 688 (c), Argosy; 688 (cr), Argosy; 688 (t), Argosy. **Chapter Thirteen:** Page 647 (t), Argosy; 650 (t), Greg Geisler; 670 (c), Greg Geisler; 671 (tr), Argosy; 673 (tr), Gary Otteson; 673 (cr), Leslie Kell; 676 (cr), Nenad Jakesevic; 677 (tl), Ortelius Design; 678 (tr), Gary Otteson. **Chapter Fourteen:** Page 690 (bl), Argosy; 690 (bl), Kim Malek; 690 (br), Argosy; 692 (cr), Ortelius Design; 696 (tr), John Etheridge; 699 (cr), Argosy; 703 (tr), Dan Vasconcellos; 705 (tr), Uhl Studios, Inc.; 712 (tr), Ortelius Design; 713 (cl), Nenad Jakesevic; 715 (c), Argosy; 720 (r), Mark Betcher; 721 (r), Ortelius Design; 722 (tr), Cindy Jeftovic.

Staff Credits

Bruce Albrecht, Ed Blake, Teresa Carrere-Paprota, Justin Collins, Marc Cooper, Kristen Darby, Higinio Dominguez, Sara Downs, Sam Dudgeon, Lauren Eischen, Kelli Flanagan, Mary Fraser, Jose Garza, Thomas Hamilton, Tessa Henry, Tim Hovde, Wilonda Leans, Jevara Jackson, John Kerwin, David Knowles, Jill Lawson, Ivania Lee, Ruth Limon, Nicole McLeod, Dick Metzger, Susan Mussey, Denise Nowotny, Patricia Platt, Manda Reid, Patrick Ricci, Curtis Riker, Eric Rupprath, John Saxe, Robyn Setzen, Chris Smith, Kristi Smith, Victoria Smith, Mimi Stockdell, Charlie Taliaferro, Elaine Tate, Tim Taylor, Holly Whittaker, Linda Wilbourn, Alison Wohlman, Lisa Woods, Glenn Worthman.

Notes

Glossary/Glosario

ENGLISH	SPANISH	EXAMPLES
absolute value The distance of a number from zero on a number line; shown by $\|\ \|$. (pp. 60, 781)	**valor absoluto** Distancia a la que está un número de 0 en una recta numérica. El símbolo del valor absoluto es $\|\ \|$.	$\|-5\| = 5$
accuracy The closeness of a given measurement or value to the actual measurement or value.	**exactitud** Cercanía de una medida o un valor a la medida o el valor real.	
acute angle An angle that measures less than 90°. (p. 223)	**ángulo agudo** Ángulo que mide menos de 90°.	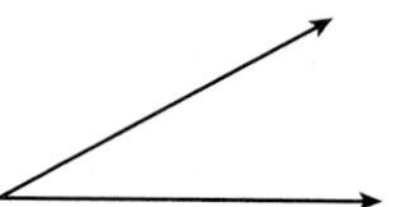
acute triangle A triangle with all angles measuring less than 90°. (p. 234)	**triángulo acutángulo** Triángulo en el que todos los ángulos miden menos de 90°.	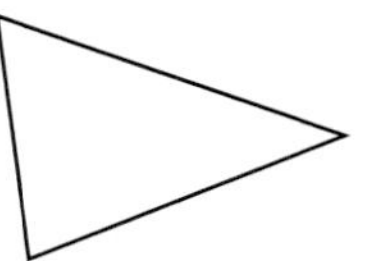
Addition Counting Principle If one group contains m objects and a second group contains n objects, and the groups have no objects in common, then there are $m + n$ total objects to choose from.	**Principio de conteo en suma** Si un grupo tiene m objetos, otro grupo tiene n objetos y los grupos no tienen objetos en común, entonces hay un total de $m + n$ objetos para elegir.	A restaurant offers 3 types of juice and 4 types of iced tea. There are 3 + 4 = 7 total drinks to choose from.
Addition Property of Equality The property that states that if you add the same number to both sides of an equation, the new equation will have the same solution. (p. 14)	**Propiedad de igualdad de la suma** Propiedad que establece que puedes sumar el mismo número a ambos lados de una ecuación y la nueva ecuación tendrá la misma solución.	$14 - 6 = 8$ $+6 \quad +6$ $14 = 14$
Addition Property of Opposites The property that states that the sum of a number and its opposite equals zero. (p. 60)	**Propiedad de la suma de los opuestos** Propiedad que establece que la suma de un número y su opuesto es cero.	$12 + (-12) = 0$
additive inverse The opposite of a number.	**inverso aditivo** El opuesto de un número.	The additive inverse of 5 is −5.
adjacent angles Angles in the same plane that have a common vertex and a common side.	**ángulos adyacentes** Ángulos en el mismo plano que comparten un vértice y un lado.	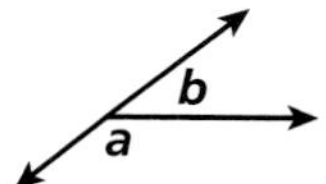

ENGLISH	SPANISH	EXAMPLES
algebraic expression An expression that contains at least one variable. (p. 4)	**expresión algebraica** Expresión que contiene al menos una variable.	$x + 8$ $4(m - b)$
algebraic inequality An inequality that contains at least one variable. (p. 23)	**desigualdad algebraica** Desigualdad que contiene al menos una variable.	$x + 3 > 10$ $5a > b + 3$
alternate exterior angles A pair of angles on the outer sides of two lines cut by a transversal that are on opposite sides of the transversal. (p. 229)	**ángulos alternos externos** Par de ángulos en los lados externos de dos líneas intersecadas por una transversal, que están en lados opuestos de la transversal.	a b c d $\angle a$ and $\angle d$ are alternate exterior angles.
alternate interior angles A pair of angles on the inner sides of two lines cut by a transversal that are on opposite sides of the transversal. (p. 229)	**ángulos alternos internos** Par de ángulos en los lados internos de dos líneas intersecadas por una transversal, que están en lados opuestos de la transversal.	r s t v $\angle r$ and $\angle v$ are alternate interior angles.
angle A figure formed by two rays with a common endpoint called the vertex. (p. 222)	**ángulo** Figura formada por dos rayos con un extremo común llamado vértice.	
angle bisector A line, segment, or ray that divides an angle into two congruent angles. (p. 227)	**bisectriz de un ángulo** Línea, segmento o rayo que divide un ángulo en dos ángulos congruentes.	N P O M
arc An unbroken part of a circle. (p. 788)	**arco** Parte continua de un círculo.	R S
area The number of square units needed to cover a given surface. (p. 281)	**área** El número de unidades cuadradas que se necesitan para cubrir una superficie dada.	5 2 The area is 10 square units.
arithmetic sequence An ordered list of numbers in which the difference between consecutive terms is always the same. (p. 590)	**sucesión aritmética** Lista ordenada de números en la que la diferencia entre términos consecutivos es siempre la misma.	The sequence 2, 5, 8, 11, 14... is an arithmetic sequence.

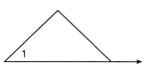

ENGLISH	SPANISH	EXAMPLES
interest The amount of money charged for borrowing or using money. (p. 428)	**interés** Cantidad de dinero que se cobra por el préstamo o uso del dinero.	
interior angles Angles on the inner sides of two lines cut by a transversal.	**ángulos internos** Ángulos en los lados internos de dos líneas intersecadas por una transversal.	1 ∠1 is an interior angle.
intersecting lines Lines that cross at exactly one point. 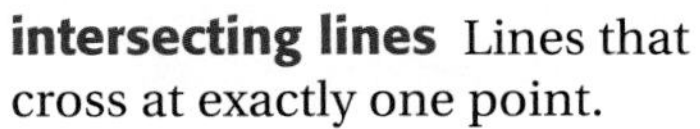	**líneas secantes** Líneas que se cruzan en un solo punto.	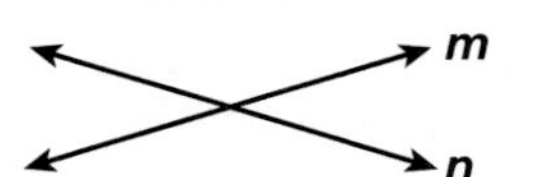
interval The space between marked values on a number line or the scale of a graph.	**intervalo** El espacio entre los valores marcados en una recta numérica o en la escala de una gráfica.	
inverse operations Operations that undo each other: addition and subtraction, or multiplication and division. (p. 14)	**operaciones inversas** Operaciones que se cancelan mutuamente: suma y resta, o multiplicación y división.	Addition and subtraction are inverse operations: $5 + 3 + 8; 8 - 3 = 5$ Multiplication and division are inverse operations: $2 \cdot 3 = 6; 6 \div 3 = 2$
inverse variation A relationship in which one variable quantity increases as another variable quantity decreases; the product of the variables is a constant. (p. 628)	**variación inversa** Relación en la que una cantidad variable aumenta a medida que otra cantidad variable disminuye; el producto de las variables es una constante.	$xy = 7, y = \frac{7}{x}$
irrational number A number that cannot be expressed as a ratio of two integers or as a repeating or terminating decimal. (p. 156)	**número irracional** Número que no se puede expresar como una razón de dos enteros ni como un decimal periódico o cerrado.	$\sqrt{2}, \pi$
isolate the variable To get a variable alone on one side of an equation or inequality in order to solve the equation or inequality. (p. 14)	**despejar la variable** Dejar sola la variable en un lado de una ecuación o desigualdad para resolverla.	$x + 7 = 22$ $\underline{\quad -7 \quad -7}$ $x \quad = 15$ $\frac{12}{3} = \frac{3x}{3}$ $4 = x$
isometric drawing A representation of a three-dimensional figure that is drawn on a grid of equilateral triangles.	**dibujo isométrico** Representación de una figura tridimensional que se dibuja sobre una cuadrícula de triángulos equiláteros.	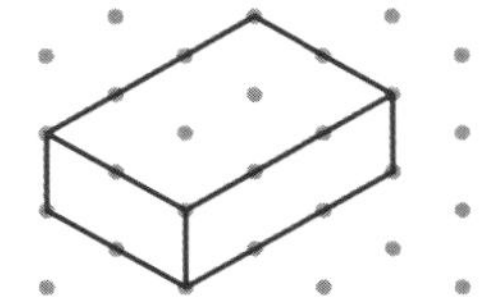
isosceles triangle A triangle with at least two congruent sides. (p. 235)	**triángulo isósceles** Triángulo que tiene al menos dos lados congruentes.	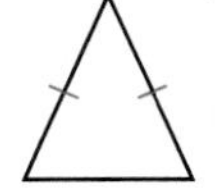

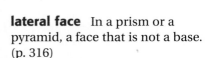

ENGLISH	SPANISH	EXAMPLES

lateral face In a prism or a pyramid, a face that is not a base. (p. 316)

cara lateral En un prisma o pirámide, una cara que no es la base.

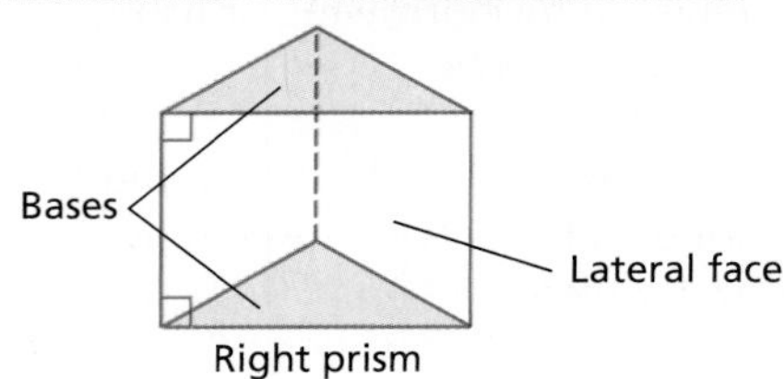

lateral surface In a cylinder, the curved surface connecting the circular bases; in a cone, the curved surface that is not a base. (p. 316)

superficie lateral En un cilindro, superficie curva que une las bases circulares; en un cono, la superficie curva que no es la base.

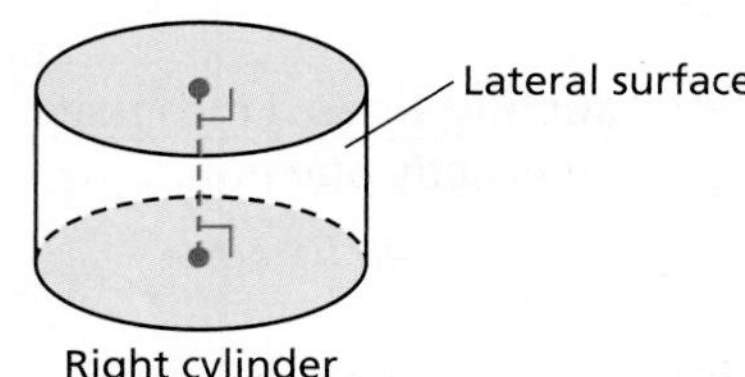

least common denominator (LCD) The least common multiple of two or more denominators.

mínimo común denominador (mcd) El mínimo común múltiplo más pequeño de dos o más denominadores.

The LCD of $\frac{3}{4}$ and $\frac{5}{6}$ is 12.

least common multiple (LCM) The smallest whole number, other than zero, that is a multiple of two or more given numbers. (p. 774)

mínimo común múltiplo (mcm) El menor de los números cabales, distinto de cero, que es múltiplo de dos o más números dados.

The LCM of 6 and 10 is 30.

legs In a right triangle, the sides that include the right angle; in an isosceles triangle, the pair of congruent sides. (p. 290)

catetos En un triángulo rectángulo, los lados adyacentes al ángulo recto. En un triángulo isósceles, el par de lados congruentes.

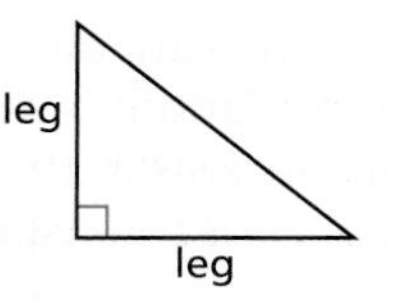

like fractions Fractions that have the same denominator.

fracciones semejantes Fracciones que tienen el mismo denominador.

$\frac{5}{12}$ and $\frac{7}{12}$ are like fractions.

like terms Two or more terms that have the same variable raised to the same power. (p. 28)

términos semejantes Dos o más términos que contienen la misma variable elevada a la misma potencia.

In the expression $3a + 5b + 12a$, $3a$ and $12a$ are like terms.

line A straight path that extends without end in opposite directions. (p. 222)

línea Trayectoria recta que se extiende de manera indefinida en direcciones opuestas.

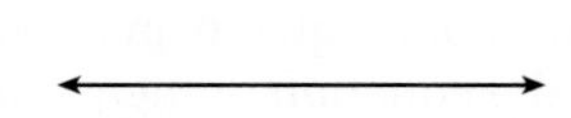

line graph A graph that uses line segments to show how data changes. (p. 197)

gráfica lineal Gráfica que muestra cómo cambian los datos mediante segmentos de recta.

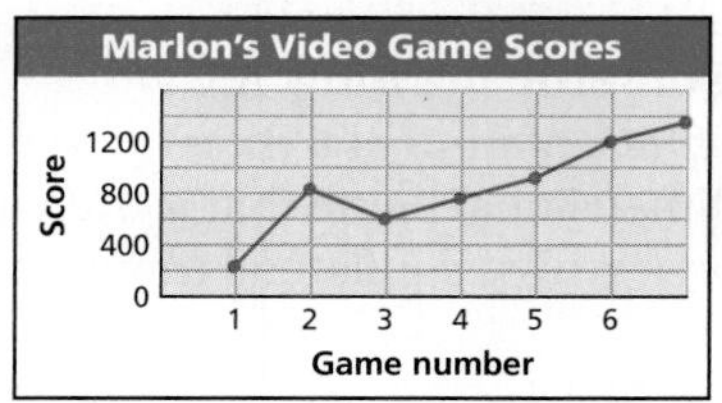

line of best fit A straight line that comes closest to the points on a scatter plot. (p. 204)

línea de mejor ajuste La línea recta que más se aproxima a los puntos de un diagrama de dispersión.

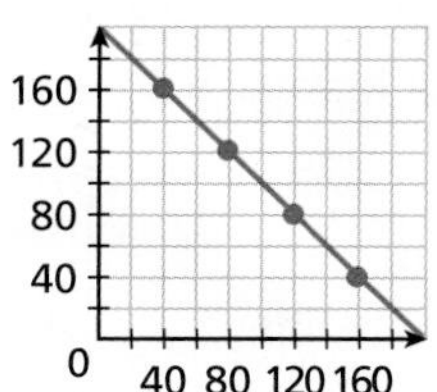

ENGLISH	SPANISH	EXAMPLES
line of reflection A line that a figure is flipped across to create a mirror image of the original figure. (p. 254)	**línea de reflexión** Línea sobre la cual se invierte una figura para crear una imagen reflejada de la figura original.	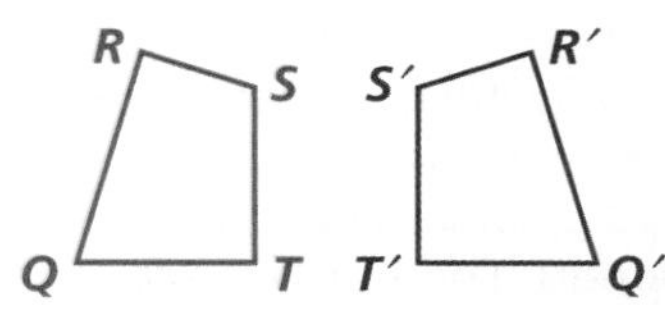
line of symmetry The imaginary "mirror" in line symmetry. (p. 259)	**eje de simetría** El "espejo" imaginario en la simetría axial.	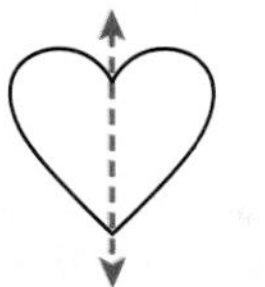
line plot A number line with marks or dots that show frequency.	**diagrama de acumulación** Recta numérica con marcas o puntos que indican la frecuencia.	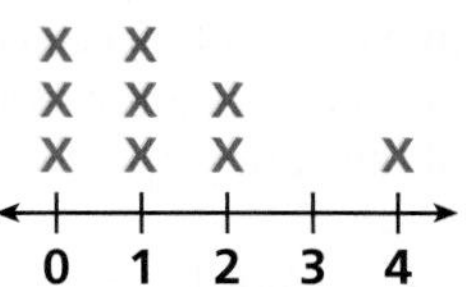
line segment A part of a line between two endpoints. (p. 222)	**segmento de recta** Parte de una línea con dos extremos.	
line symmetry A figure has line symmetry if one half is a mirror-image of the other half. (p. 259)	**simetría axial** Una figura tiene simetría axial si una de sus mitades es la imagen reflejada de la otra.	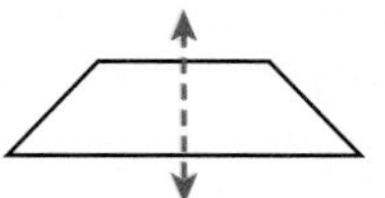
linear equation An equation whose solutions form a straight line on a coordinate plane. (p. 540)	**ecuación lineal** Ecuación cuyas soluciones forman una línea recta en un plano cartesiano.	$y = 2x + 1$
linear function A function whose graph is a straight line. (p. 613)	**función lineal** Función cuya gráfica es una línea recta.	$y = x - 1$ 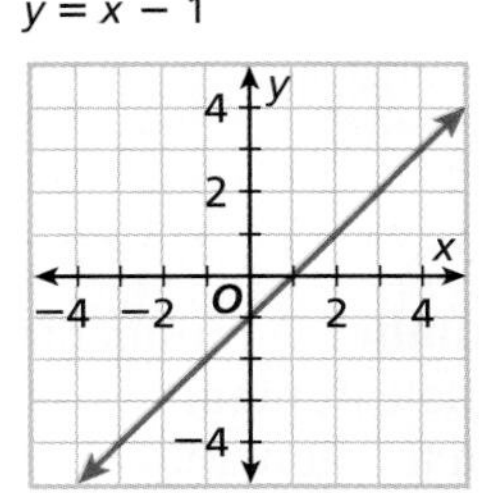
linear inequality A mathematical sentence using $<$, $>$, $\leq$, or $\geq$ whose graph is a region with a straight-line boundary. (p. 567)	**desigualdad lineal** Enunciado matemático en que se usan los símbolos $<$, $>$, $\leq$, o $\geq$ y cuya gráfica es una región con una línea de límite recta.	

M

ENGLISH	SPANISH	EXAMPLES
major arc An arc that is more than half of a circle. (p. 788)	**arco mayor** Arco que es más de la mitad de un círculo.	

ENGLISH	SPANISH	EXAMPLES
matrix A rectangular arrangement of data enclosed in brackets. (p. 789)	**matriz** Arreglo rectangular de datos encerrado entre corchetes.	$\begin{bmatrix} 1 & 0 & 3 \\ -2 & 2 & -5 \\ 7 & -6 & 3 \end{bmatrix}$
mean The sum of a set of data divided by the number of items in the data set; also called *average.* (p. 184)	**promedio** La suma de todos los elementos de un conjunto de datos dividida entre el número de elementos del conjunto. También se llama promedio.	Data set: 4, 6, 7, 8, 10 Mean: $\frac{4+6+7+8+10}{5} = \frac{35}{5} = 7$
measure of central tendency A measure used to describe the middle of a data set; the mean, median, and mode are measures of central tendency. (p. 184)	**medida de tendencia dominante** Medida que describe la parte media de un conjunto de datos; la media, la mediana y la moda son medidas de tendencia dominante.	
median The middle number, or the mean (average) of the two middle numbers, in an ordered set of data. (p. 184)	**mediana** El número intermedio o la media (el promedio) de los dos números intermedios en un conjunto ordenado de datos.	Data set: 4, 6, 7, 8, 10 Median: 7
metric system of measurement A decimal system of weights and measures that is used universally in science and commonly throughout the world.	**sistema métrico de medición** Sistema decimal de pesos y medidas empleado universalmente en las ciencias y de uso común en todo el mundo.	centimeters, meters, kilometers, gram, kilograms, milliliters, liters
midpoint The point that divides a line segment into two congruent line segments.	**punto medio** El punto que divide un segmento de recta en dos segmentos de recta congruentes.	A B C B is the midpoint of $\overline{AC}$.
minor arc An arc that is less than half of a circle. (p. 788)	**arco menor** Arco que es menor que la mitad de un círculo.	A B C $\overset{\frown}{AC}$ is the minor arc of the circle.
mixed number A number made up of a whole number that is not zero and a fraction. (p. 775)	**número mixto** Número compuesto por un número cabal distinto de cero y una fracción.	$4\frac{1}{8}$
mode The number or numbers that occur most frequently in a set of data; when all numbers occur with the same frequency, we say there is no mode. (p. 184)	**moda** Número o números más frecuentes en un conjunto de datos; si todos los números aparecen con la misma frecuencia, no hay moda.	Data set: 3, 5, 8, 8, 10 Mode: 8
monomial A number or a product of numbers and variables with exponents that are whole numbers. (p. 644)	**monomio** Un número o un producto de números y variables con exponentes que son números cabales.	$3x^2y^4$

ENGLISH	SPANISH	EXAMPLES
Multiplication Property of Equality The property that states that if you multiply both sides of an equation by the same number, the new equation will have the same solution. (p. 19)	**Propiedad de igualdad de la multiplicación** Propiedad que establece que puedes multiplicar ambos lados de una ecuación por el mismo número y la nueva ecuación tendrá la misma solución.	$3 \cdot 4 = 12$ $3 \cdot 4 \cdot 2 = 12 \cdot 2$ $24 = 24$
Multiplication Property of Zero The property that states that for all real numbers *a*, $a \cdot 0 = 0$ and $0 \cdot a = 0$. (p. 779)	**Propiedad de multiplicación del cero** Propiedad que establece que para todos los números reales *a*, $a \cdot 0 = 0$ y $0 \cdot a = 0$.	
multiplicative inverse A number times its multiplicative inverse is equal to 1; also called *reciprocal.* (p. 126)	**inverso multiplicativo** Un número multiplicado por su inverso multiplicativo es igual a 1. También se llama *recíproco.*	The multiplicative inverse of $\frac{4}{5}$ is $\frac{5}{4}$.
multiple The product of any number and a non-zero whole number is a multiple of that number. (p. 772)	**múltiplo** El producto de cualquier número y un número cabal distinto de cero es un múltiplo de ese número.	
mutually exclusive Two events are mutually exclusive if they cannot occur in the same trial of an experiment. (p. 464)	**mutuamente excluyentes** Dos sucesos son mutuamente excluyentes cuando no pueden ocurrir en la misma prueba de un experimento.	When rolling a number cube, rolling a 3 and rolling an even number are mutually exclusive events.

N

ENGLISH	SPANISH	EXAMPLES
negative correlation Two data sets have a negative correlation if one set of data values increases while the other decreases. (p. 205)	**correlación negativa** Dos conjuntos de datos tienen correlación negativa si los valores de un conjunto aumentan a medida que los valores del otro conjunto disminuyen.	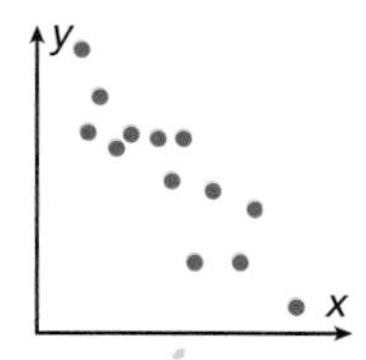
negative integer An integer less than zero. (p. 60)	**entero negativo** Entero menor que cero.	−2 is a negative integer. −4 −3 −2 −1 0 1 2 3 4
net An arrangement of two-dimensional figures that can be folded to form a polyhedron. (p. 300)	**plantilla** Arreglo de figuras bidimensionales que se doblan para formar un poliedro.	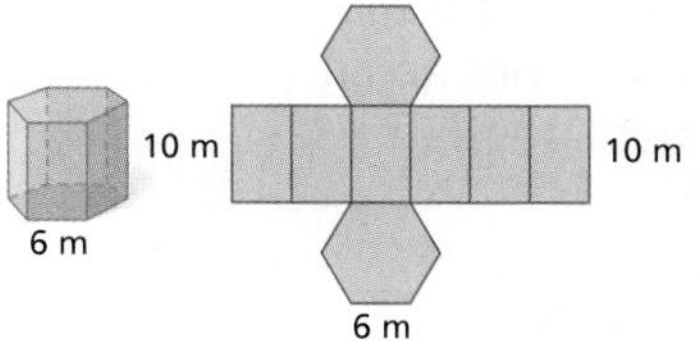
no correlation Two data sets have no correlation when there is no relationship between their data values. (p. 205)	**sin correlación** Caso en que los valores de dos conjuntos no muestran ninguna relación.	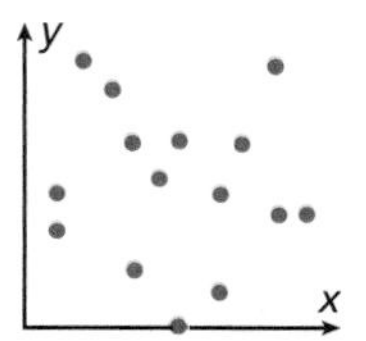

ENGLISH	SPANISH	EXAMPLES
nonlinear function A function whose graph is not a straight line.	**función no lineal** Función cuya gráfica no es una línea recta.	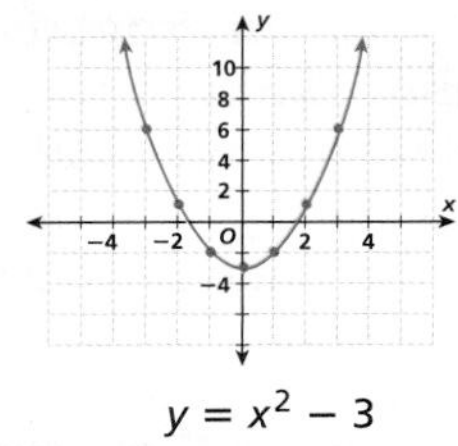 $y = x^2 - 3$
nonterminating decimal A decimal that never ends. (p. 156)	**decimal infinito** Decimal que nunca termina.	
numerator The top number of a fraction that tells how many parts of a whole are being considered. (p. 112)	**numerador** El número de arriba de una fracción; indica cuántas partes de un entero se consideran.	$\frac{4}{5}$ ← numerator
numerical expression An expression that contains only numbers and operations.	**expresión numérica** Expresión que incluye sólo números y operaciones.	$(2 \cdot 3) + 1$

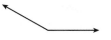

O

ENGLISH	SPANISH	EXAMPLES
obtuse angle An angle whose measure is greater than 90° but less than 180°. (p. 223)	**ángulo obtuso** Ángulo que mide más de 90° y menos de 180°.	
obtuse triangle A triangle containing one obtuse angle. (p. 234)	**triángulo obtusángulo** Triángulo que tiene un ángulo obtuso.	
octagon An eight-sided polygon. (p. 239)	**octágono** Polígono de ocho lados.	
odd number A whole number that is not divisible by two.	**número impar** Número cabal que no es divisible entre 2.	
odds A comparison of favorable outcomes and unfavorable outcomes. (p. 482)	**posibilidades** Comparación de resultados favorables y no favorables.	
odds against The ratio of the number of unfavorable outcomes to the number of favorable outcomes. (p. 482)	**posibilidades en contra** Razón del número de resultados no favorables al número de resultados favorables.	The odds against rolling a 3 on a number cube are 5:1.
odds in favor The ratio of the number of favorable outcomes to the number of unfavorable outcomes. (p. 482)	**posibilidades a favor** Razón del número de resultados favorables al número de resultados no favorables.	The odds in favor of rolling a 3 on a number cube are 1:5.

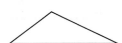

T

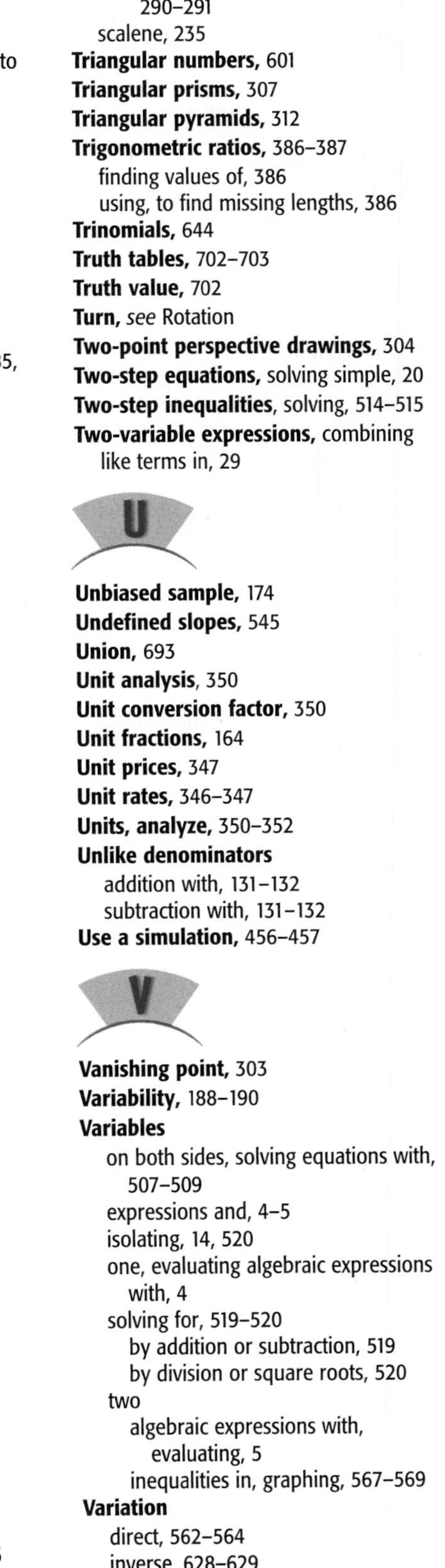

U

V

Index

W

X

Y

Z

Formulas

Perimeter

Polygon	$P =$ sum of the lengths of the sides
Rectangle	$P = 2(b + h)$
Square	$P = 4s$

Circumference

Circle	$C = 2\pi r$, or $C = \pi d$ $d = 2r$

Volume

Prism	$V = Bh$
Rectangular prism	$V = \ell wh$
Cube	$V = s^3$
Cylinder	$V = \pi r^2 h$
Pyramid	$V = \frac{1}{3}Bh$
Cone	$V = \frac{1}{3}\pi r^2 h$
Sphere	$V = \frac{4}{3}\pi r^3$

Area

Circle	$A = \pi r^2$
Parallelogram	$A = bh$
Rectangle	$A = bh$
Square	$A = s^2$
Triangle	$A = \frac{1}{2}bh$
Trapezoid	$A = \frac{1}{2}h(b_1 + b_2)$

Surface Area

Prism	$S = 2B + ph$
Rectangular prism	$S = 2\ell w + 2\ell h + 2wh$
Cube	$S = 6s^2$
Cylinder	$S = 2B + 2\pi rh$
Regular pyramid	$S = B + \frac{1}{2}p\ell$
Cone	$S = \pi r^2 + \pi r\ell$
Sphere	$S = 4\pi r^2$

Trigonometry

Sine	$\sin A = \dfrac{\text{length of side opposite } \angle A}{\text{length of hypotenuse}}$
Cosine	$\cos A = \dfrac{\text{length of side adjacent to } \angle A}{\text{length of hypotenuse}}$
Tangent	$\tan A = \dfrac{\text{length of side opposite } \angle A}{\text{length of side adjacent to } \angle A}$

Probability

Experimental	$\text{probability} \approx \dfrac{\text{number of times event occurs}}{\text{total number of trials}}$
Theoretical	$\text{probability} = \dfrac{\text{number of outcomes in the event}}{\text{number of outcomes in sample space}}$
Permutations	${}_nP_r = \dfrac{n!}{(n-r)!}$
Combinations	${}_nC_r = \dfrac{{}_nP_r}{r!} = \dfrac{n!}{r!(n-r)!}$
Dependent events	$P(A \text{ and } B) = P(A) \cdot P(B \text{ after } A)$
Independent events	$P(A \text{ and } B) = P(A) \cdot P(B)$